THE UNDERGROUND STREAM

NANCYLEE NOVELL JONZA

The Underground

THE UNIVERSITY OF GEORGIA PRESS

Athens & London

Stream

THE LIFE AND ART OF

Caroline Gordon

The paper in

this book meets

the guidelines

for permanence

and durability

of the Committee

on Production

Guidelines for

Book Longevity

of the Council

on Library

Resources.

© 1995 by the
University of Georgia Press
Athens, Georgia 30602
All rights reserved
Designed by Richard Hendel
Set in Galliard by Tseng Information Systems, Inc.
Printed and bound by Thomson-Shore
Printed in the United States of America

99 98 97 96 95 C 5 4 3 2 1

Library of Congress Cataloging in Publication Data

Jonza, Nancylee Novell.

The underground stream : the life and art of Caroline

Gordon / Nancylee Novell Jonza.

p. cm.

Includes bibliographical references and index.

ISBN 0-8203-1628-8 (alk. paper)

1. Gordon, Caroline, 1895– . 2. Women novelists, American—
20th century—Biography. 3. Southern States in literature.

I. Title.

PS3513.05765Z72   1995

813'.52—dc20

[B]   93-30366

British Library Cataloging in Publication Data available

TO JAMES & MATTHEW

CONTENTS

PREFACE

During the summer of 1935, Caroline Gordon wrote her friend Katherine Anne Porter about "a young man doing a biography of Hart Crane." "He says he wants Hart's personality to take entire possession of him before he starts writing—the idea might appall any of Hart's old friends," Gordon wrote. "Still I suppose that is the way biography gets written. Only I can't see how the biographer can ever make his way through the maze."

Any biographer of Gordon might feel the same way. Gordon lived a hectic, wandering life; she seldom dated letters, often lost important papers, and destroyed others when she felt they might be damaging to those she loved. Any biographer who wanted to let Gordon's personality "take entire possession" of her before writing would have to embrace not only her genius but also her demon: her generous spirit matched by her angry rages, her self-destructive behavior and her self-protective posturing, sometimes twin sides of the same coin.

Still, it is worthwhile to work through the maze. Until recently Caroline Gordon's literary reputation has been based in large part on misleading and inadequate portraits of her as a woman and a writer. Gordon was almost always judged in the context of her relationships—especially her marriage—and not as a woman and writer in her own right. And this is how Gordon wanted it: many, if not all, of these portraits are the result of Gordon's self-conscious posturing.

From the 1950s until her death in 1981, Gordon worked hard to establish a public myth about her life to guide interpretations of her art. According to her public myth she was a conservative southern lady married to an equally conservative southern gentleman, Allen Tate, a critic and poet who taught Gordon almost everything she knew about writing. Although her fiction was never a popular success, Gordon was known for her technical excellence. A "writer's writer," she believed in old-fashioned values: men were meant to be leaders and sometimes called to be heroes; women were always called to be submissive to men.

During her lifetime scholars and critics willingly accepted Gordon's public myth as fact. In works written during the last half of her life, Gordon was usually sketched in the shadow of her more famous husband. Some critics went as far as to suggest that she "copied" Tate's beliefs and turned them into fiction. Most misread both biography and art when discussing Gordon's marriage and her conversion to Catholicism in the 1940s. When Frederick P. W. McDowell published the first serious study of Gordon in 1966, he described her marriage as "a happy and understanding relationship" in which she was "encouraged to devote herself, without dissipation of her energies, to the artist's career." Nothing could be further from the truth. But later writers did not swerve substantially from McDowell's perspective, implying that Tate was Gordon's mentor, the "great mind" and benevolent teacher who guided her into the world of letters and into the Catholic church.

Recent biographies of Gordon managed to destroy some of these public myths, but not all. Ann Waldron's *Close Connections: Caroline Gordon and the Southern Renaissance* sketches a vivid, truthful picture of most of Gordon's life. Waldron devotes little attention, however, to Gordon's fiction and, like Veronica Makowsky after her, does not investigate Gordon's experience as a journalist. Neither one questions Gordon's assertions about her education, and in the end both biographies deemphasize the first thirty and last twenty years of Gordon's life, once again implying that Gordon is important only in her connection to Tate and other figures of the Southern Renaissance.

This is unfortunate. Gordon's marriage may have been a large portion of and controlling influence on her life, but Gordon lived more years of her life without Tate than she did with him. And he could hardly be seen as her mentor. When they first met, Gordon was twenty-eight years old, four years older than Tate. She had already nearly six years' experience as a professional journalist, a keen desire to write fiction, and a clear set of literary standards that would never change. Tate may have introduced her to new literary circles, but his influence on her writing in the early years of their relationship was minimal. While writing her first novel, Gordon told her friend and fellow writer Josephine Herbst that

Tate had "no interest whatever in the modern novel." "I never even think of showing him anything I write unless he hounds me into it," Gordon said. This state of affairs continued for some years and was confirmed by Tate as well. In a 1929 letter to John Peale Bishop, Tate admitted that Gordon knew more about the art of fiction than he did.

What caused Gordon to change her mind and call Tate her primary teacher is part of what I explore in this book, an account of Gordon's private struggle to make sense of her world in fact and fiction. This struggle began in her childhood, and it worked itself out over the next seventy years in both life and art. At its most fundamental level, the struggle involved Gordon's sense of self and her gender identity. Born into a community and culture with complex and rigidly structured gender roles, Gordon found herself at an early age negotiating the boundaries between expectations and reality. Gordon grew up with two brothers, went to school with the boys, and matched their achievements with apparent ease, but she soon discovered that her appearance and behavior often counted more in others' judgments of her. The women in Gordon's family "connection" were strong-willed and often highly educated, a force to be reckoned with in the family and community. Yet these same women often adopted more traditional public personas or hid behind figurehead men.

Far from discouraging Gordon from a literary career, many of her female relatives wrote, either professionally or as an avocation, and Gordon followed in the footsteps of one of her cousins to serve a writing apprenticeship, working for newspapers in Tennessee and West Virginia. When she abandoned journalism for fiction, Gordon continued to draw strength and inspiration from the women of her family—especially her maternal grandmother, Carrie Meriwether. "Old Miss Carrie" was perhaps the most powerful of the Meriwethers—male and female alike. She appeared as the main character in Gordon's first story, then became an instigating force in at least three of Gordon's novels and her most famous short story, "Old Red." Even when Old Miss Carrie was not physically present, her point of view—the Meriwether family mythology—animated most of Gordon's fiction.

Yet in her work both as a journalist and as a fiction writer, Gordon revealed her awareness of the complexity of her own role as woman and writer. Acutely conscious of gender distinctions and discriminations, Gordon consciously strove to write prose that was not identifiably female or feminine. This, she believed, would help others take her writing seriously. She wrote about battles and the Civil War because she felt no woman could do so; she created a fictional autobiography based on her father's life and was delighted to receive fan mail that insisted that "Caroline Gordon" had to be a pen name for a male author, because no woman could get all that fishing and hunting lore so straight. Yet she discovered that such achievements did not really resolve the conflicts she faced: she still felt torn between being a "true woman" (in the traditional sense, dependent on men) and being an artist (and therefore an independent thinker and creator). "While I am a woman I am also a freak," she wrote a friend. "The work I do is not suitable for a woman. It is unsexing."

This internal struggle was complicated by conflicting views of Gordon's family history. Ultimately the family mythology might be described more as a family feud, a battle between the Meriwethers and Caroline's father, J. M. Gordon, a battle that was waged in life before it ever became fiction. The Meriwethers had once been great landowners in the area of the Tennessee-Kentucky border. They had known power and influence, and even the devastation of the Civil War, which drained their family fortunes, could not change their exalted views of themselves and their land. Gordon grew up with their grandiose stories about Meriwether heroes and their love for the land, but these stories were always challenged, often mocked, by another great storyteller, her father, James M. Gordon, a man who had his own extended family yet fled from nothing faster than family ties.

As a child Gordon would often feel caught between conflicting loyalties. Gordon was brought up, for the most part, by her grandmother, and she loved the old woman dearly. But Gordon was her father's favorite child, and when she lived with her parents, she declared allegiance to her father, not her mother. Throughout her childhood and young adult years, Gordon struggled to negotiate her way through emotional mine fields, and the tug-of-war between Meriwether and Gordon points of view eventually became the central tension in her fiction, a tension that matched and perhaps manifested Gordon's inner struggle with gender identity. Far from being blindly celebratory of her southern heritage (personified in the Meriwether tales), Gordon could turn a sharply critical eye on its history by simply adopting her father's perspective, setting fictional members of both families in opposition.

Although this drama inspired Gordon's writing, it also complicated her personal life. Not long after their marriage, Tate aligned himself with the Gordon viewpoint, and in time he insisted that his wife abandon her

Meriwether attachments in life and fiction. The result was subterfuge and self-deception: Gordon's public myth was born, in part as an attempt to falsely reassure Tate that he was the most important influence on his wife's life and talent.

A pattern of alcoholism and abuse exacerbated the problems in Gordon's marriage. Both Tate and Gordon drank heavily from the beginning of their relationship, and their life together followed patterns clearly identified by recent empirical studies of alcoholic and abusive relationships. For Tate, excessive drinking fueled erratic behavior marked by a condescending attitude, moodiness, self-centeredness, unfaithfulness, and emotionally abusive remarks. For Gordon, alcohol combined with Tate's behavior often resulted in violent rages—toward Tate and others —and equally disastrous self-destructive behavior. Like Tate, Gordon sometimes adopted a superior stance, blaming her husband for their troubles and insisting that she knew better than he how to "fix" their lives; but more often—especially in the last half of their life together— Gordon turned on herself. Like many victims of abuse, she told herself that if only she acted differently, if only she were a different person, Tate's behavior and their life together would be different. Countless times, she declared that she (or things) had changed. Such declarations—often flying in the face of reality—gave Gordon a deceptive sense of self-control. They are typical of women in abusive and alcoholic relationships, and they may help to explain why, during the last three decades of her life, Gordon insisted that she learned everything she knew about writing from Tate and other men.

To appreciate the nature of Gordon's achievement as a woman and as a writer, it is necessary to explore these and other aspects of her life that she carefully tried to hide. To do otherwise would not only perpetuate misleading and inadequate portraits of Gordon, but it would also contribute to mistaken assessments of the writers who touched her life, including but by no means limited to Tate.

When, in 1935, Gordon heard about the prospective biography of Hart Crane, she told Porter that she felt sorry for the biographer: he would have a difficult time penetrating the polite mask that Crane sometimes wore. He had once quarreled with Tate, Gordon pointed out, but no one could tell that by reading their letters. The same can be said of Gordon. The letters and autobiographical fictions that she wrote during the last three decades of her life mask more than they reveal; they are, in fact, responsible for most of the inaccurate portraits that abound. Yet perhaps because she could sympathize with her later biographers, Gordon left a few hints in her papers to point a careful reader to another reality. This book is the result, an attempt to draw a more accurate portrait of a woman and artist by looking behind the mask of life and under the surface of Gordon's fiction to reveal both the joys and the terrors of her life and art.

ACKNOWLEDGMENTS

I would not have completed this book without the help and encouragement of many people. Caroline Gordon's daughter, Nancy Tate Wood, and her husband, Dr. Percy H. Wood, helped me in numerous ways. I appreciate their permission to quote from Gordon's unpublished papers as well as their openness in sharing their lives and memories. I will never forget their kind hospitality and the way they helped to bring the characters in this book alive for me. I am also grateful to Cleanth Brooks, Danforth and Dorothy Ross, and Elizabeth Brown, who shared their memories with me.

I began this book in early 1985 as a seminar project for a graduate course in biography, and I am deeply grateful to my professor, Stephen B. Oates, who became my dissertation director. He encouraged and challenged me, reading both critically and sympathetically, and helped me to discover my own love for the art and technique of biography. I also appreciate the work of the other members of my dissertation committee: Lucien Miller and David T. Porter.

Countless friends and colleagues supported and encouraged me along the way. I especially appreciate the help of colleagues at the University of St. Thomas: Elizabeth Parr, Joy Linsley, Kerry Jones MacArthur, Mary Kelleher, and Suzanne Shumway of the English department, and Colleen Hester of the psychology department, all of whom supplied sympathetic ears, critical insight, and often very practical support during the final revision of this manuscript. I am also grateful for the help of Sara Laidlaw and Jason Tolbert, and for a faculty development grant from the University of St. Thomas to complete certain aspects of this work. Thomas Underwood generously shared with me information from his forthcoming biography of Allen Tate, and he and Joan Givner helped me a great deal in my efforts to clarify some of my ideas about Gordon. Joanne Cavallaro and Faith Jaycox gave me personal and professional support when I needed it most, as did numerous friends who listened to my tales of triumph and woe for too many years to count: members of the St. Odilia Early Married Ministry in Shoreview, Minnesota (especially Bridget and Steve Christianson, Tim and Bonnie Elemes, Dan and MJ Moravec, and Jan and Rick Storms), Kate Bretscher, Gayle Gaskill, Cam and Reneé Murray, Jerry McCausland, Patsy Pelton, Ron and Marghe Tabar, and Maika Will. And I can never repay the kindness of friends who gave me a place to sleep, good food, and great conversation during my research trips: Chuck Bauer, Jean Curran, Michael and Karen Duni, Guerry and Karla Grune, Heidi and Geoff LeBaron, Paul and Sue Lucas, Armand and Jean Paradis, and Jerry and Toni Parmer.

In addition to Nancy Tate Wood's permission to quote from the unpublished papers of her mother and family, I appreciate Isabel Bayley's permission to quote from Katherine Anne Porter's unpublished letters; Mary Davidson Bell's permission to quote from the letters of Donald Davidson; Janice Biala's permission to quote from one of her own letters as well as those of Ford Madox Ford; Cleanth Brooks's permission to quote from one of his unpublished letters; John Burt and Eleanor Clark's permission to quote from Robert Penn Warren's unpublished letters, Robert Cowley's permission to quote from the unpublished letters of Malcolm Cowley; Helen Ransom Forman's permission to quote from the unpublished letters of John Crowe Ransom; Lincoln Kirstein's permission to quote from his unpublished letters; the Marine Midland Bank's permission to quote from the unpublished letters of Sally Wood Kohn; Danforth Ross's permission to quote from his unpublished article and notes on Gordon and Tate; Charles Scribner III's permission to quote from the unpublished business correspondence of Maxwell Perkins and Jack Wheelock; Timothy Seldes's permission to quote from an unpublished letter of Jean Stafford, and Helen H. Tate's permission to quote from Allen Tate's poetry and unpublished letters.

I also appreciate the permission of the following institutions to work in and use materials from their collections: the University of Arkansas, Bethany College, the Beinecke Rare Book and Manuscript Library of Yale University, Columbia University, Cornell University, the University of Dallas, the archives of the Disciples of Christ Historical Society in Nashville, Duke University, Emory University, the archives of the

Guggenheim Foundation, the Harry Ransom Humanities Research Center at the University of Texas, the Houghton Library, the University of Kansas, Marquette University, the University of Maryland, Memphis State University, the Newberry Library, the University of North Carolina at Chapel Hill, Princeton University, Stanford University, Syracuse University, the University of Tulsa, the Jean and Alexander Heard Library of Vanderbilt University, the University of Virginia, Washington University of St. Louis, Western Kentucky University, and Yale University. The letters from Caroline Gordon to Robert Lowell are published by permission of the Houghton Library, Harvard University. Letters and manuscripts from the William Meredith Papers, Ashley Brown Collection of Caroline Gordon Papers, Willard Thorp Papers, Allen Tate Papers, Morris Meriwether Gordon Papers, Caroline Gordon Papers, and the archives of Charles Scribner's Sons are published with permission of the Manuscripts Division, Department of Rare Books and Special Collections, Princeton University Libraries. Selections from "The Buried Lake" from *Collected Poems, 1919–1976* by Allen Tate, © 1977 by Allen Tate, are published with permission of Farrar, Straus and Giroux, Inc., and excerpts from *The Southern Mandarins: Letters of Caroline Gordon to Sally Wood, 1924–1937* are published with permission of the Louisiana State University Press.

Finally, I am grateful to Karen Orchard, Kelly Caudle, Ellen Harris, and the University of Georgia Press, and I must thank my family for years of support. Most of all, I thank my husband, James, for allowing Caroline Gordon into our lives, subsidizing my work, accompanying me on research trips, helping me search through reels of old microfilm, taking over much of the housework for several years, and, after the birth of our son, taking good care of Matthew and making it easier for me to keep writing. I could not have done this without him.

THE UNDERGROUND STREAM

THE MATRIARCH OF MERRY MONT

Even though she was not born with the Meriwether name, Caroline Champlain Ferguson revered all things Meriwether. Born in Todd County, Kentucky, in 1848, Carrie was the only daughter of John Ferguson and Nancy Minor Meriwether, and she spent her childhood at Woodstock, the home of her grandfather Charles Nicholas Meriwether. A fine estate, complete with a stable of thoroughbred horses, a racetrack, a hunting preserve, and an enclosed deer park, Woodstock represented security and stability to Carrie, a stability much needed because her father was often on the move, preaching the gospel as a Disciples of Christ circuit rider.

Woodstock also represented the achievements of the Meriwethers, and even after "the War" had taken its toll on the Meriwethers and their fortune, Carrie believed two things firmly: the Meriwether family was great, deserving of praise; and there was no better place to live than in the "Old Neighborhood" in Todd County, Kentucky.

Lest anyone disagree with her, Carrie could recite Meriwether family history as evidence. In the middle of the seventeenth century, Nicholas ("the Welshman") Meriwether had sent his sons to the colonies to settle a land grant he had received from Charles II. Before long, the descendants of Nicholas the Welshman had become numerous and important in the area around Charlottesville, Virginia. With slaves and land in abundance, they built mansions called Clover Fields, Castle Hill, and Kinloch, and counted most of Virginia's influential statesmen as neighbors or friends.

But the spirit of wanderlust that had driven the Meriwethers across an ocean would not rest forever. In 1804 Meriwether

Lewis set out to explore the area of the Louisiana Purchase with his friend William Clark, and in 1811 his cousin, Dr. Charles Meriwether, left Virginia to become one of the first to settle in the Cumberland Valley of Kentucky.

Although Meriwether Lewis certainly achieved great fame before his mysterious death in 1809, Carrie held her great-grandfather, Charles Meriwether, in equal or greater esteem. He had met and married his first wife, Lydia Laurie, in Edinburgh during his medical studies, but she and their infant daughter died on the voyage back to Virginia. His second wife, Nancy Minor, was from Virginia. According to family story she was quite a tomboy: when Dr. Charles first went to court her, he found her sitting in a cherry tree. She also died after only a few years of marriage, leaving one young son, Charles Nicholas Minor Meriwether.

After Dr. Charles married a young widow, Mary Walton, in the early 1800s, he left Piedmont Virginia with Mary and Charles Nicholas and went to Kentucky, then largely unsettled. Securing several thousand acres of land near the Tennessee border, he built a handsome home and, like his closest neighbors, the Barkers, began to raise tobacco.

In time Charles and Mary had two more sons. William Douglas Meriwether, the middle son, never married. He inherited his father's estate and became known to all as "Uncle Curious Will." Yet his younger brother, Dr. James Hunter Meriwether, far surpassed him in peculiar behavior. To pursue his medical "research," "Jeems" collected carcasses of dead cows, horses, dogs, and mules from throughout the county. According to family tradition he was often seen walking around in the moonlight by the big pile of bones heaped near the graveyard, muttering chemical formulas that sounded too much like incantations, his long white beard floating in the breezes.

The eldest son, Carrie's grandfather, Charles Nicholas Meriwether, pursued his personal pleasures just as seriously as his younger brother James pursued medical research. He built Woodstock soon after he married Caroline Huntley Barker in 1821. Named after one of the Sir Walter Scott novels Dr. Charles loved so well, Woodstock took more than five years and the profits from three crops to build, but it was magnificent.

Charles Nicholas and Caroline went on to fill their fine home with five children, all of whom married and provided them with more than twice as many grandchildren. The family prospered until the outbreak of war caused them to put aside their personal pleasures and devote themselves to a higher cause. Soon the stables were bare: Charles Nicholas willingly outfitted Confederate soldiers with Woodstock horses. The Meriwethers' youngest daughter, Caroline Douglas, organized nursing stations and filled the family ballroom with women rolling bandages and sewing uniforms. One by one, members of the family enlisted. Charles Nicholas's eldest son, Charles Edward, known as Ned, was one of the first. He recruited a company called the Meriwether Independent Rangers to serve under the Confederate leader Nathan Bedford Forrest. But Ned's military career was short. A few days after Christmas in 1861, he was killed in the Battle of Sacramento.

Carrie, like all the Meriwethers, immortalized Uncle Ned's death, speaking as if the Battle of Sacramento were one of the major battles of "the War." Actually, it was little more than a skirmish. Ned and Forrest had outridden their support and were ambushed by a regiment of Yankees just a short distance from the Meriwether family home. Forrest escaped quite miraculously. Ned died a hero, at least in the eyes of his family.

The Meriwether support of the War Between the States all but destroyed the family's fortunes. When the war ended, the glory days of Woodstock ended as well. In time the great old house was sold. For Carrie that was the greatest tragedy, akin to being cast out of Eden. Yet it did not change her perspective on either the Meriwethers or the Old Neighborhood. Instead, she championed both all the more.

And after marrying her cousin Douglas Meriwether in 1867, Carrie gradually assumed the status of family matriarch. So as not to leave the Old Neighborhood, she insisted they live not on his family land but on hers, a small farm called Merry Mont not far from Woodstock. Douglas did not, apparently, put up a fight: he was a weak-willed man, exhausted from the emotional shock and malnutrition he endured during his service in the Confederate army. Carrie brought up their four children almost single-handedly. But she was more than equal to the task. In fact, in time Carrie became known as something of a tyrant: a woman whom everyone respected but no one wanted to emulate.

Her four children all rebelled in some fashion or other, in often-futile attempts to escape their mother's clutches. Loulie, the oldest daughter, created her own religion; her brother, Rob, refused to bathe and repeatedly muttered about the tyranny of women. The youngest, Margaret, also known as Pidie because she was as "sweet as pie dough," played the part of the southern belle and surrounded herself with plenty of beaux. The middle daughter, Nancy Minor, known as Nan, retreated into fundamentalism and scholarship, marrying the family tutor, James Morris Gordon.

Carrie apparently approved of her daughter's choice because Gordon was related to the Meriwethers in a far-flung way, his family also hailing from Virginia. His great-grandfather, James Gordon of Orange, had been a member of the Virginia convention of 1788 that ratified the Constitution, and his grandfather William Fitzhugh Gordon, Sr., had been a soldier statesman known for his oratorical power and his opposition to Jacksonian democracy.

But J. M. Gordon could puzzle Miss Carrie: he did not venerate his family the way the Meriwethers did, perhaps because his own family memories were bittersweet. Although his father, William Fitzhugh Gordon, Jr., had begun his career as a lawyer, soon after his marriage to Nancy Morris he had retired to a six-hundred-acre estate in Louisa County, Virginia, and taken up a "literary life." He read Plato while sitting under the trees at Oakleigh, spouted Shakespeare to his children at the dinner table, and spent the last year of his life putting Sir Walter Scott's *The Bride of Lammermoor* into blank verse. Once a cousin found William sitting in his library at two o'clock in the morning weeping bitterly. "Don't cry, Cousin William! Cousin Nancy has just had a beautiful baby boy!" she said. Wiping his eyes, William said, "I ain't cryin' about Nancy! I'm cryin' about *Effie Dean!*"—the heroine of Scott's *Heart of Midlothian*.

J. M. Gordon did not appreciate his father's literary obsessions, and as a young man he spent a fair amount of time out West, trying perhaps to forget his family. But J. M. Gordon also had a love of great literature, especially Greek and Latin mythology. Eventually he tried to make his living as a teacher, and in 1883 that endeavor had brought him to Todd County, Kentucky, to tutor the Meriwether children. In time he fell in love with his best student, Nancy Minor Meriwether. A gifted linguist, Nan had dreaming eyes and light brown hair that framed her face in soft curls. When she was seventeen and Gordon twenty-nine, they married.

Nan apparently thought marriage would give her a reason to move away from Merry Mont and her mother's autocratic ways. Yet she did not get her wish. Although Gordon considered the Meriwethers a peculiar bunch, he did not yet mind living in the Old Neighborhood. The area had great hunting and fishing, and J. M. Gordon loved both to excess.

Miss Carrie was ecstatic, Nan far from pleased. And after her first child was born in 1891, Nan grew increasingly unhappy. At Merry Mont Miss

Carrie controlled everyone and everything. She even thought she controlled Nan's son, Morris. Every time Nan tried to care for Morris, Miss Carrie cried out, "Run, quick! Nan's got the baby."

Eager to get away, Nan began to urge her husband to consider a career in the ministry. It would not make them rich, but it would give them a reason to move, a respectable reason at that. Although originally Baptists and Methodists, many of the Meriwethers and Fergusons had experienced a religious conversion in the early 1820s when the evangelist Alexander Campbell came through Kentucky and Tennessee establishing local congregations of "Christians" or "Disciples of Christ." Several of the Ferguson men, including Miss Carrie's father, became noted Campbellite preachers. Campbell's followers believed in the supremacy of the New Testament: baptism by immersion and a regular reenactment of the Lord's Supper were the only practices they accepted as scriptural. By abolishing "human religious creeds" and by restoring the "Ancient Order of Things" recorded in the Gospels, the Disciples hoped to unite all Christians.

Although the movement was sometimes dismissed as a backwoods religion, Campbell's followers were often highly educated, and they were always outspoken and articulate in defense of their faith. And so it probably surprised no one when J. M. Gordon followed his wife's suggestion and became a Disciples of Christ minister. Although he would always be more interested in fishing for trout than in fishing for souls, J. M. Gordon was a superb preacher. Combining in his new vocation his love for teaching with his bent for scholarship, Gordon laced his sermons with classical quotations and illustrations. Before long he was making a name for himself as a preacher.

But much to his wife's dismay, Gordon had no great ambition as a minister. Instead, he was content to continue living at Merry Mont, teaching the local children and preaching only occasionally at neighborhood churches. Nan was undoubtedly upset, but she would not stop trying to flee the matriarch of Merry Mont.

1895–1924

It was a scene Nancy Meriwether Gordon would never forget and would always regret. On October 6, 1895, Nan gave birth to her second child, a little girl. Not long after the birth, an old black nurse leaned over the cradle and eyed the baby girl. "Better name this child for Miss Carrie," the old woman told Nan. "She the one going to do the most for her."

Nan must have shuddered at the idea. She and her husband, James Morris Gordon, and their four-year-old son, Morris, were still living at Merry Mont, the home of Nan's mother, Caroline Ferguson Meriwether. A short, solid woman with piercing blue eyes, a strong, determined mouth, and silvered hair pulled severely back off her face, Miss Carrie had undoubtedly presided over the baby's birth: she presided over everything at Merry Mont, often in a way that frustrated or annoyed those around her. Although Nan would expect that a namesake would please her mother, she must have feared losing control of her daughter. Four years earlier, Miss Carrie had easily established dominion over Nan's first child, Morris.

But the old nurse's suggestion fell in line with family tradition. Nan had been named for her maternal grandmother, just as Miss Carrie had been named for hers in turn. And so the baby daughter of Nan and James Morris Gordon became Carolyn Ferguson Gordon, or Little Miss Carrie for short.

The Gordon family continued to live at Merry Mont for several years. J. M. Gordon taught as well as preached occasionally, and Old Miss Carrie was happy to keep everyone related to her close at hand.

Little Miss Carrie's second brother, William Fitzhugh Gordon, known as Billy or Will, was born the following year, but the young girl remained her grandmother's favorite child. She did not look like her grandmother. Rather, Little Miss Carrie looked like her father. She had his dark coloring and bushy eyebrows, one slightly higher than the other, not the fair hair and blue eyes of the Meriwethers. Yet, as the nurse had foretold, Old Miss Carrie would do anything for her name-sake, and before long everyone, especially young Carrie, knew it. Carrie's childhood pranks and tantrums were tolerated more than those of the other children; she always got the best seat and best food at meals; and, most important, she always knew Old Miss Carrie loved and accepted her without question.

It did not take long for Nan to lose all patience with her mother as young Carrie apparently became the rope in a deadly serious tug-of-war between the two women. By the time Carrie was six years old, Nan was totally exasperated. Nan and her husband had moved away from Merry Mont to take jobs teaching at South Kentucky College, but after the Christmas holidays in 1901, young Carrie stayed at Merry Mont for an extended visit with her grandmother. Although Nan repeatedly begged her mother to send the girl back home, the old woman could not be swayed. As late as February, she was still inventing reasons why it would be "utterly impossible" to allow Carrie to leave. Nan was furious. "If I ever have another child I'll not name it after anybody," she declared.

But Nan's troubles had only just begun. As soon as Little Miss Carrie was old enough to sense the disagreements between her mother and grandmother, she was quick to take sides with her grandmother, whom she called Ma.

There were more than enough differences in temperament and personality to intensify the women's competition for the young girl. Ma would spend her days gardening and visiting kin; Nan was more likely to spend hers reading. Ma had great patience with her favorite grandchild, but Nan had increasingly high expectations for her only daughter.

Yet perhaps it was not so much a battle between the two women for young Carrie's affections as a battle between places, Merry Mont versus anyplace else. And from a very young age, Carrie preferred Merry Mont. The old gray house was cramped and ugly, but it was surrounded by wonderful fields and forests that Carrie loved to explore. There was something about the way the sunlight filtered through the leaves of the trees that made her feel happy and secure. Carrie learned to read the light and trees; she knew the way distance made the woods on the far horizon shine a different color from the trees close at hand and how the trees changed from the forest's edge to its depths. In the heart of the forest, the oaks and sycamores created a green world that Carrie loved to wander through. Often, as she wrote years later, she felt as if she were "moving through water as much as through air." When evening came, she left the woods reluctantly.

Carrie's love for Merry Mont and its environs was not unusual. Nan herself had a certain fondness for the place and brought her children back to Kentucky every summer for a long visit, no matter where the Gordons were living. But for young Carrie, a summer visit was hardly enough; she would, if given the choice, spend all her time at Merry Mont. And it was probably no small frustration for the young girl to discover that her grandmother would as willingly indulge such a decision as her own mother would readily deny the possibility of choice.

Carrie certainly felt the family tensions keenly, and sometimes the pressures were too much for her. At least once, Carrie tried to escape, and she would never forget that day. It was her first conscious memory: she thought it took place late in the afternoon of her fourth birthday, but she could never be sure. Yet Carrie remembered the rest of the details vividly. As the sun began to set, casting "a shower of gold coins upon the dark earth" outside the house, she stood alone in her grandmother's darkening bedroom. Beside one of the windows was a washstand, and on the washstand was an old tin basin, full of water someone had used and forgotten to empty. While staring at the light playing on the water, Carrie heard a hoarse cry she couldn't identify. She thought it might be a bird, or some animal being led to slaughter, or even "the muted, soaring lament" of the black field hands at work, but whatever it was, it seemed to Carrie to be "speaking of some apparently unassuageable distress."

As it sounded again, Carrie felt surrounded by shadowy companions. Suddenly she thought "it was all going to be too much" for her to take, so in a panic, she buried her head in the basin. The water seemed deep, "deep enough to drown in." But she didn't drown. Instead, against her will, she came up for air. She would never forget the surprise she felt— she was still breathing. At once, and much to her dismay, she realized "that was no way out."

DESPITE the anxiety she sometimes felt, young Carrie came to cherish her childhood at Merry Mont, seeing it as a strangely idyllic time. Life at Merry Mont was primitive. Without indoor plumbing the kin had to bathe in tubs set out each day to warm beneath the flat metal roof of the front porch. Money was often scarce or nonexistent. But there was always plenty to eat and plenty to do: horses to ride, fields and streams to explore, and a vast connection of kin with stories to tell to anyone who would listen.

By the fall of 1905, Carrie was able to spend almost as much time at Merry Mont as she pleased: her parents had set up a classical preparatory school for boys in Clarksville, Tennessee, just across the Cumberland River from Kentucky. The school was on the east side of the ground floor of a large brick house on Madison Street. The family lived in the rest of the two-story house.

Nan Gordon taught in the school with her husband, and Carrie was one of only a few girl students. The boys studied Latin, Greek, mathematics, and English literature. Carrie's program was similar, except her father let her quit studying math when she reached fractions: "No Gordon can understand Mathematics until his mind matures," he said.

Carrie had a great deal of freedom in her studies. When the boys had Latin instruction, she joined them to recite Horace and Virgil, but otherwise she worked alone on her lessons. She knew she could have "any amount of help" from either of her parents, but years later she would insist "it did not occur to them to offer it," and Carrie, fiercely independent, was not likely to ask.

Sometimes she did ask if she could go to the private girls' school in town, but J. M. Gordon would not hear of it. Carrie wouldn't learn anything there, he said; she was better off studying with the boys. So Carrie remained in her father's school, reading in the *Eclogues* of Virgil, reciting the Twelve Labors of Heracles, listening to her father declaim Shakespeare, Tennyson, Coleridge, and Scott. On her own she read poetry by Yeats and novels by George Eliot and Mary Johnston.

Classes were always over by two in the afternoon, so Carrie's father could get in some good hours fishing in Spring Creek or in the West Fork of the Red River, and Carrie indulged herself with frequent visits to Merry Mont. Sometimes Carrie would ride with her grandmother on her neighborhood rounds or go swimming in Spring Creek. Other times she roamed in the fields and woods around Merry Mont.

Sometimes Carrie composed stories that she recited to herself on her rambles. She called her stories her "work"—and years later she would marvel at how easy that "work" seemed. Usually, her stories focused on the adventures of a young girl just a few years older than Carrie. The heroine would be pretty, with fair hair and light eyes: just the way Carrie wished she could be, not homely, with eyes as black as coal. The adventures followed the pattern of Carrie's childhood reading of the stories of Uncle Remus, *The Three Musketeers,* and the Brothers Grimm. Everything took place as the fair-haired creature "wandered happily along the border of a sunlit wood," Carrie wrote later.

Yet Carrie's real education in storytelling came from her grandmother and kin during lazy spring and summer afternoons. At those times the Meriwether women could usually be found sitting on the narrow front porch at Merry Mont. The weathered gray house stood in a thick grove of sugar maples that helped to temper the bright sunlight. But nothing tempered the caustic tongues of the Meriwether women.

They talked about the kin—the "connection," they called it: the generations of Meriwethers, Fergusons, and Barkers who, after years of intermarriage, had become a tangled web of relations with more than a few eccentrics. Miss Carrie set the tone of the afternoon with acerbic observations on odd or erring kinfolk. Known for her uneven temper, Miss Carrie could wither the strongest soul with a quick, biting retort— "I don't like your blood," she might say. And once she had made up her mind, no one could change it.

During these afternoon sessions Carrie Gordon often sat listening on the steps at the edge of the porch. A small girl with dark black eyes and hair, and a slightly crooked nose, Carrie was a quiet, brooding child. To draw too close to the women's circle would invite their criticism or dismissal, but Carrie often took the risk: the women told wonderful stories, and Carrie was captivated by their tales.

Sometimes the women recounted family stories from years gone by, stories of their most famous ancestor, Meriwether Lewis, who explored the west with William Clark, or of Dr. Charles Meriwether, the first of their line to settle in the Cumberland Valley of Kentucky. Young Carrie couldn't be counted on to keep track of all the generations of Meriwethers, but she did learn to divide and classify the entire connection into its two branches: the Kinky Heads and the Anyhows. The Kinky Heads—so called because, according to some family members, they had "kinks in their heads"—went in for noble ideals and causes; they were the extremists and eccentrics. Before the Civil War, Kinky Head Meriwethers worked in the abolition movement and espoused forms of utopianism. After the war they supported the women's rights movement and took up spiritualism.

The Anyhows, on the other hand, had little interest in any organized forms or beliefs: they did "anyhow they pleased." Miss Carrie was an Anyhow, which may have accounted for a certain prejudice in the classification scheme, but the women on the porch could be equally disparaging of both branches.

Carrie was especially fond of their stories about how Great-great-great-uncle Jeems collected carcasses of dead livestock for medical research. She also loved to hear about Miss Carrie's father, John D. Ferguson, a true Kinky Head. If the Spirit moved him, John Ferguson would sacrifice home and family for the call of the gospel. The women on the porch liked to repeat one of his more memorable sayings, an apology the preacher sent his daughter when he found he could not meet her as promised but instead had to take a steamboat down the river. "In these days of steam," he said, "there is little opportunity for the manifestation of paternal affection."

These stories and many others mesmerized Carrie Gordon; she could sit for hours on the steps to the porch. While the afternoon sunlight cast a golden glow on the old gray house and dark earth, the women talked about how Cousin Garrett freed his slaves and took up silk farming, or how Susan Meriwether, one of Carrie's great-grandmothers, got her nickname "Mammy Horse" as a nurse on Civil War battlefields. The Meriwethers were no longer wealthy planters. Some even said they were all quite crazy after years of intermarriage. Still, these tales of Meriwethers past and present took on heroic, epic proportions in the young girl's dark eyes. Later in life, Carrie would think she had really seen Uncle Jeems walking around his bone pile in the moonlight.

Carrie also heard so many stories about "the War" that she began to think she had been in it. Throughout her childhood, there were a number of Civil War veterans living at Merry Mont who added to the family stories. "Cousin" Henry Hoard, deafened by cannons in the siege of Fort Donelson, was a permanent boarder in a small, one-room building behind Merry Mont. Old Mr. McEvoy, who fought with the Tenth Tennessee at the battle of Chickamauga, lived for a number of years in one of the "tenant" cabins, and Carrie would never forget the day he died. Her grandmother sent her running upstairs to get Uncle Ned's sword from one of the closets to hang above McEvoy's deathbed. "I was in the Bloody Tinth," he cried out as he died; "I was in the Bloody Tinth . . ." That phrase haunted young Carrie. She wasn't sure why the old man spoke with such pride about the "Bloody Tinth," but later she realized. The Tenth Tennessee sent 500 men into the battle of Chickamauga; only 160 came back.

Whether or not Carrie understood them, the family stories about "the War" worked powerfully on her imagination. From an early age Carrie learned from the women on the porch to love the South, hate the North, and lament the passing of the Meriwethers' glory days. In many ways that learning was epitomized in the life of Old Miss Carrie, whose story Carrie Gordon came to know well. Over and over again, she heard about her grandmother's childhood and the grandeur of Woodstock with its fine horses and life of leisure. For Old Miss Carrie—and her grand-daughter—Woodstock would always represent greatness and tragedy, a sign of the Meriwethers' stature and of the terrible price of defeat.

But rather than seeing her grandmother as a victim of that terrible time, young Carrie came to see her as a heroine. She learned how Miss Carrie was the one to deal with the aftermath of war, because her husband, Douglas Meriwether, battered by his war service, preferred to spend his time in quiet study before he committed suicide by taking an overdose of headache medicine. From the young girl's point of view, Old Miss Carrie had the strength, insight, and courage to survive. Among all the tales told and retold by the women on the porch, her grandmother's story left an indelible mark on young Carrie's mind and imagination.

But the image was a troubling one at times, because young Carrie could not avoid hearing other stories about her grandmother, other descriptions hardly flattering. When Miss Carrie was away on an errand, the rest of the women on the porch—her daughters, nieces, and cousins—would discuss the matriarch of Merry Mont with the same cutting tones she used on others. Miss Carrie, they said, was "hell on wheels," utterly capricious, sometimes vindictive, downright mean: she even shook her buggy whip at the smaller children to keep them on good behavior. And she did not treat her only son, Rob, a grown man, any better. Rob ran the farm for his mother, but it was a frustrating, thankless task, since the old woman would never really relinquish control over the place. Young Carrie adored her Uncle Rob, a kind, gentle man who was never too busy to stop and play with her, and she was disturbed by her grandmother's behavior toward him. Years later Carrie insisted that Rob regularly preached a kind of sermon in the tradition of John Knox's diatribe entitled "Against the Monstrous Regiment of Women."

The women on the porch knew some of Old Miss Carrie's meanness

was just a façade. Rob deserved some of the bad treatment he received—
he was incredibly foolish about business matters. And Old Miss Carrie
always kept a jar full of delicious sugar cookies on the dining-room
sideboard for the same children she terrorized. There was, however, no
accounting for Miss Carrie's moods or temper. When someone crossed
her, she struck out fiercely.

The family told stories about Miss Carrie with a mixture of love, fear,
and humor. Miss Carrie had more than a few absurd convictions. She
would have no screens on her windows because she didn't like to breathe
"sifted air." She believed in a natural superiority of all things Meriwether.
Miss Carrie would even ignore the taste of onions in her milk because,
she insisted, no Meriwether cow would eat onions. No one dared argue
with her, but her relatives wouldn't hesitate to talk about her behind
her back.

Carrie Gordon heard all this and more from her vantage point at
the edge of the porch. When her aunts and older cousins noticed her,
they didn't stop criticizing the child's grandmother but simply changed
their focus.

Do you think she'll grow up to be like Miss Carrie? someone would
ask. A cousin or aunt would then point out a few "Miss Carrian" traits
in the girl. Little Miss Carrie was certainly impatient, just like her grandmother. And at an early age she had developed a bad habit of angry outbursts. Once young Carrie even stood on the porch, stamping her feet,
and yelled, "Hush, dog," at her aunts. The jury on the porch wouldn't
have to deliberate long: Little Miss Carrie was doomed to follow in her
grandmother's footsteps.

Young Carrie listened to the women with a mixture of fascination,
anger, and fear. She loved her grandmother deeply and knew how lucky
she was to be Miss Carrie's namesake. Still, the young girl hated being
called Little Miss Carrie. She had seen how badly her grandmother could
treat people, and after a while the idea of growing up to be just like Miss
Carrie scared her.

The women on the porch seldom criticized the Gordon boys as they
did Carrie. With perfect manners and ingratiating airs, Carrie's older
brother, Morris, charmed most adults, and young Billy was his mother's
favorite child. Also, both boys were quite good looking. Carrie would
never forget the time she overheard one of her aunts compare her with
Morris and Billy: "it was too bad," her aunt said, "that Carrie was so
homely and both of the boys so handsome."

Carrie sometimes felt inadequate next to her brothers, and Morris liked to take advantage of that. He often tried to control his siblings at play, and he especially liked to scare Billy and Carrie with tales about Aunt Emily, a large black woman who lived at Woodstock and supposedly ate little black children for dinner. Once, Morris pointed out one little boy at Woodstock being specially fattened for her next feast. Carrie was terrified. Carrie, however, ultimately would not be cowed by anyone, and she had little patience with Morris when he tried to tell her what to do. Once Morris tried to blackmail her into mastering her Greek lessons by refusing to help her hitch up the pony until she had conjugated a Greek verb for him. Carrie would have none of that. She just learned to handle the pony by herself.

Later, when Morris flaunted his freedom to go somewhere his sister was not allowed to go, Carrie showed she could handle him as well. She locked her brother in an upstairs closet at Merry Mont and went off crowing. As was her habit, she took the fastest exit, sliding down the banister on her stomach. Yet this time Carrie's pride upset her balance: she hit the floor hard, knocking out several teeth.

Miss Carrie wasn't surprised by her granddaughter's accident; she just sent one of the kin for the doctor. But such an escapade only confirmed the suspicions of the women on the porch: the child was too impulsive, too much like Miss Carrie. Even J. M. Gordon agreed: his daughter was "too quick on the uptake," he thought. Carrie felt the mildest slights deeply, and she struck out swiftly at anyone who dared to circumscribe her world. Little Miss Carrie was a miniature tyrant of Merry Mont, sometimes playful, sometimes desperately serious.

It might have been easier for the child to leave the porch and stop listening to the women's litany of Carrian traits and destinies. But in between the indictments and sarcasm, the women told wonderful stories, and Carrie was captivated by their tales. There was only one problem: Carrie was not a full Meriwether. She did not even have the family name. As if to take a place in the family saga, she wished fervently for Meriwether as a middle name. "Caroline Meriwether Gordon"—that would be a name to treasure.

But Carrie was named for her Ferguson kin, and if folks hadn't known she was Nancy Meriwether's daughter, some might not have guessed she had any other relation to the Meriwether connection. Kinfolk inspecting the girl for signs of resemblance pronounced her "a perfect

Gordon"—which, for Carrie, "was no compliment, [but] neither was it a condemnation."

In a way it was a symbol of how Carrie was part of the Meriwether connection and yet an outsider. Both her grandmother's darling and her father's favorite child, Carrie was once again caught between warring factions, and although the players were not seriously antagonistic, Carrie felt torn by the conflict. While Old Miss Carrie championed all things Meriwether, J. M. Gordon increasingly ridiculed them. He was not at all taken in by the Meriwether family myth; in fact, sometimes Carrie's father was annoyingly proud that he wasn't a Meriwether. His habit of mocking the Meriwethers both horrified and delighted his daughter. He had no patience with their claims to greatness of any sort. "No member of the Meriwether connection . . . ever poked his head above the dull level of mediocrity," he would say.

The Meriwethers found it hard to believe someone wouldn't want a place in their connection. Miss Carrie used to say that the Meriwether name was so revered that "if a dog belonging to a Meriwether ran through the yard of a pregnant woman, the child would have Meriwether for its middle name." Sometimes, perhaps in self-defense, the Meriwethers gave J. M. Gordon a dose of his own mocking. They teased him about his tremendous size: Gordon was a large man, nearly two hundred pounds, and he could eat thirteen slices of ham for supper. They also made fun of his overwhelming passion for sport, a passion easily mistaken for laziness and lack of ambition.

At those times his daughter Carrie found herself wandering in a sort of no-man's-land between enemy camps. She loved her father as much as she loved Miss Carrie and the Meriwethers, and she would never like being forced to choose sides. When her aunts and cousins began to make fun of her father, Carrie would join in, but only if she was sure he wouldn't find out. Just as often as she sat listening to the women on the porch talk of Meriwether glories gone by, she sat listening to her father and his stories. At night, when he could no longer fish or hunt, he would be the one sitting on the porch, surrounded by the women and children, and almost everyone agreed that J. M. Gordon was the best storyteller around.

Carrie's father loved to talk about the heroes of Greek and Roman myth—Heracles, Prometheus, Aeneas, and Odysseus—but Carrie's favorite stories were her father's tales about hunting and fishing—about his battles with a sly fox named Old Red and his success with Old Speck, a lure with "powers bordering on the supernatural," Carrie believed. She would never forget the way her father held his audience captive. He had a fine voice and a sure sense of dramatic structure. He might sit quietly for a time, whittling on a stick, Carrie said later. Then suddenly, "as if borne on some current of recollection so strong that it obliterated time and space," he would begin: "Sometimes the Black Bass strikes from natural pugnacity!" Sitting on the top porch step, beside her older brother Morris, Carrie was borne along into the story with him.

J. M. Gordon's stories soon became as real to Carrie as any of the stories she heard from the Meriwethers. Yet Carrie also gained another, perhaps more valuable resource from her father, although she may not have realized it. She gradually adopted some of her father's perspective on the Meriwethers. At least, she learned to step back and observe them, to temper their sense of truth and reality with that of another, an outsider's point of view. It was a rare and troublesome gift, one that would energize and complicate her creative imagination and her emotional well-being.

Such was the case when the Meriwether connection came together for a family reunion. Thousands were invited to the summer social; sometimes as many as four or five hundred attended. "All those mediocre people, getting together to congratulate themselves on their mediocrity!" J. M. Gordon would say.

Usually they gathered at Dunbar Cave, just a short distance from Merry Mont. The kin claimed Dunbar Cave had the largest entrance in the world, much larger than the famous Mammoth Cave in middle Kentucky. In the hollow below the cave's entrance, the men set up a huge barbecue pit, loaded with hickory wood, to roast the hogs, beef, and lambs. The women brought salads, rolls, and cakes of every sort. Inside the cave the air was always cool, the smooth polished floor perfect for dancing.

Carrie would eat as much as she could, then sit back and watch as her cousins whirled around the dance floor, her uncles drank—sometimes to excess—and her aunts and grandmother made their rounds of gossip. But Carrie's most vivid memory would not be of the food or the socializing. Instead, she would always remember one "pious old cousin" who went around "grasping people's hands and peering at them out of bleary eyes."

"Do you love Jesus?" the old crone asked young Carrie and everyone else she could capture. "Do you love Jesus?"

The whole encounter was uncomfortable. Carrie wondered how the woman could go around pretending she was morally superior to everyone else. "Do you love Jesus?" The question always made Carrie "mad as hell."

From an early age Carrie apparently adopted much of her grandmother's Anyhow approach to religion. Attending Sunday services at the local Christian church was a social obligation, not necessarily a sign of spiritual commitment, and Carrie was not likely to take her faith any more seriously. According to Anyhow porch wisdom, it was foolish, perhaps even dangerous, to carry spiritual matters to extremes.

The fact that her father was a Disciples of Christ minister apparently had little impact on Carrie. J. M. Gordon seemed to take an Anyhow slant to his calling: he kept his sermons short—no more than thirty minutes—and he decided which church call to accept according to the answer to one simple question: Was there good fishing nearby?

A far greater challenge to Carrie's religious views were the spiritual convictions of her mother. Like her grandfather, Nan was deeply religious. Carrie later claimed that her mother used "the theology of the first century church . . . as her weapon of offense and defense—in the affairs of every day life." More and more often as she grew, Carrie felt that weapon being turned upon her, and she sought refuge in the most likely quarter—her grandmother.

Yet Carrie lost her refuge during the early months of 1908, when her father decided to close his school and move away from Merry Mont once again. Later Carrie would say he left looking for better fishing grounds— he was "tired of fishing the same pools over and over." But actually, her father had decided to enter the ministry full-time, perhaps in deference to his wife's desire to escape the family circle. By March of that year, the Gordons had settled in Wilmington, Ohio, where J. M. Gordon had been offered the pastorate of the Central Church of Christ.

It was not the most stable situation. During Gordon's first month as pastor, a group of the church members left to establish a new Disciples of Christ church in Wilmington—the Walnut Street Church of Christ. Gordon's predecessor, E. J. Meachem, had led the Central congregation for eight years. Gordon lasted only two years.

Carrie would never say much about the time her family spent in

Wilmington. She always claimed they lived there for four years, not two, and her most vivid memory of that time was a painful one. At the age of twelve, Carrie entered public school for the first time, and she would never forget what happened when she was first called on to translate a Latin passage, from Caesar's *Gallic Wars*. Latin was easy for her; she had studied it since she was eight. But when she read the passage smoothly, the entire class exploded in laughter. Carrie was still small for her age, and she spoke with a thick southern accent. The fact that she acted as if it wasn't any problem to translate the passage made even the teacher cry with laughter.

Carrie was mortified, but she had learned a vital lesson about appearances and the proper role for young women. After that she was careful about what she said and did in school, watching and mimicking her classmates, learning to stumble and struggle a bit when she had to translate anything.

The Gordons left Wilmington at the end of February 1910, moving to Lynchburg, Virginia. J. M. Gordon tried without much success to farm and preach at area churches. Carrie and her mother fought increasingly over what Carrie thought were rigid—even insane—pronouncements her mother made. "I would rather see you in your grave than see you smoking cigarettes," Nan might say. Such a statement would settle the matter: Carrie would eventually take up smoking.

Later Carrie claimed that her mother spent the entire time in Lynchburg talking nothing but black dialect to get back at J. M. Gordon for his lack of ambition. Carrie was sure her mother hated her; she had such unreasonably high expectations of what Carrie ought to be and do. Only her father and her grandmother really loved her and understood her, Carrie insisted.

The Gordons did not stay in Lynchburg very long. They moved to find a new school to teach at, a new church to preach at, or, perhaps, just a new stream to fish at. The more often they moved, the more they struggled on the edge of poverty, the stronger Carrie's anger with her mother grew. She couldn't blame her father: he had always treated her as his favorite, special child, and she, in turn, idolized him. Looking for a scapegoat, Carrie could blame only her mother.

Mother and daughter fought so fiercely that J. M. Gordon finally took his daughter aside when she was fifteen or sixteen and suggested a sort of "gentleman's agreement." "When she says black is white, I say black is white, and you've got to do the same thing if you are going to get along with her," Gordon told his daughter. Carrie thought it was fine for her father to act that way—he was in love with the woman—but she saw no reason to agree with her mother. Although Carrie did as her father suggested to keep the peace, she looked forward to getting away from her mother as soon as possible.

Eventually Nan herself helped assure her daughter's exodus—to college in the fall of 1912, not long after Carrie had completed her high school education at the Princeton Collegiate Institute in Princeton, Kentucky. The Gordons did not have much money, but Bethany College in Bethany, West Virginia, the private school founded by the Disciples of Christ leader Alexander Campbell in 1840, offered reduced tuition for the children of ministers. For room, board, tuition, and fees, Carrie would have to pay about $155 per year: not a small sum, but apparently manageable.

Nan Gordon was eager for her daughter to attend college, an opportunity Nan herself had to miss when she married at age seventeen. She carefully read the course and entrance requirements in the *Bethany College Bulletin* and decided Carrie should master *White's First Greek Grammar* before the fall. For once, Carrie made no argument—she enjoyed the study of languages just as much as her mother did.

Throughout the summer of 1912, in between dances and swimming parties, Carrie studied *White's Grammar*. Then in August, Nan reread the *Bulletin* and gave her daughter another task: Carrie must be able to translate all of Xenophon's *Anabasis*.

To do well, the task would take more than a summer; Carrie had less than a month. Yet Carrie was not upset at first, because she had studied and enjoyed excerpts from Xenophon in *White's Grammar*. She read just enough of the *Anabasis* to reassure herself that she could translate passages if necessary. But as the weeks went by, her confidence faltered; Carrie began to think she was not ready for college. In September she left for Bethany with a terrible sense of uneasiness.

The closer she got to the college, the more Carrie worried about her summer work. She did not know what was expected of her. Had her haphazard education prepared her for college work? Would she once again become the class laughingstock? On the long ride to Bethany, Carrie went over the last of her studies—the protases and apodoses of Greek syntax—with a gloomy, worried look in her dark eyes.

Bethany College was about fifteen miles from Wheeling, West Virginia. For the last leg of the journey over the hills, most students took a trolley car the locals called the Mountain Canary because, as Carrie would recall, it had a "habit of flying off its track under the impact of the huge boulders that now and then slid down the mountain-sides." Riders on the Canary could get a superb view of the countryside: there were endless low green hills, dotted with grazing sheep and majestic oaks, and a lovely serpentine stream—the Old Buffalo—winding through the hills.

No boulders fell when Carrie first rode on the Canary on her way to Bethany in September of 1912, but the sixteen-year-old young woman scarcely noticed the scenery. Instead, she sat brooding, rehearsing rules of Greek syntax and worrying about what lay ahead of her.

When she arrived on campus, Carrie was pleasantly surprised. Her mother had misread the catalog: knowledge of *White's First Greek Grammar* and Xenophon's *Anabasis* was recommended but by no means required. In fact, Carrie's high school studies and summer reading were enough to satisfy the requirements for the first two years of Greek offered at Bethany. She enrolled in a number of required courses in addition to what she called "Third Year Greek," the study of Homer's *Odyssey*, and quickly settled into campus life.

Carrie's first cousin, Mildred Meriwether, also attended Bethany that fall. Together, they pledged Alpha Xi Delta sorority and joined the American Literary Institute, one of four literary societies on campus. Every student pursuing a "literary" degree was required to join one of the societies and participate at least once each term by preparing an essay or speech for the monthly meetings.

Attendance at daily chapel was also required. Every morning at ten o'clock, Carrie had to listen to Scripture and a sermon, or else she would receive a one-point penalty on all her grades for each absence. But such daily doses of spiritual instruction did not apparently inspire Carrie to change her attitude about religion. She was a member of the Young Woman's Christian Association for only one year. She would never join the Young Woman's Bible Class or any of the other church-related groups on campus, even though many of her friends were active members.

The most difficult part of Carrie's freshman year turned out to be Greek. Carrie's instructor was Frank Roy Gay. He was young and handsome, with dark hair and a piercing gaze. Before joining the Bethany faculty in 1910, Gay had completed his bachelor's and master's degrees at Drake University, continued his studies at the universities of Virginia and Chicago, and taught at Virginia Christian College in Lynchburg. Soon after he began teaching at Bethany, Professor Gay had become known as one of the toughest teachers on campus. Few students were brave enough to take more than the required courses from him.

Carrie was in awe of the man. But such awe only compounded her acute sense of inadequacy. Most of the students in third-year Greek were advanced students: Carrie called them the "sharks," and even though she had been studying Greek since she was a child, she never considered herself their equal. After a few classes Carrie was sure she had gotten in over her head. She had not really "mastered" the necessary grammar, she said later, and she thought others realized it as well whenever she was called on to speak. But she kept studying with the sharks. She would not quit.

After finishing the *Odyssey* the class went on to read from Plato and from Thucydides' *Peloponnesian War*. Carrie later remembered the period as a struggle, claiming that the sharks corrected her syntax as necessary. By the end of the spring term, she was feeling "rather down-cast." But Professor Gay had seen in the small, intense, dark-eyed young woman something that she was unable to acknowledge. One day he kept Carrie after class.

Would she like to continue studying Greek? Professor Gay asked. If so, he said, he would be happy to offer an advanced class in Greek drama; the class had not been "offered for several years because there had been nobody who wanted to take it."

Carrie was dumbfounded but eager. When she told the sharks, they were equally amazed. None of them wanted to take another class with Professor Gay, and they prophesied doom. "Now he'll find out all you don't know," one of the sharks said. Carrie had no doubt her friend was right.

But once again Carrie would be surprised. Whether she spent the next summer "boning up," as she called it, on her Greek syntax or she had just been underestimating her own abilities, Carrie soon became known as one of the best language students. From then on, she took every class Professor Gay offered, even when she was the only student enrolled, reading *Prometheus Bound, Agamemnon, Oedipus Tyrannus* and *Oedipus Coloneus,* and *Antigone.* Every day she diligently translated one hundred lines. Only once did she go to class unprepared because of a late-night party. That day she tried to bluff her way through a translation of *Antigone* by using a "trot," but the cribbed translation didn't fool Professor Gay.

"Miss Gordon," he said kindly. "Jebb is the only authority who gives that word the meaning you give it. Would you care to defend his usage?"

At that point, Carrie decided that "where the Greek tragedians were concerned," Professor Gay "had second sight." She took the translation by Jebb "right back to the library and never consulted him again," she wrote later. No matter what other subjects she had to neglect, she would never again go to Greek class unprepared, and her hard work paid off. Professor Gay later said that Carrie was "the best Greek student he ever had," claiming that she "could read Greek almost as well as English" when she came to Bethany.

In addition to Greek, Carrie took classes in Latin, English literature, French, and German. Despite her success with literature and language study, Carrie had a great deal of trouble passing the required science and math classes. She flunked trigonometry and calculus at least once, and she nearly flunked physics as well. But these struggles with math and science did not prevent her from getting involved in school activities. During her sophomore year, Carrie served as assistant art editor for the college yearbook, *The Bethanian,* and she also joined the drama club.

Throughout her years at Bethany, Carrie's relationship with her grandmother remained strong. The old woman continued to give her granddaughter special treatment, sending her gifts and tokens of love. Once Carrie even received flowers from her grandmother: jonquils, carefully packed in wet cotton and probably delivered by traveling kin, arriving at Bethany as fresh as they could be.

Although Carrie remained an active member of her literary society and her sorority during the four years she was at Bethany, she apparently did not make friends easily. Her sorority sisters thought Carrie had "a brilliant mind," and they knew her as a "joyous pleasure loving" person, always eager for a party. But new pledges often found the small, dark-haired young woman rather distant, either shy or standoffish: Carrie never got actively involved in the annual "rush" for new members. Once the formalities of "rushing" were over, however, Carrie welcomed her new "sisters" warmly.

Her chief passion was the study of Greek—until she got to know George Archie Hankins during her sophomore year. Soon, when Carrie wasn't devoting herself to the study of Greek, she was involved in the favorite campus pastime—falling in love, or the "Biz," to use the campus slang.

Archie Hankins, or "Hank," as he was called, was originally from Pueblo, Colorado. Since Carrie was known to be a staunch defender of all things southern, friends teased her about her new "cosmopolitan" views. Hank would walk Carrie to Greek class, where, before he left her at the door, they "commiserated" together—both of them could think of much better ways to spend one hour and forty-five minutes. Once inside the classroom, Carrie tried to keep her attention on the lecture, but sometimes she found her mind wandering.

One day in particular, Professor Gay lectured on a scene from Aeschylus's *Agamemnon:* the Trojan war had ended, and Clytemnestra and her lover Aegisthus were planning to murder Clytemnestra's husband, Agamemnon. Professor Gay devoted the entire class session to a discussion of the carpet or tapestry Clytemnestra had prepared for her husband to walk upon. At first Carrie was bored. Professor Gay talked about the carpet and its importance to the drama; he examined every aspect of the carpet and the scene. Carrie thought the carpet "engaged far too much of Professor Gay's attention." Then, almost despite herself, she began to listen intently.

After a while Carrie could see the carpet vividly. The carpet was "woven of some dull purple stuff and ornamented with bronze-[colored] figures of birds and beasts and signs of the zodiac and it stretched from the entrance to Agamemnon's great hall to the doors at the back through which he [would] walk to his death." Carrie was fascinated by the way the poet used the figure of the carpet to foreshadow the action to come, "the blood that will soon be shed," and the attractions of Hank slipped from her mind: Carrie began to find a new passion, a passion for description and writing she would never lose.

As time passed, however, Carrie became more serious about her relationship with Archie Hankins. Hank was apparently something of a rebel, and Carrie would always be attracted to people who dared to go against convention. By their junior year she was wearing his Kappa Alpha pin. When Hank left Bethany that year, apparently expelled for disciplinary reasons, Carrie also seriously considered dropping out. Although she remained at school, Carrie evidently made plans to join Hank later. In the school yearbook that year, their names were hung together on "the Biz tree" and her classmates teased her about how she had "developed of late a remarkable fancy for Colorado" after trying " 'orful' hard to leave" school.

But by her senior year all plans for a life with Hank had apparently disappeared: in the Bethany yearbook the class prophets declared that in the years to come, Carrie would be found living in Washington, D.C., as the wife of her classmate A. E. Sims, who by 1936 would be president of the American Tobacco Company.

Years later Carrie blamed her mother for breaking up her earliest relationships with men. Nan intercepted her letters, Carrie said; once her mother even hid a telegram a lover had sent. Nan told her daughter she was doing it for her own good. Carrie must never marry, her mother said. She had "such a bad disposition," Nan said, that she "would be sure to leave [her] husband, which would be a mortal sin." Throughout this period, as the women fought fiercely with one another, Carrie longed to get away.

On June 8, 1916, she graduated from Bethany College with a bachelor's degree in classical studies and a normal certificate qualifying her to teach. But the year of Carrie's commencement was marked more by a growing gloom than by celebration. The newspapers were full of talk about the European war; by the spring of 1917, the United States had officially entered the world turmoil. Thousands of young men, including many of Carrie's friends and family, went off to fight.

Carrie wrote letters to support the men she knew in the army, but at that time, and many years later, she was haunted by two deaths totally unrelated to the war. In 1916 Carrie's cousin Mildred Meriwether committed suicide. A year later another cousin, twelve-year-old Anna Wilds, shot herself. Carrie never said much about what happened, but she was badly shaken, apparently feeling somehow responsible, as if she should have realized how Mildred and Anna were feeling and found a way to help them.

Despite a glowing recommendation from Professor Gay, Carrie had a difficult time finding a job she enjoyed. For a while, she taught school and lived with her parents in Poplar Bluffs, Missouri. Her father was again serving as pastor for a Disciples of Christ church; yet, as Carrie would recall, he spent more time fishing and hunting than preaching. As usual, the Gordons were very poor. They lived for months on the quail and wild ducks J. M. Gordon shot. But all the time on the river finally took its toll: Carrie's father got very sick with malaria. At that point her parents decided to return to the Old Neighborhood.

By 1918 the Gordons had settled in Elkton, Kentucky, not far from Merry Mont. J. M. Gordon began preaching in nearby Russellville. Carrie found another job, at the high school in Clarksville, Tennessee. She taught an assortment of classes—French, chemistry, vegetable gardening, and animal husbandry—but she did not enjoy her work. More than once her students saw her crying from either embarrassment or despair.

Worldwide hostilities ceased in November 1918 as both Germany and Austria-Hungary surrendered. But the long-standing antagonisms between Carrie and her mother did not abate. Finally, after one year of teaching in Clarksville, Carrie found the escape she had been looking for: a job writing for the *Chattanooga News*.

Carrie had no journalistic experience; she was, however, interested in writing, and at that time working for a newspaper was thought to be a good apprenticeship for anyone who wanted to pursue writing seriously. It was also, in the eyes of most Meriwethers, a pathway to fame and fortune, as Carrie's great-aunt Elizabeth Meriwether Gilmer had already demonstrated. Known to most Americans as Dorothy Dix, the celebrated advice columnist and crime reporter, Elizabeth earned more than fifty thousand dollars a year by the early 1920s, and her articles appeared in newspapers across the country, as well as in most of the major popular magazines of the time.

The kin had disapproved when Elizabeth had first gone to work as a newspaper woman: "Why couldn't Lizzie have tried something more ladylike?" they had asked. But by the time Carrie began work at the *Chattanooga News* in 1919, journalism had become a more respectable career for women, and Carrie could not escape comparisons with Cousin Lizzie. "Do you suppose Carrie will ever be as good a writer as Cousin Lizzie?" the Meriwether kin would ask. Years later Carrie would remember that "the answer was always 'No.'"

During the summer of 1919, Carrie settled into her new job and home. She lived with her favorite aunt, Pidie, her mother's younger sister, who had been widowed and had then married a prominent lawyer in Chattanooga, Paul Campbell. At that time, the Campbells had two children, a three-and-a-half-year-old son, Paul Jr., as well as nine-year-old Catherine Wilds, Pidie's daughter from her first marriage. Carrie lived in an attic room of the Campbells' home on Missionary Ridge. In exchange for her room and board, she helped her aunt with the children. She knew only a few people her age in the city, so she "lived in imagination and letters to friends" from college, she said much later. But as long as she was away from her mother, Carrie was happy.

The *Chattanooga News* was a moderate-sized daily evening paper with a few women writers covering society news and light features. Years later Carrie claimed that her editor tore up the first three pages she ever wrote, then chewed and swallowed them, before giving her "Chekhov's advice" to write about "simple things" with clarity and simplicity so the reader would be able to see those things vividly. Carrie took his advice. In July 1919 articles began to appear with her byline, "Carolyn Gordon." They were usually short vignettes about people and places around town, written in a straightforward manner with gentle humor.

Carolyn's first signed story appeared on July 10, 1919. It was about a seven-year-old boy—called Reginald "because that isn't his name"— who appeared in police court accused of stealing a bicycle. Carolyn met Reginald while visiting one of the city's "day nurseries" for children of working mothers. She told his story in his own words, noting that he took the bicycle even though he wasn't big enough to ride it. "I seen it, and I wanted it," he observed indifferently.

In the following months Carolyn went back several times to visit Reginald and his friends at the Miss Mag Day Nursery. She also explored the city, commenting on everything from the "fraternity of early birds" she had reluctantly joined as she rode the streetcars into work, to the high cost of clothes and the kind of man that "girls" wanted to marry. But Carolyn apparently wanted to do more than write short fillers, and in July she arranged an assignment more to her liking: an interview with Francis Lynde, a writer of historical fiction.

Born in New York in 1856, Lynde had been living in Chattanooga for a number of years. His novels included *The Master of Appleby, The Grafters, The Helpers,* and *Love in Transit,* what Carolyn called "novels of adventure and romance." Carolyn went to his home on Lookout Mountain, and Lynde gave her a tour of the house he and his sons had built out of stone from the mountain. Carolyn marveled over the view from the third-floor windows, but she was most interested in Lynde's career and his advice for writers.

Carolyn listened intently as Lynde described how he had to start "at the very beginning" to learn the "craft." "I did not even know how to write decent English," he said, explaining how at age thirty-five he bought a grammar and "took that grammar with me on my railroad trips and studied it until I knew it perfectly." Then, he said, "I felt that I had acquired the tools of my trade."

Lynde's beliefs about the cycles in popular fiction fascinated Carolyn. "After the historical novel came the problem novel, and at the present the sex novel holds foremost place," he explained. What would be next? Carolyn wondered. Lynde prophesied a return to the historical novel. "At the present the reading market is literally flooded with war stories," he said. "But when we get far enough away to get the perspective we will swing back to the historical novel again."

As they walked the paths around Lynde's house, Carolyn asked the writer for advice. What were "the qualities essential to a successful writer?" she wanted to know.

At first Lynde said it was "the visioning imagination," that "quality which enables me to see the thing before it is written," he said. "Next to this elusive imagination comes the ability to get down what you see," he continued. Writing was "a mingling of an art and a trade," he said. "Along with the ability to write, goes a knowledge of the tools."

But Carolyn was not satisfied. "And after that?" she asked, persistently.

"You must love it," Lynde told her. "You must love it enough to be willing to endure enormous amounts of drudgery for it. I always write a book two or three times," he said, insisting he did not mean "merely the work of revision." "I mean that I write and rewrite it until I feel that I have given it my best," he said. "Then I let it go—even though I never feel quite satisfied."

"You must love it," Lynde told Carolyn, and she took his words to heart.

ALTHOUGH years later Carolyn would insist she had always been a conservative southern lady, she hardly acted the part during her stint as a newspaper reporter. Instead she resembled many young women her age, eager for adventure and a professional career, with an apparently firm belief in equal rights for women. Both that belief and her professional aspirations would be sharply tested, however, and perhaps this is part of the reason why, years later, Carolyn would dissemble about her experiences.

If Carolyn had hopes of following in her great-aunt's footsteps as a criminal reporter, she learned quickly that such a path was not open to her at the *Chattanooga News*. In August of 1919 Chattanooga was rocked by a local scandal involving the death of eighteen-year-old Billie Crawford after an illegal abortion. The young woman made a dying confession, naming the man who had "wronged" her and had subsequently arranged for the abortion, but as soon as the confession was made public, friends of the implicated man began to come to his aid, claiming Billie Crawford was known for immoral behavior and had had numerous intimate relationships.

The Crawford case clearly demonstrated the professional and personal challenges Carolyn faced. The scandal continued to attract front-page headlines for a number of weeks, but no woman ever received a byline covering the story. "Hard news" was considered a male province; women journalists had made tremendous inroads in many areas, but at the *News* they wrote only society news and light features. Years later Carolyn suggested that her editor had tried to protect her from the seamier sides of life. Yet the protection was illusory. Carolyn knew well what was going on behind closed doors. Because Chattanooga was so close to the state line, it was not unusual for young women to go to their "ruin" after too much alcohol prompted them to dash into Georgia for a quick, often illegal marriage.

Carolyn may have been the unnamed woman reporter who went to speak with Billie Crawford's mother soon after her death and wrote several articles, including an unsigned editorial in defense of the dead woman. The editorial chastised the public attitude excusing the actions of the men involved: "The world claims to be outgrowing the false, double, moral standard. This is a time for demonstrating that the man must share the woman's punishment." Yet Carolyn herself suffered from a double standard; she never received a byline for any hard news story in the *News*.

Instead, not long after her interview with Lynde, Carolyn began a new feature, a weekly book review. Her first signed column, titled "Books— Good, Bad, Indifferent," appeared on September 27, 1919, celebrating the centennial of George Eliot's birth. George Eliot was "first of all, a pioneer," Carolyn wrote. "Living in an age which had only one standard by which to judge a woman—an age which had never heard of any education for women other than a training narrow and limited in scope to only one idea—she calmly arrogated unto herself privileges which had been monopolized by men up to that time," Carolyn wrote. "Since the spirit of the age did not admit that a woman might have anything to say which was worthy of note, Marian Evans adopted a man's name as her nom de plume." According to Carolyn, one early sign of success was that George Eliot's first published work, "Scenes from Clerical Life," had everyone but Dickens believing a man actually wrote the piece.

Carolyn went on to compare the work of Eliot, Dickens, and Sir Walter Scott. Both Eliot and Dickens were "remarkable for spirited character delineation," she said, "but Dickens' characters appear, play their parts and leave the stage unchanged," while "the growth of George Eliot's characters and the development of her plots are dependent one upon the other." Her originality and genius fared even better when compared to other novels popular at the time—especially the "prolix" novels of Scott, Carolyn wrote. "The material out of which [George Eliot] fashions her novels are love and hate and . . . virtue, and the situations brought about by these same attributes of humanity; and since her novels deal with human beings in their relation to certain immutable moral laws, she ranks with that small number of novelists whose work has an appeal which is lasting and universal," she declared.

Throughout the fall of 1919, Carolyn wrote weekly book reviews, which appeared on Saturdays. She commented on works by both established and lesser known authors: from Edith Wharton, Bernard Shaw, Theodore Dreiser, and John Galsworthy to Phyllis Bottome, Marion Harland, and Margaret Deland.

Although her remarks were necessarily brief, Carolyn regularly wrote about the technical merit of each book she reviewed: her reviews were seldom mere plot summaries, but instead judgments of the author's skill in developing character and plot. She also expected writers to have a sound command of grammar, diction, and syntax. When writers did not measure up to her criteria, she spoke out, no matter how popular the book was. That fall the best-selling author Ethel M. Dell published *The Lamp in the Desert*. Although her publishers would later call Dell a novelist who "never had a failure," Carolyn thought otherwise. The characters unconvincing, the plot little more than cliché, Dell's novel "cannot be called a success even when judged by popular standards," Carolyn wrote.

Carolyn also railed at length against another popular novel, *Mary Olivier* by May Sinclair. According to Carolyn, Sinclair had "quite obscured" her main character with "a sea of adjectives." "When one finally lays the book down, the primary feeling is one of wonder as to how the author managed to pilot [Mary] from the age of two or whenever it was she began to remember things, to the age of forty-five, with the use of such a limited quantity of verbs," Carolyn wrote.

Carolyn also identified trends in the field of modern fiction and regularly explored the distinctions between popular literature and art. Often she used humor to make her points, but she also spoke seriously about the life and duties of the artist. The nature of a career in literature was changing, Carolyn believed. Quoting Joseph C. Lincoln, a writer of Cape Cod stories, she insisted that the time "when an author had to do paperhanging on the side or calcimining or janitor work in order to make enough to live on" was "gone—almost entirely." Carolyn believed with Lincoln that those authors who could not make money were "bad authors" not likely to succeed at any other endeavor.

Yet Carolyn did not equate an author's fame with fine art. She objected to the popularity of "life" novels, like Sinclair's *Mary Olivier,* which attempted "to achieve realism by faithfully recording every thought and feeling" of the main character "from infancy to old age." "The function of the artist is to interpret," she insisted, "and, while all may be grist that comes to his mill, he ought to exercise a selective faculty which will protect a defenseless reading public from an epidemic of Mary Oliviers."

For the most part Carolyn reviewed fiction in her weekly column. The rather lengthy review of Gilbert Cannan's *The Anatomy of Society* was unusual, but Carolyn liked the way Cannan attacked "conventions and traditions alike, economic, religious and national." "The book is a protest against European civilization which the author pictures as industrialism," she wrote. Cannan "lays at the door of industrialism 'man's divorce from humanity.'" Carolyn admired the way Cannan translated "the modern doctrine of individualism" into "something higher" as he examined the relationships between men and women, and science and art.

Carolyn seldom reviewed poetry in her column; in fact, the only poets she discussed in any depth were Rudyard Kipling and Robert Burns. She admired the way Burns, "the great lyric poet of Scotland," perceived "eternal truths in the things that make up everyday life," and the way Kipling "put into words the soul of the British army" and "the swing and surge of the sea." But her literary passion remained with fiction, as did most of her reviews.

Throughout the fall Carolyn pursued her career by becoming active in the newspaper "fraternity." She apparently had few if any romantic interests, perhaps partly because of her desire to make a name for herself in journalism. Her advice for bachelors in a New Year's Day column suggests as much. Quoting Bernard Shaw, who "painted a vivid word picture of the bachelor's trials in this woman's world," Carolyn discussed the custom and laws of leap year that granted women the right to be "aggressors" in the world of love, and she offered worried, "timid" bachelors one ray of hope: "Women have secured equal suffrage and prohibition and it is quite possible that they may be so busy minding their own affairs that they will let leap year slide by unnoticed."

Carolyn continued to write book reviews, under the title "New Books," reserving some of her strongest criticism for an author she had read and loved as a child: Mary Johnston. She thought Johnston's newest novel, *Michael Forth,* suffered from the author's attempts to explore the "realm of the metaphysical." "The characters in *Michael Forth* do not exist for the reader save as the mouthpieces of the author's thought," she wrote. "They have no reality; they lack concreteness. You would not recognize 'Michael Forth' if you went home and found him sitting in your easy chair," she continued. "But then, Michael Forth probably had difficulty in recognizing himself at times, because he was so many different people."

At the end of February, Carolyn devoted some space to a discussion of southern literature. A new magazine called the *Southern Review,* "dedicated to the expression of the ideal of the new south," was being published in Asheville, North Carolina, and Carolyn thought that "those who believe that the south should support at least one standard periodical should welcome" the new review. "The south has always made generous contribution to American literature," she said, citing a long list of contemporary southern writers. Although, as Carolyn noted, "New York has ever been the mecca of southern writers," she did not think there was any reason why the region should not be able to create a more congenial environment for writers—one which would "preclude the possibility of southern ideals and traditions being lost in the writers' adaptation to a changed environment."

In her list of contemporary southern writers, Carolyn included one distant "cousin," Amélie Rives. Although her connection to the Gordons and Meriwethers was a bit tenuous, Amélie was a native of Charlottesville, Virginia, and lived in one of the first Meriwether homes, Castle Hill. Her career as a writer had been established in 1888 with the publication of what some called a scandalous novel, *The Quick or the Dead?,* about a young widow who could not decide whether to remain true to her dead husband's memory or marry his cousin. The public outcry against the novel—from pulpits and in newspaper editorials—soon made Amélie a best-selling author; her subsequent novels and her friendships with writers like Oscar Wilde, Thomas Hardy, and Henry James made her reputation as a serious artist.

Carolyn was not allowed to read "Cousin" Amélie's work until she had grown up. But by the time Carolyn wrote about southern literature for the newspaper, she had probably read more than *The Quick or the Dead?* Amélie's novels *World's End,* published in 1914, and *Shadows of Flames,* published in 1915, were both best-sellers receiving a great deal of critical acclaim. Carolyn would never say why she liked Amélie and considered her to be one of the premier southern writers of that time. Perhaps Carolyn identified with Amélie's strong, adventurous heroines. Perhaps she simply enjoyed the way Amélie set most of her stories in a large family estate like the one called World's End in the 1914 novel: Carolyn, like most Meriwether kin, would recognize Amélie's mythical estate as Castle Hill.

But more likely, Carolyn admired Amélie for her radical history and her courage. Nonconformists and dissenters of any sort always attracted Carolyn's attention, from her college beau, Archie Hankins, to Gilbert Cannan and his social theories. At that time the highest compliment Carolyn would give to a writer was to call him or her a rebel.

Carolyn became increasingly rebellious herself in pursuit of a more lucrative career. From January through April, she wrote reviews of the movies playing at local theaters, but her May 29 book review of Galsworthy's *Tatterdemalion* and *Invincible Minnie* by Elizabeth Sanxay Holding was the last signed article of any sort Carolyn published in the *News* that year. Sometime that summer or early fall, Carolyn apparently left the staff of the *News* to work for its rival paper, the *Chattanooga Times*. Great-aunt "Dorothy Dix" had launched her New York career by writing a series of thought-provoking articles for the *New Orleans Picayune,* but nothing Carolyn had written for the *News* was likely to interest New York syndicates. At the *Times* Carolyn apparently hoped to do more serious writing and perhaps find a more important position.

At some point, probably in early 1921, Carolyn came up with a scheme that just might have made the national news wires. Her friend Jane Snodgrass, another reporter for the *Times,* helped her concoct a staged news story. One day, when all the fashionable members of Chattanoogan society were assembled at the Palace, a trendy luncheonette and ice cream parlor, two women would walk in wearing lampshades to protest the high price of hats. Carolyn and Jane would just happen to be there, of course, to write up the scene for the paper.

With pictures the story might have been just odd enough to attract one of the New York syndicates. But when the *Times* publisher discovered the deception, he fired Carolyn. She couldn't have been more shocked.

Yet Carolyn was able to save face. By the beginning of March 1921, she left Chattanooga for a new job writing for the *Intelligencer* of Wheeling, West Virginia. The *Intelligencer* was not as large a paper as either the *Times* or the *News*. Carolyn, however, would be the first woman writer to receive a byline at the paper. Also, Wheeling was not far from Bethany, and several of Carolyn's friends from college had found work there. It was a congenial move.

Carolyn lived in Wheeling for little more than a year, but that year was an important one. She apparently helped to redesign the image of the *Intelligencer*; she became active in politics and women's organizations, and she continued to explore her beliefs about literature and a literary life. Before she left the city, she would acquire an impressive local reputation as a writer and book reviewer.

Although Carolyn's first signed article did not appear for several months, the newspaper reflected her presence almost immediately. Previously the *Intelligencer* had focused strictly on news: almost none of its stories had bylines, and no feature articles appeared. But at the beginning of April, less than a month after Carolyn arrived, the paper began running a series of unsigned light articles, very much like the ones Carolyn had written in Chattanooga. By the beginning of May, the *Intelligencer* included a daily features page and a weekly magazine supplement. This section, published every Saturday, continued to expand throughout the summer, although it included only syndicated material and society news.

At the end of August, Carolyn published her first signed article, a book review column. From then on, the column appeared almost every Monday or Tuesday in a prominent place on page 3 of the newspaper. Just as in Chattanooga, Carolyn wrote predominantly about fiction, and she continued to chide authors who fell short in some aspect of plot and character development or prose style. But her column became more personal and chatty: for a while Carolyn even kept her readers informed about her search for an appropriate book for her grandmother. "It is really surprising when you pause to reflect how few of the books written nowadays are suitable for perusal by one's grandmother," Carolyn wrote. Selecting a book for a grandmother was difficult: "very, very few of the books reviewed in this column . . . are recommended as gifts for anybody's grandmother," she admitted, declaring that "there is really a moral obligation involved in the protection of [a grandmother's] literary unsophistication."

Carolyn eventually decided to give her grandmother *The Charmed Circle* by Edward Alden Jewell, a pleasant story of an adventurous American boy stranded in France with an elderly guardian. But for her own reading she continued to prefer less conventional, more irreverent tales like *Gold Shod* by Newton Fuessle. *Gold Shod* was "a broadside" against "that curious tendency in the American national consciousness which makes the arts and science subsidiary to material production," Carolyn wrote, noting that Fuessle seemed "animated by a savage resentment as a man should be when fighting injustice." The book was "one of the most important books of the year," she declared.

Carolyn continued to find fault with authors who turned art into moral lessons. Although she had once appreciated Nalbro Bartley's fiction, she could not bring herself to finish her newest work, *Fair to Middling*. Bartley had a fine prose style, but her imagination was "running a bit thin, and worst of all, she has turned moralist," Carolyn lamented.

More to her liking was Sinclair Lewis's *Main Street* or Rose Macaulay's *Dangerous Ages*. Lewis wrote a best-seller despite his refusal to "compromise with magazine traditions," she declared; Macaulay was "a cynic, a rake . . . a sardonic and brilliant novelist." Carolyn delighted in sarcasm and irony, so much so that she even reversed her opinion of May Sinclair, calling her newest novel, *Mr. Waddington of Wyck,* a "delicious satire" and "probably the most immoral book that has been written in recent times."

Carolyn read voraciously throughout the fall, writing about everything from mystery stories to the first number of *Broom,* a new literary magazine edited by Harold Loeb and Alfred Kreymborg. She also wrote movie reviews, and when the actress Madame Olga Petrova visited Wheeling to perform in the play she had written, *The White Peacock,* Carolyn interviewed her. An ardent feminist, Petrova talked about how she was devoted to one "big idea"—"the ultimate economic independence of woman"—comparing her work on *The White Peacock* to that of Ibsen in *A Doll's House.* Carolyn was impressed. "We had always liked Madame Petrova in the movies," she wrote, "but we liked her even better when she was talking about her big idea."

Celebrating her twenty-sixth birthday that fall, Carolyn appeared to be finding her niche in Wheeling. Although her work for the newspaper must have kept her busy, Carolyn joined the Wheeling chapter of the League of Women Voters as well as the Wheeling Women's Club. Both were active organizations that fall. The League of Women Voters organized a local recall vote, hoping to force the resignation of the city manager and several council members accused of fraud. Carolyn served on the publicity committee for the league's state convention, held in Wheeling at the beginning of October.

Carolyn also served as a delegate to the convention of the West Virginia Federation of Women's Clubs. Held in Huntington at the end of October, this convention included one of the most spirited presidential campaigns in the federation's history. Carolyn not only participated as a delegate; she also covered the proceedings for the *Intelligencer,* garnering a series of stories that ran on the front page because the campaigners included one of Wheeling's leading citizens, Mrs. Mary Garden.

Carolyn apparently relished the convention controversy. She reported all the rumors and political maneuvering, and even called the newspaper office at two o'clock one morning with an "unofficial statement" from "a club woman close to the count of the ballots" that Mrs. Garden had lost the election. The fact that the "unofficial statement" had been wrong probably did not hurt Carolyn; if anything, it probably got her articles more attention when Mary Garden won the election after all. Carolyn did not, however, continue to write news stories for the *Intelligencer.* The front-page articles on the convention were the only ones she would ever have.

Carolyn continued to review books for the *Intelligencer* throughout the early months of 1922, and her comments revealed her growing interest in the world of literature. But at the end of April, she stopped writing her review of books. Not long after that, she apparently quit her job at the *Intelligencer* and moved back to Chattanooga to work at the *Chattanooga News.* Carolyn never said why she left Wheeling. By that time one of her college friends who had been living in Wheeling had moved as well, so perhaps Carolyn was lonely. However, the *News* was a larger paper, and Chattanooga a larger city, so Carolyn may have simply been accepting a better job offer. But in the years to come, she would suggest she worked only in Chattanooga.

Whatever the reason, Carolyn returned to the attic bedroom of her aunt's home on Missionary Ridge. At the *News* Francis Lynde had taken over as book reviewer, but Carolyn once again had a byline writing light features, investigating the demise of the flapper, exploring the Chickasaw origin of the name Chattanooga, and discussing four of Chattanooga's most talented black fortune-tellers: Aunt Savannah, "Daddy" Chisholm, Aunt Dinah, and Mrs. Coppage.

Despite the frivolous articles she wrote for the *News,* Carolyn had made a serious commitment to writing by the fall of 1922. At first her literary ambition was simply to write "as good a sentence . . . as one of Thucydides," but soon she started a novel called *Darkling I Listen,* a romance with allusions to the poem by Keats, "Ode to a Nightingale."

Carolyn approached her task with single-minded dedication. Every night after dinner, she asked the cook for a thermos bottle full of coffee. She went to bed early, setting the alarm for four o'clock in the morning. When the alarm went off, she grabbed the thermos from under the bed and drank cup after cup of coffee until she was awake and able to write. Then she worked on her novel, writing and rewriting, until eight o'clock, when she ate a quick breakfast and headed into the city for work. It was an exhausting routine, but Carolyn was ready to take Francis Lynde's advice, to toil at writing because of her love for it.

Between mid-October and December, in addition to working nearly four hours every morning on her novel, Carolyn wrote more than twenty-five signed features for the *News.* Then, at the end of December, she began editing for the Saturday *News* a new twelve-page "magazine section" similar to the *Intelligencer*'s weekly magazine. The section included syndicated features on popular science, fashion, and the home, along with an expanded report of social events and school news.

Carolyn occasionally provided a signed article, although her responsibilities included much less writing and gave her little opportunity for the sort of criticism she had contributed to either the *News* or the *Intelligencer.* But sometime in January 1923, she made plans to write at least one more review. Carolyn had noticed a new magazine of verse, the *Fugitive,* published by a group of men connected with Vanderbilt University. Many years earlier she had met one of the group's leading figures, John Crowe Ransom, a member in the English department at Vanderbilt, when he had lived near some members of the Meriwether connection, so she wrote Ransom for information about the group and its publication.

On February 10, 1923, Carolyn's review of the *Fugitive* appeared in the magazine section of the *News.* "U.S. Best Poets Here in Tennessee," Carolyn's headline proclaimed, and in her first paragraph she briefly discussed the recent "revival of interest in poetry in America" and especially in the South, evidenced by a number of new magazines: "the *Double Dealer* of New Orleans, the *Richmond Review,* the *Norfolk Lyric,* and *The Nomad* of Birmingham." But, according to Carolyn, Tennessee had "gathered the highest poetic laurels": the *Fugitive* had even managed to receive the loud acclaim of critics like H. L. Mencken, Louis Untermeyer, and John McClure, who were "oftener given to censure than praise."

Carolyn summarized the group's history, including a list of the men behind the *Fugitive,* before discussing various members of the group and other contributors to the magazine. Although Ransom was the "only member of the group who [had] published a volume of poems," Carolyn did not slight the lesser known of the circle. One member of the group in particular received special mention: Allen Tate, a "former Vanderbilt student." His poetry had been appearing in the *Wave* and other journals, Carolyn reported, adding that he was "the most radical member of the group."

Although the *Fugitive* had begun publication in April 1922, Carolyn's article was one of the first serious notices the magazine received. But Carolyn was not destined to return to writing book reviews. Instead she continued to edit the magazine section, contributing about one article a month to its pages, articles about gardens, etiquette, and weather.

That summer, however, Carolyn apparently began to explore the possibility of another job. At age twenty-seven, she knew anyone who wanted to succeed in any sort of writing had to first find recognition in New York literary circles, and Carolyn wanted that success. So after visiting her cousin "Little May" in upstate New York, Carolyn stopped in New York City. But she found no openings with the newspaper syndicates at that time and returned to Chattanooga in August to resume her exhausting routine of rising every morning at four to write for several hours before work.

In addition to her work for the *News,* Carolyn joined the Chattanooga Women's Press and Authors' Club, and began to try to make extra money as a freelance author. In the spring of 1924, she apparently sold several stories, including one to the *American* magazine about a well-known Chattanooga druggist, Jo Anderson. She was also appointed by the Chattanooga Press Club to be a delegate to the state conference of the Tennessee Federation of Women's Clubs, to be held in Clarksville in May.

But by the middle of April, the physical exhaustion that had been growing from her rigorous morning routine suddenly became too much for Carolyn. One day, a friend poked her in the ribs, teasingly. Carolyn started to cry for no reason, and then she couldn't stop. She cried and cried. It was a long time before she could get hold of herself.

Carolyn subsequently dropped out of sight for a while. Years later she claimed she had a physical and nervous breakdown. The reason for her collapse would never be completely explained. It may, in fact, have been physical. Carolyn had been consuming large amounts of coffee each morning and working long hours. But the physical explanation may have only a secondary importance. Carolyn would go on to have other "collapses," other times when she would fall into depression, retire to her bed for weeks at a time, unable to work or even move. Those times would usually come during or after a period of great stress, especially when Carolyn felt anxious about her own abilities or torn between conflicting loyalties or warring self-images.

The winter and spring of 1924 must have been one such time for Carolyn, consumed as she was by her desire to finish her first novel. Although she admired women writers like George Eliot, she must have wondered if she could write as well—or write at all, for that matter. Carolyn would always see writing as a male gift. The act of writing forced women into awkward postures, she believed: they would have to deny or mask their sex—write like men—in order to gain approval. And if, as in her later fiction, Carolyn's first novel focused on some retelling of her own family stories, the conflicting emotions she felt about being a woman and a writer could only have been intensified. Carolyn's emotional allegiances to both her father and her grandmother were traumatically at odds. A hysterical illness may have resulted from her subconscious wish to withdraw from the battles writing entailed.

Whatever the reason, Carolyn took to her bed, and for about three months Pidie and Paul nursed her in their home. Then she left Chattanooga to visit her parents, who were then living in Guthrie, not far from Merry Mont.

The action was curious, considering Carolyn's long-standing difficulties with her mother. And yet, after nearly four years living apart from her parents, Carolyn's relationship with her mother had apparently improved. At least Nan seemed eager to help her daughter. Hearing that "there were two young men who wanted to be writers visiting the area," she called her neighbor Mrs. Warren and asked if Carolyn could meet them.

Carolyn met Mrs. Warren's son, Robert Penn, and his friend Allen

Tate that afternoon. Only nineteen, Robert Penn Warren was a tall, gangly young man, with large brown eyes, curly red hair, and a powerful desire to write poetry. His former college roommate, Allen, was the one Carolyn had designated "the most radical member" of the poets publishing the *Fugitive*. Twenty-four years old, Allen was slender, with blond hair, blue taunting eyes, fair skin, and a prominent, even bulging forehead. He had a gallant, courtly manner, and Carolyn could not help but find him charming.

The three spent several hours wandering through the woods, talking about writing. Allen had just visited New York City, and Carolyn listened eagerly to his stories about the people he had met: the poets Hart Crane, e. e. cummings, Malcolm Cowley, and Matthew Josephson, all leading figures in the newest circles of New York literati.

Later, Allen would say that he immediately fell in love with Carolyn. Only five feet five inches tall, slender, with magnolia white skin, dark hair, and haunting black eyes, Carolyn was the prettiest girl he had ever seen, Allen said.

Carolyn never said whether she fell in love at first sight, but Allen certainly captivated her. After struggling to master the "male" domain of writing, she may have been eager for any relationship that would affirm the feminine side of her nature. She may also have fallen in love with the *idea* that Allen represented: he was a young man committed to writing; a southerner, like herself, who had found a way to break into New York literary circles. Carolyn both needed and wanted what Allen had to offer.

Yet perhaps need was mutual. Years later, Carolyn told her friends that when Allen first met her, he heard voices. "He heard a voice saying, 'She can save me,'" she said.

It wasn't long before Carolyn and Allen were spending all their free time together. They made love for the first time in the Guthrie churchyard, Allen said later. By the time Allen left Guthrie about a month later, Carolyn had agreed to meet him in New York City in the fall.

 1924–1930

Carolyn's move to New York City confirmed the rebellious nature she had previously displayed in more muted ways. With a new roommate, Mary Maxfield, a modern young woman eager for adventure and men, Carolyn found an apartment in Greenwich Village and set about cultivating like-minded friends.

She was well placed to do so. The area known as the Village had been a center of literary activity since the nineteenth century. In the 1800s it had been a fashionable New York City suburb. Writers like James Fenimore Cooper, Herman Melville, Edgar Allan Poe, and Samuel Clemens lived there. Edith Wharton and Henry James eventually made the Washington Square area famous in their fiction: James was born and brought up there; Wharton lived there in the 1880s. By the 1900s most of the patrician families had moved farther north of the city, and the Village had become an artists' bohemia. Tenement houses and settlements of Italian immigrants replaced the elegant mansions and old-money families. Rents were cheap, so a new wave of writers eager to be close to the center of publishing took up residence: Frank Norris, Willa Cather, John Dos Passos, Elinor Wylie, Theodore Dreiser, Eugene O'Neill, Thomas Wolfe. The Provincetown Players established a winter theater on MacDougal Street; clubs and little magazines aligned with every political and aesthetic movement of the period sprang up: the Liberal Club, the *Masses,* the *Liberator,* the *Little Review.* Even the *Dial* found its home there after 1917.

After living for a while in the Washington Square area, Carolyn and Mary moved into an apartment at 20 West Eighth Street. Later, they added a third roommate, Vivian Brown, another reporter from Chattanooga, and found a larger apartment with a private bath. Carolyn had little in common with Mary, but Carolyn and Vivian had similar goals and interests, and they both found jobs at Johnson Features, one of the newer New York newspaper syndicates.

Yet it was another rebellious young woman with a passion for writing, Sally Wood, who became Carolyn's closest friend. During the summer of 1924, Carolyn had met Sally's brother, Remsen, while visiting her cousin, and he had urged Carolyn to look Sally up when she moved to New York City, sensing, quite rightly, that Carolyn and Sally would hit it off.

Carolyn went to see Sally soon after she arrived in the Village, and Sally would never forget their first meeting. She was startled at how much she and Carolyn looked alike. If not for their coloring, they could almost pass as sisters. They were very nearly the same size; but Sally's hair was brown, and Carolyn's "gleamed blacker than a raven's wing, matching her eyes set in a masklike face," Sally said. After they had known each other for a while, Carolyn's "masklike face disappeared," and Sally realized Carolyn used the mask as "a defense always ready and often useful against 'outrageous fortune.'"

At first glance Carolyn and Sally had little in common; their histories were as different as their coloring. Sally had grown up in Rochester, New York. She went to Wellesley College with dreams of a "literary career," but in 1918, eager to do her part for the war, she became a nurse instead. After the war Sally worked as a visiting nurse and eventually married a veteran of the ambulance corps, Stephen Rauschenbush. Together they had worked for the labor movement, first living with coal miners to try to nationalize the industry, then lobbying in Washington. It wasn't until after her husband had left the labor movement, disillusioned, and they had moved to Greenwich Village that Sally even considered returning to her college dreams of a literary career. She had no practical writing experience, but she was working on a memoir she called *The Mental Voyage*.

Despite their differences Carolyn and Sally found common ground. From their first meeting they talked about writing, and it seemed as if they "had known each other for years," Sally said. Carolyn thought Sally was a bit pushy and opinionated, but they soon became fast friends.

Carolyn did not see Allen Tate again until early November. After leaving Guthrie, Allen had stopped in Washington, D.C., to see his mother, and his visit had lasted longer than he had intended. Once in

New York, Allen found an apartment on Grove Street and began work as an editorial assistant for *Telling Tales,* a pulp magazine published by Climax Publishing Company. He quickly became part of a circle of young writers that included Hart Crane and Malcolm Cowley, whom he had met on his earlier visit to the city.

Each member of the circle was a self-conscious, self-styled "man of letters," intensely interested in poetry and modern literature. They met almost every Saturday evening, and often two or three times a week, for dinner, literary talk, and raucous song at Squarcialupis, one of the many cheap Italian restaurants in the Village. Allen was the only southerner in the crowd, and he readily played the part of southern gentleman, often dressing in a dark suit, always carrying a cane. Hart and Malcolm were more typical of the Greenwich Village literati; Allen thought Hart looked like an automobile salesman and Malcolm like a truck driver.

All were writing poetry at the time, and they would read aloud, discuss their work, and make plans for new little magazines. After graduating from a Pittsburgh high school and Harvard University, Malcolm had spent a number of years in France. He had been something of a disciple of the dadaist movement, and although forced to earn his living as an advertising copywriter for *Sweets Architectural Catalogue,* he had already decided his calling was to adopt "the whole of literature" as his province, to devote himself to literature "as one might devote a life to God or the Poor."

Hart had less formal education, but his ambitions were no less lofty. Born Harold Hart Crane, he had been only seventeen when he left his home in Ohio in 1916 and moved to New York City, determined to make his way as a poet. By the fall of 1924 he had published widely in little magazines. Like Allen and Malcolm, he loved to talk and laugh, but he was also subject to quick mood swings and unexplained rages, perhaps as much due to some anxiety over his homosexuality as to his intense desire to find transcendence in his art. In the fall of 1924, Hart was at work on a poem about the Brooklyn Bridge that he thought would be a "mystical synthesis of 'America.'" He was a visionary poet, eager to explore the spiritual realm behind everyday and abstract realities.

Few women were part of this literary circle. Susan Jenkins, Allen's boss at *Telling Tales,* usually attended the Saturday evening dinners at Squarcialupis. A former classmate of Cowley and Kenneth Burke, Sue had been married to another member of the circle, Jimmy Light, the director of the Provincetown Players. Cowley's wife, Peggy Baird, and

Matty Josephson's wife, Hannah, were often part of the crowd as well. But Allen would never bring Carolyn to any of their dinners or even try to involve her in their literary projects. Carolyn was "just a newspaper-woman," with none of the literary credentials necessary to impress the rather tight-knit, snobbish group of poets and intellectuals.

Carolyn never liked being excluded from Allen's literary circle, but she continued to see him. It apparently did not matter to them that she was four years older than he. Allen acted older than his years, and Carolyn looked younger than hers. Allen was handsome, confident, and charming to a fault. Few women, least of all Carolyn, could resist him.

But by Christmas Allen's charm had worn thin, Carolyn's temper had surfaced, and they quarreled. They were both fond of drinking, and even during those Prohibition times, there was no shortage of cheap liquor in the Village. Carolyn thought Allen was drinking too much. "Don't you think you ought to cut down a little?" she asked. Allen did not agree. They fought and separated, it seemed for good.

Carolyn stayed in New York, however. There was no reason to leave. She had a growing circle of friends and an excellent job: she and Vivian served as the entire staff for Johnson Features' Sunday magazine supplement. Located in a ninth-floor office in the Manufacturers Trust Company building in Columbus Circle, Johnson Features was one of the smallest syndicates in New York, but what it lacked in size was made up in prestige, because its founder had hired one of New York's best-known literary journalists, Burton Rascoe, to write a daily column, the "Day Book of a New Yorker."

Carolyn probably met Rascoe early in January 1925, just after his return from a two-month trip to Paris. Carolyn actually worked under another editor, but she called Rascoe her boss, perhaps because she saw Rascoe as a model for her own career. His first love was literature, and in both Chicago and New York, Rascoe had made a name for himself as a candid and free-wheeling literary critic. He knew everyone with any connection to New York literary circles; he was as quick to puncture the inflated reputations of established writers as to champion unknowns.

Carolyn covered New York cultural events for Johnson Features, but in time she specialized in interviewing celebrities for the magazine. She knew that if she could get a person to start talking, her "story was half written," and usually her techniques worked. In fact, Carolyn became so adept at her trade that at least one of the people she interviewed kept in touch with her long after the story was written. Texas Guinan was a gorgeous blonde woman who operated the El Fay Club on Third Street. Guinan had starred in silent movies before getting involved in the nightclub, one of the first with a floor show full of beautiful chorus girls. Like most of the speakeasies in the village during Prohibition, the club sold carbonated cider mixed with grain alcohol for scandalous prices, and reporters flocked to interview Guinan, who was known for welcoming her customers with a "Hello, sucker!" Carolyn and Guinan must have struck up quite a conversation during their interview, because afterward the hostess began calling Carolyn at three or four in the morning to chat.

Throughout the early months of 1925, Carolyn kept busy with work, never telling her parents she had stopped seeing Allen. But after a while, Carolyn began to feel ill, nauseated. She went to several doctors, but no one was able to identify the problem. Then she went to see an osteopath and found out what was wrong: she was pregnant.

What could she do? Carolyn was twenty-nine years old, no innocent young girl, but she could not remain both unmarried and pregnant, not even in the bohemian confines of Greenwich Village, where unconventional lifestyles were accepted with few questions. It would not have been difficult to find someone to perform an abortion; but the operation cost money, which Carolyn had little of, and as she well knew, it was too often dangerous, sometimes deadly. The only safe course was one that Carolyn must have had little hope of pursuing: marriage. Still, she went to see Allen.

By the spring of 1925, Allen had begun dating other women: his interest in Carolyn had ended with their quarrel. When Carolyn confronted him with her pregnancy, he was shocked and upset. But what were their alternatives? Reluctantly Allen agreed to marriage, a temporary one. After the baby was born, Carolyn would have to divorce him.

Carolyn did not discuss her situation with her friends. Allen's friend and boss, Sue Jenkins, helped Carolyn make the arrangements, then on May 15 Carolyn told Sally. The women had planned to meet for dinner that evening; Sally was going to introduce Carolyn to an attractive male friend of hers. But Carolyn told Sally to ask Mary Maxfield instead. "I'm going to marry Allen Tate," Carolyn explained. "Ask my roommate to dinner. I don't want her to know."

Sue Jenkins and her friend William Slater Brown were the only witnesses that afternoon when Carolyn and Allen were married at City Hall. The ceremony was brief. They did not bother to exchange rings or pretend the union was anything but grim necessity. After the wedding the four went out to dinner, but Italian food did not change the day's somber tone. If there was any consolation, it was that Carolyn was already almost five months pregnant. She and Allen would have to endure only about four months of married life.

Sue gave Carolyn and Allen the use of her apartment at 30 Jones Street, and the couple began telling friends and family that they were married. To make Carolyn's pregnancy more respectable, both Carolyn and Allen claimed that they had been secretly married on December 27, 1924. It was the first of many charades in their life together. Carolyn managed to keep the notice of the actual date out of the paper, but none of Allen's close friends in New York believed their story. Carolyn's family in Kentucky did, however, and their belief was perhaps more important.

Later Carolyn and Allen would move the date of their marriage back to November 2, but Allen could never keep the story straight. Carolyn was more concerned about appearances. She would never talk about what happened, and she got extremely angry when Allen gave the wrong date.

Since Allen earned only thirty dollars a week, Carolyn continued her newspaper work after their marriage. When her colleagues wondered why she did not change her name to Carolyn Tate, she explained that she believed in women's rights and thought a married woman should keep her maiden name.

Carolyn and Allen went through the motions of married life: entertaining friends; seeing Sally Wood and her husband, Steve, almost every day; sharing cheap, home-cooked meals with them. Sally watched over Carolyn's uncertain health, and Sue Jenkins tried to ease Allen's precarious financial situation, enlisting his friends in an appeal to a local foundation for a five-hundred-dollar emergency grant.

After Sue quit her job in June to move to the country with Bill Brown, whom she would soon marry, Carolyn and Allen sometimes went to visit them on weekends. Sue and Bill bought a small house in Pawling, New York, about seventy miles from the city. Built before the American Revolution and still with no modern conveniences, the house was in an isolated section of the state near the Connecticut border. Natives called the area Tory Hill, Tory Valley, or Robber Rocks because a local cave had been used by British sympathizers during the Revolution as a refuge between ambush attacks on the carts supplying Washington's army.

Carolyn loved being back in the country. While visiting Sue and Bill over the Fourth of July, she and Allen heard about a small house nearby that could be bought for about five hundred dollars. They tried to think of a way to find the money, and Allen began telling his friends they would soon be getting a place in the country, but he was dreaming. "We couldn't buy an extra Woolworth dinner plate," Carolyn said wistfully.

In addition to the trips to Tory Valley to visit Sue and Bill, Carolyn and Allen sometimes went to spend the day with Malcolm and Peggy Cowley, who were then living on Staten Island. One evening the Cowleys took them to meet another writer from the Village, Dorothy Day, who had moved to Staten Island with her common-law husband, Forster Batterham.

Dorothy was known in the Village as much for her work as a radical journalist as for her ability to hold her drink. Only two years younger than Carolyn, she had gotten her start as a writer in 1916 as a reporter for a small socialist paper, *Call,* then gone on to work at the *Masses* and the *Liberator*. The previous spring, she had published *The Eleventh Virgin*. The partly autobiographical novel was called "truth incoherent" by a local reviewer, but the title earned Dorothy twenty-five hundred dollars—a veritable fortune—in motion-picture rights.

Carolyn didn't think much of Dorothy's writing, but she enjoyed visiting her. The Cowleys and Tates talked with Dorothy until well past midnight. Dorothy was vivacious and literate; she also envied Carolyn. "Oh, I hope *I* am pregnant!" Dorothy kept saying. This "intense desire to have a baby surprised me to no end," Carolyn said later. Carolyn felt as if her pregnancy was a millstone around her neck; it had forced her into a marriage of convenience, and it threatened her professional aspirations. Dorothy, in a similar situation, wanted nothing more than to have a child. Carolyn couldn't understand why. But as it turned out, Dorothy's suspicions were correct: she *was* already pregnant.

Dorothy also had no way of knowing that Carolyn was just pretending to be happily married, but a falsehood often repeated can sometimes pass for truth, especially for Carolyn and Allen. And as they passed months in deception, Carolyn and Allen experienced such a metamorphosis, apparently rediscovering their former affection for one another. Before long, Allen was even excited about becoming a father.

Hart Crane was also excited. He decided several months earlier to be the baby's godfather, despite the fact that a baptism was unlikely. None of the three had much faith in any religious denomination. Art was their religion, Carolyn said later, the only thing they really believed in. By the time the baby was born, Hart had left town, apparently forgetting about the whole matter.

Carolyn went into labor at the end of September. Sally sat by her side in the Sloane Lying-In Hospital, timing Carolyn's pains. Between contractions Carolyn talked about her novel: it was as good a distraction as any. She also talked about how Allen's friends, "determined to see *him* through this ordeal," took him off to drink and wait for the news. But before long Allen appeared at the hospital, "clutching his cane, . . . his face more ravaged" than Carolyn's, Sally said later. "He had escaped his friends."

On September 25, 1925, Carolyn gave birth to a daughter whom she and Allen named Nancy, after Carolyn's mother. Nancy Tate had her father's blue eyes and, originally, a "very wicked and angry expression," which delighted Allen. He wrote all his friends and both families about her birth, rejoicing in his "proud fatherhood."

Carolyn spent a short time in the hospital, then Allen brought her and the baby home to a new apartment on Morton Street. Although free to separate, Allen apparently had no interest in holding Carolyn to the promised divorce. But Sally Wood's marriage did fall apart, and she left for France unexpectedly just after Nancy was born, to Carolyn's dismay.

The first weeks after Nancy's birth were difficult for Carolyn. Laura Riding, a poet Allen had known for several years, had arrived in New York and soon became a fixture in the Tate household. Although she tried to be useful and even helped Allen clean the apartment before Carolyn returned from the hospital, Laura got on Carolyn's nerves: Carolyn christened her "Laura Riding Roughshod." Irritable and moody, Carolyn "seemed set against sparing herself full consciousness of her predicaments and bent on accepting them without feigned ease," Laura thought. When Laura left for England, Carolyn was not sorry to see her go.

But in October Carolyn's "predicaments" hardly lessened: instead, her mother arrived. At first Nan Gordon showed amazing patience, coping with the cramped quarters and a regular stream of "wild" people dropping in at all hours of the day or night, but secretly she was horrified to find Carolyn and Allen had no food in their apartment. She also had little patience with her daughter and son-in-law's "modern" notions of child raising. Whenever Nancy cried, Nan picked her up, and by the end of the month, Nan had persuaded Carolyn and Allen to let her take the baby back to Kentucky.

Carolyn felt paralyzed, unable to mount a protest and unsure she even ought to object. "It struck everybody as the 'sensible' thing to do," Carolyn observed. After all, she had no assurance Allen would not change his mind about the divorce at any time. And even if they stayed married, they had little income to live on. If Carolyn thought logically about her daughter's welfare, she had to admit Nancy would be better off with her grandparents: there she would be well fed and doted on. She would also be living near Merry Mont and her extended family, a fact sure to comfort Carolyn, who cherished her own childhood there.

Yet, logic aside, Carolyn wondered if sending Nancy to Kentucky might actually be "a very mad thing to do." Did she really want her mother bringing Nancy up? Carolyn had to fear her mother's influence on the child, and perhaps she also worried about what the decision would mean about herself. No matter how Carolyn might rationalize her choice, it would seem unnatural to send her own daughter away. Yet how would she keep writing while taking care of Nancy? At the last minute Carolyn almost refused to let her mother leave with Nancy. But she finally decided to let Nan have her way.

Carolyn claimed she made the decision because she was "afraid Allen would break down trying to work day and night too" if they kept Nancy, and she feared her mother "would have collapsed" if sent back to Kentucky alone. Yet Carolyn must have also feared her own collapse if she had to balance writing and motherhood. To mask her fears, Carolyn adopted a martyr's pose. "I feel a little like the Lamb of God taking away the sins of the generations," she wrote Sally. Nan took the baby to make up for not being "allowed to have her own babies. Now if I can just keep my hands off of Nancy's we may get back to normalcy in a generation or so!"

Carolyn tried to write herself out of the depression she felt. For a while, she felt so "rotten" she "couldn't think clearly," Carolyn said, but she kept going "through the motions." There was little else she could do.

Even at this early stage in their relationship, however, Allen had a way of complicating Carolyn's attempt to find healing through work. Soon after Nan left, he made the mistake of correcting the grammar on one of the memos the owner of Climax Publishing sent around the office. The publisher fired him. Consequently, Allen and Carolyn could no longer afford to live in New York City. Carolyn quit her job at Johnson Features; then she and Allen moved to Tory Valley, as Sue Jenkins and Bill Brown had done months earlier.

The Tates arrived in the valley on a miserable, rainy day in November. Bill met them at the railroad station in Patterson, New York, and drove them to their winter home. The roads were so muddy and full of ruts that Bill could barely get the Model T through. It was a primitive, back-woods section of New York, beautiful in the summer but rugged and foreboding most of the rest of the year.

The Tates had arranged to rent half of a large old farmhouse from Addie Turner for only eight dollars a month. They had about eight rooms, fully furnished, and more conveniences than most places in the area: there was a telephone within walking distance, some running water courtesy of a kitchen pump, and a convenient mailbox. There was also plenty of good company: Sue and Bill lived only about a half mile away, and the Cowleys had recently bought a small place nearby, in Sherman, Connecticut.

Their friends wondered how the Tates would ever "keep warm and pay for their groceries," but Carolyn and Allen both felt practically well-off, so much so that soon after moving in, they invited Hart Crane, who was in even worse financial straits, to come to Tory Valley and live with them.

Hart loved the area of Robber Rocks, as he called it, yet he hesitated to take the Tates up on their offer. He had been living for a while on what-ever he could borrow from friends, but he knew how little money Allen and Carolyn had. Then, on December 6, Otto Kahn, a banker and patron of the arts, gave Hart a thousand dollars to help him finish his long poem, "The Bridge," and he promised Hart another thousand if necessary. His financial problems solved, Hart decided to move in with the Tates. He arrived on December 12 in high spirits, bringing with him everything he owned—boxes and bundles of books, quilts, and daguerreotypes.

For a while the three writers lived together harmoniously in the ram-bling farmhouse they shared with the sixty-four-year-old Mrs. Turner and her eighty-year-old aunt. Although Carolyn was used to the rigors of country life, she had worried that Allen would not fare well, because he had never lived in the country before. Yet her fears soon appeared to be groundless. In just a short while Allen "developed a whole new set of talents": sawing, hunting, and snowshoeing. He made "a wonderful countryman," she wrote to a friend.

Hart spent most of December and January settling into three of the upstairs rooms. He wouldn't help chop the wood they needed to keep the house warm—it "constricted his imagination," he said—but he did wash dishes and help Carolyn with Christmas dinner, making cranberry sauce as well as sauce for the plum pudding. When he decided to buy a new typewriter, he helped Carolyn even more by giving her his old machine. Until that time she had to make do, using Allen's typewriter when he was not writing.

Everyone had a place for writing, although not everyone used it regularly. Hart worked in one of his rooms at an old desk; Allen had another room; Carolyn had the kitchen table. Although Carolyn tried to write every day, Allen and Hart were less rigorous about their work, preferring to wander about in the woods looking for rabbits and squirrels or to tramp over to visit Sue and Bill and drink cider by the fire.

After a while Carolyn grew bitter about the way the poets spent more time studying and meditating on their verses than writing them. She was also lonely. Sally was thousands of miles away, and Carolyn missed her dreadfully. Nancy was in Kentucky, and Carolyn's parents wrote wonderful letters about how she was gaining weight, laughing and singing and cutting teeth. They even sent "kodak pictures every now and then," but as Carolyn wrote Sally, "kodak pictures aren't much when you want your baby." She hoped Nancy might join them in the spring, but that was not assured.

January and February were bitterly cold; Carolyn got frostbite on her feet. The snow piled up with drifts as high as seven feet in some places. For six weeks even the mailman couldn't make his way to the Turner house. By mid-March tempers were short; patience with the rigors of country life in winter had about ended. As spring arrived, the snows melted. But then the dirt roads became mud holes, and the three frazzled writers were once again housebound. Before the outside weather cleared, the conditions inside Mrs. Turner's house reached a critical stage.

Hart had finished a new outline for his long poem, yet found it hard to go forward. Allen agonized over having to write another book review to get the money to eat. Carolyn was struggling to start a new novel. She had given Allen her first attempt, *Darkling I Listen,* to read, but after watching his expression as he read it, Carolyn realized the novel "wasn't any good," so she destroyed it.

Ideas for the new novel came slowly, and sometimes Carolyn could hardly write for all the distractions and interruptions. Although Allen cooked breakfast, Carolyn had to prepare lunch and dinner. Her work station, the kitchen table, had to be cleared before each meal, and the room was common ground. Frustrated, bored, and easily distracted, Hart often came clumping into the kitchen and interrupted Carolyn with a funny story to tell or some great discovery to share. Although Carolyn was often curt and in ill temper, Hart didn't realize how much his behavior bothered her. He thought he was just being friendly—and he also did not think he was interrupting anything important.

Carolyn resented Hart's patronizing attitude. With every new episode and interruption, she grew more annoyed. She also hated the way Hart had spread himself and his things throughout their house. Everywhere she looked, she saw one of Hart's knickknacks or pictures. Everything Hart did, he did with loud enthusiasm, from early morning to night.

Finally, desperate for peace and quiet, Carolyn put a lock on the kitchen door to keep Hart out while she was writing. But her action only intensified the troubles. Hart felt rejected and shunned by both Carolyn and Allen. He took to sulking in his room or spending time with the landlady, Mrs. Turner, so he wouldn't have to see the Tates.

Mrs. Turner was quite taken with Hart. Carolyn thought she "fell violently in love" with him, and the whole situation reminded Carolyn of something she might see in a Eugene O'Neill play: a "pathetic elderly person in love with a young homosexual." After a while Mrs. Turner began preparing and serving all of Hart's meals. If Carolyn or Allen dared to criticize Hart for being inconsiderate, Mrs. Turner sprang to his defense. "Mr. Crane's *so* sensitive and nervous," she said often with admiration.

Eventually no one talked to one another, except by means of angry notes slipped under each other's doors, and Hart decided to leave. Although Allen had been just as critical of Hart's behavior, Hart blamed Carolyn for the quarrel. He told his mother he could "bury [his] pride and become reconciled," but he didn't think the Tates would, "Mrs. Tate especially." His leaving was really a pity, he told friends: "My poem was progressing so beautifully until Mrs. Tate took it into her head to be so destructive."

Carolyn was glad to be rid of Hart. He was "a fine poet," she wrote Sally after he left at the end of April, "but God save me from ever having another romantic in the house with me!" Finally, she no longer had to work on the kitchen table. Instead, Carolyn set up a study for herself in a "darling little white room" Hart had used, and she was relieved to find that having a room of her own helped her to write. She thought she would have her new novel "ready to offer by fall." "I'm not bored or side tracked in the country—less so than in New York," she wrote Sally.

By the middle of May, Carolyn had written about ten thousand words of her new story. The book would have a mood of "slowly increasing madness." "A young gentleman is in love with somebody else's wife," she explained to Sally. She thought the love affair would "introduce reality into this unreal scene"; it was "the most poignant example."

Allen was also having what Carolyn called a "very fecund period" that spring. "In fact it became almost indecent the way he produced poems," she thought. "Any moment he was likely to be seized with labor pains." Yet Allen also continued to write reviews for the *Nation* and the *New Republic,* since their finances were still in disarray. "We hang on from one *Nation* check to another," Carolyn told the Cowleys; we keep "an order to Sears Roebuck or Macy's all made up ready to send the minute a check comes."

All the while, Allen searched for a publisher for a collection of his poetry. In early summer Robert M. McBride and Company, a New York publisher, told Allen it might publish his poetry if he would write a novel first. Allen tried to outline a story, but Carolyn doubted he would be able to write one. "It seems that if he could his thoughts would have turned that way long ago," Carolyn thought, wishing McBride's would take her novel instead.

In between work on her novel, Carolyn tried her hand at writing "pot-boilers." She wanted to send her mother money and get Nancy to Tory Valley for a summer visit. The Gordons continued to send Carolyn and Allen pictures and regular reports of Nancy's progress. Carolyn was glad to hear Nancy was such a model baby, but she began to be disturbed by some of her parents' comments. Carolyn's father told his daughter that Nancy could come "only for a visit." He thought Carolyn and Allen were "not prepared to take care of" their daughter, and he did not want "to jeopardize" Nancy's progress.

Carolyn's mother said they might not be able to make the trip at all: Aunt Pidie wanted to see the baby, but she could not do so until the end of July, and by August it would be too hot for them to travel. Carolyn figured her mother was only making excuses: she was "as wily and de-signing [a] female as ever lived." Yet, Carolyn wondered if they could "work out some system" to allow Nancy to spend half the year with her parents, the other half with her grandparents. For all her desire to see

Nancy, Carolyn was apparently not ready to accept full responsibility for her. Yet she said she acted out of concern for her mother and Nancy. "I'm really afraid Mother will go all to pieces if Nancy is taken away from her," she explained to Sally. Nancy would benefit from their shared care: she would "have a more varied experience than most children," Carolyn wrote.

The Cowleys held a Fourth of July party that year. Allen and Carolyn, Sue and Bill, and assorted members of the New York circle gathered in Sherman, Connecticut. Jimmy Light arrived with a manuscript of Eugene O'Neill's newest play; a sixteen-year-old flapper told stories about Hindu methods of birth control. There was less liquor than usual, but Carolyn got drunk, and Malcolm thought she and Allen gave "the impression of babes in the wood, unable to cope with the complexities of modern life." It annoyed Malcolm to see Allen working in spurts, writing only when "the grocer refuses to extend them further credit."

At the end of July, both Carolyn and Allen put aside their writing when Carolyn's mother arrived with Nancy for an extended visit. Almost a year old, Nancy was healthy and even-tempered. Carolyn thought she looked "rather like Allen" with her golden hair and deep blue eyes. Nancy "snickers to herself almost all day, occasionally breaking into a loud guffaw," Carolyn wrote a friend, adding that Allen was in "constant amazement at the uncanny things" his daughter did, since he had "never known a baby intimately."

But Carolyn and Allen could not really enjoy their daughter's visit because, as Carolyn later wrote Sally, "Mother wouldn't let us." Nan Gordon made no secret of the fact that she hoped in bringing up her granddaughter to "correct all the errors" she made rearing Carolyn. Over and over again, she turned to her son-in-law and remarked, "And you see how Carolyn turned out." Allen was embarrassed, Carolyn annoyed. Both knew what Nan meant: Carolyn had come to a "bad end"— poverty, unemployment, wild friends, and Allen.

Although Carolyn tried to approach the whole situation with her mother rationally, she couldn't get around her mother's almost "medieval" use of theology. "Lay down your mind and take up the mind of God," Nan told her daughter, but Carolyn said she wanted to "keep what little mind" she had, so they never could agree. Carolyn listened to some of her mother's statements with horror. Nan believed no one should confuse Christianity with humanitarianism because "the mind of God" was capable of cruelty. Carolyn was sure her mother would not hesitate to use cruelty "to gain her own ends, always of course within the strict letter of the law."

After several weeks Carolyn could hardly decide what to do next. She worried that her mother would collapse without Nancy, making her father suffer. Also, she feared that Nancy was actually better off with her grandparents. "When it comes to a choice between Mother and Nancy I am quite capable of being ruthless," she insisted. "But just now I honestly don't know whether it's best for Nancy to risk our uncertain fortunes. It is fiendishly cold here in the winter. Then too, there are times when we simply don't eat."

Finally, Carolyn let Nancy return to Kentucky. With a regular income of only thirty-three dollars a month, Carolyn and Allen were hard-pressed to take care of themselves, let alone a child.

As the summer ended, Carolyn gardened furiously, trying to put aside enough food for the winter months and perhaps also trying to put aside her own feelings of inadequacy as a mother. Working in the garden was always renewing for Carolyn. But Allen had no part of it. After violent quarrels with him over the garden during the early part of the summer, Carolyn had resigned herself to the fact that Allen would never share her passion for fingering the dirt. She thought he had "the strangest attitude toward the country." It was "the same appreciation you'd have for a good set in the theatre," she explained to a friend; "Allen feels toward Nature as I do toward mathematics—respectful indifference." It amazed her how he could walk "about the garden hailing each tomato and melon with amazement," never seeing "any connection between planting seeds and eating fruit." But Carolyn thought the stay in Tory Valley had made Allen "a more integrated person."

Carolyn wanted to stay there forever. With Allen's help around the house, she could devote entire mornings to her novel. By September she had twenty thousand words written, and she began to send an outline of the book to publishers. But by November the Tates had returned to New York City to live. They took a job as janitors for an apartment house at 27 Bank Street. In exchange for stoking the furnace and keeping the halls and stairways clean, they were given a basement apartment, part of which they could rent for extra money.

Years earlier in her newspaper column, Carolyn had quoted a writer who insisted that the time "when an author had to do paperhanging . . . or janitor work in order to make enough to live on" was "gone—almost entirely"; only "bad authors" would fail to make a living at their writing. But during the winter of 1926–27, Carolyn was relieved to find a job as a janitor. The work was "rather hectic at times," she said, "but better than having a steady job."

Allen was more sensitive about their situation. When Matthew Joseph-son sent a newspaper reporter to interview the "poet-janitor" of Bank Street, Allen was furious. Refusing to speak to the reporter, he started a lifelong feud with Josephson. Matty tried to placate him, at first telling him the publicity might help Allen find a rich patron, then saying it was all a dadaist prank. None of his excuses worked. Allen did not want that type of publicity; he preferred to forget his work as a janitor, or at least minimize the actual labor involved.

For the next year, in addition to her janitorial duties, Carolyn took on other odd jobs. For about a month, she did some proofreading; later, she typed for the American Society for Cultural Relations with Russia, one of many Communist-front organizations flourishing in the Village. Carolyn thought her boss "a nice girl," all too "taken up with the work," but she had no interest in the politics of "the Culture hounds." Their committees drove her mad; the nightly meetings interfered far too much with her writing.

Her best job was another secretarial position—taking dictation for the English novelist Ford Madox Ford. After arriving in New York at the end of October 1926, Ford fancied himself the darling of the American public and publishing world. Nearly fifty-three years old, he had already published more than sixty books in almost every literary genre, but his abiding passion was for the novel. Grandson of the Pre-Raphaelite Ford Madox Brown, he had become a prominent figure around London in the early 1900s as the editor of the *English Review*. More recently, he had founded and edited the *Transatlantic Review,* and he talked at length about his friendship with writers like Henry James, Joseph Conrad, D. H. Lawrence, James Joyce, and Ezra Pound.

Although none of his books were ever great financial successes, Ford's latest novel, *No More Parades,* had sold well enough to garner him a flurry of critical acclaim and lecture engagements on his first trip to America. Ford thought of himself as a Tory gentleman and ladies' man. Once described as looking "somehow like a British version of the Re-publican elephant" or a "behemoth in gray tweeds," Ford was a rotund, middle-aged man, with a double chin, prominent nose, and light, wispy hair. He had a high forehead, and "quiet, absent-looking blue eyes that seemed as if they were always pondering over something." A brilliant talker, he spoke almost incoherently, with a terrible wheeze—the result, he claimed, of being gassed in the war. That was not true—merely one of many creative fictions about his life.

For a while Ford worked in a dingy garret apartment on West Thirteenth Street. Because the apartment was always overheated, Ford, sweating profusely, wore only his undergarments while dictating to Carolyn. Yet despite his unusual behavior, Carolyn thought Ford was "awfully nice": she loved "to see him take his sentences by the tail and uncurl them—in a perfectly elegant manner." It seemed to her that he was "sought after by practically every established New York publisher," and she didn't think any other contemporary novelist wrote as elegantly as Ford.

Carolyn was amused at the way Ford would almost weep over what she called her "lapses into Americanisms." "My deah child," he once said, in all seriousness, "*do* you spell 'honour' without a u?" Carolyn soon adopted his English spellings as her own. She was greatly impressed by Ford's devotion to his art, his "deep and passionate interest in the techniques of fiction," and his endless generosity to younger writers. But for quite a while Carolyn did not show Ford her own fiction. What if he laughed or, even worse, told her she had no talent? Carolyn had little confidence in her abilities as a writer, just as years earlier, she had little confidence in her abilities as a student.

Ford spent about four months in New York during the winter of 1926–27, then returned to France. In September 1927 he returned to New York for several more months. At some point Carolyn convinced Ford to move into an apartment in their building on Bank Street. In addition to taking his dictation, Carolyn invited Ford to share their meals.

Ford admired the Tates. Allen was "such a nice fellow and a good poet," he said. Carolyn was "extraordinarily well educated and quite a lady." But he worried about them: the way they lived was "something terrible," with too much to do and only paltry sums coming in at irregular intervals. In his usual generous fashion, he tried to help Allen find a publisher for his poems.

But publishers were wary; poetry had little commercial appeal. In April of 1927, Allen finally agreed to write a biography of Stonewall Jackson for Minton, Balch, and Company. The decision marked a change in Allen's attitude toward the South. Previously he played the part of southern gentleman but professed no loyalty to southern culture or literature. Often he had attacked the parochialism of southern people and their art. But in the spring of 1927, he vowed to attack the South no more. Soon, in addition to writing a partisan biography of Stonewall Jackson, he was considering work on a volume of essays in defense of the South.

That summer Carolyn and Allen made a whirlwind tour of Virginia in a second-hand 1921 Ford they called General Jackson. In thirteen days they covered 1,150 miles, tracing Jackson's path and visiting relatives living along the way. Once they returned to New York, the Bank Street apartment became headquarters of a new Confederate movement. During the day Allen worked tirelessly on Jackson's biography. At night, talk of "the War" filled the apartment: talk of Manassas, Antietam, Fredericksburg, and Chancellorsville.

Southern friends came to New York and camped for weeks in the Tates' extra room. Red Warren, who had been doing graduate work at Berkeley, transferred to Yale University and brought his fiancée, Cinina Brescia, to meet the Tates. Carolyn enjoyed having Red around. Sometimes she and Allen would sit with him and talk from breakfast to midnight. But Carolyn took an immediate dislike to "Emma Cinina Elena Anna Clotilda Maria Borgia Venia Gasparini Brescia," a "daughter of the Borgias" and a "hell hound if I ever saw one," Carolyn said. The daughter of the conductor of the San Francisco Symphony, Cinina spent too much time bragging about her father and her family. Carolyn wanted to throw Cinina out a window after only one week, but Red and Cinina stayed about six weeks. Carolyn tried to be gracious for Red's sake.

Another frequent guest was also a student at Yale, Andrew Lytle. Although he had completed his bachelor's degree at Vanderbilt and had even published a poem in the *Fugitive,* Andrew had not known Allen before mutual friends arranged for them to meet that year. At Yale to study playwriting and drama with George Pierce Baker, Andrew had been brought up on a large plantation named Cornsilk, just outside Guntersville, Alabama. Like Carolyn, he had grown up hearing stories of the Old South and the Civil War, and he was passionate about the South. He would never forget the velvet choker his grandmother wore to conceal the scar on her throat caused by Union fire; he was "unreconstructed," a southern rebel and proud of it. When the talk about "the War" filled the Tate apartment, Andrew was a welcome participant.

In the midst of all the visitors, Carolyn worked on her novel. She also wrote two short stories, her first, in just a few sittings. When Ford Madox Ford returned that fall, she got up her courage and showed him one, "Old Mrs. Llewellyn."

"Humph, that's ver' nice," Ford said after he read the manuscript. But Carolyn realized he was only being polite. She didn't bother to show him her novel. Later she realized what was wrong: "It was not a story," Carolyn said. "Nothing happened. . . . it was simply *about* a character."

The main character in "Old Mrs. Llewellyn" was Carolyn's grandmother, thinly disguised as Ellen Llewellyn. The story line was sparse for twenty-one typewritten pages of prose: on one day in late August, Mrs. Llewellyn drove home after going on an errand and found out that her daughter Molly, who had been visiting, had decided to leave a day early for her home in Louisville. At first, Molly's sudden departure upset the old woman, but "in a moment she knew that she could bear it," Carolyn wrote. "She had borne it so many times before." Molly wanted her mother to come to Louisville for the winter, but Mrs. Llewellyn did not want to leave her home for that long: "She got sick if she stayed away from The Old Place too long," the narrator explained. "If I went away from here in the fall there'd be nothing to come back to in the spring," Mrs. Llewellyn told her daughter.

Mrs. Llewellyn was seventy-seven years old, and her children thought she had no business living alone at "the Old Place" with "all this milk and butter and chickens and all this house work without any conveniences." They also thought she was losing her wits. On one level the focus of "Old Mrs. Llewellyn" was on aging; the story was about one old lady and her foolish, stubborn refusal to change.

But on another level "Old Mrs. Llewellyn" was about creativity and independence. Carolyn did not create a dramatic plot line, but she clearly celebrated the spirit of Mrs. Llewellyn. She might be a stubborn, lonely, and fearful old woman, but, almost an artist surrogate, Mrs. Llewellyn was also strong, creative, and willing to take risks.

In a hurry to get home because she knew her hired hand would not milk the cows properly, Mrs. Llewellyn nevertheless enjoyed her drive, taking in all the sensual delights of the late August afternoon. Her eyes were failing her; she sometimes saw "very strange sights" during her drives: "the golden rod leaning over the road would suddenly leap forward like a band of men armed with spears or the twisted oak at the top of State Line hill would become a man crouching, his dog beside him." At first these sights had bothered her, but "she had grown gradually to enjoy her fantastic vision," just as she had grown to enjoy the inconveniences of living alone at the Old Place. "Old people [were] better off at home," Ellen insisted, although she usually did not think of herself as old. To keep her independence and identity, she would face her fears and create her own peculiar order out of what others saw as chaos or disintegration.

Her situation was analogous to Carolyn's own life. Almost thirty-two years old, Carolyn was sensitive about the fact that she had not yet made her mark in the literary world. Neither her husband nor his friends took her seriously as an artist, and some might say her crazy family stories were hardly suitable subjects for fiction. But in "Old Mrs. Llewellyn" Carolyn imagined one woman, her beloved grandmother, whose creative energy was stronger than the well-meaning but crippling ties of her family.

Unlike Allen, Carolyn did not have to struggle to define her southern loyalties. Although sometimes she might adopt her father's critical attitude toward the Meriwether family myth, from her earliest days she had reveled in her family stories and southern heritage. During her college years she had made no attempt to hide her strong southern sympathies; as a newspaper reviewer, she had championed southern culture and literature. Carolyn had not come to New York as an exile from the South, but as one more of a virtual stream of southerners who wanted to be writers and knew the value of the New York imprimatur. She made no attempt to hide or reject her love for the South: on Lincoln's birthday she pulled down the blinds in the apartment and declared a public fast. In her first short story Carolyn did not abandon either the South or her family; instead, she began to turn her family history into fiction. This first attempt was only a limited success, but the character and history of Ellen Llewellyn would soon reappear in her work.

Family responsibilities hampered that work for more than a year, however. In August 1927 Carolyn's mother had a mastectomy to remove a rapidly growing cancer, and soon after that Carolyn brought Nancy back to New York City for good.

J. M. Gordon warned Carolyn that she would not have an easy time. Nancy was "the worst spoiled child in the United States," he said, and in the first few weeks back in New York, Carolyn realized he had not been exaggerating. The Gordons had rocked Nancy to sleep and picked her up whenever she cried—behaviors Carolyn had no intention of continuing. Carolyn thought it was "certainly hell" for several months until they established their own routine for Nancy.

Since the Bank Street apartment, with only three rooms, was far too small for three Tates and the usual round of visitors, they eventually moved to a new apartment at 561 Hudson Street. The "fine pre-Revolutionary tenement house" had more than a few drawbacks: no hot water, for example. But Carolyn loved the place she called "The Cabinet of Dr. Caligari," referring to a movie in which "everyone was crazy although one did not realize it at first."

Nancy soon became the center of an adoring circle of "courtesy" aunts and uncles. She talked incessantly, and Carolyn was so delighted by her daughter's sayings that she regularly included them in letters to family and friends.

Realizing how her parents made their living, Nancy often encouraged them to write. "Go on, Daddy and make me a living," Nancy would say, once picking up a sheet of paper from her father's desk to ask, "Is this my living, Daddy?" When Allen said yes, Nancy's response came quickly. "It's mighty thin, Daddy," she said.

Carolyn's contribution to her daughter's "living" was even thinner, and during the winter and spring of 1928, Carolyn was in despair. "I have little to show for two—or is it three years—work," she moaned in a letter to Sally, who was still in France. Although she had finished her second novel in addition to the two stories she had written the previous summer, Carolyn could not find a publisher. When she submitted her stories to Paul Rosenfeld, editor of *American Caravan,* he told her that her "time had not come."

Allen tried to help by sending one of Carolyn's stories, called "Before Eleven," to the *Virginia Quarterly Review,* where he had published a number of poems and reviews. But by the middle of May, Carolyn had only another rejection. And Carolyn had little time to write anything new. "It is these young poets from the South," she exclaimed. Sometimes friends, often merely acquaintances of Allen, "they call us up as soon as they hit the Pennsylvania Station and they stay anywhere from a week to a month," Carolyn said bitterly.

She found some consolation in two new friends of her own: Katherine Anne Porter and Josephine Herbst. Both women wrote fiction; Katherine Anne was working on short stories, and Josie wrote novels. Katherine Anne lived one floor below Carolyn in Caligari; Josie lived not far away with her husband, John Herrmann. The three women often gathered to talk and smoke for hours. Carolyn found their friendship a great comfort during those times when Allen's circle of poets defined—

and sometimes engulfed—the Tates' world. The women reassured one another that the unfinished novels and stories would indeed be finished. No matter what the philistine publishers said, they knew they would find readers to appreciate their talents—or at least, they would tell one another that, when they weren't railing against the editors, publishers and "gents" controlling the literary world.

Five years older than Carolyn, Katherine Anne was working as a copy-editor for Macaulay and Company during the winter of 1928. After trying to work as an actress, then lecturing on the lyceum circuit and writing for newspapers in Texas and Colorado, Katherine Anne had moved to New York City in 1919. At age twenty-nine she vowed that "one day she would write as well as anyone in America." By 1923 she had published her first mature story, "María Concepción," in the *Century* magazine. But Katherine Anne wrote slowly, in spurts or not at all, and between 1923 and 1928 she had spent most of her time on hack writing jobs and failed relationships.

Like Carolyn, Katherine Anne was a southerner, brought up in Texas by her grandmother after her mother died when she was not quite two years old. Her education had been haphazard and limited, imagination her only escape from a repressive, puritanical upbringing. Although born Callie Porter, she liked to dream she was a changeling, and by changing her name—first to Katherine Russell, then to Katherine Anne—she had begun to refashion her identity and life story. She was a beautiful woman, a perpetual and accomplished flirt, with luminous gray eyes and a husky voice. Yet she was passionate about writing, so Katherine Anne and Carolyn had become close friends.

Josie Herbst was also devoted to a literary life, but she had come to New York from the Midwest, not the South. Born in Sioux City, Iowa, in 1892, she was probably the most radical member of the group. Outspoken and argumentative, she was an awkward, large-boned woman with cornflower blue eyes and a cutting sense of humor. She had struggled to escape from Sioux City, arriving in New York City in 1919 soon after finishing her bachelor's degree at the University of California at Berkeley. Always interested in politics, she had quickly gotten to know the agitators and revolutionaries of Greenwich Village, the men and women writing for and publishing the *Masses* and the *Liberator*.

Like Carolyn, Josie was married to a writer, and the marriage had been partly one of convenience: although Josie was not pregnant, John Herrmann's parents had pressured the two into marriage during the fall of 1926. But John was a novelist, not a poet, and unlike Carolyn, Josie did not have to struggle against her husband's reputation and intellectual circle to create her own niche. John's passion for writing was not at that time matched by any regular practice of the art, and his reputation was no greater than that of his wife.

Carolyn, Katherine Anne, and Josie shared identical concerns and interests despite their diverse experiences and backgrounds. All three were acutely aware that they had almost no place in the inner circle of Greenwich Village literary life: they might be friends, lovers, or wives of the men who gathered at places like Squarcialupis to talk about the world of literature, but they would never be asked to contribute to the manifestos or little magazines these men produced. As a result they had to depend on each other for support. Although Carolyn, Katherine Anne, and Josie had different styles of writing, they were all fundamentally autobiographical in approach, fashioning their fiction out of family stories and myths. They read one another's stories and gave detailed, practical, and constructive criticism.

They were not only devoted to the writing of fiction, they were crazy about cats, cooking, and country life. Josie and Katherine Anne had met during the winter of 1925–26, when they both were living in a small town in the Connecticut countryside, in situations quite similar to Carolyn's Tory Valley sojourn that same winter. All three shared dreams of settling down in the country, although, for a while, only Josie would actually be able to do so. In the spring of 1928, she and John moved out of New York to a primitive stone farmhouse in Erwinna, Bucks County, Pennsylvania. Carolyn and Katherine Anne were left in New York to write letters and share each other's company in Caligari.

Soon Carolyn knew she would also be leaving New York. After finishing his biography of Jackson, Allen was awarded a Guggenheim Fellowship. As a condition of the fellowship, Allen, Carolyn, and Nancy would have to go abroad for a year.

Carolyn could do little writing in the six frenzied months before they left for England and France that fall. Allen had agreed to write another biography, of Jefferson Davis, and for a while he hoped to finish it before they left. In the summer of 1928 the Tates took off on another whirlwind automobile tour through the South, stopping for quite a while in Richmond, Virginia, so that Allen could do research on Davis in the state library. They once again visited Civil War battlefields, and they also stopped to see Josie and John and a number of relatives, including Carolyn's parents in Guthrie. But one visit was entirely unexpected. While driving through Monteagle, Tennessee, Allen suddenly looked as if he had seen a ghost. "My God!" he cried out, "There's Mama." Carolyn had never met Mrs. Tate, but there she was, sitting on the front porch of one of the houses.

Clad all in black, Mrs. Tate never smiled, and Allen was positively un-nerved. His relationship with his mother was an awkward, confusing one. He had been the youngest of three sons; she had coddled him to the point that he wanted nothing more than to escape. Fearing he had water on the brain as a child, Allen's mother had tried to dissuade him from reading and serious study. "You are straining your mind and you know your mind isn't very strong," she had told him when he was only twelve. He had consequently worked hard to prove his mother wrong, but the sight of her could still shake him with fear and confusion. "Mama, we got to go now," Allen repeated throughout their awkward, brief meeting.

By the time the Tates returned to Caligari in August, they were flat broke. With no hope of finishing his book on Davis before they left, Allen instead tried to figure out a way to make quick money, perhaps by selling an essay twice. "Stupefied and appalled by the city," Carolyn tried to get ready for their trip abroad, sewing madly when she wasn't taking care of "a welter of young men from Vanderbilt": it was "time for the annual irruption," she observed.

Nancy adjusted as best she could to the commotion. "Now what Bill is that, Mama?" she asked one day when another young man appeared in the apartment. Only three years old, Nancy looked forward to the trip. "That is my Yurrup hat," she told visitors. "There is a lot of sand at France, and I am going to play in it." Carolyn used bribery to keep her daughter on her best behavior: when Nancy refused to take a bath, Carolyn told her the ship's captain would not let her get on the ship with-out first checking behind her ears. The threat worked almost too well.

Allen's biography of Jackson, which had been published earlier that year, sold well. By the time his book of poetry, *Mr. Pope and Other Poems,* appeared in late August, one of the New York papers said it was by the author of *Stonewall Jackson.* Although this annoyed Allen, it amused Carolyn, who almost expected the *New York Times* to announce, "The author of Stonewall Jackson tries his hand at verse."

But excellent sales of *Stonewall Jackson* promised to end the hand-to-mouth lifestyle the Tates had endured for nearly four years. They thought they might earn as much as five thousand dollars from the book, and

Allen and Carolyn knew exactly how to spend such a windfall. Like Josie and John, they would buy a home in the Pennsylvanian countryside, an old stone house near a gorgeous rock-lined pool. Carolyn knew they had to "get the place very quickly" after their return from abroad, or the money would slip through their fingers.

Only one thing tempered Carolyn's joy: her mother's failing health. For a while Carolyn felt "sort of suspended," wondering if she ought to return to Kentucky. When doctors said her mother would not live much longer, Carolyn did not want to go abroad, but eventually she decided to go to Europe without stopping in Guthrie. Nan thought her daughter had made the right decision: Carolyn's visit would be too much of a strain for everyone. "I shall probably be living when you get back and long after I am ready to go and every one else is ready for me to depart," Nan told Carolyn. "We can write to each other better than we can talk."

On September 28, 1928, the Tate family left for England on the SS *America*. With his usual flair for the theatrical, Allen walked up the gangplank carrying his grandfather's gold-headed cane and two large calf-bound volumes of *The Rise and Fall of the Confederate Government*. Following behind him, Carolyn clutched a large baby doll in one hand, a shrieking three-year-old in the other. "Where's the captain?" Nancy kept crying. "He's got to see my ears!"

It was "a fearful voyage," Carolyn said later. For four days they suffered through a near-hurricane-strength storm. No one was seasick, but everyone "got quite morbid," Carolyn admitted. Yet worse than the storm was the company, including forty Rhodes scholars. Carolyn thought most of them were "really quite terrible creatures": one young man even had "the effrontery" to refer to Carolyn as "the wife."

Carolyn's first trip abroad was marked by a confusing welter of conflicting responsibilities as a wife, mother, and writer. Her first stop—England—exemplified her troubles. Carolyn hated England, its muggy weather and plain, starchy food. But most of all she hated the fact that the high cost of living meant she could not afford to hire a nurse for Nancy. Carolyn thought she could finish revising her novel if only she could get six weeks of uninterrupted work, but that would never happen as long as she had to care for Nancy.

Carolyn had some success during their visit to Oxford, where Red Warren was studying on a Rhodes Scholarship. During those six weeks Carolyn must have found someone to help care for Nancy because she "worked like hell," revising about half of her novel and beginning another story. But at the end of November, the Tates left for Paris, where other responsibilities usurped Carolyn's time and energy.

At first Carolyn and Allen thought they might travel on to Vence or Montpellier, but Ford Madox Ford, and the high price of railroad fare, persuaded them to stay in Paris. It was an ideal place for a writer. Although they had missed the first and second waves of American artists who went into exile there and became the proverbial "lost generation," Paris was still a refuge for all manner of writers and painters and confused young Americans. Ernest Hemingway would later say Paris was "the town best organized for a writer to write in." Living was cheap; good talk was abundant at the many cafes and writer's "salons"; Sylvia Beach would loan books to a struggling young writer on credit at her famous bookshop, Shakespeare and Company. When the muse went mute, there were museums and galleries, cathedrals and monuments, and walks along the river or through the marketplace: a pastiche of smells, tastes, and sounds.

For several months, however, Carolyn saw little of Paris. Aware that her mother probably would not live through the winter, Carolyn wrote her nearly every day, sending small presents to ease her suffering along with accounts of Nancy's "bright remarks." The two women had fought most of Carolyn's life, but they could indeed write better than they could talk.

Carolyn told her mother that Nancy had no trouble getting used to their frequent moves. "Isn't this house getting old?" Nancy asked after only a few weeks in Paris. "Aren't we about through with it now?"

Another day, Nancy announced, "Mamma, I'm both of them."

"Both of what?" Carolyn asked.

"I'm a noveler and I'm a poet," Nancy explained. "I'm both of them."

As Christmas approached, Carolyn told her mother how Nancy's excitement was tempered by jealousy. Since it was the birthday of "Little Lord Jesus," Nancy was "afraid he [would] get all the toys." But Nancy got a doll and a well-equipped carriage "big enough for a young baby" and perfect for rolling through the gardens, Carolyn reported.

Less than a month later, on January 22, 1929, Nancy Gordon died, only a year and a half after her cancer had been diagnosed. Carolyn said little about her mother's death, only that she was glad that her mother "did not have to suffer any longer." Yet years later she would mark the anniversary of her mother's death with quiet reflection.

For a while the new year was full of sorrows. For weeks the Tates suffered from ear abscesses and the flu. Carolyn felt as if her head were "muffled in cotton wool all the time," and she had no sooner nursed Nancy through a round of the "grippe" or recovered herself than Allen fell ill.

By then Carolyn, Allen, and Nancy had moved once again. Off for another visit to New York, Ford had offered them his place at 32, rue de Vaugirard and refused to accept any rent, although Carolyn insisted on retyping for him a five-hundred-page manuscript that had been mangled by a French typist. The move saved them money, but the apartment was almost impossible to heat, and their quarters were very cramped. They shared the flat with "Cousin" Léonie Adams, a friend and fellow poet who had traveled with them from England. Carolyn and Allen slept on the sofa in the living room, Nancy had a small bedroom, and Léonie occupied what was actually a narrow closet.

Before long Carolyn was eager to leave Paris for a warm, open space. She felt as if they had been living for months on a combination of rum and aspirin. When they weren't shivering beside Ford's fireplace, they were "getting up every few minutes to put drops of something" in someone's ears or nose, she said.

During one of their intervals of health, Carolyn had attempted to get back to work on her novel. For about twenty dollars a month, she hired a "grand little maid" to take complete charge of both the housekeeping and Nancy, but new problems and illnesses kept cropping up to keep her away from her work. Then Allen's publisher sent an ultimatum: the biography of Jefferson Davis had to be ready for September publication if Allen did not want to lose a great deal of money to a competitor's book due out in October.

Once again Carolyn put her work on the novel aside to help Allen by "typing madly" for several months. Léonie returned to New York in mid-March, escaping secretarial labor. After a while Carolyn considered herself an expert on "the foreign relations of the Confederacy." She even wrote a section of Allen's book—the last chapter at the end of the second section, on the people's response to the war. She included in the chapter one of her favorite family stories about the old black woman, Aunt Emily, who married a young black man so she would not have to cut the firewood. But Carolyn disguised the scene, attributing it to a slave belonging to General William Quarles.

When Allen finally finished the book, it was the Fourth of July. The Tates went out and got drunk with Hart Crane to celebrate their "freedom" from "that damn book." Hart had been visiting Paris for several months, "spending his grandmother's legacy," Carolyn said. No longer angry over their winter in Tory Valley, Carolyn, Allen, and Hart even sent Mrs. Turner an affectionate postcard: Carolyn figured the card would "probably bewilder that dame a good bit." But soon Hart quarreled again with Allen. Although not quite thirty years old, Hart looked much older, his hair gray, his face red and somewhat mottled. All his drinking had caused him to put on weight, and before he left Paris, it would land him in jail. He was clearly losing control of his life.

Dazed and exhausted from too many months of nonstop work and illness, Carolyn had to struggle to regain control of her own life. She noticed with dismay that Nancy had become almost too fluent in French. One day Nancy looked at her favorite book, *Battles and Leaders of the Civil War,* and said to her mother, "There's Monsieur Stonewall Jackson." Carolyn wondered if it wasn't time to take Nancy back to New York.

Around that time Stella Bowen, Ford's former mistress, completed a portrait of the Tates that she had been working on all spring. Stella painted Allen with his head slightly cocked, his eyes and mouth almost crooked: with his high, bulging forehead and receding hairline, he looked as if he were mad or in a trance. Carolyn, captured in profile to his left, stared resolutely off into space. Only Nancy looked directly out of the portrait, but her gaze was no less intense. "Allen and I, held together in space, by Nancy, as it were," was the way Carolyn would describe it, and the description was apt, in life as well as art.

AFTER a summer in Concarneau on the Brittany coast, the Tates returned to Paris. Since Ford was once again using his apartment, the Tates stayed nearby at the Hôtel de la Place de l'Odéon. And finally, Carolyn discovered Hemingway was right: Paris was a place "organized for a writer."

Four-year-old Nancy aided that discovery by finding her own nurse that fall, Madame Gau, an elderly French woman. To Carolyn's delight, Nancy stayed with Madame Gau from ten o'clock every morning until seven o'clock each evening. Most of the time Nancy played in the Luxembourg Gardens, but, unknown to Carolyn, Madame Gau, a devout Catholic, regularly took Nancy to church and one day even had her baptized.

Carolyn managed to clear away all distractions and settle down to serious writing. Several months earlier, she had figured out what to do with the book she had been writing and revising for three years. She realized she had only been "nibbling around the edges" of a larger project, a "history of a Southern family for three or four generations, from 1800 . . . to the beginning of the industrialization of the south." It seemed as if she had been "tuning up" to write such a novel for ten years, Carolyn wrote Josie. She even had a title for the book, *The Making of Americans*, but then Carolyn realized she had "borrowed" the title from Gertrude Stein. "I . . . almost wept when I realized that it was hers, not mine," she told Josie. Nevertheless, Carolyn felt she had "the whole thing in hand now," and she expected to get "a good part of it done" before leaving France. Her new confidence allowed her to forgive Paul Rosenfeld of *American Caravan* for rejecting her work. "He was quite correct," she wrote. "My time will never come for him and his cohorts."

It also helped that Carolyn had a story published in the fall in a mimeographed little magazine called *Gyroscope*, edited by Yvor Winters. The story, called "Summer Dust," may have been the one Carolyn wrote the previous fall in Oxford, or perhaps a revision of "Before Eleven," written in 1927. Carolyn thought it was "the best piece of writing" she had ever done, although she told her friends it had been "turned down by every editor in the country on the grounds that it [was] not a short story." Winters did not call it a story either; he labeled it simply "Prose," and Carolyn gave the piece a subtitle, "Four Episodes."

In "Summer Dust" Carolyn continued to explore the possibility of turning her family stories into fiction. This time she modeled the central character, Sally Ellis, the granddaughter of old Ellen Llewellyn, on herself. Just as her grandmother had been a woman of creative imagination in Carolyn's earlier story, Sally took the role of artist-seer, sensitive to the nuances of injustice and oppression in the personal relationships that surrounded her, responsive to the flights of fancy transforming everyday appearances.

Carolyn set the episodes in the same family landscape, although she changed some of the names and the situations of the houses. In the first section Sally walked with Aunt Maria, a black woman working for her grandmother, and Maria's children, eight-year-old Olivia and eleven-year-old Sawney, called "Son." They traveled down "a dusty country road" between "the House," where Sally's grandmother lived, and "the Old Place," rented by a poor white tenant. At the Old Place they picked peaches for Sally's mother, much to the dismay of the tenant, Mrs. Wilkins. The entire episode made Sally uncomfortable: Son taunted her, giving her a worm-ridden peach; Mrs. Wilkins cursed Sally's mother; and Sally could not bring herself to pick the peaches after all.

In the next episode Sally rode deep into the woods by herself. When the trees became dense, she clung tightly to the neck of "the Black Horse," becoming almost one with the animal, amazed to discover she could "go anywhere" the horse went. Soon Sally discovered an earring in a quiet, secluded place. It belonged to a gypsy woman: Sally was so sure that she thought she could see the woman in the woods. Later, leaving her horse and walking bravely into the darkening forest, Sally discovered an owl "in the gloom beneath the branches" of "a half-fallen tree." The owl "stared at her for a moment," then "scuttled away among the leaves." Sally "watched until it was out of sight" before leaving the woods.

In the third episode Sally went on another journey, this time to a birthday party at Ellengowan, a Woodstock-like estate, with her brothers, Tom and Alec. Both of the boys pestered Sally on the drive: Alec, the younger, by poking his sister in the ribs and daring her to fight back; Tom by telling stories of the old black woman Aunt Silvy, clearly modeled on Carolyn's memory of Aunt Emily. Aunt Silvy was "a hundred and fifty years old," Tom said, as strong as "ten nigger men" because she had a habit of eating "little niggers. . . . and white chillun too if she can git 'em." Neither Alec nor Sally wanted to speak to Aunt Silvy, but once they had arrived at Ellengowan, only Sally was forced to go to the back of the house and say "howdy" to the old crone. Nearly collapsing when forced to go into Silvy's dark cabin and shake her "bird-claw hand," Sally quickly left the cabin.

In the last episode Sally was once again on the road, tagging along with her brother Tom. Once again Tom teased Sally unmercifully, trying to get her to leave him alone, but Sally would not go anywhere until her brother's friend Robert appeared. Then when Tom told her to "go down the road a piece and pick some blackberries," Sally went because she was afraid of what Tom would say to her. The boys wanted to be alone to talk: Robert had to testify in a case of statutory rape. Just out of eyesight, Sally caught snatches of Tom and Robert's conversations. When she heard them laugh about how easily their friend Virgil got off, she decided it was time to go home. Tom would not go with her, so she went herself, walking fast, "bringing the dust up around her in a cloud."

Just as in "Old Mrs. Llewellyn," Carolyn created a fully realized world with finely drawn characters. Although each section could stand individually, the parts were not at all disjointed. Several motifs bound the episodes into a coherent whole: references to eyes and sight and the dust covering the roads, quotations from the *Green Fairy Book,* and the recurring pattern of a journey. In one sense the story could be read as one young girl's retreat into fantasy, a retreat prompted by the girl's unwillingness to face the rude facts of sexual and emotional maturity. But "Summer Dust" could support a completely opposite reading. Sally, as artist-seer, was forced to confront injustice and oppression, yet she was not mastered by it. She could find delight in the natural world, in the way the sun "sent little needles of light" through the leaves of the trees; she could transcend her everyday experiences through acts of imagination. Rather than surrender to despair, she learned to rely on herself. In her final walk back to the house, Sally rejected her brother's company, surrounded herself in a cloud of dust, and rehearsed a scene, presumably from her *Green Fairy Book:*

> "But where will we go?" asked the Little Princess.
> "We will ride on this cloud," said the Fairy Godmother, "to my crystal palace in the wood. There is a gold crown laid out on the bed for you there, and silver slippers, and a veil of silver tissue, embroidered with the sun and the moon and the stars."

Although Sally may have been retreating into fantasy, she was also creating her own world, guided by the wisdom she had acquired on her recent journeys.

Most of that wisdom developed out of pain and an understanding often ignored in one of the most perplexing parts of the story. In the first section, when Sally was on the road with Aunt Maria, Olivia, and Son, she remembered how Son had looked at her earlier. "His eyes were very bright; his lower lip hung down until she could see the red part next to his teeth." At that point in her reverie, Sally exclaimed to herself, "I'm not a nigger. . . . I'm the only one who's not a nigger!" Over and over again, she repeated, "I'm not a nigger!" Nothing in the episode justified the repetition, much less the vehemence of the exclamation.

Yet the remark could be understood as the beginning of Sally's realization that, while she might not be black, she was not unlike Son. Sally even gave Son her treasured copy of the *Green Fairy Book,* instinctively understanding their common state. The discussion Sally overheard about the judge's response to statutory rape reinforced an underlying assumption: women and blacks were both vulnerable, all too dependent on the whims and considerations of others.

That Carolyn would suggest women and blacks shared a common plight was not surprising. Many southern women who wrote diaries or fiction throughout the nineteenth and early twentieth century—including one of Carolyn's relatives, Elizabeth Avery Meriwether—said or implied as much. In 1880 "Cousin Betty" had published a novel called *The Master of Red Leaf.* A southern "response" to Harriet Beecher Stowe's *Uncle Tom's Cabin,* it attempted to defend slavery by showing how well southern slaves were treated in comparison with women, who suffered terribly under their tyrannical fathers, employers, and false lovers. Carolyn had read her cousin's novel; perhaps the connection between women and blacks in "Summer Dust" was part of her meditation on the subject her distant cousin and others had long reflected on. But *The Master of Red Leaf* ended in tragedy: Hester Stanhope, daughter of a New England abolitionist, could not escape her downtrodden state. Sally in "Summer Dust" did: in self-conscious acts of imagination.

Carolyn's own act of imagination gave her new confidence about her life and work. Finally, after too many rejections, she had found an editor willing to publish her fiction. Soon she was not only writing and revising her novel but also working on four new stories based on her family.

The publication of "Summer Dust" was important for another reason: Carolyn changed the spelling of her name for the byline. Although for a while she would continue to go by the name "Carolyn" in private life, from then on she circulated and published her fiction under the name "Caroline Gordon." She would never explain the change. Perhaps she wanted to separate her journalistic writing from her serious art, or maybe she was asserting a stronger connection with her grandmother, who always spelled her name "Caroline." Some friends thought Allen was responsible: "Caroline" was more formal, more suitable for a serious writer. But for whatever reason, Carolyn made the change, at least in print. Her apprenticeship was almost at an end. Carolyn Gordon, newspaperwoman, was becoming Caroline Gordon, writer.

ENCOURAGED by the publication of "Summer Dust," Carolyn nevertheless remained precariously balanced between confidence and self-doubt throughout the fall of 1929, although she often masked the latter. Family responsibilities continued to interfere with her work, and Carolyn became quite annoyed, especially with Allen. Stubbornly refusing to take care of himself, Allen suffered from repeated and sometimes mysterious ailments. At one point he "burst out all over in enormous red splotches,"

Carolyn told Josie. "We thought he had some fell disease, but the doctor tells him what Old Doc Gordon has been telling him for four long years": Allen was drinking too much and eating the wrong kinds of foods.

Carolyn used "Old Doc Gordon" as a mask for her most cutting advice or pointed editorial commentary. When the little magazine *Transition* proclaimed a "revolution in the English language," "Old Doc Gordon" could only laugh at "their banal and ungrammatical statements." And she had even less respect for another new magazine called *Tambour*: its editor really "ought to be in school learning the parts of speech." "Although he actually cannot write a grammatical sentence he is taken quite seriously and lectures his elders sternly at times," she noted. One of his first lectures was an "attack on 'the old men of '99' (elderly creatures like Malcolm Cowley, Hart [Crane], Allen) who, doddering on the verge of the grave put out their palsied hands to strangle young talent," Carolyn said. "God, how fast we get on!"

That fall Allen was hardly trying to strangle Carolyn's talent, because Carolyn would not show him anything she had written. The previous spring Carolyn and Josie had agreed that Allen had "no interest whatever in the modern novel." When Carolyn wanted support or encouragement as a writer, she still depended primarily on Josie and Katherine Anne. But sometimes the support was not empowering but intimidating, in part because Carolyn stretched the truth.

At one point Carolyn told Katherine Anne she had finished half of her novel as well as enough stories for a collection. Before long Carolyn received a letter from an agent of Harcourt, Brace, saying he would like to see the novel Katherine Anne had told him about. Another inquiring letter from the publishing firm of Coward McCann indicated that Yvor Winters was also busy promoting Carolyn.

Carolyn took advantage of the inquiries and proposed to write a biography of Meriwether Lewis for Coward McCann. Biographies were popular with publishers at that time, so much so that even Allen, after vowing never to write another, had agreed to do a life of Robert E. Lee. Carolyn thought writing a biography of her ancestor would be "a pleasant way to make a little money," and it would also force her to read about that period in history, which would help her with a story she had planned, "Over the Mountains."

But the publishers' letters did not please Carolyn. Rather, they made her miserable. "It is certainly fine to have such active friends," she wrote to Josie, "but I get quite humiliated as the letters roll in, for my novel isn't finished and won't be for many months." Contradicting her earlier letter to Katherine Anne, Carolyn insisted she would "never have a book of short stories" ready for publication if she lived "to be a hundred." She told Josie she had written one story that summer, but it would be "the last I ever write." "I simply loathe short stories," she said. "They are all just a trick, and they simply drive me mad."

Nevertheless, Carolyn continued to work on new stories, and before the year was out, she had completed four. "The Long Day" was a horror story about a black man named Joe, his girlfriend, Sarah, and young white boy named Henry. On the day in question, each character had to endure some waiting. Henry was eager to go fishing, but he had to wait for Joe, who was unwilling to leave the cabin. Joe said he had to take care of Sarah, who had just that morning fought violently with him, but actually Joe was waiting also, expecting to be caught: inside the cabin Sarah was dead or dying—slashed by a razor that Joe insisted Sarah had turned on herself.

Carolyn probably modeled the character of Henry on her father: she had heard more than enough stories about her father's childhood, and when she finished the story, she sent it to J. M. Gordon for his reaction. He thought the whole thing "entirely true to life and setting." "You certainly have developed a 'sure touch,'" he wrote to Carolyn. "I could *see* it all: it is as clear cut as a cameo."

Another story Carolyn wrote that fall, "Funeral in Town," focused again on the Meriwether connection. But unlike the previous stories, "Funeral in Town" was not entirely sympathetic to the Meriwether family myth. Back in the Old Neighborhood for a visit, Bill Williams found himself in the middle of a fight between his friend Aleck Faylee and Faylee's wife, Barbara. Aleck's cousin, Sarah Price, had died, and the kin wanted to bury her at the Faylee graveyard on Friday afternoon at three—the same time that Barbara had planned to host a bridal shower. An outsider to the Faylee clan, Barbara had never liked the fact that her husband was responsible for tending the family graveyard, and she was furious that the death of a very distant cousin would cause her to cancel her own party. By the time the relatives of Cousin Sarah had decided to bury her in town, next to her brother, Aleck and Barbara had nearly separated in anger.

Carolyn made it hard for readers to empathize with Barbara because she was always seen through the eyes of Bill Williams, hardly an impartial witness. Yet Barbara's presence in the story indicated Carolyn's willingness to take a critical view of the Meriwether family. Like J. M. Gordon, Barbara Faylee was not sympathetic toward her relatives by marriage or toward their customs. Everyone in the community thought it mighty fine to be considered part of the Faylee connection: a black boy from the garage insisted his name was "Edward Faylee," although "some folks" called him "Edward Graham," and Bill Williams understood, saying "That's right, I call myself Faylee too." Barbara Faylee, however, found little comfort in the name: she thought the kinfolk hated her. Although Bill would not admit it, Barbara was hardly accepted into the family and community. Her objection to the funeral might seem petty, but it revealed a more serious, justifiable protest against the family structure.

Carolyn thought enough of "Funeral in Town" to show it to Ford that fall. Ford said some "very pleasing" things about the story, then made a comment which greatly annoyed Carolyn: "Of course you don't really know what you've done."

"Now really?" Carolyn exclaimed to Josie in a letter. "And I spent just three months on that piece! The things you get said to you in this life! By friend and foe!"

Carolyn did not stay angry at Ford long: he made life far too pleasant for the Tates, cooking them fine dinners, organizing parties and evenings out at various cafes. Every Saturday Ford invited the Tates and other young, admiring writers to his tiny apartment for games. Sometimes they took turns damning friends and acquaintances to the various circles in Dante's Inferno. More often, they played *bouts-rimés*, a French parlor game. After Ford supplied rhyme words from a sonnet by Shakespeare or Christina Rossetti, everyone had to try to write a new poem. The game was highly competitive: the writers were supposedly judged by how fast and how well they could write. Ford, however, did the judging, and often he declared his sonnet the best.

Ford's behavior and parties were sometimes ridiculous, but Carolyn was inclined to humor him. That fall Ford was uneasy over his declining income and the confused state of his romantic life. His long-standing relationship with Stella Bowen had ended; his latest lover, Rene Wright, whom Carolyn called the Squirrel, insisted on a marriage Ford could not give because he had never divorced his first wife. After a while, as he often did with young protégés, Ford decided he had fallen in love with Carolyn. But she knew him well enough to ignore his amorous attentions.

Between work on their writing and visits with Ford, Carolyn and Allen saw a number of other writers during their last few months in Paris. While visiting Sylvia Beach at Shakespeare and Company, Allen met Ernest Hemingway, who had recently returned to Paris, and soon the Hemingways and the Tates were spending a good deal of time together. Six feet tall, with dark hair and a ruddy complexion, Ernest had a passion for sport that should have endeared him to Carolyn: in many respects, he was not unlike her father. But Carolyn felt rather ambivalent about both Ernest and his wife, Pauline.

Carolyn respected Ernest's writing; like Allen, she thought that *A Farewell to Arms,* published that fall, was a masterpiece. She also thought Ernest and Pauline were "rather fun sometimes." Ernest introduced Allen to the weekend bicycle races; both Ernest and Pauline tried to talk the Tates into settling down in Arkansas, where Pauline had family, when they returned to the States. On Thanksgiving the Tates and Hemingways shared dinner together. But at some point Ernest looked at Carolyn in what she took to be a "subtly accusing way" and said, "I understand you have a fine prose style." Always sensitive about her writing, Carolyn found it hard to restrain her anger. When she later wrote to Katherine Anne, she complained about his "attitude towards his craft." "I get so sick of people like Hemingway who would have you believe that the stuff came down to them from heaven—or up from hell," she said. Her opinion of Ernest would never improve.

Two other celebrated writers fared no better in Carolyn's opinion: Gertrude Stein and F. Scott Fitzgerald. Carolyn met Fitzgerald and his wife, Zelda, through Allen's friend John Peale Bishop. Carolyn could not stand Scott Fitzgerald: she thought he "made himself quite a nuisance," with all his drunken lies and bad behavior. But Carolyn liked Zelda; she thought Zelda was "victim to Scott's delusions of grandeur in a silk hat."

Carolyn had less sympathy for Gertrude Stein. The Tates had met Stein soon after their arrival in Paris. Her invitation, reading more like a royal command, had been waiting for Allen when they checked into their hotel: "You and your wife will come to tea on Thursday at 27 rue de Fleurus. *Gertrude Stein.*" Their visit made little impression on Carolyn, but in the fall of 1929, she once again accompanied Allen to Stein's salon, even though she had to sit with the wives while Stein lectured the men on American literature. Carolyn listened with amazement as Stein declared herself "the flower of American genius," a genius "for ideas divorced from experience."

"That is why," Stein concluded, "street car conductors and people like that enjoy my work so much."

After that remark a polite silence filled the room. Exchanging glances with some of the other audience members, Carolyn decided they must all be thinking the same thing: "How many street car conductors had we ever known who read Miss Stein's work, much less enjoyed it?" But no one dared challenge or contradict Stein, who continued her lecture.

Later Carolyn told Sally Wood to try to visit Stein on her next trip to Paris. "She will treat you with great contempt on account of your sex," Carolyn said, "but you can see her Picassos and it will be worth going. She never addresses a remark to the women and it is rather nice, you can just wander around and look at her pictures."

In December, as the Tates prepared to leave France, Carolyn dedicated herself to one last binge of writing. She left Nancy to spend entire days and nights with Madame Gau: by that time, Carolyn noted, Nancy had acquired a "habit of rising at five o'clock and singing little French songs in a piercingly sweet voice." Free from responsibility, Carolyn worked all day, then caroused all night. She even got up her nerve and took the unfinished manuscript over to show Ford.

When Ford saw her work, he flew "into a great rage" and accused her of "concealing it from him until there [was] no time to do anything," Carolyn said. Then he took her "by the scruff of the neck," and forced her to work in his apartment every morning, dictating to him whenever she got stuck.

Sometimes Carolyn complained that "it was hard to work with everything so hurried and Christmas presents to buy."

"You have no passion for your art," Ford would reply. "It is unfortunate." He spoke "in such a sinister way," Carolyn told a friend later, that she would "reel forth sentences in a sort of panic": "Never did I see such a passion for the novel as that man has."

Carolyn's sessions with Ford did not last long, but they were fruitful. In three weeks she wrote at least five thousand words, the last she would write for many months as she once again, in what threatened to become a crippling habit, put her family's welfare before her own.

The Tates sailed for New York on December 28 on the *George Washington*. Again it was a difficult crossing, marked by rough seas, bouts of seasickness, and worry. Five days after sailing, Carolyn sat in the ship's social hall and wrote a letter to Sally. As Nancy played nearby—she and five other children were raucously "swimming" from rug to rug—Carolyn poured out her confusion and despair on paper.

"I *hated* leaving Paris," Carolyn wrote. "God, how I hated leaving Paris." It had been a "ghastly trip," and the thought of New York made Carolyn sick at heart. Life in Paris had been "all so nice and easy," she told Sally. "In spite of working like a dog," she had gained fifteen pounds: Carolyn was sure Sally wouldn't recognize her.

As she wrote, Carolyn mulled over the last months abroad and thought about their future. She knew it was certainly time for Nancy and Allen to return to the States. Allen had been restless for months. He could not find the books he needed for his research in Paris, and he was eager to work on a new project with his friends Donald Davidson, John Crowe Ransom, and Red Warren: a southern symposium, a defense of the Old South and the agrarian tradition against the forces of industrialism. Their return meant Allen could participate in the final shaping of the project. It also meant four-year-old Nancy could recover her native language before she had to go to school: she spoke almost entirely in French, having forgotten most of her English.

Carolyn alone expected little benefit from their return. In Paris Carolyn had been able to free herself from the usual pressures of earning a living, caring for Nancy, and keeping house. Carolyn doubted she could work as well in New York; she wasn't even sure where they would live. For that matter, what would they live on? "God knows when I'll finish the novel if Ford can't land me an advance," Carolyn wrote.

Carolyn told her friend that they expected to stay in New York for about three months. Then they would "go south to hunt up a farm—provided Allen's publisher isn't enough affected by the Stock Market crash to forget his magnificent promises," she wrote. It was, perhaps, too much to hope.

With the children still squealing and "swimming" from rug to rug across the social hall, Carolyn closed her letter to Sally. "*Please* write," she implored, and she signed her name "Caroline." In the months to come, she would use that spelling with increasing frequency in her personal life.

A short time after the ship docked, the Tates moved into a tiny apartment on East Twenty-sixth Street in New York City. Carolyn's fears materialized. New York was terrible; Carolyn thought she "would go mad the first week, what with the rattle and roar of everything." Over and over again, she said, "My God, I wish I was back in Paris." "I didn't want to come" home, she wrote to Léonie. "I didn't want to come, and it is all worse than I thought it would be."

Their apartment was barely livable. Carolyn and Allen slept, ate, and worked in the living room; they cooked in Nancy's bedroom and washed dishes in the bathroom. "I debate about buying a tea strainer because I don't know where I'd put it," Carolyn told Sally.

Although they had some income from Allen's biographies, Carolyn and Allen could not agree how to use it. Allen wanted to rent a suite at the Hotel Carteret for ninety dollars a month. "You can't finish your novel unless you have a comfortable place to work," he said. Carolyn said she would be damned if she did: she wanted to spend any extra money on household help. Eventually they compromised on a small, inexpensive apartment and a part-time maid. But more important questions about where and how they would live remained.

Their future plans changed almost daily. At first they thought they would spend three months in New York; next it was five, then barely two. Allen wanted to move to Virginia; Carolyn preferred Pennsylvania, but after a few weeks in New York, she decided "any place where there was room enough to turn round in twice would seem pretty swell."

Wherever they lived, Carolyn and Allen knew there would have to be a good fishing stream nearby: Carolyn's father was going to join them. Although J. M. Gordon tried to be agreeable and promised to contribute financially, he managed to complicate matters immensely. At one time they thought they might settle down in Louisa County, Virginia, but Carolyn's father objected to the plan. Allen guessed his father-in-law could not face the place of his birth: it must have reminded J. M. Gordon too much of the times when the family starved because his father had devoted his life to literature. Carolyn's father also vetoed other suggested locations because the fishing was poor or the land prices too high. After some correspondence it became apparent that it might not be easy to find a place to suit all of them.

Carolyn eventually considered asking her grandmother for some land near Merry Mont. "I know she would be anxious for me to settle down there," Carolyn told Sally. "She regards living anywhere else in the world as pure madness."

By February Carolyn and Allen had agreed only to meet J. M. Gordon at Merry Mont. From there they could search for a house while Carolyn's grandmother took care of Nancy.

Before they left New York, Carolyn and Allen both tried to arrange

publishing contracts. Allen had little trouble selling the idea of a southern symposium to Harper Brothers, but Carolyn had no luck finding a
publisher for her novel. And only Yvor Winters was willing to publish
her stories, but soon Carolyn lost even that outlet. The February issue
of Winters's *Gyroscope* included her story "The Long Day" and an official
notice that the magazine was being discontinued. Around that time a
representative of Coward McCann disappointed Carolyn as well. Apparently he had no interest in either her novel or a biography of Meriwether
Lewis. If Carolyn "didn't bring the whole book off," he said, he would
be "left with nothing but some fine writing" on his hands. Carolyn had
nothing but scorn for his views.

With every rejection Carolyn grew more and more bitter. When
Bernard Bandler of the *Hound and Horn* turned down "Funeral in Town,"
she wrote him a scathing letter, accusing him of being one in a long line
of philistine critics unable to recognize true genius. Bandler had valid
criticism of the story: Carolyn had not clarified why the Faylees disliked
Barbara, and background details were sometimes irrelevant. Yet after
Carolyn chastised him, he promised to read her story again. A second
reading did not change his opinion, however, and the *Hound and Horn*
never published the story.

Throughout the early months of 1930, Carolyn's friends sensed a "kind
of helpless fury in her." Katherine Anne and Josie agreed that "blasted
expectations" were making both Carolyn and Allen "sour," but they had
little sympathy. "What can they expect?" Katherine Anne said. "And why
not more courage and more hope. The future is something."

At age thirty-four, with only two published stories to her credit,
Carolyn could not share her friends' optimism. Josie had published a
novel the previous year; Katherine Anne had received sizable advances
from publishers. It had been ten years since Carolyn had begun making
her living as a writer, and nearly as long since she began writing fiction:
she felt she had no more time to waste. She vowed to finish her novel
"this year or come very near dying trying," but she felt desperate and
afraid she could not possibly finish it. What if she failed? What if all the
editors and publishers were right to reject her work?

Just before she left New York, Carolyn made one more effort to find
a publisher for her novel. At a going-away party the poet Louise Bogan
told Carolyn to go see Maxwell Perkins of the publishing house of
Charles Scribner's Sons. At the last minute Carolyn took Louise's advice.

Perkins was well known and respected, the editor of Hemingway, Fitzgerald, and Thomas Wolfe. Since Carolyn did not have a copy of her novel handy, she showed him two of her stories. "I . . . told him that was the way I wrote, only different," she wrote Josie later. Although nothing was decided, Carolyn felt good about their meeting. Max Perkins was "grand," Carolyn thought, "the only publishing person I ever met whom you could talk to like a human being."

Soon after that meeting the Tates left New York to meet Carolyn's father at Merry Mont. They planned to search for a home, some place where they could settle down for more than six months at a time, where there was "room enough to turn round in twice" and where both Carolyn and Allen could write.

"You have served your apprenticeship, mastered the Technique of the Trade and you ought to do something good," Carolyn's father had told her. Only one thing, in his opinion, could interfere with her talent—the lack of money. "If you and Allen can just settle the 'economic basis,'" he said, "then you can really express yourselves and write what is in you, good or bad."

 1930–1932

Carolyn's return to the Old Neighborhood in early March marked a new stage of her growth as a writer, a stage mirrored in and nourished by her surroundings. Spring had begun to turn the countryside fragrant with blossoms. Basking in the golden sunlight, Carolyn and Nancy spent entire afternoons in the garden. Jonquils colored the yard yellow; the plum trees were in bloom. In the surrounding forests and fields, Carolyn noticed a familiar fringe of smoke: tobacco farmers were getting ready for planting by burning their fields. She vowed to take bulbs, roots, and slips from Merry Mont to plant wherever they went.

While waiting for J. M. Gordon to arrive, the Tates searched for the perfect house. Soon they narrowed their prospects to two choices. One was to build a small house on the banks of the Little West Fork of the Red River. But they also considered buying an old brick house just outside Clarksville, Tennessee, not far from where Carolyn had lived as a child. Although Carolyn had no preference, Allen favored the old brick house. "That's the house where I want to live," he said the first time he saw it.

It wasn't a practical house, as Carolyn well knew. It was more than they could afford and badly in need of repair: paint peeling, porches sagging, hens roosting in the downstairs bathroom, and every set of stairs so dangerously pitched that a person could fall backward while trying to climb up them. But the two-story white brick house sat on the brow of a hill—"probably the most beautiful hill in the world," Carolyn thought, "shaped just like a crouching lion," with the house on the lion's forehead. Although the hill seemed only a gentle incline, when Carolyn stood on the porch overlooking the dark, silent waters of the Cumberland River, she suddenly realized how high the hill was and how quickly the land fell away. It was a magnificent view, she thought, especially at night, "when the lights in the town come out."

Since the house was on a river, the Tates figured Carolyn's father would be pleased, but they were wrong. Once J. M. Gordon arrived at Merry Mont, with one trunk and a bundle of fishing equipment, his choice complicated matters. He much preferred the spot on the Little West Fork, and he promised to lend Carolyn and Allen the money they would need to build there. The Little West Fork was full of fish, J. M. Gordon said, and Carolyn had to agree it was one of the loveliest places she had ever seen. Since they would pay cash and build a small, "unpretentious affair," Carolyn thought they could be settled within six weeks.

Renovations for the Clarksville house could take twice as long. And for all practical purposes, the house was on the *wrong* river. The waters of the Cumberland were muddy, hardly suitable for fishing. And the house was too close to the Old Neighborhood, just across the border from Todd County, Kentucky, a short drive from Merry Mont, Woodstock, and all the other farms of the Meriwether connection. J. M. Gordon had spent a good portion of his life in that area; he knew the woods and waters all too well—and the problem with living so close to the Meriwether connection.

Neither Carolyn nor Allen could pretend they needed eleven rooms and more than ninety acres of farmland and woods. But Clarksville was only an hour and a half's drive from Nashville, "just in the suburbs," Allen told his friends. For the first time in their life, there would be more than enough room for guests and gardens, novels and poetry. Could they possibly turn it down?

On the morning of March 11, Allen went to Cincinnati to see if he could borrow money from his brother Ben, who had become quite successful in the coal industry. Later that day, Carolyn sat with her father on the Merry Mont porch, listening once again to his stories. At sixty-nine J. M. Gordon was in excellent health, and his passion for sport had not diminished. Waiting for a decision on the house made him restless. Just as in years gone by, he spun stories about fishing to pass the time, with Carolyn his best audience.

Her father was in the middle of a "discourse on the habits of bream," Carolyn said later, when the telephone rang with a telegram. Maxwell Perkins of Scribner's had decided to take Carolyn's novel. He offered a five-hundred-dollar advance, and he said *Scribner's* magazine was interested in republishing her story "The Long Day." Carolyn immediately wrote a letter of thanks. It would be a great relief to work on the novel without interruptions; "I have actually been *afraid* to write in the snatches of time that I have had at my disposal," she told him. "But now I can go straight ahead with the book."

Allen returned from Cincinnati with more good news: Ben would lend them nearly ten thousand dollars to pay for the house and renovations. They quickly dismissed all questions of practicality, bought the ramshackle house on the Cumberland, and christened it Benfolly in honor of Ben's extravagance.

Carolyn, Allen, and four-year-old Nancy decided to stay at Merry Mont until their new home was made ready, but J. M. Gordon soon left—in search of better fishing, as Carolyn would say. Although more than willing to move in with his daughter and son-in-law, J. M. Gordon did not want the whole Meriwether connection. Before he left, he heard Allen say that Carolyn's grandmother was "one of the sweetest old ladies he had ever seen." J. M. Gordon laughed—quite cynically, Carolyn thought—and told Allen to wait: he would soon think otherwise. But Gordon did not stay around to see his son-in-law come to his senses.

It was a pleasant spring. Busy relearning "the vernacular of the country people," Nancy was a constant source of amusement to her mother. She said things like "I am a little Homerican girl now," and "He ain't never been no good since he fell off that wagon," which Caroline liked to record in letters to her friends.

While Nancy relearned English, Allen sat spellbound watching the carpenters and plasterers work on Benfolly, and Carolyn hoed and planted her garden. Corn, beets, cabbage, beans, carrots, and tomatoes: they would not starve this year, no matter how their writing went.

Life at Merry Mont was still so primitive it might have been easier and more comfortable for Carolyn and Allen to live in the chaos of Benfolly. Little had changed at Merry Mont. Carolyn's grandmother, Miss Carrie, was nearly eighty-two years old, but she still had a firm grip on everyone crossing her path. Her son Rob ran the farm, but Miss Carrie held the purse strings, tightly.

Allen soon discovered how peculiar Miss Carrie could be. One day at the time when the old woman was usually taking a nap, the bulging ceiling in Miss Carrie's bedroom gave way. "A load of plaster" crashed onto "the pillow where Ma's old white head would have been resting if she hadn't been downstairs boiling a ham," Carolyn noted. Allen rushed to congratulate Miss Carrie on her "Providential escape," but Miss Carrie did not believe him. "No plaster ever fell from any Merry Mont ceiling," she informed him. It would do no good to show her the contrary evidence: Miss Carrie would not be swayed from her beliefs by mere physical reality.

None of this surprised Carolyn, who was used to such odd behavior. Delighted to be back at Merry Mont, she sat on the porch every evening to listen again to the family stories. "I was writing my book out of ten-year-old memories of long monologues of my grandmother's," she wrote to Josie. "This spring, sitting on the porch, . . . I have gotten the detail that I needed, what they wore, and drank and so on."

Carolyn spent more time sitting on the porch than writing, but in May she helped to organize what she called a "Boosting Katherine Anne Porter campaign" with Yvor Winters. Katherine Anne had her first book of short stories coming out later in the year, but her publisher, Harcourt, Brace, had insisted on issuing only a limited edition. This humiliated Katherine Anne, who had been suffering from ill health and severe financial troubles. Yvor Winters wrote the Tates, urging them to get their friends to write Harcourt, Brace in praise of Katherine Anne's stories. According to Carolyn, "recommendations from a good many professional writers may hearten them to put out a full edition." Both Tates quickly responded to his suggestion, writing people like Josie and John Herrmann, Léonie Adams, and Edmund Wilson.

The appeal did not persuade Harcourt, Brace to issue more than the limited edition, but it did launch Katherine Anne's career as a short-story writer. Carolyn would never forget how the concerted effort of a group of writers and critics could influence a book's reception. She told Katherine Anne she was lucky to have Yvor Winters so concerned about her future. "I wish to God Allen would show half the interest in mine!" she said.

In June Carolyn nearly organized another campaign, one in defense of the South. She and Allen attended a Confederate Memorial Day celebration at the Clarksville cemetery, expecting to hear a traditional speech defending the ideals of the Lost Cause. Instead, a Baptist minister said the South had been wrong, but its error was part of God's divine providence, and the South was destined to lead the nation once again thanks to the influx of northern capital and industrialization. The minister's speech was, according to Allen, the gospel of the New South according to Henry W. Grady.

Carolyn listened in shocked silence, first to the minister's address, then to the local women congratulating the minister on his speech. Finally she went up and rebuked the minister before his admirers. His address was an affront, she said. He had made a mockery of what the veterans had done and what all had believed, she said. He had distorted the true nature of southern character.

Allen listened with pride as his wife castigated the preacher, her dark eyes flashing. On their return to Benfolly, they decided to stage another ceremony in the middle of June to pay proper tribute to the Confederate dead. They would ask Carolyn's uncle John Ferguson to give an appropriate address, followed by a more contentious speech by one of Allen's friends to chastise the Baptist minister once again. Carolyn suggested ways to gain state and national attention for the event; Allen wrote his "Confederates" in the Nashville area. But despite a positive response from Allen's friends, the event never took place. First it was delayed because the Tates had no furniture in Benfolly and therefore no way to put everyone up for the weekend. Then Ben Tate arrived to look over his "investment." The defense of the South would have to wait for a more opportune time.

By June the carpenters had finished, and the Tates moved into Benfolly. Carolyn marked the move by permanently changing the spelling of her name to Caroline, and from then on, she and Allen would pronounce the name as if it rhymed with pine. No one in the family connection paid attention to the name change: Caroline was still Carrie, or Carolyn, no matter what. But Allen took pains to correct friends and acquaintances if they dared mispronounce his wife's name.

It took the Tates two weeks to unpack: they furnished Benfolly with the furniture and knickknacks Allen had inherited from his mother. Caroline insisted her health had been permanently impaired by the move. "I developed . . . neuralgia of the heart," she wrote to Léonie Adams: "I was never meant to live with so many objects."

The irony of their situation sometimes made Caroline laugh. "Here we are," she told Josie, "absolutely broke, even broker than usual, in a magnificent house." They had two baths, and the house was "also full of electric push buttons." It was a far cry from the Cabinet of Caligari, at least on the surface. "Of course there is no water for the baths," she added, "and no electricity, until Allen's brother can work some razzle dazzle on the local light company."

Caroline quickly established a routine, rising early most mornings to walk around the house before settling down to breakfast and then her typewriter. From her breakfast table on the lower floor of Benfolly, she would watch through the dining room door as the Cumberland River valley slowly emerged from its shroud of mist. The mist was Benfolly's own peculiar feature, and Caroline loved it. By eight or nine o'clock the mist would be gone, and the sun would be blazing.

Allen and "the brethren," as Caroline called his Vanderbilt circle of friends, were busy preparing to defend the southern agrarian tradition by publishing a collection of twelve loosely related essays under the title *I'll Take My Stand: The South and the Agrarian Tradition*. Allen's contribution to the symposium would be an essay in defense of religious humanism, but in the summer of 1930 he was having a difficult time with the article, wrestling with his belief that humanism required some relationship to an established authority like that of the Catholic church. Although the history of the South had been predominantly Protestant, Allen was trying to argue that the true nature of religion in the Old South had been fundamentally Catholic. The fact that Allen could not commit himself wholeheartedly to the Catholic faith certainly must have added to his struggles with the essay. Most of the other contributors finished their essays by June, but in July Allen was still trying to make sense of his position.

Caroline did not share Allen's anxieties. Shortly after returning from France, steeped in Catholic tradition, Caroline had written to Sally about what she had experienced, referring also, perhaps, to her husband's flirtation with the faith. "I say let all of us that can turn Catholic at once," she said. "Yes, you must have plenty of servants to abandon yourself to your emotions, even to what mind you have. I can't write when I'm doing scullery work because even when I get the time my mind won't take hold of any problem."

Caroline had no role in the publication of *I'll Take My Stand*. "The brethren" briefly considered asking her to contribute an essay but never did. In fact, no woman had a voice in either the planning or the actual publication. But Caroline did not seem to mind being excluded. At that time she had her own struggles to resolve in her fictional history of the South, and the writing went slowly. There were too many distractions and demands on Caroline's time: parties with the kin to attend and Nancy to care for. As much as possible, she wrote in the mornings and left the afternoons and evenings free for picnics, swimming, gardening, and visiting with kin and guests. Although she made steady progress, Caroline still worried she would not be able to finish the novel she called *Penhally*.

The novel's title referred to the ancestral home of the Llewellyn family. Caroline's narrative began in 1826, when Nicholas Llewellyn and his brother, Ralph, separated in anger over Nicholas's refusal to divide the family property; then it flashed forward to the beginning of the Civil War. Caroline planned to take her story through four generations, into the twentieth century. It was the tale of brothers, heroes, and betrayal; the family estate was as much a character as the various Llewellyns who used and misused it. In the end the land Nicholas had struggled to keep intact would be sold to a rich northern socialite. Penhally would be turned into a hunt club, and another set of brothers would become enemies.

Although the characters, their world, and their actions were clearly modeled on those of the Kentucky Meriwethers, Caroline was not just re-telling the family legends. Like Merivale, the original Meriwether estate, Penhally was established in Kentucky at the end of the 1700s by a former Virginian. His sons, Nicholas and Ralph Llewellyn, resembled their his-torical counterparts: Caroline's great-great "Grandfather Woodstock" (Charles Nicholas Meriwether) and his brother, "Uncle Curious Will." Ralph's grand house, Mayfield, was a replica of Woodstock, right down to the ballroom, racetrack, and fine stable of studs. But Caroline switched the half-brothers' birth order and colored each character with shades of other family members.

"Old Mrs. Llewellyn" of Caroline's first story reappeared as Lucy Llewellyn, but Caroline developed the character of Lucy from her views of both her grandmother and her mother: like Old Miss Carrie, Lucy was a strong, feisty woman married to a weak-willed man; like Nan Gordon, Lucy would turn on her husband for no apparent reason, then withdraw into herself. John Llewellyn, Lucy's husband, was like Caro-line's grandfather Douglas Meriwether, but again, Caroline did not tie herself too tightly to history. Unlike Meriwether, John Llewellyn would not die from suicide, but his son Frank did—at an earlier age, for quite another reason, and in quite another way.

The twentieth-century Llewellyns would also be modeled on Caro-line's family. Chance Llewellyn, John's grandson, had many of the mannerisms of Caroline's favorite uncle, Rob. Douglas Parrish, a minor character appearing in the final chapters, bore a strong resemblance to Allen, and the Parrish house was not unlike Benfolly.

Caroline was not nostalgic about the defeat of the Old South. "It would have been better," she wrote later, "if our grandfathers had been carried off the field dead." Yet she sympathized with the southern people, trapped by a changing world. In fact, her sympathies had led her into the novel: the characters had taken hold of her before she even knew what she was writing about. That worried her at times; she didn't think it was the "right way to write a novel."

As Caroline worked on *Penhally,* she also reimmersed herself in country life, and her actions and meditations often found their way into her fiction. One such instance was "Mr. Powers," a short story she wrote in September. It was the story of a man who accidentally killed his son when he threw an ax at a hired man caught in adultery with Mrs. Powers. Caroline jokingly said she hoped the real Mr. Powers—a Mr. Suiter, apparently of local reputation—"would not sue her for libel or take after her with an ax."

But the story was about more than a freak accident; in fact, the killing happened before the story even began, and the focus was not really on Mr. Powers at all, but on Jack and Ellen Cromlie, a young city couple who had just moved to the hill farm and, unknowingly, agreed to rent a cabin to Mr. Powers and his family. The hill farm and Cromlie house was Benfolly, right down to the iris, tulip, and jonquil bulbs planted on either side of the brick walk. Like Allen, Jack was a writer with overdue articles, pestering publishers, and little practical knowledge of how things worked in the country. Ellen, the main consciousness of the story, was another of Caroline's self-portraits, just as Lucy Cromlie, the daughter, was modeled on Nancy Tate.

Ellen Cromlie knew more about country ways than her husband, but she had been away from the country for a while, and she feared the local folks would think them ignorant. Although she would have preferred to find something out about Mr. Powers before renting the cabin, Ellen trusted he was a good man. "Powers," she mused. "That's a good country name. I reckon he's all right." When she watched the family move in, she immediately sympathized with their poverty and considered helping them, but decided against it when she remembered her Aunt Molly's tenant problems. "They all said it was better not to start off being too intimate with your tenants," she reflected. "I'm going to be Christian. I hope I'll always be Christian to people, but I'm going to stand on my dignity," she said. "I believe it pays, with tenants."

When Ellen learned about Mr. Powers's infamous past, she became hysterical. Then she was forced to consider what it meant to "be Christian to people." Her meditations—on Mr. Powers, his wife, and their future—were tied to her close observation of the countryside around the small hill farm and the way the bright, flickering light covered the valley and altered one's perspective.

Caroline sold the story to *Scribner's* magazine, where it appeared in November. Although grateful for the two hundred dollars the story brought in, Caroline couldn't help being bothered by the editors' taste in stories. "They write me rather pathetically that 'it is so hard to get any stories with real emotion in them,'" Caroline told Sally, but they "take of my stories only those dealing with murder, sudden death and the like." She was glad to get back to work on *Penhally*. "Writing short stories has one advantage," she said: "it makes writing a novel seem such easy, pleasant work that you wonder why you ever took it so hard."

Much to Caroline's chagrin, she often had to interrupt her work on *Penhally* to care for the many visitors who descended upon Benfolly. In October, first Malcolm Cowley and his wife stopped by on their way to Mexico, where they were going to get a divorce, then Ford Madox Ford arrived with a few other friends. Since the weather was warm, the group spent several delightful days swimming, drinking corn liquor, and talking. Ford, however, expected more than a social visit. He made Caroline go over every bit of her manuscript, exhausting her with his careful scrutiny.

At one point in the visit, Caroline asked Ford if he would mind if she dedicated the book to him. Ford was flattered, delighted, but he tried not to let it show.

Oh, no, you mustn't do that, he told her, fully expecting her to ignore his comment. But Caroline believed he was serious. Although she wondered why he said no, she figured she had better honor his wishes and said no more.

Ford had no sooner left Benfolly than Red Warren and his new bride, Cinina, arrived for a few days' stay. Throughout the fall of 1930, the guest room "hardly got its sheets cold before another pair of guests crawled in," Caroline told a friend. As usual, most of the guests came to see Allen, especially after the Nashville brethren completed their defense of the southern agrarian tradition, *I'll Take My Stand*. In the collection of twelve essays, some sociological or economic, others historical, literary, or philosophical, Allen and his circle argued that the quality of modern life depended on one's relationship to the past, tradition, and nature. They fashioned a myth of southern agrarian life as a protest against the dehumanization of industrialism, but the myth was by no means coherent. They extolled a pastoral world where man could be truly human and truly creative, overlooking some of the more shabby or sordid aspects of the South's agrarian past: slavery and the ills of poverty, for example. The volume created quite a stir in both the South and the nation at large.

Although she had no desire to re-create the Old South, and few illusions her native land could stand as a metaphor for humanity's redemption, Caroline was proud of *I'll Take My Stand:* she thought it "worked up into quite a book"; there were only "one or two essays that might be dispensed with." Her favorite was "The Hind Tit," a defense of the yeoman farmer written by Andrew Lytle. As the Nashville brethren went to battle with all detractors, Caroline looked on with amusement, suggesting various ways the men could manipulate the press to get more attention and stir up more controversy. "The Symposiers are having a great time," Caroline wrote Sally in October. They were recriminating all turncoats "in the pages of the *Tennessean, New York Times* etc. even brawling a bit on the A. P. wires."

Later in October Andrew Lytle came for an extended visit. Having given up his idea of a career in theater, Andrew was working on a novel about the Civil War general Bedford Forrest. For a while, the War Between the States reigned supreme in Benfolly. Before Sally Wood visited Clarksville that fall, Caroline warned her that Benfolly sounded a lot like an old soldiers' home: "Our conversations are all highly military." It was a wonder, she told another friend, they weren't all "wagging long grey beards." Just as they had several years earlier in New York, the three writers gathered around the fire every night to talk about "the War." Usually Andrew began by telling some story about Forrest: Andrew admired Forrest and ignored his rather disreputable behavior as slave trader and member of the Ku Klux Klan. Not to be outdone, Allen would talk about Lee and Gettysburg; then Caroline would attempt to tell them "what a wonderful man Morgan was." At that point, Caroline said later, the men would each give her "a glassy eye," and Andrew would quickly make "some remark tending to put [Morgan] in his place."

When Sally arrived at Benfolly after Thanksgiving, she found Allen working on his biography of Robert E. Lee, Caroline reliving the battles of Shiloh and Missionary Ridge, and Andrew "pacing about the house with blank eyes, giving military orders: 'Then General Forrest said . . .'" It was amusing but restful, Sally thought. Still, as a precaution, Caroline did not allow anyone to begin a serious discussion at breakfast. That might spoil a morning's work.

Benfolly was special, Sally said later, because there "imagined things were given the same welcome [and] the same importance as . . . real things." During the winter of 1930–31, Benfolly overflowed with creatures, real and imaginary. In addition to Allen, Caroline, Nancy, a regular stream of guests, and a host of fictional characters, Benfolly sheltered Beatrice, Caroline's devoted cook and maid; Jim Hughes, an able black hired man; Mr. Perry, a poor white tenant; the dog, Freda; cats named Hind Tit, Oedipous, and Violet Emma; and assorted chickens. The "livestock" increased as strays of all sorts found their way to the place; Caroline would never send one away. Sometimes she swore the trees were raining cats, or some fiend went around dropping puppies at her gates: new ones appeared every day. But Caroline named them all and took them into the family. When Uncle Penn, a maltese cat shaped like a Boston bull terrier, joined the fold, Violet Emma was rechristened "Emma Cinina Elena Anna Roma Clotilda Borgia."

Caroline did not finish *Penhally* in the fall as planned. Because money was tight, she decided at the last minute to apply for a Guggenheim Fellowship to finish the novel. In her application she explained the "conflict of the action" in *Penhally* was "the conflict between the European idea of the preservation of the family by the handing down of property from father to son and the pioneer idea of individualism which led each man to believe that he could carve enough material goods out of the wilderness for himself and his children." Caroline described Nicholas Llewellyn as "an old time Whig," Ralph Llewellyn as "typically pioneer-minded." Although Nicholas, "being a man out of his time," would "of course" be defeated, his "ultimate defeat" would come through his heir's grandchildren: "caught in the tide of the new South," they would "become small town bankers and merchants and speedily rid themselves of the land which was the symbol of their fathers' victory over the wilderness."

In her application Caroline said her "ultimate purpose" was "the writing of prose which shall be personal and American and yet derived from classical models." She explained that her "study of creative writing began with the Greek tragedians" and that her "ideas of art form" had been influenced by the traditions of Greek tragedy "and by the early English novelists." "My method is to present an event through the eyes of several observers and then press it further in succeeding chapters," she explained, "so that members of one generation contemplate and re-value, according to their own lights, events in the lives of their fathers and grandfathers." In the novel there would be "a constant weaving back and forth until the lives of the four heroes stand out in a distinct pattern," she said.

Although she tried to put herself across in the best possible light, Caroline had little hope of success. At Ford's suggestion she did ask Max Perkins if she could turn the novel into a trilogy; if she could just finish the first part of the novel at her leisure and bring the narrative through the Civil War period, then she thought she could "knock off a few short stories" and "get through the winter in fine shape." But Scribner's did not want a trilogy, although Max agreed to defer publication of the novel.

For that much Caroline was relieved. She thought she could get the book ready for publication during the fall of 1931. "I will have very little re-writing to do," she told Max. "It is the invention, not the actual writing that comes to me so slowly and it is something I can't hurry."

The holidays came and went with the usual bustle of activity. Caroline couldn't touch her manuscript for weeks at a time, what with guests to care for and holiday parties, kin dying, others running off to get married, even a dance in the parlor one night. In January, when everyone had gone and peace returned, Caroline tried to get back to writing. Her confidence was badly shaken when Max turned down her latest story, "The Ice House." Set in Virginia in 1866, "The Ice House" was the tale of two boys hired by an enterprising Yankee to dig up the remains of Union soldiers buried four years earlier in a mass grave in the old ice house. Caroline thought it was perhaps the best story she had written so far; she painted the grim scene and the boys' contrasting reactions to their task in swift, vivid strokes.

But Max rejected the story, saying *Scribner's* had too many "tragic and gruesome stories." Caroline thought Max might have balked at some of her dialogue. "Handlin' a dead Yankee ain't no more to me than handlin' a dead hawg," one boy said early in the story. Later, when he saw the Yankee shuffling the bones to increase his profit, he laughed and said, "There ain't a whole man in ary one of them boxes. . . . If that ain't a Yankee fer ye!"

When Caroline shared the story with friends, she got mixed reactions. Katherine Anne Porter, writing from Mexico, thought it a "fine story," a "noble tale." She told Caroline she went around "reading it to people" and would be glad to "send it around a little" to see if it couldn't find a "wider circulation." "Perkins does not know what he wants," she said, pointing out how he had refused two of her own best stories, "Flowering Judas" and "The Theft." Caroline's stories were "full of light, and very firm and sure," and Katherine Anne was impressed with her use of dialogue. "No one who has not tried it can imagine what it takes to get people in stories to talk like that," she wrote. "There are other magazines besides *Scribner's*. . . . Try them."

Sally Wood was not so pleased; in fact, she thought "Caroline had treated the Yankees exceptionally badly—even for her," and for once Sally told her so. But Caroline told Sally to go and hold her "head under a pump." "You are quite off about The Ice House," Caroline said; she was not "expressing a judgment on Yankees" but "merely recording the attitude, deplorable as it is" of her characters. Insisting the attitude was historically correct, Caroline admitted she had wanted to end the story with "Thar ain't a whole man in ary one of them." Andrew Lytle and Allen had persuaded her, however, to go "a little further" than she had wanted to go to make the action clearer.

With her explanation on record, Caroline vowed to forget the story. "It has had a little private circulation and is now laid away in the old desk that I got from Merry Mont the other day," she told Sally. It didn't stay in the desk, however. Later that year, Lincoln Kirstein agreed to publish it in the *Hound and Horn*. Caroline was sure he was "the only editor in the country who would have done it" and she told him so, with profuse thanks.

As Caroline plunged back in to work on *Penhally,* she struggled with fear and pain. She had resolved to get the book to the publisher by summer, a frightening thought because she had as much left to write as she had already written. As she expected, she soon found out she would not receive a Guggenheim Fellowship. To make matters worse, she had a terrible toothache through the middle of January. As she told Sally, the "largest tooth I own, takes me by the seat of the pants and lets me see exactly how a turkey looks over a log." Because she didn't have time to have it pulled, Caroline dosed it regularly with Guaiacol and kept on writing.

Despite the disagreement over "The Ice House," she had gotten another advance on *Penhally* from Max, and she felt the pressure building. Max "persists in regarding this damn novel as almost finished, which is disconcerting," Caroline told Sally: nothing could be further from the truth. The novel was "turning out a mess," with "too much stuff," not enough organization. Still, there was "nothing to do but stagger on with it." In February she sent Max another story set during the Civil War, "Chain Ball Lightning," but he rejected that story as well, saying it did not measure up to her other published works.

Andrew Lytle, meanwhile, had nearly finished his book on Forrest, and Allen was coming out with a flurry of new poems in between work on his biography of Lee. Allen was also trying to play the part of country gentleman. New tenants had arrived at Benfolly—eighteen-year-old Jesse Rye and his bride, Florence—with only a hound dog and a kitchen stove, and Allen spent a good deal of time getting them settled.

Allen's notions of country life amused Caroline. As Allen tried to live out his "agrarian" ideas, Caroline could not help poking fun at his posturing. He was "developing the true landlord spirit," she observed. When Jesse "kept demanding all sorts of fancy things . . . like chairs" at the second-hand furniture shop, Allen was amazed. "Why Jesse," Allen said sternly, "you can sit on a box."

At first Caroline also found her new tenants entertaining. Jesse introduced her to his ten-year-old brother, who liked to stand on the brow of the hill and gaze longingly at Clarksville, only a few miles away.

"He's jist crazy to git to that town," Jesse told Caroline, "I told him hit was mighty common oncet you see it, but he ain't never been to a town."

That boy, Caroline decided, was "the one true agrarian."

Allen and the brethren may have celebrated agrarian life, but not everyone agreed with their views. Caroline herself knew the darker sides of rural life, and during the spring her experience with Jesse and Florence Rye confirmed this knowledge. Caroline had originally felt sorry for the couple: they were so young and had little to eat. But she soon realized they would steal anything they could lay their hands on. When Allen hired Jesse to do some yard work while the Tates were away, Jesse responded by going to town and running up a large charge on the Tates' grocery bill. When Caroline invited Jesse to stop by the house for some cake, he promptly let himself out by way of the kitchen, picking up two dozen eggs on his way. Eviction threats were useless: Jesse consulted a lawyer and informed Caroline, "It don't make no difference what I do. I can come up here and have a fuss with you all every morning and you can't put me off this place." Well-versed in the "system," Caroline knew how true this was.

Throughout the spring and early summer, Caroline brooded on the relationship between landlord and tenant. She felt "like one of these women who knows she is going to have another baby before the one in her arms is weaned," she told a friend, because she already had the subject for her next book: "two families, white and poor white, living on the same farm." She would look at the situation "through first the eyes of one and then of the other," she explained. "Each regards the other as his natural enemy." Caroline was sure Jesse thought it was "perfectly proper to steal" from her, and she knew she "should regard him as so much vermin." She remembered one of her kin, an uncle once or twice removed, "killed by one of his tenants." "You can just see how the situation piles up through the years," she said.

But that story had to wait; her first tale of agrarian life, *Penhally,* was still weighing heavily on Caroline's mind. By the time she had written only two-thirds of her novel, Andrew had finished his book, *Bedford Forrest and His Critter Company,* and left Benfolly. Caroline struggled on alone. At one point she almost abandoned the book: she couldn't figure out a way to move the story forward. Then she decided to have John Llewellyn reflect on the death of his son, a death he had always thought of as a hunting accident. In the midst of his reverie, John would realize the horrible truth: "the picture he had in his mind of his son's death was false"; his son had committed suicide. He would suddenly see the scene as it had actually happened; he would realize a friend had accepted the blame to save the family pain. Caroline felt a little uneasy about using such a technique. It was "a trick," she thought. But it worked; she might yet be able to finish the book.

As Caroline neared the end of her novel, Allen began to take more serious interest in her work. But his views did not always coincide with hers. Throughout the spring Allen pressed her to change the book's title. "The title does not convey enough," he insisted. Caroline thought he was wrong. The significance of the title would become apparent as the story progressed, she said, pointing out she had "a very good precedent among English novels for such a title." But then Allen or one of his friends would remind her she was "neither Charles Dickens, Jane Austen [nor] Sir Walter Scott." Finally, Caroline felt she could argue no more, and she wrote to Max suggesting a new title, *Llewellyn's Choice.*

Although content with *Penhally,* Caroline explained Allen's arguments. "A good many places were named that way, especially by people who came here from Virginia early enough to take their pick of the land," she told Max. "'Llewellyn's Choice' would have a sort of double meaning, applying to the fortunes of the family as well as to the land itself."

Max, however, preferred the original title. *Llewellyn's Choice* seemed to him "to be an old-fashioned sort of title such as was used in the eighties say, on a romantic novel." Furthermore, he said, it would "misrepresent the book" to indicate "a character's choice between alternatives." With Max on her side, Caroline could resist Allen's advice.

By May she had come within three chapters of finishing the "horrible book," as she called it, and she felt like she was in "a state of complete moral deterioration." She worked until ten or eleven o'clock each night, then she would take a heavy bromide and fall into troubled sleep, only to rise early the next day to begin again.

With such a schedule, Caroline could not relax. Her always quick temper was on an unusually short fuse; no one could calm her. Once, at a party, she even threatened to slap Andrew Lytle if he said anything soothing. It didn't help that money was scarce, Freda was about to have puppies, and the weather was gorgeous: Caroline would rather be swimming, but at her typewriter, she had to finish killing off various Llewellyns and tying up loose ends. She feared the whole novel was "rotten," but she was almost past caring. She just wanted to get rid of it.

Before she could, however, one of her aunts fell ill, and Caroline felt obliged to take in one of her displaced boarders: a cantankerous old Confederate veteran with "very set ideas on [a] woman's place in a home," Caroline complained. She wanted to lay the book aside for several months, but Max kept writing her, urging her to finish, and Uncle Rob, recalling that it took Gray only seven years to write "Elegy Written in a Country Churchyard," began calling Caroline every morning. Aren't you through with that novel yet? he'd ask. He was lucky to escape Caroline's wrath.

Allen continued to read sections of her manuscript and offer suggestions for improvement, but Caroline was not always able to handle them. At one point Allen told her point blank that the last chapter, with its carefully thought-out climax, "simply would not do." In the final section Caroline had written about how Penhally had become a hunt club. Chance Llewellyn, a younger son and a dedicated farmer, would not be able to save Penhally, and in the final scene, he would stand on the porch of the old place, surveying what he had lost. Caroline wrote the scene to end with his reflections on how the land had been destroyed, obliterated, "as if by the wave of the hand."

When Allen criticized that ending, Caroline nearly collapsed. Her hands shaking so badly she couldn't type, Caroline told Allen to write the ending himself if he wanted any more changes. Allen did—or at least tried to—but Caroline did not like his version any better. Still, she managed to settle down by editing Allen's version.

Later, when she was calm, she thought about the ending and decided "there must be some symbol of the destruction of the house and only violent action would suffice for that." Allen agreed, but Caroline had to figure out the details. She ended up taking a section from one of her earlier novels, a scene where one brother shot another. Allen approved of her choice, but added she had "a bad homicidal complex."

Yet even with the violence depicted, Caroline had to decide whether to end the scene in Chance's "consciousness or with the picture of him moving into this changed world." She eventually ended the novel with dialogue: after putting down his pistol, Chance told one of the onlookers to call the sheriff. Caroline felt a little funny, closing the scene with what she called "melodrama," but she "read the book over three or four times and each time it built up to that last gesture," she decided.

By early summer the novel was finished; exhaustion and depression replaced Caroline's nervous anxiety. Although she insisted she was through tinkering, Caroline kept rereading the manuscript. She grew increasingly worried about the first chapter in the third section, which set the stage for the last conflict between brothers. She was firmly convinced the chapter was "so bad that it may ruin the book." "The knowledge depresses me," Caroline wrote a friend, "but I am so weary I can't think of anything to do about it." She had given it to Allen and his friends, who "read and read and wrinkle[d] their brows and suggest[ed] things to do, ranging from two thousand to five thousand words," Caroline said. "I keep wondering if I could squeeze out one more sentence."

When she sent the manuscript to Scribner's in early June, Caroline was still worried about the ending. "It might be better to cut the action off a little shorter than I have," she wrote, but Max sent the book directly to the printer without responding. When he read the ending in proof a month later, Max asked Caroline to elaborate on "the state of mind in Chance that produced his act," emphasizing "the effect which the sale of the house and all, and the property, and those rich people are having on Chance."

Caroline did so, and Max was pleased. "Most novel readers are pretty quick, unreflective readers," and the new paragraphs would certainly help them catch the full significance of the ending, he wrote. But, as if to comfort her, he continued, "I do not think that genuine readers will feel any lack, even without the additional paragraphs."

Throughout the summer Caroline could not bear even to think about *Penhally:* to her its flaws were all too obvious. She felt as if she were "wandering around shakily—like a man that's just got out of the pen and thinks he might perhaps be just as well off in." "I really don't know what to do with myself," she wrote to Katherine Anne. "I can't believe it's off my chest." Although she had a number of ideas for stories and a novel, she felt almost afraid to start a new project. When Scribner's offered her a contract, however, and a five-hundred-dollar advance for a new novel on the relationship between a white landowner and his poor white tenants, she didn't hesitate. They needed the money desperately: before Caroline had written more than a paragraph of the book, the advance had been used up.

To keep her mind off *Penhally* and her inability to write her new novel, Caroline kept busy swimming, sewing dresses for Nancy (who was going to enter school in September), playing with the cats and Freda's new puppy, reading *Ivanhoe,* making beer, and playing poker once a week with friends. When she thought about *Penhally,* worry set in. She figured she had to sell three thousand copies to pay back her advance, and everyone told her it was "a frightful season" for book sales. Occasionally, feeling desperate about her new contract with Scribner's, Caroline would lock herself in her upstairs bedroom to work, but often all she wrote was long letters.

Afraid of a poor reception from relatives and critics alike, Caroline waited anxiously for *Penhally*'s publication, scheduled for September 11. There were two autographing parties planned, one at a Nashville bookstore, the other at the local drug store in Clarksville, Dickson-Sadler's. "If the kin don't come and at least stand around in the attitude of people about to buy books I shall be peeved," Caroline told Sally. "I'm nervous about it, fearing it may be like getting ready to be married and no groom turning up."

Caroline needn't have worried. The Meriwether clan rallied to support her, and Caroline thought the attendance more than respectable at both parties. "My book came out with great eclat in these parts," she declared.

The family response to *Penhally* was generally better than Caroline had expected. Miss Carrie was proud of her favorite granddaughter's accomplishment, apparently never noticing her own idiosyncrasies in the character of Lucy. Caroline's father was even more enthusiastic. Caroline had not expected him to read the book, but J. M. Gordon read it twice—he was delighted to recognize the various Meriwethers in Llewellyn garb, especially Miss Carrie. "My cows won't touch onions," he'd say, roaring with laughter.

Six-year-old Nancy was none too pleased with her mother's achievements. When Beatrice told her she would probably "write a book like Mama" when she grew up, Nancy quickly demurred. "Don't mention no books to me," Nancy said. "Mama has nearly drove me crazy, locking herself up every morning." But Allen, reading the book consecutively for the first time, was amazed and impressed.

Soon Caroline received congratulatory letters about her novel. Lincoln Kirstein called *Penhally* a "distinguished book": "amazingly vivid, how solid, how beautiful." "In no other book that I've read has been captured the superb flash and shatter of the Civil War," he wrote. He especially admired the book's structure: "The way you start a line and retract it to converge in other themes provides a fusion of immediacy and recollection that is like a cloaking atmosphere."

To Caroline's delight, Cecil Goldbeck of the *New York Evening Post* wrote her "that the book attempted to show the disintegration of the Southern ideal of life," while Yvor Winters called *Penhally* "one of the five or six best novels of the past two decades." But Winters thought "the method" was wrong. "It should have been written in an entirely different way," he said, and he graciously provided Caroline with an outline.

The newspaper and magazine reviews pleased Caroline less. Usually the reviewers criticized the novel's episodic structure and broad narrative sweep. Many connected the story to the Agrarian movement, sometimes implying *Penhally* was little more than a fictional account of the concerns Allen and his "brethren" had expressed in *I'll Take My Stand*. One critic called Caroline's work a "curious experiment . . . with much fine feeling . . . but very little judgment." Another declared "the book [was] never more than mildly moving," lacking the "fire of more personal tragedy."

Yet of all the criticism, one comment really bothered Caroline: some reviewers made a point of saying "here is a first novel which is finished work." Caroline did not think of *Penhally* as her first novel, and she thought it should surprise no one that it was "finished work." "The book is evidently a mature performance and as evidently the work of years," she wrote to Max. As she had told Katherine Anne, "three years I've been working on that damn thing, ten I've been triggering with it one way or another."

After a while Caroline gave up fighting the "first novel" perception. It did not really matter what people called her book as long as they bought it, and as sales lagged, Caroline began to consider ways to publicize her novel. Probably remembering how personal testimonies had helped Katherine Anne, Caroline suggested to Max that he use quotes from some of the more laudatory personal letters she had received in new advertisements. "I am sure that people will go on buying Mr. Galsworthy," Caroline wrote, "but after all, somebody told them what to think in the first place."

M A N Y readers saw *Penhally* as a tragedy, a lament and yearning for the days and society gone by. Caroline dedicated the novel to her great-great-great-grandfather Charles Nicholas Meriwether, as well as to her Uncle Rob, represented in the novel as Ralph and Chance Llewellyn, respectively, and this dedication seemed to be further evidence of Caroline's sympathies.

In the actual Meriwether history, however, the historical prototype of Nicholas, Caroline's "Uncle Curious Will," was not the eldest son but a middle child. His older brother, Charles Nicholas Meriwether, did not quarrel with him over distribution of the family estate: in most accounts Charles Nicholas was given the land on which he built Woodstock at the time of his marriage, while his father was still alive; Will inherited Merivale, the family estate, after his father's death. Although the distinction might seem to be minor, to read the novel purely from the perspective of family history would be a mistake.

The defeat of Penhally and the Llewellyns was prefigured from the first paragraph of the novel. But Caroline was hardly bewailing the passing of a noble society. If anything, she was turning a sharply critical eye on both her family history and that of the Old South. The criticism was covert, however; her narrative strategies tended to mask her underlying purpose. Yet even through her shifting perspectives and intricate patterns of gaps and juxtapositions, Caroline explored the conflict between male and female perspectives of family and southern history.

Perhaps her friend and fellow novelist Stark Young best described the novel's achievement in a letter he wrote Caroline in mid-December 1931. "How much I was absorbed by and admired the book," he wrote. "Once

I would have been calling it masculine, that steady mentality and purpose with which the book goes through. But now that word means less
and besides there are things in it that belong in the depth of a feminine
mind also."

This feminine mind was not immediately apparent. On the surface *Penhally* appeared to champion conventional mores and patriarchal society.
Caroline built her novel around the exploits of the Llewellyn men, her
heroes. The women of the novel appeared as little more than stereo-
types: belles, old maids, or schemers who foolishly and selfishly seemed
to bring about the destruction of the Penhally estate and, by extension,
the southern way of life.

And yet, despite these conventional images of women, Caroline
focused much of her narrative on the lives and problems of women
through the stories of her four female characters: Alice Blair, Lucy Llewellyn, Emily Kinloe, and Joan Parrish. Sometimes heroines, sometimes
harpies, these women's stories spoke of pain and misunderstanding.
Other minor female characters further emphasized Caroline's interest in
the plight of women: in fact, women's screams served as bookends to
Penhally. In the opening scenes of the novel, a black woman named Violet wailed: she was about to give birth to a mulatto child, and she thought
her world was on the edge of destruction, because her masters, Ralph
and Nicholas Llewellyn, were fighting and dividing their property. At
the end of the novel, an unnamed woman cried out at another horror,
that of brother killing brother.

There would seem to be little connection between Violet's situation
and that of the unnamed woman, much less between these scenes and
the lives of the major female characters, and yet throughout the novel,
through dialogue and interior monologue, Caroline developed their
common bond of woe, suggesting that no matter her color, a woman's
lot was desperate, her choices limited. A woman could hope only to
be pretty or wealthy, and to be able to choose wisely. An ugly or poor
woman would probably end up a spinster, living an uncertain life dependent on the munificence of others. A woman who married unwisely
might end up a grass widow, a lot far worse than that of the spinster.
Or else she might suffer the humiliation of having a profligate husband,
given to foolish spending, idle ways, or illicit affairs. In short, a woman
had little control over her own destiny.

Repeated references to women's woes surfaced also in the meditations of various men in the novel. Reflecting on news of his son's death, John Llewellyn could not overlook the fate of his son's widow, Faneuil. She had run off with a "ne'er do well cousin of the Sinclairs," he noted. "It was that girl, Faneuil, who suffered . . . all the things that women suffer when they burn their bridges behind them in that particular way," John admitted grudgingly.

Because Caroline often filtered scenes and information through the consciousness of one of her characters, a "quick, unreflective reader," to use Max Perkins's term, could misinterpret an event or misunderstand a character by failing to take into account the source of the information or judgment. Yet in the shifting perspectives, reinforced by the symbols and patterns of the narrative, another interpretation of the events and characterizations became apparent. A woman judged harshly often appeared in a more complimentary light when her own thoughts were revealed, or when her behavior was examined by other women.

One key to the interpretation of *Penhally* was Alice Blair, a character who stood in the same position with respect to the Llewellyn family that Caroline's father, J. M. Gordon, stood to the Meriwethers. In Caroline's fictional version of her family genealogy, Alice was actually *related* to the Gordons: Alice's grandfather, Judge Blair, was modeled on Caroline's paternal great-uncle James Morris, as the talk of his hounds Old Mag, Old Whiskey, and the pups indicated. Alice even referred to her great-uncle named, as Caroline's paternal grandfather was, after William Fitzhugh.

Like Caroline's father Alice was always an outsider to the Llewellyn connection, even though she was distantly related to the family. Caroline allowed almost every other character to criticize Alice, just as the Meriwethers often criticized her father. Some of the "folks sitting on the porch" called her a flirt and said she might be trying to make a fool of the men in Kentucky while she was actually engaged to someone in Virginia. Nicholas thought Alice was "a cold proposition," a "spoiled little hussy and deceitful, too." Alice's courage was foolishness, the Llewellyns believed; her wisdom selfishness. By the end of the novel, some would even think Alice had caused the destruction of the Llewellyn home and family: when her son and daughter-in-law bought Penhally and turned it into a hunt club, Chance Llewellyn murdered his brother in despair. If the elder Nicholas had still been alive, he would have blamed Alice: she had bad "blood," he often insisted.

Still, Caroline made Alice the most reliable and most perceptive commentator on the novel's events. Just as Caroline's father had often pointed out the follies of the Meriwethers, Alice was able to deflate the romanticizing pretensions of the Llewellyn family. She also articulated the tragic aspects of the lives of southern women, especially their economic dependence and fear of miscegenation. Alice feared making a poor marriage, and Caroline explained why in Alice's meditations and in the bits and pieces of her family history revealed throughout the novel. With a profligate father and a grass-widow sister, Alice knew well the price she would pay if she did not choose wisely. She also had few illusions and strong feelings about the relationships between slaves and masters: the older women tried to ignore the mulatto children around Penhally, but Alice noticed the resemblances and recoiled in disgust.

Once the war ended, Alice left the neighborhood around Penhally, to be mentioned only occasionally by John or his grandsons, who scarcely knew or understood her. From then on, the primary references to a woman's plight appeared masked in the dominant consciousness of the male "heroes." The only major female character in the last half of the novel was Lucy Llewellyn, the daughter of Ralph. Lucy occupied an even more important place in the narrative than Alice, although she was revealed only through her actions, related primarily through the meditations of her husband, John. Yet even silent, Lucy was a powerful witness to man's inhumanity to woman.

Spurned by her first suitor when her father lost his property in the Civil War, Lucy had to depend on the generosity and support of others during the period after the war. Eventually she married John, knowing full well she was not his first choice. Although she would devote herself to the land, Lucy would find little comfort in life. She hated the blacks she had to care for, some of whom apparently were her husband's children. She also thought little of herself. After caring for the house, Lucy would spend hours in the garden, and because she went without a hat even in the hottest sun, Lucy's face became "as deeply tanned as any poor white woman's." Yet, John remembered, "when some of the older ladies remonstrated with her she laughed her short, hard laugh" and said, "Well, I am a poor white woman, ain't I?"

In episode after episode, Caroline revealed Lucy's strength and her dedication to Penhally, but she only hinted at Lucy's motivations, dreams, and attitudes toward her life and the Llewellyn family. She indi-

cated that Lucy withdrew from her husband emotionally without speci-
fying any reason, but from John's meditations the reader might conclude
miscegenation had something to do with it. "Lucy was inordinately
proud," John observed. "She had perhaps thought of herself as twice
betrayed . . . by love."

In the final section of *Penhally,* two more women appeared, Emily
Kinloe and Joan Parrish, and their situations and comments extended
the critical examination of women's lives into the twentieth century.
Although Caroline once again allowed the reader access to women's
thoughts, in many ways the final section was the most confusing and the
most often misread.

When Caroline created the character of Emily Kinloe, the fiancée of
Chance, she may have been thinking of her cousin Marion Henry or
another relative, but there were enough resemblances to Caroline's life
to make Emily a rather tongue-in-cheek self-portrait. Emily was "thin
and dark, with a nervous way of flinging her hands about," not beautiful
but attractive because her "personality had a certain flavor. . . . somewhat the same quality that distinguishes a thoroughbred horse, a certain
quickness of movement, nervousness"—in a word, she was "spirited."
Although she had spent years abroad, Emily was an ardent southerner.
"They had left her too much in the library when she was a little girl, with
her grandfather. . . . you cannot let a little girl spend all her time reciting
Father Ryan with Confederate veterans without having her turn out a
little queer," Caroline wrote.

Emily's role in the narrative was that of a chorus or observer, offering insight and commentary on the characters as they moved to the final
tragic scene. She sensed the injustice and destruction the Parrishes unknowingly created in the neighborhood; she also admired Joan Parrish
at first.

This admiration was crucial, because otherwise Joan appeared as little
more than a vain, foolish, grasping female: a twentieth-century version
of her mother-in-law, Alice Blair. Emily alone thought Joan beautiful;
she sensed Joan's power, noticing the "faint, hard lines" about Joan's
mouth and guessing Joan had a more difficult life than her husband:
Douglas had "escaped into a world where important letters were found
in old shoes, or obscure Indian tribes made treaties with all the dignity
of nations," Emily thought. "But it was harder on the woman. She had,
one way or another, to live with the money." Emily realized Joan would
not be content with small-town life for long: "If she stayed here long

enough she would have to do something about Gloversville at large . . . organize a hunt club, perhaps."

Later, Emily watched Joan walk through the graveyard, "flicking with her crop at the grass that grew beside the path." To Emily it seemed there was an "air about [Joan] of having the cosmos to choose from." In the shadows of the declining day, Emily could almost see how "the gigantic woman's hand might have been swinging out to uproot the big sugar tree, or demolish that whole row of ragged cedars."

These images of power and restlessness contrasted sharply with the helplessness and despair of Joan's own meditation near the novel's end. Hints of her past were jumbled together without explanation: the reader would be hard-pressed to understand the significance of much of Joan's reflection. Yet several important facts became apparent. Although Alice Blair had remained in Paris since her marriage, she cherished her family stories—Joan would always remember her sitting in her salon, talking about places like "Silvania, The Brackets, Pleasant Grove—those places would seem to spread themselves out around you in the gray light until you would think you were in Virginia, not Paris."

Joan could appreciate their talk because of her own connection to a plantation called Kinloch (actually one of the Meriwether estates near Charlottesville, Virginia), but the nature of her connection to Kinloch was never explained. She reflected only on a scene in the Kinloch woods, a time she had received a disturbing message. It may have had to do with her affair with a married man, but that too was unclear: the affair was referred to later, in a confused memory from Paris. Throughout her reminiscences Joan was in pain. At thirty-eight she dreaded middle age, which was "coming on her." "Everything was more of an effort lately," Gordon wrote. "But that was because she so rarely slept well."

The only pleasant memory Joan could recall was of a time in Baltimore "when she had been young, seventeen, eighteen, [and] she had slept like a person drugged," and spent her days on a farm, listening to her father and a hired man "talking absorbedly, yet following with their eyes the movements of some stringy colt that was just being turned into the pasture." Joan was crazy about horses, and her memory of "a happy time" probably had much to do with her passion. But like all her reminiscences, the scene was only a confused fragment, a hint of family history shaping Joan's life.

Yet Caroline provided one key to the meaning of Joan's reflections through the juxtaposition of apparently disconnected scenes. Right after the chapter with Joan's meditations, Caroline wrote about the sale of Penhally, focusing on a scene between Chance and his brother Nicholas. Chance blamed Joan, and he wondered, "Why couldn't she amuse herself with poor land?" It never occurred to him that Joan might have been trying to create something important to her, that her actions were not simply a lark.

It also never occurred to Chance that he was also responsible for the destruction of Penhally. Although he rehearsed poignant scenes of women who would be hurt, perhaps destroyed, by what seemed to him to be nothing more than a foolish woman's whim, he kept these scenes to himself; he made no impassioned plea to his brother for the land or the people. Rather, he provoked his brother into the sale. "I'll tell you one thing," he said. "If you do keep that land you'll have to get somebody else to farm it. No hand of mine'll ever put a plow in it again."

Many readers would accept Chance's perception of the events in the final two chapters. A conventional interpretation of the story would find Alice Blair and Joan Parrish ultimately responsible for the chaos and destruction accompanying the sale of Penhally. That's what happened, the moralist would say, when women were not restrained by strong men. But more than Joan's ambition, Chance's stubbornness and selfishness brought on the defeat of both Penhally and the Llewellyn family. If Chance had spoken out for the women, Penhally might have been saved. Joan probably would have built her hunt club elsewhere; no one would have been hurt. But Chance could not think of anyone but himself, and so he brought more suffering down on the women he loved. He would kill his brother in rage, and then calmly ask someone to call the sheriff, while an unnamed woman cried out in horror. Caroline's story ended as it had begun.

Caroline's decision to filter her narrative primarily through four male heroes drew attention away from her portraits of women. But as the various characters passed judgment on one another and revealed aspects of themselves, a careful reader could reexamine the nature of the players and the events they shaped and were shaped by. No one in the novel really understood anyone else; the problems of perception and understanding multiplied as the years passed. In the end only the reader was in a position to see and understand the entire picture. It was very hard to untangle the family lines, but to some degree it was not necessary. By adopting the various perspectives, and by testing the reliability of each character in turn, the reader could assemble the pieces and understand the significance of it all. And that was part of the meaning of Caroline's story. The reader had to be the artist, creating order out of apparent chaos and tragedy.

Some reviewers compared *Penhally* to the multigenerational family sagas of John Galsworthy, but in many ways Caroline's novel was more akin to her female forebears' works. Like Elizabeth Meriwether in her novel *The Master of Redleaf*, Caroline explored the similarities between the life of a slave, Violet, and the lives of white women, whatever their station. Like Amélie Rives, Caroline created the Penhally estate as an objective correlative to the action of her narrative. And like her "Cousin" Lizzie, Dorothy Dix, Caroline refashioned family stories to launch her literary career. In fact, in *Penhally* Caroline used the same episode Cousin Lizzie had used in her first publication: the family story of how some treasure had been buried in the woods to keep it safe during the war. In the original Meriwether history, one of the slaves, named Dick, had buried the family silver inside a tomb in the family graveyard. Dorothy Dix had revised the story, making a female slave the heroine of the tale she called "How Chloe Saved the Silver." Caroline revised the story further. Nicholas's nephew and an old slave named Uncle Townsend had buried ten thousand dollars in gold in a steel box out in the woods. Lucy recovered it, even though Uncle Townsend had died and the saplings marking the burial site had long since been cut down.

In *Penhally* Caroline created a landscape peopled with characters she would use for the rest of her life. One characteristic distinguishing the landscape suggested all was not as it seemed: the underground stream. This stream was a mysterious, creative element connecting the Llewellyn family to the world beyond. It flowed, according to John Llewellyn,

through the length of the Penhally land and the Fairfields woods, crossed the big road in front of the Sycamore house and dipped into a sink hole on Cousin Rufus Llewellyn's place. After that it flowed underground for miles, to emerge in a deeper stream that ran tortuously through the bottoms to empty into Little West Fork, which was an arm of Red River. It had, too, innumerable tributaries. The little branch that flowed from the spring behind the Penhally house was one, the shallow, bright stream that came from the mouth of Crenfrew's Cave was another. And he had heard his uncle Nick identify a stream twenty miles away as part of the same system. That stream emptied into the Red River, which emptied into the Cumberland, which, in turn, emptied into the Mississippi. And at Cairo, Illinois, the Mississippi met the Ohio and flowed with it toward the gulf. They said that you could see the two rivers flowing side by side for a time, the one tawny yellow, the other greenish black.

The underground stream would be a prominent feature of Caroline's fictional neighborhood. It would also be a metaphor for Caroline's fictional technique.

"I HOPE nothing will divert you from going on with your writing," Max Perkins had written to Caroline shortly after she had finished *Penhally*. "Certainly you have every reason to believe in yourself on the basis of what you have done now. I only mention it because it is so much harder for women to write, with all the detail that they have to think about, than for a man," he said.

Caroline appreciated his concern. "It is, certainly, much harder for a woman to write than it is for a man," she responded. "It is so much harder that I am in a panic half the time fearing something will happen to prevent me from writing." But, she added, he did not have to worry about her: "I am very fierce about it, I assure you. And we have a wonderful servant who does everything she can do to help me get on with my writing."

During the fall and winter of 1931, however, Caroline found it difficult to be "fierce" about her writing. As the anxiety over *Penhally* waned, tension returned to Benfolly because Allen could not finish his biography of Robert E. Lee. For weeks after the original fall publication date had been set aside, Allen's publisher, Earle Henry Balch of Minton, Balch, and Company, pestered the Tates with long-distance telephone calls. After a while Beatrice would announce nearly every time the phone rang, "It's just Mister Balch, I reckon."

Caroline might try to be understanding, but she was getting frustrated with Allen. She agreed to write a chapter of the biography for him, and Allen asked Red Warren to draft another as well, but nothing anyone could do seemed to help. "God knows when Allen will finish that damn book," Caroline wrote a friend in early fall. "We could do almost anything this winter if he only would—he could get a sizable advance on another book he has in mind the minute he finishes Lee." Until then they had to live off the garden and run up charges in town, an uncertain existence at best.

Despite Caroline's success with *Penhally,* Allen was still the only recognized writer in the family. In October Allen, not Caroline, was invited to a conference of southern writers held in Charlottesville, Virginia. Caroline decided she would go along anyway as a "stowaway," but at the last minute, she received an official invitation.

The conference was "such a funny affair," Caroline thought, with everyone present "very anxious not to be thought Southern." Ellen Glasgow was "a grand old girl," Caroline thought, but Paul Green was a "son of a bitch." He "got up and announced that we were all going to God in a machine."

Caroline also met William Faulkner in Charlottesville. He was the "only person who conducted himself like a real he-writer, in the best Hemingway style, with some good touches of the old South," she said. "Blind drunk" most of the time, Faulkner seldom spoke more than a "Ma'am?" or "Sir," or "I dare say," in a voice Caroline thought sounded "like an indifferent weasel's." The one time Faulkner tried to say something more, Caroline suffered. She had been saying good-bye to Allen's friend, John Peale Bishop, when Faulkner opened his mouth to talk and suddenly threw up all over her. While Caroline tried not to laugh, and John Bishop looked as if "he had suddenly turned to wood," Faulkner "reeled off into a corner with a handkerchief." Realizing "the poor devil felt pretty bad about it," Caroline followed Faulkner and tried to console him. "But he just sat there staring at me like a dejected coon," Caroline told Léonie later. "Thank God it wasn't my white satin dress."

Eventually Caroline pitied Faulkner, figuring he used drink as a mask, but during the conference she was sorry he had "come out of the South and not New England": he had "combined in him all the unadmirable qualities that New Englanders [were] always ascribing to the Southern mind." Faulkner was a great writer, she decided, but he did not have the necessary "humility before his material." One of his stories, about a black cook who thought her husband was going to kill her, was "marvelous," Caroline said, "or it would be wonderful if he could let your flesh stop creeping long enough for you to feel the woman existing as a person."

Caroline thought her own novel was going to be wonderful, if she could just find the time to get it written. After the conference was over, she tried once again to get back into a routine, but there were too many distractions. At one point Nancy announced that she knew why the nuns at her Catholic school didn't marry. "It is too much trouble to cook for men," she said. Caroline was amused, but she said, "I hope [Nancy] didn't get that idea from me!"

Attending the local Catholic school encouraged Nancy's religious zeal. Every night before bed, Nancy said her prayers: three Hail Marys and an Our Father. She told her mother she was going to be a nun, and Caroline told her friends that Nancy was "much ashamed of her irreligious parents." "I'm rather glad it's hit her so early—instead of in adolescence," Caroline added, noting she had "rather dashed" Nancy's desire to become a nun "by telling her that nuns had to promise God never to have any fun. Nancy is much addicted to fun." One day Nancy shut four cats in a bureau drawer for several hours, tormented the cook, and worked "a dozen other villainies during the day" before going to bed "piously murmuring the Lord's Prayer," Caroline said.

About the only writing Caroline got done before the end of the year was her application for a Guggenheim Fellowship and a long short story about a pioneer woman named Jenny Wiley, which she entered in *Scribner's* magazine's long-short-story contest. Caroline had little hope for the Guggenheim. She proposed to write a novel showing the Llewellyn family "entirely in a contemporary light: the subject will be the clash between the land-owning family and a family of the tenant class living on the same plantation," but she did not elaborate any more in her application, perhaps because she felt her work would not get serious attention. "Allen thinks I have a chance, but I rather have an idea I have been weighed in the balance . . . and found wanting," she told a friend.

Caroline felt more optimistic about her story, originally called "To Cumberland," later retitled "The Captive." If she didn't win the prize, she thought she would at least make some money selling the story to the magazine. She based her story on a captivity narrative she had found while doing research on the pioneer period. Attacked by a roving band of Cherokees and Shawnees who had mistaken her cabin for that of a noted Indian hunter, Jenny Wiley had watched her children killed and scalped before she was carried off into the wilderness. She lived with the Indians for about eleven months before finding her way back to a white settlement.

The published account of Jenny Wiley's adventures followed the usual pattern for such stories, but Caroline thought the entire tale had an "atmosphere of tremendous excitement." After working with the story for a while, she found herself thinking that "people don't appreciate the Cherokee as they ought to." She even caught herself yelling at Nancy when she complained about her food. "Little Indian children are never allowed to eat anything hot for fear of getting soft," Caroline told her daughter. Soon after she said it, Caroline realized she was getting a bit too wrapped up in her writing, but it was hard not to, she thought: "The exploits of some of those pioneer women are things that occur usually only on battlefields."

Caroline sent the story off to *Scribner's* in mid-December. Then she and Allen spent much of the rest of the month trying to scrounge up enough money to pay their debts. Clarksville was "getting un-agrarian," Caroline decided: "the merchants are wanting their bills paid every month or so," whether or not the crops had been sold. It probably didn't help any that folks who barely knew them were saying the Tates were independently wealthy. Caroline found herself repeating the words of their new tenant, Mr. Norman, a plain-spoken, God-fearing man: "If I'm going to starve, let me starve on a farm." For a while it seemed as if the Tates would starve, but then they were able to borrow enough money to get by— "from the poorest member of the family," Caroline noted with surprise, her Aunt Loulie.

Still, Caroline was hopeful as she faced the new year. The December 1931 issue of *Bookman* included an enthusiastic review of *Penhally* by Ford Madox Ford. Calling the volume "the best constructed novel that modern America has produced," Ford compared Caroline's work to that of Henry James, Stephen Crane, and Hawthorne. "*Penhally* is the triumphant tragedy of a house and the vindication of a mode of life," he said.

Caroline felt overwhelmed by his praise. "What you have said will always endure in my memory," she told him. She appreciated it that he had noted the novel's structure and commented on one's relationship to the past. "Certain ages of the past . . . do return and loom before us," she said, "and it is not always nostalgia that makes people write about them." She was amazed that *Bookman* even ran two pictures of her—terrible pictures, she thought—but she was pleased with all the attention.

In a separate letter to her, Ford must have chided her for the book's dedication, because Caroline apologized profusely. "I see now that it was indescribably stupid in me not to know that it would please you to have had *Penhally* dedicated to you," she wrote Ford. "I can only remind you that living so long on the edge of things as I have, I have cast aside a great many amenities that some people manage to hang on to. I just have these blind spots."

In January a false spring came; forsythia, jonquils, and narcissi began to bloom. Then cold winter weather arrived; the flowers were frozen in a blanket of snow.

The Tates had barely survived their financial panic of December before they began to worry again about money. They expected the sheriff to repossess their car at any moment. In a panic Caroline wired *Scribner's* for a decision on "The Captive": two hundred dollars from the magazine publication would almost literally save their lives.

Max Perkins responded immediately, but not as Caroline wanted. "Magazine does not think Captive has enough regular story interest to publish as a long story," his telegram read. "Story interest!" Caroline exclaimed. "My rage was so great that I couldn't use my mother tongue properly," she told Red later. Nevertheless, in the return mail, she fired off a scathing letter to Max.

"If murder, rapine, and tomahawking of children, are not story-interest," Caroline wrote. "I am at a loss to know what is." She called the story an almost "literal transcript" of the life of Jenny Wiley, insisting that "the state of mind of this pioneer woman, her life and her experience, are at the spiritual foundations of thousands of Americans." "The Captive" was her best writing, she said. "I am willing to stake my reputation as a writer on it."

In the closing paragraphs of the letter, Caroline insisted she was "not a talented amateur" but "as mature" as she would ever be. "I can see no reason why my publisher should let me starve until he can catch up with my work," she said. "I am not only at my best right now; I am at my best because I am one of the few writers in this generation who have something to write about."

Caroline's protest had little effect on her editor. "The reply which came promptly back was masterly," she told a friend. "He had me roped and tied in two paragraphs and then went on to do his will." First Max praised *Penhally,* then he reminded her that "editing is not easy either." Before he finished, he had even agreed with Caroline that magazine editors might be "five years behind the mood of those who are really writing," but, Max added, "if that is true, the magazine public is ten years behind."

In between his attempts to calm Caroline, Max gave her some practical suggestions for improving the story. Roughly half of the story "had only the interest of a document," Max said. Jenny Wiley existed only as "a specimen of frontier woman" until "her past life began to come into her mind." He urged Caroline to revise the story and reveal more of her history and personality at the beginning of the story, before the Indians attacked. He also held out what Caroline called "roseate hopes," telling her that if "The Captive" fared well in the contest, *Scribner's* magazine might yet publish it.

"That Perkins is a smooth article and there is no use fooling with him," Caroline said when she read his reply. But she took his advice seriously, rewriting the first two pages of the story. Although *Hound and Horn* had agreed to publish the story, and Caroline desperately needed the money, she also followed Max's advice, deferred publication, and left the story in the contest. But it annoyed her that *Scribner's* was printing other manuscripts submitted for the contest: "Little things struck off by Edith Wharton and Sherwood Anderson in their off moments," she said with derision.

Without money for the story, the Tates were hard-pressed to get by. They lived for weeks on blackeyed peas: it was all they could afford. Caroline thought about firing her cook, Beatrice, but couldn't. "I owe her three weeks back wages, and besides, I need her to borrow money from," Caroline wrote Katherine Anne. "This all comes from putting any faith in publishers." When her royalty statement on *Penhally* arrived, and Caroline discovered she owed Scribner's ninety-six dollars, she thought things could not get any worse.

Then Caroline found out she was pregnant. The previous summer that might have been good news: Caroline had felt bad about Nancy's "solitary condition." But now it was just one more thing gone wrong. Caroline was thirty-six years old. It was all she could do to balance her writing with the care of six-year-old Nancy. What would she do with an infant?

It took little or no time for Caroline to decide to have an abortion. But the procedure did not go smoothly. While recovering, Caroline suddenly began to run a temperature of 106. Terribly frightened, she called the doctor who had performed the abortion, but he said the temperature was nothing to worry about. Not satisfied, Caroline called her family doctor, but he refused to examine her without being called in formally for a consultation. Later Caroline joked about the experience. "I was a month winding up the affair, with a stubborn old country doctor who assured me that I was the meanest patient he ever had," Caroline wrote

Sally. Yet at the time Caroline wondered if she would live through the night. Eventually her temperature broke, but not before both Caroline and Allen were scared to death.

To complicate matters, Allen came down with the flu and was bedridden for three weeks. Then Beatrice quit without warning. Caroline was shocked. Even though she had wanted to fire Beatrice, the timing could not have been worse. Still weak, Caroline had to get out of bed and take over the housework. The only thing that saved her was Andrew Lytle: when Allen wrote him, he quickly came to Benfolly and stepped in to help.

In the midst of a "rush of dish washing," Caroline found one thing to rejoice in: she won the Guggenheim Fellowship. It was, however, a mixed blessing. With so many bills to settle before they left, the Tates wondered how they would ever get away, much less live abroad on the two-thousand-dollar stipend. "We have never been as broke in our lives for we have never had as many debts before," Caroline wrote Sally in early spring. "I don't see how we'll make it at all, but we will, somehow, for we can't turn down the two thousand."

After all the pain of the last few months, Caroline was overjoyed at the chance for change. As much as she loved Benfolly, she was ready to go to a place where there was nobody to call cousin. France had been good for her before, and she was sure she would be able to write there; maybe Allen would also finally finish his biography of Lee. But if Allen couldn't work, Caroline was not going to let it bother her. If necessary, she informed Sally, she'd go off by herself and work "like hell": "I'm fed up on starving." In the last few months she and Allen had been singing a wearisome little song:

> What you going to do when the meat gives out?
> Stand in the corner with your lip poked out.
> What you going to do when the meat comes in?
> Stand in the corner with a greasy chin.

It was time for a change; Caroline was sure. As she told Sally, "The chins are immaculate as yet but we are hoping."

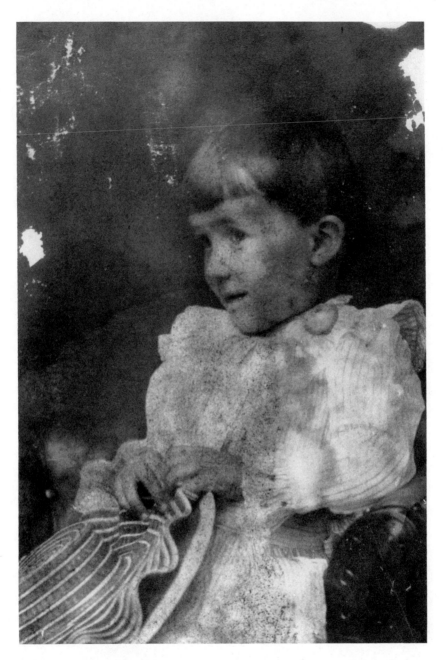

Gordon, age four (Caroline Gordon Papers, Princeton University Library, Department of Rare Books and Special Collections).

*Gordon's mother, Nancy Meriwether Gordon
(Caroline Gordon Papers, Princeton University Library,
Department of Rare Books and Special Collections).*

Gordon's father, James Morris Gordon
(Disciples of Christ Historical Society, Nashville, Tennessee).

Gordon's grandmother, Caroline Ferguson Meriwether, "Old Miss Carrie"
(Caroline Gordon Papers, Princeton University Library, Department of Rare
Books and Special Collections).

Gordon during her college years
(Caroline Gordon Papers, Princeton University Library,
Department of Rare Books and Special Collections).

Gordon as a young woman
(Caroline Gordon Papers, Princeton University Library,
Department of Rare Books and Special Collections).

Stella Bowen's portrait of the Tate family, painted in Paris in 1929:
"Allen and I, held together in space by Nancy," Gordon said (Photo from
the Princeton University Library, Department of Rare Books and Special
Collections).

Gordon, Allen Tate, and Sally Wood in France, 1932
(Caroline Gordon Papers, Princeton University Library,
Department of Rare Books and Special Collections).

A moment of relaxation during the summer of 1937 at Olivet College in Michigan: Joseph Bremer (seated), Paul Engle, Katherine Anne Porter, and Gordon (Papers of Katherine Anne Porter, Special Collections, University of Maryland at College Park Libraries).

*Gordon and Allen Tate in their New York City apartment, December 1948
(Caroline Gordon Papers, Princeton University Library, Department of Rare
Books and Special Collections).*

Portrait of Gordon with her dog, Bub, by Marcella Comès Winslow, 1944.

*Gordon, her father James Gordon, nephew Meriwether Gordon,
brother Morris Gordon, and daughter Nancy (Caroline Gordon Papers,
Princeton University Library, Department of Rare Books and Special
Collections).*

Gordon at work in bed while suffering from the flu
(Caroline Gordon Papers, Princeton University Library,
Department of Rare Books and Special Collections).

Andrew Lytle, Gordon, and Robert Fitzgerald answering questions after a panel discussion at the 1966 Southern Literary Festival at the University of Alabama (University of Alabama archives).

OPPOSITE: ABOVE
Gordon and Allen Tate during registration at the University of North Carolina at Greensboro, 1938 (Photograph Collection, University Archives, University of North Carolina at Greensboro).

OPPOSITE: BELOW
Gordon, Allen Tate, Ford Madox Ford, and Janice Biala (Photographic Archives, Vanderbilt University).

Gordon in San Cristóbal de las Casas, Mexico
(Caroline Gordon Papers, Princeton University Library,
Department of Rare Books and Special Collections).

 1932–1934

Caroline had hoped to get a good deal of her new book written in the four months before they left for France, but she eventually put it aside for another project, a fairy story called "At the Top of the Glass Mountain." Although she never found a publisher for the book she "contrived and concocted purely with the idea of making some money," Caroline used the work to explore her inner turmoil over her role and responsibilities as a woman and a writer.

That turmoil was exacerbated by the decisions Caroline had to make about her trip abroad, especially the decision of what to do with Nancy. Aunt Pidie urged Caroline to leave Nancy with her in Chattanooga so Nancy could continue with school and have a more normal life, but Caroline felt uneasy. It would certainly be easier for both mother and daughter if Nancy stayed behind. Caroline would get more writing done, and Nancy would live comfortably, surrounded by loving relatives. Yet should she once again abandon her daughter for her art? Caroline could not decide, but she explored the issue in "At the Top of the Glass Mountain."

The story was similar to the fairy tales Caroline had often read as a child. There were good fairies and wicked wizards, talking animals, and strange lands with unusual creatures. Caroline would write a section, then try it out on her daughter. When Nancy got "a certain steely glint" in her eye, Caroline felt as if she had written a "bit" that would do. Too often, however, Nancy shrieked with joy at "the most horrible spots," Caroline told a friend.

As in Caroline's childhood "writing," the plot followed a little girl, Anna Mary, who wandered into the forest and discovered adventure. This time, adventure was Wishing Land, where, of course, anything Anna Mary wished for would come true—anything except her wish to return home. In Wishing Land "you can't go backward," Caroline wrote. "You can go forward but you can't ever go backward."

Anna Mary's challenge was to find a way home by going forward. In the first chapter Anna Mary met her guide, the Wishing Beetle. In the second episode she became the Princess Rosamond, a fairy princess living in a coral palace under the sea. In the third chapter Anna Mary met "one of the most powerful witches in the whole country," the Witch of Lost Hollow, an odd, old woman who "made a point of collecting all the old, worn out things she could find." In the best fairy-tale tradition, the witch gave Anna Mary and her companions (her favorite pony, Spot, and her kitten, Tuck) some gifts to help them on their journey: an old tin whistle, a pair of carpet slippers, and a pair of spectacles. Before their adventures were complete, the travelers would use each gift, of course. The spectacles were for Anna Mary. "If you look through these glasses you will always be able to see what is going on around you," the witch said, and "that, believe an old woman, is sometimes of great advantage."

After leaving Lost Hollow the travelers had a Swiftian adventure in "The Strange Country of Parvula," a land of tiny people mourning a missing queen. In the next episode Anna Mary and her friends rescued the kidnapped queen from the Terrible Wizard of the Wood, just before the wizard could turn them all into flowers and lizards. Then Anna Mary faced the temptations of the Fairy of the Glass Mountain.

Anna Mary had the greatest need for her spectacles on the Glass Mountain. At first, she loved the place. A seemingly beautiful fairy ruled a kingdom of glass people, and because of the fairy's apparent kindness, Anna Mary almost lost sight of her desire to return home. The fairy offered to turn the travelers into glass, a great temptation since the glass children and animals had no brains or hearts; they played all day long and felt no pain.

But just before Anna Mary went under the fairy's spell, she remembered the spectacles she had been given in Lost Hollow. When she put the spectacles on, she saw beyond the blinding light of Glass Mountain. She saw her family and her home, and she realized it might be easier to live without her brain and heart, but the price she would have to pay was too great. Not willing to give up love as well as pain, Anna Mary decided at last not to let anyone turn her into glass, and with the decision she found her way home.

The story was not great art, as Caroline readily admitted. It was not even very original: she had borrowed ideas and patterns from other children's books. Yet it illustrated many of Caroline's concerns about her life.

Throughout the story, especially in the character of Anna Mary, Caroline explored the difficulty of pursuing a writing career. Like her creator, Anna Mary was fiercely independent and full of imagination, yet Anna Mary had to worry about words—about their power to liberate and their potential to wreak destruction. Soon after Anna Mary met the Wishing Beetle, he screamed, "Don't say another word—on pain of death." Later he explained that he was not telling Anna Mary to be quiet: she could ask as many questions as she liked, but she should be careful about what she wished for and careful not to "say the wrong word." Words were dangerous in Wishing Land, he said.

Imagination was also a mixed blessing, as Anna Mary discovered in the story of Princess Rosamond. The princess could never escape her royal duties. When she tried to postpone her time in "that stuffy old audience chamber where somebody [was] always coming with a tiresome story to tell," a dour prime minister and a crowd of subjects pursued her. They tried to force her to settle a dispute over a man accused of stealing a cow. Because the accused was unable to speak, the princess was commanded to "read the man's mind and tell us what he was going to say."

Anna Mary escaped from her responsibilities under the sea only to meet another artist figure, Mother Brenda, the Witch of Lost Hollow. The very source of Mother Brenda's power was her oddity: she depended on the wind to blow strange items in her path, items she would invest with magic powers and fuse into meaningful patterns with the help of "a very special kind of magic glue made according to a formula inherited from [her] dear mother." The old woman, "as might be expected, knew some very good stories," Caroline wrote. Yet she was considered to be peculiar, an attitude Caroline often held about herself.

Complicating Caroline's view of her life as a writer were the pressures and conflicting responsibilities of living in community with others, and throughout the children's story Caroline was clearly exploring her options. One could always run away, as Princess Rosamond tried to do, but too often the demands of others followed suit. Or one could find a way to go numb, to become a work of art rather than a creator of art. The choice was difficult.

In the end Anna Mary refused to give up her ability to think and feel. With the magic spectacles, she saw the value in relationships and affirmed the importance of her family ties and responsibilities. Yet Caroline's conclusion to "At the Top of the Glass Mountain" was only a temporary resolve; she continued to reflect on the issue in the coming months.

The news of Hart Crane's suicide on April 27 must not have helped her state of mind. Hart had devoted his life to art, but apparently it did not sustain him. Returning by steamer from a year in Mexico on a Guggenheim Fellowship, Hart had jumped overboard four days after sailing. Rumor had it that he had waved off a life preserver someone on the ship had thrown him. It was "all pretty sad and mad," Caroline thought, and yet Hart's suicide was "a logical end to his life": Hart "pretended to abandonment when all the time [he] knew exactly what [he was] doing."

Hart's death at sea undoubtedly added to Caroline's anxiety over whether to leave Nancy in Tennessee when she and Allen set sail for Europe. As Pidie pressured her to decide, Caroline wavered, rationalized, and worried. Over and over again she said, "It is hard to put the ocean between us." Yet Caroline increasingly felt that Nancy would be better off with Pidie, and she admitted that she "could do a hell of a lot more work" if Nancy did not come along. As if to convince herself, Caroline repeatedly rehearsed the reasons for both taking and leaving Nancy. Usually the reasons for leaving her outnumbered the reasons for taking her along.

Eventually Allen persuaded Caroline to leave Nancy behind, but by then Caroline was eager to escape. In April, after an operation to have Caroline's appendix removed, the Tates once again went to live at Merry Mont. They had rented Benfolly early in preparation for their trip abroad, figuring they would save money by living with Caroline's grandmother. But by June the tiny gray house in the grove of sugar maples was overflowing with kin: Aunt Loulie had moved in, Aunt Pidie came for an extended visit, Uncle Rob dropped in daily, and even Caroline's father, J. M. Gordon, spent a week visiting. The chaotic family circus kept Caroline from getting any work done.

Just as they always had, the kin spent long hours sitting on the porch, telling old stories, talking about one another, passing judgments, and speculating on characters and events. The women gathered on the porch in the afternoon to sit and "stare at the green fields and wonder if the old lady [was] in a good humor still," Caroline noted. Then they would go in, "eat enormous meals of country butchered mutton and then go aback and sit on the porch some more while the shadows lengthen[ed]."

At night Allen and J. M. Gordon joined the women on the porch. By then, Caroline said, "the tide of reminiscence [had] risen until we [had] called to mind most of the old time characters of these parts."

They talked about Cousin Owen, who visited the various houses in the connection and always "carried his teeth in a basket," saying, "Kisses for girls and switches for boys." Then there was "Uncle" Tom Watson and "Uncle" Joe Morris: they each kept bottles of liquor hidden, and "they too sat on the porch all day long," Caroline noted. "When they saw a man approaching they speculated on which one of them he was nearer kin to, and whose bottle he would get a drink of."

Like the old woman in her fairy tale, Caroline began collecting odd bits and pieces she could use in her fiction. Uncle Rob told Caroline about Tom Rivers, a distant member of the connection whom he had met in Texas. Caroline listened to Rob's story, to all the old tales, and she watched as new family myths took shape. With the right glue, most of what she heard and saw would be transformed into fiction in the coming months and years, especially the story of Tom Rivers.

Rivers was a cowboy during the 1890s. According to Uncle Rob, Tom was "utterly fearless, took people's guns out of their hands by the barrel and then handed them back butt first, like a lady handing somebody a tea spoon." Uncle Rob said he had no idea what became of Tom, but Caroline decided he had probably been killed "by one of those men whose guns he was always trifling with." She immediately wrote out what Rob had told her: it would make a wonderful short story.

Once again, much of the talk on the porch concerned Caroline's grandmother. Aunt Loulie had moved into Merry Mont the previous fall, thinking Miss Carrie needed someone to take care of her. But the old woman did not want Loulie around, and they had been squabbling for months. "Loulie would be a bonanza to a feeble minded person but she ain't much comfort to me," Old Miss Carrie decided.

Caroline found it amusing to watch the two women struggle for control. Sometimes Loulie seemed to wear her mother down, but Miss Carrie would not accept defeat. As Caroline stored away scenes from their battles for future use, she occasionally felt sorry for her grandmother. Yet Loulie's presence actually helped to make the Tates' stay at Merry Mont more pleasant: the old woman was too busy fighting with Loulie to criticize Allen, Caroline, or Nancy.

Another amusing struggle was the old one between J. M. Gordon and the Meriwethers. Caroline felt as if she had to take her mother's place and try to make her father "preserve a semblance of decency towards the kin" during his visit in early June. That had always been a difficult task, but Caroline discovered her father could not be controlled at all once he had enlisted an ally—Allen.

Allen wasted little time taking sides with J. M. Gordon against the Meriwethers. Earlier in the spring, Caroline had declared that "after a somewhat intensive training," Allen was "practically a Meriwether." But that June, Allen adopted his father-in-law's mocking relationship to the Meriwethers, eventually becoming more "Gordon" than J. M. Gordon himself. "The Meriwethers are all louts," Allen would say; "they are so proud of holding on to their land. But the only reason they've held on to it is that they haven't got enough sense to get along in town."

Every afternoon, while the women sat on the porch talking, the men went fishing. After a while Caroline decided Allen "would have been completely demoralized" if her father stayed any longer: Allen was "getting that care free spirit to a pronounced degree," she said. When Molly Ferguson died, neither man would attend the funeral. "Allen would have gone," Caroline thought, "but Dad instilled the spirit of rebellion in him."

"Cousin Molly Ferguson is no more kin to me than a catfish," J. M. Gordon announced grandly. "Why should I go to her funeral? No, I am going fishing. I haven't many more years to live and I have already preached four thousand funerals and some of them were the very devil."

"Allen could go," Caroline pointed out, but her father countered with what Caroline thought was "a pathetic plea for Allen's society."

"We hold high concourse on that pond," he said. "I am starved for intellectual companionship. Down in Florida I never see anybody but niggers."

Caroline laughed, a hearty guffaw which sounded so much like her father's. "As if you didn't *prefer* the society of niggers!" she said.

But the men remained adamant; the women went to the funeral alone. After J. M. Gordon left, Allen went around declaring he was not "kin" to any of the Meriwethers.

By the time the Tates left Merry Mont in early July, Caroline was ready to echo Allen's sentiments and disown her Meriwether heritage. As much as she loved her grandmother and kin, she was tired of life in the Old Neighborhood. "There is something about putting the ocean between you and your relatives," she wrote in a letter to a friend.

On July 21 the Tates left for Europe on the *Stuttgart*. Even without

Nancy there were eight people sharing two cabins, tourist third class: Allen and Caroline, Lyle and Chink Lanier and their young son, Caroline's cousin Manny Meriwether, Sally Wood, and Dorothy Ann Ross, a young girl from Clarksville on her way to school in Switzerland. It was hardly a pleasant trip. When Caroline got off the boat in France, she could barely stand upright. The rough seas, the German food, and too much coffee left her reeling for days after she arrived in Paris.

For several weeks the party stayed at Ford's apartment at 32, rue de Vaugirard. Caroline did not join the others sightseeing and cafe hopping: still sore from her appendectomy, she could not climb six flights of stairs to the apartment too often. After some bed rest she tried to polish the story of Tom Rivers into fiction, but with a steam riveter pounding beneath her window and busses roaring up and down the streets, she found it "hard to concentrate."

When Caroline did leave the apartment, she worried about bumping into Madame Gau, the old woman who had taken care of Nancy during their last visit to Paris. Madame Gau would not approve of leaving Nancy behind, Caroline was sure, and the thought of meeting her in one of their familiar haunts made Caroline uneasy. When the proprietor of the Brasserie de l'Odéon "demanded to know the whereabouts of the petite fille," Caroline felt a full measure of guilt. She comforted herself by observing how the Laniers' young son suffered, "dragged about and up till all hours" until he "flew into such a passion that he beat his French nurse."

By the middle of August, the Tates' group had dwindled to three. Dorothy Ann left for school in Switzerland, the Laniers went off on their own, and Manny Meriwether returned to her job in the States. Once Allen finished writing some articles for the *New Republic,* the Tates and Sally Wood also left Paris for Toulon in their Model A Ford.

For a while they stayed with Ford Madox Ford and his new common-law wife, Janice Biala, in their home, the Villa Paul. Ford had not changed: wheezy and fat, he still had that "pure pride of the professional" writer which made Caroline forgive him when he did those "things that enrage and alienate people." It was "too bad" he didn't "have a school," Caroline thought. "He needs one."

Since Ford had no admiring "school" of writers, Caroline was relieved to find Janice devoted to him. A Polish Jew, Janice had fine "Slavic eyes"—the most beautiful Caroline had ever seen—"and Slavic melancholy and a Jewish way of making herself unpopular," Caroline thought.

A gifted painter, Janice cared little for the luxuries of life. She "sticks to Ford through thick and thin—mostly through thin these days," Caroline observed.

Janice and Ford invited the Tates and Sally to spend a month at the Villa Paul, "the most uncomfortable villa . . . on the Riviera," Caroline thought, but with an unsurpassed view of the Mediterranean. At night the Fords, the Tates, and Sally would sit outside looking down at the sea. About halfway between the villa and the water, there was a small pond, the home of two fat frogs Ford had named Willy Seabrook and Henry James. Often, on a quiet night, Ford would listen and say, "Ah, that clear bell like note. Henry James."

Such evenings and some pleasure jaunts around Toulon helped Caroline to relax and enjoy her return to France, yet all was not peaceful. The Villa Paul was simply too small for five people, yet Ford and Janice were starved for companionship and loath to lose their guests. "There was no room even to take out one's tooth brush and no water to brush one's teeth if one had taken it out, . . . but it was very hard to make them see" that, Caroline observed wryly.

Finally, the Tates and Sally managed to get away from the Villa Paul. For several weeks they stayed at a pension on the shore; then in September they rented the Villa les Hortensias, a wonderful place surrounded by roses and mulberry trees. Both pension and villa were godsends to Caroline: it was "such a blessing to stay quiet" after months of travel and upsets, she said.

Caroline renewed her strength by gardening and taking long walks. During most afternoons Caroline and Sally explored the countryside; on one walk they discovered a charming deserted villa between the Villa les Hortensias and Ford's Villa Paul. The gate was open, and they went in to explore. The villa was enormous, surrounded by overgrown garden paths dotted with statues of Mary, benches to rest on, and roses, flowering trees, and shrubs. Like Ford's place, the villa had a seaside terrace. Caroline loved the view of the sea framed by sea pines, the grounds dotted by "flights and flights of old moss grown brick steps that go down to ruined fountains and little glades and things." It was "exactly like a child's idea of a fairy tale palace," and Caroline wished she owned it until she realized the "charm would go if somebody were living in it and all the fern and moss cleaned out of those marvelous flights of stairs."

In some ways all of Toulon took on a fairy-tale quality. For the first time in months, everyone was writing. Surrounded by novelists, Allen wrote his first short story, "The Immortal Woman," early that fall, then began his own fictional family history. Sally went back to work on the memoir she had started in the early 1920s, when she and Caroline first met in Greenwich Village. And Caroline finished "Tom Rivers," sent it off to Max Perkins, and then returned to work on her novel about the relationship between southern landowners and their poor white tenants.

Although she had "a hell of a time getting started," Caroline soon had outlined the entire book—"so that it should click into place like something by Mr. Faulkner," she said. Before too many months had passed, she had finished two chapters and slated a third.

With Allen writing and Sally for company, Caroline enjoyed her stay in Toulon for a while. She and Sally often visited the deserted villa to steal roses or wander through the paths and gardens. But after a while the quiet refuge of Toulon was disturbed by the usual financial pressures and frustrations over publishing.

Both *Scribner's* and the *Atlantic Monthly* rejected "Tom Rivers," and Caroline began to despair of ever publishing it or any other story, even though the *Hound and Horn* published "The Captive" in its fall issue. She considered "The Captive" one of her best, and it annoyed her to lose the *Scribner's* contest. The fact that Allen's friend Edmund Wilson had been one of the judges for the contest only exacerbated Caroline's frustration. Declaring Edmund an unreliable judge of art, utterly lacking in "historical imagination," she decided that the two winning stories more than demonstrated the deplorable taste of publishers and literary critics. John Herrmann's "The Big Short Trip" was about the life of a jewelry salesman; Emmett Gower's "Hill Idyll" was a love story about some poor white farmers. Neither story had much merit, Caroline thought; "knowing how to write seems to be a hindrance."

Caroline tried to get on with her novel, but she found it impossible to concentrate. With prices in France higher than in previous years, the Tates had difficulty living on the Guggenheim allowance. "We have no money at all, as usual, and I am even more depressed than usual about it," Caroline wrote Katherine Anne. "How in the hell can you write a book if you can't get your mind off finances for two hours a day even?"

Although she had little hope for sympathy, Caroline did write to Henry Allen Moe of the Guggenheim Foundation to ask if there was "any chance in the world" of getting some additional money. She told

Moe she thought she could get her novel ready for publication in the fall of 1933 if she "could only be free for a few months from pressing money worries." But several weeks went by without an answer.

Despite the financial uncertainty, Caroline would have been glad to stay in Toulon. Janice Biala began to paint both Caroline's and Allen's portraits, and Ford was his usual comfort to Caroline. But by November Allen was getting restless. Although fairly worshipped by his landlady, her daughter, and the Corsican *femme de ménage*, Allen grew increasingly annoyed with Sally: she was "constantly 'explaining' things," Allen said, and her New England mind and perspective grated on his nerves. Also, Allen felt he could not continue his work without access to a good library. Finally Allen convinced Caroline to return to Paris. Sally went by herself to Vence.

In late November Allen and Caroline drove back to Paris. At first the weather was mild, the countryside incredibly beautiful. But after they spent the night in Avignon, the weather turned bad. The skies growing darker and darker, they drove on, "crawling through a fog at about ten miles an hour," Caroline said later.

The only comfort Caroline had on the hellish trip was the promise of a studio apartment waiting for them in Paris. But when the Tates arrived, they discovered that the previous renter had decided to stay on for another month. In the drizzling rain they had to hunt for a new place to stay.

Soon they were established "like a bird on a bough," according to Caroline, in a small, ground-floor studio at 37, Denfert-Rochereau. The studio had no running water, a rather dark balcony bedroom, and a tiny, dank kitchen, but Allen loved the place. Caroline thought the rent was too high—five hundred francs a month plus expenses—yet Allen insisted it would save them money. "You can work better in a room that suits you," he said; "you save money not going to cafes."

For a while it seemed he was right, Caroline grudgingly admitted. "We are both working like hell, have settled down into one of those routines in which people do produce books," she told a friend. They stopped writing only for meals, marketing, and brief walks. One day Caroline wrote nearly three thousand words; "the glow of conscious virtue persisted" for some time after that, she said. The routine was one of those "islands" of peace which happened "about once a year for us," she wrote; "If it will only last!"

One day, while walking with Allen through the Luxembourg gardens,

Caroline spotted two remarkable dogs: a large white French poodle and a Mexican toy terrier. "My God, look at that," she said.

Allen looked, paying more attention to the dogs' owner. "Yes, it's Gertrude Stein," he replied. As Caroline noted later, Allen always had "an eye more for the ladies."

In the middle of the gardens, the Tates paused for a chat with Stein, who was more than a little surprised to find that the Tates were in Paris on Caroline's Guggenheim award.

"You?" Stein said. "And what can you do?"

"I'm trying to write a novel," Caroline replied—meekly, she told Sally later, with her usual deprecating humor. Stein's pretensions were ludicrous in Caroline's eyes.

Either at that meeting or at another that winter, Stein apparently turned to Allen and said condescendingly, "Tate, it's too bad you've stopped writing poetry." Allen later joked about her comment, saying he thought he "had scarcely begun," but the remark must have rankled him. Caroline thought it quite funny, and typical of Stein.

Soon, however, neither Caroline nor Allen was writing much of anything: islands of peace and writing never did last long. Within a few weeks Caroline and Allen had moved again, this time to a pension in the Hôtel Fleurus. Running short of money, they figured they could live more cheaply in the pension—and delay paying their bill until Caroline received her next Guggenheim installment. In December Henry Allen Moe finally responded to her plea for help, but his letter was merely a request for a detailed budget. Caroline sent one, but began to think he might never "come across" with more money: "he is a hard hearted devil," she said.

Allen might have written articles for various magazines, but he decided to put off everything else until he finished his book. Yet he was writing little of that, just "sinking into the period," according to Caroline. Although anxious to pay off their debts, Caroline agreed it was "best, even for the unfortunate debtors, for him to do that."

Caroline did receive a promise of some money before the end of the year: the *Yale Review* agreed to publish "Tom Rivers." But the *Review* did not pay until publication, and before that could happen, Caroline had to revise the story according to the editor's suggestions. The changes displeased her, but, desperate for cash, she obliged.

Caroline thought living at the Fleurus would give her more time for writing because she would not have to do housework and cooking. But then a friend's child became ill, the holiday season started, and Caroline eventually gave up all attempts at work until after the new year.

Katherine Anne Porter also helped to distract Caroline. She arrived in Paris in early December with her newest lover, Eugene Pressley, a secretary at the American Embassy. More than two years had passed since Caroline had seen her friend. During that time they had kept in touch with regular letters: Katherine Anne promising to move to Tennessee with the Tates; Caroline planning a cabin for Katherine Anne to build on their land near Benfolly. But when Katherine Anne received a Guggenheim Fellowship in the summer of 1931, she abandoned all plans and promises, and instead embarked on a trip to France that actually ended up being a trip to Germany.

During that trip Katherine Anne had written Caroline a long, detailed account of the ship, its inhabitants, and her own troubles with Gene. Caroline loved the serial letter and even copied out sections of it to share with their mutual friends. But Caroline worried about Katherine Anne's behavior. "She is one of the finest writers now living and she will kill herself very soon, by living in the wrong climate or wasting herself on idiotic people or anything else that is suicidal enough," Caroline told Ford at one point.

But now, in the winter of 1932, Caroline was relieved to see Katherine Anne had pulled herself together. Yet both Caroline and Allen found Katherine Anne changed. Only forty years old, Katherine Anne looked much older: her hair had already turned white, and she had given up the casual bobbed style she had previously worn for a more elegant *coif*. Everything about her reflected her new perception of herself as a "grande dame" or mature "femme du monde."

Although the Tates got along well with Katherine Anne and Gene during their shared time in Paris, Caroline's and Katherine Anne's relationship began to change. Both women had gotten their feelings hurt. With the best intentions Caroline had told Katherine Anne that Stringfellow Barr of the *Virginia Quarterly Review* had probably accepted one of Katherine Anne's stories because the Tates had urged him to do so. Trying to be helpful, Katherine Anne had told Caroline that one of her stories "sounded like somebody trying to write like" Caroline. "Why didn't she say it was just plain rotten?" Caroline wondered. But neither woman admitted how she had been hurt. They spent most of the holidays together, and few friends would realize the subtle breach in their friendship.

In January Caroline tried once again to get back to her writing, but she did not begin with her novel. Instead she worked on a story about her father, a nearly literal account of J. M. Gordon's last visit to Merry Mont, complete with his refusal to attend Molly Ferguson's funeral. Within the narrative Caroline wove one of her father's favorite stories about a wily old fox named Old Red, using that name for the story as well. The fox resembled her father's fictional counterpart, Alexander Maury, a wily old man who would not be caught by the snares of his family.

With gentle humor Caroline sketched in her father's rebellious stance and sardonic wit. Mr. Maury would not unpack his bags—he wanted to be ready to get away quickly from "Merry Point." At the dinner table he also made a point of tucking his napkin "well up under his chin in the way his wife had never allowed him to do," Caroline wrote. Her portrait was loving, yet laced with a critical perspective reinforced by the parallels between the old man and the fox: both made their lives out of struggle and escape.

Caroline incorporated both the Meriwether and Gordon perspectives in the story. "Aleck" Maury was both an admirable man and a pitiful escape artist. He had succeeded in taking control of his life, pursuing the art of fishing with a zest and passion. But the price he had paid for that control and the pursuit of his art was great. Like Old Red, Aleck could not relax. He found no comfort in his family; he had to be always alert, ready for escape. Yet although Aleck had only scorn for the women of Merry Point (and a bit of condescending sorrow for his son-in-law), he clearly depended on them: his independence would have meant less without the struggle, without the game.

In "Old Red" Caroline also developed her self-portrait, creating a fictional alter ego she would use repeatedly in the years to come. In many ways the portrait was an extension of Ellen Cromlie, the main character Caroline had used in "Mr. Powers" several years earlier. Like Ellen, Aleck Maury's daughter Sarah was the spitting image of Caroline: she had black eyes, a quick laugh, and a rather sharp tongue. Aleck reflected that although Sarah was thin, she "looked so much like him." Then Sarah made a sarcastic comment about one of his stories, and her father decided "she was, after all, not so much like himself as the sister whom, as a child, he had particularly disliked. A smart girl, Sarah, but too quick always on the uptake. For his part he preferred a softer-natured woman."

In addition to her self-portrait as Sarah, Caroline developed the character of Stephen, Sarah's husband, to reflect mockingly on Allen. Stephen was "infected already with the fatal germ, the *cacoethes scribendi*," Caroline wrote. He sat around thinking about sonnet forms and tried to write essays on John Skelton, but he was in many respects a ludicrous figure. Aleck Maury realized Steve didn't even know where he was, not even when he sat fishing. According to Maury, his son-in-law's face was abstracted, "like that of a person submerged." Steve was "dead to the world and would probably be that way the rest of his life," Maury realized with pity.

By the middle of January, Caroline finished "Old Red" and sent the story to Max Perkins. "I am at last convinced that *Scribner's* is no market for my stories," she wrote, "but this one is a little out of my usual line— at least it has a happy ending—so I am sending it along." She asked Max to "be charitable to any errors" she had made in fishing lore. "I'll get them out later," she promised.

To Sally, Caroline admitted that she wasn't happy with the story: "It's not one of my best," she said, "just a kind of trick." Caroline showed the story to Ford, who had recently arrived in Paris, and to John Peale Bishop. Both thought the story didn't have enough action, which Caroline knew. But she insisted she was "really more interested in rendering the character of the man than . . . the action of the story." "That always betrays you," Caroline said, and she vowed to revise the story later. "Just now the mere thought of it is too much for me," she said.

Caroline was even less satisfied with her novel about the poor white tenants. For the rest of January, she was knocked out by illness and unable to write. Even after the fever and aches had gone, Caroline could not lift her head from the pillow for two weeks. Being so horribly lazy made her uncomfortable, but she figured that some of her collapse had to do with her struggles with the novel: "the illness coincided with a problem that had come up in the plot of my novel," she admitted.

It may also have had something to do with worry. Pidie had written them that Nancy had been suffering from a fever for nine days, and Caroline waited anxiously for word of Nancy's recovery, vowing to never "put the ocean between us again, work or no work." "It's been better for her, but it's hell on me," she said. "Every night when I go to bed I am convinced that she will die before we get back. In the morning I'm not so sure, but I feel so rotten after lying awake half the night that I don't get much work done."

Finally she received another letter from Tennessee: Nancy was fine. Caroline worked herself out of her lethargy and plot problems by taking her favorite remedy—ammoniated quinine—and by simply going "through the motions of working" until she had figured out the next chapter of her novel.

As Allen began to write his book, called *Ancestors in Exile,* Caroline found herself holding her breath. "If he can just get this book written maybe we can get out from under this cloud that has hung over us, for three years now," she said.

Caroline still hoped to finish her novel in time for fall publication. But she also began to have a glimmer of an idea for another book. For several months she had been corresponding with Lincoln Kirstein of the *Hound and Horn.* Kirstein had embarked on a new writing project—a biography of Major John Pelham, an aide to General J. E. B. Stuart during the Civil War. Kirstein wanted to use Pelham's own words to create a vivid, emotionally charged panorama of the war, and Caroline was taken with his ideas. "For some years I cherished the idea of taking a soldier through four years of the war," she admitted. "I think now it can't be done—at least it can't be done by a woman," she said without explaining why. Yet when she looked at Pierre de Lannux's book on the Confederacy, *Sud,* Caroline reconsidered. She thought she could see the entire history of the South reflected in some of the portraits he had chosen. It seemed to Caroline that "there were certain things, certain heroisms if you will, that were never properly celebrated—the South, alas, was weak on poets!" The more she thought about Kirstein's book, the more she liked it. Her imagination had "taken hold" of his plan, she said. The book "seems to me a thing that will be, that must be done eventually."

But Kirstein eventually abandoned the project, and Caroline was in no position to start anything new. In February financial pressures increased. Barely able to concentrate on writing, Caroline decided she had little chance of making a fall deadline. Feeling desperate, she finally cabled the Guggenheim Foundation about her request for more money: "Decision necessary situation critical." Still there was no response.

The cloud that had been hovering broke into a storm. A series of depressing letters arrived from America. Benfolly was in disarray: the renter had forgotten to turn off the water in an unheated section, and the pipes burst with the first freeze. The county trustee wrote that the Tates were being sued for back taxes. Since they had their return tickets paid for, Caroline and Allen decided they had to return to Tennessee. Although Benfolly was rented through the summer, the Tates could camp out at Merry Mont.

Caroline hated to leave Paris, but she thought it would "be a relief to get home in a way." "If this inability to write continues," she said, "there will be other things I can do." She would be home in time to set some hens and care for the new lambs. In the fertile soil of Merry Mont, she could raise a good garden against what she was sure would be another hard winter. "I'm sure it's best for us to get home as soon as possible," she said reluctantly. "We can live at Merry Mont for practically nothing and the money we'd be spending here can go to pay debts."

On the twelfth of February, the Tates left Paris on the SS *City of Norfolk*. Ten days later they landed in Baltimore. After several days visiting Allen's friend Phelps Putnam, they went to Chattanooga to visit Nancy. It amazed Caroline to see how much her daughter had grown and how well she could read. Allen could only snicker at Nancy's slang expressions, "okay" and "hot dog." But other sights and sounds in Chattanooga were far from pleasing. All day long a stream of people went begging from house to house. Their desperation shocked Caroline—she had not realized how bad things were in the States. Not long after that, Caroline received a letter from her father. "I am saving every cent I can to buy fishing tackle when the crash comes," he said. Caroline decided the Depression was "pretty wide spread if it [had] reached" J. M. Gordon.

Caroline and Allen decided to leave Nancy in Chattanooga to finish the school year. After a few days' visit, they went on to Merry Mont. Caroline quickly immersed herself in the life of the Old Neighborhood, feeling as if she had never been away. Life at Merry Mont was "rich and strange," Caroline wrote to Sally. "I often think of you—as a man plunged into a rushing mountain stream might tread water and think of absent friends—if he was man enough." Merry Mont was a bit dirtier and more cluttered, and they could buy beer in Guthrie now, but little else had changed.

Since she had still not heard whether *Scribner's* would publish "Old Red," Caroline wrote requesting another advance on her novel. "Two hundred dollars would fall like manna," she told Max, assuring him that since she had the book "about half done," she might yet make fall publication, spring at the latest. Yet before even trying to write, Caroline planted an enormous garden: it was a relief not to have to bother with "the rocky slopes of Benfolly," she said. "If I could ever get that damn Benfolly on a self-sustaining basis then we could all just draw in our belts a little when one of these crises come along."

By the end of March, most of the Tates' financial crises had passed.

The nationwide banking "holidays" helped to ease some of their worries: "the bank had to admit sadly that they couldn't hound us about our note for awhile," Caroline said. Then the *Yale Review* paid for "Tom Rivers," and *Scribner's* magazine agreed to publish "Old Red." Max sent Caroline $200: $150 for the story, $50 as an advance on the novel. He apologized for the payment for the story. "It is a mighty low price, I know," he wrote. "I hope the time will come when we can deal more generously with you."

Around the same time, the Guggenheim Foundation also sent Caroline an unexpected $250. Caroline called the check a "godsend" and told Henry Allen Moe that it would do her "more good . . . than any of the other fellowship money" since "two hundred and fifty dollars goes as far at Merry Mont as a thousand in Paris."

Her money worries settled for the time, Caroline returned to work on her novel. With seven chapters finished and eight to go, she felt confident enough to tell Max she could make spring publication. "I find I work very well," she said. "I don't know whether it is the view from the upstairs windows or the feeling that the plastering may fall on me at any minute." By then she called the book *A Morning's Favour*. "The title would be taken from a sermon preached by a sanctified man on the vanity of this world: 'Hit's nothing. A morning's favour, that's all,'" Caroline told Max. In the novel Ote Mortimer, a poor white tenant, only half-listened to the sermon his brother-in-law preached, but it would come back to haunt him: Ote's "morning's favour," an illicit affair, would be his downfall.

"MOST people would want to cut their throats after a few weeks of Merry Mont, but I really enjoy it," Caroline said that spring. In between bouts with her typewriter, she picked strawberries and made twenty-one pints of jam, then "poisoned" the potato plants and the beans. In the afternoons and evenings she went for long walks or rides in the countryside or visited kin, often with her cousin Catherine Wilds, Pidie's twenty-three-year-old daughter, who was staying in the neighborhood at that time.

As the spring wore on, there were a lot of visitors at Merry Mont. Allen and "the brethren" got involved in a new publication, the *American Review,* a magazine launched by Seward Collins, and the Tates hosted several parties for Allen's friends. Their favorite amusement was charades. The group would split up, chose a word or words to dramatize, even dress up in costumes: Caroline saved old dresses and outfits for just that purpose.

In May Malcolm Cowley arrived to spend the summer in the Old Neighborhood. He took a room at Cloverlands, the home of Henry and Clyde Meriwether and their two young sons. Since Cloverlands was only half a mile through the woods from Merry Mont, Malcolm and the Tates spent a great deal of time together. Even Old Miss Carrie liked Malcolm and said he was "one of the nicest *northern* gentlemen" she had ever met.

Nancy also returned home in the middle of May and received her very own pony as a homecoming gift. Twenty pounds overweight, "with a perfect East Tennessee accent," Nancy had "a repertoire of songs calculated to give a parent considerable pause," Caroline said. Nancy especially loved "You go home and pack your panties, I'll go home and pack my scanties and we'll shuffle off to Buffalo."

From most appearances both Allen and Caroline were doing well that spring and early summer. But their relationship was badly strained. Individual writing problems made them both irritable. Allen was struggling with his fictionalized family history, and Caroline, making little progress with her novel, felt bitter about her own achievements. "Old Red" was scheduled to appear in *Scribner's* magazine in December, as well as in the *Criterion* in October, but Caroline complained that the *Scribner's* editors never took "any story of mine that wasn't inferior."

Caroline was also suffering from a terrible ache in her neck, an ache which had actually been bothering her off and on since November. When Caroline went to the doctor, he informed her that her neck was slightly dislocated, probably due to some unusual allergic reaction, and there was nothing to be done.

But the greatest strain on their marriage resulted from Allen's increasing dislike of the Meriwethers and his feeling that Caroline was becoming too immersed in their lives. Throughout the spring and early summer of 1933, Caroline felt more and more responsible for her family. There were routine problems to be solved which were rigorous enough —"niggers to get out of jail, turkeys to run in, and all that," according to Caroline. Also, Uncle Rob kept insisting Caroline ought to move permanently to Merry Mont to take care of her grandmother "in her declining years." Although Caroline began to realize her grandmother was a dangerous woman, actually wicked or even "sinister," she could not abandon her love for the old woman.

All this annoyed Allen, but what bothered him the most was the way

Caroline fell for the Meriwether mythology. It seemed sometimes, he said later, as if she spoke to him with a Meriwether voice, the voice of a "Sho Nuff Maywether," smug and self-absorbed—the voice of Uncle Rob. Allen hated the way Caroline worshipped her Uncle Rob. What did she see in the man? Allen could not guess. Rob was a dirty, vulgar old man, Allen thought. Rob could barely make a living farming; he had little education and rather poor manners. When Allen declared, "The Meriwethers are all louts," he was certainly referring to Rob.

Allen apparently tried without success to make Caroline see her uncle from his perspective. Caroline could never call Rob a lout. She had dedicated her first novel to him. In her eyes he was the true measure of a southern gentleman. From her childhood on, she had thought of Rob as chivalrous, generous to a fault. And when the ladies were around, Rob knew how to behave: he was never vulgar or crude.

He also told great stories Caroline could use in her fiction. That was the lure of the Meriwether mythology for Caroline, a lure Allen could not or would not understand. Caroline could poke fun at her Meriwether relatives; she had lived with her father's sardonic criticisms for too long not to see the problems with the Meriwether family. But she could never repudiate her Meriwether heritage, never see the family members with the entirely dispassionate, rational eye of an outsider like her father or Allen. Caroline was a Meriwether, at least in part. Their stories nourished her creative life. Uncle Rob, for all his warts and foibles, had filled Caroline's childhood with joy, and he now furnished her with material for fiction. Little wonder Caroline worshipped the man.

With such pressures and frustration, both Tates sought ways to escape. Allen spent a lot of time away from Merry Mont. He told Caroline he had to go to the library—he needed more information for his book, he said. That was a lie, but Caroline did not question him. She had her own diversions. To escape from her aches and from her inability to write, Caroline spent hours drinking with Uncle Rob or relaxing with Malcolm.

As the summer wore on, Caroline spent so much time with Malcolm that Old Miss Carrie began to worry. One evening, when Malcolm and Caroline were going out to Guthrie for beer and supper without Allen, the old woman stopped them. "You run around too much with married men," Old Miss Carrie said to her granddaughter, forbidding them to go.

"Well, all right, Ma, we won't go," Caroline said meekly.

Malcolm looked on with surprise: he and Caroline were simply good friends, and he didn't understand why Caroline's grandmother was objecting.

But seven-year-old Nancy knew why: she thought her mother was falling in love with Malcolm. Every afternoon, Malcolm, Caroline, and Nancy went swimming or riding around the countryside. Malcolm usually drove; Caroline sat beside him on the front seat and often sang. Nancy sat in the back seat, enjoying every minute of their jaunts.

Allen did not mind these afternoon forays. Instead, he kept having what Caroline called his "library spasms" with increasing frequency. Then one day at the end of June, Allen completely disappeared. He took the family car and left without a word.

Later, Caroline would discover that most of the time Allen said he was going to the library, he had actually been with one of Caroline's cousins, Marion Henry, with whom he had been having an affair. He had been attracted to Marion for over a year: she was very good-looking, with dark coloring, like Caroline's, and a nervous way about her. Since her father's death the previous year, Marion had run the family farm, Oakland, and her greatest wish was to regain possession of all the land her grandfather had once owned. Marion was intensely loyal to the South: she would not set foot in a Union cemetery. But for a while she was not loyal to her cousin Caroline.

It wasn't unusual for the young women in the Meriwether connection to flirt with Allen. He could be charming; they could be southern coquettes. But Allen admitted later he had wanted to hurt and humiliate Caroline for her involvement in the Meriwether mythology. What better way than to have an affair with one of Caroline's cousins?

When Marion finally ended the affair, Allen was devastated and promptly disappeared. He apparently went to stay with friends in Nashville. Only then did Caroline figure out what had been happening.

Furious and deeply hurt, Caroline nevertheless kept up appearances for several weeks while Allen was gone. Without a car she had to walk or ride horseback to go anywhere. She increasingly left Nancy with the kin at Cloverlands, spending even more time with Malcolm, who sensed something was wrong but never spoke about it. Caroline did not try to explain or explore the reasons for Allen's absence.

Yet once again Caroline must have questioned her identity as a woman and as a writer. Although she did not fully understand what had happened or what she could do to resolve their problems, Caroline must have sensed that Allen was suggesting she had to choose between his love and her art. By having an affair Allen suggested Caroline was not desirable as a woman, and he did so in part because he did not approve of the source of Caroline's creative life as a writer. When Allen came back to Merry Mont in mid-July, Caroline felt as if she were on the verge of another nervous collapse, just like the one she had in Chattanooga in 1924.

Aunt Pidie arrived at Merry Mont about that time and realized the strain her niece was under. She took one look at Caroline, said "You need a vacation," and proceeded to help Caroline and Allen pack.

Uncle Rob and Old Miss Carrie could not believe Caroline and Allen would really leave. Perhaps they didn't realize what had been happening. They kept saying, "Well, you won't leave before dinner."

"Yes," Caroline said through clenched teeth. "I am leaving this very minute."

It was time for both Caroline and Allen to escape from the Meriwethers, to try to rebuild their shattered relationship. They headed for Andrew Lytle's family farm, Cornsilk, in Guntersville, Alabama. Allen expected Caroline would forgive him. Caroline wanted to: she loved Allen more than anyone else she had ever known. But she could not take his betrayal lightly: it had shaken her to the core of her being. Forgiveness would not come easily.

CAROLINE felt rested after several weeks at Cornsilk, but she and Allen scarcely settled their differences or solved their problems. Instead, they apparently agreed to cover up the wounds, to talk no more about Marion, and to move out of Merry Mont when they returned to the Old Neighborhood in August.

Caroline told her friends Sally and Katherine Anne little about what had happened. She explained the gap in her correspondence with them in a roundabout way, writing Katherine that she had been in "a sort of spiritual slump," telling Sally she had a physical collapse, brought on by straining her back. She did not even hint that Allen had been unfaithful, but she admitted to Sally that "going to Merry Mont was a mistake." "The place has a very bad influence on me and through me on Allen," Caroline said in passing.

Aunt Loulie accompanied Allen and Caroline back to Benfolly to help with the housework, but Caroline did not know how long Loulie would last. "She has always been poor, but she had never experienced our hand to mouth, or meal to meal kind," Caroline said. "It makes her rather nervous."

Both Allen and Caroline tried to return to their overdue books. But for once, simply going through the motions did not work. Allen had told his publisher that *Ancestors in Exile* would be ready for publication in late fall, but he soon found it impossible to finish the book. He told a friend that "the discrepancy between the outward significance and the private" was too enormous to handle in the form he had chosen. Finally, by the end of October, he decided to give up the project entirely. He also informed Minton, Balch that he would never be able to complete his biography of Lee.

Caroline was relieved Allen had abandoned the biography, even if they had to pay back the advances he had received. They could no longer stand "the nervous strain, aside from the unpleasantness of slowly starving to death while Allen tried to write a book he never wanted to write," Caroline told Sally. It was "a great relief," rather like "throwing off the shackles that have bound us now these three years."

But Caroline had her own troubles with *A Morning's Favour,* not the least of which was locating a complete copy of what she had already written. In all her moving about, she had lost the first four chapters of her book. At first Caroline was not worried, because she had given a copy of the novel to one of Allen's friends, Seward Collins, who had expressed interest in serializing it in the *American Review*. But when Caroline tried to contact Collins, she found he had gone off to Europe, and his secretary had no idea where the manuscript was. Finally Caroline panicked and wrote Max Perkins, asking him to try to locate the manuscript.

Max did just that, and after reading the manuscript he told Caroline it was "extremely fine" and urged her to keep writing. But he would not see much more of *A Morning's Favour* that year. Caroline sent him only one chapter, which she had turned into a short story, hoping to make some money by publishing it in *Scribner's* magazine. Also called "A Morning's Favour," the story was about "the delights of sin in the woods triumphing over religious ecstasies," as Caroline said. But the magazine rejected the story.

By October Caroline decided to set the novel aside, at least temporarily. She had only four chapters left to write, but she felt "in no shape . . . for very difficult work," she told Sally. Instead, she had "hit on" a new book to write. The idea came to her during one of her father's brief visits.

While sitting around and listening once again to J. M. Gordon's stories, Caroline suddenly realized that her father often began a conversation in much the same way an author might begin a chapter. Remembering something Sally had said to her several years earlier, that J. M. Gordon's stories were "evidently works of art for him," Caroline decided to use her father's stories to create a fictional biography, actually an autobiography, since she would let her main character tell his own story.

The book would be "a relaxation and a sort of labor of love," Caroline told Sally. When she approached Max with her plans, she exaggerated a bit, saying she had "a book almost written . . . the autobiography of the Professor Maury," the fictional version of her father she had created for "Old Red." Max made no objections but only urged her to send him what she had written as soon as possible.

Caroline thought she would write the book in collaboration with her father. It would be "pleasant work, rather like knitting," she told Ford. Yet it would also be challenging: she could make "some experiments in timing," she thought. A first-person narrative modeled on the auto-biography of Davy Crockett, or Siegfried Sassoon's *Memoirs of a Fox Hunting Man,* it would be the "history of a life dominated by a passion for fishing."

Caroline wanted to call the book *Green Springs to White Oak* or *The Life and Passion of Alexander Maury*. The chapters would be based on her father's stories, with place names or fishing maxims for headings: "The Green Springs," "Game Fish Are Ground Nesters," or "The Spell Is on 'Em." Caroline expected to "chop" the action off "arbitrarily at some place like White Oak, some place he hopes is the perfect spot so long sought for," or at the time Maury "became a great man, the morning . . . on the Caney Fork river when he really felt there was nobody could cast any better than he did."

That fall Caroline spent several days with her father, who was living in a fishing lodge on the banks of the Caney Fork in east Tennessee. She found him in a rather sorry mood. It had not rained for weeks, and the fish were not biting. Caroline sympathized with her father, but she was secretly overjoyed. Since he could not fish, he would not really object to telling stories. After breakfast, father and daughter went out on the lodge's wide veranda. They sat side by side, looking down on the river, which was flanked by a row of pines. J. M. Gordon asked a few absent-minded questions about members of the connection, but Caroline could tell he really had no interest in any of her answers. Then, drawing on all she had learned as a newspaperwoman, she tried to get her father to talk.

"Dad," she said quite innocently, "what were the names of those hounds that Uncle James Morris had in his pack?"

Her father turned his head to look at her with what Caroline took to be "a half-indignant glance." "Why, Old Mag, Old Whiskey, and the Pups!" he said.

"Was Old Whiskey the leader of the pack?" Caroline asked, knowing full well the answer.

"Naturally," Gordon said. Caroline detected "a touch of scorn" in his voice, but she continued to ask questions. And eventually, she didn't need to prompt him any more. "My uncle, James Morris, had the finest pack of hounds in eastern Virginia," he said, and then he was off, immersed in the flow of his own recollections. He talked about the wily fox, Old Red, and a half-blind mare called Jonesboro, who would take any fence she came upon. He talked about Hawkwood, the home of his Uncle "Jeems" and Aunt Victoria, who had coached him in Latin grammar and the Catholic faith. Caroline sat by his side and took down his stories verbatim.

They sat on the veranda all morning and most of the afternoon, two accomplished storytellers, a large man with a wonderful laugh and rich voice, and a small, dark-haired woman bent over her typewriter. At four o'clock they stopped. J. M. Gordon tried to fish for a few hours until dinner, then after dinner he and Caroline returned to the veranda to work together some more.

Gordon complained that the talking and writing "upset his mind," but Caroline saw that "as time went on, he warmed to the sound of his own voice." Late that night, when most people in the lodge were sound asleep, Caroline heard her father exclaim, "Caroline! This is good, take it down."

After two and a half days, Caroline had seventy pages of notes. She spent the rest of the fall polishing the notes into an autobiography of Professor Maury. Every day she tried to write at least five pages. "It makes me very stupid but I've vowed to get on with it," Caroline told Sally.

In December "Old Red," Caroline's first story about her father, appeared in *Scribner's*. Although the story had little action, it was one of Caroline's finest stories. The characters were fully developed, the narrative perspective tightly controlled, and the conflict compelling. But

Caroline was still not satisfied with the story. "Too late now, anyhow, to speculate about what's wrong with it," she said, trying to concentrate instead on the full length "autobiography": she promised to send Max seven or eight chapters by the end of the year.

As usual, Caroline did not meet her deadline. She took some time off to write some sketches for a Methodist Sunday school magazine: the adventures of Dick and Jane earned Caroline about six dollars an episode. And she made some more money by reviewing books for the *Nation* and the *New Republic*. Then the Christmas revels, with Andrew Lytle, the Warrens, and a number of other guests, demanded time Caroline was all too willing to give. After the holidays she had to deal with a rash of problems brought on by particularly cold weather: the cook quit, the car died, the pipes froze, and Allen came down with the flu. Even with Loulie's help, Caroline spent all her time doing chores, packing coal, milking the cow, and running up and down the narrow, steep steps of Benfolly to make meals and care for Allen.

As soon as things had settled down, Caroline sent Max five chapters and an outline of the rest of the book. "I had to rewrite more of the book than I thought I would," Caroline told him apologetically, adding that she had to "check up on so many details" with her father, who said "he would rather have cramps in both legs than be a writer!"

Caroline outlined nineteen chapters, which would take Aleck Maury from childhood through his late sixties. The story of Old Red would be included early in the old man's reminiscences, but it would not have a happy ending: Aleck would reveal his part in the old fox's death. Caroline wanted to stress throughout how Aleck thought of himself as "a pretty smart fellow," always in control, able "to bring the curtain down on any scene" in his life. "He never wants to go back anywhere," she wrote: "it is always fresh fields and pastures new for him."

But, just as in "Old Red," Caroline also intended to emphasize the price Aleck would have to pay for his independence and freedom. "He relinquishes one thing after another to concentrate all his faculties on his passion for sport," she wrote. The novel would detail how Aleck became a preacher and then arranged to be called to a church near a good river for fishing. It would end with another scene of Aleck, the escape artist, fleeing from his promise to live with his daughter and her husband in much the same way J. M. Gordon had escaped once the Tates bought Benfolly.

Caroline had only one concern: she wondered if it wouldn't be better to have the book signed "by J. M. and Caroline Gordon." "It is rather a disadvantage for it to be written by a woman," she thought.

Max apparently did not think it mattered who got credit for the book since it would be published as fiction, and he was delighted with the outline. The book "shows how a man saved his independence in spite of everything," he wrote to her, and Caroline sensed she had touched a nerve in him. "People's lives are unhappy because they do what other people do, or what they think they ought to do," Max wrote. "Maury had some instinct which saved him from this, even if it only was due to the strength of a single passion. I think it is a fine theme for a novel." But he cautioned her about concentrating "too deeply upon sport."

As Caroline went back to work on the novel, she decided she had gotten herself "published on the strength of Perkins' prejudices." Just like Jenny in "The Captive," Caroline did not take any credit for her success. First Max was "crazy about old places, and now it seems about doing what you want to do," she said. "I happened to make two lucky hits or *Penhally* would even now be reposing in the bureau drawer."

Caroline tried to make spring publication but soon resigned herself to fall. She found it difficult to work "through another's mind," she told Max, but she kept writing, priming herself with Coca-Colas, sometimes five a day. They had a "marvelous effect" on the imagination, she claimed.

An automobile accident in April also set Caroline back a bit. The Tates had been on the way to a party in Nashville when another driver went through a stop sign and broadsided them. Caroline and Allen were not seriously hurt—Allen had the ignition knob imbedded in his leg; Caroline had gotten wedged between the bucket seats and sprained her shoulder—but the whole escapade cost Caroline nearly a month of work, because typing was too painful for her. And their car, with only eighteen hundred miles on it, was completely destroyed. With the cost of buying a new car exacerbating their usual financial woes, Caroline felt half out of her mind by the end of May. "All is very fecund at Benfolly, all the lower orders of creation, that is," she said.

Hoping that her father could help her finish the book, Caroline escaped at the beginning of June to east Tennessee, "where chickens, dogs, cows, and the rest of the farm cannot reach her," Allen said. Concerns about money could reach her, however, and before long Caroline was back at Benfolly, begging Max for more money. She could deliver the manuscript by July 1, but she needed one hundred dollars desperately.

Max sent the money, but he charged it against a future story because Caroline had already received nearly eight hundred dollars in advances on her novel. That "would not be a matter of importance in what we have been in the habit of calling normal times," Max wrote. "But the truth is now that the sales of books are enormously decreased." The odds were "very much heavier" against her book, "and in paying advances a publisher must look at the general situation."

Caroline wasn't satisfied. She asked Max to give her an advance on her next novel, so she could devote herself to two months of "steady work" and finish her book about her father. "The pressure on me now is so great that it will be difficult even to get the story done," she wrote. How she could write a third novel, once her advance was used to finish her second, was apparently something Caroline had not yet considered. But Max took pity on her and sent her an additional two hundred dollars, charged against her general account.

Allen also wangled another advance out of his publisher, and so, with some of their financial worries eased, Caroline returned to work on the novel she was calling *The Life and Passion of Alexander Maury*. At the beginning of July, the manuscript nearly finished, Caroline returned to Caney Fork to see her father. Allen and Cath Wilds, Caroline's cousin, went along to help her.

They met J. M. Gordon at the Hillside Inn in Walling, Tennessee. Fortunately, it was raining when the Tates and Cath arrived, so Caroline did not have to compete with the fish for her father's attention. While J. M. Gordon read the manuscript for errors, Caroline wrote a few new sections, and Cath typed the revisions. Allen also read the manuscript, groaning over her "boarding school style," sentences such as "I looked at her with something like surprise," or "I felt a little odd."

Don't "ever use the word odd again under any circumstance," Allen told Caroline. By the time he had finished going over the manuscript, Caroline figured he had "cut out about five thousand odds in all."

The other "inmates" of the Hillside Inn must have thought they were all crazy, Caroline said later. "What did you put that stuff in for?" J. M. Gordon shouted over the parts Caroline had invented on her own. The "verbatim quotations from himself" fared much better, she observed: "Daughter, this is really magnificent," he exclaimed. He was amazed that "a person as ignorant" as Caroline "got things as straight" as she did, he said. But he urged her to "stick to [her] own line" in the future.

After two days with her father, Caroline, Allen, and Cath returned home to spend two more days editing and typing the manuscript. Finally, on July 11, Caroline sent the manuscript to Max, who barely skimmed it before sending it on to the printer.

For the most part Caroline had used her father's life story with few changes. She left out one major thread of the narrative she had originally proposed: her father's experience as a preacher. The omission simplified the story line and actually enabled Caroline to cut the book down to eight chapters, but it was still about twenty-five thousand words longer than she had expected it would be.

The most significant change Caroline made involved the characterization of Molly Fayerlee, Aleck's wife. The relationship of Aleck and Molly would be strained and marked by Molly's emotional withdrawal, but Caroline offered a different reason for some of the conflict that had marked the relationship of her parents. Molly Fayerlee did not take up religion; she was overwhelmed by grief at the accidental drowning of her favorite child, Dick.

Although this change might seem minor, and perhaps was made to simplify the narrative, it reflected a corresponding change of tone and perspective in the novel. Caroline did not rail against Molly, her mother's fictional counterpart, or suggest she was responsible for unduly limiting Aleck's life. Instead, Caroline created a sympathetic portrait of Molly. Like Nan Gordon, Molly was a fine scholar. She was also quite concerned with her husband's apparent lack of ambition, a concern springing from both her practical nature and her extreme kindheartedness.

In fact, Caroline laced the entire book with gentle understanding of all characters, their needs, failures, and motivations. Aleck did not look down on his in-laws as J. M. Gordon habitually did; Molly and her family did not poke fun at Aleck as the Meriwethers did Gordon. Aleck even called his mother-in-law a "kind, motherly woman": hardly the way J. M. Gordon would describe Old Miss Carrie.

In her portrait of Aleck and the Fayerlees, Caroline for the first time reconciled the antagonisms between the Meriwether and the Gordon perspectives. Perhaps Caroline's compassion stemmed from her own recent hurt. After Allen had betrayed her, she may have realized for the first time something of the disappointment her mother had endured in marriage. But for whatever reason, Caroline wrote with understanding and appreciation of both her mother's and her father's actions and points of view.

Aleck told his own story, and much of his narrative focused on his sporting adventures. Yet the novel was not simply a chronicle of hunting and fishing. It was suitably laced with classical allusions, and Caroline would later joke that she should have called the book *Portrait of the Artist as an Angler*. That title would have been appropriate. Aleck was an artist, more concerned with the techniques of sport than the actual killing of quail or catching of fish. In devotion to his art, Aleck willingly sacrificed almost every physical comfort. The delight of learning sustained him through difficult times.

Yet Caroline's "portrait of the artist" was not blindly celebratory. Aleck gave an engaging and sympathetic account of his life's passion, but Caroline shaped the narrative to reveal another attitude towards his story. Aleck's pursuit of sport was noble and heroic; it was also foolish and selfish. Just as in "Old Red," Aleck could devote his life to sport only by deliberately cutting himself off from family and friends. He was always willing to learn something new, to sit at the feet of other "masters," but he usually refused to share what he had learned. And his dedication to his art forced him—and his family—to accept a wandering life.

Caroline made no attempt to resolve the conflicting views of Aleck and his art. She simply explored the problems and possibilities through gentle irony. Sometimes the irony was part of Aleck's narrative voice. Other times Caroline suggested a critical perspective of which Aleck seemed unaware. Just as she had in *Penhally,* she developed much of this perspective through narrative patterns and through her female characters. Aleck reported their actions and sayings honestly even when he didn't fully understand them. Often Aleck's accounts of the women in his life stood out more sharply than any instruction in fly casting or hunting.

From the opening pages of Aleck's story, Caroline emphasized the presence—and absence—of women. Aleck was a lonely child in the midst of a large, motherless family. His first home was a gloomy, barren place because "no woman's hand had tended Oakleigh" since Aleck's mother's death. When he left Oakleigh for Grassdale, it was because of another woman: Aunt Victoria. In her first appearance in Aleck's memoirs, Aunt Vic was almost overshadowed by her husband, James Morris, an ideal man. But Aleck went to Grassdale to study under Aunt Vic, and she would emerge in Aleck's memories as a truly noble woman. Aleck's father called Vic the "best Greek scholar I ever knew, woman or no woman." Aleck remembered that she was both motherly and stern, able to balance her household duties with tutoring and missionary zeal. She was "an ardent Catholic and regarded everybody, white and black, within driving distance of Grassdale as within her cure of souls," he said.

When Caroline first conceived of the novel, she had intended to tie Aleck's experiences with Aunt Vic to his career as a minister. In her original outline Caroline had noted twice that Aunt Vic would greatly influence Aleck. Even though this aspect of Aleck's life was not ultimately included in the novel, Caroline did not temper her portrait of the woman. "Dear Aunt Vic!" Aleck exclaimed at one point: "I feel a glow of pride even now when I reflect on her unfailing, her admirable sternness. It was on the scale with all her other virtues. I loved her and admired her then but it is only now after the lapse of many years that I realize what real grandeur of soul she had."

Other women made less powerful impressions in the novel but continued to suggest that Aleck's ideals, however noble, might be enlarged or modified. Molly Fayerlee was the antithesis of Aleck in many ways, conducting her life always according to "a high sense of duty." At times that sense of duty annoyed Aleck, yet Molly could be counted on to put their life into perspective. When Aleck came home one day, put away his gun, and announced he would never hunt again because he could no longer see well enough, his wife calmly told him to get his eyes checked. Although he often chafed against his wife's ambitions for him, Aleck was devastated when she died and even lost all interest in fishing.

Molly's mother was also significant in Aleck's memories. Sometimes Aleck teased Mrs. Fayerlee, but her odd country wisdom had a way of turning out to be true. And like her daughter, Mrs. Fayerlee was often able to put Aleck's life in perspective. When Molly was pregnant with her first child, Aleck stopped hunting because he did not want to be away from his wife. Mrs. Fayerlee realized how much he needed to get out and ordered him into the fields. When Molly was ready to deliver the baby, Mrs. Fayerlee took complete charge of the situation. The doctor arrived too late to be of any use, and Aleck remembered how she greeted him at the door. Mrs. Fayerlee "was pale and the lines about her mouth were deep-carved but her head had its usual confident tilt as she smiled negligently at the doctor," Aleck said. "She seemed on that night no ordinary being; I was convinced that her capabilities were far greater than the doctor's."

Mrs. Fayerlee also knew the limits of sport. When Aleck decided to use his dog-training techniques on his infant son, Mrs. Fayerlee stopped him. "That remarkable woman knew without a word what I had been up to," Aleck remembered. "She snatched the baby up and holding him tight in her arms informed me that her grandson was not a bird dog and not to be treated like one, not in her house, if she knew it."

Two other women had lesser roles in the novel but also shed a light on Aleck's passion for sport. Just as in "Old Red," Aleck's daughter, Sally, appeared at first to be made in her father's image. "She was a perfect Maury," Aleck said proudly, pointing out how her "very dark eyes" so much resembled his. She also understood his passion at an early age, because she had a similar obsession with books. In time, however, Aleck would feel that Sally was more like her mother. At the end of the novel, when Sally invited her father to come to live with her and her husband, she tried to be solicitous of Aleck's desire to spend the rest of his life fishing, but she would not carry such concern to extremes. The "perfect house" needed about three months' renovation, and Sally thought her father ought to be able to wait. "It wouldn't kill you to go without fishing three months, would it?" she asked. Aleck agreed it wouldn't kill him, but he thought she was asking too much of him. Soon he managed to escape from his daughter and son-in-law.

Caroline described Aleck's final getaway with gentle, comic tones of victory: the old man once again outwitting the young and foolish. In an earlier scene, however, Caroline suggested Aleck's immediate victory might not be entirely necessary or even desirable. Early in the novel she noted how Aleck had once studied the art of fly casting under a fishing enthusiast named Colonel Wyndham. Thirty years later, when Aleck was in his sixties and Wyndham over ninety years old, Aleck met the master fisherman again. Although most men would have been forced to quit fishing by that time, Wyndham was still as passionate as ever about his sport. He lived on the river, and every day he caught something, thanks to the help of his devoted wife, Lucy. An old woman herself, she carried his equipment down, paddled him to his post, and helped him set up his poles in a place especially rigged for him. When he reeled in a fish, she put out the landing net. Aleck watched the old couple, first with suppressed laughter, then with growing admiration.

Colonel Wyndham had adjusted to the infirmities of age and seemed capable of fishing for many years to come, but only because he could accept the help and company of another. The time would come when Aleck would need help, but he made no effort to prepare for such a day, to cultivate his relationship with his daughter or other friends. For Aleck, the present day was enough to worry about.

For all his foolishness, Aleck was a hero, a valiant soul—and lucky, as he would be the first to admit. Caroline wrote lovingly about his determination and vision, yet she did not hesitate to point out his faults and failings. She wrote the novel hoping to find relaxation and peace; the writing was supposed to be a little like knitting, something she could do almost without thinking, weaving patterns in a regular, reassuring manner. Perhaps Caroline chose to tell her father's story because he had always seemed stronger than adversity. He would not be crushed by defeat or family responsibilities; he was always free to pursue his own dreams. When Caroline adopted his voice as her own, she could imagine her own life in those terms. But, ultimately, she would not pursue her own freedom to such extremes, and her portrait of Aleck Maury included gentle criticism of the self-centered artist as sportsman. In the end it echoed her conclusion in her earlier portrait of the artist, "At the Top of the Glass Mountain": an artist needed the nourishment and support of family ties.

The "autobiography" of Aleck Maury was Caroline's best work yet. But Caroline had reservations about it. "It could have been a really good book if I'd had another two weeks to revise it," she told Andrew Lytle. Still, it was done. Caroline felt as if she had once again been let out of prison.

In August Caroline received her proofs and set about correcting factual errors that Max and others had pointed out to her. She also began debating the book's title with him. According to Max, the Scribner salesmen objected to *The Life and Passion of Alexander Maury* because it sounded "too much like a real memoir." Max suggested *The Passion of Alexander Maury,* but Caroline did not like the shortened title, so Max then suggested *The Life and Passion of a Sportsman.* It "would gain [a] special audience which will start [the] sale," he told Caroline.

"Have no selling judgment; use yours," she wired in response, and Max adopted the title. But then Caroline thought again and sent him another telegram. The title was weak, she wrote: "a sportsman" was "too indefinite" when used in conjunction with "passion." She gave him a new list to choose from—*Alexander Maury, Sportsman, The Good Sportsman, The Passionate Angler,* and *To the Victor*—saying she didn't think any of these titles were as good as the original, but the decision was his.

Max read the list, then put brackets around the first choice. At the bottom of the telegram, he wrote his choice for the new title: *Alec Maury: Sportsman*.

Caroline asked only that Max change the spelling of Maury's first name to *Aleck,* the way she had written it in the text. Yet apparently too tired to put up any more of a fight, she wrote, "If any purist in the office wants to spell it without a 'k' that's all right too."

But it really wasn't all right—nothing about the new title was all right. Caroline felt sick about the title. She could only hope it would help the book's sales: as usual, the Tates' finances were in disarray. But not so much that Caroline would forego a quick trip to New Orleans to visit some friends. On the way back she stopped for the night in Memphis. It was a hot, sultry night, "too hot to sleep," Caroline thought, so she sat reading P. G. Wodehouse. From time to time, she stopped reading and looked around the oppressive little bungalow she was staying in. "Fate had at least spared me the pain of ever having to live in a bungalow" like this, she thought.

Within a few weeks, however, Caroline found out that "Fate" had not spared her. Allen accepted an offer to teach at Southwestern College; the Tates would soon move into a Memphis bungalow not far from where Caroline had stayed that night. Caroline thought teaching might be too much for Allen, yet she knew they could not afford to turn down the position.

They couldn't rent Benfolly for any price, so they made arrangements to move their tenants into the house, then began to pack up their belongings and find homes or caretakers for the animals they had acquired. Caroline said she was "jubilant" about the move. Although she had once insisted she could always write better in the country, now Caroline declared that she wrote "so much better in town." She also said she would have much more time for writing once they exchanged Benfolly for a small apartment. But whether she believed herself remained to be seen.

The last few days before the Tates moved were busy ones. Several groups of friends dropped in for one last visit, including an old friend of Caroline's who had been recently released from a mental institution. He "kept popping in asking if any of us had seen his wife," Caroline said later. Ever the polite hostess, Caroline drew him away from the house so that he would not make a scene before other guests.

They went out to the porch overlooking the Cumberland River, and for two hours Caroline listened patiently to the man's story. He had once been a wealthy cotton speculator, before the stock-market crash and his stay in the asylum. "My hundred days," he called his hospitalization, and he insisted he had "seen God." Since then, he had been driving about the countryside, "being drawn . . . first to this place and then to that," he said.

The moonlight cast an unreal pall over their darkness, and when the man asked Caroline to go with him on a drive, she felt cold chills go down her spine. You "ought to quit writing for self exaltation and write for the glory of God," he told Caroline before he left.

As Caroline went back inside, she felt as if she had "been away from the others for years." She did not know what to make of her "insane friend." "It was a very strange experience," she said.

Soon the Tates were living in an ugly brown bungalow at 2374 Forrest Avenue in Memphis. They called their new home the Hamburger House since it rather resembled "a hamburger on the outside at least," Caroline said. But the place had "a good Confederate address," she added, and it was convenient, with large rooms, for only thirty dollars a month.

Caroline thought Memphis was still dreadfully hot and terribly dull, but she was determined to make the best of things. Allen's work load was much too heavy, but they paid one hundred dollars each month on their debts. Caroline was delighted to think that "by living very close to the knuckle all winter" they might have their "heads above water by spring."

Soon she decided there were advantages to living in a new section of the country: "a cotton country" was "so very different from a tobacco country," Caroline said. The people even seemed to walk differently, and their conversations were "pure Faulkner." "He had a better ear even than I had thought," she admitted.

Caring for the Hamburger House was not difficult, but after a week Caroline hired a cook. "It wasn't that I didn't have plenty of time," she admitted, but any sort of housework simply "constricted my imagination in Hart's memorable phrase." Then she began writing, and in about two months' time, she finished three stories.

She had more than the usual incentive: Max refused to provide Caroline with any more advances against future books. She had by that time an outstanding balance of twelve hundred dollars on her Scribner's account. Since neither Caroline nor Max expected *Aleck Maury, Sportsman* to earn that much, even if sales were brisk, Caroline agreed to write as many stories as she could for *Scribner's* magazine to discharge some of her debt. For every story the magazine accepted, Max agreed to apply part of the payment to the outstanding balance.

Caroline's first story was "To Thy Chamber Window, Sweet," another adventure of Aleck Maury. In it Aleck found himself in a quandary a month before his seventieth birthday. Unable to reel in any of the fish he hooked because the lake was covered with eelgrass, he fell prey to his own vanity and began telling stories and quoting poetry to impress a beautiful widow staying at the same boarding house. Soon Aleck was in danger of being caught by a woman bent on reforming his eating habits and dressing him up for rides about the country. But Aleck would not relinquish his freedom. He escaped once again with a new fishing partner, in search of better waters.

Just as she had in the first Aleck Maury story, Caroline used a third-person narrator, allowing the reader to appreciate both the "Gordon" and the "Meriwether" view of Aleck. But in her next story, "The Last Day in the Field," Caroline once again used Aleck as narrator of his own tale.

Caroline had originally intended to use this episode in her novel. In the tale the aging sportsman had to face his own mortality and come to grips with the fact that he was no longer physically able to hunt. He went on what would be his last day in the field with an eager but inexperienced twenty-year-old. Caroline sketched the contrast between youth and age in poignant, bittersweet tones. Aleck fought hard against his limitations but could no longer escape. His reflections almost became his own elegy. "I wished that the day could go on and not end so soon and yet I didn't see how I could make it much farther with my leg the way it was," he said to himself in the waning day, "the whole west woods ablaze with light."

She then went on to write one more story, what she thought would be her last story about Aleck Maury, called "One More Time." Again she used Aleck as a narrator to reflect on mortality. Aleck could still fish, but an old friend of his, Bob Reynolds, could not. Bob was dying. With his wife Bob came to the old lodge for one last visit. Before Aleck or anyone else realized what was happening, Bob had killed himself. What else could a true sportsman do?

After she finished the stories, Caroline tried to work on *A Morning's Favour*. She thought she could finish it with just two good months of steady work. Then she intended to write a novel about two maiden aunts who ran a girls' school and took in indigent kin, whom the elder aunt,

Julia, would eventually kill for insurance money. But Caroline would never write that story; she also did not immediately finish *A Morning's Favour*. Perhaps she still could not face her story of illicit love. For a while she grasped at any excuse to avoid the novel. At one point she even proposed what she called "another reporting job," writing the memoirs of another aged sportsman, Jim Avent, who trained bird dogs. After Max persuaded her to abandon that project, Caroline returned to the novel, but she worked halfheartedly and made little or no progress.

In October *Aleck Maury, Sportsman* appeared in print. Caroline admitted that the book looked "on the outside pretty good": she had almost reconciled herself to the title since Scribner's had emphasized the name and subordinated the label "Sportsman." But still, Caroline felt rather sick when she saw what she had written.

"Neither of my books so far has been rounded off enough," Caroline complained to Sally, adding that she did not think Aleck "got enough personal hell." That "would have made the book more dramatic," she said. But Caroline knew she always had a hard time making direct statements about her characters and the meaning of events in her writing. "It's one of my faults as a writer," she admitted, explaining that fear kept her cautious and indirect.

She compared her technique to that of Henry James, since Sally greatly admired him and had recently pressured her into reading *The Wings of the Dove*. "The thing when it is said, comes to you with a cumulative effect, a sort of rounding off of something you've already been brought to accept," Caroline explained. "It's really as if you'd been knocked down with a sledge hammer and then given one final tap."

By writing *Aleck Maury* Caroline had tried to work herself through depression. "If I was to work at all I had to work through somebody else's mind as my own had been rendered unendurable to me," she explained to Sally. "Even so it should have been a better book."

At first Caroline claimed to be pleased with Scribner's advertising. She told Max she thought the blurb struck "a fine, virile note"—"a warm hearted human book, shot through with sunlight and the ripple of mountain streams!"—so much so that she even began to regret having "such a sissy first name." But secretly she wondered if Scribner's strategy of emphasizing the sporting aspect of the book wasn't "putting the cart before the horse."

Caroline dedicated *Aleck Maury* to Ford, but she did not think he would like the book. "It marches but is flimsy in spots and you will see how I could have made a really good book out of it if I hadn't been so harried," Caroline told him. But Ford surprised her. At first he called the book "a quiet monologue addressed to someone that one likes very much and feels completely at home with." But after re-reading the novel, Ford decided the book had the "quality of Turgenev's *Sportsman's Sketches*," adding, "and you couldn't have greater praise from me!" He thought the book was "a poem rather than a novel."

In the following months others also congratulated Caroline on the book. Allen's friends Donald Davidson and John Crowe Ransom wrote glowing letters. Ransom called the book "the straightest, cleanest, most accurate and firmest piece of writing I've seen in a long time." Davidson said *Aleck Maury* was a "glorious book, a complete success . . . in every way." "Not in years have I read a piece of fiction that so satisfied, held, and touched me," he told her. "If you will keep on writing such books, you will not only be the greatest writer of fiction yet produced in the South—you will restore the Confederacy."

Although Malcolm Cowley and Red Warren also liked the book, they teased Caroline about her "masculine" prose. Red suggested Caroline's next book be titled *The Life and Passion of Caroline Gordon by J. M. Gordon*. Malcolm told her he expected to see her as "the bearded contributor to a sporting column." All their jests gave Caroline a publicity idea: she could have her picture taken wearing a false mustache and holding a large Cumberland River catfish. Folks could call her "the Hemingway of Cumberland valley," she said.

Published praise of *Aleck Maury* came slowly. The *New York Times Book Review* gave the novel "a small, inconspicuous review, written," Caroline thought, "evidently by someone who hadn't read the book." Isabel Paterson, writing in the *New York Herald Tribune Books,* said only that the novel was "serene, unpretentious, but accomplished."

Such lukewarm reviews depressed Caroline. She had thought the novel was "probably the best chance" she would ever have "of a popular sale," but sales were slow, and Caroline blamed the reviews. Even winning the second O'Henry Prize for "Old Red" could not lift her spirit: the two-hundred dollar award "melted . . . like mist before the debts," she said.

Eventually Andrew Lytle and Red Warren published more in-depth, laudatory reviews of *Aleck Maury*. Writing for the *New Republic,* Andrew called the novel "a prose Aeneid." In the *Southwest Review* Red praised Caroline for "the sense of a full and intense emotional life, which is never insisted upon, rarely stated, but implied, somehow, on almost every page" of the novel. But their reviews, though a comfort to Caroline, did not send readers running to the bookstores.

Caroline finally decided most people "missed the point" of *Aleck Maury*. It annoyed her when reviewers said "there were no 'problems' in the book." "Aleck's son was drowned, his wife got a little queer as a result, he was in danger at any moment of having to give up the thing that was more than life to him, he maintained during his seventy years the rigid spiritual discipline which would enable him to follow what he regarded as the supreme art—but with the revolution just around the corner none of these things seem real problems, of course," Caroline complained to Katherine Anne Porter.

Katherine Anne tried to comfort her. "It's a symptom of something when a man's life-long battle to preserve his personality, independence, and pursue a certain way of life precious to him, is no longer considered a problem," she wrote. Although Caroline could have "more dramatically defined" the conflict between Aleck and his wife, Katherine Anne thought she was "right not to do it, because Aleck Maury would not be the sort of man even to hint at such a state of affairs between himself and his wife. It comes out fairly subtly in incidents, . . . and if you had him speak out of character even in order to point up the dramatic conflict, it would be wrong."

All in all, Katherine Anne thought Caroline's book was "magnificent." "It reads as if a gentleman of the old south who knows not only Latin and Greek but English, had sat down and written his memories in the first words and phrases that came handily, and the kind that came handily would naturally have this sure, slightly formal and balanced rhythm," Katherine Anne said. "It's fine masculine prose, and why shouldn't it be, you writing with the sound of your father's voice, all the voices of your fore-fathers, in your ears."

Katherine Anne's description of the novel as "fine masculine prose" must have meant a great deal to Caroline. It echoed the assessment Caroline had made years earlier of George Eliot's talent: Eliot had claimed for herself the "privileges which had been monopolized by men up to that time" and had succeeded in making others believe that a man had actually written her first published work.

In the writing of *Aleck Maury, Sportsman,* Caroline did the same. Even without the male pen name, she stumped some readers into believing a man had written the story. A doctor from Rochester, New York, wrote to ask Caroline if the information she had included on training dogs was accurate because he wanted to try Aleck's methods. Another old gentleman, from Connecticut, offered to collaborate with her on her next book. And at least one man wanted to know if Caroline was really a woman. If she was, he said, he wanted to know how a woman "could write such a book."

Their offers and questions amused Caroline a great deal. How could a woman write a book like *Aleck Maury*? If the demands of sustaining a credible male narrator's voice were not enough of a challenge, the intricacies of all the hunting and fishing lore would surely baffle most women. Despite the poor sales and unenthusiastic reviews, Caroline could find comfort in the fact that she had met both challenges.

1935–1937

The Tates wore out 1934 and brought in 1935 with a wild "debauch," as Caroline called it, a brief vacation with Andrew Lytle, Red and Cinina Warren, and several of Caroline's cousins: Manny Meriwether and Rose and Manson Radford. It was a fitting tribute to the past, an unsettling hint of their life to come.

Leaving Nancy with friends in Memphis after Christmas, Caroline and Allen drove first to New Orleans, where the Radfords were living. For almost a week they feasted on oysters, drank dry martinis to excess, and did exactly what they wanted to do. On New Year's Eve they went to a small New Orleans bar for square dancing. Andrew called the figures while a black crooner pounded out "Go in and out the window." Along the edges of the dancing, several tough-looking drunks yelled, "Grab 'em, grab 'em, cowboy!" Caroline moved in a drunken haze, her dark eyes flashing with delight. She did not see Allen kissing her cousin Manny in the shadows.

After New Orleans they stopped in Baton Rouge, where Red and Cinina were living, for a few more days of reveling. By the time they had returned to Memphis in the first week of January, they were "perfectly sodden," Caroline said.

With the greatest of difficulty, Caroline returned to work. *Aleck Maury* was not selling well, but, as she wrote Ford, "There's nothing to do except go on writing other books." Yet Caroline did not intend to finish *A Morning's Favour*. Instead, she wanted to write about the defeat of the South by focusing on the life of one woman, Fanny Allard, a character in *A Morning's Favour*. Fanny would be another fictional rendering of Caroline's grandmother: a woman who loved her home, and married a poor cousin exhausted by his service under General Bedford Forrest in the war.

Caroline told Max the book would cover three generations like *Penhally* but would depend on characterization, not style and atmosphere. "I suppose I want to show not only the disintegration and corruption of the South but the spiritual confusion of the people who live through all these things," she wrote. "I am thinking of calling it *The Cup of Fury*." The title came from the Old Testament book of Jeremiah. In chapter 25, verses 15–16, the prophet said Israel had to drink a "wine cup of fury" and "cause all the nations . . . to drink it. And they shall drink, and be moved, and be mad, because of the sword that I will send among them."

"A time comes when one must sprawl a bit," Katherine Anne Porter once said. Caroline told all her friends the time to sprawl had certainly come for her: *The Cup of Fury* would be written on a grand scale. "I'm going to desert the method of narrow realism and have chapters, oh, several chapters of expository prose," she said. Using the Battle of Shiloh as the "main spectacle of the book," she intended to "interpret the Civil War in a new light, to show the Southern people just what did happen." Shiloh was "very important," Caroline said, "because to all intents the war was lost there—the Virginians were done for before they started."

When Allen said the book sounded like a southern version of *War and Peace,* Caroline said Bedford Forrest would be her Kutuzoff. Although not at all sure he was "reflective enough to stand up under the role," she decided Forrest would simply "have to": his "savagery" and "vindictiveness" would make a "splendid contrast" to the "chivalric blandness" of the other Confederate officers—they were all "little Lees."

The time had come to sprawl, Caroline said repeatedly. She thought the book would be her "major opus." It didn't take her long to set down the first sentence. "It was the nineteenth of August, a day which Fanny Allard was all her life to think of as 'Grandpa's birthday,'" she wrote. But a second sentence and a third, in fact, came more slowly.

Caroline hated the early months of every new year. "I seem to have a sort of moral collapse every year at the same time," she told Sally. Although she had the flu in February, Caroline's collapse was, as usual, probably more of an emotional withdrawal than anything else, a result of her anxiety over the new book and the trials of authorship.

For a while Caroline tried to write in bed, putting her typewriter on a pillow on her stomach. The effort was hardly worth it. She wrote what she thought was a "rotten review" of John Peale Bishop's novel, *Act of Darkness,* for the *New Republic* but could get no further than the first sentence of her own novel. Looking at the calendar panicked her. "I have only three and a half months left when I can be sure of a chance to work," she said. Since panic did not help, Caroline tried rereading southern history instead.

When Red Warren began editing a new magazine called the *Southern Review,* Caroline attempted to write some stories for him. But the only thing she could finish was a dog story called "B from Bull's Foot," written in collaboration with Nash Buckingham, a local sports enthusiast. It was hardly appropriate for the *Southern Review;* eventually *Scribner's* magazine published it.

Caroline still felt as if dark clouds loomed ominously over the Hamburger House. The only light strong enough to pierce the clouds came from Allen. After a dry spell of nearly two years, Allen had begun to write again. He not only had an idea of how to revise the novel he had begun about his family, *Ancestors in Exile,* he had written a new essay, "The Profession of Letters in the South," and two new poems. And Allen's wealthy coal-magnate brother, Ben, considered backing a new agrarian journal for Allen to edit.

"If a paralytic had suddenly thrown away his crutch to take dance steps we couldn't be more pleased," Caroline said. In her eyes Allen was not working when he was not writing, no matter how much time and energy he spent teaching. Allen felt similarly; at least, he felt despondent when unable to write poetry. One evening, some Southwestern faculty members and their wives gathered at the Tates' bungalow for a play-reading club. Allen stayed in his study for a while, trying to finish an article. "This was the first day's work he'd been able to do since we came here," Caroline said to the group to explain Allen's absence.

"What do you think he does every day?" they said accusingly, almost with one voice.

Nothing Caroline could say satisfied the other overworked faculty members. Some of Allen's friends thought Allen felt a bit overwhelmed by Caroline. "I wonder if Caroline's success hasn't had something to do with your silence," John Peale Bishop wrote Allen in February.

Nancy had little interest in her parents' writing problems or successes: the nine-year-old took "the vagaries of the artistic temperament pretty phlegmatically," Caroline said. Nancy was just pleased to be in Memphis, where she had plenty of friends her own age. Neither Caroline nor Allen paid much attention to her. They did not even realize Nancy was failing the fourth grade because she did not show them her report card and they never thought to ask to see it. As far as her parents were concerned, Nancy was "quite fat and very wily": at dance lessons Nancy looked like "an apple twirling around on her toes." It bothered Caroline to think she was not properly attentive to Nancy's needs, but she noticed with pleasure that Nancy usually managed to get "her wishes gratified in very roundabout ways."

Caroline had less success gratifying her own wishes. There was always something or someone else demanding a part of her time. Even though they had only two bedrooms in their bungalow, the Tates took in their usual stream of visitors. Sally Wood came for a short visit; so did Allen's friends John Gould Fletcher and Louis Untermeyer. Nathan Asch, another novelist they knew, stopped to see them on a cross-country bus trip: he said he was searching for material for a book, but Caroline thought he was probably "spying around" the South "on some Communist agitation."

In the spring of 1935, rumors of communism filled the air. Léonie Adams told Caroline that everyone in New York was talking about "the revolution" as if "it were just around the corner." This amazed Caroline—she had thought that "the literary vogue was much on the wane"—and she joked about Allen being put "under surveillance as a Communist."

But about forty miles from Memphis, at Marked Tree in the Arkansas delta, talk of revolution was no laughing matter. During the winter of 1934–35, members of the American Socialist party supported the attempts of the Southern Tenant Farmers' Union to organize sharecroppers. Marked Tree businessmen and local plantation owners undermined their efforts by stirring up violent action in response, inciting townspeople to attack organizers and union members, evicting tenants sympathizing with the movement. As time passed, the situation grew more and more explosive. Black sharecroppers joined the union, further upsetting the local community.

For a while Caroline, like most southerners, paid little attention to the incidents at Marked Tree, although during the spring of 1935, reporters from northern newspapers appeared in Marked Tree in droves. In April, Ford Madox Ford and Janice Biala came to visit Caroline and Allen for about ten days. Then Ford and the Tates went to Baton Rouge for a "Conference on Literature and Reading in the South and Southwest" at Louisiana State University. But shortly after returning to Memphis, Caroline got an opportunity to visit Marked Tree, an opportunity she would have just as soon missed.

James Rorty, a journalist Caroline had known in New York City, had attended the Baton Rouge conference, then stopped in Memphis to stay with the Tates while investigating the situation at Marked Tree. Before he left, he had persuaded both Caroline and Allen to accompany him on his search for information. When Rorty antagonized the Marked Tree authorities, they called the president of Southwestern College and threatened to embarrass Allen and the college publicly if Rorty published any account of his visit.

After Allen threatened to quit his job if Rorty went ahead with the story, Rorty reluctantly agreed not to publish. But before leaving he tried to convince Allen that the Agrarians needed to "develop a field technique." Allen was not persuaded. Caroline agreed with Rorty, but as she said later, she tried "in vain to make him see Allen and John Ransom and Don Davidson would make damn poor field workers." The Agrarians were "primarily artists, men of thought," lacking the "capacity for action," she said. "They've formulated the doctrine," but "somebody else would have to put it into practice."

Although she empathized with the sharecroppers' terrible situation, Caroline was relieved to forget the whole matter. She vowed never to take in "any more communists or fellow travelers": hospitality had its limits.

"As I get older I seem to give up more and more things for the sake of writing and to get less and less writing done," Caroline moaned during the summer of 1935. She had known it would be difficult to write once they left Memphis, but she had hardly expected her dry spell would continue after they had gotten settled at Benfolly.

The Tates arrived in Clarksville during the first week of June. After months of steady rain, the countryside was incredibly green. Caroline stood on the porch overlooking the river and marveled at the weeping willows and the larkspur that covered the hill. But when she turned around and went back into Benfolly, she had to face a less pleasant sight. "The whole lower floor of the house was covered with green mould, the whole middle with coal soot, and the top with honest dust," Caroline said. It took a solid week of waxing, polishing, and painting to make the house livable.

The house was no sooner clean than the guests began to arrive: first some of Caroline's relatives, then a group of Allen's friends from Southwestern College, then Ford and Janice. The cats that had gone out to forage also came straggling back: Tri-Coleur and Colonel Crocket, Blue Tato, Theseus, and Ariadne. Everyone and everything had to be fed and cared for—no small task, because the price of food was higher in Clarksville than it had been in Memphis.

Whenever Caroline could find a quiet moment, she tried to work on *The Cup of Fury*. She sat at her typewriter in the dining room on the lowest level of Benfolly and stared out at the Cumberland River, smoking cigarette after cigarette, practically praying the words would come to her. Still, she got no farther than the first sentence. In desperation, one day she typed "III" at the top of a clean sheet of paper, deciding that if she couldn't write the first or second chapter, she would try the third. But after several more cigarettes and too much time staring at her typewriter, Caroline decided it would be easier to write Katherine Anne.

"I am hoping to get my novel started before going to Olivet and yet a little afraid to get into the swing and have to cut it short," Caroline told her. "I don't suppose I need to worry—six months now I've been waiting for the right first words to come down from heaven."

The routine of writing and waiting for the words to come was getting "wearing," Caroline said, adding that she had recently been reminded how old she was, nearly forty. A young woman was writing a master's thesis on the Fugitives, and Allen had been "digging up a mass of old correspondence," Caroline wrote Katherine Anne. Another young man was trying to write a biography of Hart Crane. "He says he wants Hart's personality to take entire possession of him before he starts writing," she wrote. The idea appalled her, but Caroline figured it was the only way such a book got written. Perhaps she needed the spirit of Fanny Allard to take possession of her? Maybe then *The Cup of Fury* would flow freely.

At the end of June, Max began pestering Caroline, asking her to send him some manuscript, "even in the very rough." He wanted her to finish the book for spring publication, tempting her with grand promises. "In my own mind," Max wrote, "I am thinking of it as a leader on our list."

His words "put the fear of God" in Caroline. She figured all of Scribner's "big shots" had "just published a book" and Max was "actually looking around for a leader." Since such an opportunity might "never happen again," Caroline vowed to "try to make it," sending Max a detailed synopsis of *The Cup of Fury*.

"The life of Fanny Churchill will be the main thread of the book," Caroline told him. The story would begin in the summer of 1861, when Bedford Forrest made a secret expedition to Kentucky, stopping to visit Fanny's grandfather Fontaine Allard. Part 1 would show Fanny's love for her grandfather's home, Brackets, and introduce Fanny to her fifth cousin, Valentine Allard. Pursued by another cousin, Fanny was so much "in love with a life that just now seems so glowing and limitless" that she could not "confine herself to the attentions of one man," Caroline wrote. But when the "boys" went off to war, Fanny was left behind, restless and lonely.

Part 2 would focus on Forrest's campaigns. Caroline wanted to tamper with history and make Valentine Allard into Forrest's confidential secretary. The Battle of Shiloh would be "the grand spectacle of the book," but Caroline planned to include other battles and scenes emphasizing Val's sensitive nature. At one point, there would be "a moment when Val identifies himself wholly with Forrest." It would be an "almost mystical moment . . . a moment of exalted rage," she wrote, and it would be "a touchstone by which he measures everything" else in his life.

"This war section will alternate battle chapters with scenes at Brackets," Caroline told Max. It would end just after the fall of Fort Donelson. Fanny and her grandfather would be in Nashville when Forrest arrived to put the town under martial law. They would meet Val there, and Val, although wounded, would accompany the old man and young woman back to Brackets. Fanny and Val would fall in love.

Part 3 would begin after the war, after Fanny and Val were married. Caroline planned to closely follow her grandmother's actual experiences. The young couple would move into the overseer's cabin on land Fanny owned. Like Woodstock, the grand estate of Brackets would be sold. Fanny would oppose the sale, but Val would have no strength—either emotional or physical—to put up much resistance. Fanny would go on, "desperately trying to create an ordered life out of chaos," Caroline wrote. Even when her husband died of pneumonia, Fanny would feel "more rage than grief," feeling that he had "chosen to leave her alone in the fight."

But Fanny would be more than equal to the struggle, Caroline indicated. The final section of the novel would discuss Fanny's children, but it would still focus on Fanny's strength and determination. Caroline intended to include several of the scenes from her first story, "Old Mrs. Llewellyn." Fanny's children would succeed for a time in getting their mother away from the dilapidated house, Cabin Row, but in the final scene of the novel, Fanny would return home and reassert her independence and connection to her land, going through the rooms and walking about the grounds, "laying her hand sometimes on the trunks of the trees," and vowing "she will never leave again." Caroline wanted to contrast "the grimness of her surroundings and the joy she feels at being home." "I suppose the point I am trying to make is that a human soul can triumph by embracing its destiny, however grim that destiny may be," she told Max.

Max wrote back quickly, approving her title and plan. "Even in this outline the war material seems to me beyond anything in the way of a fictional presentation of the war that I ever heard of. It has a quality of life in it even in the outline," he said, but he cautioned Caroline that the novel might suffer a letdown once the war "fades out."

Caroline agreed the final section would be "the most difficult for it narrows down then to one woman's life." But she thought she could make it "dramatic enough." The book would be "a study of the two sides of man's nature," she wrote. "Val, representing the intellect, understands his situation completely and is defeated, partly by that knowledge. But Fanny, his wife, is the human heart, and the heart is incorrigible and cannot be defeated."

Writing the synopsis worked like magic for Caroline; soon she was writing the actual manuscript with ease. But by then it was the middle of July, and the Tates had to go teach in a school of writing at Olivet College in Michigan. "We dismissed the cook, shut up Benfolly, disposed of Nancy and all the animals and got as far as Louisville," Caroline said later. There a telegram from the president of Olivet reached them: the school was canceled because of lack of enrollment.

Since they had no idea of how to contact their cook, and no desire to reopen Benfolly for just a few weeks, Caroline and Allen decided to visit Andrew Lytle at his father's plantation, Cornsilk. The three-thousand-acre plantation just outside Guntersville, Alabama, was Caroline's idea of "the lap of luxury." The house was nothing special, just an "old dog run cabin, fixed over just enough to make it livable," she said, but it was the ideal place "for anybody writing a book." The reason was Andrew's father. "A short, white-haired man with a wide, humorous mouth and alert blue eyes," Robert Logan Lytle was "kindly disposed towards artists," Caroline said.

Although she felt guilty "visiting instead of being visited," Caroline sensed Mr. Lytle did not mind having them at Cornsilk. When she saw a monthly grocery bill for fifteen dollars, which included feed for the turkeys, she figured they were no financial burden. Caroline admired Mr. Lytle enormously: he "revels all day long in his own aesthetic pleasures so he's indulgent to other people," she told Sally.

Their work schedule was simple but almost inflexible. Every morning Mr. Lytle rose from the breakfast table and told Caroline, Allen, and Andrew that he hoped the Muse would treat them right during the day. Mr. Lytle then trotted out of the room with what Caroline thought was "the air and very much the motion of a beagle hound on a promising scent."

No one lingered after he was gone. Andrew retired to the woods to write—to get away from his father's four or five hundred turkeys. "It is hard enough to reject the world and the flesh without having to reject the turkey world anew every morning," he said.

Allen apparently courted the Muse in another part of the house, while Caroline went to a two-by-four-foot table in a secluded corner of the dining room. The table was near a window overlooking a three-acre field of tomatoes. When Caroline looked up from her typewriter, she could see Mr. Lytle in white shirt and duck trousers moving between rows of tomatoes at a rapid trot.

Around eleven o'clock each morning, Mr. Lytle and his overseer, George, came in from the fields. George had a farm of his own not far from Cornsilk, but he preferred to rent it out and live with the Lytles. "Since Mrs. Lytle's death this is a household run by men," Caroline observed. While George read the paper, Mr. Lytle nodded in the porch swing, but only briefly. In five minutes he would bounce up to prepare a grand dessert for dinner. Some days they had apricot sherbet, other days angel food cake. After dinner Mr. Lytle would ride off to take a look at his crops while George supervised some canning or other chores around the plantation, and the writers returned to their typewriters. All would work until five o'clock every day, when they quit to go swimming. After several evening drinks and an enormous supper, Caroline usually fell asleep on the front porch.

For Caroline the routine was invigorating. Within a week she had written more than fifteen thousand words, almost the entire first section of her novel. She had also begun a tribute to Mr. Lytle, called "That Man, Lytle," developed around George's stories about his boss and friend.

Life at Cornsilk got better every day, Caroline thought. But Allen

hated the Cornsilk pace. He was "right torn in his mind," Caroline observed. "As an overworked professor he ought to rest all summer but as a
writer with four overdue contracts he can't relish the rest much. Slowly
but surely he's being forced to the wall."

So the Tates left Cornsilk to visit friends in Louisville. After about a
week, however, they returned to the Lytles' plantation. Caroline began
work on the second section of her book, using the same routine:
"breakfast, work, lunch, short nap, work, swim from five to six thirty,
cocktail (one) supper, bed. Sleep like hell. Get up and go at it again."

This time, the routine worked better than expected. One morning,
"even Allen wrote two pages," Caroline said.

Caroline left for Memphis reluctantly at the end of the summer. Before long she considered returning to Cornsilk. "I know I could finish
my novel quicker there than anywhere else," she said. "But it seems too
selfish to leave Allen with the entire bag to hold." Her willingness to
put aside her own needs would increasingly hamper her work. Yet for
a while the move did not have any ill effects. After settling the family
into a new yellow bungalow on the opposite end of Forrest Avenue, and
enrolling Nancy in a private school, Caroline turned all her attentions to
her novel. Soon she was deeply immersed in the Civil War, reading book
after book about the battles and the people, fascinated by the adventures
of the soldiers and spies, Union and Confederate.

After a while she found herself living almost entirely in the past. One
day she wrote a business letter and had to ask Allen what year it was: for
Caroline it was September 1863; she was beginning work on the battle
of Chickamauga. Another evening, when Allen and Nancy complained
about dinner, Caroline was annoyed. The soldiers lived on blackberries
they picked "as they went into the line of battle," she told them.

"Mama, I don't care what those Confederate soldiers ate," Nancy responded crossly.

Caroline worked almost nonstop throughout the fall, from early in
the morning until ten or eleven o'clock every evening. "The colors in
the park are gorgeous, but I don't see much of them," she moaned. Max
wrote several times, urging her to finish the book in time for spring publication, and Caroline felt increasingly nervous. Eventually, she decided
her original plans were too comprehensive.

The problem was with the second section on the war. Caroline thought
it would be "very simple," almost a pastiche of quotes taken from books
like John Allen Wyeth's life of Forrest and *Battles and Leaders of the Civil*

War. Whenever she came across a particularly powerful sentence, she "lifted" it for her own manuscript. One of her favorites was from Wyeth: "Waving his bloody right hand high above his head he charged into the battle. 'My God, men,' he screamed, 'will you see them kill your general before your eyes?'"

But the longer Caroline worked on that section of her novel, the more she felt she needed to know. The war had to "be built up in such detail," she told Max. Some of that detail came from long talks with Confederate veterans, and Caroline decided she was lucky to live in Memphis with so many people who had known Forrest. But the process was slow, "an afternoon of an old man's talk for each detail."

By the end of October, Caroline had made significant changes in the novel. Since the battle of Shiloh did not work out, she substituted the battle of Chickamauga. She also gave her characters new names: Fanny became Lucy; Valentine became Rives. But most important, Caroline decided to "cut the book off with the Civil War," in effect, to write only half the novel—with a very different focus and greatly altered plot line. The novel would no longer be the story of the life of one woman; instead, it would be a story of the war seen through one soldier's eyes— the kind of novel Caroline had once said a woman could not write. And yet the focus of the story was not really on one man either. Using an omniscient narrator, Caroline would rove at will through the trenches and tents, listen in on strategy sessions, sweep over the dead and dying on the battlefields, and watch the men in prison plot escapes sure to end in death.

Still intending to show what happened to both soldiers and civilians, Caroline said Lucy would "participate in the war scenes." But instead of having Lucy wait until after the war to marry Rives, Caroline decided the two would marry early, then Lucy would leave her family and go to live with Rives's mother and sisters in Georgia. Rives's mother, patterned on Caroline's great-grandmother "Mammy Horse," would ride through the lines to care for the soldiers, often forcing Lucy to help. "The girl, pressed beyond her strength for weeks, comes almost to hate her mother-in-law as the incarnation of those forces which are crushing the life out of her," Caroline explained to Max.

The novel would end after Rives was badly wounded at the Battle of Murfreesboro. Lucy would take Rives home, "jolting in a wagon over remote country roads back to Brackets," Caroline said. Rives cursed and groaned "and in his delirium [killed] over again a color bearer fleeing with the standard." Lucy rode with her eyes shut, "trying not to hear him, thinking only that soon they [would] be in Kentucky."

Caroline thought the new ending would help her get around the problem of dramatizing the period of Reconstruction and also allow her to "get in enough stuff to round out the whole thing." Max approved of the changes: he had always thought the latter part of the book would be too much of an anticlimax to the war scenes. He urged her once again to finish in time for spring publication.

Caroline tried. She worked until her eyes ached, barely taking any time off for herself. But, as usual, she willingly took time to help others. She helped several Memphis women with their writing and read manuscripts Sally Wood sent her for advice. When Josie Herbst asked for a recommendation for a Guggenheim Fellowship, Caroline readily agreed, although she had not liked Josie's last novel. She knew her friend needed the Guggenheim Fellowship. Josie's marriage had ended; John was now living with another woman, and Josie was devastated. Caroline understood her pain.

Allen also agreed to write a letter of recommendation for Josie but then changed his mind. He had never liked Josie, or her radical politics, and he finally decided he could not recommend her for any fellowship because of her use of propaganda in literature. Caroline apparently tried to talk him into changing his mind: Allen seldom refused to recommend other writers, even when he objected to their politics. But this time Allen remained adamant, leaving Caroline with the uncomfortable task of informing Josie.

Usually Caroline took great pains to keep her disagreements with Allen private. But she could not conceal this difference of opinion, and she made no attempt to hide her distress. She told Josie she was writing a letter of recommendation even though Allen had refused. She also tried to comfort Josie by saying that a recommendation from the Tates might not be "much good" after all, yet Josie's political leanings might help her. "I don't think anybody who isn't communistically inclined would have much chance with the Foundation these days," Caroline wrote.

Caroline may have seen Allen's refusal to recommend Josie as a sign of more serious difficulties in their life. In another letter she discussed Josie's breakup with John in terms reflecting on her own relationship with Allen. "It's strange the way these things happen," Caroline wrote. "Successful male novelists always get rid of the partner of their lean days as soon as they hit the top. I suppose with female novelists it works just as inevitably only reversed. The unsuccessful partner can't stand the success."

Although she may not have consciously realized it, at some level Caroline sensed that her own achievements might threaten Allen. But perhaps he was threatened by more than her success; his actions suggested he was also threatened by her friendships. By repeatedly driving wedges in her relationships with others, Allen tried to isolate his wife, from family as well as friends. It was a form of emotional control, a way to ensure that Allen remained the central power in his wife's life, and Caroline was very vulnerable to it.

Caroline had congratulated her friend on beginning a new book. Josie had the "professional instinct," Caroline thought. "Sometimes it will carry you through when nothing else will," she wrote. "You have it, Old Girl, and I think it will carry you through." But Caroline was not always sure she could say the same for herself. And Allen's behavior would only increase her self-doubts.

Caroline struggled on with *The Cup of Fury* for another month, writing all day and late into the night. The routine was exhausting, far more so than she had ever expected. After living so long with battles and blood and thunder, she said it was "hard to focus on quieter scenes."

Then one day, even the routine of work failed her. Her writing seemed stale to her, and she could not find a way to work through the feeling. Finally Caroline decided she could not make spring publication.

She told Max she was "not willing to take a chance on ruining what will probably be my most important book." "If I were using the same method I used in *Penhally* I might be able to force myself more, but I'm afraid to try to go any faster than I'm going," she wrote. "The effect of the book is to be massive and cumulative—after finishing it I must have time to step back and see if all the parts are in place."

Max reluctantly agreed to delay publication until the fall of 1936. Caroline was relieved, but other pressures took the place of her anxiety about the deadline: the usual financial pressures and a tension from feelings buried but not forgotten, the feelings of betrayal Caroline had over Allen's affair. Marion Henry was gone; Caroline had probably not seen her other cousin Manny flirting with Allen, had not seen Allen kiss Manny during their trip to New Orleans the previous Christmas. But as the school year wore on, Caroline apparently began to have new suspicions.

Allen found his work at Southwestern College much easier than the previous year, and much more enjoyable also, surrounded as he was by beautiful young coeds. His mood improved; he even managed to complete a collection of essays that the Alcestis Press had agreed to publish. But Caroline was not as jubilant about his ability to write as she had been. Perhaps she sensed he was having or considering another affair. Their relationship became increasingly strained. Caroline would not confront him—she may have feared to have her suspicions confirmed—but friends began to realize that she was upset. Her temper flared much too easily.

All the tension Caroline experienced had to find an outlet, and soon Caroline created one, although it was not extremely effective. By December of 1935, the Tates adopted a new family member, a dachshund named Herr Baron Vili von Isarthal. Although meant to be Nancy's dog, Vili quickly became attached to Caroline, and she turned him into her mouthpiece, the voice of "Old Doc Gordon" camouflaged.

Vili could say all the mean and nasty things Caroline hesitated to say. She would hold Vili high in the air, so he could look into her dark eyes as he "spoke," or he would sit on her lap, like a ventriloquist's dummy. "I'm nervous and sensitive, aren't I, Mama? Like my Uncle Hart Crane," Vili liked to say. "All I am or hope to be I owe to my sainted mother." In time Caroline used Vili to bait Allen or criticize the other poets streaming through their lives.

Yet no one took Vili's comments seriously, least of all Allen. Caroline would have to find another way to effect a change in her life. The Christmas holidays came and went in confused frenzy. Early in January Caroline approached Max about publishing a volume of her short stories, but Max urged her to wait. "It is very hard to sell short stories," he said. If *The Cup of Fury* "has a marked success, the chances for a book of short stories thereafter would be greatly increased." Caroline could not have been pleased by his decision, but she offered no argument.

Not long after Christmas, Andrew Lytle and his sister Polly arrived in Memphis. Andrew was almost halfway through another novel about "the War," called *The Long Night,* but he said he was "in a dangerous psychical condition": he felt "cold" to war. So Caroline and Andrew decided to "spend the next few months together and try to whoop each other on."

The bungalow on Forrest Avenue soon became "a regular book factory," as Caroline put it. At first Allen found it difficult to live with two novelists writing on the Civil War, but soon even Allen had a writing "renascence," completing two essays in less than two months' time.

Although she worked primarily on her novel, Caroline wrote an occasional review or short story for extra money. In January she wrote a horror story, "The Enemies," a lurid tale "about a man whose enemy is about to be hanged." The enemy promised to join the man ten minutes after death, but when he did not appear, the man committed suicide to "meet the ghost on his own ground," according to Caroline. The story was eventually published by the *Southern Review*.

As both Caroline and Andrew tried to complete their Civil War novels, they once again compared battles and "symptoms," and Caroline expected that she would soon "sprout long chin whiskers or perhaps be put up for office in the Confederate Veterans." She was impressed with the progress Andrew had made as a writer, and she thought his novel might be "a sort of Wuthering Heights." "Everything he's done I'd have said couldn't be pulled off," Caroline told Sally, "It's true there are some pretty bad spots . . . but somehow he's contrived to turn out some tremendous stuff."

On February 19, 1936, Caroline received a call from Dorothy Day, the radical journalist she had met while she was pregnant with Nancy. Dorothy said she was passing through Memphis, and Caroline nearly asked her to spend the night. But the trouble at Marked Tree was still in the news. Remembering the uproar over James Rorty, Caroline decided to be honest about why she couldn't invite Dorothy over.

"I'm taking an oath not to let another Communist or fellow traveler cross my threshold because they are so unscrupulous in their dealings, particularly with southern people," Caroline told her.

Dorothy laughed. "Caroline, you don't understand," she said. "I'm not a Communist, I'm a Catholic."

"In that case," Caroline said, "I'd be delighted to have you come and spend the night."

Dorothy spent two nights with the Tates. Caroline could not believe how much Dorothy had changed. Still tall and slim, Dorothy seemed "strikingly different," Caroline said, and she wondered why. Dorothy had certainly found peace and a direction for her enormous energy. But Dorothy said little about her life; Caroline asked few questions. Instead, they spent most of their time gossiping about old friends.

Caroline probably knew that Dorothy had stopped in Marked Tree to speak in support of the tenant farmers there. But just as she had said, Dorothy was no longer a Communist sympathizer. Not long after the birth of her daughter, Dorothy had become a Catholic. After separating from Forster Batterham, she began writing for Catholic magazines like *Commonweal*. Then, in the spring of 1933, Dorothy had begun her own newspaper, *The Catholic Worker,* influenced by Peter Maurin, a French man who believed in life committed to Christian charity. Selling for only a penny, *The Catholic Worker* responded to the Communist ideology of the *Daily Worker* by promoting a gospel of Catholic teachings and social justice. By the spring of 1936, it had a circulation of over one hundred thousand. Soon Dorothy would open up "Houses of Hospitality" to care for people who had no homes or jobs.

Caroline had little interest in such activities, but once she realized Dorothy had taken a vow of poverty, she made every effort to coddle her. "I ordered a special luncheon and I saw to it that Dorothy had breakfast in bed," Caroline said later. Since, in her own words, she and Allen were "just hanging on by our toenails to our financial cliff," Caroline probably had a difficult time understanding why anyone would decide to be poor. But Dorothy did not consider her life a particular hardship; in fact, she thought Caroline was in a more perilous condition. After she left Memphis, Dorothy began to pray for Caroline's conversion.

Still devoted to her religion of art, however, Caroline hardly gave Dorothy's visit a second thought. Throughout the spring she worked almost all day and night on *The Cup of Fury,* pausing only to send several chapters of the novel around to various magazines. With Allen's salary mortgaged to pay debts, they desperately needed money. But neither *Scribner's* nor the *Southern Review* would publish two of her chapters, "Sun Sets on the Bloody River" and "The Cannon's Mouth." Caroline could only hope their financial problems would be solved by a fantastic sale of the novel in the fall.

By the end of June, Caroline had finished the book and sent it to Max before leaving Memphis. After checking on Benfolly and leaving Nancy with relatives, they hurriedly drove to Olivet College in Michigan for a two-week writers' conference. While waiting for Max's reaction to the novel, Caroline amused herself by trading battle stories with Carl Sandburg, also teaching at Olivet. She thought the students and staff at Olivet were wonderful. Everyone "worked so hard . . . that it drained us all of our vitality," Caroline said. In the morning one of the writers would get up and say to his colleagues, "Don't come near me. I've stored up some vitality. I can't waste it on you."

As Max did not respond, however, Caroline grew worried. She thought she could have used another month to polish her novel; she hoped she "didn't let it go too soon," she said.

But in a way she did not let the novel go soon enough. By the middle of July, the future success of *The Cup of Fury* was threatened by another novel about "the War." *Gone with the Wind* by Margaret Mitchell had been published on June 30, 1936, and immediately became a best-seller: within three weeks it had sold over 178,000 copies. By the end of the summer, David O. Selznick would purchase the movie rights to the novel for fifty thousand dollars, the highest price paid for a first novel at that time. The Book-of-the-Month Club offered *Gone with the Wind* as one of its regular selections, another bonanza, and Margaret Mitchell from Georgia had her work compared to that of Tolstoy, Hardy, and Dickens.

Could any other novel compete for sales with such a book? Max Perkins did not think so, and by the end of July he informed Caroline that Scribner's had postponed the publication of *The Cup of Fury*. Caroline was relieved to have time for revision, but she realized she was "too late by a season." As Mitchell became something of a folk heroine, the newspapers were full of stories about how it took her ten years to write *Gone with the Wind*. "Why couldn't it have taken her twelve?" Caroline complained to Sally. *Gone with the Wind* was little more than "a super salesman's idea, half a dozen of the best plots in the world wrapped up, with the civil war as cellophane," Caroline thought, but it had "gobbled up all the trade."

After the conference in Olivet, Caroline and Allen drove to New York City. Allen had agreed to give lectures at Columbia; Caroline met with Max about revisions to *The Cup of Fury*. Max thought Caroline needed to account for some of the minor characters. He also thought she "killed too many young men." Caroline was more than willing to revise the book according to his suggestions.

After a quick trip through New England, Caroline and Allen headed back to pick up their daughter in Kentucky. Allen could not face another year of teaching at Southwestern College of Memphis, but they also could not afford to live at Benfolly, so they went to visit Andrew Lytle and his family at the Lytles' summer cabin at Monteagle, Tennessee, an old-fashioned summer resort in the Cumberland Mountains.

For a while the Tates toyed with the idea of going in January to Mexico, where a dollar was worth nearly four times as much. But lacking the money to get there, Caroline and Allen ultimately decided to spend the winter at Monteagle. The Lytles' log cabin was enormous, built around two long intersecting halls, what Caroline called "four dog runs in the form of a cross." The halls were drafty, the kitchen only "a sort of catacomb belowstairs," but Caroline called it "the best place to work" she had ever come upon.

She and Allen and Andrew set up their typewriters on the porch that wrapped around all sides of the cabin. Andrew's sister, Polly Lytle, did all the cooking for several months, and Andrew's father came up from Cornsilk once a week with a fresh selection of eggs, butter, vegetables, and milk. "That man has a proper respect for the Muse," Caroline remarked. "Lord knows when we'll be able to tear ourselves away."

Despite the Lytles' generosity, Caroline thought mountain life would be too rough for a child, so eleven-year-old Nancy went to live in Chattanooga with her great-aunt and uncle, Pidie and Paul Campbell. "They begged to have her and it is much better for her to be there," Caroline explained to Ford, almost defensively. "Allen would have had to drive twenty five miles a day getting her back and forth."

Since Scribner's wanted the revised manuscript of *The Cup of Fury* by the first week of October, Caroline quickly returned to work. She told a friend that she "mastered details of life in Camps Chase, Douglas, Johnson's Island and Fort Lafayette," and wrote about nine thousand words in the first two weeks at Monteagle. Against Max's advice, Caroline killed another young man, gave a second chronic diarrhea, and a third a gangrenous foot. "I don't care whether he likes it or not," she exclaimed. But later she apologized to Max for her homicidal tendencies as an author. "I can't help it," she said. "All the good people in the south were killed off by the war, one way or another. . . . Only the weak or the base survive in the new conditions."

While Caroline typed madly on the porch, Vili lay beneath her desk. Caroline figured she had about twenty thousand words left to write, including a section on the Battle of Brice's Cross Roads, which would involve more research. She wrote to Sally: "When I get these thirty thousand words done I shall be through with . . . *The Cup of Fury*—and hasn't it been one?"

When Caroline finished her revision, she had "an uneasy feeling that another chapter or two might help the book." She thought she had put too much energy into "mastering maneuvers" and not enough into the actual writing. But time was short; she sent the manuscript to Scribner's anyway.

Although Caroline had tried to move between scenes of war and scenes of domestic life, she decided to end the novel without resolution. Rives died in battle, carrying the colors forward as the other Confederate soldiers fled from Union fire. The Confederate cause had been all but lost, but Forrest filled the final scene, grabbing the flag after Rives fell in death, riding forward on his great war horse, his voice "sounding back over the windy plain" as he galloped toward the Union stronghold, Caroline wrote.

Whatever happened to Lucy and the other Allards? Caroline was content to leave the reader hanging, but Max was not. When he read the revised manuscript for the first time in galleys, he urged Caroline to add "anything that might occur" to her "that would bind the book together." Above all, Max wanted an epilogue featuring Lucy. "It seems as though Lucy ought not just to fade out," he wrote. A "quiet" final chapter, even "if it were only just a scene which showed her," would "tie the book together," he told her, adding that "the danger is that it may not be sufficiently tied up."

As Caroline worked her way through the galleys, she decided Max was right. She added sentences, cut out entire paragraphs, and wrote several new chapters to be inserted within the text, as well as an epilogue. Although she felt the new material improved the novel, Caroline was still not entirely pleased. She turned her favorite chapter into a short story called "The Women on the Battlefield," and submitted it to the *Southern Review,* but when Red Warren and Cleanth Brooks asked her to revise the opening, she felt unequal to the task. "I'm sorry I was stupid about revising the story," she wrote to Red. "I am just played out."

Caroline sometimes wished she could have put the novel aside for a while before trying to improve it. Yet would it have helped? "Always before I've felt that if I could just put a little more time into a thing I could get it right," she told Red. "This time I had the feeling that I'd put all I had into it and alas, it wasn't enough."

News that at least one motion-picture company was interested in *The Cup of Fury* cheered Caroline somewhat. She didn't believe anything would come of it, but the idea was "enough to turn our imaginings towards the coast," she said. The "movie nibble," however, created new troubles. On November 27 Max Perkins sent Caroline a telegram: *The*

Cup of Fury had already been used as a title for a 1919 novel written by Rupert Hughes. Although Caroline could still use the title, Max urged her to change it because Metro Goldwyn studios already owned the rights to that phrase.

Caroline immediately began thumbing through the Bible and editions of Shakespeare, Milton, and Yeats, looking for a replacement. At the end of the day, she sent Max a list of alternate titles. Her first choice, *The Great Invasion,* was one Allen had suggested several months earlier. Caroline had not liked the title then, but when she could no longer use *The Cup of Fury,* she changed her mind. "It sounds well, is bold and makes a claim for attention," she wrote. Also, "it would make a good movie title."

Other titles she liked less included *All the Merry-Hearted, None Shall Look Back, Under the Sun,* and *Men That Ride upon Horses.* The first three were based on quotes from the Bible; the last was from a poem by Yeats, "At Galway Races." Caroline thought that only *The Great Invasion* could "stand alone": "the other titles would have to be bolstered by a quotation," she wrote.

Max thought *The Great Invasion* sounded too much like a history text. He preferred *None Shall Look Back,* from the Old Testament book of Nahum, chapter 2, verse 8: "Stand, stand, shall they cry; but none shall look back." Caroline immediately regretted suggesting it. *None Shall Look Back* sounded too much like *Gone with the Wind* and would "invite irrelevant comparison." Insisting her novel was "the real thing," not "another substitute for *Gone with the Wind,*" she once again urged Max to accept *The Great Invasion:* such a title "might set [a] style instead of trailing after one."

Max did not agree, but he proposed other titles, including *Terrible Swift Sword,* from "The Battle Hymn of the Republic." *Terrible Swift Sword* would imply "the sword of God" at the same time it referred to Forrest, he told her.

Caroline was appalled. "Even if I could swallow a title from Julia Ward Howe, other Southerners couldn't," she said. Finally, after making a few more halfhearted suggestions, Caroline accepted *None Shall Look Back.* She thought her novel was "the most ambitious novel written so far about the Civil War," and as such, "it ought to have a solid and dignified title." But she could think of nothing which sounded better than *None Shall Look Back,* "and sound is the thing in a title it seems to me," she decided reluctantly.

As the book went to press, Caroline tried to keep busy with other projects so as not to think about how the novel would be received. She helped to raise money to establish a position for Ford Madox Ford at Olivet College, and she also went to Chattanooga to see Nancy several times. Only eleven years old, Nancy had grown heavy; both her parents called her "Fat Girl." Nancy wore her hair in pigtails and looked quite cute, Caroline thought. But Nancy still had little interest in school, to her parents' dismay. That fall she was barely passing math. When Caroline chastised her, Nancy responded, "Mama can't take a joke."

Caroline found it difficult to relax about anything. For a while she tried to rest by doing typically feminine things. She made herself "a sweet little velvet jacket": it was "a great relief to do a little sewing," she told a friend, "I am so tired of cavalry maneuvers." But soon, desperate once again for money, she pulled out the abandoned manuscript for *A Morning's Favour* and decided she could finish it by February. Declaring there were "only ten chapters left to write," she asked Max for an advance. Max sent her one hundred dollars, but he warned her that she had already received an advance on the novel.

To placate him, she sent a new story, "The Brilliant Leaves," written after one of her walks around the nearly abandoned village of Monteagle. It was the "story about a girl who was a reckless climber and fell off the brow" of the mountain. Years later Caroline said she heard the tale from an old lady who "popped out of the bushes" during her walk: "I have never been sure the old lady was real, popping out at me like that. I never saw her again." Quite probably, Caroline invented both old lady and story. During the summer Monteagle was full of elderly women, but most left by December, when cold winter winds descended on the mountains. Based on fact or not, however, Caroline used childhood memories and local history in "The Brilliant Leaves."

She began the story with a favorite scene—that of two women sitting on a porch. Eighteen-year-old Jimmy listened to his mother and her sister gossip about the Monteagle regulars, especially about Sally Mainwaring. She had been wild in her youth, Jimmy's aunt said. "Highspirited," his mother conceded. But Sally had ended up an old maid: her father frightened away her lover just as she was climbing down a rope ladder to meet him.

Caroline used the opening story as a bench mark for the later action. Jimmy escaped the confines of the porch gossips to meet his lover, Evelyn, the niece of Sally Mainwaring, in the woods. There Jimmy tried to seduce Evelyn, but she wanted to explore the woods, not make love.

Even after Jimmy proposed to her, she kept her distance, eventually talking Jimmy into climbing Bridal Veil Falls. On the way, Evelyn slipped and fell. Caroline ended the story with Jimmy running for help that would be too late. Later she said she wrote the story "for the sake of the last paragraph." As a child she once had to run "a quarter of a mile on a country road to get help for a man who was dying," and she thought that road would "go on forever."

Caroline sent "The Brilliant Leaves" to *Scribner's* magazine, but the editors turned it down. Then she submitted it to the *Virginia Quarterly Review*. But the *Review's* editor, Lambert Davis, also rejected the story, feeling that the ending was not prepared for but due only to chance.

Caroline objected vehemently to his criticism. "'The Brilliant Leaves' is a story of a boy's coming of age, rather suddenly and brutally," she wrote him. "It is also a story in which Fate plays the decisive part." Evelyn was "a young Diana, in love with her own virginity, or shall we just say she is too full of herself." "If she hadn't been too full of herself she would have paid more attention to the boy's love making, wouldn't have gone climbing about on the rocks and wouldn't have been killed," she explained. "Her death comes about through too much joy of animal living."

But Davis would not be swayed by her explanations, and Caroline would not revise her work to meet his expectations. The story fared no better with Red Warren at the *Southern Review*. Finally, *Harper's Bazaar* published it. Caroline declared it was the last story she would ever write.

The story perplexed many readers. Some, like Lambert Davis, disliked the apparently random violence at the end. Others, like Red Warren, felt the story lacked focus. What connection was there between the opening scenes on the porch and the rest of the narrative? If the talk about Sally Mainwaring was to reflect on her niece Evelyn, then perhaps Evelyn was too wild and headstrong for her own good; she brought on her own death because she did not know her limits.

But perhaps Evelyn was not wild enough, or wild in the wrong way. If she had been more like her Aunt Sally, if she had paid more attention to her lover and to the conventions of courtship, then she would not have challenged the cliffs. Instead she chose to do something that young women did not generally do. She dared to act outside the norms of society, and her actions cost her life.

The story of Sally Mainwaring could also reflect on Jimmy. Sally had not been afraid to elope, but her weak-willed suitor allowed himself to be easily frightened away. Jimmy had been no more forceful in his pursuit of Evelyn. He knew the dangers of Bridal Veil Falls but did nothing to talk his girlfriend out of the climb or protect her.

Evelyn died "full of the joy of animal living," Caroline said. That was the danger a woman faced when she took risks, or the wrong kinds of risks. One false step would send the unwary climber hurtling down on the rocks.

Caroline's own footing was no more sure; she felt her life spinning out of control. Just before Christmas she went to Chattanooga and took Nancy shopping. "I leaped straight from Forrest's capture of Murfreesboro into the Christmas frenzy," she said later. "It was almost too much." Throughout the afternoon Caroline apologized to salesclerks and other shoppers. Finally Nancy whispered, "Mama, don't tell them your mind is going. They know it, anyhow."

The frenzy of shopping was mild compared to the weeks that followed. After they "ricocheted between Chattanooga, Merry Mont, Nashville and Washington," Caroline vowed to skip the entire holiday season in the future. "If I have the cash," she said, "I am going into a hospital two weeks before Christmas and emerge only when it is safely over."

But at Merry Mont Caroline realized she had another novel to write. Two aged cousins had moved in with Loulie and Old Miss Carrie: Cousin Mag and Cousin Kitty. Caroline could not believe what was going on in the old gray house. Although Cousin Mag could talk coherently on almost every subject, she believed she was a pea, small enough to roll into a crack in the floor. Cousin Kitty had no such delusions, but she paced the floor all day long, muttering and wringing her hands all the while. "Lord have mercy on me . . . Don't that dog have short legs . . . Lord have mercy on me . . . I told Loulie not to do that . . . Lord have mercy on me," Kitty said over and over again.

When the Tates went to bed after the first day of their visit, Allen put a chair against the door. "I'm not afraid of Cousin Mag," he said, "but I am afraid of Cousin Kitty."

While Mag and Kitty wandered around in imaginary worlds, Caroline's grandmother fought for her independence. Old Miss Carrie ridiculed her daughter Loulie at every opportunity. "If I didn't have any better memory than you have I'd offer myself to an institution," Old Miss Carrie said once.

"I would if I weren't already the head of one," Loulie responded.

It was "all pretty grisly," Caroline said later. "I felt ten years older when

I emerged from the fray." But she decided she could use the experience for a novel called *The Women on the Porch*. The book could explore the relationship between mother and daughter, the way two women struggled for power and control. "It will be pretty Russian," Caroline told a friend. "The two lunatics will furnish the chorus. I'll try to restrain myself when it comes to those lunatics but they are tempting."

First, however, Caroline had to finish *A Morning's Favour*. After the holidays she and Allen settled back at the Lytles' cabin at Monteagle, flat broke and grimly determined to write themselves out of their troubles.

Allen found new inspiration for his family novel, which he renamed *The Fathers*. As soon as he returned to Monteagle, he started writing. Caroline was amazed by his dedication. He displayed all the signs of a serious novelist, she said: "the glazed eye, the withdrawn look, the indifference to all worldly affairs." Soon he was "wallowing in family too," poring over old pictures and letters, muttering to himself all the while, Caroline observed.

But Caroline found it more difficult to get started. She wondered if she really had "the moral courage" to write anything new.

None Shall Look Back was published in February 1937. When Caroline received a copy of the novel, she felt "great indifference, almost repugnance to it." "The book doesn't come off," she said sadly. "It's been too hastily done," she contended. "I had to use every device I ever heard of or could invent—the material I had was so complicated and so resistant to handling."

Caroline had once again used her mother's family history as the basis of her narrative. She created the character of Cally Allard Hobart in the image of her great-great-aunt Cal, Caroline Meriwether Goodlett, who founded the United Daughters of the Confederacy. Susan Allard, like Caroline's great-grandmother Susan Meriwether, was called Mammy Horse. Even Cousin Garrett, the Meriwether kin who freed his slaves and took up silk farming, appeared in the novel.

In fact, Caroline used the same community and many of the same characters she had used in *Penhally*, although she altered some relationships and incidents. She based both Lucy Allard and Lucy Llewellyn on her grandmother; she modeled Fontaine Allard and Ralph Llewellyn after "Grandpa Woodstock," and John Llewellyn and Rives Allard on her grandfather Douglas Meriwether. Also, she created Brackets, the Allard family home, as a composite of Penhally and Mayfield, Ralph Llewellyn's house, a fictional Woodstock. In *None Shall Look Back*, however, Caroline decided to destroy Brackets: Union soldiers burned the mansion to the ground, an incident borrowed from Allen's family history.

Few reviewers noticed the similarities between *Penhally* and *None Shall Look Back,* but, as expected, many reviewers compared the novel to *Gone with the Wind.* Some critics thought *None Shall Look Back* "vastly superior" to Mitchell's novel, but many more found it lacking in power and focus, and badly in need of a sympathetic hero or heroine. "Even the thunder of guns doesn't explain the absence of someone like Scarlett O'Hara," one reviewer said.

Caroline might have pleased the critics more with her original story line: the story of Lucy Allard more closely resembled that of Mitchell's heroine. Both focused on one woman's struggle to bring order out of chaos, to survive by sheer ingenuity and strength of character. But even before *Gone with the Wind* had appeared, Caroline had virtually abandoned the story of Lucy Allard. Perhaps Caroline was afraid such a book might seem trivial, more domestic fiction than serious art. Perhaps she just wanted to test her limits again. Just as she had in *Aleck Maury, Sportsman,* Caroline seemed determined to challenge herself, to write prose not typically female. She crafted a narrative following Rives through the war, mastering the male domain of military strategy she had once thought beyond a woman's ability.

Caroline had agonized over her characterization of Lucy in the final version of the story, and her decisions about her heroine reflected her own gender anxieties. If Max had not insisted otherwise, she would have left the story of Lucy completely unresolved, perhaps because Caroline could not decide what to do with Lucy once she was no longer the focus of her story. What was appropriate? More important, what would others accept as appropriate? Max had certainly influenced Caroline's decision to abandon Lucy when he told her that the novel would not be as interesting once it focused on Lucy alone.

Like Caroline's earlier heroines, Lucy had a creative imagination and intuition sure to be her salvation. She was sensitive to the complex nature of good and evil; she recognized the terrible price of survival, the precarious lives women were forced to live. Lucy even understood her husband's headlong rush into death. Yet like her creator, she often distrusted her own strength and the intuition that enabled her to survive. Creative imagination was not enough, Caroline seemed to say. Or was it? In the end the men who survived were defeated. The women alone had strength to face the future, however bleak it might be.

On close examination Lucy and the other women in the novel were powerful figures. But for reviewers looking for a sentimental heroine, Caroline's women of silent strength were hardly sufficient. And her narrative technique—what Katherine Anne Porter would call the viewpoint of "a disembodied spectator"—confused many readers and diluted the force of the narrative. "One's blood is never stirred to the degree of rushing from chapter to chapter," a reviewer complained. "If it were not for Caroline Gordon's previous successes in fiction-writing, one might say that the author of this book is a better historian than creator of drama."

Caroline accepted the bad reviews with unusual grace. "I was due to get it in the neck this time," she said. Some of the reviews could be "disregarded on the grounds of personal prejudice," she thought: if they did not object to the novel's "ambitious plan," they were responding to Allen's notions of literature, getting even with his criticism of other works. But Caroline admitted there was "solid ground for the complaints." "The scheme is too rigid," she said, "it constricts the imagination." Although pleased with her portrayal of Forrest, she realized her "method" and the desire to make Forrest into "a demigod" had dangers. It was especially difficult to get a catharsis at the end of the story; her book wasn't "human enough." "I think Lucy ought to have been allowed to have a little more life in order to be stricken down more convincingly," she told a friend. "I didn't devote enough space to the people's private lives."

Overall, she decided that the book was "an illwritten thing." "There's writing in it would stop a clock," she told Katherine Anne, "and while it sprawls all over the place it isn't rounded out enough."

Katherine Anne said she felt otherwise. Comparisons to Margaret Mitchell were "too stupid," she told Caroline. "There are whole long passages in your book that are so piercing and so moving it seems to me nothing could be better. And so strong and direct." The characters were not only well "rounded out," they were "as alive to me as if I had known them always," Katherine Anne wrote. Also, "there is an almost intolerable vividness in the landscape and the figures of men going into and coming away from battle." But the book was not about battles or people, Katherine Anne thought. "It seems to me that again your real hero is the same as it was in *Penhally*—the Land."

In her review of the novel for the *New Republic,* Katherine Anne declared that *None Shall Look Back* was "in a great many ways a better book" than *Penhally* or *Aleck Maury, Sportsman*. Caroline felt Katherine Anne understood what she was trying to do better than anyone else, and she appreciated her friend's public and private praise. At times she found herself thinking, "Katherine Anne ought to have treated the subject rather than me."

Ford Madox Ford and John Crowe Ransom also wrote with glowing praise about the novel. Ransom called *None Shall Look Back* "an artistic revolutionary wonder," and Caroline treasured his letter. He said the novel could not be read piecemeal, "the way one trifles with most books." "It feels strange and a little harsh; has not pretty passages in it; has no episodes or complete little stories in it," he wrote; "it is a single unit, stricter than anything I know in novels off-hand" and "many times as powerful" as *Gone with the Wind*. "The old winter felt is off to you," he concluded. "I call you a Great Artist."

In his review of *None Shall Look Back*, Ford called Caroline "the most mysterious of writers," making much of her classical training: her writing was "as quiet" as that of Tibullus, better than that of Tolstoy, he wrote. Like the *Iliad*, the book was "most of all a landscape," he said; Caroline remained "mysterious, unimpassioned, almost impartial as the tragic destiny unrolls itself." "You cannot say that she writes like a man— or, for the matter of that, like a woman," Ford wrote. "It is as if she were Pallas Athene, suspended above the Grecian hosts, knowing what destiny decrees, only at moments of agonized uncertainty intervening on behalf of a hero . . . watching." The effect of the book was cumulative, he said: "It is only when you have finished the reading that you realize that you have been present at a very horrid affair and one that you will not soon forget."

His praise embarrassed yet pleased Caroline. She told Ford that he had let his imagination run away with him. "I fear the book lacks that Olympian ease you ascribe to it," she wrote. "I think it is a pretty sweaty book, but I am proud to have evoked such beautiful sentences from you."

Perhaps to comfort herself, Caroline began to dwell on the difference between popular novels and fine art. She realized her book would never have the popular appeal of Mitchell's opus. "Whether it is good or bad, it takes an effort for the reader to follow it," she admitted.

When a friend wrote that the battle scenes in *None Shall Look Back* "did not show what war is like but what war is," Caroline began to compare her novel to those of Henry James and Tolstoy. "People don't want to make an effort to see a thing, they just want to be told what it is like," she said. "Reading a great novel like *War and Peace* is an experience like falling in love or breaking your leg or going to war. One doesn't care for *War and Peace* as bed-time reading."

Max Perkins told Caroline not to worry about the bad reviews. Although most reviewers "simply muffed it," Max thought the "tone of many of the reviews" revealed Caroline's growing reputation. "They all take you as a writer of importance, as one from whom great things are expected," he said. And despite the competition from *Gone with the Wind* and a handful of other novels about the Civil War recently published, *None Shall Look Back* was selling well, in fact better than any of Caroline's other novels: about thirty-five hundred copies in the first month after publication.

Max urged Caroline to finish *A Morning's Favour* in time for fall publication. "I do not want you to be hurried," he said, "but I think that at the very worst, *None Shall Look Back* has given you a strong foundation."

How many novels does it take to "make a foundation"? Caroline wondered. "Do I really have to work harder than anybody else or is it just my persecution complex?" But she accepted the challenge and began writing furiously.

Writers are like sharecroppers, Caroline said. Publishers "furnish us and if we don't pay out we have to hunt a new home." And sometimes, even before they had the chance to "pay out," writers, like sharecroppers, had to move on. Caroline had hoped to stay in Monteagle until July. Even when she had to do the cooking and housework by herself, she thought the place was more convenient than Benfolly. And the mountain was beautiful in the spring, blooming with Japanese quince, jonquils, laurel, and violets.

By the end of April, however, the Tates had to return to Benfolly because relatives of the Lytles wanted the cabin. Caroline found the Benfolly hill greener than ever, the air sweet with wisteria and locust trees. But it took ten days to clear the debris, dirt, and dust out of Benfolly; Caroline lost four pounds in the process. Then the cook shot and killed her lover. Caroline replaced her with a young girl she hoped was not "so fast on the trigger." Soon the visitors began arriving: first Ford, Janice, and Janice's sister-in-law, Wally Tworkov, working as Ford's secretary.

Caroline had promised Ford and Janice that she would arrange things at Benfolly so that everyone could work without distractions, and she was true to her word. Within a week they had "shaken down into a routine," Caroline said: no conversation before breakfast, work all morning, swimming in the afternoon, gossiping on the porch in the evening.

Time and space were quite elastic, Caroline discovered with amazement. Even after Nancy arrived with a friend from school, there were enough beds and enough work areas for everyone. Caroline did much of the cooking, but she still found time to write five or six pages a day on her novel: she kept "one hand on the kitchen stove and one on the typewriter," she said later.

Then an unexpected visitor arrived at Benfolly: it was "the strangest visitation we ever had," Caroline said. She and Allen were standing in front of the house one afternoon, inspecting the flowers, when they heard a car stop at the bottom of the hill. They watched as a young man got out of the car and went to relieve himself. "Defense d'uriner," they nearly shouted. As the young man climbed up the driveway, they eyed him sternly. He was tall and slim, dressed in dirty white linens and badly knotted moccasins. With pale skin and dark curly hair, he looked like a choirboy or a matinee idol. When he stood before Allen and muttered something about Ford, they asked him in.

"Something made us treat him more gently," Caroline said later. Soon they realized that the young man who answered to the nickname "Cal" was a struggling young poet named Robert Lowell, the grandnephew of James Russell Lowell. After Cal had quarreled with his parents, a family friend suggested he go away for a while. Cal had heard Ford lecture in Boston, and Ford had suggested he study writing in the South, so Cal followed Ford to Tennessee. "Imagine one coming all the way from Boston to sit at Southern feet," Caroline quipped.

The Tates put Cal up overnight, then sent him to Nashville, suggesting he study under John Crowe Ransom. But he came back after a short while and asked to stay at Benfolly. Too polite to refuse, Allen lied and said they had no place to put him unless he wanted to pitch a tent on the lawn. Not easily dissuaded, Cal purchased an olive green umbrella tent from Sears Roebuck and established himself on the front lawn, staying several months.

Cal thought the Tates were "stately yet bohemian, leisurely yet dedicated." Although Allen thought "the Lowell boy" might become something of a nuisance, Caroline decided the nineteen-year-old was "such a nice boy"—"the handiest" she "ever knew." He would drive her over to Merry Mont, haul the buttermilk, even "flit" the dining room: much more than the other guests at Benfolly would think of doing.

Only Ford really objected to the earnest young man's presence. He was "enraged at being taken literally," Caroline said. For a while Ford even refused to speak to Cal at the dinner table. But Caroline would not tolerate such behavior, and in no uncertain terms she told Ford to behave. From then on, Ford acknowledged Cal's presence, although he said little more than "Young man."

The summer heat scorched all the land around Benfolly, and then the cistern ran dry. Since Allen had to bring in all their water, he became quite testy about how his guests used it. Ford decided he could help, so he built a dew pond: a washtub set in the front yard, filled with twigs. According to Ford, the twigs would get moist in the morning, then the water would drip into the basin for use later in the day. But the basin and twigs remained as dry as the cistern.

As the temperatures rose, tempers grew short. Ford declared that "consorting with the Tates" was like "living with intellectual desperadoes" on the Sargasso Sea. Caroline did not think living with Ford was any easier. He had "insomnia, indigestion, and gout to boot," and he spent many days confined to the middle level of Benfolly. Only Janice's help made Ford bearable, Caroline thought.

Despite the heat and hardships, the manuscript pages and works of art piled up steadily. Janice painted when she wasn't caring for Ford; Allen worked on *The Fathers*. Ford wrote his history of world literature, dictating a thousand words each day to Wally, who was, Caroline thought, "a sweet child and very agreeable." Cal Lowell sat in his tent when he wasn't running errands, writing what he thought were "grimly unromantic poems" and reading Andrew Marvell aloud to get the scansion.

Caroline worked on her novel about the poor whites, although she was tempted to lay the book aside. An editor at Houghton Mifflin had approached her with a new project, a popular history of the Cherokee nation. Yet Caroline knew Max would never release her from her contract, so she turned down the assignment. By early summer she had finished nearly two-thirds of her novel and had chosen a new title, *The Garden of Adonis*, taken from James G. Frazer's *The Golden Bough*. The title referred to vegetation rites honoring the Greek god Adonis. "The women put earth in pots and plant wheat and other grain but the plants, . . . in pots and not in the earth itself, wither and have to be thrown out," Caroline explained. She thought the title appropriate since the Antaean theme ran through all her books: the land was a source of strength, and those who lost touch with it usually withered and died.

Caroline developed this theme through two parallel stories of illicit love. The first story focused on Ote Mortimer and Idelle Sheeler, two tenants at Hanging Tree, the farm of Ben Allard. The second story involved the affair of Ben's daughter, Letty Allard, and Jim Carter, a married man.

Caroline emphasized in each story how her characters had lost touch with their agrarian roots. Letty had grown up at Hanging Tree, but she knew little about her home and cared even less. Although her father was having financial troubles, Letty did not scruple to take all the money he could give to buy clothes and visit the city. Throughout the novel Caroline stressed Letty's shallow nature and self-absorption: she was a "garden of Adonis" in miniature.

Letty's lover, Jim Carter, apparently knew and understood more about life at Hanging Tree after a brief visit. Caroline devoted a great deal of the novel to a description of Jim's childhood in the country, a childhood very much like that of Aleck Maury, devoted to sport. But Caroline spared little sympathy in her characterization of Jim: he was an Aleck Maury gone wrong. Forced to abandon country pleasures for life as an advertising writer, Jim had little moral fiber. He would spend the rest of his life blaming women for his troubles: first his mother, who insisted he take a job at age seventeen; then his wife and her family, who expected him to solve their business problems. Even though he recognized the vital rhythms of life at Hanging Tree, he would not respect them.

Caroline obviously intended the story of Letty and Jim to reflect on her original narrative of Ote and Idelle. At first the life and love of poor white tenants appeared to have an advantage over that of the more wealthy city dwellers. Although Ote had been away in Detroit for several years working in a factory, he had not lost his love for or understanding of the land. Idelle came from shiftless stock, but like Ote, she was industrious, destined, it would seem, to make something of herself. Caroline underscored the pastoral innocence of Ote and Idelle's love, their respect for the land and willingness to work for their future. But ultimately Caroline revealed the shallowness of their love. When Idelle found herself pregnant, Ote would resort to violence. Desperate for money to marry, he would destroy crops and in the end would kill his boss and friend, Ben Allard.

Caroline continued to develop her fictional family connection in this novel. She made Ben a neighbor and relative of Chance Llewellyn, and explained that the Mortimers were related to Jerry O'Donnell, a character who had fought alongside John Llewellyn and spent the rest of his life living near Penhally. But Caroline did not trouble to work out inconsistencies. Both Fanny Allard and Lucy Llewellyn had been modeled on Caroline's grandmother.

As she wrote *The Garden of Adonis,* Caroline remembered incidents she had heard about while working as a reporter: how young people in Chattanooga got drunk and drove across the Georgia border to get married. After checking out the legal limits, she had Jim marry in just that manner.

Caroline worked diligently, trying to make her July deadline for the book. After a while, her brain felt "a little like a muffin," she said. When she wasn't wrestling with her own writing, she was helping another writer. Brainard "Lon" Cheney, a newspaper reporter from Nashville, had completed his first novel. Caroline went over his manuscript sentence by sentence that summer. She thought he had talent.

Although she insisted that her "method of never stopping work" entailed "less suffering" than others' attempts to work in spurts, Caroline began to think she needed more time to complete her novel. Ford and other friends wrote to Max Perkins, asking him to delay publication, but Max said the book had already been announced for the fall list and should not be withdrawn.

Caroline was not pleased, but once again she did not try to argue with him. Instead, she wrote an article for the *Chattanooga News* about southern fiction and subtitled it "Hasty Writing No Spur to True Art." Although she never referred to her own situation, she must have hoped Max would read the article and realize the error of his ways.

She began her article with the story of "a certain metropolitan critic" about to publish a novel he had spent "almost a year" writing. "Knowing the kind of life that young metropolitan critics lead I realized how valuable—in dollars and cents—were the hours that Mr. X must have devoted to the writing of his novel," Caroline wrote. But she stifled her desire to applaud, remembering "another man, a half-legendary figure" who lived in "the pine barrens of South Georgia" and raised free-ranging razorback hogs.

According to Caroline, that farmer had a visit from a northerner who did not realize "that the razorback produces the most delicious of all bacon and a well-flavored though small ham, to boot." The northern visitor urged the Georgian to "get rid of all the razorbacks and buy Poland China." It would save time, he said, but "the Georgian shook his head and spat. 'Stranger,' he said, 'what's time to a hog?'"

According to Caroline, the southern novelist was like the razorback hogs: "he has a wide territory to range over, so wide that the metropolitan critics are often bewildered by the many different pictures that are emerging." Also "the Southern novelist, the regional novelist in particular, is often accused of burying himself in the past." But for the southern novelist to "survive for posterity," he will have to "emulate the razorback hog and wallow still deeper in the mire of his nostalgia," Caroline insisted.

"It will not hurt him to spend whole days, months, years—if the exigencies of modern publishing will allow it—brooding on the past," she insisted. "If the Southern novelist is far-sighted he will continue to emulate the razorback hog. He will turn his back on time and range farther and root deeper into the past until he has turned up all the heritage which was plowed under so recklessly and so wantonly in Reconstruction times." The southern writer was "in a peculiarly fortunate situation" because "he has something to write about." Americans "manufacture pasts with a rapidity which makes Europeans dizzy," she wrote: "our past has, in a sense, been taken from us." But most of all, she insisted, a writer needed time, time "to loaf and invite his wilful, razorback soul."

But that was time Caroline would not get. Soon even the organized chaos of the Benfolly ménage had to end: Caroline, Allen, and Ford had agreed to teach at another two-week school of writing at Olivet College in Michigan. Caroline hated to go. She still had several chapters left to write on *The Garden of Adonis,* and she thought teaching for the Olivet school was "like being put under glass and having all the air pumped out of your lungs." But the Tates desperately needed the money, so Caroline packed up her manuscript with everything else—including Nancy. "She is beginning to be a little bitter about being parked off somewhere away from her parents," Caroline admitted.

Once they arrived at Olivet, Caroline worked nearly nonstop, finishing her novel between sessions and after hours. Katherine Anne Porter arrived toward the end of the first week to give some of the lectures, but Caroline had little time to talk to her or anyone. Finally, on July 28, Caroline mailed *The Garden of Adonis* to Scribner's. It was rotten, she thought, but she didn't care. She vowed to take a long rest. "I can't keep this up," she said. "I write more and more like the late John Galsworthy."

When Caroline, Allen, and Nancy returned to Benfolly in August, Katherine Anne went with them. Katherine Anne had been promising to visit Benfolly for a long time, but in August 1937 she was not paying a visit as much as making an escape. She could not return to her apartment in New York City: Gene Pressley was waiting for her there. They had been married for several years, but Katherine Anne was tired of him. "If I mean to do any work, I have to renounce the world, the flesh, and embrace my Demon in poverty, chastity and obedience," Katherine Anne had proudly proclaimed.

Caroline was not fooled. She knew Katherine Anne could never be satisfied with a long-term commitment. She "cast Gene off, with a twist of the wrist, as it were," Caroline observed; "I'm surprised he lasted as long as he did." But that did not mean Katherine Anne would actually settle down and start writing. She was merely ready for another adventure, another conquest perhaps. What would Katherine Anne do when she no longer had "any ties to sever"? "Will she be able to work then?" Caroline doubted it.

Still, Caroline was glad to see Katherine Anne. They both pampered themselves: Caroline took two naps a day and read detective stories to recover her "moral health," and Katherine Anne reveled in domestic pleasures. Between playing with the cats and milking the cow, Katherine Anne went on a canning binge. She made apple butter, mint liqueur, and elderberry wine; she preserved whole peaches and brandied peaches, "and would have brandied and preserved bushels more if I had provided her with them," Caroline said later—"all this, of course, partly out of domestic passions, partly out of charitable concern for our welfare and a good part I wickedly believe just to get out of work."

Katherine Anne thought Benfolly was "an island of peace and vast green landscape," but she knew Caroline could not enjoy the place as much as she did. Caroline had the daily responsibility of keeping everything running and everyone in his or her place. Allen helped: he ironed his own shirts and sometimes Caroline's dresses as well, and he handled all the family finances. But Caroline had to tend to the garden and cooking and hired help, and Katherine Anne appreciated how the demands of daily life could make Caroline irritable. When Caroline lost her temper over something Ida, the cook, did, Katherine Anne admired her forbearance. If Ida "had belonged to me," Katherine Anne said later, "there were times when she would have thought Ole Miz Tate's temper was like the angels in heaven." "You *are* a kind of saint, Caroline," Katherine Anne said, "one of the more turbulent ones."

Katherine Anne got no writing done during the five weeks she stayed at Benfolly, but Caroline could not afford to stay idle that long. By mid-August she had already begun to plan her next novel. At first she thought she would write the novel about her grandmother and Aunt Loulie, which she had titled *The Women on the Porch*. "I am really a sort of reporter of my family," Caroline told Katherine Anne.

She worked up a plot synopsis colored with her own experience. The fictional mother, Ellen Archbold, "did not scruple to interfere in [her daughter] Anne's life, separating her from the man she loved," Caroline wrote in her notes. "Anne has enough imagination to know what sort of person she would have been if her mother had let her alone—she feels that her mother robbed her of life when she was too young to fight." Caroline decided the novel would focus on the daughter's dilemma one winter. Anne would return home to care for her aging mother, and gradually she would assert her power over her mother. But when Ellen died, Anne would realize "that she has lost," Caroline observed, "for in order to kill her mother she had to destroy herself."

Caroline sent the synopsis to Max, and he liked it well enough, but he persuaded her to try another historical novel, one set in Cherokee times. Although Caroline had no idea what she would call the novel, and hardly more than a glimmer of what the book might be about, she readily agreed to try. She considered it "a good omen" that Katherine Anne was visiting: she was "the great great granddaughter of Daniel Boone," Caroline told Max. At least, Katherine Anne liked to pretend she was somehow related to that great pioneer.

In keeping with her ancestry, Katherine Anne soon left Benfolly on another adventure. A family wedding in New Orleans with a six-piece Mexican band lured her away, but not before she met a young man named Albert Erskine, who stopped at Benfolly for a brief visit. While completing an M.A. degree at Louisiana State University, Albert was serving as the business manager of the *Southern Review*. He was twenty-six; Katherine Anne was forty-seven. But Katherine Anne could not resist flirting and paid no attention to their age differences. Albert was enchanted with her husky voice and confident air: he overlooked her white hair. Late at night, long after the Tates had gone to bed, Albert and Katherine Anne sat on the porch overlooking the river and talked.

Overhearing snatches of their conversation, Allen worried. All the signs were right: Katherine Anne would not renounce the world and the flesh, but leave one lover and acquire another. It was all part of the pattern of her life, but still Allen felt uneasy. Even Katherine Anne could not expect romance with a man young enough to be her son—or could she?

Although neither Allen nor Caroline realized it for a while, Katherine Anne and Albert carried on their romantic interlude by mail after they left Benfolly for New Orleans and Baton Rouge, respectively.

Soon after Katherine Anne had left, Caroline began reading proof for *The Garden of Adonis*. When she finished, she settled down for a quiet autumn of puttering around the house. Every morning, she luxuriated in an hour's work in the yard, planting wisteria and late vegetables, raking, and carrying manure from one place to another—"a very soothing occupation after writing fiction," she told a friend. After a while she felt thoroughly rested for the first time in four years, "a sort of super feeling," like "a cat that has just been thoroughly wormed."

Caroline was only mildly curious to see *The Garden of Adonis;* at times she forgot all about it as she slowly reacquainted herself with Indian lore and the history of the pioneer period. She began by reading the journal of Dr. Thomas Walker, one of the first explorers of "Kaintuck." Then she went on to read works by Adair and Timberlake.

As she read, she reflected on a curious coincidence: Castle Hill, a Meriwether estate near Charlottesville, Virginia, had been the starting point for both Dr. Walker's exploration of Kentucky and Meriwether Lewis's exploration of the West. The fact appealed to Caroline: it elevated her family mythology to epic proportions.

After several months of reading, Caroline began to formulate a narrative line, but she hesitated to spell anything out in a synopsis. She wanted to give herself time, time to brood on the past. All she knew for sure was that she wanted to "get the Indian side of it" into the narrative. She planned to use something of the story of John Sevier, a "frontier hero," who "was a perfect Attila to the Indians," and she thought she might have "a boy captured and brought up by the Cherokee nation." But her main character would be "a frontiersman who settles on the Cumberland," she told Max.

Once again Caroline would emphasize the importance of the land. The pioneers "would endure hardships to establish themselves on a piece of land, then move on to land that was no richer," she said. "And from the time they began to pour over the mountains most of them thought of land as something to be bought and sold, not to be lived on." She told Max she thought she might call the book *Beyond the Mountains*.

Before she began the novel, Caroline found herself writing a new short story. She got the idea for "Frankie and Thomas and Bud Asbury" from her brother Bill, who had moved back into the neighborhood to farm. During one of his infrequent visits to Benfolly, Bill told her about "Mister Lee Jones, the confirmed drunkard who [was] a genius at firing tobacco." Once, when Bill's wife was away, Bill brought Jones home to take care of his dark-fired tobacco. According to Bill, Lee Jones "took a fancy" to the black cook, Frankie. When Edward, Frankie's husband, "objected strenuously," Bill finally had to choose "between genius and Frankie," and he "took up a tobacco stick and told Lee he would make knots on his head if he didn't go on down the big road." "You'll regret this," Lee went off yelling. "You don't know how to fire tobacco. You'll ruin your whole crop!"

Caroline used Bill's story with few changes; she even used her brother as the first-person narrator. She switched some of the names: Lee Jones became "Bud Asbury," Edward became "Tom Doty," but Frankie's name remained unchanged. "Frankie was well named," Caroline wrote; "She and Tom were just like the niggers in the song. They were willing to work but loving came first." Caroline included the character of her grandmother, called "Miss Jinny" in the story, for additional comic relief, and she told the story simply, indicating in the first paragraph that the story would end with the crop being ruined. But by using the first-person narrator, "Jim," Caroline explored the ironies and problems of the situation. In the end Jim chased Bud off the property, and by doing so, destroyed his crop of prime leaf tobacco. He knew he had to do the noble deed, to protect the honor of a woman and the sanctity of a marriage, even if that woman was "that yellow wife of Tom Doty," but he still felt uncomfortable, unsure. "A man has to fight if somebody tries to take his woman," Jim said at the end of the story. "It struck me as a funny business. Always has."

Caroline first published the story of "Frankie and Thomas and Bud Asbury" in the *Southern Review;* later she would change the title of the story to "Her Quaint Honor." It was a gentle, comic look at the relationships between whites and blacks, men and women, in the modern South.

In the late fall *The Garden of Adonis* appeared, but it garnered little critical attention. A writer in the *Saturday Review* said the novel was "thoughtful, intelligent, restrained; but . . . never quite good enough to be memorable." Caroline had not worked out the parallel plot lines, he said. Also, the novel failed to reach "tragic depths of passion and defeat." Ultimately, "technical excellence in the details is made an unconscious substitute for the organic demands of art of the first order."

Augusta Tucker in the *New York Times Book Review* called the book "a provocative study" as a "sociological document," but she thought Caroline failed as a novelist. The characters did not come to life, she said. Ote's murder of Ben was "a Faulknerian twist, but without the Faulknerian wrist," and the entire ensemble little more than "an unstable conglomeration of boring and irresponsible people." Caroline was "best at old men," Tucker said, "but she can only tell you what happened to them, and never, with that indefinable insight, permit you to *know* them as they once were."

Caroline ignored the reviews: she expected the novel would "deal a sad blow to what little reputation" she had. But when Scribner's seemed to take little interest in promoting the novel, she got angry. Max said "the trade" was "all against books about share croppers or poor whites." Why, then, did he press her to finish? she asked.

For a while even the Scribner salesmen seemed to be working against her. They were supposed to send copies of *The Garden of Adonis* to a local bookstore for Caroline to autograph; instead, they sent copies of Ernest Hemingway's new book, *To Have and Have Not*. Caroline said she would just as soon autograph Ernest's book: "I seem always to fall into the troughs made by these leviathans like Ernest—and Margaret," she said. But a special-delivery shipment got the correct books to the store in time.

Caroline's friends tried to reassure her that the novel had merit despite its faults. Katherine Anne called *Adonis* "a good bold live book." "The first fourth equals anything you ever did," she said. "There was the pure desperation of hopeless poverty in that simple sounding narrative."

Robert Penn Warren agreed. "When the novel is in the country, it's absolutely at your best level," he wrote. "The whole handling of the story of the croppers is very strong and moving, and the countryside is rendered as well as possible." Only the sections that took place in town, the story of Letty Allard and Jim Carter, had "a certain sketchiness" and should have been developed further, he said. "Were they pressing you for publication?"

Caroline would never find much good in the novel. The people came "nearer being real characters than any" others she had created, she said. Still, she thought the book was a failure, a failure because she had been pressed for time. But perhaps even time would not have helped. Once again the struggle between the Gordon and Meriwether views colored *The Garden of Adonis,* but this time Caroline could not sort out her sympathies in the fictional world. In turn, Caroline embraced and rejected both perspectives of her family mythology. Jim Carter, the Aleck Maury/ Gordon figure, was threatened by the aggressive women aligned with the Meriwether connection; yet he was also a dangerous threat to them because he was fundamentally shallow and selfish. Caroline attempted to portray Ben Allard and Ote Mortimer as men sensitive to the natural world, as men also threatened by women like Letty and Idelle who were out of control. But she also hinted at the terrible problems Letty and Idelle faced: problems brought on by men like Ben and Ote.

Although Caroline attempted to weave the novel together by moving back and forth between the characters, she never clearly established her perspective on the action. Ben Allard was the only link between the two stories, but Caroline did not use Ben to reflect on what had happened. Once again, she created a novel that, when read from a conventional, moralistic point of view, seemed to suggest that the irrational nature of women threatened both men and the overall state of society. But in the undercurrent of women's concerns, Caroline almost turned such conventions upside down. Perhaps the destruction of society was not due so much to the irrational power of women, but the unrestrained, unreflective passions of men?

Caroline figured that her years of turmoil had ended with the publication of *The Garden of Adonis*. The novel, which had taken nearly five years to write, clearly showed the suffering she had endured during that time, the private cup of fury she had been forced to drink time and again. The world of *The Garden of Adonis* was in chaos; even the land offered no hope of regeneration, parched by drought, seemingly forgotten by a capricious deity.

But Caroline's turmoil did not end. Instead, tragedy struck her family again. On November 12, 1937, Cath Wilds, Caroline's first cousin, committed suicide in New York City. She turned on the gas in her apartment and left a note for her lover that said she "just couldn't stand any more." Only twenty-seven years old, Cath was the third of Caroline's cousins to end her life violently.

The entire Meriwether connection was devastated. And Caroline felt terribly guilty, full of self-reproach. She remembered one of the last times she had spoken to Cath. It had been almost a year earlier; Cath had been living in Chattanooga, seeing Harold Cash, a promising young sculptor who was separated from his wife. Because people in Chattanooga were beginning to talk about the affair, Caroline had urged Cath to go to New York. Looking back, Caroline wondered if she had done the right thing.

After Cath and Harold had moved to New York, Caroline had urged Ford and others to look in on her cousin. When Cath found a job in the religion department of Harper's, Caroline had rejoiced. But she had owed Cath a letter since August, and the thought tormented her. When the family found a note to Allen in Cath's effects, Caroline's guilt was complete. Cath complained about Caroline's long silence, urging Allen not to let Caroline give him a bad opinion of Harold. "I talked too harshly to her," Caroline decided.

Thanksgiving was quiet and sad. The Tate family went to visit Lon and Fannie Cheney in Nashville and lost Caroline's dachshund, Vili. Caroline and Allen walked up and down the streets near their apartment calling out "Vili, Vili," and later they even put up advertisements, but the little dog was never found, which only added to Caroline's sorrow.

Then in December Caroline received good news. Officials from the Women's College of the University of North Carolina at Greensboro wrote Allen about a new position they were creating for a professor of creative writing, and they invited him to bring Caroline along with him. After a visit to the campus, and some negotiations, both Caroline and Allen received offers to teach at Greensboro. They would be hired at the rank of professor in the Department of English. For twenty-four hundred dollars each per year, they would have to teach only one class apiece each semester, Allen's on poetry and literary criticism, Caroline's on the novel.

Caroline was ecstatic. Although she called Greensboro "a frightful place," many of the locations she wanted to use in her novel were close by: the French Broad River, the Yadkin, the battlefield of Guilford Courthouse. She would start her book in the "Old Watauga section" of the state. She could use the excellent collection of material on the pioneer period at the university library in Chapel Hill, and the teaching would not interfere too much with her work. It might even help, she thought: for the first time in years, she would not have to worry about money.

This was her "first big chance" to write a truly good book, Caroline told Max. "I'd rather be in North Carolina right now than anywhere else." It was "just the kind of job every impecunious writer would like to have," she crowed. Perhaps the cup of fury had been emptied for the last time.

⤳ 1938–1944

Caroline had been eager to take the job in Greensboro, but as she settled down to work on her novel during the first half of 1938, she found herself dwelling on an observation the naturalist François André Michaux made during his 1793 journey to America. According to Michaux, "the long habit of a wandering and idle life" prevented the first inhabitants of Kentucky and Tennessee from "enjoying the fruits of their labours." Caroline agreed and decided to use the quote as a headnote for her novel. But it was also an appropriate commentary on her own life at that time.

In fact, Caroline's experience in North Carolina was marked by tension between settling down and moving on. Perhaps because she knew they would not live there long, she did not name their first home in Greensboro, a red brick house with fake colonial columns at 112 Arden Place. But she threw herself into teaching with great enthusiasm, even offering her help to would-be writers outside class.

Allen took another path. He figured he had been hired more for appearances than for teaching, and he resolved to "work the racket" as long as possible. He cultivated his reputation as a writer and, for the first time in years, worked on his physique, exercising every afternoon at the YMCA. But he put little effort into teaching, and privately he sneered at the people and students of Greensboro.

Greensboro was a nearly perfect place to write—for Allen. Vowing to finish his novel *The Fathers* during the spring or summer at the latest, Allen spent every morning secluded in his study, but Caroline could find time only for reading and planning. Most of her energy was spent on teaching and smoothing the way for Allen's work: even the slightest disturbance put him off his writing.

By May Caroline had prepared an outline of her novel, but before she could start writing, Allen decided they had to move. Their academic responsibilities ended at commencement, and Allen did not want to spend any more time than necessary in Greensboro. Yet he had no intention of going to Benfolly: he could not write there, he said.

Instead, they would go to Cornwall, Connecticut. Mark and Dorothy Van Doren found them a house on a lake to rent for the summer. It was primitive—no electricity or running water—but Allen thought he could finish the novel there.

Caroline was eager to do whatever it took to help Allen finish his book. But she hated the way Allen was "jerking" them around. "I am getting so sick of packing up and moving I sometimes think I will go out to Merry Mont and curl up around some tree trunk," she wrote in one letter. Although Caroline was relieved "not to have to open Benfolly and get it running this summer," that did not make their migrations any easier. "I'm so tired of moving," she exclaimed.

Allen finished *The Fathers* at Cornwall. But Caroline did not even attempt to write: she thought it was "too risky to have two novelists going at it at the same time in one house." In September the Tates returned to Greensboro, to a new house, actually a furnished six-room cottage, on Winston Road just outside town. Caroline loved the place. She called it the Gadget House and declared that it was "the most comfortable of all the houses we've ever lived in." She had a feeling they wouldn't stay there long, but she told Katherine Anne that if they "ever did stay anywhere this would be a good spot to stay in." The house was surrounded by a small forest of mimosa and fig trees, a magnificent array of pomegranates, quince, gardenias, roses, petunias, marigolds, and snapdragons. Caroline planned to relax in the garden when she wasn't writing or teaching.

On September 23, the day Nancy turned thirteen, *The Fathers* was published. Caroline thought the novel was quite good. Nancy always thought it was remarkable, "one of the best novels ever written," and much better than most of her mother's novels. "Mama just uses the time shift business in her novels because she never can get anything straight," Nancy declared after reading *Penhally*.

In *The Fathers* Allen told the story of the Buchan family through the reminiscences of Lacy Buchan, a sixty-five-year-old doctor retired from practice. The narrative had three sections: "Pleasant Hill," "The Crisis," and "The Abyss." From the vantage point of 1910, Lacy tried to make sense of his family's history and his own relationship to George Posey, the brother-in-law whom he loved. Just as Caroline had used family myth as the basis of her fiction, Allen explored his own genealogy in the novel. And like Caroline, Allen focused on the tension between pioneers and aristocrats in southern society. His tale covered the years immediately before and after the Civil War. But there the similarity to Caroline's fiction ended. Allen's writing focused on more abstract intellectual concerns; his first-person narrative depended not on scene painting and character development but on interior monologues and symbolism.

Both Caroline and Allen were ecstatic over the book's sale. The prepublication sale of five thousand copies covered the advances Allen had received; all subsequent sales gave them hope of a year free from debt. The critical response was favorable, but Allen said he couldn't take the compliments too seriously: he just didn't consider himself a novelist.

With Allen settled Caroline could resume writing, and on October 27 she began her novel about the Indians and pioneers. Although eager to return to her typewriter, she still found it difficult. Life was "just starting in on one long, hard, damned job after another," she said. "The jobs are hard enough, but the starting is the worst."

She called the novel *Weep for the Mountains*. The title referred to the Old Testament book of Jeremiah, chapter 9, verse 10, in which God told the Israelites to weep and wail for the mountains, to lament for "the habitations of the wilderness," because "they are burned up so that none can pass through them, neither can men hear the voice of the cattle; both the fowl of the heavens and the beast are fled, they are gone." In Caroline's narrative the mountains and the wilderness of Tennessee and Kentucky, like the Promised Land of Israel, would be laid waste because the pioneers did not respect one another and the land they had been given.

Caroline had summarized the story for Max several months earlier, although she did not want to work out too many of the details, fearing the book would "harden" on her. Her hero, Orion Outlaw, would travel from Salisbury, North Carolina, to the Old Watauga section of Tennessee with his parents, his wife, Margaret, and a younger brother, Archy. On the way Archy would be captured by the Cherokees; in time he would become a "linguister."

Adopted by the tribe, Archy would go on the warpath with Dragging Canoe, a great Cherokee chief. Meanwhile, Rion would take his wife on to Old Watauga, clearing land to build a home, becoming one of the leading men in the valley and an accomplished Indian fighter. But his prowess would not protect his family: two of his children would die after an attack by a band of marauding Indians, and his wife would go insane out of fear and despair. After she died, Rion would marry again, and the settlers' problems would continue.

Caroline was not entirely sure how to end the novel. She wanted to stop the story shortly after the deaths of Archy and Dragging Canoe: Rion would listen to his neighbors talk about the new land farther west, "The Cumberland," and decide that it was time to move on. "Aye," he would say, "we'll have everything we want. In Cumberland."

Such an ending would illustrate the tragedy of the Cherokee nation as well as the unsettled, insatiable life of the pioneers, Caroline thought. But she might also end the book with Rion realizing with despair that he no longer had any enthusiasm for new lands. "He may realize that he is done for and so may stay" in Watauga, perhaps as his wife goes on with another man, Caroline told Max.

Yet whatever ending she used, Caroline knew the book would resolve "into a study of sin." After participating in the massacre of several Cherokee chiefs who had voluntarily given themselves up as hostages, Rion would become a moral leper. Failing both his wives and his community, he would forsake "his very self and so [come] to grief," she wrote.

The only problems Caroline foresaw concerned the double plot and historical framework. By telling the story through two brothers, she hoped to revise the settlers' perspective on the Cherokees. Archy would be "Rion Outlaw's other self," someone to "bridge the gap between the Indians and whites." Yet Caroline feared Archy's story might weaken the book's structure. And to use Dragging Canoe's death as the climax, she would have to "kill him off" twelve years early and change other incidents as well. She worried such "historical inaccuracy" would "make a disagreeable impression."

Max's only concern, however, was that Caroline include "some sort of a love story." "It ought to be quite a prominent one," he wrote. "I realize that you would have women in the book necessarily, but you must have one at any rate what used to be called a 'heroine.'"

His comments annoyed Caroline. "You can't expect a *sentimental* heroine from *me,*" she responded. "A sentimental heroine doesn't fit in with my conception of the book." But there would be "a love interest," she told him: either one of Rion's wives, Margaret or Polly, would "fill the role of a heroine all right." Just as Rion and Archy were paired as opposites, Margaret and Polly would represent two extremes. Margaret belonged "to the old, conservative order"; she had a horror of the wilderness and the wandering life, whereas Polly would be "a girl of true pioneer stock," eager to give herself up to the wilderness and to the "handsome Indian bucks," she wrote. The novel's conflict would revolve around Rion's struggle with his wives as well as his own personal demons. "The pioneer spirit" would betray Rion, making him "a wanderer whether he stays in the Watauga valley or goes on moving for the rest of his life," Caroline told Max.

Caroline's plans for the women satisfied Max. But from the beginning she was more interested in the men in the novel. All fall and winter Caroline worked at bringing Daniel Boone, Rion Outlaw, and his family to life. She found it especially convenient to be in North Carolina. Early in the fall, she went to Salisbury, about sixty miles away, and tried to "get hold of those Boones." She also explored the old "Trading Path" crossing the Yadkin river at Salisbury, "once the artery of commerce for the continent," Caroline said. Over the Thanksgiving holiday, she explored the area around Kingsport, Tennessee, including Long Island on the South Fork River, where Daniel Boone had begun his journey through the Cumberland Gap. By December Caroline had gotten a good understanding of the local geography, and she had written three long chapters. "Lousier chapters I never read," she declared, but she kept writing. By the following spring, she had finished two more chapters, although she did not feel as if she was making any progress, and she feared her book would be "one of the dullest novels ever published."

She put aside her work for two writers' conferences during the spring. Caroline hated the one held in Savannah over Easter: the conference came near killing them, she said, and they never got paid for their efforts. But a smaller affair held in Greensboro in early March was a great success. Ford Madox Ford and Janice Biala came down to visit the Tates so that Ford could speak at the two-day conference.

When Caroline first saw "the Master," she wondered whether he really ought to be allowed to talk. At age sixty-five, he seemed pretty feeble. The next morning, as they climbed the stairs to one of the classrooms on campus, Caroline noticed how quickly Ford's "veined rubicund face" went ashen. Once inside the classroom, he sat behind a long table, skimming a copy of the *Saturday Evening Post*, waiting for the session to begin. Caroline looked at him sadly. "His chair pushed well back in order to accommodate his great paunch, his legs spread wide to support his great weight," she thought he "looked like a big white whale . . . , forcing breaths through his wide open mouth." But then Ford looked up at her and his blue eyes brightened. The story he had just read was written in an impressionistic style. "I see that our method has reached the *Post*," he said with a chuckle. Caroline realized that however feeble the body was, his spirit had not changed.

"Nobody heard much he said, owing to his deplorable habit of chewing up three-fourths of every sentence," Caroline said later. But whether because of his physical stature or his personal history, Ford impressed everyone anyway. "It was a good thing for them to look at him, even if they couldn't hear them," a college dean said to her.

Caroline expected to return to work after Ford and Janice left, but another visitor arrived to turn the Tates' lives upside down. Christian Gauss, a dean at Princeton University, came to Greensboro to ask Allen to participate in an experimental program in the creative arts funded by the Carnegie Foundation. All but promising Allen the position as head of the literature program, although the formal offer could not be made until early April, Gauss assured Allen that the teaching would be light, the money good. But Gauss would not guarantee more than a year's appointment.

While the Tates waited for an official notice from Princeton, a telegram arrived from Merry Mont: Caroline's grandmother had died on March 27. She was ninety years old and had been in failing health for several years, but Caroline could not believe she was really gone. Why, for the last ten years Old Miss Carrie had been threatening to die just to exert her control over the connection. "You had better come see me; I may not be around next year," she would say. Remembering her grandmother's tyrannies, Caroline felt rather bewildered. "She kept us hopping so long," Caroline said. Who would have believed she would really die?

Caroline did not go to the funeral. Perhaps she felt she could not abandon her teaching; perhaps she simply could not face the loss of her grandmother. Instead, she sent the kin a check for the amount of her railroad fare to help with expenses. Allen thought the Meriwethers needed the money more than a visit from Caroline.

Soon after Old Miss Carrie's death, Allen received the official offer to teach in the Princeton Creative Arts Experiment. More and more unhappy with the people and life of Greensboro, Allen was eager for a change, even a temporary one, so he arranged for a leave of absence from the Woman's College. Caroline would not teach in Princeton, but that was no great hardship: Allen's salary of five thousand dollars was two hundred dollars more than the Tates' combined salaries in North Carolina.

At first Caroline did not mind taking a sabbatical. "The teaching does take it out of you, if you take it seriously, and I can't seem to take it any other way," she said. Then Dean Gauss suggested Allen would be able to teach at Princeton for at least two years. But since they could not get a leave of absence for two years, both Caroline and Allen would have to resign their positions at Greensboro.

Allen was enthusiastic. Even if he could wangle no more than two years at Princeton, he thought the move a smart one. Princeton had more prestige than the Woman's College. Also, some faculty members at the University of North Carolina at Chapel Hill had expressed an interest in having Allen teach there, but they were reluctant to "steal" him from another branch of the state university system. Going to Princeton might make it easier for Allen to go on to Chapel Hill later.

On April 17 Allen resigned both his and Caroline's positions at Greensboro. He said he could not pass up the complete freedom that the Princeton program would offer. Although he did not want to leave the South, he said he had to follow the advice of Milton: "Artists being homeless people . . . must go where their fullest capacities are employed." Also, he insisted that the move was necessary for Caroline: teaching was too great a burden on her.

Caroline agreed that teaching was getting her down: as the school year ended, she felt crazed by the welter of other people's manuscripts. But she did not want to move. "I will hate like the devil to give up this house," she wrote to Katherine Anne. "Allen can hardly afford—or thinks he can hardly afford to turn down the offer. Dang it."

The idea of giving up "a permanent thing" at Greensboro for "what may be in the end only another Guggenheim fellowship" worried Caroline. And the fact that she had just planted gourds in the garden annoyed her: Caroline began to feel as if she never got to see the fruits of her labor. Every time she planted something permanent, they moved.

They spent the summer in Monteagle, in a cabin they called Wormwood, next door to the cabin of Andrew Lytle and his new wife, Edna. Caroline arrived exhausted, calling herself "Dragging Canoe," but the summer proved to be "a little breathing space," she said. They got up at six o'clock almost every morning, then spent most of the day writing. It was a "wonderful routine," Caroline thought. "The day is so long that you can make a failure of the morning and still retrieve the afternoon."

But the summer was not without sorrow. At the end of June, Caroline found out that Ford Madox Ford had died. Convinced that a quick trip to France would restore his health, Ford and Janice had returned to his adopted country, but the ocean crossing had been too much for the old man. Suffering from uremia, he had been hospitalized in a Catholic clinic in Deauville. He died there on June 26.

Badly shaken, Caroline could not write a letter to Janice until the next morning. Even then, she could barely type. "I wish we could be with you," she wrote. But it was a good thing Ford died in France, "for he loved it so." Perhaps "an instinct took him there," she said. Perhaps "after a while . . . we can all be glad that he died in harness." Caroline thought Ford would not have been able to stand "growing old and not being able to work."

Caroline offered Janice a place to stay whenever she returned to America; she also cabled fifty dollars to Janice—"just in chance it might be needed," she wrote. But for the second time in just four months, Caroline could not believe that someone she loved so dearly had died.

During the summer the Tates paid two brief visits to the Old Neighborhood. Caroline thought Merry Mont seemed "very strange and hushed without Miss Carrie." After picking up her "share of the loot," including the sword Great-uncle Ned had used in the Civil War, Caroline hurried away.

The situation at Benfolly was no different. The hill looked marvelous, Caroline said later, but when she opened the front door, "memories of the Master rushed out and overpowered us."

At the end of the summer, the Tates left Monteagle for Princeton: Allen, Caroline, thirteen-year-old Nancy, a new dachshund named Bibi, and his son Heros von Borcke, commonly called Bub. Disturbed by the deaths of her grandmother and Ford, Caroline was almost glad to be moving to yet another house for another unspecified, but undoubtedly short, duration. "An artist was not meant to have a fixed habitation," Caroline thought. "He is meant to wander."

But the drive north was exhausting, and when they reached Pennsylvania, both Caroline and Allen began to feel numb. "That trapped feeling" Caroline remembered so well from their earlier life in New York "closed in" on them.

The feeling did not easily lift after they arrived in Princeton. Caroline liked the house they had rented at 16 Linden Lane better than she had expected. It was an old-fashioned, two-story house on a quiet side street, convenient to campus, with plenty of beautiful trees: maples and crabapple, dogwood and cherry. But ladies' leagues and tea parties regularly interrupted her work, and the magnitude of her project sometimes overwhelmed her.

A visit to the World's Fair gave her unexpected insight into the novel. Standing before Pieter Bruegel's "Wedding Dance" at the exhibit of the old masters, Caroline realized with a start that she was trying to achieve the same effect in her prose. The peasants in the picture whirled wildly, surrendering themselves to their baser instincts, seemingly forgetting the more solemn nature of celebration. Yet Bruegel gave order to his canvas, suggesting in subtle ways the nature of the relationships among the revelers. The thought of doing the same in her fiction appalled Caroline: "I don't see how I can ever do what I am trying to do," she exclaimed. But she pressed on.

By the end of October, Caroline had nearly gotten Rion Outlaw out of North Carolina, on his journey to Old Watauga. Always her own toughest critic, she got into the habit of starting her day with curses. "What in the hell made you do this?" she would say as she looked over the writing she had finished the day before. "If you can't do any better than this you'd better throw the whole thing away."

After a while, quite unconsciously, Caroline began to use that tone to address her friends. After reading a story Lon Cheney had sent her, she dashed off a two-page letter detailing the story's weaknesses. "There are some good moments in this story," she wrote, "but it is all wrong structurally."

Allen read the letter—a "nasty habit he has," Caroline said—and told her it sounded rude, so she added a postscript apologizing for the letter's tone. "I was thinking entirely of the story and not so much of what was good in it as what was wrong," she explained. Confident Lon could handle her criticisms, she proclaimed, "That, Brother Cheney, is art."

In Caroline's mind the demands of art were their own reward. In the early months of 1940, however, she fell into what she thought was an especially severe "spiritual collapse," and neither art nor play could ease her despair. She loathed "all forms of human activity," she said, "except drinking." Every evening she would get "a little ease" by "tanking up just before supper but that would wear off and by bed-time despair would set in again," she said. Blaming her gloom on the weather, Caroline fantasized about getting on "all fours financially" and going south in the winter. "I believe we would get twice as much done with the sun shining on us," she said. But she knew it was an idle fancy.

Having just weathered his own minor depression, Allen told Caroline not to worry. She had the same collapse every year in January, he said. It would pass. But it was March before Caroline was able to rouse herself to work again.

And even then Caroline was easily distracted. She was drinking too much, eager for any diversion. When an old friend, William Slater Brown, came to visit, Caroline found a drinking partner and a reason to avoid writing.

Caroline and Allen had seen Bill only occasionally since they had lived as neighbors in Patterson, New York, in the 1920s. Separated from his wife, Sue Jenkins, Bill had been drifting aimlessly through life. He had started at least six novels but never finished even one: he preferred to finish himself with drink. Still, the Tates enjoyed his company. Caroline thought Bill was "one of the most charming men that ever lived, and one of the most soothing." He shared her passion for gardening and cooking, and he could talk a good story, even if he never got around to writing one.

Since Bill was still living in Patterson, he and Caroline often discussed Tory Valley. One evening when they had both had too much to drink, Caroline sat listening to Bill go on and on about the place. He "hates and loves and is obsessed by it," she realized. "Bill," she said, "why don't you write a novel about the valley?"

"I will do it, Caroline," Bill said, twirling his mustache. All the drink made him earnest, in a silly sort of way. "I will write it at once," he said. "I will write a thousand words every day and hand them to you every evening."

Caroline did not give much thought to his promise: she was too drunk. The next day they both had frightful hangovers. Dosing herself with Anacin, Caroline paid no attention to Bill, but that evening he gave her an outline for his novel. "The whole action fell into place almost in one movement," she said later, with amazement.

Bill decided to stay with the Tates until at least June. He began writing immediately, turning out a thousand words every day, even when drunk. Caroline thought it was "*marvelous* stuff." She figured the writing came so easily because he had little research to do; the details had "been in his head for years and have got that kind of lustre that they get from being brooded over."

"It is a risk to urge him on," Allen said. If Bill did not finish the book, he would be "dreadfully demoralized."

But Caroline did not intend to let Bill abandon the novel. "I have got so interested in the book that I don't care what happens to the man," she said. "Besides, you have got to take risks in this our life."

So Bill stayed with the Tates, working steadily—and soberly—for most of the summer. In July Edna and Andrew Lytle arrived for an extended visit. Although Andrew was in almost continual despair as he worked on his novel about de Soto, and Caroline suffered intermittently as she turned Archy into a Cherokee warrior, they had a good summer. "It was easier suffering together," Caroline said later.

Yet Caroline still found ways to avoid writing, especially after Bill got her interested in mushroom hunting. Caroline thought collecting mushrooms was the most wonderful sport containing just the right mixture of excitement and danger. In a short while she declared herself an expert, talking knowingly on the *Clavariae,* the *Boleti,* the Morels, the *Fistulinae*. She roamed the grounds of the Rockefeller Institute to gather them up. "There's really nothing pleasanter than stealing those little pearls, all glistening with dew, off Rockefeller grounds," Caroline exclaimed.

Allen did not approve of his wife's newest hobby. He read one of her books on mushrooms and then started quoting admonitions. "The beginner cannot be too cautious," he said over and over. Caroline ignored him. "Bill and I were not at all reckless," she insisted. "Allen will never make a mushroom hunter. He lacks the spirit of adventure."

The first fall frost helped to turn Caroline's enthusiasm back to fiction. By then the Lytles had ended their sojourn in Princeton. Bill Brown worked in Princeton for a few more months, but eventually he retired to Tory Valley to wrestle with his muse alone. It felt very strange to Caroline to have no one in the house except the Tates.

Caroline continued to worry a great deal about Bill Brown. She did not think it was good for him to be working alone. He got a two-hundred-dollar advance from Bobbs-Merrill, but he could not be trusted with the money, so Caroline agreed to act as his "banker." With Malcolm Cowley's help, she made sure that he spent the money on food, not liquor.

Caroline also worried about Katherine Anne Porter. When she saw her friend the previous spring, Katherine Anne had said she was "still head over heels in love with Albert," whom she had married. Caroline thought her friend "was looking fine and very full of beans." But by the winter of 1940–41, the marriage of Katherine Anne and Albert had ended, although not in the usual pattern. Too much bothered by the difference in their ages, Albert decided to end the relationship.

When Caroline heard the news, she could not believe it. The story sounded like something Katherine Anne might invent "in order to make her exit commendable," Caroline thought, and although she tried to offer her friend some consolation, she could not hold her tongue. "I never expected it to last," she wrote Katherine Anne. "Really, darling, he *was* not dry behind the ears and you must realize that now."

In between worrying about her friends, Caroline worked steadily on her novel *Weep for the Mountains*. She had over four hundred pages written, but she knew that she still had a lot left to write. To her dismay, the writing went slowly. She thought the novel was the biggest job she had ever tackled. But she figured out that if she wrote a page every day until the following May, making allowances for her usual collapse in January and February, she would be able to finish the novel in time for publication during the fall of 1941.

One evening when Caroline was working, Nancy and Allen began to make a bit too much of a racket. "A little less noise," Caroline pleaded. "I am writing a book."

"I can not remember a moment you weren't writing a book," Nancy responded; "except the three months that Daddy was finishing his novel and you were scared to start one."

"It has been hard on the poor child—to say nothing of me," Caroline realized. "My path is very plain before me," she decided. "Just one novel after another."

By early 1941 Caroline had finished nearly three-quarters of her novel, about 170,000 words. With only sixteen chapters, about 60,000 words, left to write, she felt like she could "see a little light." Yet working steadily all winter and spring wore Caroline out. She sometimes felt isolated, as if she were in the wilderness with her Indians. The Princeton women were "great callers," she said, but that did not help matters. One day, she planned to kill twenty-six of her Cherokees, but she had to "stop the bloody work" early "to go and pour tea at a ladies gathering," she said. "If they know who you are they call on you because they like to know writers. If they don't know who you are they call more than ever to console you for being so obscure."

With Allen's reputation beginning to eclipse her own, Caroline figured that she fit into the latter category. "I am known in [Princeton] as a writer of mystery stories under a nom de plume," she joked. "I hope they think I'm Mignon C. Eberhart."

Yet Caroline got quite upset when friends slighted her work. In the spring she was angry with Cleanth Brooks. The last time she had sent a story to the *Southern Review,* Brooks had written her a rather belated and formal rejection letter. According to Caroline it was the kind of letter "that might have been written by the editor of the *Atlantic Monthly.*" "Maybe we are making a mistake," Brooks had said, "but we just don't feel that this is the one." In other letters he had infuriated her by saying things like "It doesn't quite jell." Caroline thought he was really trying to say, "We wish you wouldn't send anything else but we are determined to be polite about it." When Brooks came to lecture at Princeton, Caroline took advantage of his visit to tell him off. Then she vowed to never write another story.

Instead Caroline focused on her novel, supplementing her writing with painstaking research. She went to the opening of an exhibit of Native American art at the Museum of Modern Art in New York to get a few ideas for Dragging Canoe's costume, and she read an entire volume of George Bancroft's *History of the United States* for two sentences of dialogue between Rion Outlaw and an old Cherokee trader. "If I don't get them right it will worry me to death," she said.

After a while the unceasing toil and violence of her narrative took its toll on Caroline. After she "tomahawked" Rion's children and his brother-in-law, she felt like crying. Then her dachshund, Bibi, was hit by a car and killed instantly; Caroline was dejected. She wrapped him in one of her nightgowns and buried him in the back of the garage, beneath the compost heap.

When she reached the closing chapters of her novel, Caroline felt as if her muse had deserted her. By that time she had made significant changes in the narrative. Omitting the massacre of the Cherokee chiefs, she decided Rion would recognize his dead brother Archy during his final encounter with the Cherokees. And at some point she changed the name of her first heroine from Margaret to Nancy, then finally to Jocasta, or Cassy for short. Eventually she abandoned the story of her second heroine, Polly, altogether.

But Caroline still had not worked out the ending of the novel. In the original synopsis Cassy died from grief over the death of her children at the end of the fourth section; then Rion married Polly in the final part of the book. But once Caroline altered the end of the novel, she reconsidered Cassy's fate. Perhaps she would die, perhaps not.

When she could delay no longer, Caroline decided to spare Cassy's life. But after she figured out the details, the words refused to come. She wondered whether it was "coffee, fatigue, old age, [or] moral degeneration" causing her writer's block. She tried every trick she knew to get herself through the spell; she read the entire manuscript over and "resorted to every kind of fetichism" she had ever practiced, she said. Still, no words came.

After a week of agony, Caroline began to consider alternate endings for the book. Maybe she had taken the wrong tack. Would Cassy be able to survive her children's death? She was strong; she had traveled through the wilderness; but she longed for stability, feared chaos. She might blame herself: the Cherokee who killed the children would look at her and smile, as if she were an accomplice.

Perhaps in time Cassy would get over her guilt, but what if she did not have time? What if she stumbled across Rion and another woman just as she was recovering? Would she be able to forgive him and go on with her life? Or would the image of the two of them haunt her, cause her to recoil, accuse herself even more? Then she might try to escape somehow, from him, from herself.

Yes, Caroline decided, Cassy had to die—not so much from grief as betrayal. In much the same way as Caroline's mother had retreated from her disappointments in life, Cassy would survive her children's deaths by retreating into religion. But then she would realize Rion was having an affair. Although she would die from pneumonia brought on by an ill-fated drive through a storm, Cassy was actually destroyed by Rion's adultery. "She had told herself that she could forgive, that she could make it be as if it had never happened," Caroline wrote. But then, "lying there beside him, thinking of that woman, she had gone cold as stone."

To Caroline's surprise, the writing went smoothly once she decided Cassy's end: just as suddenly as the words had disappeared, they returned. "My Muse turned the inspiration on again as if I had been a bath tub and she the keeper of the faucet," she said later; rather than abandoning her, the Muse had stayed "on the job, just turning the power off the minute I got on the wrong track and switching her on again when I started right."

By the beginning of June, Caroline was finishing the last chapter and revising the manuscript. She decided to dedicate the novel to Max Perkins because he had suggested the project to her. She also chose a new title for her book, *Green Centuries,* borrowing from a poem by John Peale Bishop.

Before Caroline took the novel into Scribner's, Allen went over the manuscript, "taking out the 'thens,' 'theres' and 'nows'" which were "thick as fleas on a dog's back," Caroline admitted. He also urged her to "take out some of the dialect, or at least make it less homely, particularly towards the last." Caroline appreciated his thorough reading. The manuscript was so bulky that revision was "a dreadful chore," she said. In the last chapter she got "off on the wrong foot, striking the folksy note, using too much clinical detail." But "Allen stepped in, took a look and pulled the whole thing together with a passage that works in the symbolism of the constellation Orion." As Cassy lay dying, Rion would look out the window, catch sight of the constellation, and compare himself to the mythical hunter:

> It seemed that a man had to flee farther each time and leave more behind him and when he got to the new place he looked up and saw Orion fixed upon his burning wheel, always pursuing the bull but never making the kill. Did Orion will any longer the westward chase? No more than himself. Like the mighty hunter he had lost himself in the turning. Before him lay the empty west, behind him the loved things of which he was made. Those old tales of Frank's! Were not men raised into the westward turning stars only after they had destroyed themselves?

Caroline told Edna Lytle that Allen "practically wrote the last chapter." But the references to the constellation and the idea behind Rion's final meditation had been a part of the narrative from the start. As in her earlier novels, Caroline was emphasizing the importance of a proper relationship to the land and to the past, both individual and communal. Using phrases from and allusions to several of John Peale Bishop's poems, Allen suggested a bold, compelling way to reiterate the themes Caroline had established.

Rion's final meditation achieved its power through the stark contrast of his life with that of his brother Archy. Through descriptions of the life of the Cherokees and their adopted son, Caroline explored the darker, troubling side of her story, the destructive alienation from community plaguing the pioneers. The powerful images of redemption in the Native American rituals stood in contrast to Rion's proud, ignorant individualism. The warriors honored their dead, even those whose names were lost to the ages, by pausing to place a stone on the burial site; Rion dismantled those stones to build his hearth.

The Cherokees' ceremonial storytelling served not only to celebrate their heritage but to guide future actions. Dark Lanthorn, both artist and historian, painted a carpet to honor her husband and to demonstrate his place in the history of his people. But Rion ignored his heritage, even blotted from his memory his own misdeeds. And since he could not read, he was cut off from the lessons of history, forced to repeat the mistakes of his ancestors. In addition, where the Cherokees nurtured community rituals, Rion rejected them. He made fun of a friend's wedding festivities and refused to have his relationship with Cassy recognized by church or legal authorities. Most of all, he was willing to live outside time and society: only his love for Cassy kept him from a life of constant wandering.

Yet Caroline was not simply writing about life in the latter part of the eighteenth century. Through symbolism, classical allusions, and a series of quotes from Michaux, Thucydides, Daniel Boone, and Flaubert used as headnotes for the four sections of her book, she was able to expand the scope of her narrative into a study of the perils of *all* wanderers. Forced to become something of a nomad herself, first by her father and then by Allen, Caroline used the novel to explore the tensions of the life she knew all too well. And ultimately she suggested a way to resolve the tensions: the wanderer, like the artist, needed to adopt various perspectives, to understand the way the past operated on the present, and to assert a connection either in time or in space to other human beings.

Caroline revealed a great deal about herself and her views on love, marriage, and betrayal in *Green Centuries*. This time, however, she was not primarily interested in retelling the Meriwether family myth. Instead, she seemed to be offering a fictional version of Gordon family history. At one point Rion would even be accused of being a Gordon.

Actually Rion was a descendant of the clan MacGregor, the most famous in Scotland, which Sir Walter Scott had immortalized in his fiction. While the details of the Outlaw/MacGregor history did not exactly correspond to those of the Gordons, Caroline developed the connections to the Gordon perspective through her fictional alter ego, Cassy Dawson. The daughter of a minister, Cassy was small and dark, like Caroline and all the Gordons, and like Caroline she was born in the month of October. Even Cassy's relationship with Rion resembled Caroline's relationship with Allen. Both would fall deeply and passionately in love, then suffer the betrayal of adultery.

As she had in other novels, Caroline gave prominence to the story of her hero, but for the first time she explored her heroine's perspective fully. Like many of the earlier heroines, Cassy Dawson was fiercely independent and intuitive, sensitive to nuances in relationships and nature. Unlike Rion, Cassy understood the importance of community; she respected the sanctity of individuals and views other than her own. A type of artist, Cassy could usually create a stable, nurturing order in her life.

Yet, like Caroline's other female characters, Cassy could not articulate her feelings beyond the level of imagery and myth. Often she did not fully understand why she would act as she did. And like her mythical namesakes, Cassandra and Jocasta, Cassy was destined for a tragic end. Her wisdom would often be ignored, her strength no match for the larger forces in her world.

In a way, however, Cassy would not go mutely into death without understanding. Once again, borrowing a technique from her "cousin" Amélie Rives, Caroline used a storm as the setting for the final revelation of her heroine's situation. Then she created a final emotional storm at Cassy's deathbed to allow for a brief moment of reconciliation, a chance for Rion to understand what had happened. After Cassy had died, Rion would make his first stumbling attempt to join the community he had so long held at arm's length.

By the middle of June, Caroline finished her revision of *Green Centuries*. On Friday, June 13, she braved a downpour and took the completed manuscript to Scribner's. It ran to sixty-six chapters and 613 pages: whenever Caroline thought about the numbers, she became uneasy. But she was too relieved to get rid of the manuscript to succumb to foolish superstition.

Caroline was determined to "pleasure" herself for at least six months after she finished the novel; she told Katherine Anne that she had "thousands of things saved up" that she wanted to do: "study Greek and Spanish, read the Bible and Shakespeare, sew, garden, hunt mushrooms, fix the house up a bit." She even bought a sewing machine and made four garments. It had almost become a habit: Caroline would finish a novel and then take up sewing. Sewing was restorative, utterly domestic and feminine: it helped her reestablish the proper rhythms in her life.

But eventually Caroline had to put aside her personal pleasures and take care of family responsibilities. Early in the summer Nancy was stricken with pains resembling appendicitis, but the doctor determined that Nancy's appendix was sound. Caroline thought her daughter was actually suffering from malnutrition. "Greensickness" was the "old fashioned phrase for it," she said. "She diets too much."

Nancy was also studying too little at Miss Fine's School for Girls. At fifteen, having shed her extra weight to become a slim and quite pretty young lady, Nancy was more interested in boyfriends than school work. At the end of the school year, her teachers voted to expel Nancy, and neither Caroline nor Allen knew what to do with her. Caroline liked to blame Nancy's behavior on Allen, insisting that "poet's daughters are likely to be that way." But Nancy certainly had more than her share of her mother's rebellious nature.

After growing up with the idea that she was a homely girl, Caroline thought "it would be fun to have a daughter who just mowed the men down." Yet Nancy was "so headstrong and so precocious" that she kept her parents "worried stiff," and Caroline was alternately supportive of and hysterical about her daughter. Once, when Allen refused to allow Nancy to attend Princeton University house parties with upperclassmen, Caroline sneaked outside to stand below Nancy's window and hold a ladder steady to help her escape from her room unseen. But whenever Nancy came in late, Caroline would fly into a rage. Sometimes she even insisted that Allen go to search for Nancy through the streets of Princeton.

When she was not worrying about Nancy, Caroline found herself taking care of Allen and their cook, Beatrice. Both fell ill about the same time. Beatrice had to have an operation to remove a benign tumor; Allen took to his bed with bursitis and various other ailments. In some ways Beatrice healed much more quickly, probably because Allen began to enjoy the attention his illness generated.

Caroline was sure that much of Allen's suffering was psychosomatic. Earlier that year he had begun to see Dr. Max Wolf, a recent émigré from Vienna who had established a practice in New York City. Although some said Dr. Wolf was a quack, many others thought he was a genius. Writers like Stark Young and Ellen Glasgow raved about the man; wealthy patients like Alfred Vanderbilt and Marshall Field paid high fees to consult him. Allen got a reduced rate and what appeared to be a complete cure for the migraine headaches that had plagued him. "Hurrah for Doctor Wolf!" Caroline exclaimed. "I have always thought that Allen was one of the laziest people I ever knew, and now I begin to think he has been a hero all these years."

But then Allen began to suffer from what he called "my nervous spells." The first spell happened when he was out on an errand. Feeling faint, he promptly abandoned the car, took a taxi home, and climbed into bed, all set for a day of invalidism. But Dr. Wolf told him that the problem was "certainly circulatory," and he suggested exercise.

The next time Allen felt a spell coming on, he followed Dr. Wolf's prescription, but he still wanted more attention. Caroline and Nancy could not help laughing at the way he jogged through the house, yelling instructions as he went, stopping at intervals to look in the mirror.

"Call Rainey, call Burbidge, call Summers . . . no call Wolf!" Allen cried out as he ran. "I am dying," he insisted. "I am numb to the knees, have no feeling in my fingers now. Call Rainey, call Burbidge."

Caroline managed to get Dr. Rainey of Princeton to make a house call. He looked at Allen, "pinched his ears which he said were the color of a healthy baby," and told Allen "to behave himself," Caroline noted. After giving Allen every conceivable test, Rainey insisted that there was nothing the matter with him. Allen thought otherwise, and Caroline figured that it was "either the thwarted migraine headache" or "his subconscious protesting against writing the [second] novel which he [was] trying to start."

To get Allen's mind off his symptoms, Caroline agreed to take a short vacation. They spent ten days in August at the First Colony Inn in Nags Head, North Carolina, with Willard and Margaret Thorp, before going to Monteagle to visit the Lytles and help Andrew finish his novel on de Soto. Then, since Allen had negotiated a third, and probably final, year at Princeton, the Tates returned to 16 Linden Lane.

The fall was relatively quiet, despite the usual stream of company. When the faculty at Miss Fine's School for Girls agreed to readmit Nancy, she was suitably chastened. To Caroline's amazement, Nancy became "a perfect angel": she even began to speak "kindly to her parents and [act] so considerate[ly] around the house."

The Tates started to make plans for the future, "trying to save some money against the time when we're out on the well worn ear," according to Caroline. If Allen did not find a new teaching job, he thought he might get a position as a "cultural ambassador" to South America. Barring that, Caroline suggested they put Nancy in boarding school and go to Florida. But their plans were tentative at best.

Caroline tried to continue pleasuring herself in Princeton, but soon she was overwhelmed by housework. She told herself that dusting, scrubbing, and waxing were good exercise, but she felt increasingly harried and inadequate. When she woke up one morning and found she could not stand up, Caroline thought she was having a relapse of the trouble that put her in bed for three months in 1924. For a week she was convinced that she had polio. Eventually she discovered that she was suffering from a low-grade infection caused when an osteopath tried to treat her for backaches.

As she recovered, Caroline realized she would have to start another novel. "The life of a person who is not writing a book is too strenuous for me," she said repeatedly. Compared to scrubbing floors and doing laundry, writing a novel was easy, pleasant work. At the very least, it was an escape from that feeling of inadequacy. "If I am writing a novel I have an excuse for letting other things go," she explained to a friend. "If I'm not my conscience hurts."

At first Caroline thought she might write a story on bloodhounds, or a detective story set in Sewanee. But she decided to return to work on the novel she had outlined several years earlier, *The Women on the Porch*. The main action of the novel would take place at Merry Mont; the women in the title would be her grandmother and aunts.

As she prepared to write, Caroline decided to take a new angle on the story. The main characters would no longer be a mother and daughter, caught in a death struggle for power and control. Rather, the story would focus on the marriage of Jim Chapman, a professor of history from Columbia, and his wife, Laurie. The narrative would begin with Laurie's flight from New York. Caroline was not sure why she would flee. She might discover Jim had been unfaithful, or she might be running away from her own infidelity. Whatever the reason, Caroline knew "Laurie must be wounded unto death." She would flee to Swan Quarter, her grandmother's home, and find her grandmother and elderly kin sitting on the porch.

Once again Caroline would be writing about the Meriwether family. But this time she would delve into the shadows; the Swan Quarter porch would be "a sort of stoa to hell, or not hell so much as Hades, or Orchos," she said. Using the myth of Orpheus and Eurydice, she would explore "the deeps that underlie family life."

WHEN *Green Centuries* appeared in October 1941, Caroline felt none of her usual publication anxieties. For the first time she had not been unduly rushed; she had given herself and her novel enough time and attention, revising the novel to her own satisfaction, thoroughly mastering both the historical background and the fictional techniques.

But newspaper and magazine reviewers were not impressed by the novel. Writing for the *New York Times Book Review,* Edith Walton called *Green Centuries* "a superbly rich and authentic picture of life on the frontier, and the kind of men who made it what it was." However, she criticized Caroline for failing "to interest one crucially in any of her characters." According to Walton, the novel suffered from the same weakness as *None Shall Look Back:* it sometimes lacked "human warmth"; it was "a little chill and austere."

In his brief review in the *New Yorker,* Clifton Fadiman congratulated Caroline for "the realness of the scene" which she had created, but he too found the novel sadly lacking. "Her historical novels don't have much pace," he wrote; the story was "not exciting nor . . . the characters complex."

Only Stephen Vincent Benét, writing for the *New York Herald Tribune,* had extensive praise for the book. He thought "too many catastrophes" befell the characters in the closing section, and Rion's unfaithfulness was contrived, but otherwise the novel was "excellent, sensitive, . . . distinguished, vivid and continuously readable."

Such reviews upset Caroline, but she might have been able to dismiss them if the novel had sold well, or other more complimentary notices had appeared. However, as no new reviews appeared and sales were half-hearted at best, she soon felt that Scribner's was not doing enough to promote *Green Centuries:* the book had fallen into obscurity.

On a trip into New York City one day in early November, Caroline made a tour of the bookstores. When she did not see *Green Centuries* on display in any of them, she became increasingly incensed. Finally, she went to the Scribner's bookstore on Fifth Avenue and Forty-eighth Street. Two novels offered by other publishers, *The Saratoga Trunk* by Edna Ferber and *The Sun Is My Undoing* by Marguerite Steen, were displayed prominently, but Caroline could not find her novel. When she asked a clerk for help, he took her to a table of gardening books and handed her one on growing herbs.

That was the final straw. Her dark eyes glowering, Caroline tore upstairs to the Scribner's offices to launch a "Put Gordon Over" campaign. Cornering Bill Weber, an advertising executive at Scribner's, she insisted something had to be done to encourage the sale of her novel. When he told her he welcomed her suggestions, she went home and wrote him a long letter detailing her grievances.

Her writing had changed, Caroline wrote, "steadily growing more human, easier to read," yet the novel's advertisements did "not reflect this." In fact, she said, "it seems to me that ten days after it was out Scribner's had forgotten they had published" *Green Centuries*. She told him she had "helped in the creating of a good many reputations." She and Yvor Winters had convinced Katherine Anne Porter's publisher to take her work seriously: it was all a matter of "telling the book store women what to think about her work."

Comparing her novel to Allen's, Caroline pointed out how well *The Fathers* sold. It was "higher-browed than anything I will ever write," yet it was popular because Allen's publisher promoted it vigorously, she told Weber. "You ought to let the book store people know that you think you have got something pretty good in me," Caroline declared. "I assure you that it would be quite a surprise to them."

To buttress her arguments, Caroline sent Weber a letter Mark Van Doren had written her about the book. She also told him how various people had criticized the way *Green Centuries* had been handled. After reminding Weber how Scribner's had once sent copies of Hemingway's *To Have and Have Not* for her to autograph, Caroline insisted she was not trying to make Scribner's "spend more money on advertising," but to take "a different tone towards" her work. She firmly believed proper advertising was the key.

For all her agitating, however, Caroline never had much success with her "Put Gordon Over" campaign. Whitney Darrow of Scribner's insisted that *Green Centuries* was "offered for sale in all sizable book stores." Caroline disagreed. "When you go into a store and ask for a book and twenty minutes' search doesn't reveal it on any counter it can't be said to be offered for sale," she argued. But Darrow said that her view was "a common delusion with authors," and Caroline finally decided it wasn't worth fighting any longer.

Scribner's did come up with a new advertisement for the novel, but

Caroline called it "awfully dull." Only one new review of the novel appeared in a major publication, but it was far from positive. Writing for the *New Republic,* Max Gissen accused Caroline of being "blind to faults that any first novelist wouldn't have been guilty of in his first draft," although he did not really explain what faults he was referring to. "The book is dedicated to Maxwell Perkins, but why wasn't he around?" Gissen wrote.

Caroline's friends wrote her letters about *Green Centuries,* but little of what they said pleased her. A friend from Sewanee warned Caroline not to send the novel to his mother-in-law: it was too obscene, he said; "she would burn it." Another friend, who had written a scholarly history of the Cherokees, agreed: the book was not something he wanted either his wife or his daughter to read.

When John Crowe Ransom wrote Caroline to congratulate her on the novel, he offered "a little friendly scolding from a great and veteran admirer." "I think you are becoming such a realist that you're almost a *naturalist,*" he wrote.

Caroline would never forget or forgive him for that comment. How could he call her work naturalistic? Had he missed the extensive symbolism? She decided he did not "know or care to know anything about fiction." As she had told Katherine Anne, "He can't bear for women to be serious about their art. If a woman writes anything let it be phony, says he in his inmost soul."

Max tried to console Caroline about the poor book sales, but nothing he could say was any comfort at all. Instead his perspective began to annoy her. Caroline "ought to be braver under misfortune," he said, suggesting she "was never meant to make a living by [her] writing."

Caroline did not try to argue with Max, but she began to think about finding a new publisher. Soon she realized that she was in the depths of despair, "sunk fathoms deep."

Then, on December 7, the Japanese bombed Pearl Harbor. The United States immediately declared war on Japan; within days the United States would also be at war with Germany and Italy. As the nation rallied to the cry "Remember Pearl Harbor," Caroline plunged deeper and deeper into despair. She felt "as if some horrible Grendel were lurking in the marshes, bellowing for the sacrifice of young men, and that all our business nowadays will be to pack them up and ship them off to him properly."

It wasn't that Caroline objected to the war; she actually thought it was "spiritually necessary." But the "fol de rol, the asininity, the hypocrisy that accompanies it," she exclaimed to a friend. "I don't believe that when they were sending the youths off to the Minotaur each year the Athenian women went on about how nice it was for them to see the world. I believe they wept."

Throughout the early months of 1942, Caroline felt as if she were choking. She tried to work on her novel, but the work went slowly. She was not entirely sure about what would happen to her characters, but she decided that she would simply try to imagine in detail the lives of her characters, then select and arrange the incidents into a coherent whole.

As part of her search for a new publisher, Caroline prepared a tentative synopsis of the novel. She also wrote a draft of the first chapter, along with two installments of a serial potboiler she called "Violette et Cie," which an agent tried to sell. She vowed to put herself and *The Women on the Porch* on the auction block and "take the highest bidder," but she did not think the bidding would "go very high in view of *Green Centuries'* failure." If no one bid, she said, she would write crossword puzzles for Simon and Schuster, or "fall back on Max Perkins and starve to death."

In the end Caroline stayed with Scribner's. Max offered her an advance of twelve hundred dollars, even though she still owed a thousand dollars on unmet advances from *Green Centuries*. No other publisher would offer enough to make a move practical; in fact, one editor said Caroline was on the wrong track with *The Women on the Porch*. He feared the book would be "light and popular and not one of the author's major works."

Caroline objected at first. How could a book "be very light in tone with half of the characters shades from the underworld," she wondered. Yet eventually she agreed she had made a wrong start. The first chapter did not have "psychic distance," she said, so she destroyed it and began again.

She completed all the research she intended to do in one trip to New York City. Since her hero, Jim Chapman, would be a professor of history at Columbia University, she went to explore the campus. "I had to find him an office," she said, "so I'd know what he looked at, how the light fell, etc."

On the way home, Caroline passed the *Normandie,* a former French ocean liner destroyed by fire while it was being converted into a U.S. Navy transport ship. The *Normandie* lay on its side, "the funnels pointing downward, the whole hull exposed": Caroline thought it looked like "a great, wounded animal" that had "crawled off to die." The sight moved and haunted her. She wondered if the United States *could* win the war, and for weeks after that she would wake up in the middle of the night, gasping for breath.

But the ludicrous and incongruous excesses of the war mentality did not escape her. For her "war work" she sat out in a field in a small hut and looked for airplanes. Whenever a plane passed overhead, she was supposed to use a code number and alert the army, giving information such as how many motors the plane had. "They could hardly have picked a worse spotter," Allen said. Caroline agreed: no matter what she saw, she always said it had two motors. She figured the actual intelligence gathered from such activities was minimal; its value was "in disciplining idle women."

Allen registered for the draft that spring, but there was little chance he would see combat. At the age of forty-two, he suffered intermittently from a pulled shoulder muscle, and he was also still having his "spells," insisting he was about to collapse or explode, making Caroline call a doctor at two in the morning. Caroline finally decided not to bother any doctor. When Allen demanded help, she would just "hold down the receiver and pass on to him an imaginary line from the doctor," she said; "I know all the responses by this time."

Healthy or not, Allen knew he had to find something to do in the coming year. As expected, he would not be rehired for a fourth year. For a while Allen tried to lobby for another academic appointment, an editorship, or a commission in the public relations or intelligence sectors of the navy. But all chances for an editorial position fell through, and Allen quickly discovered he had too many enemies in high places in the government for a navy commission.

Caroline applied for a part-time position teaching journalism at Sarah Lawrence, asking her old boss, Burton Rascoe, for a recommendation. With the help of publishers' advances, they could live on her salary, although they would have to live in New York. Caroline eventually withdrew her application, however, because the people she talked to at Sarah Lawrence were "so insulting to Allen," she said.

Finally, Louisiana State University offered Allen a position in the English department to replace Red Warren, who was going to teach at the University of Minnesota. Allen seriously considered the offer but decided to take a year off to write the novel he had been thinking about. Caroline thought he made the right decision. Allen "realizes that if he doesn't start using his mind again pretty soon it may atrophy on him," she said. With advances from both their publishers, they could put Nancy in a boarding school and live simply at Monteagle for a year.

They left Princeton at the end of the school year. Caroline noted that Allen was gloomy, convinced he would be "drafted as a buck private." "Things will be like this the rest of our natural lives," he said. But Caroline was ecstatic. She had gone through farewell parties "grinning like a chipmunk," she told a friend. "The feather bed was nice while it was under us," she said, but she was "almost hysterically anxious to be in the South again."

The year at Monteagle went by too swiftly for Caroline. She and Allen arrived in Tennessee in the middle of June 1942 and made only a brief stop in Clarksville. As usual, Caroline thought Benfolly looked "mighty pretty," the lion-shaped hill fragrant with blossoming hollyhocks, but she knew that Allen would never get any writing done if they stayed in that house. Hardening their hearts, the Tates put Benfolly up for sale and went on to Monteagle.

On the way up the mountain, Caroline and Allen could hardly contain their excitement. Monteagle had little natural beauty left to it: most of the trees had been cut down, and the houses were dilapidated affairs. Yet there was a magic to the place; both Caroline and Allen were certain that they could write there.

And they *did* write, although Caroline got a slow start. First she had to settle the family into New Wormwood, their hideous three-level Victorian cottage on the south end of town. Then she fell under the spell of the mushrooms. She spent days combing the woods for new specimens and even took a trip to Knoxville—180 miles by bus—to have an expert identify what she had gathered.

By the time Caroline's mycological fever had subsided, she had picked up a persistent virus, her weight falling from 139 to 125 pounds in a few months. But a visit to Dr. Wolf in New York City cured her, and soon she was writing in earnest.

Allen also began writing his new novel, although he eventually abandoned the project to work on new poetry. He experienced "a regular renaissance" that fall and winter, the first such flurry of poetry in almost ten years, Caroline said. It was quite a relief: "when one is married to a poet one always feels a little guilty when he isn't writing poetry," she said. The "supposition" was "that he might be writing if he were married to somebody else."

Having failed Latin, Nancy did not enter boarding school as expected.

Instead she enrolled in a private school on the mountain. She never did shine as a student, which annoyed Allen. "He can't understand how a daughter of his could make such grades," Caroline said. But seventeen-year-old Nancy was content: she had a steady supply of beaux from the University of the South in Sewanee. Before the year was out, she was serious enough about one young man from Memphis, Percy Hoxie Wood, Jr., to worry her parents. They feared she would make a hasty wartime marriage.

The circle at New Wormwood was completed by two other writers: Cal Lowell and his new wife, Jean Stafford. They arrived in the fall and shared the third floor of the cottage with Nancy. A year after his marriage to Jean in April 1940, Cal had converted to Catholicism, and Allen feared that Cal's newfound faith "would tie him up in even more knots than he [was] already tied in," but Cal soon set all fears to rest. He was still the considerate and affable young man who had lived in a tent on their lawn, Caroline thought.

Jean was equally pleasant to live with. Jean had grown up in the West, but as soon as she could, she "hotfooted it across the Rocky Mountains and across the Atlantic Ocean," she said. She spent two years at a university in Germany before completing a master's degree at the University of Colorado at Boulder, where she met Cal in 1937.

In a near-fatal car accident with Cal, Jean's nose had been badly broken, and even a series of operations could not completely restore her face. Her eyes looked always if she had been crying or was about ready to burst into tears, but Jean was far from morose. In fact, she was very much like Caroline. Both had sharp tongues and rather wicked senses of humor. Both were passionately devoted to the writing of fiction and also fond of embroidering on the truth. The two women got along well: they were "poets' wives," and as a mutual friend observed, "poets' wives, like coal miners' wives, or the wives of other men engaged in dangerous occupations, feel a certain solidarity."

Cal and Jean also began writing almost immediately after they arrived in Monteagle. Cal planned to write a biography of his great-great-grandfather Jonathan Edwards, but he actually spent most of his time writing poetry. Jean worked on a novel she would call *Boston Adventure*.

Throughout the fall and winter they all wrote furiously. Some days the "surges of creative energy" seemed to "shake the house," Caroline said. Cal and Allen did not make much of a clamor, doing most of their work in longhand, but sitting before the typewriter in her bedroom on the second floor, Caroline could hear Jean working on the floor above her: she always seemed to be writing at a fever pitch; her typing sounded like a small explosion, or as if some sea had swept over Monteagle and was crashing on to the rocks. Jean assured Caroline that her typing sounded just as "sustained and rhythmical."

At times theirs was such "an idyllic existence" that Caroline felt guilty. Around them the world was in dire straits. It was like one of Botticelli's pictures, she said: "the year in which fury broke loose." Thousands died in Europe and on islands in the Pacific; in America foodstuffs and gas were rationed, and other staples were in short supply. The war touched everyone in one way or another.

Caroline's only nephew, Meriwether Gordon, had been drafted, along with a host of other young writers and teachers the Tates had known, so once again Caroline found herself writing letters to soldiers. She also tried her hand at a story and an essay about the war.

The story, called "The Peaks of Otter," was a collaborative effort. Caroline got the idea from a soldier she met on a train while returning from her visit to New York, and she enlisted William Meredith, a young friend from Princeton who had joined the army air force, for help with the technical details. It was a meditation on heroism seen through the eyes of a young flying instructor who had to accompany the body of a decorated hero back to his family in a small town in Virginia. Caroline tried to sell the piece to the *New Yorker* but had no success. The narrative dragged; the symbolism was too heavy and a bit obscure.

She had more fun and much better success with "We Were Ready," an essay published in *Mademoiselle* in February 1943. It was a lyrical reflection on the war, on patriotism and sectional pride. She recalled her exposure as a child to the songs and the veterans of the Civil War; she celebrated the work of her great-grandmother Susan Meriwether, who had served tirelessly on the Civil War battlefields, and compared it to that of the present-day Susans, the women who served as stretcher bearers, riveters, and welders.

In the essay Caroline declared that "these days" it was perhaps "an advantage to have been born a Southerner." Southerners were "born to an awareness of war, something people living in other parts of the country are having to learn slowly and grimly," she wrote. They knew the destruction of war; their poverty made them "resourceful—and realistic."

They were able to imagine defeat and so could concentrate their efforts without hysteria.

Without embarrassment Caroline extolled her sectional pride. In "sectional differences" there "lies the strength of American nationalism," she said: "deprive" the southerner "of his loyalty to Lee and Forrest and you weaken his zeal to overcome the enemies of his whole country, for he participates in the whole country through his immediate devotion to his own region."

Yet despite her words of hope, her public celebration of patriotism, Caroline never lost the private feeling that "the dark ages" were closing in on them. "With all our energies going into material things there are not going to be many people left capable of asserting spiritual values," she wrote in one letter to a friend.

Only the congenial fellowship at Monteagle and an early spring gave Caroline any solace. The writers stopped working most days at about four o'clock. They would get together for a walk in the woods or a trek across the grounds to pick up the mail and have a soda at the village drugstore. In the evening Allen, Cal, and Jean might play bridge—three-handed because Caroline refused to learn—or they would all sit drinking around the fire, sharing a bit of "amiable venom," gossiping about their friends, enemies, and acquaintances, sometimes quite savagely. "Let's see, who should it be tonight?" Allen or Caroline would say to begin the discussion. "What about John Berryman?"

The victim would change, but the tone would not. Both Allen and Caroline could be cruel; they would retell the most embarrassing stories, point out character flaws of friends and enemies alike without hesitation. Yet they saw it only as entertainment, the best way to relax after writing.

Occasionally Cal and Jean would take over the discussion with stories told by their favorite fictional creatures: an odd assortment of bears called the Berts. Cal had invented "the Berts" several years earlier. His chief bear, called Arms of the Law, was his personal alter ego; the others were caricatures of friends and family. In a singsong whine Cal told their stories to tease, using Arms as a sheriff to scold or arrest the other bears, who usually behaved outrageously.

Similarly, Caroline would let her dachshund, Bub, gossip for her. Just as she had done with Vili years earlier, she held Bub erect in her lap like a ventriloquist's dummy, and he would "speak" in a high, squeaky voice. If Bub did not have something cutting to say about the various writers they knew, he often shared poems he had "written": "doggerel,

of course," Caroline said; "he has a strong sense of the fitness of things."
The first poem he wrote was "quite properly dedicated to his mother,"
according to Caroline:

> If you loved me like I love you,
> You wouldn't treat me the way you do.

He also said,

> Sometimes I roll in manure
> Just to increase my glamour.

But with increasing frequency Bub criticized Allen, saying things Caroline wanted to say but could not. Allen had been christened Zov, a short version of Karamazov, and Bub would often intone:

> Zov, zov,
> He don't know
> What he's thinking of.

Allen hated both the nickname and the poem, and Nancy was annoyed at the way her mother kept goading her father. When Nancy's boyfriend, Percy, visited, he decided the Tate marriage would not last: Allen and Caroline could agree only when they were criticizing Nancy, he said. Once she had left home, they would have nothing to keep them together.

But Allen certainly did plenty to deserve the teasing and carping he received. From the first days of their relationship, Allen had adopted a lofty and condescending attitude toward Caroline's abilities. He praised her fiction highly but suggested she could not write much else. "All novelists have the minds of six year old children," he said more than once. Caroline "had as little intellect as any human he had ever encountered," he told her.

Caroline said she took these remarks as compliments, but over time she had become convinced that she lacked the ability to think and analyze. When she had to write a book review, she declared herself unequal to the task. When Mark Van Doren published a new poem, she said that she wanted to tell him what she thought of the poem but could not. "I know (thanks to association with Mr. Tate) that I don't know anything about poetry," she said.

Of course, Allen may not have consciously intended to destroy Caroline's self-esteem, but he did little to improve it or to preserve her emotional well-being. Once again he was engaging in extramarital affairs, and visitors to Monteagle during the winter and spring of 1943 often knew it. At least once Allen even arranged a romantic interlude in his own house. Going to bed early with Caroline, he later slipped out to meet one of their guests. The sound of creaking bedsprings mixed with the cries of Allen and his lady friend woke one of the other house guests.

Did Caroline know? Perhaps. She never said anything directly to friends or family members. She may have had suspicions that she preferred to ignore or to voice only through Bub, using his poems to needle and to warn Allen.

> If you loved me like I love you,
> You wouldn't treat me the way you do.

Although Caroline had tried to forgive Allen for his affair with her cousin in 1933, she could not forget it, and she would not want to experience the agony and betrayal again. She might joke about other people's sexual indiscretions, but she expected nothing less than absolute fidelity from Allen.

She also expected her closest friends to behave likewise. During the spring of 1943, when she realized Edna Lytle was having an affair with a college student from Sewanee, Caroline insisted Allen inform Andrew. But telling Andrew only made a bad situation worse.

For several months relationships had been strained between the Tates and Lytles. The previous year Andrew had become the editor of the *Sewanee Review*. Allen thought his friend was hardly qualified for the position, so he made a special effort to help Andrew, and the two men became rivals in the process. Then in February Andrew's father had died, which added to Andrew's emotional strain. When the Tates confronted Andrew with Edna's affair, the split was complete.

Caroline was sorry to lose such treasured friends, but she did not understand why the breakup occurred. She wrote Andrew what she thought would be a final letter, saying he and Edna need no longer feign fellowship. "I don't expect, really, ever to be friends with you and Edna again," she said, "for art is long and life is shorter even than we can imagine and time is rarely given for the kind of adjustments and readjustments that would have to be made in this case."

After urging Andrew not to cut himself off from the fellowship of other writers, Caroline reiterated her love and gave more advice: "Remember what I say about your talent. It is the great thing in your life, the thing to which everything else must be subordinated if you are not to rot—and lilies that fester smell far worse than weeds, you know."

It was a strange, loving, scolding letter, and Andrew never answered it. Years later he was still chuckling over the last line; he knew the way Caroline's temper flared for moments and then disappeared. And perhaps he also realized Caroline wrote the advice as much for herself as for him.

Soon after the Lytles and Tates parted company, Allen was invited to become a consultant in poetry at the Library of Congress. Not only was Caroline loath to leave Monteagle; she also hated the idea of living in Washington, D.C. It was "the very last place I'd choose to be these days and times," she said. But once again Allen felt he could not turn down the job, and so at the end of July, Caroline and Allen left the mountain, just a few weeks after Jean and Cal left for Yaddo and New York City. Nancy stayed behind to finish some course work for her high school diploma.

There was little available housing in Washington, but Lon Cheney, who was already working there, helped the Tates find a small house to rent at 3418 Highwood Drive. Caroline called the place the Bird Cage: gaudy and undersized, it reminded her of a whorehouse by that name in one of Lon's novels. Before the year ended, almost every available perch in the house would be taken.

Caroline did not mind the cramped quarters. There were some woods nearby, "as good as the woods around Monteagle," she said, which helped to reconcile her to the neighborhood. Every day she took Bub on a walk through the woods. When she found mushrooms there, her joy was complete.

In August Lon and Fannie Cheney came to live in the Bird Cage: Allen had hired Fannie as his assistant, and to Caroline's delight, Fannie insisted on doing the shopping and many of the household chores. "Living with Fannie is very demoralizing," Caroline told Jean Stafford. "She does, without grumbling or apparent effort, all the things that I am accustomed to do with clenched teeth and curses." Caroline said she could not "go on living on such a low moral plane," but she would enjoy it while finishing her novel.

In September Nancy rejoined her parents, diploma in hand, and immediately tried to talk them into letting her move in with friends in Princeton. But Allen and Caroline knew their daughter wanted to go to

New Jersey only so she could be closer to Percy Wood: Nancy and Percy were already talking about getting married, and Caroline figured they would "hop off" together as soon as Percy got enough money to support a wife. To forestall such behavior, Allen arranged for Nancy to get a job as a desk attendant at the Library of Congress. It was a very good position: Nancy had plenty of free time, and she made $140 a month. In fact, Caroline was a bit jealous. "It is the job I'd like to have if Allen would let me apply," Caroline told a friend.

But before she could think about a job, Caroline had to finish her novel *The Women on the Porch*. During the year at Monteagle, she had worked out most of her plot difficulties and written a major portion of the novel. Renaming her main character Catherine Chapman, Caroline decided the novel would hinge on Catherine's discovery of her husband's infidelity. Setting the novel in the summer and fall of 1940, she used references to the war to heighten her exploration of personal and marital turmoil. But ultimately Caroline was not interested in presenting a realistic account of either conflict. Instead, she experimented with a more subjective narrative which became almost hallucinatory in nature through the use of myth and modified streams of consciousness. Her goal was to bring what she called the "circumnatural" into fiction, those "intangible verities that lie about us and are yet not supernatural"—the mythic past, an individual's history, a society's collective spirit, all just as real as any other event, she thought. As a "dramatic force," the circumnatural acted on the present, shaping the outcome of narrative and character in significant ways, she believed. Her challenge would be to control its use and revelation.

"This novel will not be like any other that I have written," she told a friend. A major portion of it developed through interior monologues. Almost every character would lapse into reverie, and Caroline interspersed the interior monologues with flashbacks. Old Mrs. Lewis, Catherine's grandmother, would begin her monologue in bed, reflecting on the sights and sounds around her, but as she went back into memory, her stream of consciousness would dissolve, and scenes from the past would take over. In this way Caroline was able to mix meditation with drama, reveal the past, and intensify the mood of madness and isolation.

As Caroline worked on her novel, she often carried on typewritten conversations with herself about the characters and their motivations, about her techniques and themes. "Your difficulty will be to keep the pressure of the pasts dramatic," she told herself. No, "Jim Chapman is your difficulty," she went on. "He is not the man you conceived him to be." Repeatedly Caroline rehearsed the way her story would turn out. It would take "the masculine mind to deliver the constatation at the last," she thought. Chapman was "the interesting, the important person in this book"; the women would be interesting and important only in relation to him.

The women were the living dead, doomed from the start. They were frivolous, frustrated, and "raging, with the impulse to order things but not knowing how to order them," Caroline noted. They had the capability for action, but it was "unconsidered action and never the kind of action" that would extricate them from difficulties, but only plunge them deeper into the mire. The women needed to be "held in subjection," she told herself. Barring that, they needed to be rescued—by the man.

But did Caroline believe that or was she trying to talk herself into the idea? For all her pronouncements, she could not always keep her characters from taking on lives of their own. The women on the porch— Old Mrs. Lewis, Aunt Willy, and Cousin Daphne—would not remain "shades from the underworld," perhaps because Caroline allowed them to tell their own stories, stories of disappointment and of survival. The women would not be "held in subjection," and they would not really be rescued by men; they would either rescue themselves or accept their lot with grim resolution.

Caroline finished a complete draft of her novel in late October, then gave the manuscript to Allen and Lon to read. More and more she depended on Allen's editorial judgment. When he told her that the two chapters introducing Jim Chapman were "perfectly foul," she did not hesitate to rewrite them. But her revisions did not please Allen any better; they had "exactly the same faults as the original," he told her, so she tried again, and she would no sooner finish one section than Allen or Lon would point out other things which needed work. Still, Caroline was grateful for their comments: Lon and Allen "saved my life, that is to say, my book, several times," she told Jean Stafford.

As Caroline worked on her manuscript, she found herself thinking about Katherine Anne Porter. Writing Max Perkins to tell him that she was nearly finished, she said her friend was "the most fortunate woman" because whenever Katherine Anne got "into a press of work," she would throw "her current husband, her whole menage out of the window." Unfortunately, Caroline wrote, "one can hardly do that with Allen."

Instead of throwing everyone "out of the window," Caroline actually found herself putting aside her novel to deal with family crises. Allen's friend John Peale Bishop arrived in early November to take a job in the Library of Congress, but poor health made him an invalid in the Bird Cage for a short while before he realized he had serious heart trouble and returned to his family in Massachusetts. Then the Tates' cook, Jessie, took to her bed and began hemorrhaging. Without complaint Caroline took care of Jessie, even washing her bloody sheets, and when Jessie refused to be operated on in Washington, Caroline took her home to her family in Tennessee.

On returning to Washington, Caroline found a letter from Max urging her to finish the novel quickly if she wanted to make spring publication. Caroline sat down at her desk and worked eight days straight. Finishing everything but two chapters introducing Jim Chapman, she sent the manuscript off to Scribner's, then took to her bed. Exhausted, she swore her exertions had given her a "white streak up the front of [her] hair that wasn't there two weeks" earlier.

But Caroline's rest was brief. Before she could complete her work, she had to go to Orlando, Florida, to see her father, who was hospitalized with an enlarged prostate gland and related kidney trouble. When she arrived at Orange General Hospital, Caroline discovered that her father might actually be dying. The urologist refused to operate: he said that Gordon would not survive the surgery.

J. M. Gordon was relieved to see Caroline—or at least to hear her voice: his eyesight was clouded by the toxins in his system. "I don't believe I could have stood it if you hadn't come," he said. "You think I'm going to die?"

Assuring him he would not die, Caroline tried to ease his anxieties. But suffering from hallucinations brought on by kidney disease, J. M. Gordon became increasingly difficult to handle. He saw strange beasts and lambs above his bed, and he did not want to remain lying down. Sometimes he bellowed like a bull; other times he snarled like a tiger. "His lifelong study of animal life enable[d] him to make the sounds quite realistic," Caroline said.

Since there was a shortage of nurses, Caroline found a room near the hospital and spent most of her time at her father's bedside, "attending to his real and imaginary wants," she said. She could ease his anxiety somewhat by humoring him. When he wanted to "float up to the ceiling" to get at the animals which were hovering over his bed, she simply cranked up his bed. But often he raged and cursed quite horribly, and there was nothing Caroline could do.

Even during his lucid intervals, J. M. Gordon sometimes behaved badly. Never before hospitalized in his eighty-three years, he insulted the nurses, calling them "God damned little runaway girls," and he wanted no part of the various tubes the doctors had put into his body. He was constantly tugging off the bandage on his abdomen, and sometimes he called for a knife, "to cut the whole works out," he said.

Yet J. M. Gordon did not wholly lose his wonderful spirit of play. Occasionally he teased the nurses and urged his daughter to help him escape. "Douse the lights, so we can make a break for it," he declared one evening. Another time, he asked if they had to stay much longer in the hospital. When Caroline said yes, he responded mournfully, "Then I am the most unfortunate of Mortimers."

Caroline was glad that her father was fundamentally "so sweet-tempered": she did not think she could manage him otherwise. But his sufferings were intense; some days he vomited all day long. Caroline began to hope that for his own sake he would die quickly. If he survived, he would need constant attention, and Caroline thought her father would not like such enforced dependence on others.

While Caroline kept her death watch, the inhabitants of the Bird Cage had other concerns on their minds: on December 29 Nancy and Percy announced they were going to leave for Sewanee in two days to get married. After mounting a few weak attempts to dissuade them, Allen persuaded the lovers to be married in a nearby Episcopal chapel. Years later Nancy said that her father "agreed to the wedding because he was bored" and because he "liked to buy cases of champagne."

Of course, Caroline would not be able to attend any ceremony, and when Allen telephoned her with the news, she was perfectly appalled. On the day of the wedding, she sat in her father's hospital room writing a letter to Jean Stafford. "If I had been there I think I could have talked them out of it," she said. Nancy was only eighteen years old; Percy had several years of the navy and then medical school ahead of him before he would be able to support a wife and family. But Caroline realized she might be exaggerating her powers of persuasion. "Certainly no two young things were ever more determined to get married," she wrote another friend. With her father bellowing and snarling his way to death, she decided not to worry about Nancy and Percy.

Caroline tried to finish her novel while her father slept, but she had to write in snatches. At first she wrote longhand, standing at the dresser in her father's room. Later the hospital superintendent allowed Caroline to use her typewriter at night, after J. M. Gordon had fallen into a drugged sleep. But Caroline found it difficult to work at the superintendent's desk. She could ignore the women going into labor around her, "but when they bring in a baby that has been asphyxiated to put it in an iron lung it gives you pause," she said.

Finally Caroline rented a typewriter to use in her father's room. "Now be good, I am going to work on my book," she would say to her father, and he would stay quiet for nearly twenty minutes.

When she had done as much as she could, she sent the new pages to Allen with a plea for help. He should find a quotation from Ovid—"something about love," she said—and insert it in the manuscript. "You will have to read the manuscript carefully to see where it fits," she said. "The bum murmurs one or two words of it, looks away, makes another effort, and comes finally with the whole quotation."

Caroline also asked Allen to change the name of the bum's university. If he wished, he could even change the bum's name. "Fill in anything that needs to be filled in," she wrote. "Punctuate or change in any way you want to, but get it off to Max." Allen obliged.

On January 10 James Morris Gordon died. Caroline went through the ensuing days in a shocked state of relief. She accompanied her father's body back to the Old Neighborhood. He had always poked fun at the Meriwethers, but he was buried in the family graveyard at Merivale.

Nancy joined her mother for the funeral, then Caroline spent a night visiting the newlyweds, who had taken a cabin at Monteagle. By the time Caroline returned to Washington, she had passed beyond grief and exhaustion. Fannie Cheney said Caroline reminded her "of one of those old bird dogs that have been off on a three day binge and come home with their coats all matted and full of burrs." Caroline was sure the description was accurate. "Things just all happened too fast for me," she said.

Caroline needed rest desperately, but she could not or would not stop pushing herself. Through the end of January and the beginning of February, she had to proofread galleys of *The Women on the Porch*. As soon as the galleys were done, Caroline devoted herself to painting, her newest hobby. She had started using pastels the previous spring but had since progressed to oils, and the desire to paint worked like madness in her veins. "It is the worst thing that has ever come my way—worse than gardening, worse than sewing, worse even than mushrooms," Caroline declared.

Her enthusiasm far surpassed her talent: her turtles looked more like gourds, and one nude rather resembled a corset ad. Believing that all she needed was practice and a few lessons, however, Caroline signed up for classes at the Phillips Gallery in Washington. Her instructors told her that she was "not a true Primitive, just naive," but she continued to work at her painting: putting brush to canvas helped Caroline to relax.

By this time Katherine Anne Porter had arrived in Washington to take John Peale Bishop's place as a resident fellow in comparative literature at the Library of Congress. Since housing was still scarce, Katherine Anne took up residence in the basement game room of the Bird Cage. Having her old friend around might have helped Caroline to relax and recover from the stress she had been under, but instead the opposite occurred: Katherine Anne quickly got on her nerves. Although her job at the Library of Congress made few demands on her, Katherine Anne was not writing. Instead she devoted herself to making good appearances. She primped before the mirror for hours; she monopolized almost every conversation, and she flirted with every male who appeared—young and old alike.

Caroline had come to expect such behavior. She had always thought Katherine Anne flighty and unreliable. During the previous summer she had even called Katherine Anne "an actress who happens to have a talent for setting down her emotions in felicitous prose." Yet usually Caroline was willing to make allowances for her friend. Katherine Anne's "histrionic gifts" served as "a protective bit of colouring" that enabled her to work, Caroline had said.

But during the spring of 1944, she became less indulgent and forgiving. A writer had an obligation to her talent, she felt: talent was "the great thing" in a writer's life, "the thing to which everything else must be subordinated." Didn't Katherine Anne realize that?

Bit by bit, Caroline lost patience with her friend. Once when Katherine Anne slept late, Caroline went downstairs to rouse her. "Get up, get up," she shouted as she stood beside the bed and shook her friend, "You have a God-given talent. Get up and use it."

Another time Caroline tried to shame Katherine Anne back to work. During a conversation with the Tates, Katherine Anne read a quotation she found on the destructive effect of early fame. "Well, that's one thing you need not worry about, Katherine Anne," Caroline said rudely.

Katherine Anne was offended but not likely to take anything her friend said too seriously, which must have only increased Caroline's frustration. Eventually Caroline could not control her irritation. One day the two women had a trivial disagreement over some childhood rhyme about a turkey "so cool and ca'm" who "did not give a damn." When Katherine Anne insisted Caroline did not remember the rhyme correctly, Caroline exploded. In an instant the old friends were enemies, both screaming about everything and nothing at all.

Nancy, who was visiting her parents at the time, listened with amazement as her mother launched into a tirade that had little or no connection to the disagreement which had started it. "If you say that, I'll never speak to you again," Caroline screamed. "Anybody who says that is morally degraded, degenerate, corrupt . . ."

Fannie Cheney came into the room at one point and tried to make peace. "Now, now, Caroline," she began.

"Don't now now Caroline me," Caroline shouted back. She continued to rant and rave for several hours. At first Katherine Anne made "some feeble remarks" in response, Nancy said later, but after a while, Katherine Anne just sat silently, listening in shock.

In time Caroline's rage was spent. In fact, in a few days she acted as if nothing had happened. But Katherine Anne would not forget the scene. Various rumors circulated among their friends about the quarrel, some suggesting Caroline saw Katherine Anne as a rival for Allen's attention.

Allen himself thought Caroline's anger was not so much due to Katherine Anne's behavior as to Caroline's own inner frustrations. Realizing there was no way the two women could continue to live together, he found Katherine Anne a place to stay in Georgetown with a friend, Marcella Comès Winslow.

It was an ideal situation for everyone involved. In the Winslow house Katherine Anne no longer had to compete for attention. Reveling in the indulgent care of a new circle of admirers, she could be gracious to Caroline, keeping up the appearance of friendship, inviting the Tates to parties, seeing Caroline on a purely social basis.

But both women nursed their hurt in secret. Katherine Anne decided Caroline was insane, and, although she would not admit it for quite a while, Caroline remained quite jealous of Katherine Anne. That spring Marcella Winslow painted portraits of them both, and Caroline would never forget how different the portraits were. As time went on, the differences became symbolic to Caroline of the problems in her relationship with Katherine Anne.

Marcella chose a soft, romantic gray and rose color scheme for Katherine Anne's portrait; she created an atmosphere of mature beauty and infinite sadness. But for Caroline's portrait she took a harder, less feminine line. She painted Caroline in a henna-colored dress and one of Allen's family heirlooms, "the Lewis shawl," a bit of brownish red silk embellished with a border of autumn leaves.

The portrait was stunning, an excellent likeness. In it Caroline sat with Bub on her lap, leaning on her elbow, her hand against the side of her face, deep in thought. But sure that Marcella was trying to make her "look very masculine," Caroline greatly disliked the painting. It was typical, she came to believe, of how people misunderstood and misjudged them. Caroline wanted to be painted in blue; she thought she—not Katherine Anne—needed "glamourizing." It did not seem fair: people always made a fuss over Katherine Anne because of her beauty and charm. Condoning frivolous actions and tolerating thoughtlessness, they encouraged her romantic image at the expense of her art. In short, they did not look beyond the surface.

Caroline came to feel that Katherine Anne was "the little sister who sits on Papa's knee and gets the sugar plums," while she was forced to wash the dishes. Caroline thought that because she did not have the surface glamour, or Katherine Anne's ability to put the best face possible on everything she did, she did not get the support, understanding, and encouragement she deserved, and she greatly resented that fact.

But also Caroline worried about Katherine Anne—and feared her. Katherine Anne had the freedom Caroline longed for, yet she seemed to willingly squander her time and creative energy. Was it possible that Caroline would do the same thing and abandon her art if she did not have to struggle against the demands and responsibilities of friends and family? Were both critical respect and popularity actually dependent on the image one portrayed, the public persona, not the actual work one produced?

Caroline did not know how to separate her concern for Katherine Anne from her personal anxieties, to put aside her fears and resentments and rebuild her twenty-year friendship. So, for a time, she tried to do what she always did: bury her hurt, pretend nothing had happened, try to forget. But Caroline could never forget anything for long.

1944–1947

In May 1944 *The Women on the Porch* was published. It was a subtle yet scathing analysis of her relationship with Allen, and Caroline would always feel that the book contained some of her best writing. Yet Allen claimed that Caroline could not explain why her hero was unfaithful, and that only demonstrated how little she understood any marriage relationship. But perhaps Caroline understood too well the nature of their life together. Although she would always downplay the autobiographical parallels in her novels, *The Women on the Porch* was a profoundly personal book, richly haunting and difficult to read for all its deceptive simplicity.

When Caroline saw her work in print, she decided the novel was not "round enough": she should have devoted more space to defining the problems between Catherine and Jim Chapman. But she was pleased to think she had achieved some of her desired effects through the use of myth and her modified stream of consciousness. She knew she had a long way to go to perfect her techniques, but she believed she had begun to make "a real contribution to the art of fiction."

The first reviews of *The Women on the Porch* seemed to agree that Caroline had written a different sort of book, one creating atmosphere "in part by echoes and excerpts out of the race's poetic past," according to Florence Haxton Bullock in the *New York Herald Tribune Weekly Book Review*. Marion Strobel, writing for the *Chicago Sun Times Book Week*, even compared the book favorably to the novels of Virginia Woolf.

Reviewers could not agree, however, that Caroline's techniques were entirely successful. Nathan Rothman compared the novel to that of Joyce and D. H. Lawrence in his article for the *Saturday Review,* insisting one could forgive the limitations of *The Women on the Porch:* it was "fine and evocative writing" ranging "far out to the periphery of experience." But in the *New York Times Book Review* Lorine Pruette argued that "shadows of the past" sometimes obscured "the lineaments of the present." Another newspaper reviewer dismissed the novel as "warmed-over O'Neill."

Caroline was not disturbed by their comments. She admitted to friends that she *was* obsessed by the past, and consequently, the present in her fiction seemed pale in comparison. Accepting the reviews with uncustomary good humor, she said the past would take its place better when she had gotten more control of her method.

But when Edmund Wilson wrote to say he would not review *The Women on the Porch* for the *New Yorker,* Caroline was not inclined to be charitable. According to Caroline, Edmund had not read the novel, but "he felt sure that it was not any good," mired as it was in local details. His letter made Caroline furious. She immediately sat down and wrote a letter to "let him have it," she said later.

Challenging him to find one detail in her book "used for picturesque effect, and not to give immediate reality to the scene of action," Caroline chided Edmund for his condescending attitude toward her work. She had listened to him talk about literature for nearly twenty years. "I don't think it ever occurred to you during that time that I might possibly have something interesting to say," she wrote. But it might do him some good "to listen occasionally to what fiction writers have to say," she went on: "you show great interest in novelty of subject and almost no interest in technique." Implying this was wrongheaded, she begged him not to have her book "reviewed in the *New Yorker* at all."

Edmund did not answer Caroline's letter; in fact, neither of them communicated with one another for nearly five years. Caroline later said she should not have sent the letter. But at the time she was fed up with Edmund and, although she would not admit it, with most of Allen's friends. They would sit and talk about writing as if they were the only ones who understood it, and through their reviews and essays they promoted their personal preferences as if they were eternal, unswerving truths.

For years Caroline had been willing to listen, even though she often thought their pronouncements about fiction mistaken, sometimes ludicrous. But after publishing six novels, Caroline felt her fiction deserved serious critical attention, and she was beginning to realize such attention would not be forthcoming because, for her, the literary world might be divided into two camps: Allen's friends and Allen's enemies. Caroline did not expect the latter camp to give her writing its due: indeed, she felt that writers and critics who had suffered from Allen's acerbic essays or political machinations often took out their frustrations on her novels. No, Allen's friends were the only hope she had for serious analysis of her achievements. And, as Edmund's letter revealed, such hope was slim indeed.

Caroline did receive some thoughtful appraisals of *The Women on the Porch*. Red Warren compared the book to her other near masterpiece, *Aleck Maury, Sportsman*. The earlier novel was "a classic and here to stay for quite a spell," he said, but *The Women on the Porch* was its equal in sustained effect, more than its equal, perhaps, since it had "depths of implication" not found in *Aleck Maury*. He felt Caroline ought to have developed Jim and Catherine's relationship more fully, and he chided her for her characterization of Roy Miller, one of the minor characters, yet he said "the writing is perfection, line by line." The book "has to be read in the spirit in which one reads a poem, with that kind of attention to detail and movement," Red wrote.

Caroline appreciated Red's letter but thought the only valid criticism she received came from another friend, Sally Wood. It had been a long time since the two women had been together, and both had been too busy to keep in touch regularly with letters. But Sally remained a devoted friend, one who instinctively understood what Caroline was doing, sometimes better than Caroline understood herself.

"You've done it this time," Sally wrote. "It's a major novel." The balance of present and past was masterful; the novel took on "a sort of Greek feeling" through Caroline's descriptions of ordinary events, foliage, and shadows, Sally said. Her chief criticism was that Caroline had been "more than a little unfair" to Catherine Chapman. "You do your best to make her banal," Sally wrote. "Perhaps it is that you do not say a word *for* her in the beginning of the book."

Sally thought Caroline had exaggerated or even lied about Catherine's character. "She is so sensitive, so strong," Sally wrote; "that she did nothing, not one single thing to show what she was really like during fifteen years of married life does seem contrived. If true, one sees why Jim felt like a change, and I suppose that's why you did it. But it seems much more likely to be just plain untrue, or rather that the writer concealed from us the character that Catherine must somehow or other have shown."

So challenged, Caroline agreed with her. "There was always in the back of my mind the feeling that she in herself didn't amount to much, but that the thing she had back of her, even in its decadence, made her in a way, the equal of her intelligent, gifted husband," Caroline admitted. "The woman represents the earth. It may be fine, rich soil or it may be barren. But any way, it is earth. The man represents the mind of the modern, rootless American."

Caroline suggested as much in the novel, although much of her sympathy for Catherine was implied, not expressed. Consequently, many readers, including Allen, missed the nuances of characterization and complained that Catherine's actions lacked motivation. But the novel included ample justification for the separation and estrangement of the Chapmans, justification drawn from Caroline's own marriage. Jim had an affair out of jealousy and fear: fear of his wife's independence and ability to create a life without him. To get even, to assert his own independence, Jim pursued another woman. His adultery was not an act of passion or even lust, but of retribution and the desire for possession.

Although Catherine withdrew from Jim emotionally, Caroline suggested that Jim brought this withdrawal on himself. By making fun of the way Catherine talked, by belittling her friends and teaching her to see the world in terms of abstractions instead of relationships, Jim had systematically destroyed Catherine's self-esteem. He had stripped her of the feeling of independence, of choice, in much the same way that Allen had belittled Caroline.

Yet through fiction Caroline could imagine another type of relationship. She always insisted that she was inverting the myth of Orpheus and Eurydice, following the pattern of Gluck's opera *Orfeo ed Euridice*. But Caroline's inversion went beyond Gluck's happy ending. Below the surface pattern of Jim rescuing Catherine, Orpheus rescuing Eurydice from the shades of the underworld, Caroline suggested that Eurydice alone actually had the power and responsibility to save her husband. Caroline created a menacing land of shadows, not Hades but "No Man's Land," a land at once empowering and terrifying because it was so entirely feminine.

Caroline shared this idea of a "No Man's Land" with many of her contemporaries, but she advanced it with her usual indirection. Through imagery and delicate foreshadowing, she emphasized how Jim had no hope of salvation until he abandoned his analytical powers and relied on a more feminine, instinctual nature. Caroline revealed Catherine's unfolding understanding of herself and her power. And finally, she proposed that Jim would not find his true self without Catherine's help. When, succumbing to absolute fear, he attempted to strangle her, she would rescue them both, the fulfillment of a dream prophecy given early in the novel.

Consciously or not, Caroline also included references to her female forebears, weaving patterns that her cousin Amélie Rives and other writers like Charlotte Perkins Gilman and Kate Chopin used in similar narratives of marriages gone awry. And finally, in the novel's final pages, Caroline created a powerfully disturbing scene in which Jim would become convinced that the land that was his only hope for redemption was ruled by Cleena, "an ancient goddess whom men have awakened from an evil dream." Implying that Cleena or some other goddess had put the land under an enchantment, dooming all to a bitter life of wandering, Jim beseeched her for help. His perspective was unreliable—he was literally and metaphorically lost in the wood—but Caroline used his frenzied outburst to complete her revision of the Orpheus and Eurydice myth. In place of the Greek god Hades, she offered a female deity, who actually was no menacing presence but a Danaan maiden, a champion of the arts, whose ancestors had once reigned over an idyllic civilization.

Caroline closed her story of *The Women on the Porch* with one final image of reconciliation: Jim bending down to kiss Catherine's bare foot. The scene resolved both the surface and the underground patterns of meaning: Jim appeared to be leading his wife away from her underground world, but at the same time he was humbling himself, becoming a suppliant to her unacknowledged power.

Many readers would comprehend only the conventional surface patterns of the book, dismissing the women as lonely neurotics or people without hope. Those who sensed the personal dramas and subtext of Caroline's narrative too often settled for easy interpretations: Catherine Chapman was Caroline; Jim was Allen; the Lewis family was yet another version of the Meriwethers. But Cousin Daphne was also a fictional self-portrait: like Caroline, she had a passion for mushroom hunting that most people misconstrued as a death wish. Caroline's fondness for Daphne led her to write another short story about a similar character,

Miss Fuqua of "All Lovers Love the Spring." A middle-aged woman whose family had once been wealthy, Miss Fuqua appeared to be an eccentric spinster; she lived with her mother and devoted herself to collecting mushrooms. Her first-person monologue revealed she was a woman who celebrated life through her humor and creativity. Daphne's monologues did not go as far, but Caroline developed the character in her own image.

Similarly, several of the male characters in *The Women on the Porch* had complex parallels to the men in Caroline's life. Jim Chapman may have been yet another fictionalized version of Allen, but he was also cast in the physical image of James M. Gordon. Tom Manigault, Catherine's lover in the novel, had more than a few connections to another J. M. Gordon figure, Jim Carter of *The Garden of Adonis*. Like Carter, Tom Manigault was an Aleck Maury gone wrong. Yet he was also a fictional portrayal of Allen Tate: a man almost possessed by his abnormal relationship with his mother.

In the end, in highly complex and evasive ways, Caroline was once again dramatizing the struggle between the Meriwethers and the Gordons, symbolized as an almost primeval struggle between men and women. Perhaps she was trying to resolve in her art the growing tension in her own marriage. But just as she was unwilling or unable to admit to problems with Allen, she was unwilling or unable to make her narrative insights explicit. In life as well as in fiction, she had to deny her heroine's wisdom and strength.

In one of Jim Chapman's monologues, Caroline compared her hero's rootless wandering to that of a more sinister figure, Count Dracula. Remembering how his mother's house had been sold and his keepsakes packed away for storage, Jim wondered if he would do better to carry the remnants of his family with him, "like the boxes of his native Carpathian earth that Count Dracula took with him to London."

The image haunted Caroline. She had moved too often; she realized how dangerous it was to end up without roots and homes. But did she really have any choice but to become a wanderer herself? Soon after the publication of *The Women on the Porch,* Caroline had to pack up all her belongings once again. In the summer of 1944, after less than a year in Washington, the Tates moved to Sewanee, Tennessee, so Allen could become editor of the *Sewanee Review.*

When Caroline and Allen stopped in Clarksville to check on Benfolly, the kin were shocked to see how old and tired Caroline looked. "Isn't it awful the way they move around?" Aunt Pidie wrote to another member of the connection. "No wonder Carolyn's head is turning gray."

Caroline would have agreed: it was awful the way they moved around, three houses in as many years. But she was relieved that they were at least moving back to the country. "Washington life takes its toll and there's no use denying it," she said. "What a damned nuisance it is that we don't all have independent incomes so we could live exactly where and how we please, instead of being driven here and there."

The Tates rented the only house available in Sewanee, an enormous white colonial built in 1890. Situated on the forest's edge, the house had bay windows and a curved front porch: Caroline thought it looked "as if it were steaming down the Mississippi," so they called the place the Robert E. Lee. With five bedrooms, the house was far too big for them, and Caroline thought it was also "far too good," "the most comfortable house" they had ever lived in.

Since her husband, Percy, was off at midshipman's school, Nancy joined her parents: she was expecting a baby in October. She and Caroline spent the first month settling in, sewing curtains from plant-bed canvas, searching for furniture to fill up the nobly proportioned rooms.

Then Caroline devoted herself to "sucking on country pleasures." "The mountain certainly looked good to us after a year in Washington," she said. Only a quarter of a mile from the house was a magnificent bluff: on a clear day Caroline could look out and see more than thirty miles. Although the mountaintop was "pretty tame, having been lumbered off a generation ago," Caroline said, there were "primeval trees" in the gorges: enormous hemlocks and wild magnolia, near "marvelous pools to bathe in, fed by waterfalls."

Usually the weather was pleasantly cool. The garden cried out for attention, so Caroline toted manure to revive anemic clematis vines and raked leaves for a compost pile. When mushroom season began, she found an old friend, Fuzzy Ware, and a new one, Dr. Ned MacCready, a biology professor. Together they scoured the area for *boleti* and other delicacies. Caroline had "legs of steel," Fuzzy said. She also ran "like a pointer dog."

When Allen could be lured away from the office of the *Sewanee Review,* they often went on picnics. One day Dr. MacCready came over to tell them about a fine discovery he had made in a nearby cave with Henry Kirby-Smith, one of the Tates' neighbors: the remains of what was surely a saber-toothed tiger. Caroline was fascinated. "Imagine what fun, finding a saber tooth tiger some day when you were picnicking!" she wrote to Jean Stafford. "Why couldn't it be me instead of Henry Kirby-Smith?"

When not out in the woods or garden, Caroline continued to pursue her newest passion, painting. Although she toyed with several ideas for a new novel, she wrote little. Allen borrowed a violin from a neighbor and began playing it every afternoon and late into the night. The noise was more than Caroline could stand.

On October 6, Caroline's forty-ninth birthday, Percy Hoxie Wood III was born. The family soon started calling him P-3. While vowing to be one of those "grandmothers who don't interfere," Caroline was ecstatic over her first grandson. She and Allen sent out telegrams announcing P-3's birth to friends, and Caroline filled her letters with descriptions of him: his feet looked as if they were "covered with the best quality of purple satin"; he had "very large smoky blue eyes" and an "extremely sly," knowing look.

Nancy called her mother "the most wonderful grandmother that ever existed, and quite old-fashioned too." After Nancy and P-3 returned home to the Robert E. Lee, Nancy often found Caroline rocking and singing to P-3. "That, of course, is all wrong according to modern baby-lore," Nancy said. But since it stopped "the howling," Nancy did not mind.

When P-3 came down with ringworm, however, Nancy decided that Caroline was not so good a grandmother as she ought to be. That fall nearly every living creature in the Tate household suffered from the skin disease. Nancy blamed her mother: she brought home the mangy cat that had infected the family. But after P-3 recovered, Nancy did not hesitate to leave him with her mother while she went to visit Percy.

Caroline spent several weeks caring for her grandson, and soon, with Caroline's help, P-3 could "talk." His sayings included "Damn the torpedoes, grandma, full steam ahead and don't let the boilers cool," which meant, "Get the bottle hot, I'm hungry, and don't relax for an instant."

By December Nancy and Percy were settled in a small apartment in Boston, so Caroline took her grandson by train to rejoin his parents. On the way back she stopped in Washington to see her Aunt Loulie, who was living with her daughter Manny.

The family knew Loulie was dying of lung cancer, but they had decided it was best not to tell Loulie: perhaps she would die of heart trouble before her sufferings became acute, they reasoned. Realizing that Manny did not have the time for the kind of nursing Loulie would soon require, and rather dreading to find the nursery empty in Sewanee, Caroline persuaded her aunt to return with her to Tennessee.

The trip back to Sewanee was a nightmare, a portent of things to come. "Travelling with a two months old infant is child's play compared to travelling with a reduced gentlewoman," Caroline later said. The *Tennessean* was delayed because of a wreck just outside Washington: eight hours passed before the train even left the station.

Once the track was cleared and they were en route, Loulie refused to lie down. She said she wanted "to be on her feet quick in case of a wreck." Caroline tried to reassure her, but whenever Loulie looked out her window, she saw wreckage from other trains and refused to believe her.

When it came time to eat, Caroline had another battle on her hands. "Armed with sea biscuits and cheese, which she intended to munch in the ladies' room," Loulie refused to go to the dining car, Caroline said. At one point, Caroline wondered if either one of them would survive the ordeal.

Loulie was soon established in the nursery at the Robert E. Lee, however, and Caroline found it hard to believe her aunt was really dying: Loulie seemed "so chipper every morning." Although she tried to force Loulie to relax, there was no way to restrain the old woman without letting on about her condition, so Caroline decided it would be best for everyone to allow Loulie to do whatever she wanted, for "as long as she could stand up to do it."

As the year ended, Caroline found out that her profit on *The Women on the Porch* would be only thirteen dollars: unexpected charges for corrections and other miscellaneous fees totaling five hundred dollars had been taken out of her account. Desperate for more money, Caroline offered to write a novel for another publisher, Morrow: a horror story about Dracula, set in Princeton, New Jersey. She also wrote Max Perkins a bitter letter. After complaining about the fees charged against her earnings on *The Women on the Porch,* Caroline asked if Scribner's was ready to publish her short stories as promised. If not, she threatened, she would give them to Prentice-Hall, and she told Max that he was a bit like the British foreign minister Lord John Russell, who always said to the Confederate generals, "Give us a victory and then we'll help you." Caroline knew Scribner's contracts were "the most generous of any to authors." But "what good does it do the author if he never sells enough to take advantage of all the benefits they offer?" she wondered.

Max immediately agreed to publish her short stories in the fall. Caroline chose seventeen stories for the volume, including "The Captive" and five stories about Aleck Maury: "The Burning Eyes," "To Thy Chamber Window, Sweet," "One More Time," "The Last Day in the Field," and "Old Red."

Most of the stories had been written and published in the 1920s and 1930s, but three were new, or nearly so: "The Forest of the South," "Hear the Nightingale Sing," and her story about Miss Fuqua, "All Lovers Love the Spring." Caroline had written "The Forest of the South" while living in Greensboro in the late 1930s, but the story had not been published until 1944. An account of Yankee occupation and the courtship of a Union officer and a southern girl, "The Forest of the South" inverted the typical patterns: the marriage of blue and gray led not to reconciliation but to terror, because the southern belle had gone mad.

"Hear the Nightingale Sing" described another encounter between North and South: this time the northern soldier would be killed when he tried to take a cherished mule named Lightning from a seemingly defenseless southern girl. Caroline had written the story, originally called "Chain Ball Lightning," in the late 1920s, but she had never been able to sell it. When Max agreed to publish her stories, she revised it according to suggestions Allen made. Revising something written more than fifteen years earlier was "a grisly business," Caroline said, but she was pleased with the result, and before the story collection appeared in print, she sold "Hear the Nightingale Sing" to *Harper's*.

At Max's urging Caroline called her collection *The Forest of the South*. The title worked on several levels. The book began with "The Captive," the story of Jinny Wiley's agony in the forest; it ended with Miss Fuqua in another forest, hunting mushrooms in "All Lovers Love the Spring." Yet more than background and setting throughout the tales, the forest served as a measure and reflection of society in Caroline's fictional world. It was at once the source of inspiration and madness, a refuge and a place of terror.

During the winter and spring of 1945, the Robert E. Lee, which stood at the edge of yet another southern forest, became not unlike a scene in one of Caroline's stories. Not at all pleased to have one of Caroline's eccentric aunts dying in the nursery, Allen distanced himself from the house and its inhabitants: he buried himself in his work, played the violin to all hours, and took trips to New York and Washington whenever possible. Caroline hardly saw him.

She did see Nancy and Percy and P-3, sometimes all too frequently. In early February Nancy and Percy arrived in Sewanee for a visit. When Percy was called to duty, Nancy went to South Carolina to see him off, leaving P-3 behind.

Caroline did not mind, but taking care of a grandson and an ailing aunt almost proved to be too much for her. Although Loulie's strength slowly slipped away from her, she struggled valiantly against her decline. Every morning for several months, Loulie crept downstairs, holding on to the banisters, to cook the midday meal. When she could no longer manage the stairs, Loulie tried to take charge of P-3. Caroline had to shadow every move her aunt made. At one point she caught Loulie hiding the baby's bottles. Convinced that his stomach was in the same condition as hers, Loulie insisted that P-3 "would sleep so much better on an empty stomach."

Still ignorant of the cause of her decline, Loulie thought the mountain fogs caused her illness, and she threatened to leave for Florida, by herself if necessary. A disciple of a church of her own making, Loulie claimed all knowledge had been revealed to her, especially medical knowledge, and she refused to take any aspirin, much less the medication prescribed for her. The doctor was drunk when he wrote the prescription, Loulie said; "they say that people with heart trouble should never take aspirin."

By March both Caroline and Loulie were ready to collapse. When her daughter Manny arrived to help, Loulie took to her bed. As soon as Nancy returned to take care of P-3, Caroline collapsed with the flu.

While recuperating, Caroline found herself meditating on a phrase which came to her mysteriously: "and rear the olive garden for the nightingale." Almost without thinking she got out of bed and began to write, only vaguely aware of the tumult going on around her in the house: Allen playing his violin, Manny squealing over P-3. Later Caroline said she felt as if she were taking dictation: a story lurked behind the phrase, "already shaped, to the last detail."

Called "The Olive Garden," the story was about Edward Dabney, a professor of English, who returned to France after the war and revisited favorite haunts, especially the abandoned Villa Agatha, which he had discovered with his first love, Susan. Although Caroline never used the mysterious line which started her writing, she used both the olive trees and the nightingale within the story as a subtle metaphor for the creation of art out of chaos. The olive trees could not be tamed or domesticated in the garden. Yet beneath the tangle of their limbs, the nightingales created their nests, often startling the unknowing visitor with a burst of song.

In "The Olive Garden" Caroline recreated scenes from her memories of Toulon in 1932. Experimenting with mood and setting, she again inverted traditional patterns. While Edward wandered through the Villa Agatha and the surrounding countryside, he remembered people from his past, so vividly the reader might expect the story to end with a reunion. But all the people Edward had known and loved were long dead, just as the villa had long been deserted, and Edward's only reunion was with his memories and shades from the underworld.

Caroline closed the story by extending the metaphor of the nightingales hidden in the olive grove. Looking at the sea, Edward remembered the legend that Ulysses had found refuge in one of the nearby caves during the course of his wanderings. Wallowing in his own loneliness, Edward also thought about another hero, one "lonelier than ever Ulysses had been on his wanderings," Deucalion. And suddenly Edward no longer wished to meet someone during his walk through the garden: he realized that he was not alone. "Far below, in the rocky caves, that would always furnish refuge, that could, if they were needed, bring forth a new race of men, he could hear the heroes murmuring to each other," Caroline wrote. Like the underground stream of Caroline's early fiction, or the nightingale in the olive grove, the subterranean world was a source of inspiration, and the heroes of myth were comforting companions for lonely wanderers.

Caroline finished a draft of "The Olive Garden" in just two days. But too exhausted to type the finished manuscript, she nearly threw the story away. It could not be "any good," she thought. Allen put aside his violin long enough to read what Caroline had written, however, and he persuaded her not to destroy the manuscript. He thought that the story was "one of the best" she had ever written. Caroline was quite surprised; she had thought her writing "daimon" was "asleep or gone forever," she said. With the help of a new agent, Caroline sold the story to *Harper's*.

Bed rest and the successful completion of a story helped to renew Caroline's strength; before long, however, the situation in Sewanee once more taxed her to her limit. Loulie's condition worsened, but she showed no signs of surrendering to death. In fact, she made life increasingly difficult for the Tates. Manny spent most of her waking hours at her mother's bedside, but she was overwhelmed with grief and the feeling of helplessness, and Caroline found it necessary to support her cousin as well as care for the invalid.

Once Loulie finally realized what was wrong with her, she decided that she wanted to commit suicide. When Caroline refused to help, Loulie told her to call Uncle Rob and ask him to bring some poison for her.

Caroline refused. "It would be a sin to poison you," she said.

Glaring at her, Loulie declared that there was "no such thing as sin"; there was "only what pleased or displeased" her. Rob "will gladly do it for me," Loulie said. "You are afraid of a little electric plate on your head."

Eventually, Loulie realized that she could not bully anyone into helping her, but that did not prevent her from concocting other schemes to end her life, all the while refusing to take any medication for her pain. Later, Caroline said that Loulie "got madder and madder, until we cut loose almost entirely and floated in a world of our own." Various relatives traveled to Sewanee to say good-bye to the dying woman. Caroline and Manny sat for hours at Loulie's bedside, talking about the kin, re-telling the family stories. Often, the atmosphere became so oppressively "Meriwether" that Nancy and Allen felt driven to escape.

By the end of May, everyone in the Robert E. Lee teetered on the edge of sanity, and nothing could restore balance. Convinced traveling might hasten her end, Loulie finally decided to go to Chattanooga to stay with her sister Pidie. When they could not change her mind, Caroline and Manny loaded Loulie into the only available vehicle, a hearse, and took her down the mountain.

Loulie died in the middle of June, about two weeks after she left. But her death brought little peace to Caroline, who was more exhausted than she had ever been. For a long time she felt as if she were waiting "for some energy to well up" in her; some days even the simplest tasks were too much for her.

For a long time Caroline reflected on how her aunt's life ended. Looking for some way to understand it all, Caroline began to read Hindu philosophy, especially Shankara's commentaries of the Upanishads.

Written between 800 and 600 B.C., the Upanishads explored the problem of death using metaphors and parables. Shankara, a south Indian philosopher, had turned the rather wild speculations into a more rigid system in which a soul had to journey through the illusion and trickery of the world to an ultimate union with an impersonal absolute.

Such beliefs coincided neatly with what Caroline called her "intuitive certainties." It was reassuring to know what had happened to "poor, dear Loulie": she was "in the moon, where she will stay, enjoying the society of gods, as long as she can pay her hotel bill, which she pays with all the good deeds . . . which she did in this life," Caroline said over and over again. When Loulie had "used up all but a certain percent of her credit," she would leave the moon and embark on "another existence," Caroline thought. "None of the Meriwether have much mind," and Loulie lacked "the higher cognition," but she was "treading the path of the Fathers."

Allen thought Caroline's theories were nonsense. He did not like to see his wife reading Hindu philosophy: he did not think that she could learn anything from it. "Caroline has neither the scholarship nor the kind of mind necessary to enlarge her consciousness through the Vedas," he declared. But Allen could offer Caroline no other consolation, and she was not about to surrender what little hope she had.

Throughout the summer Caroline and Allen fought quite fiercely, sometimes over trivial matters but increasingly over something Allen had or had not done. Later Caroline admitted she had been possessed by fear that summer—fear that Allen no longer loved her. Allen was having affairs with several women, something Caroline may not have realized, but she sensed something was wrong and deliberately provoked him, hoping perhaps that he would reaffirm his love for her.

"Mama threw something every night," Nancy said later. The house was "a sea of broken pottery," she said. Once Nancy even saw her mother shaking a knife at Allen. "I'm going to cut your heart out," Caroline shouted.

Nancy did not understand what was bothering her parents, and she wondered why her father did not restrain her mother more forcefully. Once she saw Allen grab Caroline and shake her hard. "Caroline, you've got to stop this, stop this," he said. But usually he just tried to stay out of her way.

Caroline did try to keep her temper under control, her growing anger and uncertainty veiled, but frustration almost overwhelmed her. Too exhausted to hunt mushrooms, work in the garden, or even go on picnics for most of the summer, Caroline amused herself with her painting. Her favorite was one of Allen: a painting of his head trapped between two planes, one dark red, the other dark blue-green. She said she had tried to capture "that same glazed look he so often turns on friend and family":

his eyes had no pupils; they were pale greenish blue, the same color as the background. She called it "Trapped in the Infinite Void," or "Thinking Nothing, Nothing, Nothing All the Day."

Although Caroline had already imagined the end of the war in fiction, and the war in Europe had ended in early May, the United States was still fighting against Japan through the summer of 1945. Then, in August, the United States dropped two atomic bombs on the Japanese cities of Hiroshima and Nagasaki. On September 2 Japan formally surrendered. The church bells rang out in Sewanee and in nearly every other city and town across America, and Caroline went with the rest of the mountain's inhabitants to sing "Rejoice" in the Church of All Saints. "God, it is wonderful not to have to lie awake nights, worrying about boys!" she said.

Soon, as Caroline put it, "the landscape was thick with figures hurrying towards the Tates, expecting a little fun and frolic": Willard and Margaret Thorp, friends from Princeton coming in mid-September; Eleanor and Peter Taylor and Sam Monk, the men recently discharged from the army; Jean and Cal Lowell, eager to begin another winter of work.

Caroline warned everyone that she was still too exhausted to offer any hospitality. "I don't feel equal to keeping house for a flea right now," she told Margaret Thorp. But Caroline rented rooms and apartments for her friends and looked forward to the visitors. "A little stimulating society is what we need for a complete cure," she said.

There were signs her strength was returning. At harvest time Caroline began a rash of canning—tomatoes and jam. She also began writing again, another story of the war, picked up from a veteran who was in Sewanee to attend college.

When the Thorps arrived, however, they sensed trouble lurking beneath the calm façades both Tates put forth. But Allen left Sewanee on a lecture trip soon after the Thorps arrived, and Caroline did not discuss her troubles, so neither Willard nor Margaret could do anything to help.

During the week Allen was away, Caroline suffered from an inner-ear disturbance. One morning she got out of bed only to crash to the floor. "The room whirled around for four days," she said later. When she could walk again, she staggered and lurched uncontrollably at times: Caroline was sure folks around Sewanee would think she was drunk. Her doctor told her she had Ménière's syndrome, probably caused by an extreme allergy to coffee. Ménière's syndrome often caused deafness, vertigo, and loss of vision; Caroline likened it to seasickness, "only worse." Although she did not realize it, the allergy explained several other collapses: in Chattanooga in 1924, Paris in 1932, and Princeton in 1941.

After taking regular doses of nicotinic acid, Caroline felt better. Then Allen returned from New York City and dealt her another blow that set her reeling again. She had just returned home after seeing a movie. Allen met her at the door and told her he wanted a divorce.

She "must leave town on the next train," he said. They would get a divorce so that they could be happy again.

Not understanding, Caroline pressed him for "a more sensible explanation." But he gave her one that seemed even more irrational at the time.

"You admire me too much," he said.

Caroline would never speak about what happened after that. Years later she would remember and rehearse the events of that night; it was a violent scene, emotionally if not physically, unexpected and almost incomprehensible. Allen later conceded that he "forced the issue with sudden violence." Caroline should have realized what he was going to do, he insisted, but she acted as if she did not have any idea divorce was imminent.

Years later Sally Wood insisted that Allen had actually tried to kill Caroline just before they separated. In a letter he wrote to Sally during the fall of 1945, Allen admitted that he was afraid of continuing to live with Caroline because he could not trust his own reactions.

Whatever happened that night, Caroline believed she had no choice but to do as Allen asked. Early the next morning, her dark eyes still drowning in tears, she asked Willard Thorp to drive her to Winchester, the county seat, so that she could file for a divorce. Soon after the papers were filed, Caroline left Sewanee.

As she rode the swiftly moving train northward, Caroline wondered what she would do next. Where would she go? What would she tell her friends? Since Jean Stafford and Cal Lowell were expected to arrive in Sewanee soon, she decided to write them a letter, but she could not admit what had happened. Instead, she concocted a plausible fiction: "Nancy and Allen got tired of having me tottering about, with this and that ailment and have shipped me off to New York for a vacation, or rather, a rest," she wrote. "Part of the cure is being foot-loose and irresponsible!" she said. "I feel positively wicked, acting this loose way!"

Caroline said she did not know where she would go: she might stay in New York City, or she might visit college friends in Connecticut. She pretended everything was fine; she would be back in Sewanee before long. She claimed she was eager for the change. But as she wrote, her handwriting lapsing into an illegible scrawl, Caroline must have felt a rising panic. She thought about the house at Sewanee, the friends due to arrive, the glories of fall on the mountain. "I hate to not be there in October!" she wrote. But she never let on that anything was really wrong.

When Caroline arrived in New York, she could no longer put up a good front. Frightened and sick, she called Allen and asked if she could return to Sewanee. But Allen refused to talk about it. He wanted her to stay in New York City at least until he arrived in the middle of October.

But Caroline could not face the city's whirl and chaos. She spent the weekend of her fiftieth birthday, October 6, with Malcolm and Muriel Cowley in Connecticut, then visited her college friends before returning to the city. Allen came to New York as planned, but he decided he could not face talking with Caroline and left without seeing her.

Caroline finally decided to rent a room in Princeton. With a good library nearby, and friends like the Thorps and Samuel Monk willing to help her master "the arts" of living alone, Caroline thought she could settle down and get some work done. Her goal was simple: "to become financially independent of Allen as soon as possible," she said.

Caroline immediately began to look for a teaching job, and she arranged for a release from Scribner's to write the book about Dracula she had proposed to Morrow months earlier. Max Perkins was furious, but Caroline did not think he had any reason to be upset with her. She said that she "had to have a special kind of job to pull [herself] together." She also needed the seven-hundred-dollar advance desperately.

The Forest of the South appeared that fall to better than expected reviews. Then a French publisher expressed an interest in bringing out *Green Centuries* and *The Women on the Porch* in translation. Caroline began to feel that she was at least on the road to financial independence.

Becoming emotionally independent of Allen, however, was not so easy a task. Caroline felt as if she had "had both legs cut off," but she thought she could still "learn to get around quite spryly on crutches." She began to tell her friends what had happened, and although she alternately raged or denied the truth, she slowly began to put what had happened into perspective.

Caroline continued to try to ignore rumors of Allen's infidelity. Perhaps she knew he had been seeing several women, including Elizabeth Hardwick, a young writer whose stories he had published in the *Sewanee*

Review, but Caroline was not at all certain. She did fear, however, that fiction had unconsciously played the prophet to life, that Allen was having an affair with his secretary, Mildred Haun, just as Jim Chapman in *The Women on the Porch* had taken up with a woman he worked with.

But no matter what, Caroline sensed, quite rightly, that Allen's behavior could not be simply explained by a new love affair. Allen was suffering from the delusion that he could "have a new life if he [could] only get a new wife," Caroline told a friend. "Occasionally it works, but for the most part it's a dreary procession."

The "other women" in Allen's life were actually two spirits, Caroline thought: his mother and Caroline's muse. "I'd have done better if I hadn't been so absorbed in my work and so drained by it," she told Malcolm Cowley. "But Allen's mother looms larger in the picture": she "so tortured him when he was a child that he is literally afraid to commit himself to any woman." Caroline thought she might have been able to do something to change that situation, if she had been wiser years earlier, but it was "too late now," she said. "It's a wonder that we've lasted this long."

Above all, Caroline realized that Allen was once again reacting to her family. "None of this would have happened but for my aunt's being there this year," she decided. Loulie "exuded a poison which is still hanging over the place, all that hasn't entered into Allen," she said. "He has conceived a violent hatred of the Meriwethers."

Although Caroline had always thought her family bored Allen, she began to understand "it wasn't boredom as much as deep-seated resentment" motivating his attitude. Allen resented the fact that the Meriwethers, "louts as they are," still had "something that his family has lost," Caroline decided. "That deep sense of insecurity is the real motif" of Allen's novel, *The Fathers*.

Gaining a tenuous peace through reflection, Caroline vowed to stop thinking about Allen. Friends gave her terrifying reports of his behavior, but she said there was "absolutely nothing" she could "do for him."

Unfortunately for Caroline, Allen did not agree: he did not seem to want Caroline to go on with her life. Throughout October he wrote her letters almost every day, "perfectly wild letters," Caroline said: "long analyses of my character. . . . sometimes contradicting himself in every paragraph."

According to Caroline, Allen claimed that she "did not bolster his ego" as she ought to have, that she had "too high an opinion of him, an opinion he [could] not live up to." At one point Allen said he wanted her to divorce him and then "marry him again," Caroline said. In another letter he insisted they could never live together again.

Caroline did not trust anything he said. "I do not think he understands himself, or is frank with himself," she told Jean Stafford. "Twice before I have seen him like this, completely irrational. When it is over he has demanded that I make these seizures be as if they had never been."

Late in October Caroline received a letter Katherine Anne Porter had written while still unaware of Allen and Caroline's separation. Writing on Caroline's birthday, Katherine Anne seemed to be reaching out a hand of reconciliation. "May this be the best year of your life until now, and may you have near you only the things and people you want and love, and good health, and time to write exactly what you mean to write; and every other good and blessed thing, to your own taste and desire," Katherine Anne said. "May everything you have planted sprout forth and flourish. The year just past has been so specially difficult."

Caroline appreciated Katherine Anne's words and wishes. "It *has* been a year," she wrote in response. When she looked back over the year, she could see the many mistakes she had made. But still, she could not blame herself entirely, she said; "there is a kind of fate pursuing me through it all."

Allen was afraid Caroline would find herself alone and without friends once news of their separation became widely known. He thought she had alienated most of their literary friends. But Caroline did not lack for company or support at first. Malcolm and Muriel Cowley offered advice and encouragement, Sally Wood visited, and Jean Stafford and Cal Lowell invited Caroline to join them for the winter in their new home in Maine. Such an outpouring of love almost overwhelmed Caroline. "One of the hardest things has been the concern our friends have shown," she told Malcolm.

In November Caroline decided to take Cal and Jean up on their offer of a place to stay in Damariscotta Mills, Maine. She told some of her friends that she was leaving Princeton because she could not "set up a routine for work there": there were too many friends to distract her, and her landlady had gotten to be "a bit of a bore."

But to Katherine Anne, Caroline admitted two more serious reasons for moving to Maine. First of all, she felt that Cal and Jean needed her. "They couldn't face the winter without company," Caroline said, "and I wasn't needed anywhere else and yet had to be somewhere." But perhaps more important, Caroline had heard that Allen's boss, Vice Chancellor Alexander Guerry, would be coming to visit her in Princeton. To help Allen protect his job in the fairly conservative Episcopalian university, Caroline had written Guerry an outright lie, claiming full responsibility for the separation. But Guerry was "cagy," Caroline said. "He feels sure that he can persuade me to come back if he can only see me." Knowing she "couldn't keep up the fiction" if she "saw him face to face," Caroline had to flee.

She did not stay long in Maine, however. Although she had intended to travel to Damariscotta Mills with the Lowells, she went up alone after Cal had to have an emergency appendectomy. The house was "perfectly beautiful," Caroline said, surrounded by a dark forest of hemlock and spruce, set on a hill overlooking Damariscotta Lake on one side and a tidal river on the other. But the weather was bitterly cold. At night the winds shook the old house till it rattled, and Caroline had to sleep at a neighbor's house to stay warm.

She spent her days feeding an old stove in a makeshift study she had set up at the Lowells'. The woods were wonderfully inviting, but it was hunting season, and Caroline said she was afraid "to go very far into them, for fear" that she would be "shot for a deer."

For several weeks Caroline braved the cold. When she completed the first chapter of her novel about Dracula, she felt considerably cheered. "If Allen will just leave me alone I can finish this book very quickly," she said.

One morning, while struggling to light a fire in "a recalcitrant stove," she remembered something an acquaintance had said several years earlier. "You would go on writing novels if you had to strike matches in a cave to do it," Ward Dorrance had told her. All through the day Caroline hugged the remark close to her, remembering the young man who had appeared without warning on their doorstep during the summer of 1939 in Monteagle. Where was he now? she wondered. Still in the army or navy? Alive or dead? Late that evening she sat down to write him.

As she wrote, she wondered why she was writing. She barely knew Ward; he had spent a summer at Monteagle, had proved to be a charming companion, if a bit of a dilettante, then had passed out of Caroline's life. Finally, she decided that she was writing Ward partly because she did not have the courage to write her brother, Morris, whom Ward had known. Perhaps Caroline was remembering her mother's comments years earlier: Nan Gordon had insisted her daughter should never marry because she had "such a bad disposition" and "would be sure to leave [her] husband, which would be a mortal sin."

At any rate, Caroline gave Ward a quick summary of all that had happened since they had last seen one another, explaining that she just did not have "the nerve to write to Morris." As she wrote, Caroline tried to sound optimistic, but she could not help reaching out for comfort. "If you were here I'd probably weep on your shoulder and try to tell you all about it," she said. "But I really can't explain it as yet and probably never will be able to." She urged Ward to visit, to write and tell her where he was and what he had been doing. Somehow, she sensed Ward would understand.

Just after Thanksgiving Jean arrived in Maine. But Caroline got no comfort from her presence, only heartache. One day Jean referred to one of Allen's more recent affairs, perhaps after Caroline mentioned her suspicions about Allen's infidelity. Caroline pressed Jean for more information, which Jean too willingly gave.

The more she listened, the more upset Caroline became. She was furious with Allen: all fall he had been chastising her about her reaction to his affair with her cousin Marion Henry in 1933. He insisted that Caroline had been punishing him for a single indiscretion: she had refused to forget what he implied was an isolated incident. But once again he had lied. Caroline had suspected as much, yet she liked to pretend her suspicions were false. Confronted with the truth—Allen had betrayed her not once but several times—she felt her world collapsing before her.

Jean did not realize how devastating her words were. All of a sudden, Caroline exploded, throwing a glass of water in Jean's face, shouting, "You've probably ruined the lives of two people by what you've done to me."

Stunned, Jean went to get a towel to wipe her face. Caroline responded by throwing the empty glass at her; it shattered on the wall just above Jean's head.

"I'm going to break every goddamned thing in your goddamned house," Caroline shouted. Grabbing dishes and glasses, jars of mayonnaise and peanut butter, everything and anything within reach, Caroline raged on. After Caroline broke a window, Jean ran for help. Eventually, the sheriff arrived. Calm by that time, Caroline insisted that everything was fine: she had a slight temper tantrum, nothing serious. Jean spent the night at a neighbor's house, afraid Caroline might kill her.

Later Caroline remembered little of what had happened: primarily that Jean had told her the horrible truth about Allen. She insisted that she did not throw water at Jean: "Some water must have flown in her direction, but at that time my thoughts were not of Jean," she said. "I had, in fact, forgotten her existence."

Eventually, Caroline apologized to Cal for speaking "rather harshly at times," but she never apologized to Jean. Instead, she insisted that Jean had allowed her imagination to run away with her. "I do not believe that she was frightened in the way that she maintains she was," Caroline told Cal. "I think that after she realized that what she had done might have extremely unpleasant consequences, she grew frightened. But that is a different kind of fright from the kind she maintains she had."

Soon after the incident Caroline went back to New York City, where she met Allen. Later she told other friends that she left Maine only because Allen asked to see her and "talk things over again." Despite her shattered illusions, and the months of mutual recriminations, Caroline and Allen were soon heading back to Sewanee together.

They resumed their married life most "warily," Caroline said. Neither one accepted responsibility for what had happened; each insisted the other did not understand the true nature of their problems. Yet they did agree that the Meriwether connection was at the root of their difficulties. Allen still blamed Caroline for embracing the Meriwether mythology too readily. He felt she ought to distance herself from her family, but instead, she penalized him for failing to become a Meriwether, even though she knew that if he had been a member of her connection, she would never have married him. Allen suggested she had mistakenly glorified her family in fiction. "Your basic theme is the primal innocence of Merry Mont betrayed," Allen told Caroline.

Caroline was stung by his accusations, but she had already recognized the underlying resentment in Allen's response to her family, and that made it easier for her to stand up to his comments. She knew as soon as she arrived in Sewanee that their attempt at reconciliation might not work, not because she had "any reservations" about their mutual love, but because she felt the issue between them was "so deep that it may be no human affection can resolve it."

As Caroline reflected on all that had happened, she realized that she was in the same state that Catherine Chapman had been in *The Women on the Porch*. She had denied her own interests for years, "foregone many friendships" she "would have enjoyed," and tried to keep her life "as uncomplicated as possible" because "Allen's reactions to life" had been "so complicated." "It seemed better for me to have as little personal life as possible," Caroline observed. "I think now that that was a mistake and did neither of us any good." She resolved that "no matter how things turn[ed] out," she would "take more time" for "friendships, for personal correspondence," for herself. "It has been years since I enjoyed that luxury!" she exclaimed.

But Caroline found it hard to live out her resolution. Although she loved being back at Sewanee, Allen had grown to dislike the place, and Caroline felt his attitude kept her "from enjoying it as much as" she "otherwise would." Within two weeks old quarrels flared up again, and both Caroline and Allen decided they could not live together.

Caroline prepared once again to leave Allen. She resolved to stay with friends in Nashville until the divorce was final in early January. But before she could get off the mountain, an ice storm hit, trapping them together. Caroline spent as much time alone as she could manage, writing old friends like Léonie Adams and Janice Biala about what had happened, asking them to help her find a place to go after the divorce. "This, of course, is the worst time in the world to split up a menage," she said to Léonie. "There just don't seem to be any quarters available for wanderers."

When the ice cleared, another complication delayed Caroline's departure: the arrival of her nephew, Meriwether Gordon, recently released from the armed services. Caroline tried to "put on the best show" she could muster, but she could not sustain the charade for long. After dinner she told him the truth. "I simply couldn't face breaking it to him in the morning," she said later. "Mornings are so grim."

Meriwether was shocked, but he quickly rallied to her aid. The next morning, he drove Caroline's dachshund, Bub, to a cousin's home in Elkton, Kentucky, and then dropped Caroline off with friends in Nashville.

As she waited out the final days of 1945, Caroline tried to reassemble her composure and peace of mind, all but destroyed by the abortive reconciliation attempt with Allen. She did not know where she would be living in the new year, or even what she would find herself doing, but she comforted herself by thinking about what she had achieved so far in her fiction, and what she had left to accomplish.

Ward Dorrance responded to the letter she had written him from Maine, so Caroline wrote him again and again, long letters reflecting on her art. "I've been on the rack ever since I started writing," she told him. "I've always felt that I hadn't an hour to lose—and I still know damn well that I haven't, though I'm beginning to see that hours may be put in different ways to bring good results."

She realized that one thing kept her "more on the rack" than perhaps had been necessary: her "determination not to let [her] family cushion [her] the way some women writers are cushioned." "Nancy has never hesitated to interrupt me at a crucial moment," Caroline wrote to Ward. "Nobody ever thought of not having people staying in the house when I was at a crucial stage in a book. And that was the way I wanted it." Caroline realized that she had been "trying to do something that was impossible."

To be starting over again at age fifty must have been frightening. Caroline found it difficult to get back to work, to find a writing routine that would restore her as in years past. "But I am certain of one thing," she said. "That reaction to the patterns of sunlight on leaves, that delight in the visible world is one of the greatest gifts a writer can have. It is one of the reasons you write: to communicate it. I have had it, or had it—it is [in] abeyance just now—but I will have it again."

On January 8 Caroline went to court to finalize the divorce. Allen did not appear. He was in the hospital with the flu, and the symbolism of his situation bothered him. But his presence was not necessary. The court proceedings took only fifteen minutes. "They do these things very well in Tennessee," Caroline quipped.

Feeling "almost gay," Caroline left immediately for New York. Janice Biala had found her a small apartment, and Caroline was eager to get on with her life. "It is such a relief to have that over, to be convinced that there is absolutely nothing I can do for Allen anymore, and am at liberty to pick up the pieces of my own life," she told Ward in a letter written later that day. "Please don't lie awake any more nights, thinking of my worries," she said. "I feel better today than I've been in months."

But others were not sure Caroline was ready to begin again. Janice especially worried about Caroline. It was "an unhappy time of life for her to be divorcing Allen," Janice told a mutual friend. Also, if Caroline wasn't "already mad, she is very near to it," Janice thought. "I tremble for the future for her and everyone concerned with her."

WHEN Caroline got to New York, her optimism faltered and collapsed. How could she start over? It was disconcerting to be back in the city after twenty years. Her entire world was shattered, but her friends' lives seemed unchanged. They were "all doing just about the same things they were doing twenty years ago, in much the same way," she said. "New York seems to preserve people like flies in its own amber."

Unable at first to write, Caroline hunted up part-time jobs, teaching creative writing at Columbia and New York University, reading manuscripts for Macmillan. With Sally Wood's help she found furniture and settled into her cold-water flat at 108 Perry Street. She thought she could finish her Dracula book by May 15. She had to keep busy to keep the horrors away, she said: she was setting up "a routine to struggle against," "treading water" as best she could.

For a while she avoided Max Perkins. She figured he had to listen to too many sad stories about separations and divorce; she would not add to his burdens. But Max asked her to meet him, and Caroline was relieved to see him again.

By the end of January, she was quite proud of herself. "Here I am, a slip of a girl of fifty, only been out in the world alone two months and I think I have enough jobs lined up to get by on," she told Margaret Thorp.

Caroline's friends still worried, however, realizing she was under a lot of stress. Sally Wood feared Caroline did not have the strength to resist the most likely danger: Allen working his way back into Caroline's life. Sally knew Caroline was too much in love with Allen to forget him.

Allen was in a bad state after the divorce. At first he felt "paralyzed morally and intellectually," then he realized the divorce created more problems than it solved. The vice chancellor of the University of the South asked him to resign in February. Allen did not know what he would do next.

At the end of February, Allen visited Caroline in New York. Just as Sally had feared, he set out at once to seduce Caroline again, insisting he still loved her, claiming he no longer harbored any resentment against her. He urged her to marry him again, and Caroline did not hesitate to say yes. Despite her success at starting life anew, Caroline must have felt uncomfortable living alone. In twenty years she had come to depend on Allen, to shape her world around him. He was still the most charming, most exciting man she had ever met. She could never resist his charms or promises.

When Caroline told Sally about their plans to remarry, Sally tried to talk both Caroline and Allen out of it. She urged them to wait, to "live in sin" if necessary until they were both sure they were ready for a genuine commitment, not merely escaping from loneliness and insecurity. But Allen would not be swayed. Completely rejecting Sally's suggestion

that he live with Caroline for a while without marriage, he insisted that
the divorce and separation had removed all obstacles to their happiness.
Although he said he could not guarantee there would never again be violence between them, he assured Sally that he would not marry Caroline
again if he thought they would only revert to their former misery.

Caroline also resisted Sally's advice. She knew their whirlwind divorce and remarriage sounded foolish, yet if things went wrong again,
she thought a second divorce would not be as difficult. Since they were
"quite wretched apart," it was best for them to remarry immediately, she
told Sally. Their reunion was all part of the pattern Allen had once said
they had to follow: they would have to separate and "shatter everything
and start fresh," he had told her. "Of course a lot of other things got
shattered in the process, alas, but not my affection for him," Caroline
said. "I'd have that, no matter what happened to the poor devil."

Realizing they would never again be able to live in Tennessee, Allen
sold Benfolly and disposed of most of the furniture and household belongings. At first Caroline was relieved she did not have to oversee the
packing, but later she regretted her decision to let Allen handle the move.
He sold Benfolly for less than it was worth, and he lost, sold, or destroyed some of Caroline's family heirlooms. He also left their house in
Sewanee in disarray, full of furniture and a trunk of manuscripts and
correspondence. Nancy and Percy had to clean the house and put things
into storage.

While Allen prepared for his move north, Caroline returned to her
writing and teaching with new energy. She worried a bit that her book
about Dracula would "show the scars" of "one divorce and two reunions," but still she was able to write. In addition to work on her novel,
Caroline wrote a review of Malcolm Cowley's edition of *The Portable
Faulkner* for the *New York Times Book Review*.

On April 8 Allen and Caroline were married again. Although Caroline
had tried to talk Allen into another quick ceremony before a justice of
the peace in some city hall, Allen insisted they marry in Princeton. He
wanted to share their celebration with friends, and Caroline was glad he
did. So much was different from their first grim ceremony twenty years
earlier. Margaret and Willard Thorp hosted the ceremony and prepared
a wedding breakfast for the guests. Reverend Wood Carper, the Episcopal chaplain for Princeton University who had married Nancy and Percy
only two years earlier, officiated, and Allen gave Caroline a ring that she
treasured as a reminder of their commitment. Glowing from the love

of her friends and the beauty of the ceremony, Caroline predicted that she and Allen were "going to be very peaceable and quiet for a long time now!"

During their first months of remarriage, Caroline meditated deeply on the nature of love, in part to write an article for *Mademoiselle*. As if she were responding to Nancy's marriage several years earlier, Caroline drafted a fictional letter for "Vocabulary of Love." The mother-author expressed sadness at missing her daughter Mary's marriage because she had to care for an ailing relative. She could construct a picture of Mary's wedding with her "maternal imagination," yet she did not "have the conviction of having been present at the ceremony." "Ceremony has its uses," Caroline wrote. "I think part of that use is presenting us with symbols that are such tangible evidence of the important happenings of our lives that we can never forget them."

Mary wanted her mother's advice about cooking, but the mother realized that her request for recipes and advice was "in its modest way, symbolic," and she searched for more meaningful, valuable counsel to share with her daughter, passing along stories that must have been part of Caroline's own history—stories about Cousin Emma Anderson, who believed in the romance of a lace nightgown, and about why Great-great-uncle Will remained a bachelor. The tales not only reaffirmed the importance of ceremony and symbol; they also pointed out how absurd lovers sometimes appeared.

Yet after reflecting on the way courtship had changed, Caroline's fictional mother concluded that any advice she could give her daughter was not likely to be heeded. "Love has a different vocabulary in every age," Caroline wrote. "But never think that the words are unimportant. Love is eternally busy, creating its language. I am convinced that it is the most important in the world."

Lovers had to follow their own path, Caroline seemed to be saying, confident the creative power of their love would forge the right words, ones appropriate to their situation. Those words might seem foolish to others, just like Caroline and Allen's hasty remarriage, but that did not matter: love had its own logic and could not be judged by externals. It could only be celebrated, in ceremony and symbol.

In June Caroline left New York City to celebrate a ceremony of another sort: she returned to Bethany College in West Virginia to receive an honorary doctor of letters degree. Caroline took the train to Wheeling, then traveled by bus the rest of the way. She knew several of her college friends who still lived in Bethany would have been glad to pick her up at the train station, but as she said later, her trip was "a journey back into the past," and Caroline wanted to approach Bethany alone, as she had that first day.

"The Mountain Canary" was no longer operating; the roads had been widened and the mountains tunneled through, but as Caroline rode over the low, green hills, she thought about the first ride into town, how worried and insecure she had been. She also remembered how Professor Gay had encouraged her and built up her confidence, and she vowed to find him as soon as she got to Bethany and thank him heartily. But when Caroline arrived at the college, she discovered Professor Gay was no longer teaching there: he had been fired for "having his head in the clouds," Caroline's friends said. So Caroline decided to praise Professor Gay in the talk she had to give at an alumni luncheon. Before the event she browsed through the library stacks, searching for classical allusions to embellish her talk. When she came upon an edition of *Agamemnon*, she could barely bring herself to open it. "The very sight of its dull, reddish covers brought the past back with a rush," she wrote later. After a few moments, she began to page through the book, but she could only recognize isolated words and phrases: she could not "make out the whole of a single sentence."

Then she came to the section about Agamemnon and the purple tapestry, the scene Professor Gay had so thoroughly explicated in years past. To Caroline's amazement, she could read and understand the Greek at that point, and at that instant she realized how much she owed Professor Gay. "Standing there between the stacks, in the somewhat musty air of the little brick building, I suddenly realized where I had first been initiated into . . . [the] secrets of my craft—not in the works of Flaubert or Chekhov or James Joyce, but in Aeschylus' great play," she wrote later.

On June 9 Caroline received her honorary degree. She was praised as "one of Bethany's favorite daughters," a "teacher of youth, a successful author with the rare ability to make places and people of her imagination real and beloved to those who read her words." But for Caroline the highlight of her return to Bethany became her realization of the important role Professor Gay had played in her life. She decided Professor Gay was "a brilliant teacher of creative writing," and she increasingly attributed her success as a writer to his tutelage. The fact that Professor

Gay had been fired for "having his head in the clouds" only increased his stature in her eyes: he became a symbol of the artist, misunderstood and judged by inappropriate standards.

IT took Caroline a while to readjust to life in "double harness," as she put it, and she could never be completely reconciled to life in the city. Since they could not find or afford another apartment, Allen and Caroline had renovated the cold-water flat on Perry Street, adding a tub, turning a small, dank bedroom into a kitchen, and transforming the old kitchen into a combined study and dining room. The apartment was small, but Caroline insisted it was the kind of place she had always wanted: it was "rather primitive but with plenty of light and really enough space for just the two of us."

But often there was not enough space, especially when Allen played his violin or guests arrived, as they often did during the summer and fall of 1946. Sometimes the strains of Bach were so overpowering in their apartment that Caroline could not even concentrate on writing a letter.

To Caroline's delight, her dachshund, Bub, rejoined them early in the fall, but he too was not used to city living, and so he added to the chaos of life on Perry Street, howling in accompaniment to Allen's music, barking whenever Caroline left him alone for too long. Caroline escaped often, spending weekends in Tory Valley with Sue Jenkins.

During the week Caroline continued teaching at Columbia, two classes in the fall of 1946. The students in her class on the novel wore her down with their enthusiasm. She felt like they were "vampire bats, every one of them, sitting there, waiting for the drops of lifeblood to fall." When she tried to give them a ten-minute break in the middle of their two-hour class, they refused. "We can't take the time, Dr. Gordon," they said.

"Teaching is getting me down," Caroline said repeatedly, but secretly she was pleased with her students' dedication; she tried to give them as much of her lifeblood as she could spare. Sometimes she gave so much that her students felt overwhelmed. Every student in her course was trying to write a novel, and Caroline responded to each manuscript with detailed analysis, sometimes pages of typed comments.

Caroline spoke informally in the classroom, often sitting on the desk, sometimes sharing stories about her own education as a writer. But despite her informal manner, Caroline was actually quite dogmatic in her approach to teaching. As one student observed years later, Caroline was "very sure of her direction and the minute a student [started] eating grass over at the side of the road she just about [jerked] his neck off." Another student compared her to a modern pioneer woman. Dressing simply, with her hair drawn back tightly into a knot at the nape of her neck, Caroline sometimes looked a bit like Jenny Wiley or Cassy Outlaw, and she was always armed and ready to defend herself and fight for her beliefs.

"I'm not going to waste my breath discussing that until you show some glimmer of getting this," Caroline told one recalcitrant student. Another time she chastised the entire class. "Flaubert and Crane are not dated," she said, "but some of the manuscript in this class is definitely dated."

Students sometimes rebelled against her severe style. And yet many more respected her. Caroline challenged her students to master the techniques of fiction, stressing above all the writer's need to render details clearly. "You can't say that men ate rats at Vicksburg and make the reader see it," Caroline would say. "You have to show a specific man eating a specific rat. And it should be good eating too."

With all her teaching responsibilities, Caroline found it difficult to write. Since she had already missed the first deadline for her book about Dracula, she tried to force her way through the rest of the book. But the words refused to come. The character of Dracula kept "changing under my hands," she said. Eventually, Caroline thought of Dracula as a manifestation of the devil, and that created more problems for her. "I find that I don't know nearly as much as I need to know about the Devil," she told her friends. Yet after reading *The Cloud of Unknowing,* the work of an unknown English mystic writing in the thirteenth or fourteenth century, Caroline considered turning her mystery story into a more philosophical book, almost an abstract study of evil.

But Caroline was not able to return to the novel she called *Mr. Voivoide.* During the winter and spring of 1947, the old problems between Caroline and Allen resurfaced and multiplied: jealousy, resentment, fear, anger. Caroline seldom spoke about what had happened: she wanted to protect their reputations. When she did write to Lon and Fannie Cheney about that time, she asked them to destroy her letter after reading it. "Allen and I have been going through another of our tail spins," she said. "This one makes the antics of the past two years look like child's play."

In another letter to Mark Van Doren, Caroline suggested their troubles were due in part to Allen's unhappiness with his job at Holt. Years later, however, she suggested that the crisis began because Allen had gotten involved with a student of Léonie Adams, their old friend from their Paris days. But Bill Brown thought Caroline had actually caught Allen flirting with Léonie. One night after a party, Bill saw the Tates had been fighting. "Allen's face was scratched," Bill said later. "Caroline had a satanic expression on her face, as though possessed."

The rumors circulating about the Tates' problems in the spring of 1947 often cast Allen in the role of victim, Caroline as the aggressor: mad, possessed, dangerous. Late at night the Perry Street neighbors heard Caroline scream, heard dishes crashing against the walls of the apartment. By the end of March, Allen had moved into the Hotel Brevoort, perhaps to escape the midnight rages. This time the crisis was acute and not complicated by extraneous matters, Allen said. Caroline said only that they had gotten "to the point where it was impossible—literally impossible"—for them to live in the same apartment.

Caroline could always justify her anger; she seldom thought her tantrums were excessive or inappropriate. Instead she increasingly believed Allen was possessed or mad; she had to "assemble defenses" against his "antics." That spring he again began to act erratically; he even tried to sell their car without telling her.

When Sally Wood heard about the Tates' troubles, she arranged for them to see a psychoanalyst, Dr. Lawrence Kubie. As Caroline reexamined their relationship, she wondered if she had failed Allen, but finally she decided she was not solely to blame. Allen was "incapable of making the kind of marriage that most people make," she said. He could "never fall in love with any woman who couldn't have real power over him," but "his neurosis forbids him to give himself up so completely to any woman, for committing himself wholly to me would be a kind of self relinquishment," she concluded.

Although Caroline realized she had complicated their problems with her "jealous, suspicious nature and violent temper," she felt Allen needed help with his "mother fixation." "He finally turned on me all the hate he had been bottling up all these years," hate originally fostered by his mother, she said. "I have become so identified with his mother that he simply couldn't disentangle us."

Caroline hoped they would be able to work through their problems, but once again she began to plan for a life without Allen. She decided she could share an apartment in New York with Sue Jenkins and spend weekends in the country. Yet Caroline was not able to make the final decision to go through with another divorce. She felt Allen still loved her, as much as he was capable of loving anyone. She also thought Allen needed her, and so she deluded herself into a sort of martyrdom. Believing she would destroy Allen if she left him, she willingly sacrificed herself, and in doing so, she avoided facing her own fear of life as a single person. "I think I would step out of his life, if I thought it would not do him harm," she said.

All the while she struggled to save her marriage, Caroline felt rather like a broken reed. She cut herself off from friends, partly because she had neither time nor energy for visiting or writing letters, partly because she wanted to protect Allen's reputation, and also because she did not want to burden anyone. Yet she continued to reach out to help others, and she continued to teach and critique students' manuscripts. "Artists are tough—a lot tougher than ordinary people," Caroline said. "The thing that so complicates your ordinary life stands by you in times of stress."

In time, with Dr. Kubie's help, Allen and Caroline began to resolve their problems. Caroline was enthusiastic about the counseling at first. Psychoanalysis gave her new alibis and new avenues to explore, and Caroline had an incredible ability to fool herself. She decided that both she and Allen ought to have had counseling years ago. They were "victims of too little learning": "we feel that we know all about the mechanics of the unconscious because we have read a little Freud or Jung. But we really don't," she said. Allen needed "a Father Confessor," she thought. "This damn modern world takes such a heavy toll of us. I suppose we have to have psychic aids, even people like us, just as we have to use the automobile or the telephone—though we don't really believe in people covering so much ground or communicating with each other so often or on such a level."

But eventually Caroline became disenchanted with psychoanalysis. "This modern substitute for prayer is not really an improvement," she told friends. "You stood some chance of getting hold of God when all you had to do was kneel down at your bedside, but getting hold of your psychiatrist takes all the energy and skill you can muster. And then he can only give you an hour."

When Dr. Kubie suggested that both Allen and Caroline suffered from latent homosexuality, the Tates were enraged enough to end their sessions. Neither of them could accept, or even consider, such a possibility. "There is an abyss at the bottom of every human soul, I feel sure, . . . [but] it ought to remain unplumbed," Caroline decided.

Sometime in early summer Allen moved back into the Perry Street apartment, and he soon arranged to reduce his work at Holt's to half-time status. Caroline was relieved. She thought Allen needed to devote more time to his own writing. When Allen was writing, he was confident and calm. It was only when he could not write that he would try to turn his world upside down, according to Caroline.

During the upheavals of the spring, Caroline could not work on her novel about Dracula, but once she and Allen had settled their affairs somewhat, she returned to work with a new understanding of how she could resolve her problems with the narrative. The book had to be more like Samuel Coleridge's poem "The Ancient Mariner," Caroline decided: it had to have a firm surface pattern of events; those events could be symbolic, but they had to be "presented as events as baldly as the slaying of the albatross [was] presented."

Caroline decided on a new title for the book, *The Walker,* a reference to the devil's propensity to walking about the earth, and a fairly simple story. Disguised as a visiting scholar, the devil would appear in Princeton and wreak great havoc. Two men would realize what was happening, but one of those men would be "always falling away from his real knowledge and trying to explain things by the play of his 'curious wits,'" Caroline explained to a friend. "The other man never swerved from what he had announced at the start: that he had just seen the Devil," but he would disappear at the same time the devil disappeared, and people would wonder "just what sort of man he was, after all."

Having a clear understanding of how she could finish the novel cheered Caroline considerably. She began to consider what she would work on next, and when she had one project clearly defined, she went to see Max Perkins.

Max had been fighting against poor health and utter exhaustion for some time, but Caroline did not realize just how ill he was. His hands trembled, yet his tight-lipped, wry smile seemed the same, and Max listened supportively as she outlined her idea for a book called *The Figure at the Window.* It would be a book about the art of fiction, based on her teaching at Columbia and her own experience as a writer. She took the title from Henry James's metaphor about fiction: it was a house with many windows, dependent on an individual's unique angle of vision.

Max liked the idea, but he told Caroline that he might not be able to be her editor for such a project: it would probably have to be handled by the textbook department of Scribner's. Not long after their meeting, Caroline received the official approval for her book, and the promise of a five-hundred-dollar advance. She would have to collaborate with Allen, however: Scribner's thought the book would sell better that way.

On Friday, June 13, Caroline stopped in to see Max once again. Buoyed by his interest, she asked him if she could get a larger advance on the book. "No," Max said firmly but kindly, shaking his head.

Struck by his gentleness, Caroline backed down. "All right, Max," she said. "I don't really need it."

Less than a week later, the telephone rang at 108 Perry Street. When Caroline answered it, she found it was Charles Scribner, Jr., calling. Maxwell Perkins had died on June 17, of a sudden bout of pneumonia, Scribner said.

Caroline was shocked. In the weeks that followed, she kept thinking about how her last conversation with Max had been about money. She was glad something had made her back down, but she wished she had not asked him for more money. She wished she had talked with him about more important things, about all those ideas she had for other books, about what his support had meant to her.

Caroline's grief overwhelmed her at times. Max's death reminded her of her father's death; it seemed somehow worse than her father's death, perhaps because of its suddenness and because it had occurred while she was recovering from her most recent crisis with Allen. During the day Caroline could muster up an appearance of control, sitting at the typewriter, pretending to write, but at night, her routine failed her. She could not sleep; she could only think about Max and about what she and Allen had been through.

One evening, after Allen had fallen asleep, Caroline decided to compose a letter to Ward Dorrance. Writing in pencil, so as not to wake Allen with her typewriter, she began by commenting on Ward's talent, but soon she dropped the pretense of offering advice and admitted how she was suffering. "I simply cannot realize that Max is dead," she wrote. "I am still talking to him. I mean we both understand that we were terribly occupied and all that, but we saved up things to tell each other, and now he is dead, and all sorts of things—some of them rather silly—I can never tell anybody else."

Caroline knew Max had never been "terribly interested" in her work. "He liked better people like Tom Wolfe or Marcia Davenport," she told Ward; "they gave him an opportunity to exercise his extraordinary talent." Still, she knew she could always appeal to Max for help, "and then he'd put his whole mind on it and tell you what he thought." During the twenty years she had Max as her editor, he had given her four "damn good" suggestions, she thought.

Caroline's hand shook and her writing sprawled, almost illegibly at times, but she tried to hide some of the confusion and pain she was feeling. "Don't think I am in any particularly feeble state," she wrote. "It's simply that in the last few months I have had to do—simultaneously—a lot of things that I would have regarded as impossible at one time. I've had to re-make my own life," she wrote. "But, as if that weren't enough I've had to simply take Allen's life in my two hands and make it over."

Caroline explained how she had admired Allen too much, but then thought better of her confession and crossed out what she had written. "All this has been very exhausting," she wrote. "But you'll understand, and destroy this letter, *please*. I don't like to leave my tracks in the snow."

From the summer of 1947 on, Caroline increasingly preferred to hide behind a mask, to protect and promote a conventional public image. Before their divorce and remarriage, she had frequently teased Allen in public, making fun of his idiosyncrasies and inadequacies just as she mocked other young poets and writers, while in private she had admired Allen without bounds and depended more and more on his judgment and guidance. Now, after two years of separations and reunions, Caroline's approach to her relationship with Allen had changed.

Although she would struggle to live out her new understanding, Caroline realized she could not depend on Allen to create order and stability in her life. Too often, he was simply hanging "by a hair," and whenever that slim lifeline was cut, he fell "into the depths," she said. What he needed was a "satisfactory relation with the sensuous world," she thought, but Allen never seemed "to be able to refresh himself or renew himself through Nature—or even through other people."

When Caroline could finally admit that Allen might actually need psychiatric help, she began to recognize how she had mistakenly cast him, and other men in her life, in exalted positions. Yet she found it extremely difficult to break the patterns of dependence she had created in her life, to rely on her own strength and judgment. As if to compensate for her new understanding, she became more determined than ever to guard and champion Allen's reputation, no matter the cost.

Caroline's masquerade took place in fiction as well as life. Sometime between the euphoria of remarriage and the despair of a near second divorce, she wrote another story about marriage, called "The Petrified Woman." The story revealed her growing desire to conceal the true nature of any conflict, or perhaps her inability to see or admit that the problems that plagued any marriage relationship were not black and white—all his fault, or hers. In the story Caroline also demonstrated how willing she was to blame herself to protect the image of one she loved.

Caroline dedicated the story to Eudora Welty, whom she had recently gotten to know. Eudora had written a story called "Petrified Man." The tale was set in a beauty parlor of a small Mississippi town. In between perms and colorings, the women gossiped about everything, including a man one of them saw in a traveling freak show. He was supposedly turning to stone, but actually he was hiding from the law: he had raped four women in California. Eudora used the discovery of the petrified man to satirize the unnatural relationships between men and women. The man's crimes were monstrous, but the actions of the women in the beauty shop were less than admirable. In fact, Eudora suggested women might be responsible for turning men to stone.

Caroline's companion piece, "The Petrified Woman," was the story of the appearance of another freak-show character at a reunion of the "Fayerlee" connection. According to Caroline's notes, the petrified woman named Hazel "shot seven men in Alabama" but masqueraded in a carnival wagon as the virginal Stella, a petrified sixteen-year-old beauty. Caroline wrote two versions of the story, but she did not reveal Stella's misdeeds in either version. Rather, she concentrated on the effect Stella's appearance had on one marriage, that of Tom and Eleanor Fayerlee.

In several respects the story of the Fayerlees resembled one of Caroline's first tales, "Funeral in Town." Modeled on Uncle Rob, Tom Fayerlee was a genial drunk; Eleanor was his second wife, originally from Birmingham and an outsider to the ways of the connection. She could not tolerate Tom's behavior when he was drunk, and his family did not appreciate her. After seeing the "petrified" Stella, Tom made a fool of himself at a family dinner party, declaring that he loved Stella to torment Eleanor. By the time Tom collapsed in a drunken stupor, his marriage was all but over.

Caroline told the story through the eyes of her fictive alter ego, Sally Maury, the young daughter of Professor Aleck Maury. Using the child's innocent eye allowed Caroline to explore the way point of view affected one's understanding: Sally worshipped Tom but she also admired

Eleanor, and she did not fully understand what was happening around her or whom she should sympathize with. "It's all in the way you look at it," as Tom said early in the story.

In Caroline's first version of the story, a careful reader would undoubtedly sympathize with Eleanor, who clearly suffered from her husband's behavior and his family's narrow-mindedness. But Caroline did not publish that version. Instead she covered her tracks and revised the story, creating a much more enigmatic account, one in which she muted the criticism of Tom and greatly altered the character of his wife, suggesting Eleanor was the true petrified woman because of her cold heart and intolerance of the Fayerlees. Caroline also cut Tom's comment, "It's all in the way you look at it," and added the thread of a fairy tale. Just as in Caroline's first published story, "Summer Dust" Sally remembered snatches of a fairy tale and began to see Tom and Eleanor as characters in such a tale. But in "Summer Dust," Sally's fondness for fairy tales was a creative fiction; in "The Petrified Woman" her fondness had become an escape, a way for Sally to block out the unpleasant realities of life.

Caroline's two versions of "The Petrified Woman" revealed a new split between her public image and her private self. Previously in her fiction, she had undermined conventional surface patterns with underground streams of meaning sympathetic to women's concerns. In "The Petrified Woman," however, Caroline ultimately diverted or destroyed the underground stream of meaning, perhaps because she began to realize that she was leaving "tracks in the snow." In the final version of the story, published in the September 1947 issue of *Mademoiselle,* Caroline deliberately masked and inverted her sympathies. She did not destroy the original version, however, but saved it, one of the few manuscripts she preserved over the years.

Throughout the summer and fall of 1947, Caroline reorganized her life according to new patterns. After teaching at the Utah Writers' Conference in July, she divided her time between New York City and Tory Valley. The valley was her refuge: Caroline could dig in the dirt, study the light filtering through the trees, renew her strength.

During one such visit to Tory Valley during the summer of 1947, Caroline found another source of strength, order, and stability—Christian faith. She had been idly thumbing through an old calf-bound Bible she found on the shelf in Sue's house, when suddenly the familiar words spoke to her in a new way. Before long, she had reread the entire Bible, and she knew she not only believed in God but also wanted to join the Catholic church.

On November 24, 1947, the feast day of St. John of the Cross, Caroline was baptized at the Church of St. Francis Xavier, on West Sixteenth Street in New York City. Immediately after her baptism Caroline began to read avidly in Catholic theology and to study the lives of the saints. She attended Our Lady of Pompeii Church, an Italian parish on Bleecker Street, and prepared for her confirmation with Father Martin J. Scott, a Jesuit priest.

The history, ritual, and mystical life of the Catholic church appealed to Caroline. She approached the mystery of the sacraments slowly, however, astonishing Father Scott several weeks after her baptism by saying that she was not taking communion because she did not "feel worthy."

"You never will be!" he snorted. "That's the reason you take it."

At first Caroline struggled to explain her faith. "I would really like to tell you what being in the Church is like, but can't," she wrote to a friend. "It's like suddenly being given authority to believe all the things you've surmised." Yet soon she was not shy about trying to bring others into the church with her, passing out tracts, sharing copies of her daily missal, copying quotations from Catholic writers in letters to her "heretic" friends. When she was confirmed, she chose Monica as her patron: Monica had brought her son, St. Augustine, into the church with her prayers.

Although many of Caroline's friends thought her new-found faith was shocking, still others sensed her conversion was inevitable. Especially since her aunt's death, Caroline had been meditating on the nature of good and evil, reading the works of Christian mystics as well as Hindu philosophers. She had suffered through too many deaths, disappointments, and upheavals in recent years, and her sufferings left her shaken and searching for something to believe in. Becoming a Catholic gave Caroline a sense of security and answers to her questions about the purpose of her life and the nature of death.

It also gave her a thoroughly respectable mask to hide behind. In the Catholic church Caroline found conservative ideology well suited to her life and fictional techniques. By declaring herself a dutiful daughter to Catholic teaching, Caroline could wield moral authority over recalcitrant "sinners," most notably and frequently Allen. She might have to mouth patriarchal pieties, but she could readily identify with strong women like

Dorothy Day and many female saints who could exert power and gain a measure of prestige and prominence in the world.

Caroline had known several zealous converts to the Catholic faith, among them Cal Lowell and Dorothy, and when she joined the church, it was experiencing a wave of popularity. Yet some of the Tates' friends believed Allen had in fact led Caroline to the church. Since the early 1920s he had been flirting with the idea of Catholicism, and at one point in late 1945, he had said the success of their marriage might depend on Caroline's having a religious conversion of some sort.

But when Caroline first explored the reasons she joined the church, she never referred to Allen. In fact, she suggested a few years after her conversion that Allen had the opposite effect on her faith: by approaching the church almost as an intellectual exercise, he had actually been an obstacle to her conversion.

Caroline gave a number of explanations for her becoming a Catholic. Once she claimed the Gospel of St. Mark spoke to her; another time she said quotes from the book of Jeremiah or the book of Psalms convicted her. Sometimes she credited the prayers of Dorothy Day; various books she had read, like Sigrid Undset's novels; or even the example of piety that some of her Benfolly tenants had shown.

But ultimately Caroline believed the act of writing revealed the nature of faith to her. She felt she had been approaching the Catholic church her entire life. "I have lived most of my life on the evidence of things not seen—what else is writing a novel but that?—and my work has progressed slowly and steadily in one direction," she said. "At a certain point I found the Church squarely in the path. I couldn't jump over it and wouldn't go around it, so had to go into it." All artists were fundamentally religious, Caroline decided. The writing of fiction was, "in essence, a religious act." "We are moved to imitate our Creator, to do as he did, and create a world," she said.

One of the first things Caroline did after her conversion was to return to her favorite fictional world and write what would be the final story about Aleck Maury, "The Presence." In the story seventy-five-year-old Aleck was living in a boardinghouse run by Jenny and Jim Mowbray. Conscious only of his own needs and desires, Aleck did not realize Jim was having an affair with another boarder. Only after Jenny discovered her husband's infidelity and collapsed in agony did Aleck understand what had been happening. But at first all he thought about was how he would be left without a home if Jenny went through with her plans to divorce Jim and sell the boardinghouse.

Yet Aleck Maury was saved from selfishness by memory and faith, or rather, by the memory of faith. When another boarder, Miss Gilbert, began to spout pieties and platitudes, Aleck began to reflect on how women would "rock the world." His sour musings carried him back to his childhood and his favorite aunt, Victoria. Recalling Aunt Vic's desire "to save his immortal soul," Aleck remembered praying at her death bed. He had been "mumbling the Angelic Salutation"—"Hail, Mary, full of grace . . ."—when Aunt Vic cried out, rose as if she saw a vision, and then collapsed in death.

At that time "he turned and saw nothing," and "he had wondered what it was that he could not see," Caroline wrote. But at the end of "The Presence," Caroline suggested that Aleck had begun to understand his aunt's life of faith, and that the vision may have been of an angel, or of Mary herself, appearing at Vic's bedside, joining in Aleck's halfhearted prayer.

Although Caroline ended the story at the moment of Aleck's understanding, she knew most readers would think he was on the verge of conversion to Catholicism. It would shock some readers, undoubtedly, and yet, there was nothing in "The Presence" that had not been foreshadowed in Caroline's earlier works. The character of Aunt Vic, the depth of her Catholic faith, and her commitment to converting Aleck, even Aleck's ultimate dependence on others: all had been referred to in *Aleck Maury, Sportsman*. Also, the idea of a woman bringing salvation to the misguided man had been developed in Caroline's last novel, *The Women on the Porch*. In these and so many other ways, "The Presence" demonstrated how, in Caroline's own words, her work had "progressed slowly and steadily in one direction"—toward the Catholic faith.

But another thread of the story suggested that Caroline's faith would be eclectic and inclusive. Aleck identified his aunt with both Mary and the Greek "Queen of Heaven," Juno. "In his childish mind pagan and Christian symbols had mingled," Caroline wrote. When, as an adult, Aleck described Jenny Mowbray in both terms, as Junoesque and as the virtuous woman of the Old Testament, the readers of "The Presence" would also find it hard to separate the pagan and Christian symbols. Jim and Jenny Mowbray were like Zeus and Juno, the philandering man and his jealous, raging wife. Yet in another of Caroline's inversions, Jenny, and not Jim, would be the victor in conflict, just as Mary, not Christ or God the Father, would lead Aleck to faith.

"It is at a time like this, when the hard core of the personality is shattered, that the real self has a chance to emerge," Miss Gilbert told Aleck at the end of "The Presence." Caroline had experienced such a shattering; all that remained for her was to discover how, or if, her "real self" would emerge.

 1947–1953

For a while Caroline's faith was the only fixed point in her life. The winter of 1947–48 was brutally cold, and Caroline found it difficult to keep their apartment on Perry Street warm. She also struggled, with limited success, to balance teaching, writing, and entertaining. As soon as spring arrived, she replenished her strength by spending weekends in the country, digging like mad in the garden.

Caroline thought Allen was beginning to settle down, and that made life easier for both of them. She persuaded him to quit his job at Henry Holt and Company at the end of January and begin teaching part-time at New York University. During the spring of 1948, Allen considered following Caroline into the church. Caroline was ecstatic, but he was not baptized then: the priest instructing Allen sensed he did not have the right attitude of humility. He told Allen to wait.

Caroline and Allen spent the summer of 1948 on what Caroline called one long "barnstorming tour" through Tennessee, Missouri, Kansas, and Ohio, visiting friends and relatives, teaching at writing conferences. Caroline enjoyed most of her stay at the University of Kansas Writers' Conference. She thought the students were unusually good, if demanding, and her lectures and roundtable sessions went well. She knew she had her audience under her spell. "I must say I wowed them," she wrote a friend. "It's . . . a relief to know that if you have to do it you can take an audience up and do pretty much what you want to do with it."

Despite her short stature Caroline had an imposing presence as a lecturer. Several months earlier she had cut her own hair, giving herself bangs, which she thought made her "look like a cross between Alice B. Toklas and John the Baptist." She spoke forcefully and tolerated no nonsense: when one participant objected to her criticism of Somerset Maugham's short story "Rain," Caroline reiterated her opinion and dismissed his. The students realized Caroline might look like a rather sweet, good-natured grandmother, but she was not at all shy and retiring: rather, she was a strong woman who did not hesitate to speak her mind.

Caroline's enjoyment of Kansas was marred by a health problem, however. During the last week of the Kansas conference, she began to hemorrhage. When Caroline consulted a gynecologist, he told her he would have to operate to determine the reason. Allen urged her to wait until she joined him in Gambier, Ohio, to have the surgery. Caroline agreed, but while she finished her sessions in Lawrence and traveled to Ohio, she suffered greatly, sure she had developed cancer like her mother and aunt.

Caroline had to wait only about two weeks for the diagnosis, but those weeks were both the happiest and most agonizing, she later said. She imagined what her death from cancer would be like; she also reviewed what she had accomplished and what she might yet be able to complete.

Could she finish *The Walker,* several years overdue already? She had completed about six chapters, more than half the manuscript, and outlined the rest: a first-person narrative by Stephen Fane, a young novelist, of how he and his wife, Veronica, came to know Mr. Voivoide, who brought terror to their university town. But she could not find the right tone for the final chapters. She wanted to close the novel with Fane's realization that the devil or Dracula figure would be "an incarnation of Fane's own nature, and hence, always in danger of becoming dear to him," Caroline wrote in her notes. Fane's "devil merely looses the dark forces that lie at the centre of every man's being." Yet Caroline did not know how she could make the spiritual realm clear. She was also not sure that she really understood her narrator well enough. Finally she decided to abandon *The Walker.* "I ought never to have started" it, she decided. It was not only a relief, but "a major economy" to heave it overboard, she said later.

Much to Caroline's relief, the exploratory surgery revealed no malignancy, only a fibroid tumor; Caroline had a second operation to remove the tumor. When they returned to New York at the end of the summer, Caroline restored her strength with trips to the country. Allen went along, and, for a change, he was able to establish a writing routine.

Eager for a permanent home and a more stable way of life, Caroline decided that Tory Valley was an ideal place for Allen. "He has to have, in order to really work, a certain amount of money, a certain amount of solitude and a certain amount of society," she told Ward Dorrance. In Tory Valley Allen could have all three, Caroline thought, and she began to make surreptitious plans for the future. When she sold an article to *Mademoiselle* called "How Not to Write a Short Story," she gave Sue Jenkins three hundred dollars as a down payment for three acres of her land, part of an old orchard surrounded by stone walls, just out of sight of Sue's house.

Caroline told all her friends that she wanted to build a house with rammed earth walls on her acreage. But she would settle for a house made of cinder blocks, or even some arrangement with Sue to use her house from spring through fall in exchange for help with the repairs and Sue's use of the Perry Street apartment: Caroline would agree to anything if it meant she would have a permanent country escape.

Throughout the fall of 1948, Caroline worked on the textbook for Scribner's, which she and Allen had decided to call *The House of Fiction*, a tribute to Henry James. They chose thirty stories to include in the book: from American writers like Hawthorne, Melville, and Edgar Allan Poe to European artists like Chekhov, Kafka, and Flaubert. Allen wanted to include one of Caroline's stories, but she thought that would be inappropriate. They did, however, include a number of southern writers in the anthology: Katherine Anne Porter, Eudora Welty, William Faulkner, Peter Taylor, Andrew Lytle, and "Red" Warren.

The Tates planned to include commentaries for half the stories in *The House of Fiction*. They also would include two appendices: "The Arts of Fiction" and "Faults of the Amateur." Caroline expected to do most of the work, and she did. In addition to writing part of the appendices, she wrote commentaries for twelve of the fifteen stories. Allen provided the analysis for three of the stories: "The Dead" by James Joyce, "The Beast in the Jungle" by Henry James, and "The Fall of the House of Usher" by Edgar Allan Poe.

Caroline used many of the stories included in *The House of Fiction* to illustrate principles of good and bad writing in her classes at Columbia. She believed that teaching had helped her to articulate her criteria for good writing and that everything she had learned could be summarized in two sentences. First, an object did not exist in fiction "until it has either acted upon or been acted upon by" some other object. Second, a character also did not exist in isolation but had to act or be acted upon by some other character.

Although the principles might seem easy, Caroline thought most beginning writers did not grasp them. She stressed the basic tenets in all her classes and based the article she had sold to *Mademoiselle,* "How Not to Write A Short Story," on those principles as well. For *The House of Fiction* she revised the *Mademoiselle* article only slightly and used it for the appendix, "Faults of the Amateur."

In *The House of Fiction* and "How Not to Write A Short Story," Caroline wrote with compassion about the difficulties that beginning writers faced. But during the fall of 1948, she began to tire of teaching, and she admitted privately that she had begun to construct barriers and "set up some defense against the pupils." Teaching creative writing was very depleting, deceptively so, she thought. "I regard myself as a hired gladiator and make it a point to spill considerable of my lifeblood every week," she told Ward Dorrance. "Anybody who satisfies the entrance requirements and pays his sixty bucks is privileged to come and lap up all he wants. But I find that students—usually the least talented[—]prefer a private veinletting and will try to make me repeat the performance in conference." She decided she could no longer accommodate "those gentry": if she spilled too much of her lifeblood for the students, she would not have enough left for her own work.

Caroline got a much-needed break from teaching between January and May 1949, since Allen had accepted a one-semester position at the University of Chicago. At first everything went splendidly in Chicago. Caroline liked the city much better than New York. "One has always the consciousness of wide fields outside the city," she observed soon after she arrived. "Life here is just one grand sweet song."

The university had found them a spacious and comfortably furnished apartment on Kenwood Avenue, a beautiful tree-lined street in the heart of the city. Caroline set aside one room for painting and another for writing, and she pursued both activities with vigor, glorying in the "quantities of leisure" she had. She painted pictures of dachshunds and various saints and martyrs, all quite primitive. Painting was relaxing, "rather like knitting or embroidery," she said, something she could do "in the intervals of writing."

By the middle of February, the Tates had finished *The House of Fiction,* and Caroline had begun a new novel she had been meditating on for several months. At first Caroline thought she would call her book *The Bush Arbour Meeting,* but she soon changed the title to *The Strange Children,* a reference to Psalm 144: "Rid me, and deliver me from the hand of strange children, whose mouth speaketh vanity."

Caroline decided to use Benfolly for the setting of her story, and she chose an eight-year-old girl named Lucy for her heroine. As she worked on her novel, Caroline realized that Lucy was the granddaughter of Aleck Maury. Lucy's parents were Sarah and Stephen Lewis, Caroline's fictional version of herself and Allen; the other characters were composites of various friends and family members.

Caroline created Uncle Tubby, whom she sometimes called the villain of her tale, to resemble Edmund Wilson, Ford Madox Ford, Malcolm Cowley, Andrew Lytle, and Robert Penn Warren in turn. One of Lucy's "courtesy uncles," he was a large man with curly chestnut-colored hair, a poet who had written a long narrative poem, *If It Takes All Summer,* which he had sold to Hollywood for fifty thousand dollars.

Caroline developed the character of Isabel Reardon as the villainess, a mad woman poet originally from Minnesota with whom Tubby had fallen in love. Caroline used incidents from the lives of Katherine Anne Porter, Louise Bogan, Laura Riding, Jean Stafford, Mary McCarthy, and even Zelda Fitzgerald to fashion Isabel's personality and history.

Caroline also planned to use her Benfolly tenants, the Normans, thinly disguised as the MacDonoughs, in her novel. Since the book was ultimately about the need for religious faith, the MacDonoughs would have a pentecostal revival, called a brush-arbor meeting, that would attract the attention of the Lewis family and their friends, and dramatize the true nature of the "strange children."

Caroline later realized that she had gotten "the germ" of the story and much of the plot from several incidents in the 1930s, especially her memories of how the tenants would act whenever she and Allen had visitors at Benfolly. "Let's go up the hill and watch," the Normans used to say, and then they would "crouch in the bushes and observe the goings on in the big house, (much the way we go to the zoo,) while the guests would hang over the balcony of the big house and observe the Normans with an equal amount of curiosity and lack of comprehension," Caroline recalled. Other episodes which would find their way into her story included a time Nancy had stolen Andrew Lytle's watch and one of Edmund Wilson's visits to Benfolly, when he sneaked off for a romantic tryst with another guest.

After some false starts Caroline decided to tell her story through Lucy. She wanted to use Henry James's technique of a central intelligence, and she thought Lucy's perspective was "superior to that of the grown people because it [was] *pure*." Lucy might hear things she could not understand, but she would still "register" the important things happening around her, much the way Nancy used to mimic her great-grandmother. Caroline vividly remembered a time when she overheard four-year-old Nancy talking to herself. "I've got to die some time. I've got to die some time," Nancy said, quite gaily, but Caroline heard the grim tone of Old Miss Carrie's voice beneath the child's unconscious chatter. To create that undertone in her prose, Caroline decided to use an omniscient observer at times during the narrative. "After all, we all speak Jonsonian English when communing with our souls, as Faulkner has shown many times," she told a friend.

After she had finished the first two chapters of the book, Caroline realized that she was once again working with the metaphor of an underground stream in her fiction. Two phrases from Keats's poem "La Belle Dame sans Merci" served as the figurative underground stream for the opening scenes: Uncle Tubby spoke one phrase, Lucy remembered another, and the phrases would "emerge at the denouement like . . . a waterfall dashing over black rocks," Caroline wrote. To extend the analogy, she had Lucy and Tubby walking beside a literal waterfall and underground stream.

Much to Caroline's dismay, her work on *The Strange Children* was interrupted almost as soon as it was begun. In the beginning of March, Caroline and Allen were diverted by a series of strange phone calls and telegrams from Cal Lowell. Having divorced Jean Stafford and left the Catholic church, Cal had been acting erratically for some time. During the spring of 1949, however, he suddenly reclaimed his Catholic faith and began to have visions that made him act even more peculiar. He helped mount a crusade to fire the director of Yaddo for being a Communist sympathizer, and when that failed, he embarked on another campaign against the general state of evil in the world. He implored Allen to come to New York to help him fight, but Allen refused. Instead Caroline invited Cal to visit them in Chicago, but neither she nor Allen minded when Cal kept postponing the trip.

In March the Tates went to Memphis to visit Nancy, Percy, and their two grandsons, "Baby Allen," born in the spring of 1947, and P-3, who had, by age four, grown into a new nickname, Peto. After returning to

Chicago, Caroline and Allen moved to a new apartment at 5521 South Kimbark Avenue. Then, on March 29, Cal Lowell appeared.

When Caroline and Allen first saw their young friend, they sensed Cal was in "a dangerous state of elation." After only twenty-four hours, they realized Cal was probably on the verge of a psychotic breakdown. Kissing Caroline almost every five minutes, Cal kept saying that Allen had to tell him what the will of God was for his life. When Caroline was alone with the young poet, she began to fear for her own safety. Allen later told a friend that Cal was especially dangerous around women and children: Cal had a purification mania that might at any time turn homicidal, Allen thought.

Cal calmed down briefly after a day or so before becoming more aggressive. He insisted that Allen had to repent of his sins, and to help Allen, he gave Caroline a list of all the women with whom Allen had had affairs. Later Cal began kissing Allen as well, and grabbing him from behind in a fierce bear hug, jerking him up in the air. Caroline realized that Allen was helpless in his grasp: Cal was nearly twice as big as Allen and much stronger.

Cal stayed with the Tates for five days. On his last evening he created a scene in a restaurant, then returned to the Tates' apartment, opened a window, and began shouting obscenities at passersby. It took four policemen to restrain Cal, and then all the finesse Allen could muster to keep Cal out of jail or a psychiatric hospital. Later a mutual friend would insist that Cal had actually held Allen "at arm's length out of his second-floor apartment window . . . [and] forced [Allen] to listen to a bear's voice recitation" of "Ode to the Confederate Dead."

By the time the Tates escorted Cal to the train the next morning, they both felt as if they had been "run over by a steam roller," Caroline said. They called Cal's friend Peter Taylor and warned him that Cal was headed to see him. Before two days had passed, Cal was once again in restraints, this time a straitjacket: he had been running through the streets of Bloomington, Indiana, shouting tirades against devils and homosexuals, trying to stop cars with only the force of his spirit. By the end of the week, Cal was locked in a padded cell of a private hospital in Massachusetts.

Caroline was relieved to hear that Cal was receiving medical attention, but she was badly shaken by the entire affair. It was almost as if she had been the one placed in police custody, she told a friend. Her muscles were "tied in knots"; she walked as if she had a bad attack of rheumatism.

She could not write or even edit her own writing; she could only sit at her desk and go through the motions of work, all the while wondering what had caused Cal's collapse and if she could have done anything different to help him.

In the end Caroline blamed Cal's illness on his "meteoric success": in 1947 alone, he had won a Guggenheim Fellowship, a Pulitzer Prize, and an award from the American Academy of Arts and Letters. This rush of attention had in some way brought about his "rapid decline," she thought. It was small comfort, she said, but perhaps she was lucky "to be only moderately famous."

Before Caroline completely recovered her equilibrium, Allen finished his term in Chicago. The Tates spent the summer of 1949 on yet another barnstorming tour, which took them to Minnesota, Missouri, Kansas, and Ohio. Caroline got little writing done. By the end of the summer, she said she could hardly even "visualize the process" of work. "It is all this racketing around," she exclaimed. "One would have to be Somerset Maugham or a Herbert Agar to survive it."

The only thing sustaining Caroline was the promise of a new home to return to in Princeton, New Jersey. During the spring, between the crises and upheavals, the Tates had heard about a perfect little house for sale. After Allen's brother Ben agreed to help them out again, they arranged to buy the house at 465 Nassau Street, not far from the center of town and Princeton University, but seemingly in the country, with an acre of land.

When the Tates moved into their new home that fall, Caroline could hardly contain her enthusiasm. "This is It!" she yelped. "This is the house for us." They had lived in six different houses in about as many months, she figured. "One more would push me over some edge," she said.

Built sometime in the eighteenth century as the gatehouse for a larger estate, the two-story white house resembled a fairy-tale cottage, Caroline thought: "the upper story over-hangs the lower story, which gives it that old world, fairy tale look." It had "touches of Benfolly" although everything was "on a Lilliputian scale," and the front was ornamented with brackets, so the Tates called the place Benbrackets. The rooms were tiny but pleasantly proportioned, the stairs steep and narrow. "It's all most inconvenient, but full of charm," Caroline insisted.

Most of all, Caroline was thrilled she could "nip outdoors and be in the wildest kind of spot in ten minutes." There was a small country lane beside the house, and plenty of open fields, not to mention many fine trees around Benbrackets. Although the grounds surrounding the house needed a great deal of attention, Caroline did not mind but instead immediately began to plan her garden.

"It's heavenly to be out here, where I can set my foot on the ground any minute I please," she said repeatedly. Before long she was planting fall bulbs: she expected to stay at Benbrackets for a long time.

The only drawback to living in Princeton was that Caroline and Allen were still working in New York. The first time Caroline took the train into New York, she nearly did not make it back: a conductor took her entire round-trip ticket on the way into the city, and Caroline had to borrow thirty cents from another conductor to buy a new ticket home. After a while the commuting became routine, exhausting but well worth it, according to Caroline.

Although she sometimes felt overwhelmed by the demands of house-keeping and teaching, Caroline was able to get a great deal of writing done. She even attended "Holy Roller meetings" with her former cook, Beatrice, and Beatrice's husband, Mose. The black pentecostal church services were not unlike the revivals of the southern poor whites that Caroline wanted to portray in *The Strange Children,* so she sat at the meetings and brazenly took notes.

In addition to her work on *The Strange Children,* Caroline wrote a preface to Flaubert's *Madame Bovary* for Harper that fall. Not long after she finished the preface, she found herself identifying with Flaubert. Andrew Lytle had written an article evaluating Caroline's fiction for the *Sewanee Review.* When Caroline read the article, she decided that she felt just as Flaubert must have felt when he read what Baudelaire wrote about *Madame Bovary:* Andrew had understood what she had been trying to do, perhaps better than she ever understood herself.

In "Caroline Gordon and the Historic Image," Andrew discussed the way Caroline had completely assimilated the "accidental restraints of manners and customs" of various historical periods in order to repre-sent "what is constant in human behavior." According to Andrew, "This makes the period at once the setting and the choral comment," and such a technique was "literary irony at a high level," the "nearest substitute for the religious image."

Caroline was delighted with almost everything Andrew said, probably because Andrew discussed her work in her own terms. "If she did not sign her name, it would be at first hard to know her sex," Andrew had written. Caroline responded immediately with a letter of thanks. "It is a wonderful thing . . . to be really *read,* as you have read my work," she wrote to Andrew. "Perhaps a piece of fiction never really exists until it finds such a reader. And one is enough. All one wants is to be really *read*—once."

But she did disagree rather vehemently with Andrew's discussion of her female characters. Quite rightly, Andrew identified the theme of Caroline's work as "what Life, the sly deceiver, does to womankind but particularly to the woman of great passion and sensibility." But to Caroline's dismay, Andrew had insisted that Caroline's women were patterned on a prehistoric, matriarchal theology, popularized as the White Goddess in recent years by the poet and scholar Robert Graves. According to Andrew, "Very subtly the White Goddess reasserts herself as Miss Gordon's Muse."

Caroline could not accept such a theory. "Oh, that Robert Graves!" she exclaimed. Graves did not "understand Mary's place in the supernatural order," she insisted. "Those women of mine aren't followers of The White Goddess. They are simply unregenerate." To cast them in the image of Graves's White Goddess would be to give them too much credit for insight and power. According to Caroline, her women "look for perfection in the natural order and—naturally—never find it." But "perhaps we are just saying the same thing in different ways," she admitted.

Years later Caroline would not be so agreeable. In fact, she eventually felt that Andrew had completely misread her work. But in the fall of 1949, she was genuinely quite pleased by his insights. She felt that he had illuminated aspects of her fiction that she herself had struggled to articulate. "I shall read your essay often again," she wrote Andrew. "I can learn a good deal from it, I know."

Caroline felt secure and optimistic, having a home of her own for the first time in years. In November she organized a huge celebration for Allen's fiftieth birthday. Friends were amazed that so many people could fit in the tiny living room, but everyone had a grand time, eating and drinking to excess. Caroline made a laurel wreath for Allen to wear. As the night went on, the wreath slipped down over his right eye, but Allen was apparently too drunk to fix it.

Once the birthday cake had been eaten and innumerable toasts had been made, Caroline organized a game of charades, just as they had always done in Benfolly. Although some of the guests tried to avoid the game out of shyness, others threw themselves into the act with abandon.

Caroline thought the hit of the night came when John Berryman and

Helen Blackmur took their turn. First Helen appeared and draped herself sensuously on the couch. Then John rushed into the room. Around his neck he wore a napkin folded to resemble a Roman collar. Dropping down beside Helen, John rested his head on her lap. The scene shocked the other guests; they fell silent.

After a few moments someone ventured a guess. "Passion, is that the word?"

John looked up and made an encouraging gesture.

"Demimondaine?"

"Affair?"

"Infidelity?"

No, no, no, John signaled, pointing to his collar.

"Actress?" —No.

"Theater?" —No.

Finally, no one had any more guesses. "Give up? Give up?" John cried out triumphantly. "The word is 'parnel'—a priest's mistress."

Caroline loved it. The next day most of Princeton was buzzing about how John and Helen had acted, and Caroline had a new scene for her novel. She had intended to include a game of charades in *The Strange Children,* and she decided that *parnel* was the perfect word.

The Tates entertained frequently that year and through the spring of 1950, and Caroline decided it was "awfully nice being in Princeton without any academic responsibilities." She made new friends, like the Catholic theologian Jacques Maritain and his wife, Raissa, and she renewed acquaintances with old ones, most notably with Edmund Wilson.

Caroline would not have initiated any reconciliation with Edmund, but she also would not oppose it if he made the first effort. He appeared at Benbrackets one afternoon and told the Tates he had missed them. Caroline thought Edmund had even been "prepared to say that he had misjudged" her writing, but she "never gave him a chance," she said later. "I found that I hadn't the slightest interest in what he thinks of my work," she told a friend. "I have come to realize that he literally does not know how to read fiction."

Feeling more and more sure of herself, Caroline could accept Edmund's friendship without reservations. She also began to appraise other friends of Allen's more fairly, realizing she had sometimes given herself an inferiority complex unnecessarily. One day, while listening to Malcolm Cowley lecture, Caroline decided "that he just did not know how to take hold of any of the writers he was discussing." Since Malcolm

could not "grapple with the book itself," he "fell back on a trick classification—the year each one was born in," she noted, and the observation cheered and affirmed her. Caroline had always thought that Allen's
friends lacked a fundamental understanding of the art of fiction, but she
could never before articulate the reasons why.

As Caroline continued to work on *The Strange Children,* she became
convinced that the book would "define and, in a sense, crown the body"
of her novels. The writing went slowly, however. At first she had hoped
to finish the novel by June of 1950, but early in the year she realized that
she could never make such a deadline. It was some consolation when her
new editor at Scribner's, John Hall Wheelock, assured her that she could
take as much time as she needed to finish the novel. "This sort of thing
can't be hurried," he told her. "I have so strong a feeling that it is going
to be the finest thing you've ever done."

In the spring of 1950, Scribner's published *The House of Fiction.*
Although the immediate response to the book was good, several aspects
of the text did not escape censure. As Robert Gorham Davis pointed
out in the *New York Times Book Review,* the Tates' literary standards were
"moral as well as artistic," and all the stories included in the volume were
concerned in some way "with Man's relationship to God," as Caroline
noted in her commentary on a story by Kafka.

While Davis did not object to the Tates' fundamental belief that
"failures of form are usually also failures in moral sensibility or moral
intelligence," other reviewers did, including William Peden, writing for
the *Saturday Review of Literature.* "The editors tend to identify their
own critical evaluations with absolute facts and consequently are often
unnecessarily dogmatic," Peden said.

Other readers pointed out discrepancies between the translation of
the first story included in the anthology, Flaubert's "A Simple Heart,"
and the quotations Caroline used in the commentary, as well as a host
of proofreading and factual errors in the textbook's biographical notes.
Allen and Caroline were furious about the problem with "A Simple
Heart," but they had simply not paid enough attention to the production
of the volume. Most of the errors, as well as the inconsistent transla-
tions, could have been caught by careful proofreading. Scribner's, however, quickly interrupted the first press run to correct the most egregious
errors. And errors and criticisms notwithstanding, *The House of Fiction*
became a standard textbook in many college classrooms, influencing several generations of students and teachers.

Strong sales of *The House of Fiction* may have been part of the reason Caroline and Allen decided to spend about six thousand dollars on an addition to Benbrackets. Construction began in the fall, after they returned from a writers' conference in Indiana. By tearing open one side of the house, Caroline and Allen were able to add an ell housing a combined kitchen and dining room downstairs and a bedroom and bath upstairs. But for several months they had to live in chaos.

Caroline felt as if they were living in Pompeii: everything was covered with a layer of plaster dust an inch thick. Or rather, she told a friend, "it was as if we were being stirred up by a giant spoon ever and anon." Caroline would no sooner "establish some rough camp order" than the construction workers would tear open another portion of the house and the Tates would have to rearrange themselves again. They had no running water for six weeks, and they had to move the refrigerator into Allen's study, cook in the living room, and store almost everything else in Caroline's study.

Allen began getting up before five o'clock in the morning to write before the workmen began to hammer. Caroline tried to follow suit, but she found it hard to concentrate. She did manage to finish an article on Ford Madox Ford commissioned for the *New York Times Book Review,* but only because the editor hounded her with telegrams.

Although ostensibly reviewing a new edition of Ford's four war novels, published under the collective title *Parade's End,* Caroline wanted to evaluate Ford's entire career and pay tribute to her old friend and mentor. Yet even without the distraction of plaster dust and hammering, she found the article difficult to write. Caroline felt that she had "to calculate and translate" her insights "into language for the simple-minded," and she agonized over whether she ought to mention the scandals that had tarnished Ford's personal and professional reputation. Caroline wanted to concentrate on his art, yet she realized that Ford's personal life could hardly be separated from his fictional preoccupations. Ford had been married and had a number of affairs, yet he had never learned anything about the relationships between men and women, and that was evident in his novels. "He had only one story—a version of the antics of the lady whom Robert Graves calls 'The White Goddess,'" she noted.

Caroline eventually decided to refer to Ford's life story only in passing, discussing Ford's preoccupation with "those life-giving and death-dealing attributes of woman" without drawing biographical connections. And she argued that his obscurity as a writer was due primarily to his excessive demands on his readers. According to Caroline, Ford was "one of the most brilliant and faithful recorders of his time." "There is no one, not even [Henry] James, who can bring a scene before us with more vividness," she wrote. But "in some of Ford's writing, . . . there is too much going on," and the readers failed to appreciate the complexity of his vision.

Caroline did not complete much more than the review that fall, because the work on the Benbrackets addition continued through October. "If the carpenters aren't hammering we are nervous as cats, fearing we will never get through," she wrote to her daughter. When the addition was finished in early November, Caroline was ecstatic. But then she began to wonder if living in such luxury wouldn't wreak havoc on her prose style. "Artists aren't meant to be too comfortable in this life," she said. "However, the Lord has always taken care of that for us, so I am not worrying too much."

Dorothy Day was one of the first visitors to stay with the Tates after the addition was completed. Although Dorothy had put on a lot of weight and wore only second-hand clothes, Caroline thought she looked magnificent. Dorothy's face did not really look any different from the way it had years earlier, but her features had been somehow "transformed because they have been put to such a different use."

Most of all, Caroline could not get over how much Dorothy's life had changed since she was "just a forlorn girl, somewhat raddled from knocking about Greenwich Village." The *Catholic Worker* had grown to a circulation of over sixty-five thousand; it was "read with attention by cardinals and no doubt, the Pope himself," Caroline noted. Also, Dorothy had established "Houses of Hospitality" throughout the country to minister to the homeless and downtrodden. In New York alone, Dorothy's volunteers fed five hundred men a day. Caroline thought Dorothy was "certainly an example of seeking first the Kingdom of God and getting everything else thrown in."

After spending time with Dorothy, Caroline decided that she would not worry about her old age. Instead, she would just go to live with Dorothy and her followers when she got too feeble to write and teach. At Maryfarm, a Catholic Worker community just outside of New York City, Dorothy was "fixing up cells in the barn, any one of which would suit me to a T," Caroline told her daughter. Allen could "live there, too, if he wants to," she said. "No doubt he will be converted to Catholicism by that time."

To Caroline's great joy, she did not have to wait long for Allen's conversion. Soon after Dorothy's visit Allen again began to seriously consider joining the church. He prepared for the occasion in "characteristic fashion," Caroline noted: he "got himself two huge tomes entitled 'The Catholic Faith' and plowed through them." Always a stickler for details, Allen often stopped reading to accuse Caroline of various heresies or inform her about obscure points of church teachings or history. After a while Caroline began to call Allen the Grand Inquisitor, but she did not mind his outbursts in the least. "The things he knows now about The Holy Ghost and Original Sin!" she exclaimed to a friend.

On December 22, 1950, Caroline witnessed Allen's baptism at St. Mary's Priory in Morristown, New Jersey. Jacques and Raissa Maritain served as Allen's godparents, and Caroline was in what she called "a dither of delight." Nancy, Percy, and their sons had driven up from Washington, where Percy was finishing medical studies, to help celebrate the occasion, and they also planned to join the church. The prayers of Caroline Monica Gordon had brought her family to faith.

But as Caroline soon discovered, "entering the Church doesn't change one's nature overnight," and Allen had no intention of abandoning his controversial disposition. When Cardinal Spellman tried to suppress the movie *The Miracle,* Allen wrote a letter to the *New York Times* criticizing the cardinal. Censorship was not necessary or possible, he argued, because bad art would not endure and good art could not be suppressed.

Allen's friends joked that Allen had joined the Catholic church just to write the letter. He should have begun his letter, "As a Catholic of many weeks," one friend quipped. Another wondered how Cardinal Spellman felt being called a heretic, but he decided "he might as well get used to it."

Caroline thought Allen related to Cardinal Spellman just as he related to his former Vanderbilt professor, Dr. Mims, rebelling against both, seeing them as rigid authority figures. She believed Allen's pride and intellect got in the way of his relationship to the Catholic church, and once Allen admitted as much. He said "he would have joined the Church years ago if he had not understood the dogma as well as he did, or as well as he thought he did," Caroline noted. "He didn't really understand it, but the fact that he *thought* he did kept him out of the church for years."

Caroline felt Allen's comment confirmed her fictional instincts. *The Strange Children* had become the story of one man's conversion, because, Caroline believed, the spiritual fate of the Lewis family depended on its patriarch, Stephen, Caroline's fictional version of Allen. Stephen's wife, Sarah Lewis, "would like to have some religion but her life [was] shaped by her husband who [was] too much of an intellectual" to approach the church with humility, Caroline said.

It would take several sets of strange children, including a friend who saw visions, to move Stephen out of his arid intellectual world into a life of faith. Yet as Caroline worked on the final chapter of the novel in the early months of 1951, she struggled to dramatize Stephen's religious awakening. Throughout the novel Caroline tried to emphasize how important Stephen's faith or lack of faith was to those around him, but she could do so only by rendering dramatic scenes through the consciousness of her "central intelligence," Lucy. When it came time to reveal Stephen's turn toward faith, Caroline decided she needed "more range" than she "could get through the child's intelligence or sensations," but she was not sure how to get that range. Finally she decided to end the novel by switching to Stephen's point of view and consciousness.

Caroline finished her novel at the end of February 1951, just before Nancy and Percy and their sons, Baby Allen and Peto, arrived in Princeton for an extended visit. Although their arrival made living at Benbrackets rather like living through a two-hundred-mile-an-hour gale, Caroline was delighted to see the Woods. Percy read her manuscript for "psychiatric errors," and Caroline spent time with her grandsons, when she wasn't cooking or cleaning.

Caroline also tried to help her son-in-law settle his future. Having completed his internship, Percy wanted to find a residency in psychiatry, but he was not pursuing his goal with any vigor. Instead, he decided he was dying from Hodgkin's disease. Caroline realized he was not ill but afraid. She invited Ken Wallis, a Princeton psychiatrist, to dinner to talk with Percy about job possibilities, and she launched a spiritual campaign, promising God she would quit smoking if Percy did not have the disease.

Although she had been a chain smoker for more than thirty years, Caroline kept her vow and never smoked again. Percy did not have Hodgkin's disease after all—just a bad case of cold feet—and he was soon admitted to a psychiatric residency program at the nearby Trenton State Hospital, a program he found out about at the dinner with Ken Wallis.

All was not well at Benbrackets, however. Baby Allen and Peto were normal, rambunctious little boys, and their noisy play disturbed Allen's work on a long poem. "It is the short, sharp yelps that are the worst," he said. Yet Allen did not really want the Woods to move out. They could be a buffer between him and Caroline, he said, insisting that Caroline had gotten especially difficult to live with.

Perhaps because she had given up smoking and because their financial woes were considerable, Caroline was especially short-tempered and irritable that winter. She was also drinking to excess, perhaps to escape lingering depression over and fears for her marriage. Once, during a visit to New York City, she collapsed in a drunken stupor, and friends had to put her to bed at Sue Jenkins's apartment. When Caroline awoke the next morning, she could barely remember what had happened. "The truth is, I am a bit of an alcoholic," she confessed. "I have had to give up whiskey entirely. I see that sherry will have to go, too."

Nancy and Percy realized that Allen and Caroline's marriage was badly strained, but even if the Woods had been willing to serve as mediators, they would not get the chance. By the end of March, the Tates knew they would be moving to Minnesota in the fall. Allen had accepted a tenured position at the University of Minnesota. Caroline knew it was too good a job for Allen to turn down, yet she was very sorry to leave Benbrackets. "I knew I ought not to have planted those wood hyacinths," she exclaimed. "Every time I have ever planted a bulb we have had to move the next season."

That summer, between the usual round of writing conferences, Caroline reviewed the galleys of *The Strange Children* and indulged in "a debauch" of painting. In early August she and Allen returned to Benbrackets for six more weeks of packing and gardening, then loaded up the car and began the drive west. They took what Allen called the direct route, visiting West Virginia and Ohio before actually setting their sights on Minneapolis and St. Paul.

As they drove through Wisconsin, Caroline marveled at how large the country seemed to be. The fields seemed "to soar up into the sky"; the earth was so black Caroline thought it was "covered with fine cinders." And everyone and everything they passed looked healthy and prosperous: the farmers had round, red faces, not the gaunt, sallow look of southern farmers, she noted.

Caroline was still impressed on arriving in Minneapolis. There was "a feeling of largeness everywhere," she said; "the sky is the highest and widest I ever saw and the cleanest blue." Caroline was delighted to find that she could walk to most of the places she wanted to go, and the house they rented at 1801 University Avenue was "a sizeable chunk of all right," she said: it was "all dark wood and stucco," with four bedrooms and "plenty of waste space—the kind that keeps people from bumping into each other."

Caroline claimed the sunniest bedroom for her study and quickly settled down to work. She claimed to have "achieved her worldly ambition" that fall when she began to teach writing at the College of St. Catherine, a small women's college in St. Paul. Tired of "having to set the whole universe up for each seminar," Caroline thought it was "positively luxurious to teach Catholics—even Catholic *jeune filles*." She even arrived at the campus early each day so that she could spend a half hour praying in the chapel.

Although Allen had been prepared to dislike Minnesota, he too gave the place ecstatic reviews and settled down to work without a struggle. He found other music lovers to accompany him as he played his fiddle, and he made friends almost indiscriminately. Most of all, he was pleased that Caroline seemed to be enjoying herself.

The Tates quickly became known as somewhat eccentric artists. Caroline painted and took up mushroom hunting again: she found that the Lake of the Isles in Minneapolis was the perfect place to find shaggy manes and *Coprinus atramentarius*. Allen shocked the younger professors and graduate students at the university by drinking cheap blended whiskey. Both Caroline and Allen lived a rather "'You-Can't-Take-It-With-You' existence," according to Wendell Weed, a newspaper reporter from the *Minneapolis Star* who interviewed the Tates shortly after their arrival. "It takes a lot of fiddle playing and plenty of dabbling in water colors to produce literature," Weed wrote.

The fall publication of *The Strange Children* did little to alter most people's perceptions of the Tates. Caroline had used so many identifiable incidents and characters from her own life that many readers thought the novel was little more than thinly disguised autobiography. Caroline would always insist that she was creating fiction, not recounting her life, but there were numerous similarities between Allen and Stephen Lewis, herself and Sarah Lewis. And however much she might dissemble in life, in the autobiographical fictions of *The Strange Children*, Caroline had written a devastating analysis of Allen and of their marriage.

Throughout the novel Stephen Lewis belittled his wife's intelligence and mocked his wife's family, just as Allen did. He used his intellect as a weapon and a shield: to inflict pain on people who annoyed him, like Sarah, and to ward off any direct encounter with life. He could "keep things from happening," Sarah thought, by simply turning every person and event into an abstraction to be analyzed.

Although he never voiced any direct objection, Allen was probably not comfortable with Caroline's fictional portrait of him. Sometimes he would joke with his friends about how dangerous it was to be married to a novelist who might include uncomplimentary portraits in her fiction. But if Allen was seriously upset, he hid it well.

Perhaps Allen could afford to be gracious, since Caroline did not treat herself any better in fiction. Unlike Caroline, Sarah Lewis was a mere shadow of her husband: she had no intellectual life of her own. When not organizing the household or trying, in vain, to keep the peace between her husband and her neighbors and family, Sarah attempted to paint, but she never thought her work was good enough and so she often destroyed it. Like Caroline's earlier heroines, Sarah was an intuitive woman, sensitive to the spiritual side of life, but unlike Caroline's earlier heroines, she was helpless to respond to those intuitions.

Caroline was equally harsh toward the other women in her story. Jenny, the cook, had secret knowledge that she longed to share with Lucy, but she did not have the ability. Lucy, perceptive and precocious, realized she would turn out to be no better than the parents she often scorned. Isabel Reardon was the proverbial madwoman in the attic: she could no longer write poetry, and she could not be cured of her mysterious mental illness; she could only escape from the Lewises' third-floor bedroom into a life of sadness.

The only person to appear in a sympathetic light was Kevin Reardon, who, in some respects, also resembled Allen: diagnosed as suffering from latent homosexuality, he could never work with a psychiatrist because he had "read as much as the fellow had." The only peace he could find was in the Catholic church, but even his faith did not give him the strength and wisdom to deal with his wife and her madness.

How Caroline expected anyone to ignore autobiographical parallels amazed even her sympathetic readers. Caroline's friend Sally Wood had a difficult time reading *The Strange Children*. Sarah Lewis resembled Caroline too closely, Sally thought; she could not view the novel dispassionately.

Far from anticipating such responses, Caroline thought the religious theme of her novel would alienate most reviewers. Few critics, however, objected to the novel's pervasive Catholicism. In fact, one writer for the *Christian Science Monitor* thought *The Strange Children* lacked "a concrete moral focus," and other reviewers faulted Caroline for diffusing the novel's impact by creating too many lines of development. According to Robert Gorham Davis in the *New York Times Book Review,* the novel had more "symbolism, high dramatics, and elaborate interweaving" than it could handle, and more than seemed "imaginatively necessary."

The other objections to the novel concerned the character of Lucy. Not only did some reviewers criticize Caroline for abandoning Lucy's viewpoint at the end of the novel, but others found Lucy an insufficient narrator. A writer for the *New Yorker* called Lucy "something of a pest," her observations "more stupid than childlike." In *Commonweal* Anne Fremantle declared that Lucy was odious: "Of all American brats in fiction she is outnastied only by Carson McCullers' megalomaniac heroine in *The Member of the Wedding.*"

Caroline, however, believed she had made a "modest contribution to the form of the novel" by combining Henry James's technique of the "central intelligence" with "the innocent eye" of a child. Yet as time passed, she agreed reluctantly that there were problems with the book, most significantly the final shift to Stephen's consciousness.

The ending of *The Strange Children* revealed Caroline's willingness to fashion her work in support of a more conservative ideology. In accord with her Catholic faith, she dramatized her belief that the man must be the head of the house, the woman and any children submissive to his will.

Yet once again and perhaps unconsciously, she undercut her conservative message with a literal and figurative underground stream. The literal stream defined the boundaries of Caroline's fiction world, the same world she wrote of in her first novel, *Penhally.* It also served as symbol of the unconscious, of creativity, and of life itself. Those who were sensitive to the presence of the underground stream—Sarah and Lucy, primarily— were also sensitive to spiritual forces. Those who ignored the stream— most notably, Uncle Tubby—did so at their own peril.

The figurative underground stream was one of saints and images of feminine power. Just as in *The Women on the Porch,* Caroline created an unusual path to salvation, concentrating on two female guides who brought the message of faith to the world: St. Martha and the Virgin Mary. St. Martha brought about Kevin Reardon's conversion and continued to sustain his faith: he sometimes tried to "put the woman out of his mind," but then he felt "a kind of severing pain" and "a period of desolation" until St. Martha rejoined him.

In the novel Stephen Lewis scoffed at the idea of such a vision, but Sarah believed. In a sense Sarah was a modern-day St. Martha, constantly caring for the needs of others at the expense of her own soul. Caroline described in the novel how the original St. Martha had subdued the dragon, the archetypal villain of fairy-tale worlds. Caroline also hinted that Sarah had similar power. Kevin sensed Sarah's affinity to the saint, or at least her perceptive nature. He consulted her about what he ought to do with his statue of St. Martha, and he revealed his vision to her. But at the novel's end Sarah had not yet come to understand or exercise her power. In life Caroline could respond to her spiritual promptings and, ultimately, lead her family to faith, but in fiction Sarah could not, at least not until her husband stopped ridiculing the spiritual life.

When he was not scoffing at visions, Stephen Lewis often ignored or avoided confronting questions of faith. Caroline demonstrated this in a long and apparently disconnected scene near the end of the novel, a confrontation between Stephen and Sarah's uncle Fillinger Fayerlee, a lonely old man who wanted to believe in the Virgin Birth. Needing a rational explanation of the mystery, and sensing Stephen would be a worthy colleague for such an intellectual exercise, Uncle Fill attempted to draw Stephen into the argument. But to his wife's embarrassment and annoyance, Stephen scorned the old man: he did not dare to question.

Belief in the Virgin Mary and in saints like Martha was an important part of the Catholic faith. In *The Strange Children* Caroline made that belief the key to faith. She invested her female characters with knowledge, sensitivity, and untapped power. She even gave one of her female characters the most important voice of narrator and central intelligence. But she also took away that voice.

Caroline often found herself defending her decision to end *The Strange Children* in the mind of Stephen Lewis. Inevitably she would point out the various incidents in the novel where Lucy looked to her father for consolation. She would also account for how Sarah Lewis was "full of natural grace" and "marked for death." But sensing perhaps that her explanations did not adequately account for what she had written, she eventually resorted to a plea that her reader consider the theological context of her work. "Anybody reading my work from now on will get more out of it, I believe, if he takes into consideration the fact that I am a

Catholic," Caroline said, "for any book I write during the rest of my life
will be some kind of testimony of faith."

IN the winter of 1951, Caroline began a new novel, *The Malefactors,* a
story of one man's journey of faith, "the old story that is or ought to be
the story of every human being." But the women in her story occupied
most of her time and energy. They represented Caroline's struggle to
find wholeness, her failure to reconcile her ambitions as a writer with her
expectations of proper feminine behavior.

From the start Caroline knew the basic plot she wanted to use in
her novel. Her hero was the poet Thomas Claiborne, who lived with
his wife, Vera, in an old Pennsylvania Dutch farmhouse. Although Tom
struggled to write, he had no trouble adopting an attitude of conde-
scension toward his wife and friends. When Vera's sister appeared, Tom
would be easily led into adultery. Vera's sister would also be a poet, and
Tom would be drawn into the affair in part by his better nature, his desire
to help her with her poetry. Relying too much on his pride, wits, and
intellect, Thomas would nearly destroy himself before he found the path
to salvation, returning to his true mate and a life of faith.

As always, Caroline borrowed from her own history in fashioning
her characters. She modeled Tom after Allen, made Catherine Pollard a
thinly disguised version of Dorothy Day, and patterned a number of Tom
Claiborne's companions after Allen's friends, especially Horne Watts, a
fictional version of Hart Crane. But Caroline split her own self-image
into pieces: she was part Vera, part Vera's sister, and even part Tom. And
the fractured images caused her no end of trouble.

Caroline crafted Vera with a loving hand, and the character descriptions reveal Caroline's perspective on her own behavior. Although, unlike Caroline, Vera would be a wealthy woman and not an artist of any
sort, Vera had a similar psychological history. She had lived in many
places as a child, "always craving to live in one place and craving, too,
a settled home life," Caroline wrote in her notes. "She is a person who
wanted very much to live, but was brought up in circumstances that frustrated her every impulse." Often subject to what others thought were
inexplicable rages, Vera was "seeking love desperately through the creature." Her rages resulted from suspicions that her husband did not really
love her.

Caroline was not as generous to Vera's sister. Just as in her earlier writings, she thought of the women as opposites or mirror images. Vera was

the submissive wife, the nurturing homemaker; she had no intellect, just intuition. Her sister was the adventuring artist, the selfish home wrecker. She had a considerable intellect, which had been "sharpened by the help of her father, the Devil," Caroline wrote.

Yet even after she had cast the women as opposites, Caroline was not especially comfortable with her characterizations, especially that of Vera's sister. She questioned her motivations and struggled at length to name her. At first she called her Laura, then she christened her Cynthia, but neither name pleased Caroline. After calling her character Zenia for a while, Caroline reluctantly settled on the name of Cynthia. Like the moon, she would be a false light, a "Lilith or Night Monster," a strange woman with "movable ways," as Caroline put it.

Despite her sense of the novel's shape, Caroline's work went slowly. By early November she had written only the first chapter, revising it four times without finding what she thought was the right approach. Yet she was not at all distressed. "The business of a fiction writer is, in its humble way, the same as the Almighty's: incarnation," she said, "and it has to proceed at an even slower pace."

In addition to writing, Caroline continued to teach, formally at the College of St. Catherine, informally through letters to aspiring writers who dared to ask for her help. The formal instruction at the College of St. Catherine had an auspicious beginning: Caroline had twelve students and a large circle of auditors, including several of the college's alumnae and most of the Sisters of St. Joseph of Carondolet who taught in the English Department. But before long the students and auditors dwindled away, and by the end of the fall semester, only three students remained. Caroline was not rehired to teach another course.

Caroline's informal teaching bore better fruit. In fact, by the end of the year, she decided she might not have to write many more novels. "I have got me a disciple who is going to be able to do everything I have ever been able to do and a lot more," she exclaimed. Actually, she had two disciples: Walker Percy and Flannery O'Connor.

Caroline got to know Flannery through mutual friends, Robert and Sally Fitzgerald. Born in Georgia in 1925, Flannery had met the Fitzgeralds in 1949, about a year after completing her studies at the University of Iowa Writers' Workshop. She spent a year living with them in Connecticut, working on her first novel, *Wise Blood,* before an attack of lupus erythematosus, a degenerative autoimmune disease, forced her return to her family in Milledgeville, Georgia.

While Flannery was recovering her strength and completing the novel, Robert Fitzgerald sent a copy of the manuscript to Caroline. He thought she would appreciate Flannery's fiercely Catholic, often comic tale about Hazel Motes, a young southerner struggling against belief, preaching in "The Church without Christ."

Caroline recognized Flannery's talent immediately. "I wish that I had as firm a grasp on my subject matter when I was her age!" Caroline wrote to Robert Fitzgerald; Flannery was "already a rare phenomenon: a Catholic novelist with a real dramatic sense, one who relies more on her technique than her piety." Eager as always to nurture talent, Caroline suggested several ways to revise the manuscript.

Flannery appreciated Caroline's suggestions, and when she completed her revision of *Wise Blood* during the fall of 1951, she asked Caroline if she would reread the book. Caroline readily agreed. She wrote Flannery, "There are so few Catholic novelists who seem possessed of a literary conscience—not to mention skill—that I feel that your novel is very important."

Around the same time Caroline received a letter from Walker Percy, a young man she had met many years earlier at Monteagle. Walker wanted her advice. The nephew of William Alexander Percy, a lawyer and poet who had written a well-known memoir, *Lanterns on the Levee,* Walker had been pursuing a career as a doctor until tuberculosis forced him to adopt a less strenuous lifestyle. He had spent several years reading, thinking, and writing, and he had also converted to Catholicism. Finally, he had completed what he thought was "a Catholic novel, though it [had] no conversion or priests in it," he said. Would Caroline read it? Of course.

When Caroline received Walker's five-hundred-page manuscript, *The Charterhouse,* her heart sank. "I feared that a Wolfe had got into that fold," she said later. As she read, however, her fears subsided. Walker had a lot to learn, she thought, almost everything in fact, but Caroline thought the novel was one of the best first novels she had ever read, "a sample of what the next development in the novel" would be. "Reading that novel was like suddenly getting down on your knees on a long, dusty walk to drink from a fresh, cold spring," she said later. Believing she could help him, Caroline wrote him a thirty-page single-spaced letter full of specific suggestions for revision.

She gave Flannery O'Connor's revised manuscript the same careful attention. Flannery was a writer "of the first order," Caroline decided. But Caroline was never content merely to praise a piece of writing.

Although she told Flannery that she could "let this manuscript go with good conscience," Caroline offered what she called "a few suggestions and comments"—roughly nine pages of single-spaced typing. "They are really suggestions for your future work, but I have to have something to pin them to, so I am going to take passages from 'Wise Blood' as illustrations," she wrote.

Flannery appreciated the detailed and practical criticism; it was just what she needed, she told Caroline. Although they would not meet for some time, the women became friends. Flannery trusted Caroline's judgment and was eager to learn whatever she could from Caroline.

Having two talented young writers seek her advice and approval greatly flattered Caroline. "I am walking on air these days," she kept saying, insisting it was no accident that both novelists were Catholic. "People who don't have to set the universe up fresh for every performance, people who don't have to spend time trying to figure out what moral order prevails in the universe," necessarily had "more energy for spontaneous creation," she declared.

Allen was delighted to see his wife so happy, and he conspired to keep her that way. As the new year began, the Tates were once again facing severe financial difficulties, but Allen tried to keep Caroline from finding out. They were overextended on all their charge accounts, in part because they had been sending Nancy and Percy regular sums of money all fall, nearly four hundred dollars total, to help the Woods get by on Percy's modest salary and to maintain Benbrackets, where the Woods were living. Worst of all, Allen had discovered that he had not filed their 1946 income taxes correctly. He owed nearly nine hundred dollars in back taxes, and at one point the agents from the Internal Revenue Service threatened to take away Allen's car if he did not come up with four hundred dollars immediately.

Allen postdated checks and apparently borrowed money from friends: at least he did not lose his car. Still, by early February 1952 several stores had cut off Allen's credit, and the Tates were over two thousand dollars in debt, but Caroline had little idea of the crisis. Then Allen intercepted a letter Sue Jenkins had written to Caroline. Sue mentioned the land Caroline had bought from her in Tory Valley, and asked, as she often did, if Caroline would be interested in selling the land back to her. Without telling Caroline, Allen sold the land to Sue.

Caroline did not find out until Sue's check arrived. Then, as Allen had anticipated, she could scarcely argue against the accomplished fact. But she did force Allen to sit down and explain their financial problems in detail. She was not devastated as Allen had expected, but she was upset. She wanted to do more to help Nancy, who had just had her third child at the end of January, a girl named Caroline after her grandmother. She also wanted to hold on to the Tory Valley land. Neither was possible.

When Nancy found out about her parents' financial problems, she worried they would sell Benbrackets. She urged her mother against such a move. Benbrackets was their most valuable financial asset, Nancy argued; there was no telling when Caroline and Allen might need the place.

Caroline agreed that they should not sell Benbrackets, but for another reason. She thought she and Allen would "stay put in Minnesota" since they were both over fifty years old. "We can't keep moving every two years," Caroline wrote. "At least I hope to heaven we don't have to." But even if they did not return to New Jersey, Caroline wanted to keep Benbrackets for as long as Nancy and Percy wanted to live in it. She wanted her grandchildren to have "some fixed point of location," she said. It was one of the most valuable things a child could have while growing up, she believed.

With one more financial crisis averted, the rest of the winter and spring of 1952 went by quickly for Caroline. She worked only intermittently on her novel. Three young boarders lived with Caroline and Allen for part of the spring, and Caroline was also teaching one course at Hamline University, another small private institution in St. Paul, and lecturing occasionally to other groups. When Allen heard her speak on "The Art and Mystery of Faith" at the Newman Club of the University of Minnesota, he was amazed and proud of her. Caroline appreciated his compliments, but she thought Allen had no sense of her abilities. "The truth is he hasn't heard me make any speeches since I got professional and didn't know that I really was," she remarked.

Caroline's accomplishments surprised Allen several times that winter and spring. He was impressed, most of all, that she continued to write novels despite her history of poor sales and lukewarm critical reception. Her novels were excellent, he thought, and they would be appreciated more keenly in years to come, when readers and scholars had gotten some perspective on her art. But "it *is* a little rough on her now," he observed. "If she didn't have as much character as talent she would probably have given up long ago."

Far from giving up, Caroline had embarked on a new scholarly endeavor. After rereading all of Henry James's novels and his critical prefaces, she thought she had discovered a new insight into James's techniques and achievements. His fiction had been misread, she believed. Critics had imposed Freudian, historical, or sociological interpretations on his novels; they had not read his work systematically or sympathetically. Most of all, they had not recognized the religious significance of James's work. According to Caroline, consciously or not, James was exploring questions of faith in his fiction.

Allen encouraged Caroline to write an essay on her ideas. Caroline wanted to, but she rather doubted herself. "As Allen remarks I haven't got the kind of skill it takes," she wrote Nancy; "Still, I've made such a terrific discovery that I have to try to put it into words."

Caroline decided to illustrate her thesis by examining James's last great novel, *The Golden Bowl*. The book invoked and celebrated *caritas*, Christian charity, Caroline believed. It was a comedy, the only one of James's major works "in which virtue is wholly triumphant over vice," she argued.

After working for several weeks on the essay, Caroline felt that her own prose style was deteriorating under the influence of James, his critics, and his father. As soon as she finished a draft of the essay, "The Figure at the Window on the Carpet," she escaped to the library, picked up "a green book bag full of trash"—writers such as Angela Thirkell and Nancy Mitford—then went home to wallow in bed reading until she had "returned to normalcy," she said.

Allen also returned to writing that fall and winter. In a short time he had completed several new lectures and two sections of a long poem. Caroline thought his poetry was the best he had ever done. "It lacks that unmotivated violence that his work has so often had heretofore," she observed.

Caroline believed that Allen's return to poetry signaled the end to their difficulties and the beginning of new years of promise. "What a wonderful thing it is that he is in the Church," she wrote to Nancy. Allen was "even resigned to his periods of desolation," she thought: he no longer felt "that he has to tear up his whole universe every time he can't write any poetry, but is actually resigned to waiting until the Spirit moves him." Caroline was sure that everyone could see the change in Allen; he was a new man, she thought, and it was all "the result of the exercise of faith."

But Allen had not really changed at all, no matter what Caroline thought or hoped. In May 1952 Allen went to Paris as one of the literary representatives of the United States at a celebration of the arts sponsored by the Congress for Cultural Freedom. Because of their financial worries, Caroline stayed in Minnesota and gave the Phi Beta Kappa address Allen had promised to deliver at the College of St. Catherine. The trip was the beginning of a new round of sorrows for Caroline.

Allen wrote Caroline regularly during the month he was abroad. He mentioned people he was seeing, like Katherine Anne Porter and William Faulkner; he said he desperately missed her and longed to see her. Caroline was delighted he was having a wonderful time; she did not even worry when Allen said he had been taking long walks with Natasha Spender, the wife of the British poet Stephen Spender. Quite naïvely, Caroline thought Allen was trying to convert Natasha. He "hopes to have her in the Church in a few months," Caroline told a friend.

But Allen actually had other plans for Natasha, and none of them were religious. That spring he began an affair with her, and before long Caroline was one of the few people who did not know about it. Like a schoolboy with a first crush, Allen confided freely in his friends, especially Katherine Anne, about his new love, declaring that he and Natasha were joined together for life. What he would do about his marriage to Caroline, he never said.

Allen returned to Minneapolis in the beginning of June, but his stay was brief. Within a week he left again for a summer writers' conference in Vermont. After closing up their rented house, Caroline left Minnesota as well, for another conference at the University of Utah.

Caroline saw little of Allen that summer. In early July they got back together in Princeton, but by the third week of August, Allen was heading back to Europe, this time to Venice for an international literary conference sponsored by UNESCO. Once again Caroline remained behind, still with no idea of Allen's feelings for Natasha.

Caroline spent the rest of August in Princeton, with visits to Tory Valley and to Maryfarm, Dorothy Day's retreat house in Newburgh, New York; then she went to see Ward Dorrance in Columbia, Missouri. The visit was disastrous. Caroline tried to help Ward with a story he was writing, and he apparently took offense. After Caroline returned to Minnesota in September, she wrote a vicious one-act play about their disagreement called "Under the Mulberry Tree."

Caroline attacked both herself and Ward in the play, which was set on the terrace at Confederate Hill, Ward's home. Her two main characters were "C.G.T.," a fat, ill-tempered old woman in an alcoholic haze, and "W.A.D.," a narrow-minded, self-centered prig who shut himself off from life by wearing a suit of chain armor, too small to be comfortable, and a rather obscene muzzle, a "snufflicator," which restricted his breathing and freedom of movement.

Throughout the play, C.G.T. tried, without success, to talk W.A.D. out of his complacency, his armor, and the snufflicator. Often she lost her temper, grimacing and clenching her fists, and then her guardian angel, who stood behind C.G.T. throughout the play, would reprove her silently. But after a while, even the angel could not keep C.G.T. calm. At the end of the play, C.G.T. howled loudly, stamped her foot, then rushed off stage. As W.A.D. began to read his "Essay on Constipation," she could be heard off-stage "howling and tearing up the shrubbery."

After she finished it, Caroline did not attempt to publish or perform "Under the Mulberry Tree." The play was not a serious attempt at art, but more a private temper tantrum. Through her sketch she voiced her frustration with a friend she had come to depend on. She also admitted that her own behavior was excessive, that many saw her as little more than a foul-tempered, alcoholic old woman. Yet Caroline was not ready to change. She filed the play away and tried to maintain a calm façade before the rest of the world.

Exhausted from her travels and the rigors of living out of suitcases, Caroline kept to herself for several weeks after she returned to Minnesota. Since Allen was not expected back until just before the fall quarter started in October, Caroline thought she could hibernate without hurting anyone's feelings. Telling only two friends that she was back, she seldom ventured out of the new house she had rented at 1908 Selby Street in St. Paul. She did not even bother to pick up the mail. "It is just heavenly to sit down every morning at your own desk, with your clothes hanging up in your closet, and at least one clean dress ready to put on if you have to go out—and then just not go anywhere," Caroline wrote in a letter to her daughter.

The house on Selby Street delighted Caroline, as much as any rented house could. She was extremely tired of "tenting about" in one place after another. "A new house every year if it can be managed seems to be our motto!" she mused. Caroline was glad to be living in a predominantly Catholic neighborhood, with her church, St. Mark's, only a few blocks away. Best of all, she had a small herb garden: basil, thyme, savory, and lemon verbena. It did not matter where she lived as long as she could work the soil, even a little bit. "What I crave is the opportunity to garden," she said. "I am really hardly human without it."

While Caroline settled into a routine at Selby Street, Allen jaunted about Italy. In addition to giving lectures in Venice, he visited Florence and Rome, had a disappointing audience with the pope, and continued to see Natasha. All the while he wrote Caroline love letters, insisting he could not live without her.

Caroline believed and trusted him. But when Allen returned in the first week of October, she began to worry. Allen arrived in a dangerous state of exhaustion, yet he allowed himself little time to rest. He was in the grip of "the greatest poetic seizure" he had ever experienced, she observed. He got up at four o'clock every morning for several weeks so he could work on the long poem he had begun the previous spring. It was a poem called "The Buried Lake," addressed to a "lady of light."

Throughout the fall and winter of 1952, Allen's writing seizure continued. After a while friends began to take Caroline aside. Allen looked tired, they said. Caroline agreed, but she said she could not help him, even if she wanted to. "You are damn lucky to hear that wild syrinx cry at any hour of the day or night," she said.

Caroline also spent a lot of time listening to her muse during the fall of 1952, although her writing routine was not as maniacal. Eventually she decided that her original draft of the book did not work, so she threw it out and returned to making notes on the incidents she wanted to use. Throughout the fall she worked in fits and starts; new characters kept appearing, and old ones demanded greater attention.

In early November a source for one of her characters arrived in St. Paul for a visit: Dorothy Day. Caroline felt as if she were entertaining a saint. Traveling across the country by bus to visit her Houses of Hospitality, Dorothy looked every inch the pilgrim. She carried a small suitcase, a "brief case bulging with books," and a box of reliquaries, "which she will leave with anybody who needs them," Caroline noted. Dorothy gave Allen "a bit of flesh" from Pope Pius X. It would help Allen finish his poem, she said.

Caroline got no reliquary, but she did get new inspiration for her character Catherine Pollard, the religious woman in *The Malefactors* who was based on Dorothy. But sensing perhaps that Dorothy would not be pleased to see herself in fiction, Caroline never told her what she was writing. Instead, she just spent hours talking to and watching her friend.

Dorothy awed and impressed Caroline: she had made such a radical commitment to live the Christian message. "You strip yourself in order to put on Christ," Dorothy said, and both Caroline and Allen felt certain Dorothy was "on the way to sainthood."

After Dorothy left, Caroline tried to return to her writing, but she had other interruptions. First she had to read a revision of Walker Percy's novel *The Charterhouse*. It was extremely long but well rounded and greatly improved, she thought. When she sent the manuscript to Scribner's, she proclaimed that Walker was "the most important talent to come out of the South since Faulkner." Unfortunately, Caroline's editor, Jack Wheelock, did not agree, and Walker never did find a publisher for the novel.

After reading Walker's novel, Caroline had a round of lectures, one at the University of Iowa, another at the College of St. Thomas in St. Paul. Her talk at St. Thomas was unexpected. Allen had originally agreed to give a lecture on Catholic writers, but his poetic seizure proved to be too great for him, and he bowed out at the last minute. Caroline agreed to take his place: giving a lecture was an effort and a distraction, but she wanted to send the money she earned to Nancy.

Caroline based her talk on ideas from Jacques Maritain's *Art and Scholasticism*, especially his belief that "wherever art . . . has attained a certain grandeur and purity, it is already Christian . . . Christian in hope, for every spiritual splendour is a promise and a symbol of the divine harmonies of the Gospel." According to Caroline, James Joyce was "a more Christian writer than Francois Mauriac" because he was a better writer. The following year she published the lecture as "Some Readings and Misreadings" in the *Sewanee Review*.

After the lectures came the Christmas season. Allen and Caroline both drank too much and worked hardly at all. In January they struggled mightily to get back to regular writing routines. Caroline finished a review of two books about the novelist Willa Cather for the *New York Times Book Review*, but she found it difficult to get anything written on *The Malefactors* because she was not entirely sure how all the people and incidents would come together. Tom's cousin George, a psychiatrist, had crept into the novel, and Caroline felt as if she had to struggle to keep him in a minor role. George was "always threatening to run away with the show," she wrote to her son-in-law. "I would throw the fellow out, but I am superstitious," she said. "When a character acts like that it is nearly always a sign that he is going to be needed at some crucial moment."

Another difficult character also appeared: Tom's Aunt Virginia, an elderly woman determined to die in the upstairs room. "The stage gets more crowded all the time," Caroline wrote to her daughter. "It is really going to be one hell of a big novel—but if you can't write a big novel at the age of fifty-eight I think you might as well shut up shop."

Deciding Vera would raise Red Poll cattle, much to Tom's annoyance, Caroline did research on the Red Poll breeds. She also haunted the campus of the University of Minnesota agricultural school, not far from her home in St. Paul. The school was "the fountain-head of artificial insemination," Caroline noted, and she wanted to use the conflict between nature and science in the novel.

In a local paper Caroline found a story to dramatize the conflict. A farmer from Wisconsin was suing his neighbor because the neighbor's purebred bull had crashed through a pasture fence to mate with two of the farmer's heifers. A firm believer in artificial insemination, the farmer claimed that natural mating had ruined his heifers. For her novel Caroline made Vera's prize bull, Bud, the aggressor. How Vera and Tom reacted to Bud's escapades would reveal their fundamentally different perspectives on life and love.

Although she continued to follow her overall plan for the novel, Caroline was still not satisfied with her description of Vera and Cynthia. She repeatedly tried to resolve her lingering questions, to avoid turning Vera into just another Sarah Lewis, or Cynthia into a madwoman. When she could not write narrative and dialogue, Caroline would often insert a clean sheet of paper into her typewriter and begin to question her own intuitions about her characters.

As a young girl Vera must have had a nervous break-down, but Caroline was not sure what might have caused it. Perhaps Vera suffered from being separated from her father, or from the trauma of her parents' divorce. Cynthia would be the older sister, and yet, was she really Vera's sister? After a while Caroline decided that her narrative might make better sense if Vera and Cynthia were only half sisters. "The fact that they have different fathers will account for several things: differences between Vera and Cynthia, Vera's having control of the family money, Cynthia's latent jealousy of Vera, her failure to understand what a blow it is to Vera to lose her father," Caroline wrote.

Whenever Caroline compared Vera and Cynthia, she concentrated on the differences between the two women. And yet Vera and Cynthia were similar. Although she exaggerated their tendencies and disguised their appearances, Caroline continued to fashion them in her own image. She gave Vera most of her best qualities: Vera loved nature and animals; she was intuitive and generous to a fault, naïve and trusting. Cynthia did not fare so well. Caroline gave the elder sister most of the personality traits she disliked in her own life. Cynthia was "outwardly very demure and feminine," but she was wily and egotistical. She was "perhaps too direct, too brusque," Caroline noted. Cynthia would become angry and defensive about her writing. Although Caroline endowed the woman with talent and a fine intellect, she suggested Cynthia would be better off without either. "Cynthia has missed out on everything that makes life worth while to a woman," Caroline wrote in her notes. "Therefore her ambition grows larger. Life must make up to her for what she has missed."

Caroline's attitude toward Cynthia was no different from her attitude toward herself. She increasingly believed writing was "not suitable for a woman." It was "unsexing"; it turned her into "a freak," she said. Writing a passage "so that it will be hard enough and firm enough to hang [a] whole book on" took "a kind of masculine virtue," Caroline thought. George Eliot had it; Jane Austen did not; Caroline struggled to master it.

Worst of all, Caroline noted, even if a woman mastered her art, she would often have to dissemble. "I have got to stop writing and dress myself up and go to dinner at a dean's house and spend the evening persuading the man who sits next to me to talk about himself and if I don't do it with a fair degree of skill he will be telling people that Mrs. Tate is up-stage and conceited," she noted bitterly. Perhaps Dr. Johnson was right, she said: "a woman at intellectual labor is always a dog walking on its hind legs."

IN the spring of 1953, Caroline was still struggling to write *The Malefactors*. She had better luck with poetry, writing one short verse that aptly captured her feelings:

> 'Twas ever thus from childhood's hour
> I've seen my fondest hopes decay
> I never loved a tree or flower
> > But when it got ready to bloom
> > I had to go away.

Before the apple tree in the back yard blossomed, or the patio tomato plants bore ripe fruit, Caroline had to leave for Seattle. She had been hired as the Walker Ames Lecturer for the spring term at the University of Washington.

When Caroline left Minnesota at the end of March, she knew she would probably not be returning for at least a year. After several months in Seattle, she would teach at the Utah Writers' Conference in Salt Lake City, then go to Princeton for the summer. In the fall they might go to Italy: Allen thought he would be awarded a Fulbright for a year at the American Academy in Rome. The logistics of such a schedule daunted Caroline. "I consider myself a specialist in moving but this move is one of the damnedest yet," she said.

Caroline found a place to stay in Seattle with the help of friends. Located at 4337 Fifteenth Avenue, the apartment was convenient but dark. Caroline thought she could work better if she took her typewriter up to the rooftop garden. From there, when the sun was out and the skies clear, she could see Mount Rainier and Mount Baker. That did not happen often, Caroline quickly learned, but it was impressive.

Equally impressive was the lush vegetation; Caroline delighted in the flowering fruit trees, rhododendron, and azaleas that seemed to cover every available inch of ground. Every morning on her way to mass at the Blessed Sacrament Church, Caroline walked the back alleys and inspected the terraces and rock gardens, becoming more and more homesick for a garden of her own.

But her garden yearnings did not interfere with her work. Soon after she settled into her apartment, Caroline made another sort of move she had been contemplating for some time: she switched publishers. For years she had been unhappy with the way Scribner's handled her books, but she could not afford to make any change: she had always drawn advances beyond her sales. In the spring of 1953, however, she received a financial windfall: Scribner's sold the paperback rights for *Green Centuries* to Bantam. Caroline received two thousand dollars for the sale, which settled not only her own debts to Scribner's but those Allen had incurred as well. On Allen's advice Caroline signed a contract with Denver Lindley of Harcourt, Brace for *The Malefactors*. She also negotiated a contract with Viking for a book called *How to Read a Novel*, based in part on her essay about Henry James.

Still unsure about some aspects of her novel, Caroline thought she would write *How to Read a Novel* first. Three days after she arrived, however, she began a new short story called "Emmanuele! Emmanuele!" According to Caroline, the title was supposed to sound "like a cry of anguish." It was the story of Guillaume Fay, a fictional rendering of the writer André Gide. Emmanuele of the title referred to Fay's wife: her name was Therese Gabrielle, but Fay called her Emmanuele in the daily letters he wrote her while staring at a mirror. Those letters were to be his secret journal, published after his death. To Fay's horror, however, his wife did not save the letters but burned them.

Caroline sometimes compared the story to her earlier work, "The Captive": much of her work was done for her since she based her account on Gide's writings and correspondence. But she made the story her own by adding the perspective of Robert Heyward, a young poet and scholar who had gotten a job attending to Fay's correspondence. In awe of Fay, Heyward overlooked his employer's failings. He argued with anyone who suggested that Fay was not a great artist. "An artist's first duty is to confront himself," Heyward said.

Caroline wanted to implicate Heyward in the tale: he was an unreliable judge of character, on the edge of the same abyss of self-exploration to which Fay had abandoned himself. Like Fay, he could only be saved by understanding that the artist's first duty was "the same as any other man's—to serve, praise, and worship God."

When Caroline finished the story, she could not tell if she had brought it off. She thought it was good, perhaps the best thing she had ever done, but she was too exhausted to trust her own judgments. Perhaps it was too complex for a short story. Caroline considered turning it into a short novel, but first she sent it to Allen for his opinion.

Allen did not like "Emmanuele! Emmanuele!" The story was entirely different from any of Caroline's earlier works, and perhaps Allen also objected to the tale because, consciously or not, Caroline had woven autobiographical parallels into Gide's story. The young poet Robert Heyward and the character of Guillaume Fay resembled Allen in some respects; Fay's long-suffering wife, Emmanuele, had more than a few similarities to Caroline. Allen would not have to read much into the story to see the warning beneath the story of André Gide. If Allen did not abandon his false companions and his introspective tendencies, he would destroy himself and his art, Caroline seemed to be saying. He needed to cherish and respect the true source of creative life, the life his wife embraced so heartily.

The admonitory note of "Emmanuele! Emmanuele!" may have been intentional. As she wrote the story, Caroline had become increasingly upset over Allen's behavior. Saying he was "too lonesome" to stay by himself, Allen had moved out of the house they had rented in St. Paul and went to stay with one of his colleagues, Hunt Brown. Caroline thought it was ridiculous for him to be living in someone's guest suite while they were still paying $170 a month to rent the house on Selby Street. Then she heard that Allen had gone on a short vacation with Natasha Spender. She was furious and, once again, quite fearful.

Yet Caroline still could not admit the true nature of her fear. She approached Allen cautiously, writing, "Darling, there is something I want you to do for me, without getting angry about it—because I love you. I want you to examine your conscience about the Spenders. . . . They seem to come on the scene every time we have a reconciliation." Although she must have suspected that Allen and Natasha were having an affair, Caroline focused her disapproval on Stephen Spender. She explained that she felt uneasy about him, although she was not sure why. Yet despite her worries, or perhaps because she feared her husband's wrath, Caroline told Allen that she would accept his views on the Spenders. "If you tell me you think I ought to be friendly with them I shall certainly meet any overture," she wrote.

Much to Caroline's relief, Allen said she had nothing to worry about. But he admitted to some of his friends that he was not doing very well that spring. He was tired; he spent most of the spring lecturing at various colleges, trying to make enough money to help Nancy and Percy, and to support what Caroline called "the Bottomless Pit at Princeton." After a while, Allen began drinking so much that he suffered from blackouts. Although he sometimes insisted that he was in better shape than ever before, he felt severely depressed. He told friends that his marriage was an empty shell because Caroline did not love him unconditionally.

But Allen said none of this to Caroline, and she did not press any suspicions she might have. Caroline knew her instinctive reactions and intuitions were often absolutely right and necessary. But she told herself she reacted too harshly, in an almost paranoid way, against people she suspected might hurt her. Caroline wanted to believe in Allen, to trust him. She forced herself to do so.

In the same way she forced herself to accept Allen's view of "Emmanuele! Emmanuele!" It was a good thing Allen did not like the story, she thought. "If it's not as good as 'Old Red' it would seem there's not much use in my writing any more stories," she wrote. "This one nearly killed me. The thought of another one positively paralyzes me." Although she continued to revise the story, Caroline abandoned the idea of turning it into a short novel.

In the middle of June, Caroline left Seattle. After teaching for one week at the Utah Writers' Conference, she went to Princeton, but her stay there was brief. Caroline began to feel that her presence at Benbrackets annoyed her son-in-law: she "stirred up" Percy's "mother complex," Caroline said. Worried about Nancy, who had been suffering from an ulcer, Caroline decided to keep her distance. She went to Sue Jenkins's home in Tory Valley, vowing to let her daughter work things out for herself.

But Caroline did continue to support the Woods financially. She knew Nancy found it difficult to raise three children on Percy's salary as a resident, and she willingly shared with her daughter whatever money she had. When Monroe Spears of the *Sewanee Review* bought "Emmanuele! Emmanuele!" Caroline sent her pay to Nancy, urging her to use it for household help. She also began to revise the first chapter of *The Malefactors* into a short story called "Feast of St. Eustace." If it sold, Caroline promised that Nancy could have whatever she earned.

Although the Tates had planned to travel together to Europe, they ended up going separately. Allen left in early July: he had been asked by the State Department to teach an additional six-week seminar at Oxford. Caroline followed at the end of the month. She went by ship, to save money, sharing a cabin with three other women. The voyage was uneventful, giving Caroline plenty of time to think about her relationship with Allen. The more she thought about his recent behavior, the worse she felt. She was determined to protect Allen, even from himself. He had been ill, she thought, otherwise he would not act so irrationally. They were both Catholics, and no matter their difficulties, they had to stay together—Caroline believed that wholeheartedly. But what if Allen continued to have these attacks? Could she continue to protect him and his reputation, much less hers?

Realizing Allen had been leaving his "tracks in the snow," Caroline wrote Nancy and Percy and asked them to destroy any of the letters Allen had written them "during one of his attacks." "I have been trying for the last few years to do what I can to undo the harm he has done for himself while he was ill," she wrote. "I'll have much less heart for the effort if I feel that people are preserving records of the way he behaved when he was ill."

Allen was not as concerned about appearances. The Spenders were in England that July, and before Caroline arrived, Allen managed to go off with Natasha at least once. He even went to lunch with Natasha before he went to meet Caroline on the day her boat docked in Southampton. Caroline had no idea, or else she continued to will herself into ignorance. At the age of fifty-seven, after nearly twenty-eight years of marriage, Caroline could not envision life without Allen. Also, although she seldom admitted it, she knew Allen was emotionally incapable of remaining faithful to her. In willed ignorance Caroline could find some measure of security: by burying her fears she could exert control over her life, however fragile and temporary.

The Tates stayed in Oxford until the middle of August, then went to London for a week before leaving for Paris. It had been about twenty years since Caroline was in Paris; the city had changed a lot. For ten days Caroline and Allen spent most of their time doing just what they used to do: sitting around in cafés, drinking, and talking. On the day before they left, Allen and Caroline went on a sentimental pilgrimage, revisiting some of the places they had lived.

Caroline hated to leave Paris the next day; the city held so many happy memories. But, beginning to feel guilty about not working, she was eager to get to Rome and establish a routine. They arrived in Rome in early September and settled into an apartment on the Janiculum, in part of the Villa Aurelia, the home of Laurance Roberts, director of the American Academy. For only forty-five dollars a month in rent, the Tates had a large apartment with marble floors, high ceilings, "a perfectly divine terrace" overlooking the city, and free use of the villa's garden, much to Caroline's delight. They also had household help for less than ten dollars a month—Assunta, the wife of the villa's gatekeeper, Giuseppe. Although at first Assunta spoke no English and Caroline no Italian, they got along splendidly, communicating through pantomime or through Giuseppe, who spoke French. Caroline called Assunta a "benevolent domestic tyrant." Assunta insisted on doing all the washing and cooking. "You do not love Assunta," she said if Caroline even tried to wash out a pair of socks.

Relieved to be free of household chores, Caroline wasted no time getting back to work on her novel. On the second day after they arrived, she pulled out her typewriter and began to write. From then on her schedule was set: write all morning, take a siesta after lunch, then go out sightseeing in the late afternoon and evening, using two books, *The Wonders of*

Italy and *Pilgrims and Martyrs of Rome,* to guide her through the winding streets, ruins, and cathedrals.

As Caroline got to know the city, she remembered something Stark Young had once told her: Rome was "earthy, mystical, universal, gross and golden." Caroline decided he was right. In colors ranging from saffron yellow to Pompeian red, the city was "out of this world while heavy with relics of the pomps of this world," she said.

Walking down the Via Aurelia, past the ancient wall that used to surround the city, Caroline thought of the pilgrims who had gone before her. She saw trees growing out of the crumbling wall, marble shields with the insignia of various popes decorating the wall at intervals, and an amazing combination of old world and new. Since the government had laws against disturbing any remains, "layers on top of layers" of history were all jumbled together. Fragments of the past covered the stark white plaster walls of modern apartment buildings: "a broken frieze of animals from some sacred procession, the head of a bull and half the head of the man who has his knife raised to sacrifice the bull to Mithras," Caroline noted.

The effect was oddly beautiful, rather "like walking down the street with your brother or sister to find that your father and mother are walking along with you, too, then stumbling and falling into a hole in the pavement and there are your grandpa and grandma and great grandpa and great grandma, too," Caroline said.

Sometimes she walked to St. Peter's at the bottom of the Janiculum. She stood in awe before Bernini's famous colonnade. The figures of Christ and his apostles were twelve feet tall, but Caroline thought they looked only life size, their outlines stark against the deep blue sky. The view from inside the church just as incredible, everything glittering "in a way to take your breath," she wrote to her daughter.

Although Allen did not enjoy walking as much as Caroline did, he sometimes went along with her. Caroline was sure he did more walking in his first weeks in Rome than "in all his life put together." She enjoyed exploring the city with Allen, and she was especially glad to see how fresh air and exercise improved his appearance: Allen's cheeks even began to lose their sickly, sunken look.

When the Fulbright officials advanced Allen money to buy a new Austin, most of their walks ended; however, they were able to get around much easier. They drove along the Appian Way, spent weekends in

Pompeii, Naples, Florence, Venice, and Ravello. Everywhere they went, Caroline found something to exclaim about: broken statues and ruins full of cats, high mountains terraced with crops and ancient frescoes and mosaics. In a short time Caroline had decided that she and Allen would spend their retirement in Italy. "I simply love every inch of the country," she declared.

Before long, however, Allen became ill, not for lack of exercise but because he once again refused to eat balanced meals. According to Caroline he had engaged in "an ancient and . . . losing warfare with the vegetable kingdom." In addition to eating only pasta and meat, no vegetables or fruits, he drank plenty of espresso, and then he wondered why he had stomach problems and other related afflictions.

"Old Doc Gordon" told him how to cure his ills, but Allen would not listen. He preferred to go "doctoring" elsewhere, although none of the Italian physicians understood "Allen's peculiar notions of diet," Caroline grumbled. They had to cancel several trips because Allen's "attacks" continued throughout most of the fall.

Although Allen found it difficult to return to work on his long poem, Caroline wrote steadily on her novel *The Malefactors*. At first, she was frustrated by her slow progress: Caroline felt as if she were carving the novel "out of the solid rock." By the middle of November, however, she had hit her stride and completed roughly half of the novel in addition to outlining the rest.

Caroline continued to question the motives and actions of her characters, especially those of Cynthia. Then in early December she decided that she had been wrong about Cynthia. She was not Vera's older sister but her younger, first cousin, a married woman about to divorce her husband, a university professor, Caroline realized. Tom would have met Cynthia only once before, briefly, around the time of his marriage to Vera.

Caroline was relieved to settle Cynthia's relationship to Vera, but her greatest struggle during the fall and winter of 1953 was one of technique, not character. She had to simultaneously juggle past, present, and future, revealing not only the characters and personal histories of Tom, Vera, and Cynthia, but the lives of three others who had died long before the narrative began: Tom's father, Vera's father, and Horne Watts, Caroline's fictional version of Hart Crane.

In a way Caroline's technique in *The Malefactors* would resemble the blended architecture of Rome. While following the main action, Thomas

Claiborne's struggle for faith, the reader would stumble across fragments of the past, like the broken friezes preserved in the walls of modern apartment buildings. When those fragments were examined, their stories revealed through careful excavating, they would illuminate and deepen the present scene.

To some degree Caroline had used a similar technique in *The Women on the Porch*. But in *The Malefactors* she would go one step further. In *The Women on the Porch* the past operated on the present through the dramatic monologues of the old women and through a visionary appearance at the end of the novel. But in *The Malefactors* the past would be a more steady presence in the narrative. The stories of the dead characters had to "unfold chronologically, counter-clockwise to the main action," Caroline explained to a friend. Tom and Vera's fathers and Horne Watts would never really appear in the novel, and yet they had to be as fully developed as any of the living characters. Their life stories would run parallel to and serve as a sort of choral comment on the rest of the narrative.

Caroline knew her plan to use the lives of the dead in the novel was ambitious; sometimes she thought it was too ambitious. "Flaubert had some such idea once, for *one* person, but had sense enough to leave it alone," she noted. Yet Caroline knew she could not change her course. "I never asked these dead people to stalk on to my stage, but now they're there I have to deal with them," she told a friend.

As Caroline wrestled with technique and characters, living and dead, she found several new sources of inspiration and relaxation. Not far from her apartment she discovered the Convent of the Perpetual Rosary, a cloistered community of American nuns who prayed the rosary constantly. Caroline liked to visit the convent to meditate before the Blessed Sacrament, and when she woke up in the middle of the night, she found it comforting to "tune in on the Rosary with the sisters instead of taking phenobarbital."

Caroline believed that living near the convent helped her to understand "what a prodigious mystery Mary's life" was, and she looked forward to the new liturgical year, beginning on December 8, 1953, and centered around devotion to Mary. Caroline felt that writing cut her off from "female identification," but she began to think that reverence for Mary and other female saints would restore her and her family. She prayed fervently for her family, certain that the coming year would be a very important time for them.

1954–1959

Caroline wanted to place her trust in spiritual aid, but by the beginning of 1954, she was forced to look elsewhere for help. Allen's drinking was out of control, and Caroline felt both powerless and put upon. Nearly every other day Allen had to sleep off a hangover. When he did, Caroline had to forego typing in the apartment. Fearing she would never finish her novel, and worried about Allen and their marriage, Caroline turned once again to psychiatry. She wanted answers to two questions: Why did Allen have "these spells of maniacal drinking"? And why did they make her "so damn mad," she wondered. But the answers she found were both liberating and confining. They directed her to new "underground streams" of knowledge while reinforcing patterns of submission and self-sacrifice. Caroline would be hard-pressed to put her insights into practice.

Her guide for the journey was Dora Bernhard, a Jungian analyst. Born in Austria and brought up in Germany, the *dotoressa* lived in Rome with her husband, who was also a psychiatrist. Although Caroline would have preferred a Catholic doctor, she liked the idea of working with a Jungian. They saw each other weekly throughout the early months of 1954.

At first Caroline tried to spend her time with Dr. Bernhard talking about Allen's behavior. The *dotoressa* listened amiably, but she was not really interested in what Caroline had to say about her marital problems. Instead, Dr. Bernhard wanted Caroline to focus on herself through analysis of her dreams. This annoyed Caroline—especially since she thought she did not dream or would not remember her dreams enough to talk about them. Yet shortly after their first meeting, Caroline began to remember her dreams. Soon, abandoning even the appearance of trying to work on her novel, she typed up her dreams for discussion.

Caroline felt right at home with the *dotoressa*'s discussion of archetypes and dreams, "the text which gives a true report from the unconscious." While preparing to write *The Malefactors*, Caroline had read and enjoyed Jung's "Integration of the Personality." His belief that the human psyche had "the powers necessary to heal itself" at "its deepest level" appealed to her; his idea of the collective unconscious, an underground stream of memory of the history of the society, coincided with Caroline's ideas about art.

From the first Caroline's dreams spoke of her anxiety about appropriate gender roles, and her lack of self-confidence resulting from Allen's treatment of her. Once Caroline dreamed that she and Allen were out on one of the archeological excavations that abounded throughout Italy. As they watched the men dig, they talked about a large stone face that had just been found. The expression on the face was archaic and serene, not smiling or sad, looking out as if into eternity. Both Allen and Caroline agreed it was best to put the face away, perhaps in a box. Then Caroline looked up and saw a little goat with twisted black horns creeping along a wall, cropping the grasses. "This animal, too, had been kept away somewhere, for the sake of convenience," but she was delighted to see him again. "Look, we don't need to put him away," Caroline said. "He can make his own living."

Another time, Caroline dreamed that she was in a large, crowded room, standing beside Allen, who was seated on a throne. Allen gave advice to a stream of people standing before him. All the while he kept talking to Caroline in a low voice. Then a procession entered the room: Jesus Christ astride an ass on his way to Jerusalem. Caroline wanted to join the procession, but Allen said no. "This procession or symbol is all right for other people," he said, but it was not right for her. If she followed it, or imitated it, the action would come from her "dark" side, he said. "That is not our kind of word."

When Caroline shared her dreams, Dr. Bernhard showed her how to "read" them, and Caroline respected the *dotoressa*'s passion "for underground exploration." Dr. Bernhard had "one of the subtlest intellects or imaginations" that she had ever encountered, Caroline said. The *dotoressa* helped her realize she had not paid enough attention to her own nature, her "true self" symbolized in the first dream as the great stone face. Caroline was a "feeling-intuition type," but she was always being asked to deny her intuitions, to put them away, the *dotoressa* said. Yet denying her true nature solved nothing, as the appearance of the little goat attested. Caroline could stop drinking in the hope that her outbursts against Allen would cease, but then her "violence, which was a form of self-assertion and also justified resentment toward Allen, only went underground to reappear in another form," the doctor explained.

With Dr. Bernhard's help, Caroline admitted that Allen was too impatient with her intuitive nature; often he was wrong to be so imperious. "My instinctual nature, whatever its flaws, is *my* instinctual nature, the only one I've got," Caroline wrote in her notes. "I should rely more on it instead of identifying myself so with Allen and trying to do everything the way he wants it done."

Yet Caroline wondered if Allen did not have the key to her happiness, and the *dotoressa* supported such a limiting point of view. She told Caroline that Allen was her animus, her lover, guide, and mentor. Just as in the dream when he warned her not to join the procession, in life Allen could warn her against "the danger implicit in a certain side" of her nature, Caroline wrote: "I am impulsive and violent and these traits might make me lose myself in certain aesthetic sides of the church, to the neglect of its real wisdom."

As she delved deeper into Jungian ideas, Caroline started having dreams about her grandmother and her cousins Mildred, Anna, and Catherine, who had committed suicide. Once she even woke up shouting, "Mother!" after dreaming about almost being mugged. She tried to come to terms with her ambivalent feelings toward these women. Several times Caroline dreamed that a veiled woman stood at the foot of her bed, looking at her with disapproval.

Caroline remembered how her grandmother had often embarrassed her, giving her favored status while treating Caroline's cousins quite badly. Yet the *dotoressa* helped Caroline realize how much her grandmother had done for her: she was "the first person who ever 'recognized' me—that is, recognized me as an individual, the way we all want to be recognized," Caroline wrote in her notes.

The *dotoressa* also tried to help Caroline forgive her mother. According to Dr. Bernhard, Caroline had saved herself by distancing herself from her mother and cultivating the talents she had inherited from her father, but suppressing the more feminine side of her personality exacted "a heavy price." The time had come for Caroline to acknowledge the problems she had with her mother.

Slowly Caroline began to realize how much she owed the women in her life. In her dreams she began to accept her mother, to recognize her and her gifts. Once Caroline dreamed that she was working in an underground cavern when her mother arrived with a beautiful desk she had found at an antique shop. Caroline thought it was the perfect desk, "exactly the desk [she had] always longed for." But as she gazed at the desk, she decided to give it to her mother: it was "so wonderful" that Caroline wanted her to have it.

In another dream a young friend helped Caroline climb up into a loft bedroom. She cleared away a circle of men and urged Caroline to climb up on a square wooden chest. When some of the men volunteered to help, Caroline's young woman companion told them no: Caroline had to do it by herself, she insisted. The chest represented "the substantial female under-pinning on which I must stand in order to get up into 'a room of my own,'" Caroline wrote.

Yet as long as she depended on Allen to be her animus, guide, and mentor, Caroline would find it difficult to find that room of her own. However she was delighted with her discoveries and saw no conflict in the advice she was given. Dr. Bernhard was "a real 'new critic'" of dreams, Caroline told her friends. "Meeting this woman, at least becoming acquainted with the Jungian technique is the most tremendous experience of my life, next to falling in love and being converted, and of a piece with both," she wrote.

Delighted that Caroline was seeing the *dotoressa*, Allen applied for an extension of his Fulbright to allow them to stay in Italy through the summer. Unable to work on his poetry, Allen went around quoting Hawthorne: "I fear this Italian air does not favor close toil." However, he did manage to stop his "maniacal drinking" soon after Caroline began her counseling sessions. Before long he was eager to consult with Dr. Bernhard himself. But the *dotoressa* told him that she wanted to finish her work with Caroline first. "We still have a lot of work to do," the *dotoressa* said.

In between the sessions with Dr. Bernhard, Caroline continued to explore Italy. She also saw William Faulkner, who was briefly vacationing in Rome. The first time they had dinner with Faulkner, Caroline was disappointed. "He was sunk in a trance so deep that when spoken to he would answer three or four minutes later," she told her daughter.

But when they met again several days later, Faulkner seemed livelier and pleased to see Caroline. Over dinner at Galeassi's, he kept referring to "Mr. Morey."

"Where is Mr. Morey?" Faulkner would ask.

Caroline thought he meant Rufus Morey. "He spends his days in the Vatican, cataloguing the Pope's collection of gold-glass medallions," she responded.

"I wish I could have met that man," Faulkner kept saying. "That is a wonderful story."

After several such discussions about "Mr. Morey," Caroline discovered that she had misunderstood Faulkner. He wasn't interested in Rufus Morey, she realized. He was talking about Aleck Maury!

By early spring Allen found out that his Fulbright had been extended, and the Tates made plans to rent a studio apartment in Florence. Then on April 5, 1954, the Tates received an emergency cable from their son-in-law, Percy Wood. Nancy was extremely ill, Percy said. He needed help: could Caroline come back to Princeton at once?

Caroline left Rome the next day by plane. When she arrived in New Jersey, Percy assured her that Nancy was much better. Still Caroline was horrified at what she saw. Nancy greeted her with tears, Caroline claimed months later.

"Mama, I'm sick of penis envy . . . and latent homosexuality, too," Nancy said. "And I don't believe the atom bomb is the most powerful weapon ever devised by man." No, she said, "the castration complex" was more powerful than the atom bomb: "with the castration complex a man can have his way about everything in this life," Nancy wailed.

Nancy had been suffering from what Percy called a psychotic episode. She had been "detached from reality," he said, and perhaps having hallucinations. Before her actual breakdown, she had also been spending large sums of money. Percy had tried to help her by taking time off from his last year of psychiatric residency at the University of Pennsylvania in Philadelphia. For about a week before he contacted the Tates, he had taken care of the children and the housework as best he could, hoping that his wife would cure herself with time and relaxation. Nancy had improved. But she was still not herself, and he considered placing Nancy under formal psychiatric care.

Caroline tried to squelch that idea from the start. Her daughter and grandchildren had already had too much informal counseling at home, Caroline believed. Nancy had had an old-fashioned nervous breakdown, the result of fatigue and worry. According to Caroline, Nancy just needed rest, help around the house, and a more steady source of income.

Caroline wanted to make life easier for her daughter. But at first, there seemed to be little Caroline could do. Nancy was angry with both Percy and her mother. She was especially furious that Percy had even called her mother.

Although Caroline did not realize it, Nancy felt torn between her parents. For several years Allen had been confiding in his daughter. He told her that he loved Natasha Spender and insisted that after she got a divorce, he would divorce Caroline to marry Natasha. But Nancy discovered that Natasha had no plans for a divorce. She felt sorry for her father, angry with her mother for making life so difficult for him, and caught in the middle of their battles. Having Caroline around that spring was little comfort to Nancy.

Caroline realized Nancy was upset with her, but she thought their money worries were to blame. Percy's salary as a resident was just not sufficient for a family with three children under the age of nine, and Caroline felt guilty that she had not been able to give her daughter more money. She also wondered if Nancy's spending orgies weren't inherited: Allen's mother had similar sprees.

When Caroline wrote Allen about her feelings, Allen urged her not to let guilt cloud her thinking. He insisted they had already been overly generous with money and said spending sprees were not likely to be hereditary. Allen believed Percy had caused Nancy's collapse. He wanted Caroline to send Nancy to Rome to work with the *dotoressa*.

No one in Princeton thought Nancy ought to travel to Rome. Instead, Caroline tried to help her daughter around the house, and Nancy continued to improve. After a while Caroline began to think she would be able to return to Italy for the summer.

Before she would make definite plans, however, Caroline wanted to make permanent changes around Benbrackets to make life easier for Nancy. Although the tiny house had been perfect for her and Allen, Caroline thought it was "a torture chamber" for Nancy. "There was no place even to sort the mountains of laundry," she said later. "They all just walked around on top of it and dived under from time to time to bring up a diaper or a pair of shorts."

Caroline wanted to build a new addition to the house or a prefabricated garage to give the Woods more room. When she went to the bank to inquire about a loan, however, she discovered that they would be more willing to finance the purchase of a larger house. It did not take Caroline, Nancy, and Percy long to decide what to do: they bought a ramshackle mansion located at 54 Hodge Road.

Nancy and Percy had discovered the house on Hodge Road about five months earlier. It was "the house of our dreams," Nancy told her mother at that time. Located in what Nancy called "the who's who in Princeton part of town," the house had been built in 1900 by a Princeton University professor. It was "the ugliest house" Caroline ever saw: "late Victorian gone pazza," she called it. It had a circular front driveway and a Moorish archway for a front entrance, lots of stained glass, and a pointed bay window. The side porch was "shaped exactly like the band stand at the county fair and wreathed in wisteria so thick the boys [could] climb upstairs on it," Caroline said.

The house had been rented for years, and it was badly in need of attention. Yet it had six bedrooms, three and a half bathrooms, and a back entrance for the children to use. Percy could run his private practice from the house, and Caroline and Allen could have a suite upstairs without crowding the Woods at all. For only twenty-three thousand dollars the house seemed ideal. The family called the place Dulce Domum, from the inscription on the chimney, or Hodge Horror.

Caroline spent the rest of the spring and early summer helping the Woods move and settle into their new home. She sold Benbrackets for twenty thousand dollars, impressing Allen with her financial genius. Since they had a smaller mortgage on Dulce Domum, he figured they had made a profit on the deal.

But despite Caroline's willingness to help with the cooking and get up on stepladders to paint, all was not well in Dulce Domum. To Caroline's dismay, Nancy stopped attending services at the Catholic church. Nancy's mental state continued to improve, but her anger at her parents did not wane. In fact, Caroline thought it increased.

For a long while Percy debated over whether Nancy needed psychiatric treatment. Encouraged by Allen, Caroline gave Percy what she called an "inter office memo," arguing that Nancy would be irreparably harmed if Percy attempted to label and diagnose her problem. But the memo backfired: Nancy began to feel that her parents were in league against Percy, and Nancy blamed her mother all the more.

Friends who saw Caroline during the early summer of 1954 were impressed with her vitality and control over everything that was happening. They did not realize Caroline was often acting. The regimen at Dulce

Domum was sometimes too much for her. And Caroline worried about what Allen was doing in Italy. He continually reassured her in his letters that he was fine, but he mentioned seeing Natasha and Stephen Spender and another woman with whom he had had an affair.

Caroline and Allen carried on long conversations by mail about their relationship throughout the first part of the summer. Caroline decided that she could not continue their marriage if she did not believe that, despite his behavior, Allen was more gifted and intelligent than she was. Allen disagreed. "You are more gifted but less intelligent, and have not been able, for that reason, to use your resources in the most concentrated way," he told her.

As they discussed their marriage, Allen insisted they were ready to begin again, almost as if they were starting new, but Caroline worried about women like Natasha Spender. She was sure Allen would always be attracted to women like her—women somehow unattainable and generally undemanding.

Allen agreed he was vulnerable around other women, but he urged Caroline to trust him. He reminded her of their troubles in the summer of 1933, and insisted Caroline had been wrong then, wrong to speak to him as a Sho Nuff Maywether. When she talked like that, she reminded him of his mother, and he could only rebel, he insisted.

Allen's letters appeared optimistic and comforting on the surface, but Caroline did not have to read deeply to find the threat. "Don't ask so much of me, or I will continue to seek other women who will ask less," Allen seemed to say.

Caroline suffered under the strain of caring for her daughter and three grandchildren while worrying about Allen. Soon her anxiety found a destructive outlet. One evening, while the Woods were out for dinner, Caroline surrendered to exhaustion and depression, destroying a picture of Nancy.

When Percy and Nancy came home and discovered what Caroline had done, they were furious. Caroline tried to explain that she had burnt the picture because it reminded her of an unhappy time, a time when Nancy had been a great trial to her parents, but her explanation fell on deaf ears. Nancy and Percy would not forgive her.

Increasingly, Nancy and Percy did not trust Caroline. Once they found a letter which she had written, then discarded, describing something which had happened in Dulce Domum. Caroline's account of the events bore very little resemblance to the truth, they said later. Of course, she had thrown the letter away, so perhaps she realized she was writing fiction, but would any of Caroline's observations and letters be any more accurate? Nancy and Percy doubted it.

By the first of July, Percy had completed his residency and entered into private practice. This pleased both Nancy and Caroline, but it also added to the tension around the house because, Caroline claimed, Percy did not have the slightest idea about housework and child care. Once he even intentionally woke his baby daughter from a sound sleep. Suitably chastened by her subsequent cries, Percy vowed he would "never do that again."

"Can you imagine doing it the first time?" Caroline wondered. "This place is like a short order restaurant at lunch hour, if you can imagine the waitresses giving three deeply disturbed patients therapy while preparing and serving the food," she told a friend.

Allen returned to Princeton in the middle of July. He and Caroline spent the rest of the summer at Dulce Domum, since Allen had work to do at the Princeton University Library. Everything seemed harmonious, but actually the Woods and the Tates were fighting what Allen called "the Battle of Princeton," a battle neither side won. At the end of the summer, Caroline and Allen left for Minneapolis "stuck full of arrows of hostility," according to Caroline. Nancy and Percy and their children left also: they had to rent the house on Hodge Road because Percy had been offered a well-paying job with the Carrier Clinic. Although the psychiatric hospital was located just outside Princeton, Percy was required to live in a house on the clinic's grounds.

Since the house Caroline had rented in Minnesota for the new academic year would not be available until sometime in November, the Tates spent a number of weeks living with friends that fall. When they finally settled into 1409 East River Road in Minneapolis, their fourth address in a year, Caroline was feeling bitter. She had left Rome and spent nearly five thousand dollars trying to get Nancy and Percy settled, only to have them move away, angry. She should have stayed in Rome and sent Nancy the money to hire a maid, Caroline thought.

Allen disagreed. "Dire calamity would have befallen" Nancy if Caroline had not gone to Princeton, he said.

"Well, I have done all I could to help them," Caroline said. "It's better for us all to be separated now."

As Caroline reflected on her stay with Nancy, she realized that five months in Princeton taught her things she "could never have learned in any other way," especially that no one worked harder than Nancy.

Percy's actions bothered Caroline: he seemed to her "like a man standing on his head and looking at the universe through his spread legs," she wrote a friend. "Everything goes into the Freudian meat-grinder to emerge as pap suitable to be fed invalids."

After some time had passed, however, Caroline concluded that Percy had acted as wisely as he could, and that the Tates had not always made life easy for their daughter and son-in-law. "It is hard for Allen and me, with all our flaws of character and infantilisms, to realize that as parents-in-law we are rather formidable, simply because of our achievements," Caroline admitted. Percy was "a wonderful fellow, with something like genius," she decided. He had "dived right into the abyss," and she was proud of him.

Both Caroline and Allen looked forward to a quiet winter of work in Minneapolis, and they had just that. After nearly a year of writer's block, Allen returned to work on a poetry anthology and gave a number of lectures in addition to his regular teaching. Caroline decided that Allen was a wanderer because he was "a listener, not a looker." He worked best in Minnesota with the landscape "veiled in snow . . . obliterated, for seven months of the year," she observed. With nothing to look at, Allen could listen to his muse.

Caroline did not usually need enforced isolation for writing, but during the winter of 1954–55, she appreciated their retreat. She locked herself in what she sometimes called a "death cell" of writing, determined to finish her novel by the first of May.

The Tates went to parties given by Allen's colleagues at the University of Minnesota, but they did not entertain much. Caroline did not even write many letters. All her energy went into *The Malefactors*. To relax, she read regularly in the Italian edition of the *Seraphic Dialogues* of St. Catherine of Siena: she wanted to be ready to return to Italy with a better command of the language. Next to the Virgin Mary, St. Catherine was "the most wonderful woman that ever lived," Caroline believed. "She never learned to read till three years before she died, but she licked two popes and one emperor into shape natheless."

With Allen, Caroline also continued to explore the theories of Jung. She was especially interested in Jung's *Religion and Alchemy*, and she tried to apply what she was learning to fiction and her own life. In *The Male-*

factors Caroline would have Horne Watts and Catherine Pollard approach Christianity through alchemy.

Caroline believed that Jung helped her to understood Allen better. She thought Jung's notion of "the shadow"—"man's darker side which grows more and more menacing until it is confronted and come to terms with"—explained many of Allen's problems. As Caroline saw it, Allen had never dealt with a "mother-fixation" that had originated in childhood, and over time it had become his shadow, threatening their marriage. Allen did not always agree with Caroline's diagnosis of their problems, but he similarly felt that through Jung they would be able to forge a better pattern for their life together. Neither of the Tates could apply their understanding of Jung or one another in practical ways, however. They continued to drink too much, to fight, to struggle against one another, although they tried to keep up appearances as a happily married couple.

Sometimes Caroline lost her struggle with appearances. At one party for members of the English department at the university, Caroline broke into a tirade against her friend Danforth Ross. Caroline loved Dan: he was a native of Clarksville, Tennessee, and a part of her family connection by marriage, as well as one of her former students at Columbia. But that night she lost her temper without warning when Dan mentioned an article he had read by Samuel Monk in the winter edition of the *Sewanee Review*.

The *Sewanee Review* had published Caroline's article on Henry James, "Mr. Verver, Our National Hero," in that same issue, and Caroline seemed to think that Dan was slighting her by referring to Monk's work. "I have worked all my life to write this essay," she said. "It's got everything I have ever learned in it. Everything I have learned and you talk to me about Sam Monk."

When Caroline was angry, she held nothing back. Dan did not get a chance to speak. "That essay was written for you and you haven't read it," she said. "I have spent all my life writing it and you talk to me about Sam Monk's article on *Gulliver*. Cousin Caroline has spent all her life on that one little essay and Dan Ross talks to me about something Sam Monk has written on *Gulliver*."

As Caroline continued to scold him, Dan listened in silence. He knew it would do no good to defend himself.

"Old Caroline Gordon is just not going to worry," she went on to say. "I'm so damn glad I don't have to write another essay. I've spent all my life writing this essay and now I'm so damn glad I don't have to write another essay. For I'm through. Old Caroline Gordon's washed her hands of all of you. And I'm so damned glad. Talking to her about Sam Monk's article on Gulliver."

Dan Ross never forgot the scene Caroline made. But he realized that Caroline was insecure at times and yearned for recognition, and he did not hold her outburst against her.

Despite her tirade against Dan, Caroline tried not to lose her temper in public. She did, however, give free reign to frustration in her novel. In the marriage of Vera and Tom Claiborne, she dramatized the problems in her own marriage. Just like Allen, Tom accused Vera of being too much of a romantic, of expecting too much from him. Vera "frightened me, the way she thought I could change the whole world," Tom said. Vera assumed "he had powers that he had never thought of himself as possessing," Caroline wrote. "She had come to him as to a physician—or magician. He was to give her everything she had ever wanted and never got. When she found that he could not do it (what man could?) she had turned away from him (for she could not deny that in the last few years she had turned away from him!) to lose herself in frenetic activity." Like Allen, Tom would have preferred his wife to be a little less demanding. "If only she had been content to remain what she was when he found her," Caroline wrote: "a bird fluttering on a terrace that a man might pick up and warm in his bosom, a bird that would nestle tamely, grateful for any warmth it might come by, and not be always turning its fierce, golden eye on yours, not always be beating its maimed wing against your breast!"

Caroline wrote her novel from Tom's perspective. In the past she had sometimes used a male narrator to prove her expertise as a writer, but this time she may have also done so to veil some of her harshest criticism of Allen. Throughout the novel Caroline suggested through dramatic irony that Tom destroyed his marriage because he was a cold, all-too-conceited intellectual. Like Allen, Tom considered himself the expert on all things, and he consequently looked down on his wife, her activities, and many of her friends. Although shocked when Vera lied to him, Tom did not hesitate to tell her falsehoods and shut her out of his life. He precipitated their marriage problems by being too introspective and self-centered while accusing his wife of withdrawing from him emotionally.

"These things—follow patterns," Cynthia told Tom after Vera attempted suicide, and Caroline concentrated on developing family patterns to explain some of her characters' actions. Yet Caroline also complicated her novel by transposing some of the autobiographical patterns. Caroline drew Vera in her own image. She had Tom accuse Vera of having an "uncritical attachment to her family." "I always knew they were crazy. . . . But *she* doesn't," Tom said. Allen often said the same thing about Caroline. Vera, however, was not a southerner, and unlike Caroline she did not even have an extended family connection. But Tom did. Although Caroline created Tom to resemble Allen, she actually gave him much of her own family history.

In *The Malefactors* the Claiborne family was related to the Fayerlees and the Allards, Caroline's fictional version of the Meriwether-Barker connection. There were "Anyhow" Claibornes and "Kinky Head" Claibornes, as well as family homes near Gloversville with names like Eupedon and Sycamore.

Once again, however, Caroline did not create simple genealogical lines. In fact, she even had Tom Claiborne's father resemble several of her Gordon relatives, especially her father in his love of classical heroes. She also gave Tom Claiborne some of her own attributes and experiences. He had lived in a lonely third-floor room of his uncle's home while going to law school by day and writing poetry at night, just as Caroline had lived with her aunt and uncle and wrote her first novel before work at the newspaper. He was sensitive to the way light filtered through the trees.

By reversing the family histories Caroline may have simply been trying to disguise Tom's relationship to Allen. Or she may have been trying to reconcile her love for Allen with her loyalty to her family. Even though they no longer lived near the Old Neighborhood and seldom saw any of the Meriwether connection, Caroline still had to defend herself from Allen's attacks. Allen wanted her to see the Meriwethers as he saw them: they were all louts, all crazy. But Caroline's life as an artist depended on the Meriwether family myth. She could not adopt his point of view.

Increasingly, Allen suggested to Caroline that her attachment to her family would destroy them. He could not forget the time she turned on him with the tone of a Sho Nuff Maywether. He could not forgive her, perhaps because, as Caroline had realized long ago, he was a bit jealous of her family. No, Allen insisted that Caroline would have to choose between her marriage and the Meriwether family myth. But by creating Tom Claiborne as a fictional representation of Allen *and* as a member of her own family connection, Caroline may have been attempting to demonstrate that such a choice would surely destroy them both.

Often in her notes for *The Malefactors,* Caroline analyzed Vera's relationship with her family, and how that relationship affected her marriage. In doing so she offered a key to her own relationship with Allen. She wrote about how Vera identified herself with her father's struggles. "When he goes out of her life she knows the loss of the relationship and also sees unconsciously the defeat of something that she already feels is dearer than life," Caroline wrote. But by associating her husband's struggles with those of her father, Vera hoped to "see the good fight fought again—and won." That was one of the reasons Vera married Tom, Caroline wrote in her notes. It was also part of the reason Caroline remained married to Allen.

Claiborne, like Allen, wanted his wife to reject her family because he felt that she was "making him over in her father's image," Caroline wrote. However, if Vera were to distance herself from her family, she would also be cutting the heart out of her marriage. Consciously or not, Caroline suggested that the same was true for her.

By the beginning of March 1955, Caroline had nearly finished *The Malefactors.* With only the final chapter to write before beginning to revise the novel, she felt sure she would make her May 1 deadline. She had the last chapter completely plotted: it would be an account of Tom and Vera's reconciliation, or at least of Tom's movement toward faith and reconciliation. Tom would beg Vera to take him back. "I will do what the Church tells me to do," Vera would respond. And the church, in the figure of a broken-down priest, would remind them they were married once for all time.

Allen left on a West Coast lecture tour, so Caroline had no distractions and unlimited time to write. But by the end of March, she was in despair. The words would not come. Every day she went through the motions, trying to write, but after three weeks she had only a page and a half to show. And she was not sure she could even use that.

What was wrong? Caroline did not know, and she wished Allen were around to help her. He was infallible on tone, and Caroline began to think she had not struck the right one for the chapter. But perhaps the events she had planned to use were throwing her off? Caroline was not sure. Her deadline for fall publication drew near, adding to her anxiety. But there was nothing she could do. "I will just have to wait for more light," she said.

Caroline was still struggling with the chapter when Allen returned to Minneapolis in early April. His trip had been a critical and financial success; Allen had earned enough to get them out of debt and through the summer. But three weeks of lectures took a lot out of Allen. Caroline realized he was dangerously fatigued.

Allen did not stay in Minnesota long. He and Caroline attended a symposium of Catholic educators in Milwaukee, and then Allen left on another lecture trip. Caroline could not depend on his help with her novel, but Allen performed one valuable service for her: he wrote her editor at Harcourt, Brace. "Caroline can't possibly make Fall publication," Allen told him, "so pay no attention to her if she tells you she thinks she can."

Getting out from under the pressure of a deadline freed Caroline to work with new energy. Within a month she had finished the last chapter, but it bore little resemblance to her original notes. Instead of constructing a reconciliation scene in which Vera would submit to the church's teaching, Caroline created in her final paragraphs a scene reminiscent of the ending of *The Women on the Porch*. Tom would have to humble himself to rebuild his marriage and reclaim his life. Late at night he would drive to Mary Farm, where Vera was staying. As he drove, he would decide that he would sleep with the rest of the derelicts who had found refuge there. "He could sleep in the hay if there was no bed," Caroline wrote. "He could be sitting there on the bench with the other bums when she came down in the morning."

"A wife is subject to her husband, as the Church is subject to Christ," Catherine Pollard, Caroline's fictional version of Dorothy Day, would tell Tom just before he left for Mary Farm. The reader might expect Tom to remind Vera of her duty when she found him in the morning, but Caroline ended the novel with Tom speeding to the farm. Overtly, Caroline appeared to be championing the traditional patriarchal values in the closing scenes of *The Malefactors*. She even chose an epigraph from an essay by Jacques Maritain to reinforce these values: "It is for Adam to interpret the voices that Eve hears."

And yet once again, consciously or not, Caroline suggested another level of meaning and interpretation for those beliefs. A wife may be subject to her husband, but he must first be stripped of his pride and truly solicitous of his wife. He must recognize and respect the "voices" that she hears, accept her as his muse. Far from relegating the woman to a minor, subservient role, Caroline once again could be said to be elevating her. Just as in *The Women on the Porch*, the man's salvation depended on the woman.

Throughout the novel Caroline used her female characters to guide Tom. Although he scorned them and considered them fools, the women in his life actually knew him better than he knew himself. Their wisdom would lead him to a proper reverence for his family, his wife, and his god. Although Caroline developed this theme in her usual subterranean way, she nevertheless implied that if Tom ignored the women's advice, he was doomed to be a rootless wanderer in the depths of hell.

The images and messages in *The Malefactors* were strident because Caroline knew all too well what it was like to be damned as a rootless wanderer. Although she hardly needed any reminder of the horrors of that life, she continued to live like a gypsy during the summer of 1955. At the end of May, she left Minnesota. She spent several weeks in Tory Valley, a weekend at Dorothy Day's retreat center in Newburgh, New York, then visited friends and family in Tennessee, and taught at the Indiana Writers' Conference in Bloomington—all before the end of July. It was a confused and hectic summer.

Caroline saw little of Allen: whether by accident or design, their paths crossed only once, in Bloomington, where Allen had gone at the beginning of the summer to teach at the School of Letters. Caroline joined him there in July, but by the beginning of August, they had separated again. Allen went to Italy for an international conference. Caroline went to Princeton to finish her novel and visit her grandchildren.

To her surprise, Caroline enjoyed her stay in Princeton. The Woods were moving back into Dulce Domum, since Percy's job no longer required him to live on the hospital grounds, and Caroline was amazed at how much her relationship with her daughter and son-in-law had changed. After a year of anger and silence, she once again felt that Nancy and Percy loved her. Nancy even helped her mother revise *The Malefactors,* suggesting that Caroline put a lot of background information that had been revealed through dialogue into one of Tom Claiborne's soliloquies. It was a brilliant suggestion, Caroline thought, and she did so.

In the middle of September, Caroline gave a final version of *The Malefactors* to her editor, Denver Lindley of Harcourt, Brace. She thought the novel marked the end of thirty-three years' work; it would be "the dividing line" in her work. "I have learned almost as much as I will ever learn about [the writing of fiction] in writing this book," she wrote to Allen. "From now on I will be writing about the same things—the same thing, there being only one—but I will use a different method of attack."

Although Caroline did not explain what that method would be, she insisted she might never "have written any fiction" if she "had envisioned [that] method of attack" at the start of her career. "But the Lord has to use even our blindness his wonders to perform," she told Allen. "James hit his stride when he was older than I am but he was never married and was never a parent or a grandparent."

Two days after Caroline turned in her novel, she left for Rome. She and Allen had decided that she needed to continue her work with Dr. Bernhard. After meditating on her shortcomings all summer, Caroline had begun to feel that the source of all her troubles was her lack of faith. "If I had faith in the promises of Christ I would never be disturbed and would never do things that disturb other people," she wrote to Allen. "The psychologists say that when a person is frightened it's 'fight or flight.' I don't flee but I am too quick to fight. If I had enough faith I wouldn't feel that I had to fight. I wouldn't feel menaced."

Allen flew back to Minneapolis on the day Caroline's ship sailed, so they never saw one another. Although Caroline would later insist that Allen had forced her to go to Rome, she was not upset about the trip at the time. She knew she and Allen would not be able to live together. It would be better for her to go to Rome and try to learn from Dr. Bernhard, she thought.

"I think that if I could learn not to get angry no matter what happened our life would be different," Caroline wrote to Allen. "And if you could forgo deception at the same time I was forgoing anger we'd probably be as happy as any two people could be."

Arriving in Rome late in September, Caroline settled into a pension on the Via Nicola Fabrizi, not far from where she and Allen had stayed two years earlier. She ate her breakfast at the pension, her dinner at the American Academy, a few blocks up the Janiculum, and skipped lunch, claiming she needed to slim down.

Caroline went to see Dr. Bernhard soon after her arrival. The *dotoressa* thought Caroline seemed better, less hostile and more content than she had been in the spring of 1954. They agreed to meet twice a week to continue their underground explorations.

In between sessions Caroline worked on an article called "How I Learned to Write Novels," a tribute to Professor Gay and an indictment of modern education. Resuming her walking tours of the city, she explored the Appian Way, delved into the catacombs, and rambled through fields around the city. She also found herself a garden to work in at the

Convent of the Perpetual Rosary. Using money that friends from Princeton had sent to her, Caroline planted a rosary of rose bushes, each of the fifteen bushes named for a friend or loved one.

Gardening renewed Caroline, but it reminded her of the restless, wandering nature of her life. She had worked in four gardens in four months, none of them really her own. In her dreams and subsequent sessions with Dr. Bernhard, Caroline began to articulate her desire to settle down in one place. She realized her mother had felt the same way: it was her father, not Nan Gordon, who was to blame for "keeping the ground always shifting" under their feet when Caroline was a child. Living with Allen repeated the pattern from Caroline's childhood, the *dotoressa* pointed out. Caroline agreed that she probably used Allen as "a 'screen' on which to project that long-cherished resentment" against her father.

Encouraged by the *dotoressa*, Caroline wrote Allen about her discoveries. "More and more I feel handicapped, both in my work and in my life, by not knowing . . . where I'll be tomorrow," she wrote. "My longing to have ground under my feet represents that most feminine side of my nature, a side which has been dangerously suppressed and frustrated by our wandering lives."

Caroline wanted a home of her own—"or, at least, a desk of my own, under my typewriter," she wrote. When Nancy and Percy offered to pay them ten thousand dollars for Dulce Domum, Caroline thought she might have her wish. But while she was making plans for the future, Allen was seeing other women. Some friends in Minneapolis even heard rumors that Allen had promised to divorce Caroline and marry someone else.

The rumors may not have traveled as far as Italy, but Caroline soon had other reasons to be upset: she discovered that Dr. Bernhard had been writing Allen, telling him things Caroline had told her in confidence. Feeling she could not trust either her husband or her analyst, Caroline lost her temper with a vengeance.

Shocked by Caroline's violent reaction, the *dotoressa* lied and tried to make Caroline believe she had only written Allen to respond to one of his dreams. But Caroline would not be entirely taken in by the lie. With her usual explosive wrath, she accused the *dotoressa* of betraying her.

Despite Caroline's fury the *dotoressa* continued to write Allen reports of their sessions. By the time Caroline's initial rage was spent, she had found other reasons for anger. Caroline reacted to rumors she heard about Allen's behavior in Minnesota; she feared for their future; she became jealous and suspicious about his past, especially of the women Allen had referred to in his poem "The Buried Lake," written in 1953.

Allen thought Caroline saw herself in the poem. In the middle of his poem, Allen wrote about seeing "a stately woman who in sorrow shone" with "coiled black hair." They had once made love together under a blooming dogwood tree, and on being reunited, they renewed their vows. "My Love," the narrator said, "I'm back to give you all." However, instead of giving the dark-haired woman love, he cut her head off with a hidden knife. Then he discovered that he had cut the wrong head, "another's searching skull whose drying teeth / Crumbled me all night long and I was dead." The scene Allen wrote about was violent and accusatory. "You have destroyed me," he seemed to be saying.

Caroline insisted that she did not see herself in "The Buried Lake" but another woman "pictured as the object" of Allen's desire. Later she apologized for her "violent reaction." "I have betrayed you on a higher level," she wrote to Allen. "It was a worse betrayal, coming from me, who am myself an artist, than it would have been coming from another woman, but it came from a level where I am not an artist, but just a woman."

Caroline began to feel that her own life as an artist complicated her marriage. Yet, she wrote Allen, "I had little choice: art was for me a way of surviving, of going on drawing my breath. If I hadn't become an artist I'd have gone under under the family pressures, the dotoressa says."

Caroline told Allen that he had helped her; he had, in fact, saved her life, she insisted. "I never could have done what little I've done without your help." But as if to assure him that their troubles were over, Caroline declared, "My work as a novelist is over." "I feel a little relieved," she wrote, "as if somebody had told me I didn't need to sit around, waiting for messages any longer but could go on and do something else."

Part of what she could do was help Allen, Caroline thought, even if that meant she would have to continue living apart from him. Shortly before she left Rome, Caroline admitted that the problems between her and Allen were "even more profound" than she had realized, and she began to agree with Allen. "You have been sorely tried and in ways more intangible and hence in some ways harder to bear than in the ways in which I have been tried," she wrote him. Yet Caroline thought that she now had some understanding, enough, perhaps, to keep her from reverting to childish fears.

Allen was not so sure, but Caroline would not be put to the test immediately. When she left Rome in December, she saw Allen only briefly during a visit with Nancy and Percy in Princeton. In January Allen returned to Minnesota alone. Caroline had agreed to teach during the spring semester at the University of Kansas in Lawrence.

Since she did not have to start teaching immediately, Caroline stayed in Princeton for several weeks during January. Much to Caroline's relief, she got along well with her daughter and son-in-law. Caroline did not, however, really have a pleasant visit. Her health was poor: during her last weeks in Rome, she had suffered greatly from the bitter cold and from stomach ailments, and while she was in Princeton, she caught the flu from her grandchildren.

Yet Caroline continued to put the best face on her affairs. When George Clay, one of her former students, saw Caroline at a cocktail party, he could not believe her exuberance. She smiled brightly and talked with everyone at the party. When George asked her if she was working on a new novel, she said no, she was too tired and too old, but George did not believe her. There was an undercurrent in her voice that belied her words. He thought it more likely that she would begin her next novel that very evening.

CAROLINE had a difficult time in Lawrence. She was still suffering from the flu when she arrived in January, and the first apartment she rented gave her nightmares. It was in a house full of talkative old ladies; the thermostat was set at an uncomfortable eighty degrees, and the walls of her rooms were covered with large, gaudy flowers. Caroline tried to ignore her surroundings, but by the beginning of March, she had to move to a new apartment.

She needed all the strength she could muster to teach, and often she could not muster enough. Caroline had three classes at the University of Kansas. On Wednesday afternoons she conducted a seminar on modern American and British writers; on Thursday afternoons she ran a writers' workshop, and on Tuesday evenings she gave a series of lectures on the art of fiction. The lectures were broadcast on a local radio as well as open to the public. "Everybody in Town and Gown can come, and does," she noted.

Caroline found her students in the seminar and writers' workshop demanding. But she thought the weekly lectures nearly killed her. Although she could recycle some of the talks from previous teaching experiences,

Caroline had to write a great deal of new material, so she decided to use the series to prepare for the book she still owed Viking, *How to Read a Novel*. In her first lecture, "Constants in the Techniques of Fiction," she advanced her basic thesis: "the only way to learn how to write novels is to learn how to read novels." She demonstrated the "constants" in the following lectures, but she did not confine her remarks to the study of serious fiction. One week Caroline analyzed the structure of *Oedipus Rex*. The next week, she compared Sophocles' techniques to those of Beatrix Potter's *Jemima Puddle-Duck*.

Preparing for the lectures took a lot out of Caroline: "it was really like writing a book in fifteen weeks and one would hardly attempt that," she said. But Caroline suffered more from the publication of her novel that spring, and from her continued struggle with Allen.

Allen visited Caroline soon after she arrived in Lawrence, and they corresponded regularly. For a while both believed they could conquer their most difficult problems. They vowed once again to stop drinking, and they made plans for the future, renting a house in Princeton for the summer and discussing ways to renovate an apartment in Minneapolis for next fall. Allen worked on his poetry and began to see a spiritual advisor, which greatly pleased Caroline. When Allen said he never again wanted to live apart from her for a long period, Caroline believed him. "Hope springs eternal in this breast, of course, (and a damned good thing, too!)," she wrote to her daughter.

But even in their euphoric declarations of faith, there were signs of tension. Caroline gave Allen all the credit for their achievements and most of the responsibility for their future. "We were born, as it were, in a jungle of misinformation and prejudices and lies," she wrote him. "You took machete in hand and hacked a way out for both of us when we were young but you have got to hack another trail in the next few years, or, I think, we are both lost."

Allen not only urged Caroline to accept responsibility for their future, but he tried to make her see that she had done more to clear away the jungle than he had ever done. Caroline could agree to the first but not the second. She needed to trust and believe in Allen.

Allen eventually felt that Caroline asked too much of him. But in the early months of 1956, he supported Caroline through several crises over the publication of *The Malefactors*. The first arose before the novel had even gone to press. Caroline wanted to dedicate the book to Dorothy Day, but she had never told Dorothy what she was writing about. "A

Still, Small Voice had warned me long ago that I better not," Caroline said later. When Denver Lindley, Caroline's editor, sent Dorothy a set of the novel's page proofs, Dorothy found out how Caroline had based the character of Catherine Pollard on her. She was furious.

Dorothy wanted Caroline to make major changes. She did not like seeing herself or her ministry depicted in such detail in the book, and she did not think Caroline should have portrayed the mental and physical decline of Joseph Tardieu, a fictional version of Dorothy's mentor, Peter Maurin. Most of all, Dorothy objected to a reference Caroline had made to a black mass that Catherine Pollard had participated in during her wild youth.

Caroline's publisher could not make all the changes Dorothy wanted, and even if time had allowed, Caroline would not. But she placated her friend somewhat by removing the dedication page, and by having Catherine participate in alchemical experiments instead of a black mass. Dorothy decided to adopt a Christian attitude toward the book: it did not injure her but forced her to do penance, she said.

Although not really surprised at her friend's reaction, Caroline was deeply hurt. Allen comforted her, insisting that Dorothy did not understand the demands of fiction or its relationship to life, and Caroline ended up invoking the spirit of Henry James in her defense. When his brother rebuked him for caricaturing an old woman from Boston in his novel *The Bostonians,* Henry James had insisted that similarities between his character and any living person were inconsequential: "Miss Birdseye was evolved entirely from my moral consciousness, like every person I have ever drawn," James insisted. Caroline often quoted his remarks. "*My* moral consciousness is, naturally, a small affair, compared to Uncle Henry's," she said. "Still, I've got one." The characters she had taken "identifiably from life" were either dead or "a saint" and that "makes their inclusion in the book very different from what it would be if they were living," she declared.

But once the novel was published that spring, Dorothy's criticism was not the only trial Caroline had to bear. Most reviewers panned it. An unnamed writer for *Time* magazine called the book a "moral and intellectual striptease": "one of those Mary McCarthy–like exercises in intellectual cattiness in which one claws one's literary coterie in public." Rosemary G. Benét in the *Saturday Review* said that the "picture of sick intellectuals" was "indeed a bitter dose . . . despite some spots of excellent writing."

Only a few reviewers praised the novel, and most of them were friends of either Caroline or Allen. Writing for the *New York Times Book Review,* Arthur Mizener called *The Malefactors* Caroline's "most ambitious novel," a work of "great intelligence," and he lamented the way Caroline's novels had been overlooked. In an article published in the *Southern Review,* Vivienne Koch called Caroline "the best woman novelist we have in this country at this time." *The Malefactors* was a "profoundly conceived, incandescent story," Koch insisted. Writing for the *New Republic,* Willard Thorp proclaimed that the novel was Caroline's best to date, although he admitted that some readers might not be able to appreciate it in all its depth.

More than any of the published reviews, Caroline cherished a letter that Jacques Maritain sent her about the novel. Jacques had profuse praise for *The Malefactors.* He did not think the book ought to be called a *roman à clé:* rather Caroline had created "overtones" that were "very new and bold, and very successful," he wrote.

Caroline made a number of copies of Jacques's letter. From then on, whenever anyone dared to call her book a *roman à clé* or ask her about the biographical parallels, she sent them a copy of the letter, as if Jacques's words not only justified what she had done but somehow transformed it.

Cal Lowell was one of the first people to receive a copy of Jacques's letter: he made the mistake of asking whom Tom Claiborne was supposed to represent. Although most people took Tom's similarity to Allen for granted, Cal probably realized that Caroline had put a lot of herself into his character. Perhaps Cal was also trying to find out Allen's opinion of the novel. Some friends thought Allen did not really like Caroline's novel because she seemed to denigrate him in her characterization of Tom Claiborne.

Caroline ignored Cal's question and every other suggestion that Tom was a fictional representation of her husband. In a letter to Allen, however, she admitted that Tom was "a pale reflection" of him, but she insisted she had tried to portray Tom admirably. She pointed out how Tom was "nearly always right, even when he didn't know it, even when he [was] doing the wrong thing," and she said the rest of her characters paid tribute to Tom because "all of them not only liked him but recognized that he had remarkable qualities."

For his part, Allen called the book a masterpiece, equal to the writing of Virginia Woolf, and he tried to protect Caroline from adverse criticism throughout the spring. Although Caroline insisted she did not take the bad reviews seriously, Allen realized how much she was suffering. When a friend wrote her a letter criticizing the novel, Allen intercepted and destroyed it to save her further pain.

The combination of a rigorous teaching schedule, the poor reception of her novel, and the difficulties of living alone soon proved to be too much for Caroline. When she visited Allen in Minneapolis during her spring break, they quarreled. Later Caroline apologized, saying that she had been "unsympathetic and hard" because she had been drunk. She was "worried to death" about Allen, but she begged him to help her, to be patient. "I am going through a strange and terrible time," she wrote. "A certain enthusiasm, a kind of vigorous response to life which I held on to through all sorts of trials has left me. I can hardly face each day. I long only for the night."

At the beginning of May, Caroline and Allen got together again for a reunion of the Fugitives in Nashville. Although Caroline would later insist that they had a wonderful time, Allen disagreed. Caroline had brought some friends from Kansas City with her, perhaps to serve as a buffer, and Allen found their presence annoying and exhausting.

After Caroline and Allen had returned to Lawrence and Minneapolis respectively, new problems arose. Reacting to rumors she apparently heard about Allen's behavior, Caroline reviled him over the telephone. Allen did not have the strength or patience to reassure her; he was suffering from an ulcer and circulatory trouble in his legs. He insisted she was asking too much of him.

Caroline tried to be sympathetic and reasonable, but she once again felt stretched to her limit. "My life here is unnatural and repugnant to my deepest instincts," she wrote. "Here I am only the professor. I have no house-keeping, no garden—no means of escape into the feminine world."

Although Caroline wanted to save her marriage, she felt she could not keep living on hope. "These separations that we have had keep me suspended in a sort of half-life, forcing me to live alone and to live in a way that I would never choose," she told Allen. "I'd rather live with you than with anybody in the world but if we can't live together then I must set about arranging some way of life for myself."

At the end of May, Caroline finished her work at the University of Kansas. She felt as if she were "just crawling out from under a big rock" that had "all but crushed" her, but she looked forward to spending the summer in Princeton in the house they had rented from one of Nancy's friends, Anne Fremantle. When Caroline arrived in New Jersey, however, she discovered that she could not move in as planned. Anne had somehow forgotten that the Institute of Advanced Study had already rented the house through the summer.

Caroline nearly collapsed in anger and despair. She stayed at Dulce Domum and searched for another place to rent. Allen joined her in June, and before long, they discovered the ideal house at 145 Ewing Street. It was small, red farmhouse, "sort of a glorified two storey cabin," Caroline called it. Part of it built in 1780, the house was in one of the poorer sections of Princeton, on the corner of Ewing and Harrison streets. There was no front yard to speak of, but behind the house was nearly an acre of land, complete with a brook at the foot of the garden, and a small wooded area beyond that. When Caroline stood in the back yard, she felt like she was in "the depths of the country."

But the owners wanted to sell the house, not rent it. The Tates did not think they could find money for the down payment. While Allen went off to teach in a summer program at Harvard, Caroline remained in Princeton, trying not to get her hopes up. "I am not going to cry if we don't get it but I'll sing paeans of praise if we do," she said.

Once again Caroline was putting up a good front. She desperately wanted to settle down in a place of her own. Still exhausted from her stint in Lawrence, she had only a tenuous hold on her composure, and when she went away with Allen to spend a weekend at the New Jersey shore, she cracked. For no apparent reason Caroline screamed at Allen all night long; she tore the bed sheets to shreds.

They were visiting Franklin and Ida Watkins that weekend, a couple they had met in Rome. Allen had once had an affair with Ida, and Caroline may have been responding to jealous suspicions. But later Caroline insisted that she had lost her temper only because she was frustrated over missing mass. Allen realized Caroline was worried about the future; he hoped her outbursts would stop if they bought the house.

A short while later, some friends from Minnesota offered to lend the Tates the money they lacked. The Tates accepted. Although Caroline had to move into the house by herself since Allen was still teaching at Harvard, she did not mind. She caught up on her correspondence and spent long hours outside in the garden. Every evening she sat on the terrace, half enclosed in lilacs and syringas. As she watched the rabbits gambol in the backyard, she felt at peace for the first time in years. She felt she had come home.

Caroline decided to call the place the Sabine Close, a reference to a farm belonging to the poet Horace in the Sabine country. "This place is as near a farm as folks like us can get," Caroline wrote to Flannery O'Connor.

It's "our last house," the "house of my dreams," Caroline wrote over and over again in letters to family and friends. The house reminded her of Benfolly, in miniature, but it was infinitely more practical, she wrote, "utterly suited to our ages and conditions of servitude."

Her friends had heard it all before. "What of it?" Stark Young wrote. "You will buy another house in a year or so, differing from this house only in being more expensive. That kind of thing would run me crazy."

Caroline hoped he was wrong. At age sixty she couldn't think of moving again in a year. She vowed to hang on to the place as long as she lived.

Weeks went by at the Sabine Close without a word from Allen. Caroline seldom left home, preferring to dig in the garden or unpack boxes. In the parlor, over the mantel, she hung the Tate family portrait Stella Bowen had painted in Paris more than twenty-five years earlier: Allen, Caroline, and Nancy, "grimly facing our respective fates," she mused.

When Allen returned to Princeton in late August, he was tired and on edge. Caroline was deeply hurt over Allen's failure to write or call from Cambridge. They both wanted to try to work things out, but it had been over a year since they had lived together, more than five years since they had lived happily together. Reconciliation had become a cautious series of maneuvers, an endless rhythm of advances and retreats, actions and reactions. Caroline and Allen tried to talk their way to another understanding, each vowing to forgive, forget, trust one another, hope again.

After a great many talks Caroline thought they had found peace. Around that time she invited her cousin Kate Radford, who lived in Toms River, New Jersey, to come for an overnight visit. Allen promised to drive Kate home if she could arrange her own ride to Princeton.

Kate arrived around four o'clock one afternoon, about an hour after Allen had left to work in the Princeton University library. She and Caroline spent the rest of the afternoon talking. They expected Allen to return for dinner, but hours went by. Allen did not return. He did not call.

Caroline began to wonder what happened to him. She made up excuses to cover his absence. He might have lost track of the time. He might have run into someone from the English department, or an old student. Maybe he decided to talk over a drink or something to eat. He ought to appear any moment.

Still the time passed without any sign of Allen. Around seven o'clock Caroline decided to stop waiting and start dinner. When she went into the kitchen, she found a special delivery letter lying on the floor. It was from Allen.

Caroline read the letter in shock. "There is no good way to do what I am doing. I am going away for a few days to try to recover my equilibrium," he had written. "I simply haven't the courage to tell you to your face, particularly after our understanding talk before lunch."

Allen insisted that he could not "any longer live under the threat of . . . reproaches and disapproval." He suggested that their mutual love would not suffice any more, although he declared himself unwilling "to take total responsibility" for any separation. "Marriage is a sacrament, and I am bound to you for life," he wrote. "I want you to consider whether the supernatural level of the sacrament is not lowered by our conduct towards each other."

Caroline would never forget the horror of that evening. Kate spent the night as planned: she had no way to leave. Before the sun rose the next morning, the Sabine Close, the house of Caroline's dreams, had become a place of nightmares. Sometime that evening a trap Allen had set just a day earlier snapped, catching a mouse. Unwilling to touch the trap, Caroline and Kate spent the night listening to the mouse struggle, its back broken but its strength unfailing. It would have been a good idea to kill the poor creature, put it out of its misery, but neither woman was able to do so. Instead, they could only listen to the struggle and wait for the light.

When morning came, Caroline called Pleasant Phox, an old black handyman she knew. He came and killed the animal. Years later Caroline would remember that night and blame Allen for two cruelties. He had left her and left the mouse, and it was a fate neither one of them deserved.

Allen called Caroline a few days later, and the reconciliation dance began again, but this time promises of trust, hope, and forgiveness were not enough. Allen was afraid he could never live in the same house with Caroline again. He said her anger would always send him fleeing into the arms of some other woman. The best they could hope for was to live apart—she in Princeton, he in Minneapolis. Allen thought he was strong enough to face life alone.

Caroline was not so sure. She had been through so many episodes with him that she could even spot the linguistic clues. Whenever Allen asked her to "ponder" something, she knew he was in a bad way, and throughout the fall Allen pondered deeply. Caroline thought he was in the middle of another manic attack.

Throughout September Caroline and Allen exchanged letters and re-criminations. When Allen decided to take a Fulbright offer to lecture in India, Caroline worried that he would jeopardize his job in Minnesota. But Allen became furious whenever Caroline expressed concern for him. He was fine, he said; she was letting her imagination run wild.

Eventually Caroline began to tell friends that she and Allen had sepa-rated for good. Yet, deep down, she believed Allen was just having another of his "seizures." It was an especially severe one, to be sure, but with any luck and some time, the seizure would pass and they would be reunited. In the meantime Caroline worried about Allen's health. The Indian curries would do him no good, but perhaps, "since his ills [were] mostly psychic," he would survive the trip, she wrote to Malcolm Cowley.

Malcolm could not have been surprised at the Tates' separation, but he tried to reassure Caroline. "I refuse to believe that this time, or any other time, 'the separation must be permanent,'" Malcolm wrote. "Permanent is a long time, but not so long, in our lifetimes, as you and Allen have been together." He thought Allen needed to "settle down at Princeton for a whole year" without academic responsibilities. "You haven't had much of a life for the past, is it six? years," he said. "No wonder Allen has psychic ills."

Allen was not ready to settle down, however. He left for India during the first week of October. Caroline feared she would not have enough money to live on and pay the mortgage, but Allen reassured her that she would be fine even though he would be earning only two-thirds of his normal salary. He said he had arranged for his paycheck, about four hundred dollars a month, to be directly deposited in their joint account at the Princeton bank.

Taking him at his word, Caroline tried to put Allen out of her mind and settle down to work: she had promised Viking that she would de-liver the manuscript for *How to Read a Novel* by December. That was not much time, but Caroline felt certain that she could make her deadline. The book was practically written, she thought; she just had to "assemble the parts" and finish writing an introductory chapter.

Before long, however, Caroline had no time or mind for writing. She found herself facing two years of accumulated bills Allen had forgotten to tell her about. When she wrote some checks, they bounced, and Caroline discovered that Allen's paycheck for October had not been deposited in her account as promised. Caroline cabled Allen in New Delhi, and he responded with more assurances. The money was coming, he said; he would not touch it.

Caroline wrote new checks, and the checks continued to bounce. Finally, Caroline called the English department at the University of Minnesota. The secretary told her that Allen had instructed them to deposit his checks in a Minnesota account.

Allen later insisted that it was all a misunderstanding; he had forgotten about the old bills and had borrowed the money he had promised to Caroline because he hadn't realized he would not be paid for the Fulbright until his return to the States. But Caroline knew better. She was furious; she was also terribly frightened.

Allen promised to work things out, but Caroline was through trusting him. Afraid she might lose the house if something wasn't done quickly, she looked for work, anything to help balance the checkbook. Not sure what she needed or wanted, she took every job offered her—a couple of writing classes at Columbia, another at City College. She appealed to Sally Wood for help, and Sally loaned Caroline five hundred dollars until her first paycheck came. Other friends helped out with smaller sums.

Once the immediate financial crisis had been averted, Caroline tried to make sense of what had happened. She decided it was all part of the pattern of his seizures: when Allen was in one of his "states," he was "not capable of attending to business," she thought. His psychology that fall was "that of the absconding bank teller," she said later. Somehow, Caroline could always forgive Allen by labeling him as mentally disturbed.

Forgiveness did not mean Caroline was ready to go through another financial panic, however. When Allen returned in December, she finished putting her financial affairs in order. With the support of her son-in-law, Caroline marched Allen over to her lawyer's office and insisted he sign a "separate maintenance" agreement guaranteeing her three hundred dollars a month and insurance benefits.

Allen was badly shaken by the permanence of the agreement, and after he had time to think about it, he worried about how he would ever manage the monthly allowance. But Caroline felt nothing but relief. This was the "first financial security" she ever had, she said. The arrangement was just as much for Allen's protection as her own, she insisted: "It doesn't look good for me to have to telephone the head of the English department for money."

Allen spent four days with Caroline before Christmas. Caroline thought he looked terrible: weighing only 135 pounds, he could not eat or sleep, and he was "twitching with nerves." She persuaded him to go to see Dr. Wolf, and Wolf's diagnosis—an enlarged liver—scared Allen. He swore off liquor for life, but Caroline doubted that Allen could keep his pledge, especially living alone in Minnesota.

Still, when Allen left Princeton on Christmas day, Caroline was not without hope. "His mania has spent itself, for the time being—if long and sad experience qualifies me to judge," Caroline wrote a friend. "I just don't know what is going to become of Allen," she wrote. "This seizure has been the worst of all, in a way." But she knew what she wished would become of her: "I hope I can stay right here in this house for the rest of my life."

Caroline gave a talk on André Gide at the annual meeting of the Modern Language Association at the end of December, then threw herself wholeheartedly into her work. Having missed her original deadline for *How to Read a Novel,* she had not only to teach but to write. Before long her schedule overwhelmed her. Even though Sue Jenkins Brown offered to help type the manuscript, Malcolm Cowley agreed to edit it, and Caroline arranged to be let out of her teaching at Columbia for several weeks, she could not make her new March deadline. Fresh rumors and worries about Allen's behavior set her off. Sometimes she called him to yell about gossip she had heard; other times she chided him by letter. "I think that you have a great deal of intellectual pride," she wrote once. "You have not yet become the little child that one has to become in order to enter the kingdom of heaven."

Money problems also plagued both Caroline and Allen again, despite their legal agreement. At one point Caroline had to cook breakfast on the fireplace: the gas had been turned off because she had missed a payment. Yet through all the hardships and emotional outbursts, Caroline said she still believed they could work things out. As if to reinforce the ties between them, she reminded Allen of how much she had learned from him. She even insisted that he had taught her everything she knew about writing, and that this was as it should be. "Man is supposed to lead, woman to follow," she told him.

When Caroline finally completed a draft of *How to Read a Novel* in

April, Malcolm urged her to make major revisions. Caroline did not finish until the end of June. By then she was exhausted and almost completely disenchanted with the book. She realized Malcolm had helped her improve her prose immensely, but even so, she thought the manuscript was not "rounded out properly."

The book was iconoclastic, she reluctantly admitted: "relegating Maugham to a foot-note, dismissing Gide as an amateur, contradicting Eliot, etc." She did not, however, think she was entirely to blame. "Allen and I, between us, have botched a really important book," she told Malcolm. She had "written it under the most damnable conditions."

How to Read a Novel had twelve chapters, dealing primarily with the techniques of fiction, for example, "Complication and Resolution," "The Scene of a Novel," "The Center of Vision," and "The Effaced Narrator." Adopting a conversational tone, Caroline often quoted other critics and writers, creating a sort of patchwork-quilt effect. Her manuscript was not highly original or even systematic, but it was interesting, especially her first two and final chapters, called "How Not to Read a Novel," "The Novel as an Art Form," and "Reading for Enjoyment." In these Caroline defined and defended her beliefs about what a novel ought to be and in doing so chastised many of the reviewers who had misread her novels.

Caroline believed that the best parts of the book were her chapters on Henry James. "I think that I am the only person who knows what James accomplished as a novelist, who, at the same time, can write decent English," she declared. Even though her arguments were not "solidly buttressed," Caroline thought that with the proper publicity, her book might still be a success. She urged Viking to tell the public "what to think about it." If the book failed, she said, "the bright boys will take over my ideas and in a few years they will be in literary circulation, uncredited to me, of course."

For the rest of the summer in Princeton, Caroline wrote nothing but letters. She worked in her garden, commuted to New York to teach, entertained guests, and resumed painting. Allen visited the Sabine Close briefly, and Caroline thought they might yet reconcile, but unknown to her, Allen was seeing other women. In his mind there was no chance he and Caroline would ever live together again.

In the fall *How to Read a Novel* was published, without the publicity campaign Caroline desired. The reviews were damningly pleasant at best. At worst they were patronizing. William Bittner, writing for the *Saturday Review,* called the book "a series of lectures aimed at the kind of women's club whose members want to be 'challenged' without having their ignorance remotely violated."

Allen reassured Caroline that *How to Read a Novel* was a wonderful book. But then he probably realized Caroline was in no mood to hear criticism from him. They continued to fight with one another by mail and phone. Allen felt Caroline expected too much of him; he also thought she would not forgive him for past infidelities. Caroline felt the same way.

"You demand more of me than I can give at the moment you demand it," she told him. "What you are really asking is that I strip myself completely of self-love and go forward entirely in faith." The problem was, Caroline pointed out, that Allen kept changing his mind. "One day I am sharing a life with you. The next thing I know you are out of the picture and I have to learn the techniques of living alone. Then you intimate that you might like to come back into the picture. The nervous strain, alone, would have put some women in a sanitarium," she wrote.

Still, Caroline thought that the hardest trial she had to bear was Allen's accusation that she had not forgiven him for past offenses. "It may be possible that you have the matter in part reversed," she said. Perhaps "it is you who cannot yet forgive me—for offenses committed by another woman when you were too young and tender to defend yourself."

Searching for consolation and guidance, Caroline read numerous religious texts, especially the writings of St. John of the Cross and Jean-Pierre de Caussade. She tried to conquer her fears, telling herself that her trials were God's will, that she did not need to look to others for love and acceptance.

But no matter how hard she tried, Caroline often found her fears too strong to suppress. She turned sixty-two years old that fall, and her anxieties about old age were exacerbated by the threat of being left alone and financially destitute. Yet, Caroline wondered, was there any security left in her marriage? In December 1957 she and Allen spent the Christmas holiday together visiting Lon and Fannie Cheney in Tennessee. Caroline once again brought a friend with her, Kitty Morgan, perhaps as a buffer against unpleasantness. But the presence of friends did not work. Before she left Tennessee, Caroline had another angry outburst.

Allen was furious, but Fannie later insisted that Caroline's tantrum did not amount to much. On returning to Princeton, Caroline was immediately contrite. She apologized to the Cheneys, explaining that "the Devil" had been tempting her "to try to get a formal separation from Allen." "I get so weary of his antics sometimes that I feel I simply can't stand any more of them," she wrote. Then she reassured the Cheneys that their visit did Allen "worlds of good." She would try to "push the temptation in to the background and try to behave" herself "a little better from now on."

Later, however, Caroline gave Fannie and Lon a different picture of what had happened and why. She claimed that Allen provoked her: he was having another of his manic seizures, and her subsequent "attack of hysterics" was "a frantic plea for help, an admission that [she] was about to go under."

THROUGHOUT the winter and spring of 1958, Caroline struggled to exert control over her world. She vowed to stop judging other people harshly, especially Allen; she claimed that most of her anxieties and outbursts stemmed from a desire to be loved and an excess of self-love. "I see my own life . . . as largely a conflict with daimons," she wrote Allen, and she prayed fervently for supernatural aid.

Part of her prayer became a formal study of St. Teresa of Avila: Caroline wanted to become a Carmelite tertiary, a lay member of the order, devoted to charitable works. "I may not make it but I am going to try hard," she said. "I feel that a person with my faults—and my kinds of family—badly needs some spiritual discipline to practice every day in order to have it backing me up in times of trouble."

Yet for all of Caroline's attempts to develop independent strength and peace, she continued to pin her hopes for the future on Allen. She was ecstatic when Allen said he would consider taking a job at Columbia University so they could try to live together again at the Sabine Close. But the job never materialized. Caroline told herself it was just as well: Allen did not need to be involved in the academic politics that always accompanied such positions.

What he needed was time to work on his own writing, Caroline thought, and she began to count on Allen's spending his sabbatical year, the fall of 1958 and spring of 1959, in Princeton. She thought everything would be fine between them if Allen could just stop traveling so much and devote one year to poetry. Allen apparently agreed. In the spring the State Department offered him a Fulbright appointment to England for the 1958–59 academic year. Allen told Caroline he had turned it down.

But by the summer of 1958, Allen had no intention of spending his sabbatical year in Princeton. For several months he had been seeing the

poet Isabella Gardner. In July he and Isabella consummated their relationship, and Allen immediately began to promise marriage. Although
he said nothing to Caroline, Allen tried to figure out a way to spend the
year with Isabella. He apparently even considered a full-scale deception:
he would pretend to take the Fulbright but actually live in hiding with
Isabella. But lacking the money to finance such a scheme, Allen accepted
the Fulbright offer and made plans to leave for England.

Caroline had no idea of Allen's decisions, amours, and deceptions. But
almost instinctively she realized something was wrong, and several times
during the summer, she reacted with violence. Once she refused to see
some of Allen's friends because she apparently felt they knew all about
her problems with Allen and would take sides with him against her. Then
two young friends called Caroline from Massachusetts to tell her that
they had heard Allen was going to England. Caroline could not believe
it, but they insisted they had heard the news from another acquaintance,
Sally Sidgwick, who lived in Boston.

A bit drunk and very angry, Caroline immediately called Sally and
bawled her out for spreading vicious rumors. When Caroline sobered up
and realized what she had done, she called Sally back and apologized.
But the damage was done—to both Caroline and Allen. As Caroline
later wrote a friend, "Allen's familiar had at last accomplished what he
had planned and took complete charge from then on."

Caroline tried to talk Allen out of his trip. When that failed, she chastised him for his treatment of her and tried to justify her episode with
Sally Sidgwick. "I would not blow my top like that if I did not go always
in such fear of receiving a mortal wound," she wrote.

But Allen thought Caroline's behavior appalling, and he exploited her
outburst as much as he could. Acting the part of an injured but devoted
spouse, he declared it was his prerogative as Caroline's husband to determine their activities and friends. He even scolded Caroline for her pride,
while insisting she could rejoin him in Minnesota in the fall of 1959.

Caroline did not believe him. Tell me the truth, she implored. But
Allen was too deep in deception. At the same time he was promising Isabella they would ultimately live together as man and wife, Allen vowed
his unwavering love for Caroline.

At the end of September, Allen left for England. Caroline was sure
he was once again in the midst of a manic seizure, and she blamed his
condition on his high-paying job in Minnesota and on his Fulbright

fellowships. "Necessity and poverty kept him anchored to reality for a good many years but now that he can fly around the world at the tax-payers' expense he whirls like an autumn leaf," she wrote a friend. "But there is order in his madness. His mother moved four times a year. He follows faithfully in her foot-steps, slipping in a writers conference, even, no matter how tired he is so that the sacred numbers work out in the pattern."

Trying to keep busy while Allen was away, Caroline worked on a new edition of *The House of Fiction* for Scribner's and taught at various universities in New York City. But the stress of not knowing what Allen would do next proved to be too much for her. She started to think Allen had turned all their mutual friends against her, just as he had turned their daughter, Nancy, against her. She also began having memory lapses. Once she gave the wrong lecture to one of her classes and feared she would be fired for incompetence.

For a while Caroline did not bother writing Allen. But in early November she broke her silence. Urged on by friends, several priests, and a Catholic psychiatrist, Caroline wrote Allen that she would no longer stand for his irresponsible behavior. She had just passed her sixty-third birthday; Allen was about to turn fifty-nine. He could not continue to come and go as he pleased. As her psychiatrist had said, Allen was hurting himself when he treated his wife so poorly.

Allen responded by filing for divorce. But, as Caroline guessed, her letter did not really precipitate Allen's actions. Allen had been in contact with his lawyer since early October. He had also been telling friends about his plans to divorce Caroline. He hoped the divorce would go through quickly so that he could marry Isabella in January.

Caroline did not know what to do. She hired Robert Barnett, a lawyer from Minneapolis, to represent her, but at first she thought she would simply accept the divorce and Allen's offer of $350 a month alimony. She felt certain that if she told Allen she would not contest the divorce, he would change his mind and drop his suit. Even if he persisted, she thought his settlement offer would be better than anything the court might decide on. Since in seven years she would face mandatory retirement at age seventy, Caroline knew she had little hope of earning enough to support herself.

Yet the religious aspect of divorce bothered Caroline. Catholics did not believe in divorce: would she be guilty of sin if she allowed Allen his way? She consulted one priest after another, looking for answers, looking, perhaps, for someone to make the decision for her. Finally she decided she could not sit by passively, and she wrote Allen.

Each priest "has said unhesitatingly that it is my duty to actively oppose a divorce, so I feel that I have no choice," Caroline wrote. "I find myself inclined to make less and less emotional demands on you, as time goes. You are perfectly free to live apart from me if that is your wish. But do you feel that it is morally right to inflict considerable hardship on me in my old age?"

Allen did not respond.

In the middle of December, Caroline wrote again, this time to enclose copies of some of her revisions to their anthology, *The House of Fiction*. She wanted Allen's opinion on several decisions she had to make for the book. She also asked Allen to do her another favor: sign the Sabine Close over to her.

In the letter Caroline explained that a friend had offered to take over the eight-thousand-dollar mortgage on the house. This friend would give Caroline three thousand dollars as a gift, then allow Caroline to pay the remainder off in small sums. "It would be a great relief because I know she wouldn't foreclose if I defaulted on the payments," Caroline wrote Allen. "But there is, as always, a catch. She won't take the mortgage over as long as the place is owned jointly."

Caroline's unnamed friend, Grace Lambert from Princeton, hoped to keep Allen from ever taking the house away from her. Yet Caroline promised Allen that she would always "consider the place as belonging to us both just as jointly as if a paper hadn't been signed."

Once again, however, Allen refused to answer Caroline's letter. Yet he did talk and write freely to friends about his plans for a divorce, and his story changed with every letter. He told one friend he did not intend to marry anyone else because he could not afford it. He told another he did not even intend to go through with the divorce: he filed the suit to scare Caroline into treating him better.

But at the same time Allen promised Isabella that they would marry soon, that they were already married in spirit, in fact. If necessary, Allen thought, he could get a quick Mexican or Parisian divorce. He told Isabella he was even willing to face charges of bigamy: he did not think Caroline would want to humiliate herself and take him to court.

Caroline knew nothing of all this; throughout the early months of 1959, she did not even realize Allen was having an affair with Isabella. But she suspected Allen would get involved with some woman if his actions ran true to form. As she waited anxiously for him to send her the deed to the house, she began to suffer from a severe attack of inflammatory arthritis brought on by worry.

She found herself looking back over more than thirty years of her relationship with Allen, rehearsing all the sacrifices she had made. She had lived a vagabond life, cut herself off from friends to please or protect Allen, even willingly subordinated her career to his. Suddenly all the sacrifices seemed meaningless, and Caroline feared it was too late for her to strike out alone.

As the months passed, her worries increased. At one point she discovered that Allen had intercepted her monthly allowance. Overdrawn at the bank, she once again had to contact the English department in Minnesota to figure out what money she had coming to her. She became increasingly eager to accept Grace Lambert's offer for the mortgage, and finally, in early March, she cabled Allen for his decision.

She also appealed to both her own lawyer and Allen's. "A man who communicates with his wife only through his lawyer ought not to have a joint checking account with her," she argued. "And nobody ought to sign a contract for the joint revision of a book when he refuses to communicate with his collaborator."

Allen continued to refuse to communicate directly with Caroline, but he sent word back that he had already signed the house over to her: the deed had been waiting for her for several months in the Princeton office of their former lawyer, Douglas Smith. Caroline was furious. "This affair of the missing deed is clearly the work of the Devil!" she exclaimed. But her joy at owning the house outright calmed her mind. She asked her cousin Manny Meriwether to come to stay with her. "I really need you," Caroline wrote. "I've gone through a lot in the last year or two and I need the companionship and support of some member of my family."

Manny could not or would not come, however, and Caroline soon had more need than ever for her. In May Cal Lowell told Caroline about Isabella.

Her worst suspicions confirmed, Caroline went to talk with her priest, Father Horace McCoy. She still wanted to do what was right in the eyes of the Catholic church, but Caroline was no longer sure she wanted to oppose the divorce. Father McCoy agreed with her. When Caroline condoned Allen's adulterous behavior, she "helped to create evil," he said.

Caroline subsequently wrote both her lawyer and Allen that she would no longer contest the divorce, but agreeing to the divorce did not mean she had abandoned hope—or self-deception. Although she could no longer pretend Allen's infidelities did not exist, she did begin to delude herself with another idea: if she stopped resisting Allen, perhaps he would change his mind and drop the divorce proceedings, or else he would repeat his behavior of 1946 and return to her as soon as the divorce was final. Caroline still believed Allen loved her as much as she loved him. She had to believe this: it made all the years of sacrifice meaningful. "The quickest and best way" to bring Allen "to his senses—and therefore back to the Church—would be to give him what he asks for: a divorce," she told her lawyer.

Advised by her lawyer and friends to file a countersuit, Caroline began to look for evidence she could use against Allen. Although it would have been easy and effective to cite adultery as the grounds for divorce, she refused to have Isabella's name—or the names of any of the other women Allen had had affairs with—mentioned in her suit. Instead she filed for divorce on the same grounds Allen had cited: cruel and inhuman treatment.

Most of the friends whom she asked for help readily agreed to provide affidavits of Allen's behavior. But Malcolm Cowley demurred. He said he did not remember any incidents clearly, and he thought it would be difficult to compile enough evidence of Allen's cruelty. "He never meant to be cruel," Malcolm wrote. "All the cruelty was incidental to something else."

When Caroline read his letter, she felt sick. She wrote back as politely as possible. "You are quite right," she told Malcolm. "Allen never means to be cruel to anybody—he merely acts under compulsions that are evidently too strong for him to withstand." The charge was only "a legal fiction," adopted "in large part for his protection," she wrote, apologizing for her request. But inwardly seething, Caroline mentally crossed Malcolm off her list of friends. To Malcolm's surprise, she would never forgive him.

Caroline turned her anger and frustration on many friends and acquaintances that spring and summer. Feeling abandoned and helpless, insecure and suspicious, she tottered on the brink of an abyss. If friends disagreed with her in any way, she suspected they had taken Allen's side. Allen was a consummate liar, Caroline knew, and she believed he could deceive almost anyone. "His plausibility is his curse," she said. Her friends often reassured Caroline that they were not taken in, but little they could say would change her mind.

When friends urged Caroline to assert herself and fight Allen more forcefully, she also objected. She began signing her letters "Caroline Tate" or "Caroline Gordon Tate," a symbol perhaps of her willingness to be a submissive wife. She was also more anxious than ever to protect Allen's reputation. When she wrote her friends for evidence of Allen's cruelty, she asked them to send her letters back: she did not want to leave any public admissions of their problems.

But despite all of her fears and often-destructive behavior, Caroline did not surrender herself to the abyss. Instead she bought a white wig to give herself a new look, and she wore it frequently, delighted when she could scare her friends or surprise them. Many did not recognize her: one friend said the wig made Caroline look like one of "the mothers of chorus girls who stroll up and down Broadway."

Caroline also returned to her typewriter and found she could write again. She had not intended to do so; she thought she was too exhausted for any work. But one morning while she was lounging in bed, determined not to get up, she caught sight of her typewriter on the night table beside the bed. She remembered some scenes from her childhood: the world around Merry Mont, and how she tried to kill herself as a young child. Caroline decided to type up some of the memories. Before she knew it, she had written eight pages. Later she reread what she had written and found herself adding more. By the time she had twelve pages of manuscript, she knew she had begun another book. "The gaff, as my father would say, has been slipped home," she told friends.

She decided to call her work *The Narrow Heart*. Later she changed the title to *A Narrow Heart: The Portrait of a Woman*. The book would be part novel, part autobiography. It would operate on several levels: from one perspective it would be the story of "a woman's life from childhood to old age"; from another it would be a story of both a woman's and a family's lifelong "struggle with the daimonic."

Caroline felt enthusiastic and confident as she developed her plan for the novel. She thought she could include a wide array of characters—Meriwether kin from generations gone—to dramatize the family's struggles, shifting her focus frequently for effect. The idea pleased her so much that Caroline decided to apply for another Guggenheim Fellowship. Although she soon found out she had missed the deadline for a fellowship, Caroline did not let anything deter her from writing. As always, she found strength in the routine of writing, strength she badly needed.

Throughout the summer Caroline fought panic as her lawyer attempted to negotiate an acceptable divorce settlement. At one point Allen tried to tie Caroline's alimony to the mortgage payments for her house in Princeton. Caroline refused to accept such an arrangement. Then she discovered Allen had allowed most of his insurance policies to lapse, and she feared she would become a pauper if Allen died before her. "The insurance carried in his name represents the only money I was ever able to save and until recently he always referred to it as joint savings," Caroline wrote her lawyer. "I have so considered it in any plans for the future."

Little could be done to ensure that Allen would maintain any future life-insurance policies to benefit Caroline, but the lawyers and the Tates finally agreed on a settlement. Allen promised to pay Caroline permanent alimony: $375 a month for twelve years, then $300 a month for the rest of her life. In the middle of August, Caroline flew to Minneapolis. On August 18 Caroline and Allen went to court and finalized their divorce.

Caroline was devastated. But three days after the divorce, she wrote Allen another letter. She told him she still loved him. In the eyes of the Catholic church, they would always be married. Caroline apparently still hoped Allen would come back to her; she could not believe otherwise. She had built her life around Allen, denied her own dreams, needs, and talents in efforts to please him. Once before Allen had divorced her, only to land back on her doorstep within a few months. Perhaps this time he would do the same.

Allen did not respond to Caroline's letter immediately. On August 27 he married Isabella Gardner. Then early in September he answered Caroline's letter. "I pray to God for forgiveness of the wrong I have done, but it is not so great a wrong as what I *was* doing, and not so great as the wrongness of my interior self in the past year and a half," he said. "For the rest, I am not telling you goodbye. If your feeling for me had been what your phrase, in your last letter, conveys—'My dearly loved Allen'— I should be with you now. We shall always be together in a sense that nobody but you and me can understand. And I shall so try to live as to deserve seeing you in the next life."

Caroline could not have received a more bitter pill to swallow. In utter despair, she raged—against Allen, against her friends, against herself.

 1959–1981

For a while Caroline wallowed in her pain. She cut herself off from many of her friends, suspecting them of siding with Allen, of falling for his lies and encouraging his delusions. No one could convince her otherwise. "I have a deep, instinctive revulsion against people who lend themselves to Allen's machinations," she exclaimed. "I feel as if there is almost nothing he can't manoeuvre them into doing."

Even when Caroline did not abandon her friends, she held them at a distance. She often invited Eileen Simpson over for dinner, yet she would not allow Eileen to comfort her. Caroline wanted an audience; she did not want consolation.

Throughout their dinners together, Caroline would rehearse her agonies. Eileen listened willingly. Having suffered greatly after her own divorce from the poet John Berryman, Eileen tried to let Caroline know that she understood her anguish. But Caroline could not believe Eileen or anyone else could fathom what she was feeling.

Their situations were not the same, Caroline would say. John did not leave Eileen for another woman—she left him.

"Only because he drove me to it," Eileen would point out, but Caroline ignored her. She thought Eileen had "the satisfaction of knowing that John . . . suffered greatly; whereas, from all reports, Allen was shamelessly happy."

There was nothing Eileen could say. "Any word of comfort I offered Caroline was certain to be the wrong word," she said later. Caroline was inconsolable.

Yet Caroline did not surrender herself to bitterness; she did not even withdraw completely from life. Slowly, deliberately, she rebuilt her world. She finished revising *The House of Fiction* and tried to persuade Scribner's to reissue some of her novels. She took in a series of lodgers and changed the name of her home: it would no longer be called the Sabine Close but the Red House, a tribute to Grace Lambert, who called her home the Pink House. And although Caroline had once sworn that her artistic life was over, she returned to writing.

By the spring of 1960, Caroline had completed the prologue to *A Narrow Heart* and most of the first chapter. She published the prologue, under the novel's title, in the *Transatlantic Review*. "My life, my secret, conscious life, which is the only life worth telling about, began on a summer day," Caroline wrote. Actually it was a day in late summer or perhaps early fall, the fourth birthday of Carrie Gordon. The actual time did not matter; Caroline moved freely between past and present in the story, one of her best.

Caroline wrote about her childhood world of Merry Mont and her adult life in Paris and Rome. She sketched vivid pictures of her grandfather, Aunt Pidie, her brother Morris, and Old Miss Carrie. But most of all, Caroline re-created her childhood self: a young storyteller with a penchant for fairy tales, a "thin, undersized child with a slightly crooked nose" and too-black eyes, an intense, gifted child, who sensed the presence of shadowy companions and, in a fit of panic, tried to drown herself in a basin of water.

Caroline prefaced her story with an open letter to Ford Madox Ford in which she wrote of Ford's "pursuit of good letters," his "search for *le mot juste*," and his incredible generosity to younger writers. In private letters to friends, Caroline admitted that she did not know "whether you *could* address a letter to a dead man," but she wanted to pay homage to Ford. *A Narrow Heart* was "the kind of novel" he prophesied she "would one day write," she said.

Yet Caroline found it increasingly difficult to write her autobiographical novel while continuing to teach at Columbia and the New School and to speak at seminars and writing conferences. In the fall of 1960, hoping to get a year off from teaching, Caroline applied for a Guggenheim Fellowship. She thought her chances were good; she even made tentative reservations to spend her fellowship in Greece.

Her application, however, was rejected. Caroline figured the judges feared she would write a scathing memoir, attacking former friends, and she may have been right. Although she intended to write no such book,

Caroline was known for her quick temper and biting sarcasm. She had lost more than a few friends with her blunt, often rude behavior, and she continued to make influential enemies.

One such time occurred in late October 1960, when Caroline participated in a panel discussion on recent southern fiction at Wesleyan College in Macon, Georgia. Katherine Anne Porter, Flannery O'Connor, and Madison Jones were also on the panel, which was moderated by Louis D. Rubin, Jr., a scholar of southern literature from Hollins College in Virginia. Caroline got along well with Jones and O'Connor. She even had a pleasant visit with Katherine Anne. Although both women still nursed grudges in private over their falling out in Washington in 1944, they had declared a public truce which would not be broken. But without realizing it, Caroline alienated Rubin. As he became increasingly powerful in southern literary studies in the years to come, Caroline felt she suffered from his enmity.

The animosity began to develop at a small party on the night before the seminar. Rubin sat listening with the other guests along the periphery of the living room while Katherine Anne and Caroline sat together on a settee in the center of the room and discussed other writers. Although seventy years old, Katherine Anne still played the part of grande dame, her white hair coifed to perfection, her manners elegant, her comments always gracious. At age sixty-five, Caroline affected no such airs. She looked like a sweet-tempered grandmother—with white hair curled tightly around a face lined with wrinkles—but her jet black eyes still sparkled brightly, and her sarcastic wit had not mellowed at all. When Katherine Anne mentioned a writer whom Caroline disliked, Caroline said so. After a while Rubin decided she could not say anything nice about anyone. He found her manner abrasive and derogatory.

The next day Rubin challenged some of Caroline's remarks. When she criticized Erskine Caldwell's fiction, he praised it. When she talked about naturalism in southern fiction, he argued another perspective. When Caroline insisted she was not writing another historical novel, Rubin refused to believe her. They quibbled over definitions; they exchanged patronizing comments. And Caroline felt that from that day on Louis Rubin did not like her, but she did not know why. She only knew she did not trust him as a critic of southern writing.

It apparently never occurred to Caroline that she might hurt her reputation by alienating scholars like Rubin. Even if it had, she was not likely to dissemble her feelings. Age had not mellowed Caroline: if anything it made her all the more fierce. Although she had once dreaded becoming just like her grandmother, Caroline certainly resembled Old Miss Carrie in spirit if not appearance. Behind the white hair and soft-spoken, sometimes cloyingly feminine demeanor lurked a sharp tongue given to quick, harsh judgments.

As the years passed, Caroline became increasingly controversial in an arch-conservative way. She deplored the use of the vernacular in the Catholic church, and she declared women ought not be allowed to vote. She also disapproved of the zip code: "this computerization of human beings" would be "a step towards the gas chambers of the future," she said. She even raged against structural grammar. "It is my sober and long considered conclusion that this movement is a new sort of Communist front, one that goes deeper underground in a way than any of them has ever gone," she said. "Destroying a people's language is a pretty effective way of brain-washing them."

Caroline apparently uttered some of her eccentric pronouncements just for fun. She got a perverse pleasure out of shocking people, of seeing their reactions to absurd or extreme statements. But she was serious in her devotion to the Latin mass and her objection to structural grammar. Teaching so many creative-writing workshops had reinforced Caroline's appreciation of her own classical education. Aspiring writers needed a knowledge of mythology as well as "the *habit* of writing sentences which are, at once, forceful and grammatical," Caroline believed. What better preparation could there be than study of Greek and Latin?

Caroline immersed herself in the world of myth during the winter and spring of 1960–61. She taught a class in Greek and Norse mythology at the New School and began to write an essay called "No Snake Has All the Lines; or, The Apotheosis of Heracles." She felt she had discovered "things about Heracles that nobody else seems to have noticed." According to Caroline, the story of Heracles was "one of the best stories that the imagination of man has ever conceived." Heracles was the greatest of the Greek heroes, the only one to triumph over the powers of darkness and get to heaven, a prefiguration of Christ.

Caroline found it difficult to write the essay. She kept remembering Allen's disparaging comments about her intellectual abilities. But passion for her subject consumed her. She not only wrote the essay—a celebration of the powers of myth and a creative retelling of Heracles' story—but she decided to include Heracles in her novel *A Narrow Heart*. Heracles' life would serve as an archetype of her protagonist's struggle against the daimonic.

Caroline had grown up reciting the labors of Heracles, yet she would not write her account of his exploits without careful research. Neither would she begin composing other historical sections of *A Narrow Heart* —sections on Calvin, Lord Byron, Sir Walter Scott, and others—without extensive study. She revised her first story, "Summer Dust," into a more traditional narrative, "The Dragon's Teeth," for the second chapter of the novel but wrote little else on it during the spring and summer of 1961. Instead she kept busy "discovering some of the joys of scholarship late in life," she said, reveling in odd facts and minutiae she picked up.

Although she had gone through similar library binges years earlier while writing *Green Centuries* and *None Shall Look Back,* Caroline's scholarly ardor soon became obsessive. Throughout the fall and winter of 1961, she compiled enough material for two books. Soon she began to despair of ever finishing her work. Perhaps she involved herself in research so that she would not have to write. Or perhaps she was trying to prove that she did have the intellectual abilities that Allen had so often claimed she did not have.

During the spring and summer of 1962, Caroline began to consider switching publishers. But before she could make any decision, she began to hear disturbing rumors about her former publisher, Scribner's. According to some friends, Scribner's was refusing offers to reissue some of her stories and novels in paperback edition, without even consulting her.

Eager to see her old work back in print, Caroline wrote Charles Scribner, Jr., in July, asking if her copyrights could revert to her, since they apparently had no intention of ever republishing her work. Scribner quickly responded with an offer to publish a new collection of her short stories in the fall of 1963. He made no mention of her copyrights, and Caroline was so glad to have a new story collection in print that she did not pursue the issue. As she told a friend, she was rather relieved not to have the responsibility of her copyrights. "I'd let them lapse out of sheer forgetfulness," she said.

In the fall of 1962, Caroline celebrated her sixty-seventh birthday in Davis, California. She had agreed to spend a year teaching writing and American literature at the University of California at Davis. It did not take her long to fall madly in love with California. She took up bird watching and marveled at the fabulous cork-trunk oak trees. When she walked across campus, she crushed unshelled almonds beneath her feet. Everything about the place pleased her. "I never saw anything in Europe as grand as these valleys," she exclaimed. "I never saw mountains before that look as if they were composed of velvet."

Being in California reminded Caroline of her distant cousin Meriwether Lewis, his journey to the Pacific Ocean with William Clark, and his mysterious death. At first Caroline decided that Lewis had been "going back to Virginia to persuade all the kinfolks to move on out instead of sticking in that red clay when he succumbed to despair and committed suicide." Later, adopting the Meriwether point of view, she concluded that Lewis had not committed suicide; he had been murdered. Caroline thought she even knew who killed him, and she decided to include his story in *A Narrow Heart*.

Caroline completed several chapters on her novel while in California, but not as much as she had hoped. Instead she devoted a great deal of time to writing about Ford Madox Ford, giving a lecture on his novels, then revising her work into a formal essay. In it she argued that Ford's fiction was "inspired by one vision": "that goddess who is larger than life and even more terrible than she is beautiful," a lamia, "White Goddess," or "belle dame sans merci."

When she finished the essay, she sent it to Allen for his comments. Her bitterness toward him had abated; she even wanted to get an annulment of their marriage so Allen would no longer be living "in sin." Allen would not agree to an annulment because he said he could never deny his marriage to Caroline. But he was genuinely glad to help her with her writing. After cutting several anecdotal sections of her essay, he sent it to Graham Greene, who was involved in republishing some of Ford's novels. Allen thought Greene might like to use it as a preface for one of Ford's novels, but by the spring of 1963, the Library of the University of California, Davis, had offered to publish Caroline's essay as a separate chapbook, *A Good Soldier: A Key to the Novels of Ford Madox Ford*.

Caroline left California in early summer, but she did not spend much time in Princeton. In the fall of 1963, she went to West Lafayette, Indiana, to teach at Purdue University. She hated to be away from home for another year, but she could not turn down any positions that paid well. She used the money she made at Davis to build a new wing for the Red House; she expected her earnings from Purdue to finance the completion of her novel.

Even though she longed to be gardening in Princeton, Caroline generally enjoyed her stay in Indiana. New sights and people always captured her imagination, and just as in California, she liked everything she looked on: the small farms outside the city, the tiny, late Victorian houses full of scrollwork and turrets, the woodlots ablaze with fall foliage, even the pigs, which seemed more numerous than the human inhabitants. "I adore Indiana," she exclaimed repeatedly.

In addition to teaching at Purdue, Caroline gave four lectures at St. Mary's College at Notre Dame University in South Bend. In the lectures she not only asserted the importance of myth and explored the influence of the classics on modern literature, she told story after story about the heroes and heroines of Greek myth. And in her favorite lecture, "The Shape of the River," she explained the source of her own strength, hope, and faith.

Caroline took her title from the words of one of Mark Twain's characters, the pilot called Mr. Bixby in *Life on the Mississippi*. When a young man asked him for advice on becoming a riverboat pilot, Bixby said: "My Boy, you've got to know the *shape* of the river perfectly. It is all there is left to steer by on a very dark night. Everything else is blotted out and gone."

For Caroline, Bixby's words had far-reaching implications. She connected his advice to other river imagery that Dante had used in *The Divine Comedy,* as well as to a letter Ford Madox Ford had written to Joseph Conrad, comparing a writer's struggle for recognition to a life spent on a boat "on an immense river, in impenetrable fog. . . . And you row and never, never will you see a mark on the invisible banks that will tell you if you are going upstream or if the current bears you along."

According to Caroline, "The young man or woman who aspires to write fiction professionally has a hard and dangerous voyage before him." Yet, "the knowledge of the *shape* of the river, by day or night, in fog, in mist, going up the river or coming down, will stand him in better stead on this voyage than any other knowledge he can acquire," she declared, and she spoke with authority. Caroline's personal knowledge of the shape of the river had enabled her to recover from the devastation of divorce. In the years to come it would sustain her through other griefs and disappointments.

Caroline enjoyed her work at Purdue and St. Mary's, yet by the spring of 1964, she was eager to quit teaching altogether. She felt that creative-writing programs were "not only useless but vicious, almost criminal in their waste and misdirection of youthful 'creative' energies." A better system would be to require anyone who wanted to enroll in a creative-writing course to first complete a more traditional course of study, she argued: an intensive course in grammar and syntax, as well as courses in elementary logic, mythology, and Greek drama.

After Caroline completed her stay in Indiana, she flew down to Georgia to visit Flannery O'Connor as well as one of her extracurricular students, who was a Trappist monk. Flannery had been hospitalized for most of the spring: a minor operation had reactivated her lupus. When Caroline saw her friend in the hospital in Atlanta, she realized Flannery did not have long to live. Flannery looked quite weak, but as soon as the nurse left the room, she grinned at Caroline and pulled a notebook out from under her pillow. Caroline would never forget her friend's wry comment.

"The doctor says I mustn't do any work," Flannery said. "But he says it's all right for me to write a little fiction."

Caroline was allowed to stay only twenty minutes. Flannery talked a bit more about her writing: she had seven stories finished for a new collection, but she wanted eight, and she was working on one, she said, "whenever they aren't doing something to me." Caroline talked about her newest idea for a book about creative writing and education. It would be called *Creative Writing or Craft Ebbing?* Flannery was amused and a bit awed by Caroline's enthusiasm and seemingly boundless energy.

Caroline returned to New Jersey, and sometime in July Flannery sent her a copy of her newest story, "Parker's Back." It was an odd tale about a man fond of tattoos who tried to appease his fundamentalist wife by getting a tattoo of Christ on his back. Feeling that the story still needed work, Caroline wrote Flannery a letter from "Old Dr. Gordon." The story was one of her best, Old Dr. Gordon thought, but it had "a tendency to rely on statement rather than rendition, also lack of preparation for interior monologue."

Flannery would not respond to these criticisms; she could not. Caroline later admitted that she "did not realize, or perhaps . . . was unwilling to admit" that Flannery was "so near death." Nevertheless, soon after she mailed the letter, Caroline regretted her comments and sent Flannery a telegram. "Congratulations on having succeeded where the great Flaubert failed!" Caroline wrote.

Not long after this, on August 3, 1964, Flannery O'Connor died. Caroline was not able to attend her funeral, but she had a mass said for her at a nearby Carmelite monastery. She spent the rest of the summer and fall of 1964 trying without success to write an appropriate tribute to Flannery.

She also worked on *A Narrow Heart, Craft Ebbing?*, a new article about Ford Madox Ford, and an appraisal of Katherine Anne Porter's work, actually a review of a book by William L. Nance, *Katherine Anne Porter and the Art of Rejection.*

Published in *Harper's* magazine, Caroline's essay, "Katherine Anne Porter and the ICM," revealed just as much of Caroline's ideas about the proper perspective on her own art as it did her ideas on Katherine Anne. She chastised Nance for what she called an "erroneous belief that the Old South was predominantly matriarchal." She also insisted that Nance had made a grave mistake by relying on Freudian critical "apparatus," a "Procrustean couch" or "International Critical Machine."

Both Caroline and Katherine Anne had been strongly influenced by the presence and absence of their female ancestors. Many of Katherine Anne's stories revolved around the relationship between her fictional alter ego, Miranda, and Miranda's grandmother. But Caroline asserted that a more important relationship was that of Miranda and her father. It was the same assertion she was trying to make in her autobiographical stories for *A Narrow Heart:* even though she had come to recognize how important her grandmother and mother had been in shaping her character, Caroline preferred to define her life in relationship to her father and other male relatives.

A writer deserved to have his or her intentions considered in any analysis, Caroline believed, and she argued that Nance had misunderstood Katherine Anne's intentions. Miranda was not an adventurer but a pilgrim, Caroline insisted, in terms she would have liked applied to her own life. "A pilgrim, by the nature of his calling, sees more of the world than he would have seen if he had stayed at home," she wrote. "But if he settles down in any one place he ceases to be a pilgrim."

Caroline settled down at the Red House, but she made little progress on *A Narrow Heart*. The only chapter she finished was a lyrical mixture of autobiography and mythology entitled "Cock-Crow," which she published during the summer of 1965 in the *Southern Review*. In "Cock-Crow" Caroline combined her impressions of her childhood at Merry Mont with her love for Greek mythology to explain her plan for the novel: she would retell the stories of heroes and heroines she had known in life or myth, stories of how these people fought their mortal enemy while standing on the edge of an abyss. "Women, of course, are always on the look-out for heroes," she wrote. "Every one of us has his ghostly company, of course. And they are all heroes."

Caroline tried to work on other chapters, about John Calvin and Lord Byron, but she was not able to complete anything, and she blamed most of her writing problems on the young professors who kept asking her about the other writers she had known, or former students who kept writing her, asking her to read one more manuscript. "These days an aging novelist has a hell of a time getting any writing done," she complained.

Caroline, however, was her own worst enemy. She would seldom refuse a request for help, and she apparently could not curb her enthusiasm for research: in just four years she had accumulated about twenty-five pounds of notes. Also, increasingly worried about her financial security, she spent time she could have been writing looking for ways to earn extra money. She signed up with University Speakers Bureau and began lecturing at various colleges on the East Coast and in the Midwest. She even volunteered to teach writing at Emory University from January through March 1966. Every interruption made her increasingly crotchety, and her antipathy for creative-writing classes grew, but she did not feel that she could afford to turn down any job.

Caroline's financial situation was uncertain at best. Although she had four books in print for the first time in many years, she had little or no savings against her old age or illness, and the cost of living in Princeton increased every year. With only her Social Security allowance, a small pension from her year of teaching in California, and a modest amount of money for renting out part of the Red House, Caroline feared she would not have enough money to live on when she could no longer work.

Allen was required to pay alimony for life, but Caroline did not trust him. By the spring of 1966, he had divorced Isabella Gardner and had become involved with a young woman named Helen Heinz, a former student and a former nun. In July 1966 he married her. Before long he was asking Caroline if he could temporarily stop his monthly payments to her.

Although Caroline did not realize it, Allen had been getting the money to pay her from his wealthy brother, Ben. Not long before Allen divorced Isabella, Ben had become mentally incompetent, and the secret payments ceased. Allen was in a great panic: he did not know how he would ever be able to afford the alimony on his own. But all he told

Caroline was that he was building a house in Sewanee, Tennessee, and was temporarily short of cash.

Later Allen blamed his financial hardships on his wife's unexpected pregnancy. Helen had twins, several months premature, in the summer of 1967. Caroline was not at all surprised. "Of course, sixty year old men who marry young women nearly always have a baby if they can," she noted, and despite her previous fears about money, she allowed Allen to stop paying her alimony for a time. She felt very sorry for him; she thought his marriage to Helen was the result of another manic "episode."

Caroline did not, however, suffer for her generosity at that time. In the fall of 1966, she had received a ten-thousand-dollar grant from the National Endowment for the Arts, and in the spring of 1967 she had signed up with a new publisher, Doubleday and Company, and received half of a six-thousand-dollar advance for her next novel.

Caroline's new editor at Doubleday, Stewart Richardson, expected that novel to be autobiographical, but by the summer of 1967 Caroline had realized that she was in fact writing two novels: one, the "upper half" of her story, would be somewhat autobiographical; the other, a "lower half," would be the dramatic retelling of the story of Heracles as a prefiguration of Christ. Without telling Richardson Caroline decided to finish the "lower half" novel first. She called the book *The Glory of Hera,* since Heracles ultimately owed his fame and his ascension into the heavens to Hera's machinations.

Caroline had been doing research on Heracles for a number of years, but she thought that she could not finish the book without making a trip to Greece. She decided to go in the fall of 1967 with her friend and housemate, Cary Peebles. Cary was an editor at Rutgers University Press; Caroline claimed her as a sixth cousin several times removed.

They left for Greece in the first week of September with Caroline's favorite grandchild and namesake, Caroline Wood. The fifteen-year-old spent most of September with her grandmother, visiting Athens and Delphi, before leaving to spend the year at a private school in Switzerland. Caroline and Cary stayed on in Greece for about two more months.

They spent most of their time in a small hotel in Vivari, a fishing village just outside of Nauplion. Every morning Caroline worked on *The Glory of Hera.* Every afternoon she and Cary went sightseeing. Celebrating her seventy-second birthday in October, Caroline thought Greece was magnificent, everything she expected it to be. The colors fascinated her: the sea ranged in color from indigo to cerulean blue, the soil was either red or black or purple, and the mountains, which reminded Caroline of Utah, looked pink or purple, like "great pre-historic beasts that have just lain down for a nap."

Cary bought a Volkswagen, which gave them the freedom to explore the countryside. They not only drove north to Thessalonica, where one of Cary's authors lived, but they visited almost every area around Vivari, trying to find locations that Caroline wanted to use in her novel. They saw Tiryns, where the infant Heracles strangled the snakes in his cradle, and Mycenae, a city thought to have been fortified by the Cyclops. They surveyed the marsh areas around the Lerna River where, according to legend, Heracles killed the hydra, and they had a picnic lunch in Nemea, where he killed the lion.

Halfway between Nauplion and Vivari, Caroline discovered the spring Kanathis, thought to be the place where Hera had bathed each year to renew her virginity. But she had a more difficult time finding the stone which the Delphic sibyl had sat upon in preparation for her prophetic frenzies and the spring Cadmus had camped near before asking the sibyl's advice. Persistence, and an active imagination, eventually paid off: Caroline decided that it was a good thing to be "so highly gifted in credulity."

After about two and a half months in Greece, Cary and Caroline went back to Italy to spend a week in Rome and some time visiting friends in Siena, Florence, and other cities nearby. In January they flew back to America. Caroline was glad to get settled back in her Red House, but for months afterward she longed to return to Greece.

She could only do so in her fiction, however, and that she did most diligently. Throughout the spring and summer of 1968 she worked furiously, trying, she said, "to finish that novel before the Grim Reaper—or some form of imbecility"—overtook her.

Yet Caroline was still her own worst enemy, finding many dodges that kept her progress minimal. One such diversion was an article called "Twiggy, or the Well-Connected Shoots," which she wrote with Cary Peebles. In the uneven and confusing article she examined the recent popularity of the British model Twiggy and her promoter, Justin de Villeneuve, in the context of Celtic and Greek mythology.

When she was not trying to show off her newfound scholarly erudition, Caroline sometimes drank too much. At one point she even fell down in a drunken haze and broke three ribs. Caroline insisted, however, that she was not an alcoholic, only an occasional drunk. The difference between the drunk and the alcoholic was "partly a matter of rhythm," she told a friend. "The alcoholic just goes nuts when he gets around the stuff. The drunk it seems to me, keeps a rhythm of his own."

For Caroline the rhythm included a bit of game playing. When her doctor told her that she should have no more than two ounces a day of alcohol, Caroline was glad to oblige, in a fashion. Although she would not stop drinking at cocktail parties, she did limit herself. "Just two ounces please," she said coyly each time the host came around to refill her glass.

Yet even without the diversions Caroline often had difficulty working, because she increasingly had to fight against arthritis. At times the pain was so great she could not even type. "Arthritis is a wild beast which makes first one, then another lair in the body," she said. Throughout the fall and winter of 1968, the beast was practically a leopard, raging always in her brow. She bought an electric typewriter, but sometimes she could not use it. She wondered if she would ever finish the novel. "If only I hadn't bitten off such a sizable chunk of the universe," she exclaimed.

Caroline wanted to finish *The Glory of Hera* before the spring of 1969, but by that April she realized that she still had about forty thousand more words to write. She sent the first chapter, "Cloud Nine," around to several magazines, "somewhat diffidently," she said, because she was just not sure if it was "suitable for publication by itself." "I am too close to the stuff to be able to judge," she wrote.

"Cloud Nine" appeared in the fall 1969 issue of the *Sewanee Review*. It was a long, discursive account of how Zeus, the father of gods and men, spent one afternoon. Although concerned about the "woeful condition of mortals," Zeus could not keep his mind on a solution to their problem. Rather, he reminisced about the many women, mortal and goddess, whom he had courted, and he rehearsed the histories of his various progeny and relatives.

With its rambling style, "Cloud Nine" confused many readers and bored others, but Caroline had only cast her usual underground stream of meaning into new garb. Little happened in the course of the narrative except that Zeus had an unsatisfactory talk with Apollo, and Hera called all the Olympians to a midafternoon conference in which she interrogated the mortal seer Teiresias. Yet Caroline tied the apparent digressions together by referring to the powers, threats, and pleasures of women. Although Zeus was all-powerful and far-seeing, Hera and the other female deities obviously had far-reaching influence over the ways of both gods and mortals, and "Cloud Nine" closed with a hint that Hera's power, and feminine wiles, would be more than sufficient to achieve whatever she desired.

In the fall of 1969 Caroline worked on *The Glory of Hera* in three shifts a day. She woke up each morning around three or four o'clock—not by choice but because a chronic heart condition roused her then "as if an alarm clock had been rung," she said. After working for several hours, she would eat breakfast, then go back to sleep. At nine o'clock in the morning she would rise again, work for three more hours, then eat lunch. After another nap she would work for two more hours in the afternoon. "It is a damn dull life and I am sick of it but I know that I have to have one uninterrupted push if I am going to get through this book," she wrote her brother.

In the intervals of writing, eating, and napping, Caroline amused herself with the exploits of her daughter and grandchildren. Nancy had become involved in politics, and she tried to teach her mother what she learned about "politicalese." Caroline shuddered whenever Nancy used the "barbarous jargon," turning "elite" into a verb or padding her speech with words like "pragmatical" and "function," but she admired her daughter's passion and enjoyed her stories immensely.

Caroline also enjoyed watching her grandchildren grow up. Although she was fondest of Caroline Wood, during the winter of 1969 she was most fascinated by her second grandson, twenty-two-year-old Allen Tate Wood. She even dedicated part of her novel to him. Called "A Walk with the Accuser (Who Is the God of This World)," it was an account of John Calvin's misguided religious zeal, and Caroline may have meant her grandson to read the story as a loving warning: young Allen had dropped out of college and joined the Unification Church, run by the Reverend Moon.

His actions infuriated and frustrated his parents, but Caroline was able to have long theological talks with him, and she sensed that he would not get lost in the life of the cult. He was just like most young people, "a real lost generation," searching for something to believe in, Caroline thought.

Caroline had sympathy for her grandson, even when his behavior cut him off from the rest of the family, but she had no sympathy for his namesake when he began to act up again. Although the elder Allen had resumed his monthly alimony payments, at a reduced rate, not long after Caroline's return from Greece, he still feared for his own financial security and that of his new family. By the spring of 1970, he had apparently decided to solve his financial ills by getting Caroline to give him some interest in the Red House.

With the growth of Princeton, the house had appreciated in worth, and Allen must have realized that Caroline would make a nice profit if she ever had to sell it. He repeatedly tried to convince her to put his name back on the deed, or to rewrite her will to leave him some part of the house, or the use of it if she died before him. And he tried to press his point by reminding her that she had gotten him to sign the house over to her by promising him that she would always consider the house as jointly owned by them.

Caroline did not fall for his schemes. She remembered telling him that she would think of the house as belonging to both of them, but claimed she had made no promises. They had still been married when Allen signed the house over to her; since then, he had treated her terribly, abandoned her, divorced her, and even reneged on his alimony obligations. She did not think that he deserved any part of the Red House. Allen kept trying to get her to change her mind, but Caroline remained firm.

Despite Allen's machinations and smaller family crises, Caroline finally finished *The Glory of Hera* during the summer of 1970. She was embarrassed to discover that she had written almost a thousand typed pages; the revised manuscript that she delivered to Doubleday in September was nine hundred pages long.

Embarrassment quickly gave way to fear and depression. "What one had thought of as a load on the chest turns out to be the raft which held one up," Caroline remarked wryly. Although she tried to justify the length of the book, claiming that she "had to deal with an out-sized character," she began to worry that no one would want to read such a long novel. She also worried that her editor, Stewart Richardson, would not like the book, much less recognize it as the one she had agreed to write. "My books never have sold and doubtless never will—at least in my lifetime," she observed. "But I hope the publishers will like it well enough to give it a decent send off."

Caroline tried to shake her depression by getting to work on the other book she had in mind, *Creative Writing or Craft Ebbing?* But she felt as if she had sprained her brain writing *The Glory of Hera,* and as Richardson failed to respond to her manuscript, her gloom deepened.

Then a host of family tragedies struck. In October, just before Caroline was to celebrate her seventy-fifth birthday, her favorite aunt, Pidie, died. Later that fall Caroline's oldest brother, Morris, became very ill. In January, just as Caroline was ready to go to Florida to help her sister-in-law Polly take care of Morris, Allen announced that he could no longer afford to pay Caroline any alimony.

Caroline went to Florida anyway and spent a month there. It was a time not unlike her vigil at her father's deathbed; Morris was "clear out of his head" the entire time, Caroline noted, and his hallucinations made the Gordon home "a kind of Kafka's Castle." Finally, the two old women could not handle Morris and had to put him in a nursing home. Caroline returned to Princeton in February. Morris died in April.

Caroline spent part of the spring sorting out her papers for sale to the Princeton Library. For some time she had worried about what to do with Allen's letters. At one point she even considered destroying everything that cast Allen in a bad light. But eventually she decided to leave Allen's correspondence intact. "Allen's psychosis carries with it a strong streak of exhibitionism," and he was "an important figure in the contemporary world of letters—so important that even his decline is of interest," she noted. "Also, years of writing fiction have taught me that everybody always knows everything there is to know, anyhow—unless it is something good."

Caroline, however, was not as generous with her own correspondence. She apparently destroyed a large number of letters that an old friend from Bethany College had returned to her. Caroline had written the letters while she was working on the Chattanooga and Wheeling newspapers. Why she did not save them puzzled her friend, but letters about Caroline's involvement in the League of Women Voters and other such experiences would hardly fit the conservative public image that Caroline had crafted for herself.

Before long, however, she was contemplating action that could hardly be called conservative. Without warning she had received a letter from Cooper Square Publishers informing her that Scribner's had sold them all rights to her first seven novels and one collection of her short stories for sixteen hundred dollars. Under the new contract the books would be reprinted in hardcover editions; Caroline would get eight hundred dollars initially and a minimal royalty payment on all subsequent sales.

Caroline was horrified. At first she could not believe that Charles Scribner, Jr., the president of the firm, had arranged such a contract without telling her. But he had done just that. Throughout the summer she tried to reason her way out of the arrangements, to negotiate her own deal, to no avail. At one point she got so furious that she considered picketing in front of the Scribner headquarters. She thought she would wear a sandwich board with an appropriate slogan, something like

Old Women's Liberation Movement
Chas. Scribner's Sons Refuse to
Liberate Caroline Gordon so she can
Earn Her Living In Her Old Age.

On the advice of others who understood the publishing world better, Caroline tried less radical tactics first. In August, when Cooper Square sent her initial "advance royalty" payment of eight hundred dollars, she tried to refuse it, hoping that her action would nullify the contract. But Charles Scribner, Jr., informed her that the contracts were legal whether or not she approved. He also told her that if she had requested her copyrights before the Cooper Square Contracts were signed, he would have given them to her. He did not, however, think the letter she had written him in the summer of 1962 such a request.

Caroline hired several lawyers to help her fight both Cooper Square and Scribner's, and she threatened to take her story to the Author's Guild. But even after much research and negotiation, little could be done. Caroline's original contracts gave Scribner's some authority to arrange such reprints, and Caroline had once accepted a contract they negotiated with Bantam for a paperback reprint of *Green Centuries*. Caroline's lawyer did not think they had a strong enough case to fight Cooper Square and Scribner's.

After Scribner's agreed to give Caroline the entire sixteen-hundred-dollar payment they had received for the rights to her books, Caroline had no recourse but to accept the settlement and a five-year contract, but she did complain vehemently. The president of Scribner's "sold me down the river," she said over and over again.

CAROLINE spent much of the fall of 1971 proofreading galleys of *The Glory of Hera*. After a lengthy delay the novel was finally slated for publication in the spring of 1972. After she finished her proofreading, she spent several months traveling, giving lectures and visiting friends and family in Tennessee. Since Allen had cut off her major source of income, Caroline could not afford to fly but took the bus, much to the dismay of some of her friends. She decided it was the best thing that could have happened to her. "I saw and heard things I never would have encountered going by plane," she said later. "I don't want to lose my ear for our vernacular and one who stays away too long is in danger of doing so."

After her bus trip Caroline went on to Mexico with her daughter and son-in-law. Nancy and Percy liked to explore picturesque corners of the world; Caroline believed that Percy had to go somewhere without telephones once a year to get away from the demands of his patients and the stress of family crises. In the course of their travels, Nancy and Percy had discovered a quaint Mexican town called San Cristóbal de las Casas. Located in Chiapas province in southern Mexico, San Cristóbal was nestled in the mountains, two hours by car from the nearest airport.

Caroline thought the city heavenly. The oldest Spanish settlement in Chiapas, San Cristóbal was once known as the Royal City. It was a bustling, crowded place, where old world and new existed side by side. Many descendants of the Mayan Indians still lived in the area—the Chamulas, the Zinacantecos, and the Tenejapans—and they still wore their native costumes and lived much as they had for centuries.

Caroline visited some of the Mayan ruins and archeological digs in the area, as well as the Indian villages and the daily market in town. When she wasn't basking in the sun, wandering about in the gardens and local shops, she began to work again on the "upper half" of her autobiographical novel, *A Narrow Heart*. In a small hardbound notebook, she searched her memories, trying to find the meaning in her story, but she decided it was "next to impossible to determine what [was] important."

Searching for a key, Caroline tried on different perspectives. At one point she declared that her life was shaped by the need to escape from her grandmother. Another time she insisted that life at Merry Mont was not really a matriarchy. "A woman's life, I suspect, is defined by the men she has known," she wrote. "They, as it were, *edit* her life."

Before she left Mexico, Caroline had filled her small notebook with tentative outlines and scenes she might include. But she had an uneasy feeling about what she had left to do. Would she be able to write the novel after all? Caroline was not sure. She had invaded the consciousness of others, but she found she could not invade her own.

Soon after she returned to Princeton, *The Glory of Hera* was published. Of course, Caroline's friends praised the novel. Allen called it "a masterpiece, one of the great books of the twentieth century, a much greater work than Joyce's *Ulysses*." But *The Glory of Hera* received little or no public recognition: the *New York Times* did not even bother to review it.

And as Caroline expected, it did not sell well. The novel was too long and tedious for most readers. Caroline used the perspectives of several characters to retell the story of Heracles, and she moved back, forth, and, in some sense, even beyond time in the narrative: an unwary reader could easily get lost in her labyrinthine tale.

Caroline pretended at first that she couldn't have cared less about the success of her book. "Nowadays I feel about *Hera* the way Mary Hamilton, in the ballad, felt towards her infant," she wrote in one letter. "Sink ye, or swim, my bonnie babe. Ye'll get nae mair fra me!" But later, Caroline admitted that she was devastated by the commercial failure of her work. She had counted on making some money on it, but the novel did not even sell enough to cover the advance she had received.

After a while Caroline hardly mentioned *The Glory of Hera*. Sometimes she would even leave it off lists she made of her fiction. Later critics and friends would suggest that the novel demonstrated Caroline's failing powers as a novelist, or perhaps her dependence on Allen's editorial judgment. And yet *The Glory of Hera* contained brilliant sections of writing, and the story more than repaid careful reading. It was not only a creative retelling of the life and labors of Heracles as a prefigurement of Christ, but it was Caroline's last story about the saving power of women.

In the character of Hera, Caroline created one more autobiographical fiction. Like Caroline, Hera was a long-suffering wife of a philandering husband. And yet Zeus could not truly frustrate Hera or render her silent or inactive. Instead, Hera had the peculiar gift of being able to put words into the mouths of mortals and gods, just like her creator, Caroline. Although Hera might sometimes appear to be little more than a vindictive harpy, she would actually use her wisdom and talents to accomplish the salvation of the human race. After all, as Hermes observed at the end of the novel, "heroes have ever been her particular concern."

Caroline did find one small comfort in the failure of *The Glory of Hera*: it made it easy for her to change publishers. Throughout her fight against Cooper Square and Scribner's, Caroline had gotten advice from another editor she had known for a while, Robert Giroux of Farrar, Straus, and Giroux. She decided at that time that she would leave Doubleday as soon as possible after her novel was published. Bob Giroux was a Catholic, an honorable man, and eager to have Caroline under contract: he would not sell her "down the river," Caroline believed. "The Lord has tempered the wind to this shorn goat," she wrote to a friend after signing her new contract. "I am very happy to be in this safe harbour after the recent storms."

Caroline assured Bob Giroux that she did not have much left to write of *A Narrow Heart,* only about four or five chapters as of the summer of 1972. But she did admit she was a bit concerned about how she would knit together the seemingly disconnected chapters of autobiography, history, and mythology. "Again I am trying—or think I am trying—to do something that hasn't been done before," she wrote. "Some days I think I am going to bring it off."

The previous year, Caroline had published a new autobiographical section of the novel, called "Always Summer," in the *Southern Review*. In the fall of 1972, she published another section of autobiography in the *Sewanee Review,* "A Visit to the Grove," originally intended as the first chapter of the novel. Both sections focused on Caroline's childhood at Merry Mont. In "Always Summer" she wrote about the strong-willed characters who filled the old house, especially her grandmother, her uncle Rob, and her great-aunt Caroline Meriwether Goodlett, founder of the United Daughters of the Confederacy. In "A Visit to the Grove," Caroline described the Old Neighborhood and her childhood games in the woods and fields around the house.

Caroline had intended to take her story beyond her childhood; she made notes on her life at Bethany, Chattanooga, and New York. But she apparently found it difficult to write these sections, perhaps for the same reasons she had destroyed some of her letters from these periods. If she wrote about her experiences at that time, she might have to tell the truth, admit she had not learned everything she knew about writing from Allen or Ford, admit she had once been the kind of woman she now so roundly denounced—a shrewd, intelligent woman, a bit of a rebel, hardly an irrational creature who needed to be "restrained by the proper masculine authority," as she wrote in "Cock-Crow."

By concentrating on her childhood, Caroline did not have to face her more difficult memories or come to terms with the discrepancies between fact and fiction in her various accounts of her life. But not long after the publication of *The Glory of Hera,* Caroline received from her old friend Sally Wood a letter that posed a threat to her myth making. While cleaning her attic Sally had found a great many letters that Caroline had written her during the 1920s and 1930s, letters about the early years of Caroline and Allen's marriage, their travels to Europe and move to Benfolly. Reading them over, Sally became convinced that the letters ought to be published, and she wrote Caroline about her idea.

"These early letters would be valuable for historians because they show the Fugitives and the Agrarians as they really were," Sally explained. "My plan would be to quit before the strains between you and Allen became apparent. What ought to show is the years when you and Allen meant so much to people together, as you used to say."

Much to Sally's surprise, Caroline did not like her plan at all. The letters were "juvenilia," Caroline responded, and she urged Sally to send them back to her. But Sally refused, realizing perhaps that Caroline might lose or destroy the letters. "I am afraid to send them to you without being there to argue against your reluctance," she wrote Caroline. "They are far from juvenilia. They are a Portrait of the Artist as a Young Woman."

Trying to argue her case forcibly by mail, Sally pointed out that Caroline had never gotten "the least bit of credit" for what she did for Allen's "brethren." "Without Benfolly and your family country the Agrarians would have lacked any embodiment for their ideas," Sally wrote. "Andrew's connection with the soil was real but not as real as yours by a long shot. You did all the work and Allen sat around being pleasant to people so he got all the credit and you none."

Nothing Sally could say or write at that time would convince Caroline to publish the letters. In fact, Sally's arguments probably guaranteed her friend's refusal: the last thing Caroline wanted was to publish letters which would "quite unconsciously" reveal a true portrait of "the Artist as a Young Woman." But Sally would not be permanently put off by Caroline's resistance. She kept the letters safe and apparently began to put them in some kind of order—no easy task, since Caroline seldom dated her correspondence.

Reacting perhaps to Sally's pressures, Caroline became increasingly adamant about how people ought to read her fiction and interpret her life. She was quite pleased with a book that William Stuckey, her colleague from Purdue, wrote about her life and fiction for the Twayne United States Authors Series, probably because Bill had stressed the conservative nature of her work and her artistic debts to Ford Madox Ford and Allen.

She also admired the work of Ashley Brown, who in his 1958 dissertation and later articles had called Caroline "a conscious heiress to what is probably the central tradition of modern fiction . . . the Impressionist novel." But she continued to rail against other scholars who tried to pry into her personal life or describe her fiction in terms of "regional literature." In the fall of 1972, when one graduate student dared to stray from the prescribed point of view, Caroline rebuked her sharply: "It seems to me that if you persist in writing about my work you should acquaint yourself with the writings of critics whom I find capable of judging my work instead of relying on judgments which I find unsound."

THROUGHOUT the fall of 1972, Caroline worked on *A Narrow Heart*. Yet even though she insisted she was eager to finish the book, she welcomed every interruption to her writing routine, and in November she put aside the novel altogether. Dr. Louise Cowan from the University of Dallas invited Caroline to teach a January seminar in creative writing, and Caroline did not hesitate to accept. She had lectured at the university the previous year and had been extremely impressed by the students and faculty at the small Catholic institution located in Irving, just outside Dallas.

To prepare for the seminar, Caroline resumed her old routine of getting up before sunrise and working three shifts each day interspersed with meals and naps. Although she complained that she did not like such a rigorous schedule, Caroline was ecstatic over the chance to return to the university. And her enthusiasm did not wane after she arrived in Texas. Instead, it increased, despite the fact that for almost three weeks, Caroline taught three hours a day, six days a week. Everything about the University of Dallas pleased her, especially her students. "I work every morning until my brain gets numb but I have the best class I ever had anywhere—the class I have dreamed of having," Caroline wrote her daughter.

Compared to Texas, Princeton seemed like a "Great Dismal Swamp," and Caroline began to dread returning there. She was convinced that the University of Dallas came "nearer the ideal of Christian education—or just plain education—than any institution" she knew of, and she wanted to become permanently affiliated with the place. Over long talks with Louise Cowan and her husband Don, the president of the university, Caroline concocted a plan for a "center for fictional studies in prose and poetry." Although she said she could not make any commitments until she finished *A Narrow Heart,* Caroline offered to help organize the center and return to teach when she was able, perhaps in the spring of 1974.

When Caroline returned to Princeton, she changed her mind. She did not want to wait a year to return to Texas, she wanted to move as soon as possible. Texas was wonderful, "a foretaste of heavenly bliss," she said, and she owed it to Bob Giroux to move because she could work so much better there.

When Caroline told her daughter and son-in-law about her plans, they were shocked. Caroline was seventy-seven years old, hardly the age to begin teaching again. "Mama, you have just gone ape over Texas," Nancy said. "You'll get over it."

"If it is a question of money," Percy murmured.

"No," Caroline said firmly. In Texas she would have a chance to do the kind of teaching she liked to do, she explained. In addition, she said, she would have "the opportunity of landing in a kind of nursing home where I will have a chance to try to save my immortal soul."

Nancy and Percy realized it would be futile to argue. But to their surprise, Caroline's enthusiasm for the University of Dallas proved to be contagious. The next morning, their twenty-one-year-old daughter, Caroline, announced that she wanted to attend the University of Dallas as well. Her grandmother made some phone calls to get her admitted, and within days young Caroline went off to begin the spring semester in Texas.

If the Cowans were surprised by the elder Caroline's sudden change of plans, they never showed it. Instead, they quickly made arrangements for her to begin work at the University of Dallas in the fall of 1973. Caroline told them that she did not want a large salary, just enough to get by, roughly three thousand dollars a year plus lodging, but the Cowans thought it would be better if she had a regular salary and took care of her own living expenses. They offered her ten thousand dollars a year for teaching one course each semester.

Caroline spent the spring and summer getting ready for the move. She lined up many of her friends to serve as advisors for the creative-writing program, including Seán O'Faoláin, Robert Fitzgerald, Madeleine L'Engle, J. F. Powers, and Eudora Welty, and she prepared a new course she wanted to teach, "Creative Grammar." Over and over again, she spoke and wrote glowing praise of the University of Dallas. The fall could not come too soon. "Just a slip of a septuagenarian, setting out on a pedagogical career!" she exclaimed.

In the intervals of packing and planning, Caroline worked on *A Narrow Heart*. She had gotten to a section on Meriwether Lewis; for months she toiled on the Pacific Coast with him and his partner, William Clark.

Yet she could not finish the book, or even her section on Lewis. The question of his death had captured her attention, and she began to write other scholars of Meriwether Lewis—the "Mountain Men," she called them: Richard Dillon, his biographer; Jonathan Daniels; and others. She thought she had solved the mystery of his death, and she said that she wanted their opinion and approval. But perhaps she wanted only one more diversion to keep her from finishing the book: she kept telling her friends that she could not work in the Red House, but she was sure she would be able to write in Texas.

In August Caroline left the Red House after a flurry of farewell parties. She was not at all sorry to leave. "The Red House was a wonderful refuge for me for fifteen years," she told a friend. "It was the first time in my life I had ever been able to stay in one place that long. That, in itself, was bliss. But the worship of mediocrity is almost a religion in Princeton," she insisted. "I was sick of the place after fifteen years. Boredom—honest to God boredom—is a kind of living death for an artist."

At first Caroline had no time to get bored in Texas. Even moving into her apartment proved to be an adventure: for a while she thought she had lost her notes and manuscripts for her novel. But eventually she located the missing papers and began to settle into her two-bedroom apartment at 1744 East Northgate Drive in Irving. She called her new home the Labyrinth. Located just across the street from campus, and in the shadow of Cowboy Stadium, the apartment complex seemed as confusing as the great maze Daedalus had built for King Minos of Crete, she thought.

Caroline missed the fireplaces at the Red House, the garden, and, most of all, the trees—or rather, "the shadows of leaves on grass or walls," she said. But she quickly acquired an indoor garden of ferns and laurel trees in tubs, which passed as an acceptable substitute, and she delighted in the brilliant sunshine and magnificent skies. Collecting odd bits of Texas trivia and examples of the rivalry between Fort Worth and Dallas, she declared that she had moved to Irving because she was a "professional gambler." It was, she insisted, most appropriate: "writing a novel is a gamble always," and Irving had once been called "the bedroom of Dallas" because it was where the "old time professional gamblers . . . kept their wives and children . . . while they operated their gambling 'hells' in Dallas," she explained.

At first her gamble seemed to pay off. In September she began teaching "Creative Grammar," and even the challenge of lecturing on prepositional phrases and compound sentences did not faze her. "You and I are trying to do something that never has been done before," she told her students. "It is possible that we may make academic history."

Caroline celebrated her seventy-eighth birthday in October, amazing some of her students with almost youthful enthusiasm. Although her face was covered with deep wrinkles, her throat heavy with folds of extra skin, she did not hesitate to wear the latest styles: a body suit and wrap-around skirt. But Caroline's energy was not equal to her enthusiasm, and her students could not meet her high expectations. By December, exhausted and irritable, she began scolding her students and rebuking her friends. For no apparent reason, she even told Sally Wood to give herself "a good sock in the jaw" and stop interfering in her life. "In my old age I make it an inflexible rule never to take advice from any woman," she wrote. "Women are irrational creatures, (thank God. Novelists would have to shut up shop, otherwise.) I have been inundated by advice from women all my life. It boils down to two pieces of advice: 1. Stop writing fiction. 2. Be just like me. I wouldn't follow the advice if I could and I couldn't follow it if [I] would."

Sally was not put off by her friend's tantrums, and most of Caroline's students accepted her occasionally irascible behavior. One student, however, got so angry with Caroline that he stormed out in the middle of class. He was a "red-headed firebrand who [had] to be handled with kid gloves," Caroline noted. "The kid gloves wore thin, I guess."

Refusing to join her family in Princeton for the holidays, Caroline spent most of January working on her novel, which she had renamed *Behold My Trembling Heart,* from the writings of St. Augustine. In the spring, she taught "Techniques of Fiction," the kind of class she had taught for years at Columbia. Although she insisted she was teaching "a perfect dream-boat of a course" with some of the best students she had ever had, she once again found it difficult to balance the demands of teaching and writing.

Since the only time she could find to write without being interrupted was early in the morning before sunrise, she got up each morning at four o'clock. The schedule surely added to her ill humor, but Caroline had begun to feel desperate about her novel, and she would not let up. "I am trying hard to get in as many licks as I can before senility comes to my relief," she told a friend.

After a while the constant toil took its toll, and Caroline apparently began to suffer from delusions and hallucinations. One day she called her daughter with a strange tale about how an elderly cousin in Kentucky had been raped by a burglar who had broken into her house. When Nancy tried to get more information and find out how the old woman was, Caroline became evasive and quickly ended the conversation.

Not long after that, Caroline traveled down to Milledgeville, Georgia, to speak at a festival honoring Flannery O'Connor. After she returned, she called Nancy again. The strangest thing happened, she said. One morning, while she was dressing, two black youths had entered her hotel room. They acted rudely, then attacked her, Caroline said, implying that she, too, had been raped.

Are you all right? Nancy asked. What did you do?

Caroline insisted that she was fine. She did not tell anyone, she said; she simply told the boys to leave her room, then she dressed, called a cab, went to the airport, and took the first plane home.

Nancy was horrified but also suspicious. Caroline's story sounded too much like her account of the rape of her elderly cousin, and she kept insisting that she was fine, that there was no need to talk to anyone or see a doctor. After her mother hung up, Nancy told her husband Percy about the strange conversation. "It didn't happen," Percy said.

Nancy thought he was probably right, and some time later, when she was visiting her mother in Texas, Nancy was sure. Caroline told her the same story again, as if she had never mentioned it before, but she told it slyly, almost as if she were testing Nancy, trying to see whether her daughter would believe her tall tale. Nancy remembered that Caroline had once behaved the same way on another occasion, insisting that the Electrolux salesman in Princeton was a devil: she had seen his cloven foot, Caroline had said.

Clearly, Caroline was having hallucinatory spells, but since she seemed otherwise healthy, there was little Nancy could do. Caroline refused to move back to Princeton.

DURING the summer of 1974, Matthew Bruccoli of the Southern Illinois University Press expressed an interest in publishing *Aleck Maury* in their "Lost American Fiction Series." Even though Caroline was eager to have her books reissued in paperback editions, she objected vehemently to his offer. "I do not believe that *Aleck Maury* belongs in your category of 'Lost Fiction,'" she wrote. "It has been a classic for over twenty-five years and well-known in discriminating literary circles."

Caroline took the same haughty tone to rebuke Sally Wood when she appealed once again for permission to publish the letters Caroline had written her. Sally said that she was afraid that she would lose the letters, or that "they won't interest the public when everyone in them is not only dead but temporarily forgotten." Caroline insisted that she would not be forgotten, that she had a loyal following of "discriminating critics." If Sally did not realize that, she was not qualified to write about her, Caroline insisted.

Caroline's teaching that fall fared no better. She felt that her students did not appreciate her methods. They felt frustrated as well by her often arbitrary and capricious fits of temper. Caroline seemed to expect them to go beyond her assignments, but when some students read more than the assigned sections of Aristotle's *Poetics,* she scolded them. Although she devoted much of her class to a study of Henry James's method of the "central intelligence," she became angry when students attempted to use the method. They should wait, she said. "What I'm teaching you, you won't need for eight years," she insisted, and she told her students to imagine eight years had passed and take notes for that time.

By the middle of the semester, everyone sensed that Caroline should not continue teaching. When Louise Cowan offered to teach "Techniques of Fiction" in the spring, Caroline reluctantly agreed to take a sabbatical. As it turned out, the rest was a medical and emotional necessity. Caroline had been suffering from poor health all fall; she lost thirty pounds but kept her problems a secret from her daughter because she did not want to have to return to Princeton. Finally, she became so ill that in February she had to be hospitalized. Nancy came out to care for her for a while, then a friend from Princeton, Kitty Morgan, took Nancy's place.

By the end of March, Kitty had to return to Princeton. But before she left, she helped Caroline move into a new apartment in the Labyrinth, one with "twice as much sunshine and twice as much ground," and a magnificent "vista" of meadow and several large trees, Caroline noted with delight. The Cowans arranged for Mary Mombach, a graduate student at the university, to move in with Caroline and look after her—"to check on my continued existence each morning," Caroline noted wryly.

Caroline liked Mary and did not mind having a "keeper," but she began to worry even more that she would not live to finish her novel. Yet she began teaching again in the fall of 1975, and before the year had ended, she had created another obstacle for herself: she decided to abandon her plans for *Behold My Trembling Heart* and turn her section on Meriwether

Lewis into a separate novel on his journey and subsequent murder called *Joy of the Mountains*.

In the novel Meriwether Lewis would reenact the role of Heracles, Caroline believed. She persuaded Bob Giroux to go along with her plans, even though such a novel, requiring more research, could not possibly be published within a year as he hoped. Caroline could be quite persuasive, and she also consistently overestimated her own abilities, promising Bob that she did not really have much to write. She could be finished by April, she said.

But Caroline continued to teach, and then she began to suffer from eye problems. She insisted that there was "nothing like a deadline to galvanize a person," but her April deadline passed with the novel still unfinished. Although she vowed to finish her book by the following spring, she did not cut back on her teaching, and in the winter of 1976–77 she also suffered from a bad case of shingles, which kept her from her typewriter. Finally she asked Bob Giroux if she could postpone her deadline yet again, and Bob agreed.

Having her deadline postponed should have taken the pressure off Caroline, but little cheered her during the spring of 1977. She hated her students so much that she wrote an "Ode on Vampire Bats," and she complained bitterly that her life as a teacher consisted of "sustaining, with as much equanimity as one can muster, repeated kicks in the teeth."

The University of Dallas honored Caroline with a symposium on March 25, 1977, but Caroline could not enjoy it. Sally Wood was visiting her at the same time, recovering from the death of her husband, and Caroline felt like she had to be in two places at once. Suffering from an unexpected bout of deafness, which turned out to be nothing more serious than plugged ears, Caroline got confused and frustrated. She wanted to comfort Sally, but she also wanted to visit with her old friends Howard Baker, Radcliffe Squires, William Stuckey, and Ashley Brown, who had flown into town for the symposium. Before the day was over, she lost her temper for no reason at all.

Not long after that, Caroline found herself once again fighting with Allen over ownership of the Red House. Seventy-eight years old and suffering from acute emphysema and other ailments, Allen was apparently trying to get his financial affairs in order. He had dropped most of his insurance before he realized that the income he received from his brother Ben's estate would not continue after his death to support his

young family, and although he had won a number of literary prizes totaling more than twenty thousand dollars in 1975 alone, he had not been
able to save much. So he appealed once again to Caroline for some share
of the Red House.

Caroline refused, but Allen continued to pester her throughout the
summer. He thought his share of the house would be no more than one-
fourth or one-third its current worth, he said, and he implied that she
did not need the money as much as he did. Still Caroline refused, but his
arguments did not make her life any easier.

Don Cowan, the retiring president of the University of Dallas, tried
to persuade Caroline to take a year-long sabbatical at half pay during
the 1977–78 academic year. He also suggested that Caroline return to
Princeton, but she persuaded him and her daughter to allow her to spend
one more year in Texas. She still dreaded "the *boredom* of Princeton," and
she thought she could still do some good for the university.

After only a few weeks of teaching in September, Caroline was exhausted. In October she turned eighty-two. Before long she faced a task
more demanding than teaching: she had to write a reflection on *Aleck
Maury, Sportsman,* because Bob Giroux had persuaded her to allow the
Southern Illinois University Press to go ahead with their publication of
the novel. Caroline later insisted that writing the afterword was one of
the hardest tasks she had ever faced; "I cursed loud and deep when I realized that I had no choice in the matter," she told Bob. Yet Caroline's final
version, in which she invoked the memory of Henry James and Turgenev
to explain how she got the idea for the novel, showed no sign of her
anguish. It was a gentle, loving look back, as poignant and captivating
as the masterpiece Caroline had written more than four decades earlier.

When Caroline agreed to move back to Princeton, she also agreed
to sell the Red House: she needed more convenient quarters and more
supervision than she could have in her ramshackle house on Ewing
Street. After selling the Red House for a nice profit, Nancy began preparing a special suite for Caroline in the Woods' house on Hodge Road.
But by the early months of 1978, Nancy and Percy realized they would
probably be moving to Mexico after Percy retired. They had bought a
house in San Cristóbal de las Casas. If Caroline was still living at that
time, she would have to join them, so they urged her to go with them in
February for a vacation.

Caroline did not want to go; she had already seen San Cristóbal, and
she liked it well enough. Why bother going back? "I am so tired and there

is so much involved in any trip and I hate air planes," she complained. But Nancy and Percy insisted, and Caroline agreed. "One's needs must be put aside when the younger generations drive," she ruefully observed.

Once in Mexico Caroline saw things differently. From the courtyard of Nancy and Percy's house in San Cristóbal, she could look down on the bright, tiled roofs of the city or out at a towering ring of cloud-shrouded mountains: the house was "on a slope, commanding what seems to be a vision of infinity," Caroline said. Although the weather was cool at night and often rainy by day in February, the countryside was lush and green, a gardener's delight. In fact, the area was sometimes called the "garden of Eden," apparently because specimens of almost every kind of plant had been found there. Caroline did not believe that, but she suddenly fell in love with San Cristóbal de las Casas and knew that she wanted to spend the rest of her life there. "My eyes were opened," she wrote later. "I beheld my 'Promised Land.'"

Certain that she would be quite happy spending her last years in Mexico, Caroline bought a small house next door to her daughter and son-in-law's home and made plans to restore a common enclosed patio between the two houses. Nancy and Percy called their two-story white stucco home El Jacarandal after one of the native flowering bushes; Caroline named her one-story pink stucco abode Chenk-Ku, a "place for several wild animals."

With little to tie her to Texas or Princeton, Caroline was eager to start her new life, but both El Jacarandal and Chenk-Ku needed extensive renovations before anyone could comfortably live there, and Nancy and Percy were not yet ready to retire to Mexico. Caroline would not be able to move in until the beginning of summer at the earliest, but she wasted no time making preparations for the move. Immediately after her return to Texas, she began to pack and to study Spanish. She told all her friends about her "Promised Land" and invited them to visit her after she moved.

Caroline had no trouble imagining what her life would be like in Chenk-Ku. She thought she could live comfortably in one large room and keep several other rooms available for guests. She would work every morning, then appear at lunch time to eat and entertain, work in the gardens, and perhaps even visit with the pigs that the cook would raise. And she would never leave San Cristóbal, "except for lecture trips made in the line of duty," she declared.

But Caroline's roseate visions soon dimmed considerably. Hoping to explore some of the sights around Mexico that she could not otherwise visit before her cataracts matured or her health failed completely, she bought a small motor home to travel in. "I want to *see* as much as I can before I have to depend on that 'inner eye' which, according to Wordsworth, is 'the bliss of solitude,'" she wrote a friend. Nancy and Percy, however, knew there would be no place to store such a vehicle in San Cristóbal, and they doubted that Caroline would get much use out of it, so they insisted that she sell it. Caroline resisted them at first, but eventually she had to acquiesce to their wishes. As she repented of her self-indulgence, Caroline sensed that her world was closing in on her. "Have already seen as many sights as I need to see," she told Percy. "Sorry to give you trouble undoing my blunder."

Not long after the uproar over the motor home, two new crises rocked Caroline and the Woods. First fire ravaged Nancy and Percy's home in Princeton: no one was hurt, but damage was extensive. Then Allen called Nancy and asked her to help him leave his wife. He said that he wanted to move into a nursing home in Princeton so that he could be near her and Percy.

Nancy told him that they were moving to Mexico, but Allen could join them there. When Caroline found out about Allen's request, she urged Nancy to give him Chenk-Ku. "I think this house is much too fancy for me," Caroline told her daughter. "Find me a hovel and give my house" to Allen.

Absolutely furious, Nancy threatened to have her mother declared mentally incompetent if she dared repeat her suggestion. But Nancy need not have worried. Even if Caroline had given him her house, Allen would not move to Mexico. "Who would I talk to in Mexico—the Indians?" he asked Nancy. "Who would know who I am?"

Caroline did not share Allen's worries, and not long after Allen made his plea for deliverance, she insisted that Nancy fly to Texas and help her move immediately to Mexico. Still trying to sort out the insurance claims for the fire in Princeton, Nancy wanted her mother to wait. But Caroline was adamant. Everything was packed, she said. Her furniture had all been sent away; she could not stay in Texas.

Nancy finally gave in. When she arrived in Texas, however, she discovered that Caroline had lied. Suitcases and boxes were strewn all about the apartment, but many had only one or two items in them. Nothing was ready.

Although Nancy had less than a day to get everything packed, they left early the next morning: Caroline, Nancy, two dogs in traveling carriers, fourteen suitcases, and all the hand luggage they could carry. The dogs annoyed Nancy the most: she did not know how Caroline would ever be able to take care of them, and she tried to persuade her mother to leave them behind. But Caroline refused.

When they arrived in Mexico City, it took two station wagons to transport them and their luggage to the hotel where they had a reservation. Once they got there, the hotel refused to accept them because of the dogs. They tried another hotel and got the same response: no dogs allowed. At her wits' end, Nancy told Caroline to sit in the hotel lobby with the dogs and luggage and wait for her to find another hotel. "If you say a word to me, I'm going to slap you," Nancy said.

They spent the night in a ghastly hotel, then went on to San Cristóbal in the morning. Since the renovations had not yet been completed at El Jacarandal or Chenk-Ku, they went to stay in a guest home called Na Balom.

Nancy hoped that her mother's behavior would improve once they settled down, but the horrors of the trip were just a portent of things to come. Caroline had stayed at Na Balom before and had always liked it, but after a short while she began to refuse to eat there. Then one day she passed out while walking in the garden. Nancy thought her mother had suffered a stroke or a heart attack, but a doctor's examination revealed a less serious problem: Caroline had passed out from taking too many drugs for her various physical ailments.

Once she was weaned from her excess medications, Caroline's health improved, but her mental state did not. By then, however, Nancy had to go back to Princeton, so she arranged for her mother to move into the finished section of El Jacarandal with her namesake and favorite granddaughter, Caroline, who was married by that time to a young man named Chris Fallon.

With their small son, Toby, young Caroline and Chris tried to help Caroline get settled into her new home. But Caroline did not want to get settled, she wanted to escape. "I am not going to be able to stay here," she wrote her daughter. "I cannot work here," she complained to Percy. "The language barrier makes it difficult for me to order my life so I can work. The cold makes my arthritis unbearable."

Time and again, Caroline begged to be allowed to leave Mexico. But her pleas would not be answered, indeed, could not be answered. Not only did Caroline have nowhere else to go, but she probably would never have survived the flight back to the States, and she knew that. "My ignorance—or indifference—to the oncoming rigours of old age has landed me in quite a jam," she wrote in her notebook. "My stupid heart won't stand air-plane travel at an elevation of thirty feet."

"I am a prisoner of these mountains—indeed, ring upon top of ring of these mountains," Caroline declared. "This place is beautiful, the mountains pile up seemingly higher than the cumulus clouds that hang over them," she wrote to a friend. "I am the only thing that is vile around here."

Caroline did try to write during the first year she was in San Cristóbal; she even developed an elaborate working routine, setting up four desks in one of her rooms with a typewriter and a different manuscript at each desk. She had enough unfinished manuscripts to do that: she had written most of *Joy of the Mountains,* her novel about Meriwether Lewis, as well as a significant amount of her autobiographical novel and her treatise on the problems with education in creative writing, *Craft Ebbing?* She also wanted to revise *A House of Fiction* for a third time. But Caroline could not finish any of these books. Her arthritis worsened until she could barely type, and her mind often wandered.

Bit by bit, Caroline lost interest in the world around her. She would not attend church, perhaps because she could never understand Spanish, and she would not work in the garden. She would not even take pleasure in supervising anyone else's gardening. When she sat in the courtyard, she would keep her back to the mountains and her eyes on the front door. She kept waiting for visitors, but only a few of her friends could make the long journey to San Cristóbal. Most of the time, her guest rooms were empty.

In the fall of 1978, Caroline celebrated her eighty-third birthday. Shortly afterward Sally Wood wrote to ask once again for permission to publish Caroline's letters. This time she got no arguments. Go ahead, Caroline responded. "I am too ill to give the matter any more thought."

Sometimes Caroline did go out sightseeing with her granddaughter, but the effort brought her little pleasure, and after attending one Indian festival in honor of San Lorenzo, Caroline vowed never again. "The people here are so desperately poor it is painful to see them," she wrote.

On February 9, 1979, Allen died. When Caroline got the news, she was relieved. "Well, thank God," she said to Nancy, who was back in Mexico by that time. "Now he can get to work." Caroline then heaved a great sigh, but she did not shed a tear. Nancy did not know exactly what her mother meant by "now he can get to work." At his salvation? For some time after that, she often overheard Caroline talking in the garden, addressing Allen as if he were beside her, having a friendly conversation.

Several months later, Caroline found out that Farrar, Straus, and Giroux wanted to publish a collected edition of her stories. "Bob Giroux is launching a Caroline Gordon Renascence campaign," she wrote to Sally Wood. "I ought to be pleased. But I am too old and too feeble to take any pleasure in it."

Later that summer Caroline had what she thought was a slight stroke that left her hand partially paralyzed. In the fall she was diagnosed as having pneumonia, pericarditis, and arteriosclerosis. Nancy thought Caroline would die, but she recovered, almost despite herself. "I've seen all I want to see and I want to get out of this world," she told a friend. "My doctor is determined I shan't."

In February 1980 the jacaranda bloomed, nearly three months early. Caroline continued to insist that she was "weary of this world," but her spirits and her health improved noticeably, in part because her son-in-law, Percy, had arrived in San Cristóbal to stay. Caroline got along with Percy much better than with anyone else. Together they would walk about the patio or sit on the terrace in the evening to watch the sun set. With her dark eyes and shoulder-length white hair pulled back off her thin, weathered face, Caroline sometimes rather resembled the natives of San Cristóbal. She would tell stories about the Old Neighborhood, or Percy and she would quote poetry to one another—Tennyson, Wordsworth, Browning, Hopkins, Donne: Caroline had a great memory for the old poetry her father had taught her.

During the summer of 1980, the *Southern Review* printed a selection of the letters that Sally Wood had edited and would later publish as *The Southern Mandarins*. Caroline was pleased when she saw what Sally had done. "What good times we seem to have had in those days!" Caroline wrote. "I am glad that the letters are in print."

Still Caroline felt as if she were swimming in a sea of fatigue. "Everything I do demands more strength than I have got," she said. If she went out to lunch, she was exhausted for two days afterward. And she was also bored. "I have got so I dislike books," she told Sally. "I read nothing but detective stories."

Nancy tried to help encourage her mother to take an interest in the local Catholic church; for a while she even brought a priest in to hear Caroline's confessions. But Caroline only got more frustrated. "He just doesn't understand my sins," she said. "He gives me absolution which I don't deserve."

The only cleric she trusted was Jean de Vos, a Jesuit priest and anthropologist from Belgium, who served a small parish in a remote mountain section. A friend of Nancy and Percy, Jean visited Caroline whenever he was in town. He realized that Caroline was lonely and full of anger, and he tried to bring her some comfort. Caroline loved him. "I like to look at him," she told Nancy. "He's like one of those implacable Flemish angels."

Caroline suffered a fairly severe stroke during the spring of 1981. When Howard Baker and his wife, Virginia, visited her in March, they could tell she was failing rapidly. Caroline could not get around very well, and she had to have regular massages and hot-pack applications to fight against circulatory trouble. Nancy had hired a full-time nurse to care for her: the nurse not only bathed and dressed Caroline each morning, but she also followed her around with a portable chair.

Yet Caroline still had a fairly clear mind and her usual caustic sense of humor, and she was delighted to see the Bakers. She had known Howard for more than sixty years: in the 1920s they had both lived in Paris near Ford Madox Ford. They spent several afternoons drinking and chatting on the terrace, Caroline with her back to the mountains as usual, her dark eyes still shining in the mass of wrinkles which creased her face.

Shortly after the Bakers left, however, Caroline's health turned suddenly worse. Although she was on the highest possible dosage of medicine to prevent circulatory failure, Caroline had developed gangrene in her right foot. During the first week of April she had to go into the local hospital to have her leg amputated above the knee.

Nancy hoped that her mother would die mercifully during the surgery. She knew that Caroline would not like becoming even more dependent on others, being further restricted to bed or a wheelchair. But to everyone's surprise Caroline survived the operation. She came out of the surgery with a remarkably tranquil face, Nancy said later: it was almost as if every line of age and worry had been erased.

Four days later Nancy realized that her mother had decided to die. Caroline refused to speak or eat or take medicine of any sort. She remained perfectly conscious, her jet black eyes following whoever appeared in her room, but she would not open her mouth for anything.

The doctors told Nancy and Percy to take Caroline home, where she would be more comfortable; there was little else they could do for her. Three days later, late in the afternoon of Saturday, April 11, 1981, Percy realized that Caroline was dying, and he went to get Jean de Vos, who happened to be in town at the time.

When Jean arrived, Caroline was lying in her bed, visibly agitated but still refusing to speak. Nancy sat on one side of the bed, Jean sat on the other, and Caroline looked quickly from one to the other, her breath coming in quick gasps.

When Jean told Caroline that he had come to give her the last rites of the Catholic church, the panic in her eyes left. Nancy held her hand, but Caroline stared resolutely into Jean's eyes as he blessed her and prayed for her. "I know you can't speak anymore," Jean said soothingly. "I know you would like to speak. It's as good as if you make a confession."

As Jean finished giving her the sacraments, Caroline had "this look of absolute bliss," Nancy said later. When he finished the last prayer, he kissed her on her forehead. Then Caroline gasped for air three times and died.

It was late on a Saturday evening. Caroline could not be buried immediately, but her Mexican servants did not leave her alone. All night long they sat in her room, saying the rosary and setting out beside her body small glasses of rum, which they would periodically drink and then refill. "To warm Doña Carolina as she begins her dark journey," one of the women explained to Nancy.

The next morning the women gathered armloads of flowers to fill her room and then prepared to dress her body for burial. Nancy suddenly realized that she could not face such a task, so an acquaintance who had stopped by unexpectedly for a visit volunteered to take over. "Listen, Nancy, we're going to dress her in that purple velvet dinner dress," she said after looking at Caroline's wardrobe. "Purple is best because she was a royal sort of person."

After they had dressed Caroline and put her in her coffin, the Mexican women continued their vigil throughout that day and night. The next morning they went out to the market and brought back even more flowers, calla lilies and white roses, wild orchids and carnations to fill the courtyard. Jean de Vos celebrated mass in Caroline's living room; then the family and friends prepared to take Caroline's body to the cemetery.

Just as Percy and the gardener were about to lift the coffin, one of the maids shouted, "Stop." While Nancy and Percy looked on in amazement, the young woman ran down to the clothesline, snatched up all of Caroline's underwear, and put it in the coffin. "It's the custom here," she explained.

They buried Caroline at the Panteon, in the shadow of the mountains. While the grave diggers did their work, their sons played leapfrog nearby. It was a scene Caroline would have loved, Nancy thought. Percy read Caroline's favorite poem, "The Windhover," by Gerard Manley Hopkins, and when the coffin was lowered and covered, the Mexican servants put pottery jars of water in the earth and filled them with flowers. They also buried ritual packages of food and drink at the grave site, to sustain Caroline on her final journey home.

ABBREVIATIONS

The following abbreviations are used in the notes.

MANUSCRIPT COLLECTIONS

BPPU   Ashley Brown Collection of Caroline Gordon Papers. Published with permission of the Manuscripts Division, Department of Rare Books and Special Collections, Princeton University Libraries, Princeton, New Jersey.

CGLT   Caroline Gordon Letters to Jean Stafford. Department of Special Collections, McFarlin Library, University of Tulsa, Tulsa.

CGPU   Caroline Gordon Papers. Published with permission of the Manuscripts Division, Department of Rare Books and Special Collections, Princeton University Libraries, Princeton, New Jersey.

CPNL   Malcolm Cowley Papers. Newberry Library, Chicago.

CPVU   Brainard and Frances Cheney Papers. Jean and Alexander Heard Library, Vanderbilt University, Nashville.

DDCW   Dorothy Day–Catholic Worker Archives. Marquette University Library, Milwaukee.

DPVU   Donald Davidson Papers. Jean and Alexander Heard Library, Vanderbilt University, Nashville.

DUNC   Ward Dorrance Papers. Southern Historical Collection, Library of the University of North Carolina at Chapel Hill.

EWBL   Edmund Wilson Papers. Yale Collection of American Literature, Beinecke Rare Book and Manuscript Library, Yale University, New Haven.

FMFC   Ford Madox Ford Collection. Courtesy of the Division of Rare and Manuscript Collections, Cornell University Library, Ithaca, New York.

FPUA   John Gould Fletcher Papers. Special Collections, University Libraries, University of Arkansas, Fayetteville.

GUNC   Paul Green Papers. Southern Historical Collection, Library of the University of North Carolina at Chapel Hill.

HHBU   *Hound and Horn* Papers. Yale Collection of American Literature, Beinecke Rare Book and Manuscript Library, Yale University, New Haven.

HPBL   Josephine Herbst Papers. Yale Collection of American Literature, Beinecke Rare Book and Manuscript Library, Yale University, New Haven.

JSGF   John S. Guggenheim Foundation Archives. New York.

KAPM   Papers of Katherine Anne Porter. Rare Books and Literary Manuscripts Department, University of Maryland at College Park Libraries.

LABL   Léonie Adams and Bill Troy Papers. Yale Collection of American Literature, Beinecke Rare Book and Manuscript Library, Yale University, New Haven.

LPVU   Andrew Lytle Papers. Jean and Alexander Heard Library, Vanderbilt University, Nashville.

McDY   Dwight Macdonald Papers. Manuscripts and Archives, Yale University Library, New Haven.

MERP   William Meredith Papers. Published with permission of the Manuscripts Division, Department of Rare Books and Special Collections, Princeton University Libraries, Princeton, New Jersey.

MFPK   Letters of Caroline Gordon and the Meriwethers. Department of Library Special Collections, Western Kentucky University, Bowling Green.

MGPU   Morris Meriwether Gordon Papers. Published with permission of the Manuscripts Division, Department of Rare Books and Special Collections, Princeton University Libraries, Princeton, New Jersey.

MPVU   Arthur Mizener Papers. Jean and Alexander Heard Library, Vanderbilt University, Nashville.

ODWU   George Marion O'Donnell Papers. Special Collections, Washington University, St. Louis.

RLHU   Robert Lowell Papers (bMs Am 1905 [513–522]). By permission of the Houghton Library, Harvard University, Cambridge, Massachusetts.

RPWB   Robert Penn Warren Papers. Yale Collection of American Literature, Beinecke Rare Book and Manuscript Library, Yale University, New Haven.

SAPU   Archives of Charles Scribner's Sons. Published with permission of the Manuscripts Division, Department of Rare Books and Special Collections, Princeton University Libraries, Princeton, New Jersey.

SPWU   Radcliffe Squires Papers. Special Collections, Washington University, St. Louis.

SRBL   *Southern Review* Papers. Yale Collection of American Literature, Beinecke Rare Book and Manuscript Library, Yale University, New Haven.

SWKP   Sally Wood Kohn Special Gift. Published with permission of the Manuscripts Division, Department of Rare Books and Special Collections, Princeton University Libraries, Princeton, New Jersey.

SYPT   Stark Young Papers. Harry Ransom Humanities Research Center, University of Texas at Austin.

TPPU   Allen Tate Papers. Published with permission of the Manuscripts Division, Department of Rare Books and Special Collections, Princeton University Libraries, Princeton, New Jersey.

TPUV   Virginia Tunstall Papers (#8606). Manuscripts Division, Special Collections Department, University of Virginia Library, Charlottesville.

VDPC   Mark Van Doren Papers. Rare Book and Manuscript Library, Columbia University, New York.

VQUV   *Virginia Quarterly Review* Papers (#292-a). Manuscripts Division, Special Collections Department, University of Virginia Library, Charlottesville.

WPMS   Anne G. Winslow Papers. Mississippi Valley Collection, John Willard Brister Library, Memphis State University, Memphis.

WTPU   Willard Thorp Papers. Published with permission of the Manuscripts Division, Department of Rare Books and Special Collections, Princeton University Libraries, Princeton, New Jersey.

ZPNL   Morton D. Zabel Papers. Newberry Library, Chicago.

PEOPLE

AB	Ashley Brown
AGW	Anne Goodwin Winslow
AL	Andrew Lytle
AT	Allen Tate
BT	Bill Troy
CG	Caroline Gordon
EL	Edna Lytle
FC	Frances ("Fannie") Cheney
FMF	Ford Madox Ford
JB	Janice Biala
JCR	John Crowe Ransom
JH	Josephine Herbst
JMG	James M. Gordon
JS	Jean Stafford
KAP	Katherine Anne Porter
LA	Léonie Adams
LC	Brainard ("Lon") Cheney
MC	Malcolm Cowley
MG	Morris Gordon
MP	Maxwell Perkins
MT	Margaret Thorp
NTW	Nancy Tate Wood
PG	Paul Green
PW	Percy H. Wood, Jr.
RL	Robert Lowell
RPW	Robert Penn Warren
RS	Radcliffe Squires

SWK   Sally Wood Kohn
SY   Stark Young
WD   Ward Dorrance
WM   William Meredith
WT   Willard Thorp

PUBLICATIONS

AM   Caroline Gordon, *Aleck Maury, Sportsman*. 1934; reprint, Carbondale: Southern Illinois University Press, 1980.

"AS"   Caroline Gordon, "Always Summer." *Southern Review,* n.s., 7 (1971): 430–46.

CC   Ann Waldron, *Close Connections: Caroline Gordon and the Southern Renaissance*. New York: G. P. Putnam's Sons, 1987.

CN   *Chattanooga News*.

CS   Caroline Gordon, *The Collected Stories of Caroline Gordon*. New York: Farrar, Straus and Giroux, 1981.

GC   Caroline Gordon, *Green Centuries*. 1941; reprint, New York: Cooper Square, 1971.

GH   Caroline Gordon, *The Glory of Hera*. Garden City, N.Y.: Doubleday, 1972.

"GM"   Caroline Gordon, "At the Top of the Glass Mountain." Typescript, undated, Box 16, Folder 3, Caroline Gordon Papers. Published with permission of the Manuscripts Division, Department of Rare Books and Special Collections, Princeton University Libraries, Princeton, New Jersey.

"HI"   Caroline Gordon, "How I Learned to Write Novels." *Books on Trial* 15, no. 3 (November 1956): 111–12, 160–63.

"LW"   Caroline Gordon, "Learning to Write on the University Campus." Typescript, Box 19, Folder 7, Caroline Gordon Papers. Published with permission of the Manuscripts Division, Department of Rare Books and Special Collections, Princeton University Libraries, Princeton, New Jersey.

Mal   Caroline Gordon, *The Malefactors*. New York: Harcourt, Brace, 1956.

NB   Caroline Gordon, *None Shall Look Back*. New York: Charles Scribner's Sons, 1937.

"NH"   Caroline Gordon, "A Narrow Heart: The Portrait of a Woman." *Transatlantic Review* 3 (Spring 1960): 7–19.

PN   Caroline Gordon, *Penhally*. 1931; reprint, New York: Cooper Square, 1971.

PY   Eileen Simpson, *Poets in Their Youth: A Memoir*. New York: Random House, 1982.

RG   Mary C. Sullivan and Robert E. Golden, *Flannery O'Connor and Caroline Gordon: A Reference Guide*. Boston: G. K. Hall, 1977.

SC Caroline Gordon, *The Strange Children*. 1951; reprint, New York: Cooper Square, 1971.

SM Sally Wood, ed., *The Southern Mandarins: Letters of Caroline Gordon to Sally Wood, 1924–1937*. Baton Rouge: Louisiana State University Press, 1984.

"VG" Caroline Gordon, "A Visit to the Grove." *Sewanee Review* 80, no. 4 (Fall 1972): 509–54.

WI *Wheeling Intelligencer*.

WP Caroline Gordon, *The Women on the Porch*. 1944; reprint, New York: Cooper Square, 1971.

"WR" Caroline Gordon, "We Were Ready." *Mademoiselle*, February 1943, 77, 124, 126, 128.

NOTES

PREFACE

ix   "A young man" to "Still I suppose": CG to KAP, undated, KAPM.

x   "A happy and understanding": Frederick P. W. McDowell, *Caroline Gordon* (Minneapolis: University of Minnesota Press, 1966), 7.

x   Recent biographies: see *CC* and Veronica Makowsky, *Caroline Gordon: A Biography* (New York: Oxford University Press, 1989).

xi   "No interest whatever," "I never even": CG to JH, February 11, 1929, HPBL.

xi   In a 1929 letter to John Peale Bishop: see Thomas Daniel Young and John J. Hindle, eds., *The Republic of Letters in America: The Correspondence of John Peale Bishop and Allen Tate* (Lexington: University Press of Kentucky, 1981), 13.

xii   "While I am a woman": CG to WD, undated, DUNC.

PROLOGUE: THE MATRIARCH OF MERRY MONT

1–3   Meriwether family history: compiled from Nelson Heath Meriwether, *The Meriwethers and Their Connections* (Columbia, Mo.: Artcraft Press, 1964); Louisa H. A. Minor, *The Meriwethers and Their Connections* (Albany, N.Y.: Joel Munsell's Sons, 1892); Frances Marion Williams, *The Story of Todd County, Kentucky, 1820–1970* (Nashville: Parthenon Press, 1972); CG, *Narrow Heart* notebooks, CGPU; Caroline Gordon, "That Strange Welsh Look," *Michigan Quarterly Review* 15, no. 3 (Summer 1976): 268–69; CG to NTW, August 16, 1977, CGPU; and "VG."

4   Gordon family history: compiled from Armistead C. Gordon, *William Fitzhugh Gordon* (New York: Neale, 1909); CG, notebooks and lectures, CGPU; "AS"; *AM*; materials from the Disciples of Christ Archives, Nashville; Veronica Makowsky, *Caroline Gordon: A Biography* (New York: Oxford University Press, 1989); and *CC*.

4   "Don't cry, Cousin William!" to "I ain't cryin'": CG, typescript lecture notes, undated, CGPU.

5   "Run, quick!": "NH," 9.

5   "Human religious creeds": Louis Cochran and Bess White Cochran, *Captives of the Word* (Garden City, N.Y.: Doubleday, 1969), ix.

CHAPTER 1: BATTLES AND LEADERS

6   "Better name this child": "NH," 8.

7   "Utterly impossible" and "If I ever": Nancy Gordon to Miss Ella, February 9, 1902, CGPU.

8   "Moving through water": "VG," 519.

8   "A shower of gold coins" to "that was no way out": "NH," 18–19.

9   The Gordon preparatory school: compiled from "Cumberland Lore," *Clarksville [Tenn.] Leaf-Chronicle*, Monday, October 7, 1985, p. 8, cols. 1–2; CG, *Narrow Heart* notebook, CGPU; *AM*, 168–71; and *CC*, 35.

9   "No Gordon can" to "it did not occur to them": CG, *Narrow Heart* notebook, CGPU.

9   Gordon's childhood reading: compiled from CG to RS, May 4, 1971, SPWU; CG to LC, February 4, 1953, CPVU; CG to NTW, undated [January 1953 and fall 1953], CGPU.

10   "Wandered happily along": "NH," 12.

10   They talked about the kin: general information about these scenes on the porch and Caroline Ferguson Meriwether compiled from *Narrow Heart* notebook, CGPU; *SM*; and Danforth Ross, "Caroline Gordon, Uncle Rob, and My Mother," *Southern Quarterly* 28, no. 3 (Summer 1990): 9–22.

10–11   "I don't like your blood" to "anyhow they pleased": CG, *Narrow Heart* notebook, undated, CGPU.

11   "In these days of steam": CG, *Narrow Heart* notebook, CGPU.

11   "I was in the Bloody Tinth": "WR," 124.

12   "Hell on wheels": CG to WD, undated [February 1948], DUNC.

12   "Against the Monstrous": "AS," 433.

13   "Sifted air," no Meriwether cow: *SM*, 6.

13   Do you think, "Miss Carrian": CG to WD, undated [February 1948], DUNC.

13   "Hush dog": CG to SWK, undated, CGPU.

13   "It was too bad": CG to WD, undated, DUNC.

14   Morris tried to blackmail: CG to F. P. W. McDowell, January 22, [1966], CGPU; "HI," 160.

14   Later, when Morris flaunted: CG to MG, March 1, 1963, and August 1, 1965, MGPU.

14   "Too quick on the uptake": CG, *Narrow Heart* notebook, CGPU.

14   "Caroline Meriwether Gordon": "NH," 9.

14–15   "A perfect Gordon": "VG," 521.

15   "No member": CG, notes for *Joy of the Mountains*, February 5, 1975, CGPU.

15   "If a dog": "NH," 9.

15–16   On J. M. Gordon: compiled from "NH"; CG, *Narrow Heart* notebook, CGPU; and *SM*, 143.

16   "Powers bordering": *AM*, 295.

16   "As if borne" to "Sometimes the Black Bass": *AM*, 293.

16   "All those mediocre people": *CS*, 6. Information on the family re-
      unions compiled from Harnett T. Kane and Ella Bentley Arthur,
      Dear Dorothy Dix (New York: Doubleday, 1952), 229–30.

16–17 "Pious old cousin" to "mad as hell": CG to WD, undated [1950–
      55?], DUNC.

17   On Gordon's religious upbringing and her father's ministry: com-
      piled from the archives of the Disciples of Christ Historical Society,
      Nashville, Tenn.; "VG," 3; interview with NTW, September 11,
      1988, San Cristóbal de las Casas, Chiapas, Mexico.

17   "The theology of the first century": *SM*, 29.

17   "Tired of fishing the same pools": *AM*, 182. Information about
      J. M. Gordon's tenure in Wheeling taken from a typescript by Mar-
      jorie Murphy, "History of the First Christian Church, Wilmington,"
      held in the Clinton County Historical Society, Wilmington, Ohio.

18   Carrie was mortified: W. J. Stuckey, *Caroline Gordon* (New York:
      Twayne, 1972), 12.

18   "I would rather see you": CG, Notes on Dreams, undated, CGPU.

18   Talking nothing but black dialect: CG to AT, September 10, 1955,
      CGPU.

18   "Gentlemen's agreement": *SM*, 30.

18–19 "When she says": CG, Notes on Dreams, undated, CGPU.

19   According to the *Bethany College Bulletin, 1911–1912*, the yearly
      cost for a student at Bethany was between $164.50 and $168.50;
      this included $15.00 in fees, $36.00 for tuition, between $21.00 and
      $25.00 for room rent, and $92.50 for board. Children of ministers
      received a one-third discount off tuition.

19–20 On Gordon's summer studies and arrival at Bethany: "HI," 111–12.

20–21 On Professor Gay: see the *Bethany College Bulletin* and the *Bethanian*
      from 1913 and 1916; "HI," 160.

21   "Sharks," "mastered": "HI," 160. When Gordon began to study
      Greek or Latin, and how proficient she was when she entered col-
      lege, is unclear. According to an article in the *Bethany College Bulle-
      tin*, J. M. Gordon had begun to teach his daughter Greek "when she
      was but six years old." See "Interesting Bits Heard About Bethany
      People," *Bethany College Bulletin* 29 (April 1936). Years later, Gordon
      said she began to learn Latin "around the age of eight" and "began
      to study Greek much later," but she admitted at that time that she
      had a poor memory for dates and often made up numbers just to
      satisfy other people. See her letter to Frederick P. W. McDowell,
      January 22, [1966], CGPU.

21   "Rather down-cast" to "trot": "HI," 160.

21   "Miss Gordon" to "defend his usage": CG, "Learning to Write on
      the University Campus," lecture typescript, CGPU, 22.

22 "Where the Greek tragedians" to "right back to the library": "HI," 160.

22 "The best Greek student": "Interesting Bits Heard About Bethany People," *Bethany College Bulletin* 29 (April 1936).

22 Carrie even received flowers: CG to WD, undated [1949–50], DUNC.

22 "A brilliant mind" to "sisters": Maurine Lappin Coleman, "Alpha Xi Deltas You Would Like to Know: Caroline Gordon Tate," *Alpha Xi Delta* 29, no. 3 (May 1932): 305.

22 "Biz": *Bethanian*, 1915, 162–63.

23 "Commiserated" to "the blood that will": CG, "Learning to Write on the University Campus," lecture typescript, CGPU, 20–21.

23 "Developed of late" to "'orful' hard to leave": *Bethanian*, 1915, 39. Little is known about George Archie Hankins. Although in the 1914 and 1915 Bethany yearbooks, he is listed as a member of the class of 1916, there is no picture of him. Gordon lists only his initials in her notes for her unfinished autobiographical novel. In a letter from her daughter, Nancy Tate Wood, to Allen Tate Wood, October 17, 1966, CGPU, there is a passing reference to the fact that Gordon was once "pinned to a KA." Wood, in an interview in September 1988, remembered that her mother was always very secretive about any past boyfriends. Although Wood did not know the name of her mother's college boyfriend, her husband, Dr. Percy H. Wood, did know that he had been something of a radical student, and he thought that Hankins had been expelled from school for writing something derogatory about Bethany College in the local newspaper.

23–24 The class prophets: ALR and SFB, "Senior Class Prophecy," *Bethanian*, 1916, 119.

24 "Such a bad disposition" to "a mortal sin": CG, Notes on Dreams, undated, CGPU.

24 She was haunted by two deaths: CG, Notes on Dreams, CGPU.

24–25 Despite a glowing recommendation: information about Gordon's activities after graduation compiled from the following: CG to JH, undated [fall 1929], HPBL; *CC*, 36; and Veronica Makowsky, *Caroline Gordon: A Biography* (New York: Oxford University Press, 1989), 40–42.

25 "Why couldn't Lizzie": Kane and Arthur, *Dear Dorothy Dix*, 54.

25 "Do you suppose Carrie": Frances Marion Williams, *The Story of Todd County, Kentucky, 1820–1970* (Nashville: Parthenon Press, 1972), 326.

25–26 "Lived in imagination," "Chekhov's advice": CG, *Narrow Heart* notebook, CGPU.

26 "Because that isn't his name" to "I seen it": CG, "Renews an Acquaintance in Crowded Police Court," *CN*, July 10, 1919, p. 6, cols. 5–6.

26–27 "Novels of adventure" to "You must love it": CG, "Historical Novels Will Again Be Vogue in Short Time, Predicts Francis Lynde," *CN*, July 26, 1919, p. 10, cols. 1–4.

28 Years later Carolyn suggested: *AM*, 228.

28 "The world claims": "Were Billie Crawford's Lips Unsealed: Defense of Dead Girl and Argument for Single Standard of Virtue by Chattanooga Woman," *CN*, August 22, 1919, p. 5, cols. 5–6.

28–29 "First of all, a pioneer" to "lasting and universal": CG, "Books—Good, Bad, Indifferent," *CN*, September 27, 1919, p. 2, cols. 1–3.

29 "Never had a failure": CG, "Book Reviews," *WI*, December 5, 1921, p. 3, col. 1.

29 "Cannot be called a success": CG, "Books—Good, Bad, Indifferent," *CN*, November 15, 1919, p. 10, cols. 3–5.

29 "Quite obscured" to "limited quantity of verbs": CG, "Books—Good, Bad, Indifferent," *CN*, November 8, 1919, p. 6, cols. 6–8.

30 Quoting Joseph C. Lincoln: CG, "Books—Good, Bad, Indifferent," *CN*, October 25, 1919, p. 11, cols. 1–3.

30 "To achieve realism" to "The function of the artist": CG, "Books—Good, Bad, Indifferent," *CN*, November 15, 1919, p. 10, cols. 3–5.

30 "Conventions and traditions" to "something higher": CG, "Books—Good, Bad, Indifferent," *CN*, November 8, 1919, p. 6, cols. 6–8.

30 "The great lyric poet" and "eternal truths": CG, "The Newest Books," *CN*, January 24, 1920, p. 7, col. 2.

30 "Put into words" and "the swing and surge": CG, "Is Kipling True Poet? Is Debatable Point," *CN*, February 7, 1920, p. 5, cols. 5–6.

30 Active in the newspaper fraternity: see "Billy Sunday and His Party Guests of Fourth Estate," *CN*, November 29, 1919, p. 5, cols. 4–5; "Newspaper Men to Play Old Santa Claus to Poor Children," *CN*, November 12, 1919, p. 26, cols. 6–7; "4,000 Enjoy Scribes Huge Christmas Tree," *CN*, December 25, 1919, p. 5, cols. 1–2.

30–31 "Painted a vivid" to "Women have secured": CG, "Wary Bachelors, Lay Low!" *CN*, January 1, 1920, p. 12, cols. 4–7.

31 "Realm of the metaphysical" to "But then, Michael Forth": CG, "New Books," *CN*, January 17, 1920, p. 4, cols. 4–5.

31 "Dedicated to the expression" to "preclude the possibility": CG, "New Books," *CN*, February 28, 1920, p. 8, col. 1.

31–32 On Amélie Rives: Gordon referred to reading Rives in a letter to Francis Fife, August 16, 1977, CGPU. Additional information about Rives is compiled from Welford Dunaway Taylor's *Amélie Rives (Princess Troubetzkoy)* (New York: Twayne, 1973).

32 Carolyn came up with a scheme: according to Ann Waldron, *CC*, 36–37, Gordon was not fired until the spring of 1924. However, I have discovered that Gordon was working for the *News* throughout the spring of 1924. During that period, there is no reference to Jane Snodgrass in any of the reports of the newspaper frater-

nity meetings. Snodgrass is mentioned, however, as being present at meetings during 1919 and 1920. Although I have not discovered any signed articles in the *Times* during the fall of 1920, Carolyn was not working for the *News* yet continued to associate with the newspaper fraternity, according to reports in the *News*. From these stories, and references in the "Society Notes" about her new job at the *Intelligencer* of Wheeling, W.V., I conclude that she joined the *Times* during the summer of 1920 and was fired by the early months of 1921. See "Society Notes," *CN*, March 1, 1921, p. 6, col. 2.

33   An impressive local reputation: many decades after Gordon left Wheeling, articles about her in Bethany College publications referred to her work for the *Intelligencer*. By that time, Gordon had begun to hide or obscure this period of her life. See, for example, "Novelist Visits Campus," *Bethany College Bulletin*, August 1937, 7.

33–34   "It is really surprising" to "there is really a moral obligation": CG, "Book Reviews," *WI*, November 15, 1921, p. 3, cols. 4–7.

34   "A broadside" to "one of the most important": CG, "Book Reviews," *WI*, November 7, 1921, p. 3, cols. 3–4.

34   "Running a bit thin": CG, "Book Reviews," *WI*, October 3, 1921, p. 3, cols. 3–4.

34   "Compromise with magazine traditions": CG, "Book Reviews," *WI*, February 27, 1922, p. 3, cols. 3–5.

34   "A cynic, a rake": CG, "Book Reviews," *WI*, September 19, 1921, p. 3, cols. 4–7.

34   "Delicious satire" and "probably the most immoral": CG, "Book Reviews," *WI*, October 24, 1921, p. 3, cols. 3–4.

34   "We had always liked Madame Petrova": CG, "Madame Petrova Tells Her Idea," *WI*, November 19, 1921, p. 3, col. 2.

35   Carolyn served on the publicity committee: "Women Voters Favor Recall of Council and City Manager," *WI*, September 28, 1921, p. 4, cols. 3–5.

35   "Unofficial statement" and "a club woman": CG, "Club Women Waging Warm Contest for the Presidency," *WI*, October 28, 1921, p. 1, cols. 3–5.

35–36   Carolyn once again had a byline: see, for example, "Has Flapper Gone Forever?" *CN*, October 14, 1922, p. 11, cols. 1–2; "Say 'Chattanooga' of Chickasaw Origin," *CN*, December 9, 1922, p. 4, cols. 5–6; "Chattanooga's Soothsayers," *CN*, November 13, 1922, p. 8, cols. 1–3.

36   "As good a sentence": CG, *Narrow Heart* notebook, CGPU. Information about Gordon's work on her first novel also taken from Makowsky, *Caroline Gordon*, 43.

36   Every night after dinner: CG, Notes on Dreams, March 9, 1954, CGPU.

36 So she wrote Ransom: Louise Cowan, *The Fugitive Group: A Literary History* (Baton Rouge: Louisiana State University Press, 1959), 98.

36–37 "Revival of interest" to "the most radical": CG, "U.S. Best Poets Here in Tennessee," *Chattanooga News*, February 10, 1923, Magazine Section, p. 11, cols. 6–7.

37 That summer: News of Gordon's travels is reported in "Social Notes," *CN*, July 5, 1923, p. 6, col. 5; and August 2, 1923, p. 6, col. 3. Gordon knew no one in New York City except a distant cousin, Walter ("Skip") Meriwether, who was also a newspaperman.

37 In the spring of 1924: "Story in Magazine about Jo Anderson," *Chattanooga Times*, March 8, 1924, p. 6, col. 2; "Readings Heard by the Press Club," *Chattanooga Times*, April 1, 1924, p. 7, cols. 5–7.

38 Carolyn started to cry: CG, *Narrow Heart* notebook, February 1972, CGPU.

38 Years later she claimed: Gordon wrote about her collapse in letters to friends in the summer of 1933. See for example, *SM*, 144. Announcements in the Chattanooga newspapers help to date this illness. According to stories in early April, Gordon was supposed to arrange a luncheon for the Chattanooga Press Club on April 11. But Gordon was relieved of these arrangements shortly before this date, and her signed articles for the *News* stop in mid-April. See "Announcements for Week," *Chattanooga Times*, April 6, 1924, p. 32, cols. 3–4; "Press Club Luncheon," *Chattanooga Times*, April 11, 1924, p. 7, col. 6. Although there was never any reference to Gordon's illness, according to notices in the *News* ("Among the Sick," May 3, 1924, p. 6, col. 4, and May 7, 1924, p. 6, col. 5) the entire Campbell household was sick at this time, the children suffering from whooping cough and Paul Campbell from bronchitis.

38 "There were two": *CC*, 31.

39 On Tate and Warren: information about Warren compiled from Radcliffe Squires, *Allen Tate: A Literary Biography* (New York: Pegasus, Bobbs-Merrill, 1971), 46, 51–53; and Daniel Joseph Singal, *The War Within: From Victorian to Modernist Thought in the South, 1919–1945* (Chapel Hill: University of North Carolina Press, 1982), 342. Information about Tate compiled from Squires, *Allen Tate*, 13–19, 21–30; Allen Tate, *Memoirs and Opinions, 1926–1974* (Chicago: Swallow Press, 1975), 7–8, 16–17, 21; *SM*, 59–60; Danforth Ross, "Memories of Allen Tate," unpublished article, 14.

39 The three spent: *CC*, 30–31.

39 Later, Allen would say: Ross, "Memories of Allen Tate," 8.

39 "He heard": CG to Father William Lynch, undated [1959], CGPU.

39 They made love: *CC*, 32.

CHAPTER 2: FANTASTIC VISION AND
VERY STRANGE SIGHTS

40 The area known as the Village: information compiled from Susan
Edmiston and Linda D. Cirino, eds., *Literary New York: A History
and Guide* (Boston: Houghton Mifflin, 1976), 35–110.

41 "Gleamed blacker": *SM*, 12–13.

41 "Masklike face disappeared" to "a defense": *SM*, 15.

41 "Had known each other": *SM*, 14.

41 Carolyn thought Sally: CG to SWK, undated [1970s], CGPU. Background on Wood compiled from *SM*, 13–15, 146.

42 Allen thought Hart: John Tyree Fain and Thomas Daniel Young,
eds., *The Literary Correspondence of Donald Davidson and Allen Tate*
(Athens: University of Georgia Press, 1974), 120–21.

42 "The whole of literature": Malcolm Cowley, *Exile's Return: A Literary Odyssey of the 1920's* (New York: Viking Press, 1951), 160.

42 "Mystical synthesis": Brom Weber, ed., *The Letters of Hart Crane,
1916–1932* (Berkeley and Los Angeles: University of California
Press, 1965), 124. Information about Crane compiled from Susan
Jenkins Brown, *Robber Rocks: Letters and Memories of Hart Crane*
(Middletown, Conn.: Wesleyan University Press, 1970); Malcolm
Cowley, "Two Winters with Hart Crane," *Sewanee Review* 67 (1959):
549; Cowley, *Exile's Return*, 222.

43 On Gordon's relationship with Tate's literary friends: see the AT and
MC correspondence, as well as letters between MC and Kenneth
Burke, summer 1925, CPNL.

43 "Don't you think": CG to LC and FC, First Sunday in Advent, 1958,
CGPU.

43 On Johnson Features and Rascoe: see Burton Rascoe's autobiographical account, *We Were Interrupted* (Garden City, N.Y.: Doubleday, 1947), 194; Donald M. Hensley, *Burton Rascoe* (New York:
Twayne, 1970), 21–29; and Cowley, *Exile's Return*, 176–77.

43 "Story was half written": *AM*, 295.

43–44 On Texas Guinan: see *SM*, 13; Rascoe, *We Were Interrupted*, 222,
224.

44 Throughout the early months: see *CC*, 40–41.

44 "I'm going to marry": *SM*, 15.

45 None of Allen's close friends: see, for example, letters between MC
and Kenneth Burke during this period, CPNL.

45 When her colleagues wondered: *CC*, 41.

45 Sue Jenkins tried: unsigned, undated letter to Mrs. Anna B. Davis,
"Secretary of the Personal Service Fund," CPNL.

46 "We couldn't buy": Brown, *Robber Rocks*, 31.

46 "Truth incoherent": quoted in William D. Miller, *Dorothy Day: A
Biography* (New York: Harper and Row, 1982), 162. Information

about Day compiled from Miller's book as well as CG interview with Deane Mowrer, May 19, 1970, DDCW; and CG to Dwight McDonald, St. Cyril's Day, 1951, McDY.

46 "Oh, I hope": CG interview with Deane Mowrer, May 19, 1970, DDCW.

46 "Intense desire": CG to Dwight McDonald, St. Cyril's Day, 1951, McDY.

46 Allen was even excited: CG to EL, October 31, 1939, LPVU.

46 Art was their religion: CG interview with Deane Mowrer, May 19, 1970, DDCW; Brown, *Robber Rocks*, 34.

47 "Determined to see *him*" to "He had escaped": *SM*, 16.

47 "Very wicked" and "proud fatherhood": Fain and Young, *Correspondence of Davidson and Tate*, 144–45.

47 "Seemed set against": *CC*, 43.

48 "It struck everybody" to "allowed to have her own": *SM*, 17.

48 "Rotten" to "through the motions": *SM*, 18.

49 "Keep warm and pay": Cowley, "Two Winters," 550.

49 Hart loved the area: John Unterecker, *Voyager: A Life of Hart Crane* (New York: Farrar, Straus and Giroux, 1969), 417–19.

49 "Developed a whole new set" to "a wonderful countryman": *SM*, 19.

49 "Constricted his imagination": Unterecker, *Voyager*, 433.

50 "Kodak pictures": *SM*, 19.

50 "Wasn't any good": Veronica Makowsky, *Caroline Gordon: A Biography* (New York: Oxford University Press, 1989), 71.

51 "Fell violently in love" to "pathetic elderly person": *SM*, 24.

51 "Mr. Crane's *so* sensitive": Brown, *Robber Rocks*, 56.

51 "Bury [his] pride" to "my poem was progressing": Unterecker, *Voyager*, 434.

51 "A fine poet . . . but God save me": *SM*, 21–22.

51–52 "Darling little white room" to "I'm not bored": *SM*, 22.

52 "Slowly increasing madness" to "Any moment": *SM*, 21.

52 "We hang on": CG to MC and Peggy Cowley, undated [spring 1926], CPNL.

52 "It seems that": *SM*, 24.

52 "Only for a visit" to "to jeopardize": *SM*, 22.

52 "As wily and designing": *SM*, 24.

52–53 "Work out some system" to "have a more varied": *SM*, 22.

53 "The impression of babes" to "the grocer refuses": MC to Kenneth Burke, July 26, 1926, CPNL.

53 "Rather like Allen" to "bad end": *SM*, 27.

53–54 "Medieval" to "to gain her own ends": *SM*, 29.

54 "When it comes": *SM*, 27.

54 "The strangest attitude" to "a more integrated person": *SM*, 30.

54–55 "When an author": CG, "Books—Good, Bad, Indifferent," *CN*, October 25, 1919, p. 11, cols. 1–3.

55　"Rather hectic": *SM*, 31.

55　Allen was more sensitive: see letters between AT, Josephson, and MC in CPNL, as well as AT to Arthur Mizener, August 7, 1968, MPVU.

55　"A nice girl" to "the Culture hounds": CG to SWK, undated [1927], CGPU.

55　"Somehow like a British version": Robert Lowell's description, quoted in Arthur Mizener, *The Saddest Story* (New York: World, 1971), xx.

55　"Behemoth in gray tweeds": Herbert Gorman, "Ford Madox Ford: A Portrait in Impressions," *Bookman* 67 (March 1928): 56.

55–56　"Quiet, absent-looking blue eyes": Mizener, *The Saddest Story*, 21. All information about Ford's activities is compiled from Mizener's biography. According to Mizener, Gordon did not begin to work for Ford until the fall of 1927; letters from Gordon to Sally Wood, CGPU, suggest, however, that she began to work for Ford in the late fall or winter of 1926–27.

56　"Awfully nice" to "elegant manner": *SM*, 31. Although this letter is dated fall 1927 by Sally Wood, it was more likely written in late 1926 or early 1927: Gordon refers to Ford's plans to return to France in February.

56　"Sought after": CG to Arthur Mizener, September 23, 1968, FMFC. See also Mizener, *The Saddest Story*, 359.

56　"Lapses into Americanisms" to "*do* you spell": *SM*, 31.

56　"Deep and passionate interest": CG to AB, undated [August 2, 1956], BPPU.

56　"Such a nice fellow" to "something terrible": Mizener, *The Saddest Story*, 359.

57　"Emma Cinina Elena": *SM*, 33.

57　"Hell hound": CG to SWK, November 20, 1927, CGPU.

57　On Andrew Lytle: see James Kilgo, "Andrew Lytle," in *Dictionary of Literary Biography*, ed. James E. Kibler, Jr. (Detroit: Gale Research, 1980), 6:183–92; as well as Paul K. Conkin, *The Southern Agrarians* (Knoxville: University of Tennessee Press, 1988), 61.

58　"Humph, that's ver' nice" to "Nothing happened": William J. Stuckey, *Caroline Gordon* (New York: Twayne, 1972), 13. Stuckey mistakenly says that this incident occurred while Gordon was a secretary to Ford in 1924. Notes found in CGPU indicate that "Old Mrs. Llewellyn" was the first story she wrote. The return address of "Carolyn Gordon, 27 Bank Street," dates this story, and comments in letters to Sally Wood confirm that she must have written it during the summer of 1927. Since Ford returned to New York during the fall of 1927, it is likely she showed him "Old Mrs. Llewellyn" at this time.

58–59　"In a moment she knew" to "old people [were] better" CG, "Old

Mrs. Llewellyn," typescript, CGPU.

59−60 "The worst spoiled child" to "fine pre-Revolutionary": *SM*, 35.

60 "The Cabinet of Dr. Caligari" to "everyone was crazy": *SM*, 34.

60 "Go on, Daddy" to "It's mighty thin": *SM*, 35.

60 "I have little to show": *SM*, 36.

60 "Time had not come": CG to JH, February 11, 1929, HPBL.

60 Allen tried to help: AT to James S. Wilson, May 8, 1928, and James S. Wilson to CG, May 16, 1928, VQUV.

60 "It is these young poets" to "they call us up": *SM*, 36.

61 No matter what the philistine: see Elinor Langer, *Josephine Herbst: The Story She Could Never Tell* (Boston: Little, Brown, 1983), 89−92. Langer does not mention Gordon in this instance, but other sources for this period indicate that she was a part of many of these discussions. Although Gordon destroyed Herbst's letters, Herbst preserved the letters that Gordon wrote to her, and a number of these letters (and letters between Gordon and Porter) indicate that Gordon shared these women's views at this time in her life. All subsequent biographical information about Herbst is compiled from Langer's biography.

61 "One day she would write": Joan Givner, *Katherine Anne Porter: A Life* (New York: Simon and Schuster, 1982), 18. All subsequent biographical information about Porter is compiled from this book.

63 "My God!": *CC*, 61.

63 "You are straining your mind": Allen Tate, *Memoirs and Opinions, 1926−1974* (Chicago: Swallow Press, 1975), 16−17.

63 "Mama, we got to go now": *CC*, 61.

63 "Stupefied and appalled": *SM*, 37.

63 "Time for the annual irruption" to "That is my Yurrup hat": *SM*, 39.

63 Carolyn used bribery: CG to Virginia Tunstall, undated [fall 1928], TPUV.

63 "The author of Stonewall Jackson": *SM*, 39.

64 "Get the place" to "sort of suspended": *SM*, 41.

64 "I shall probably be living": Nancy Gordon to CG, undated [fall 1928], CGPU.

64 "Where's the captain?": CG to Virginia Tunstall, undated [fall 1928], TPUV.

64 "A fearful voyage" and "got quite morbid": *SM*, 41.

64 "Really quite terrible creatures" to "the wife": *SM*, 42.

64 "Worked like hell": *SM*, 44.

65 "The town best organized": Ernest Hemingway, *A Moveable Feast* (New York: Charles Scribner's Sons, 1964), 182.

65 "Bright remarks" to "big enough for a young baby": CG to Nancy Gordon, December 19, [1928], CGPU.

65−66 "Did not have to suffer" and "muffled in cotton": CG to JH, February 11, 1929, HPBL.

66 "Getting up": CG to KAP, undated [November 1931], KAPM.

66 "Grand little maid," "typing madly": *SM*, 46.

66 "The foreign relations of the Confederacy": CG to May Morse, undated [summer 1929], CGPU.

67 "Freedom" from "that damn book": *SM*, 46. In *Memoirs and Opinions*, 56, Tate said he finished the book on Bastille Day, but he was writing in the late 1960s or early 1970s. I believe Gordon's date is more reliable, because she referred to it in several letters written during the summer of 1929.

67 "Spending his grandmother's legacy": *SM*, 46.

67 "Probably bewilder that dame a good bit": CG to JH, March 22, 1929, HPBL. See also *CC*, 69; and Brown, *Robber Rocks*, 117.

67 "There's Monsieur": *SM*, 45.

67 "Allen and I": *SM*, 47.

68 "Nibbling around the edges" to "My time": CG to JH, February 11, 1929, HPBL.

68 "The best piece of writing": *SM*, 48.

68 "Turned down": CG to KAP, undated [spring/summer 1930], KAPM.

68–70 "A dusty country road" to "I'm not a nigger!": CG, "Summer Dust," *Gyroscope* 1 (November 1929).

71–72 "Burst out" to "We thought": CG to JH, undated [fall 1929], HPBL.

72 "Revolution in the English language": Cowley, *Exile's Return*, 276.

72 "Their banal and ungrammatical" to "God, how fast": *SM*, 47.

72 "No interest": CG to JH, February 11, 1929, HPBL.

72–73 "A pleasant way" to "They are all just a trick": CG to JH, October 6, 1929, and undated [late fall 1929], HPBL.

73 "Entirely true to life": JMG to CG, December 12, 1929, CGPU.

74 "Edward Faylee" to "That's right": CG, "Funeral in Town," *Westminster Magazine*, 1935, 278–94.

74 "Very pleasing" to "And I spent": CG to JH, undated [fall 1929], HPBL.

74 Ford decided he had fallen in love with Carolyn: according to Makowsky, Ford actually "proposed to Caroline in a Parisian church, of all places." See *Caroline Gordon*, 87. However, Makowsky's source for this information is an interview with Gordon shortly before her death in 1981. Gordon never mentioned this proposal to anyone at any other time, and at the end of her life, she had a tendency to glamorize and elaborate on old stories. She also told bald-faced lies. For example, she claimed to have burnt all the letters which Ford sent her, but a fairly complete collection of these letters is on deposit in the Princeton University Library. These letters do indicate that Ford was in love with her, but there is no mention of any proposal. There is also evidence in letters to her friends written between 1929

and 1930 that Gordon knew better than to take Ford's attentions seriously.

75   "Rather fun sometimes" to "I get so sick": CG to KAP, undated [November 1931] and undated [spring 1932], KAPM.

75   "Made himself quite a nuisance" to "victim to Scott's delusions": as reported in Thomas Daniel Young and John J. Hindle, eds., *The Republic of Letters in America: The Correspondence of John Peale Bishop and Allen Tate* (Lexington: University Press of Kentucky, 1981), 16.

75   "You and your wife": Tate, *Memoirs and Opinions*, 47.

75–76   "The flower of American genius" to "how many street car": CG, "A Certain Man . . . A Certain Woman," lecture typescript, CGPU. See also Tate, *Memoirs and Opinions*, 64–66.

76   "She will treat you": *SM*, 127.

76   "Habit of rising" to "Never did I see": *SM*, 51.

77   "I *hated* leaving" to "*Please* write": *SM*, 49.

77–78   "Would go mad" to "I didn't want to": CG to LA, undated [January–March 1930], LABL.

78   "I debate": *SM*, 52.

78   "You can't finish": CG to LA, undated [January–February 1930], LABL.

78   "Any place where": *SM*, 50.

78   Although J. M. Gordon: see letters from JMG to the Tates in CGPU, as well as letters from CG to JH, undated, HPBL; and AT to AL, June 16, 1929, LPVU.

78   "I know she" to "She regards living": *SM*, 50–51.

79   "Didn't bring the whole book": CG to JH, undated [spring 1930], HPBL.

79   When Bernard Bandler: CG's letter to Bandler does not survive. See Bandler's letters to CG about the story and her response to its rejection, January 21, 1930, and January 24, 1930, HHBU.

79   "Kind of helpless fury" to "And why not more courage": KAP to JH, undated [spring 1930], KAPM.

79   "This year or come very near dying": CG to LA, undated [January–February 1930], LABL. See also FMF to CG, February 24, 1930, CGPU.

80   "I . . . told him" to "the only publishing person": CG to JH, undated [spring 1930], HPBL.

80   "You have served your apprenticeship" to "If you & Allen": JMG to CG, December 12, 1929, CGPU.

CHAPTER 3: THE CHINS ARE IMMACULATE

81   "That's the house": CG to JH, undated, HPBL.

81–82   "Probably the most beautiful hill" to "when the lights": *SM*, 54.

82 "Unpretentious affair": CG to KAP, March 11, 1930, KAPM.

82 "Just in the suburbs": AT to MC, May 3, 1930, CPNL.

82 "Discourse on the habits of bream": CG to KAP, March 11, 1930, KAPM.

83 "I have actually been *afraid*": CG to MP, March 11, 1930, SAPU.

83 "One of the sweetest": CG to JH, undated [spring 1930], HPBL.

83 "I am a little Homerican": *SM*, 55.

83–84 "A load of plaster" to "No plaster": CG to MG and Polly Gordon, February 16, 1967, MGPU.

84 "I was writing": CG to JH, undated, HPBL.

84 "Recommendations from a good many": CG to JH, May 13, 1930, HPBL. See also AT to Edmund Wilson, May 13, 1930, EWBL; CG to LA, undated, LABL; AT to KAP, January 21, 1962, KAPM.

84 "I wish to God": CG to KAP, undated [spring 1930], KAPM.

84–85 On Confederate Memorial Day: see AT to "Confederates," with postscript by CG, June 5, 1930, DPVU; AT to Donald Davidson, June 9, 1930, DPVU; AT to AL, June 9, 1930, LPVU.

85 "I developed": CG to LA, undated [summer 1930], LABL.

85 "Here we are": CG to JH, undated, HPBL.

86 "I say let all": *SM*, 52.

86 On Gordon's role in *I'll Take My Stand*, see Conkin, 94.

87 But Caroline switched: for example, Ralph is heavy, too heavy, finally, to ride the horses he loves so well, like Gordon's own father. Nicholas is known to sit beneath the silver poplar in the front of Penhally, just as Gordon's grandfather, Douglas Meriwether, often did.

88 "It would have been better": Mitzi Berger Hamovitch, *The "Hound and Horn" Letters* (Athens: University of Georgia Press, 1982), 107.

88 "Right way to write a novel": *SM*, 91.

88 "Would not sue her": *SM*, 60.

88–89 "Powers," she mused. "That's a good" and "They all said": *CS*, 239.

89 "They write me," "take of my stories": *SM*, 62.

89 "Writing short stories": *SM*, 61.

89 Oh, no, you mustn't: CG to FMF, undated, FMFC.

89 "Hardly got its sheets": *SM*, 62.

90 "Worked up into quite a book": *SM*, 64.

90 "One or two essays that might be dispensed with": CG to KAP, undated, KAPM.

90 "The Symposiers are having a great time": *SM*, 60.

90 "Our conversations are all highly military": *SM*, 64.

90 "Wagging long grey beards": CG to Mark Van Doren, undated [November 14, 1930], VDPC.

90 "What a wonderful man" to "some remark tending": CG to KAP, undated [fall 1930], KAPM.

91 "Pacing about the house": *SM*, 64–65.

91 "Imagined things were given": SWK to CG, undated, CGPU.

91 "Emma Cinina Elena": *SM*, 60.

91–92 "Conflict of the action" to "a constant weaving": CG, "Plans for Study," 1930 Guggenheim application, JSGF.

92 "Knock off a few short stories": *SM*, 62. See also MP to CG, November 14, 1930, SAPU.

92 "I will have": CG to MP, November 17, 1930, SAPU.

92 "Tragic and gruesome": MP to CG, January 5, 1931, SAPU.

92 "Handlin' a dead Yankee": *CS*, 168.

92 "There ain't a whole man in ary one": *CS*, 174.

92–93 "Fine story," a "noble tale" to "There are other magazines": KAP to CG, January 12, 1931, CGPU.

93 "Caroline had treated": *SM*, 71.

93 "Head under a pump" to "a little further": *SM*, 71–72.

93 "It has had a little private circulation": *SM*, 72.

93 "The only editor in the country": CG to Lincoln Kirstein, undated [1931], CGPU.

93 "Largest tooth I own": *SM*, 68.

93–94 "Persists in regarding this damn novel" to "nothing to do": *SM*, 70.

94 On "Chain Ball Lightning": MP to CG, February 6, 1931, SAPU.

94 "Developing the true landlord spirit" to "the one true agrarian": *SM*, 68–69.

94 "It don't make no difference": *SM*, 75.

95 "Like one of these women" to "You can just see": *SM*, 76.

95 "The picture he had" to "a trick": CG to JH, undated, HPBL.

95–96 "The title does not convey" to "'Llewellyn's Choice' would": CG to MP, undated, SAPU.

96 "To be an old-fashioned sort of title" to "a character's choice": MP to CG, April 3, 1931, SAPU.

96 "Horrible book": *SM*, 76.

96 "A state of complete moral deterioration": *SM*, 78.

96 "Very set ideas": CG to FMF, undated, FMFC.

96 "Simply would not do": *SM*, 78.

96 "As if by the wave": CG to FMF, undated, FMFC. No drafts of this novel survive, but Gordon described her original ending in this letter.

97 "There must be some symbol" to "read the book over": CG to FMF, undated, FMFC.

97 "So bad" to "I keep wondering": *SM*, 80.

97 "It might be better": CG to MP, June 8, 1931, SAPU.

97 "The state of mind in Chance": MP to CG, July 15, 1931, SAPU.

97–98 "Most novel readers": MP to CG, July 27, 1931, SAPU.

98 "Wandering around shakily" to "I can't believe": CG to KAP, undated, KAPM.

98 "A frightful season": *SM*, 82.

98 "If the kin don't come" to "I'm nervous": *SM*, 86.

98 "My book came out": *SM*, 87.

99 "My cows won't touch onions": *SM*, 91.

99 "Write a book like Mama" to "Mama has nearly": *SM*, 89. For Tate's opinions of the novel, see AT to AL, July 28, 1931, LPVU; AT to Don Davidson, August 1, 1931, DPVU; AT to RPW, August 16, 1931, RPWB.

99 "Distinguished book" to "the way you start": Lincoln Kirstein to CG, September 5, 1931, CGPU.

99 "That the book attempted to show" to "It should have been written": *SM*, 88.

99 "Curious experiment": anonymous review, *Boston Transcript*, November 18, 1931, 2.

99 "The book [was] never more than mildly moving": anonymous review, "A Southern Mansion," *New York Times Book Review*, September 20, 1931, 6–7.

99 "Here is a first novel" to "The book is evidently": CG to MP, undated, SAPU.

99–100 "Three years I've been working": CG to KAP, undated, KAPM.

100 "I am sure": CG to MP, undated, SAPU.

100–101 "How much I was absorbed": SY to CG, Friday [December 18, 1931], in John Pilkington, ed., *Stark Young: A Life in the Arts* (Baton Rouge: Louisiana State University Press, 1975), 1:382–83.

101 Women's screams served as bookends: see Anne M. Boyle, "The Unendurable Feminine Consciousness: A Study of the Fiction of Caroline Gordon" (Ph.D. dissertation, University of Rochester, 1983), 24.

102 "Ne'er do well": *PN*, 203.

102 "Folks sitting on the porch": *PN*, 42.

102 "A cold proposition": *PN*, 143.

102 "Spoiled little hussy": *PN*, 147.

102 She had bad "blood": *PN*, 181.

103 "As deeply tanned" to "Well, I am a poor white": *PN*, 185.

104 "Lucy was inordinately proud": *PN*, 196.

104 "Thin and dark" to "spirited": *PN*, 214.

104 "They had left her": *PN*, 253.

104 "Faint, hard lines" to "But it was harder": *PN*, 251.

104–5 "If she stayed here": *PN*, 249.

105 "Flicking with her crop": *PN*, 256.

105 "Silvania, The Brackets": *PN*, 261.

105 "Coming on her" to "a happy time": *PN*, 262–63.

106 "Why couldn't she amuse": *PN*, 267.

106 "I'll tell you": *PN*, 269.

107–8 "Through the length": *PN*, 43–44.

108   "I hope nothing": MP to CG, July 28, 1931, SAPU.

108   "It is, certainly, much harder" to "I am very fierce": CG to MP, August 1, 1931, SAPU.

108–9   "It's just Mister Balch" to "stowaway": *SM*, 87. For information on Gordon's and Warren's proposed contribution to the Lee biography, see AT to RPW, August 9, 1931, and August 16, 1931, RPWB.

109   "Such a funny affair" to "got up and announced": *SM*, 91.

109   "Only person who conducted himself" to "Thank God it wasn't": CG to LA, undated, LABL. Additional information about Faulkner's behavior at the conference compiled from Stephen B. Oates, *William Faulkner: The Man and the Artist* (New York: Harper and Row, 1987), 108–9.

109   "Come out of the South" to "or it would be wonderful": CG to FMF, undated [December 1931], FMFC.

110   "It is too much trouble": CG to LA, undated, LABL.

110   "Much ashamed" to "by telling her": CG to JH, undated, HPBL.

110   "A dozen other villainies" to "piously murmuring": CG to RPW, undated, RPWB.

110   "Entirely in a contemporary light": CG, 1932 Guggenheim application, JSGF.

110   "Allen thinks I have a chance": *SM*, 92.

110   "Atmosphere of tremendous excitement": CG to FMF, undated, FMFC.

111   "People don't appreciate the Cherokee" to "Little Indian children": CG to LA, undated, LABL.

111   "The exploits of some of those pioneer women": CG to FMF, undated, FMFC.

111   "Getting un-agrarian": CG to LA, undated, LABL.

111   The Tates were independently wealthy: Lutie Jones to James Gordon Hackett, November 27, 1931, James Gordon Hackett Papers, Duke University, Durham, N.C.

111   "If I'm going to starve": CG to KAP, undated, KAPM.

111   "From the poorest member of the family": CG to RPW, undated [December 1931], RPWB.

111   "The best constructed novel": Ford Madox Ford, "A Stage in American Literature," *Bookman* 74 (1931): 373.

111   "*Penhally* is the triumphant tragedy": Ford, "Stage," 374.

111–12   "What you have said" to "I can only remind you": CG to FMF, undated, FMFC.

112   "Magazine does not think": telegram from MP to CG, January 13, 1932, SAPU.

112   "Story interest!": CG to RPW, undated, RPWB. According to this letter, Tate wrote to Perkins for Gordon. The letter that Gordon signed, however, said nothing that Gordon had not said elsewhere.

Also, it is not dated, which is typical for Gordon but very unusual for Allen Tate. It is likely that Gordon wrote at least part, if not all, of the letter.

112   "If murder" to "I am not only": CG to MP, undated [January 13, 1932], SAPU.

112   "The reply which came": CG to RPW, undated, RPWB.

112–13   "Editing is not easy either" to "her past life began": MP to CG, January 16, 1932, SAPU.

113   "Roseate hopes" to "little things struck off": CG to RPW, undated, RPWB.

113   "I owe her three weeks back wages" and "This all comes": CG to KAP, undated, KAPM.

113   Things could not get any worse: CG to FMF, February 28, [1932], FMFC.

113   "Solitary condition": CG to SWK, undated [early summer 1931], CGPU.

113   "I was a month": CG to SWK, undated [March 12, 1932], CGPU. This letter was published in *SM*, but reference to Gordon's pregnancy and abortion was omitted.

114   "Rush of dish washing" to "I'm fed up": *SM*, 100.

114   "What you going to do" to "The chins are immaculate": *SM*, 99–100.

CHAPTER 4: PORTRAITS OF THE ARTIST

115   "Contrived and concocted": *SM*, 112.

115   "A certain steely glint": CG to KAP, undated, KAPM.

115   "The most horrible spots": *SM*, 112.

116   "You can't go backward": "GM," 22.

116   "One of the most powerful": "GM," 25.

116   "Made a point": "GM," 27.

116   "If you look": "GM," 33.

117   "Don't say another word": "GM," 6.

117   "Say the wrong word": "GM," 8.

117   "That stuffy old": "GM," 19.

117   "Read the man's mind": "GM," 21.

117   "A very special kind" to "as might be expected": "GM," 28–29.

118   "All pretty sad and mad" to "pretended to abandonment": CG to KAP, undated, KAPM.

118   "It is hard to put," "could do a hell": *SM*, 114.

118–19   "Stare at the green fields" to "by one of those men": CG to KAP, undated, KAPM.

119   "Loulie would be": *SM*, 118.

120   "Preserve a semblance": CG to FMF, June 18, [1932], FMFC.

120   "After a somewhat intensive training" and "practically a Meriwether": *SM*, 102.

120   "The Meriwethers are all louts": CG, *Narrow Heart* notebook, CGPU.

120   "Would have been completely demoralized" to "As if you didn't *prefer*": *SM*, 115.

120   "There is something about putting the ocean": *SM*, 111.

121   "Hard to concentrate": CG to KAP, undated, KAPM.

121   "Demanded to know" to "flew into such a passion": CG to RPW and Cinina Warren, undated, RPWB.

121   "Pure pride of the professional" to "He needs one": CG to KAP, undated, KAPM.

121–22   "Slavic eyes" to "Ah, that clear bell like": CG to LA, undated, LABL.

122–23   "There was no room" to "a hell of a time": CG to KAP, undated, KAPM.

123   "So that it should click into place": CG to JB, undated, FMFC.

123   "Historical imagination": see Thomas Daniel Young and John J. Hindle, eds., *The Republic of Letters in America: The Correspondence of John Peale Bishop and Allen Tate* (Lexington: University Press of Kentucky, 1981), 76.

123   "Knowing how to write": *SM*, 135.

123   "We have no money at all, as usual": CG to KAP, undated, KAPM.

123–24   "Any chance in the world" to "could only be free": CG to Henry Allen Moe, November 2, 1932, JSGF.

124   "Constantly 'explaining' things": Thomas Daniel Young and Elizabeth Sarcone, eds., *The Lytle-Tate Letters: The Correspondence of Andrew Lytle and Allen Tate* (Jackson: University Press of Mississippi, 1987), 70.

124   "Crawling through a fog": CG to JB and FMF, undated, FMFC.

124   "Like a bird on a bough": CG to KAP, undated, KAPM.

124   "You can work better" to "We are both working like hell": *SM*, 124.

124   "The glow of conscious virtue": *SM*, 125.

124   "Islands" of peace which happened "about once a year": *SM*, 124.

125   "My God, look": *SM*, 126.

125   "Yes, it's Gertrude Stein" to "I'm trying to write a novel": *SM*, 127.

125   "Tate, it's too bad you've stopped writing poetry": see Allen Tate, *Memoirs and Opinions, 1926–1974* (Chicago: Swallow Press, 1975), 58; and CG to JB, undated, FMFC.

125   "Come across," "he is a hard hearted devil": *SM*, 128.

125   "Sinking into the period": *SM*, 130.

125   "Best, even for the unfortunate debtors": *SM*, 126.

126   "She is one": CG to FMF, undated, FMFC.

126   "Grande dame," "femme du monde": Joan Givner, *Katherine Anne Porter: A Life* (New York: Simon and Schuster, 1982), 275.

126   "Sounded like somebody" and "Why didn't she": *SM*, 131.

127   "Well up under his chin": *CS*, 43.

127   "Looked so much like him": *CS*, 43.

127   "She was, after all": *CS*, 47.

128   "Infected already": *CS*, 43.

128   "Like that of a person submerged": *CS*, 53.

128   "I am at last convinced": CG to MP, January 15, 1933, SAPU.

128   "It's not one of my best": *SM*, 133.

128   "Really more interested": *SM*, 137.

128   "The illness coincided": *SM*, 131.

128   "Put the ocean": *SM*, 132.

129   "Through the motions": *SM*, 131.

129   "If he can just get": *SM*, 133.

129   "For some years" to "seems to me a thing": CG to Kirstein, undated, HHBU.

129   "Decision necessary": telegram from CG to Henry Allen Moe, February 8, 1933, JSGF.

130   "Be a relief to get home in a way" to "We can live at Merry Mont": *SM*, 139–40.

130   "Okay" and "hot dog": *SM*, 140–41.

130   "I am saving" to "pretty wide spread": CG to MP, undated, SAPU.

130   "Rich and strange": *SM*, 141.

130   "Two hundred dollars": CG to MP, March 4, 1933, SAPU.

130   "The rocky slopes of Benfolly": CG to JH, undated, HPBL.

130   "If I could ever get": CG to JB, undated, FMFC.

131   "The bank had to admit": CG to JB, March 15, [1933], FMFC.

131   "It is a mighty low price": MP to CG, March 23, 1933, SAPU.

131   "More good than any": CG to Henry Allen Moe, March 23, 1933, JSGF.

131   "I find I work very well": CG to MP, March 30, 1933, SAPU.

131   "Most people would": CG to MC, undated, CPNL.

132   "One of the nicest *northern*": Young and Sarcone, *The Lytle-Tate Letters*, 84.

132   "With a perfect East Tennessee accent": CG to FMF, undated, FMFC.

132   "Any story of mine": *SM*, 142.

132   "Niggers to get" to "sinister": *SM*, 144–45.

132–33   What bothered him the most: see Tate's letters to SWK during the fall and winter of 1945–46, CGPU.

133   "You run around" to "Well, all right": *SM*, 145.

134   On Marion Henry: compiled from interviews with NTW, September 1988, San Cristóbal de las Casas, Chiapas, Mexico; AT to AL, November 4, 1932, LPVU; *CC*, 127.

135   "You need a vacation" to "I am leaving": *SM*, 144–45.

135   "A sort of spiritual slump": CG to KAP, undated, KAPM.

135   "Going to Merry Mont was a mistake": *SM*, 144. This letter is misdated by Wood; it was probably written in August.

135–36   "She has always been poor": CG to FMF, undated, FMFC.

136   "The discrepancy between the outward significance and the private": Young and Hindle, *Republic of Letters*, 84.

136   "The nervous strain" to "throwing off the shackles": *SM*, 151–52.

136   "Extremely fine": MP to CG, August 21, 1933, SAPU.

136   "The delights of sin": *SM*, 149.

136–37   "In no shape" to "evidently works of art": *SM*, 146.

137   "A relaxation and a sort of labor of love": *SM*, 146.

137   "A book almost written": CG to MP, undated, SAPU. MP's response is dated October 17, 1933.

137   "Pleasant work, rather like knitting": CG to FMF, undated, FMFC.

137   "History of a life": CG to MP, undated, SAPU.

137   "Arbitrarily at some place like White Oak": *SM*, 146.

137   "Became a great man": CG to FMF, undated, FMFC.

138   "What were the names" to "a touch of scorn": *AM*, 296.

138   "My uncle, James Morris": CG to KAP, undated, KAPM.

138   "Upset his mind": *SM*, 150.

138   "As time went on" to "Caroline! This is good": *AM*, 297. He probably yelled, "Carolyn!" since he always addressed his daughter in that fashion. See also *SM*, 150.

138   "It makes me very stupid": *SM*, 152.

139   "Too late now": *SM*, 153. When "Old Red" appeared in the December issue of *Scribner's*, it had already been published in England in the *Criterion*, which T. S. Eliot edited. For the *Scribner's* publication, Gordon "lopped off the ending" of the story, "finishing it up with the fox taking to earth," although she didn't know if shortening the story helped any.

139–40   "I had to rewrite" to "It is rather a disadvantage": letter and outline from CG to MP, undated, SAPU.

140   "Shows how a man" to "too deeply upon sport": MP to CG, January 16, 1934, SAPU.

140   "Published on the strength" to "I happened to make": *SM*, 161.

140   "Through another's mind," "marvelous effect": CG to LA, undated, LABL.

140   "All is very fecund": *SM*, 164.

140   "Where chickens, dogs, cows": Young and Hindle, *Republic of Letters*, 99.

140   She could deliver: telegram from CG to MP, June 7, 1934, SAPU.

141   "Would not be a matter" to "in paying advances": MP to CG, June 7, 1934, SAPU.

141   "Steady work," "The pressure on me": CG to MP, undated, SAPU.

141   "Boarding school style" to "inmates": CG to AL, undated [July 12–13, 1934], LPVU.

141 "What did you put" to "Daughter, this is": CG to KAP, undated, KAPM.

141 "A person as ignorant" to "stick to [her] own": CG to AL, undated [July 12–13, 1934], LPVU.

142 "Kind, motherly woman": *AM*, 73.

143 Caroline would later joke: CG to FMF, undated, FMFC. In a letter to KAP, undated, KAPM, Gordon suggested another version of the title: *Portrait of the Artist as Sportsman*.

143 "No woman's hand had tended Oakleigh": *AM*, 5.

143 "Best Greek scholar": *AM*, 28.

144 "An ardent Catholic": *AM*, 53–54.

144 "Dear Aunt Vic!": *AM*, 55.

144 "A high sense of duty": *AM*, 59.

144 "Was pale and the lines around her mouth were deep-carved": *AM*, 126–27.

145 "That remarkable woman knew": *AM*, 130.

145 "She was a perfect Maury": *AM*, 130.

145 "It wouldn't kill you": *AM*, 285.

146 "It could have been": CG to AL, undated [July 12–13, 1934], LPVU.

146 "Too much like a real memoir": MP to CG, August 7, 1934, SAPU.

146 "Would gain [a] special audience": telegram from MP to CG, August 21, 1934, SAPU.

146 "Have no selling judgment": telegram from CG to MP, August 22, 1934, SAPU.

146 "A sportsman," "too indefinite," "passion": telegram from CG to MP, August 23, 1934, SAPU.

147 "If any purist": CG to MP, undated, SAPU.

147 Caroline felt sick about the title: *SM*, 168.

147 "Too hot to sleep": *SM*, 165.

147 "Fate had at least spared me": CG to KAP, undated, KAPM.

147 "Jubilant," "so much better in town": CG to MP, undated, SAPU.

147–48 "Kept popping in" to "It was a very strange experience": CG to AL, October 24, 1934, LPVU.

148 Hamburger House, "a hamburger on the outside": CG to LA, undated, LABL.

148 "A good Confederate address": *SM*, 166.

148 "By living very close to the knuckle all winter": CG to FMF, undated, FMFC.

148 "A cotton country" to "He had a better ear": CG to LA, undated, LABL.

148 "It wasn't that I didn't have plenty of time": CG to KAP, undated, KAPM.

149 "I wished that the day": *CS*, 103.

150 "Another reporting job": CG to RPW, undated, RPWB.

150 "On the outside pretty good": *SM*, 168.

150   "Neither of my books" to "would have made the book": *SM*, 172.

150   "It's one of my faults as a writer": *SM*, 171.

150   "The thing when it is said" to "Even so it should have": *SM*, 172.

150   "A fine, virile note": CG to MP, undated, SAPU.

150   "A warm hearted human book": *SM*, 169.

150   "Such a sissy first name": CG to MP, undated, SAPU.

150   "Putting the cart before the horse": CG to JB and FMF, undated, FMFC.

150–51   "It marches but is flimsy": CG to FMF, undated, FMFC.

151   "A quiet monologue": FMF to CG, Lord Mayor's Day, 1934, CGPU.

151   "Quality of Turgenev's *Sportsman's Sketches*": FMF to CG, December 4, 1934, CGPU.

151   "The straightest, cleanest, most accurate": JCR to CG, January 24, [1935], CGPU.

151   "Glorious book, a complete success": Davidson to CG, January 6, 1935, CGPU.

151   "The bearded contributor" to "the Hemingway of Cumberland valley": CG to LA, undated, LABL.

151   "A small, inconspicuous review": CG to RPW, undated, RPWB.

151   "Serene, unpretentious, but accomplished": Isabel Paterson quoted in *RG*, 208.

151   "Probably the best chance": CG to KAP, undated, KAPM.

151   "Melted . . . like mist before the debts": *SM*, 173.

151   "A prose Aeneid": Andrew Lytle, "The Passion of Alec [*sic*] Maury," *New Republic*, January 2, 1935, 227.

151–52   "The sense of a full and intense emotional life": Robert Penn Warren, "The Fiction of Caroline Gordon," *Southwest Review* 20 (January 1935): 8.

152   "Missed the point": CG to Donald Davidson, undated, DPVU.

152   "There were no 'problems' in the book": CG to KAP, undated, KAPM. See also CG to LA, undated, LABL, in which Gordon says that the novel "suffered" from the Communist literary vogue.

152   "It's a symptom" to "It's fine masculine prose": KAP to CG, first day of spring, 1935, KAPM.

152   "Privileges which had been monopolized": Caroline Gordon, "Books—Good, Bad, Indifferent," *CN*, September 27, 1919, p. 2, cols. 1–3.

153   "Could write such a book": CG to KAP, undated, KAPM.

CHAPTER 5: THE CUP OF FURY

154   "Go in and out the window," "Grab 'em": CG to KAP, undated, KAPM.

154   Allen kissing her cousin Manny: *CC*, 145.

154 "Perfectly sodden": CG to RPW, undated, RPWB.

154 "There's nothing to do": CG to FMF, undated, FMFC.

155 "I suppose I want to show": CG to MP, December 15, 1934, SAPU.

155 "A time comes": CG to LA, undated, LABL.

155 "I'm going to desert": CG to KAP, undated, KAPM.

155 "The main spectacle" to "because to all intents": CG to MP, undated, SAPU.

155 "Reflective enough to stand up": CG to KAP, undated, KAPM.

155 "Savagery" and "vindictiveness" to "little Lees": CG to MP, undated, SAPU.

155 "Major opus": CG to LA, undated, LABL.

155 "It was the nineteenth of August": quoted in CG to RPW, undated, RPWB.

155 "I seem to have a sort of moral collapse": *SM*, 181.

156 "Rotten review": *SM*, 177. See Caroline Gordon, "The Shadow of Defeat," review of *Act of Darkness*, by John Peale Bishop, *New Republic*, March 27, 1935, 192.

156 "I have only three": *SM*, 175.

156 "If a paralytic": *SM*, 180.

156 "This was the first" to "What do you think": *SM*, 178.

156 "I wonder if Caroline's success": Young and Hindle, *Republic of Letters*, 112.

156 "The vagaries of the artistic": CG to FMF, undated, FMFC.

157 "Quite fat and very wily" to "her wishes gratified": CG to LA, undated, LABL.

157 "Spying around": *SM*, 177.

157 "The revolution" to "under surveillance": CG to KAP, undated, KAPM.

157 On Marked Tree: see *SM*, 182–85; *CC*, 149; CG to AL, undated, LPVU.

158 After Allen threatened: CG to AL, undated, LPVU.

158 "Develop a field technique," "in vain to make him": *SM*, 185.

158 "Primarily artists": CG to John Gould Fletcher, undated, FPUA.

158 "They've formulated the doctrine": *SM*, 185.

158 "Any more communists": CG interview with Deane Mowrer, May 19, 1970, DDCW.

158 "As I get older": CG to KAP, undated, KAPM.

158 "The whole lower floor": CG to AL, undated, LPVU.

159 "I am hoping" to "He says he wants Hart's": CG to KAP, undated, KAPM.

159 "Even in the very rough" to "leader on our list": MP to CG, June 24, 1935, SAPU.

159 "Put the fear of God" to "try to make it": *SM*, 192–93.

160-61 "The life of Fanny Churchill" to "I suppose the point I am trying": CG, synopsis, *The Cup of Fury*, SAPU.

161 "Even in this outline" to "fades out": MP to CG, July 8, 1935, SAPU.

161 "The most difficult for it narrows" to "Val, representing the intellect": CG to MP, undated, SAPU.

161 "We dismissed the cook": CG to LA, undated, LABL.

161 "The lap of luxury": *SM*, 194.

161 "Old dog run cabin": *SM*, 145.

161 "For anybody writing a book": *SM*, 194.

161 "A short, white-haired man," "kindly disposed towards artists": CG, "That Man, Lytle," typescript, 1, CGPU.

161–62 "Visiting instead of being visited" to "revels all day": *SM*, 193.

162 "The air and very much the motion": CG, "That Man, Lytle," 1.

162 "It is hard enough to reject": *SM*, 191–92.

162 "Since Mrs. Lytle's": CG, "That Man, Lytle," 3.

163 "Right torn," "As an overworked professor": *SM*, 193.

163 "Breakfast, work, lunch" to "even Allen wrote": *SM*, 194.

163 "I know I could": CG to AL, September 16, 1935, LPVU.

163 "As they went into the line," "Mama, I don't care": *SM*, 197.

163 "The colors in the park": *SM*, 196.

163–64 "Very simple" to "Waving his bloody right hand": *SM*, 192.

164 "Be built up" to "an afternoon": CG to MP, undated, SAPU.

164–65 "Cut the book off" to "get in enough stuff": CG to MP, undated, SAPU. MP's response is dated October 31, 1935, SAPU.

165–66 "Much good" to "You have it, Old Girl": letters from CG to JH, undated, HPBL.

166 "Hard to focus": CG to JH, undated, HPBL.

166 "Not willing to take a chance": CG to MP, undated, SAPU.

166 "If I were using": CG to MP, December 20, 1935, SAPU.

166 "The effect of the book": CG to MP, November 10, 1935, SAPU.

167 "I'm nervous and sensitive": *PY*, 141.

167 "All I am or hope to be": *SM*, 204.

167 "It is very hard": MP to CG, January 15, 1936, SAPU.

167 "In a dangerous psychical condition" to "spend the next few months": *SM*, 198.

167–68 "A regular book factory": CG to RPW, undated, SRBL.

168 "About a man whose enemy": CG to RPW, undated, SRBL.

168 "Sprout long chin whiskers": letters from CG to RPW, undated, SRBL.

168 "A sort of Wuthering Heights" to "It's true": *SM*, 199.

168 "I'm taking an oath" to "I'd be delighted": CG interview with Deane Mowrer, May 19, 1970, DDCW.

168 "Strikingly different": CG to Dwight Macdonald, St. Cyril's Day, 1951, McDY.

169 On Dorothy Day and the *Catholic Worker*: information compiled from William D. Miller, *Dorothy Day: A Biography* (New York: Harper and Row, 1982).

169 "I ordered a special luncheon" to "just hanging on": CG interview with Deane Mowrer, May 19, 1970, DDCW.

169 Dorothy began to pray for Caroline's conversion: CG to Dwight Macdonald, St. Cyril's Day, 1951, McDY.

169-70 "Worked so hard" to "Don't come near": *SM*, 201.

170 "Didn't let it go too soon": CG to MP, undated, SAPU.

170 On *Gone with the Wind*: information compiled from Anne Edwards, *Road to Tara* (New Haven: Ticknor and Fields, 1983).

170 "Too late by a season": CG to FMF, undated, FMFC.

170 "Why couldn't it have taken her twelve?": *SM*, 202.

170 "A super salesman's idea": CG to MP, undated, SAPU.

170 "Gobbled up all the trade": CG to FMF, undated, FMFC.

170 "Killed too many young men": *SM*, 201.

171 "Four dog runs," "a sort of catacomb": CG to LA, undated, LABL.

171 "The best place to work": CG to RPW, undated, SRBL.

171 "That man has a proper respect for the Muse": CG to RPW, undated, SRBL.

171 "They begged to have her": CG to FMF, undated, FMFC.

171 "Mastered details of life": *SM*, 201.

171 "I don't care": *SM*, 202.

171 "I can't help it": CG to MP, undated, SAPU.

171 "When I get these thirty": *SM*, 201.

171 "An uneasy feeling": CG to MP, undated, SAPU.

172 "Mastering maneuvers": CG to FMF, undated, FMFC.

172 "Sounding back over": *NB*, 375.

172 "Anything that might occur" to "the danger is": MP to CG, November 16, 1936, SAPU.

172 "I'm sorry I was stupid" to "This time": CG to RPW, undated, SRBL.

172 "Enough to turn our imaginings": CG to JB and FMF, undated, FMFC.

173 "It sounds well" to "the other titles": CG to MP, undated [November 27, 1936], SAPU.

173 "Invite irrelevant comparisons" to "might set [a] style": telegram from CG to MP, December 1, 1936, SAPU.

173 "The sword of God": MP to CG, December 2, 1936, SAPU.

173 "Even if I could swallow" to "and sound is the thing": letters from CG to MP, undated, SAPU.

174 "Mama can't take a joke": CG to Robert Lytle, undated, LPVU.

174 "A sweet little velvet jacket": CG to LA, undated, LABL.

174 "Only ten chapters": CG to MP, undated, SAPU.

174 "Story about a girl" to "I have never been sure": CG to May Morse, undated, MFPK.

174 "High-spirited": Caroline Gordon, "The Brilliant Leaves," *Harper's Bazaar*, November 1937, 81.

175 "For the sake of the last paragraph": CG to RPW, undated, SRBL.

175 "'The Brilliant Leaves' is" to "Her death comes about": CG to Davis, undated, VQUV.

175 Caroline declared it was the last story: CG to RPW, undated, SRBL.

176 "I leaped straight" to "Mama, don't tell them": CG to LA, undated, LABL.

176 "Ricocheted between": *SM*, 202.

176 "If I have the cash" to "Lord have mercy": *SM*, 203.

176–77 "I'm not afraid" to "The two lunatics": *SM*, 204.

177 "The glazed eye" to "wallowing in family": CG to KAP, undated, KAPM.

177 "The moral courage," "great indifference": CG to LC, January 28, 1937, CPVU.

177 "The book doesn't come off": *SM*, 204.

177 "It's been too hastily done," "I had to use": CG to FMF, undated, FMFC.

178 "Vastly superior": Edith H. Walton, "Miss Gordon's Civil War Novel," *New York Times Book Review*, February 21, 1937, 6.

178 "Even the thunder of guns": review of *None Shall Look Back*, *Newsweek*, February 20, 1937, 39.

179 "A disembodied spectator": Katherine Anne Porter, "Dulce et Decorum Est," review of *None Shall Look Back*, *New Republic*, March 31, 1937, 245.

179 "One's blood is never stirred": review of *None Shall Look Back*, *Tucson [Ariz.] Citizen*, March 6, 1937 (clipping in CGPU).

179 "I was due to get it": CG to FMF, undated, FMFC.

179 "Disregarded on the grounds" to "it constricts the imagination": CG to MP, undated, SAPU.

179 "A demigod": CG to LC, undated, CPVU.

179 "I think Lucy ought to have been allowed" to "I didn't devote": *SM*, 208.

179 "An illwritten thing": CG to KAP, undated, KAPM.

179 "Too stupid" to "It seems to me": KAP to CG, February 22, 1937, KAPM.

179 "In a great many ways": Porter, "Dulce et Decorum Est," 245.

180 "Katherine Anne ought to": CG to KAP, undated, KAPM.

180 "An artistic revolutionary wonder" to "I call you": JCR to CG, April 6, [1937], CGPU.

180 "The most mysterious of writers" to "It is only when you have finished": FMF, Scribner in-house review of books, SAPU.

180 "I fear the book lacks that Olympian ease": CG to FMF, undated, FMFC.

180–81 "Whether it is good or bad" to "Reading a great novel": CG to LC, undated, CPVU.

181 "Simply muffed it" to "They all take you": MP to CG, March 4, 1937, SAPU.

181 "I do not want you to be hurried": MP to CG, March 24, 1937, SAPU.

181 "Make a foundation": CG to LA, undated, LABL.

181 "Furnish us": CG to LC, March 12, 1937, CPVU.

181 "So fast on the trigger": CG to MP, undated, SAPU.

181 "Shaken down into a routine": *SM*, 208.

182 "One hand on the kitchen stove": CG to AGW, undated, WPMS.

182 "The strangest visitation" to "Imagine one": *SM*, 209. In Lowell's account of this visit, "Visiting the Tates," *Sewanee Review* 67 (October–December 1959): 557, he claimed that he hit the Tates' mailbox and got out of the car to "disguise the damage," not, as Gordon insisted, to answer "the calls of Nature."

182 "Stately yet bohemian": Lowell, "Visiting the Tates," 557.

182–83 "The Lowell boy" to "Young man": *SM*, 211.

183 "Consorting with the Tates": Ian Hamilton, *Robert Lowell: A Biography* (New York: Random House, 1982), 50.

183 "Insomnia, indigestion": *SM*, 210.

183 "A sweet child and very agreeable": *SM*, 209–10.

183 "Grimly unromantic poems": Lowell, "Visiting the Tates," 559.

183 "The women put earth": CG to MP, undated, SAPU.

185 "A little like a muffin" to "less suffering": CG to KAP, undated, KAPM.

185–86 "A certain metropolitan critic" to "to loaf and invite": Caroline Gordon, "Some Thoughts on Southern Novels: Hasty Writing No Spur to True Art," *CN*, June 26, 1937.

186 "Like being put under glass": *SM*, 210.

186 "She is beginning to be a little bitter": CG to JB, undated, FMFC.

186 "I can't keep this up": *SM*, 211.

187 "If I mean to do any work": KAP to CG, February 22, 1937, KAPM.

187 "Cast Gene off": CG to RPW, undated, SRBL.

187 "Any ties to sever": *SM*, 214.

187 "Moral health" to "all this, of course": *SM*, 214.

187 "An island of peace" to "one of the more turbulent": KAP to CG, September 20, 1937, KAPM.

188 "I am really": CG to KAP, undated, KAPM.

188 "Did not scruple" to "that she has lost": CG, undated synopsis, *WP*, SAPU.

188 "A good omen": CG to MP, undated, SAPU.

189 "A very soothing occupation": *SM*, 215.

189 "A sort of super feeling": CG to KAP, undated, KAPM.

189 "Get the Indian side" to "And from the time": letters from CG to MP, undated, SAPU.

190 "Took a fancy" to "You don't know how": CG to AL, November 11, 1937, LPVU.

190 "Frankie was well named": *CS*, 228.

190 "That yellow wife of Tom Doty": *CS*, 222.

190 "A man has to fight," "It struck me": *CS*, 237.

190 "Thoughtful, intelligent" to "technical excellence": HMJ, review of *The Garden of Adonis*, *Saturday Review of Literature*, November 6, 1937, 20.

190–91 "A provocative study" to "but she can only": Augusta Tucker, "Southern Conflicts," *New York Times Book Review*, November 7, 1937, 7.

191 "Deal a sad blow": *SM*, 206.

191 "The trade" was "all against books": MP to CG, December 21, 1937, SAPU.

191 "I seem always to fall": CG to MP, undated, SAPU.

191 "A good bold live book" to "There was the pure desperation": KAP to CG, January 16, 1938, CGPU.

191 "When the novel" to "Were they pressing": RPW to CG, undated, CGPU.

191 "Nearer being real characters": CG to MP, undated, SAPU.

191 The book was a failure: *SM*, 206; and CG to AL, undated, LPVU.

192–93 "Just couldn't stand any more" to "I talked too harshly": CG to KAP, undated, KAPM.

193 "A frightful place" to "I'd rather be": CG to MP, undated, SAPU.

193 "Just the kind of job": CG to AGW, undated, WPMS.

CHAPTER 6: A WANDERING AND IDLE LIFE

194 "The long habit": *GC*, 217.

194 "Work the racket": CG to KAP, undated, KAPM.

195 He could not write there: CG to JB, undated, FMFC.

195 "Jerking": CG to Elizabeth Green, undated, GUNC.

195 "I am getting so sick" to "I'm so tired": CG to KAP, undated [spring 1938], KAPM.

195 "Too risky" to "ever did stay anywhere": CG to KAP, undated, KAPM.

195 "One of the best novels": interview with NTW, September 12, 1988, San Cristóbal de las Casas, Chiapas, Mexico.

195 "Mama just uses": CG to KAP, undated, KAPM.

196 Allen said he couldn't take the compliments: AT to BT, October 7, 1938, LABL.

196 "Just starting in": CG to KAP, undated, KAPM.

196–97 "The habitations of the wilderness" to "make a disagreeable impression": CG to MP, undated, SAPU.

197 "Some sort of a love story" to "I realize": MP to CG, May 24, 1938, SAPU.

197–98 "You can't expect" to "a wanderer whether he stays": CG to MP, undated, SAPU.

198 "Get hold of those Boones," "once the artery": CG to KAP, undated, KAPM.

198 "Lousier chapters" to "one of the dullest": CG to LC, March 27, 1939, CPVU.

198–99 "Veined rubicund face" to "I see that": Arthur Mizener, *The Saddest Story* (New York: World, 1971), 460.

199 "Nobody heard much" to "It was a good thing": CG to George Marion O'Donnell, March 14, 1939, ODWU.

199 "You had better come" to "She kept us hopping": CG to KAP, undated, KAPM.

199 Allen thought the Meriwethers: AT to AL, March 28, 1939, LPVU.

200 "The teaching does take": CG to KAP, undated, KAPM.

200 Allen was enthusiastic: CG to AL and EL, April 18, 1939, LPVU.

200 "Artists being homeless": AT to W. C. Jackson, April 17, 1939, TPPU.

200 Also, he insisted: AT to AL, March 22, 1939, LPVU; AT to Frank P. Graham, May 1, 1939, TPPU.

200 Caroline agreed: CG to EL, May 23, 1939, LPVU.

200 "I will hate" to "what may be in the end": CG to KAP, undated, KAPM.

200 "Dragging Canoe": CG to LC, May 26, 1939, CPVU.

200–201 "A little breathing space," "wonderful routine": CG to KAP, undated, KAPM.

201 "The day is so long": CG to George Marion O'Donnell, undated [June 26, 1939], ODWU.

201 "I wish we could" to "just in chance": CG to JB, undated, FMFC.

201 "Very strange and hushed," "share of the loot": CG to EL, September 16, 1939, LPVU.

201 "Memories of the Master" to "He is meant to wander": CG to KAP, undated, KAPM.

201 "That trapped feeling": CG to EL, September 16, 1939, LPVU.

202 "I don't see how": CG to AL and EL, September 30, 1939, LPVU. Gordon never explained what she thought Bruegel was doing in his picture. This explanation is taken from Wolfgang Stechow's *Pieter Bruegel, the Elder* (London: Library of Great Painters, 1970), 116.

202 "What in the hell" to "that, Brother Cheney": CG to LC, December 20, 1939, CPVU.

202 "Spiritual collapse": CG to LC, February 29, 1940, CPVU.

202–3   "All forms of human activity" to "tanking up": CG to AL and EL, March 6, 1940, LPVU.

203   "All fours financially," "I believe we would": CG to AL, undated, LPVU.

203   Allen told Caroline not to worry: AT to PG, January 26, 1940, GUNC.

203–4   "One of the most charming men" to "been in his head": CG to EL, April 27, 1940, LPVU.

204   "It is a risk" to "Besides, you have got": CG to WD, undated, DUNC.

204   "It was easier": CG to KAP, undated, KAPM.

204   "There's really nothing": CG to Mary Wilson, undated, EWBL.

204   "The beginner cannot be" to "Allen will never": CG to KAP, undated, KAPM.

205   "Still head over heels," "was looking fine": CG to EL, April 27, 1940, LPVU.

205   "In order to make her exit": CG to LC, undated, CPVU.

205   "I never expected": CG to KAP, undated, KAPM.

205   "A little less noise" to "Just one novel": CG to KAP, undated, KAPM.

205   "See a little light": CG to Rosemary Mizener, February 27, 1941, MPVU.

205   She sometimes felt isolated: CG to KAP, undated, KAPM.

205–6   "Great callers" to "I hope they think": CG to MC, undated, CPNL.

206   "That might have been written": CG to EL, undated, LPVU.

206   "Maybe we are making": Cleanth Brooks to CG, October 26, 1939, SRBL.

206   "It doesn't quite jell," "We wish you wouldn't": CG to EL, undated, LPVU.

206   "If I don't get them right": CG to AL and EL, April 14, 1941, LPVU.

206   "Tomahawked": CG to EL, May 4, 1941, LPVU.

207   "Coffee, fatigue, old age" to "resorted to every kind": CG to KAP, undated, KAPM.

207   "She had told herself": *GC*, 458.

207–8   "My Muse turned": CG to EL, June 17, 1941, LPVU.

208   "On the job": CG to KAP, undated, KAPM.

208   "Taking out the 'thens'" to "Allen stepped in": CG to EL, June 17, 1941, LPVU.

208   "It seemed that a man": *GC*, 468–69.

208   "Practically wrote": CG to EL, June 17, 1941, LPVU.

210   "Pleasure" herself: CG to MC, undated, CPNL.

210–11   "Thousands of things": CG to KAP, undated, KAPM.

211   "Greensickness" to "worried stiff": CG to MC, undated, CPNL. In-

formation about Gordon's relationship with her daughter is drawn from interviews with NTW, September 1988, San Cristóbal de las Casas; and *CC*, 193–94.

212 "Hurrah for Doctor Wolf!": CG to KAP, undated, KAPM. Background on Dr. Wolf is drawn from *CC*, 197.

212 "My nervous spells": CG to EL, July 26, 1941, LPVU.

212 "Certainly circulatory": CG to EL, June 17, 1941, LPVU.

212 "Call Rainey" to "his subconscious protesting": CG to EL, July 26, 1941, LPVU.

212 "A perfect angel": CG to AL and EL, October 15, 1941, LPVU.

212–13 "Trying to save": CG to MC, undated, CPNL.

213 "The life of a person": CG to May Morse, undated, MFPK.

213 "If I am writing": CG to Mark and Dorothy Van Doren, undated, VDPC.

213 "Laurie must be wounded": CG, notes for *WP*, CGPU.

214 "A sort of stoa" to "the deeps that underlie": CG to KAP, undated, KAPM.

214 "A superbly rich" to "a little chill": Edith H. Walton, "The Frontier South," *New York Times Book Review*, November 2, 1941, 4–5.

214 "Her historical novels": Clifton Fadiman, review of *Green Centuries*, *New Yorker*, November 1, 1941, 70.

214 "Too many catastrophes": Stephen Vincent Benét, "Land Beyond the Mountains," *New York Herald Tribune Books*, November 1941, 4.

215 "Put Gordon Over": CG to Mark Van Doren, November 8, 1941, VDPC.

215 "Steadily growing" to "a different tone": CG to Bill Weber, undated, CGPU.

215 "Offered for sale" to "a common delusion": CG to KAP, undated, KAPM.

216 "Awfully dull": CG to LC, November 21, 1941, CPVU.

216 "Blind to faults": Max Gissen, "Two with Indians, One Without," *New Republic*, January 5, 1942, 27.

216 "She would burn it": CG to EL, November 22, 1941, LPVU.

216 Another friend: CG to WD, undated, DUNC.

216 "A little friendly scolding": JCR to CG, March 10, 1942, CGPU.

216 "Know or care": CG to AL, undated, LPVU.

216 "He can't bear": CG to KAP, undated, KAPM.

216 "Ought to be braver" to "sunk fathoms deep": CG to KAP, undated, KAPM.

216–17 "As if some horrible" to "I don't believe": CG to WD, undated, DUNC.

217 "Take the highest bidder": CG to LC, January 13, 1942, CPVU.

217 "Fall back on Max": CG to KAP, January 16, 1942, KAPM.

217 "Light and popular" to "psychic distance": CG to AL and EL, undated, LPVU.

217 "I had to find": CG to WD, undated, DUNC.

217 "A great, wounded animal": CG to May Morse, undated, MFPK.

218 "War work" to "in disciplining idle women": CG to KAP, undated, KAPM.

218 "Hold down the receiver": CG to AL and EL, undated, LPVU.

218 "So insulting to Allen": CG to Mark Van Doren, undated [spring 1942], VDPC.

218 "Realizes that if he doesn't": CG to AL and EL, May 19, 1942, LPVU.

219 "Drafted as a buck private": CG to EL, undated, LPVU.

219 "Grinning like a chipmunk" to "almost hysterically anxious": CG to MC, undated, CPNL.

219 "Mighty pretty": CG to MC, undated, CPNL.

219–20 "A regular renaissance" to "He can't understand": CG to KAP, undated, KAPM.

220 They feared: AT to PG, March 8, 1943, GUNC.

220 "Would tie him up": CG to KAP, undated, KAPM.

220 "Hotfooted it across": Ian Hamilton, *Robert Lowell: A Biography* (New York: Random House, 1982), 51.

220 "Poets' wives": *PY*, 198.

220–21 "Surges of creative energy" to "the year in which fury": CG to KAP, undated, KAPM.

221 "These days" to "resourceful—and realistic": "WR," 124.

222 "Sectional differences" to "of his loyalty": "WR," 126.

222 "The dark ages" to "With all our energies": CG to Morton Zabel, February 25, 1943, ZPNL.

222 "Amiable venom" to "What about John Berryman?": *PY*, 136.

222 "The Berts": information about Lowell's mythical bear friends compiled from Hamilton, *Robert Lowell*, 55–56; *PY*, 126–27; and Charlotte M. Goodman, *Jean Stafford: The Savage Heart* (Austin: University of Texas Press, 1990), 124.

222–23 "Doggerel, of course" to "Sometimes I roll": CG to KAP, undated, KAPM.

223 "Zov, zov" to "Once she had left home": interview with NTW, September 1988, San Cristóbal de las Casas, and interview with PW.

223 "All novelists," "had as little intellect": Gordon mentioned these remarks in numerous letters. For example, see her letter to Ben Toledano, October 31, 1977, CGPU.

223 When she had to write a book review: *SM*, 156.

223 "I know": CG to Mark and Dorothy Van Doren, undated [1941], VDPC.

223–24 On Allen's affairs: Walter Sullivan, *Allen Tate: A Recollection* (Baton Rouge: Louisiana State University Press, 1988), 4–5.

224–25 "I don't expect" to "Remember what I say": CG to AL, March 15, 1943, LPVU.

225 "The very last place": CG to KAP, undated, KAPM.

225 The Bird Cage: *CC*, 216.

225 "As good as the woods" to "go on living": CG to JS, undated, CGLT.

226 "Hop off": CG to MT, undated, WTPU.

226 "It is the job": CG to JS, undated, CGLT.

226 "Circumnatural" to "dramatic force": CG to SWK, undated [August 1944], CGPU.

226 "This novel will not": CG to WM, undated [January 19, 1943], MERP.

226–27 "Your difficulty" to "held in subjection": CG, notes from *WP*, CGPU.

227 "Perfectly foul" to "saved my life": CG to JS, undated, CGLT.

227 "The most fortunate woman" to "one can hardly": CG to MP, undated, SAPU.

228 "White streak up the front": CG to JS, undated, CGLT.

228 "I don't believe": CG to AT, undated, CGPU.

228 "His lifelong study" to "float up to the ceiling": CG to JS, undated, CGLT.

229 "God damned little": CG to MT, undated, WTPU.

229 "To cut the whole works" to "Douse the lights": CG to AT, LC, and FC, undated, CGPU.

229 "Then I am" to "so sweet-tempered": CG to AT, undated, CGPU.

229 "Agreed to the wedding": *CC*, 219.

229 "If I had been there": CG to JS, undated, CGLT.

229 "Certainly no two": CG to MT, undated, WTPU.

230 "But when they bring": CG to LC and AT, undated, CGPU.

230 "Now be good": CG to AT, LC, and FC, undated, CGPU.

230 "Something about love" to "Punctuate or change": CG to AT, undated, CGPU.

230 "Of one of those" to "Things just all happened": CG to MT, undated, WTPU.

230–31 "It is the worse thing": CG to KAP, undated, KAPM.

231 "Not a true Primitive": CG to JS, undated, CGLT.

231 "An actress who happens" to "a protective bit": CG to JS, undated [August 14, 1943], CGLT.

231 "The great thing": CG to AL, March 15, 1943, LPVU.

231 "Get up, get up": *CC*, 222.

231 "Well, that's one thing": Joan Givner, *Katherine Anne Porter: A Life* (New York: Simon and Schuster, 1982), 331.

232 "So cool and ca'm" to "some feeble remarks": interview with NTW, September 12, 1988, San Cristóbal de las Casas.

232 Allen himself thought: for AT's view, see his letter to KAP, November 16, 1945, KAPM. For KAP's view of the scene, see Givner, *Katherine Anne Porter*, 331–33.

246 "For some energy": CG to MT, undated, WTPU.

247 "Intuitive certainties," "poor, dear Loulie": CG to JS, undated, CGLT.

247 "In the moon": CG to KAP, undated, KAPM.

247 "Used up all" to "treading the path": CG to JS, undated, CGLT.

247 "Caroline has neither": AT to SWK, October 27, 1945, SWKP.

247 "Mama threw" to "Caroline, you've got to": interview with NTW, September 11, 1988, San Cristóbal de las Casas.

247–48 "That same glazed" to "Thinking Nothing": Gordon describes this picture in letters to KAP, undated, KAPM, and to JS, undated, CGLT.

248 "God, it is," "the landscape": CG to KAP, undated, KAPM.

248 "I don't feel," "A little stimulating": CG to MT, undated, WTPU.

248 "The room whirled" to "only worse": CG to KAP, undated, KAPM.

249 "Must leave town," "a more sensible": CG to Robert Barnett, June 8, 1959, CGPU.

249 "You admire me": CG to Father William Lynch, undated [1959], CGPU.

249 "Forced the issue," Allen admitted: AT to SWK, October 20, 1945, SWKP.

249–50 "Nancy and Allen" to "I hate to": CG to JS and RL, undated, CGLT.

250 "The arts," "to become financially": CG to MC, undated, CPNL.

250 "Had to have" to "learn to get around": CG to KAP, undated, KAPM.

251 She did fear: see AT to SWK, November 1, 1945, SWKP.

251 "Have a new life": CG to KAP, undated, KAPM.

251 "Other women" to "It's a wonder": CG to MC, undated, CPNL.

251 "None of this" to "That deep sense": CG to KAP, undated, KAPM.

251 "Absolutely nothing": CG to JS, undated, CGLT.

251 "Perfectly wild letters": CG to KAP, undated, KAPM.

251–52 "Did not bolster," "too high an opinion": CG to JS, undated, CGLT.

252 "Marry him again": CG to KAP, undated, KAPM.

252 "I do not think he": CG to JS, undated, CGLT.

252 "May this be": KAP to CG, October 6, 1945, CGPU.

252 "It has been": CG to KAP, undated, KAPM.

252 Allen was afraid: AT to SWK, October 27, 1945, SWKP.

252 "One of the hardest": CG to MC, undated, CPNL.

252 "Set up a routine": CG to KAP, undated, KAPM.

252 "A bit of a bore": CG to WT and MT, undated, WTPU.

252–53 "They couldn't face" to "saw him face to face": CG to KAP, undated, KAPM.

253 "Perfectly beautiful": CG to WD, undated [November 13, 1945], DUNC.

253 "To go very far": CG to WD, December 7, 1945, DUNC.

253 "If Allen will": CG to KAP, undated, KAPM.

253–54 "A recalcitrant stove" to "But I really": CG to WD, undated [November 13, 1945], DUNC.

254 "You've probably ruined" to "I'm going to break": JS to AT, December 16, [1945], TPPU.

255 "Some water" to "I think that": CG to RL, undated, CGLT.

255 "Talk things over" to "warily": CG to WD, December 7, 1945, DUNC.

255 Allen still blamed: see his letters to SWK, October 27, 1945, and November 22, 1945, SWKP.

255 "Your basic theme": CG to WD, undated, DUNC.

255–56 "Any reservations" to "otherwise would": CG to WD, December 7, 1945, DUNC.

256 Within two weeks: CG to WD, December 17, 1945, DUNC.

256 "This, of course": CG to LA, undated, LABL.

256–57 "Put on the best" to "That reaction to": CG to WD, undated, DUNC.

257 The symbolism: AT to KAP, January 9, 1946, KAPM.

257 "They do these" to "I feel better": CG to WD, January 8, 1946, DUNC.

257 "An unhappy time" to "I tremble": JB to KAP, December 27, 1945, KAPM.

257–58 "All doing" to "treading water": CG to WD, undated, DUNC.

258 "Here I am": CG to MT, undated, WTPU.

258 Sally Wood feared: SWK to MC, February 9, 1946, CPNL.

258 "Paralyzed morally": AT to WT, January 23, 1946, WTPU.

258 "Live in sin": SWK to AT, March 20, 1946, CGPU.

258 Allen would not be swayed: AT to SWK, April 4, 1946, CGPU.

259 "Quite wretched" to "the poor devil": letters from CG to SWK, undated [spring 1946], SWKP.

259 "Show the scars": CG to MT, undated, WTPU.

260 "Going to be": CG to MT, undated, WTPU.

260 "Maternal imagination" to "in its modest way": Caroline Gordon, "Vocabulary of Love," *Mademoiselle*, September 1946, 155.

260 "Love has a different," "But never think": Gordon, "Vocabulary of Love," 278.

261 "A journey back": "HI," 111.

261 "Having his head": CG to Frederick P. W. McDowell, January 22, 1965, CGPU.

261 "The very sight" to "make out the whole": "HI," 160.

261 "Standing there": "HI," 161.

261 "One of Bethany's," "teacher of youth": honorary degree from Bethany College, June 9, 1946; housed in CGPU.

261 "A brilliant teacher": "HI," 161–62.

262 "Double harness": CG to WD, June 30, 1946, DUNC.

262 "Rather primitive": CG to MT, undated, WTPU.

262 "Vampire bats": CG to WD, undated, DUNC.

262 "We can't take": CG to LC and FC, undated, CPVU.

262 "Teaching is getting": CG to WD, undated, DUNC.

262–63 "Very sure": Danforth Ross, "Caroline Gordon's Golden Ball," *Critique* 1, no. 1 (Winter 1956): 69.

263 A modern pioneer woman: see George R. Clay's letter to Denver Lindley, February 25, 1956, CGPU.

263 "I'm not going" to "Flaubert and Crane": Ross, "Caroline Gordon's Golden Ball," 69.

263 "You can't say," "You have to show": Ross, "Caroline Gordon's Golden Ball," 73.

263 "Changing under my hands" to "I find that": CG to LC and FC, undated, CPVU.

263 "Allen and I": CG to LC and FC, undated [April 21, 1947], CPVU.

264 "Allen's face was scratched": CC, 252. See also CG to Mark Van Doren, undated, VDPC; CG to LA, undated, LABL.

264 This time the crisis: AT to MC, April 1, 1947, CPNL.

264 "To the point": CG to WD, undated, DUNC.

264 "Assemble defenses": CG to WD, undated [April 1947], DUNC.

264 "Antics": CG to LC and FC, undated [April 21, 1947], CPVU.

264 "Incapable of making" to "his neurosis": CG to WD, undated [April 1947], DUNC.

264 "Jealous, suspicious" to "I have become": CG to LC and FC, undated [April 21, 1947], CPVU.

265 "I think I would" to "The thing that so complicates": CG to WD, undated, DUNC.

265 Both she and Allen ought: CG to LC and FC, undated [April 21, 1947], CPVU.

265 "Victims of too little" to "This damn modern world": CG to WD, undated, DUNC.

265 "This modern substitute": CG to LC and FC, undated [April 21, 1947], CPVU.

265 "There is an abyss": CG to WD, undated [April 1947], DUNC.

266 "Presented as events" to "just what sort of man": CG to LC and FC, undated [April 21, 1947], CPVU.

267 "All right, Max": CG to LA, June 24, [1947], LABL. Several years later, Gordon also spoke of this meeting to MC, in an undated letter [1957], CPNL.

267–68 "I simply cannot realize" to "But you'll understand": CG to WD, undated, DUNC. This letter has no salutation and may in fact be a fragment.

268 "By a hair" to "to be able to refresh": CG to WD, undated, DUNC.

269 Eudora suggested: see Ruth M. Vande Kieft's discussion of this story in *Eudora Welty* (Boston: Twayne, 1987), 62–65.

269–70 "Shot seven men" to "It's all in the way you look at it": CG, first version of "The Petrified Woman," typescript, CGPU. See also CG to RPW, undated, from 1606 West Twenty-eighth Street, Minneapolis, RPWB, for more information on the story.

271   "Feel worthy" to "That's the reason": CG to LC, February 4, 1953, CPVU.

271   "I would really like": CG to WD, undated, DUNC.

271-72   On Gordon's conversion: Alexandra Michos's unpublished essay "Conservatism and Empowerment: Caroline Gordon's Identity as Fiction Writer and Literary Critic" has helped me to clarify my views on Gordon's conversion.

272   At one point in late 1945: AT to SWK, November 22, 1945, CGPU.

272   Allen had the opposite effect: CG to LC, February 23, 1951, CPVU.

272   "I have lived most" to "At a certain point": CG to WD, undated, DUNC.

272   "In essence, a religious act," "We are moved": Caroline Gordon, "The Art and Mystery of Faith," *Newman Annual*, 1953, 56.

273   "Rock the world": *CS*, 119.

273   "To save his immortal soul" to "he had wondered": *CS*, 120.

273   "In his childish": *CS*, 114.

274   "It is at a time": *CS*, 119.

CHAPTER 8: TESTIMONIES OF FAITH

275   The priest instructing Allen: CG to WD, May 21, 1948, DUNC.

275-76   "Barnstorming tour" to "look like a cross": CG to WD, undated, DUNC.

276   She spoke forcefully: Veronica Makowsky, *Caroline Gordon: A Biography* (New York: Oxford University Press, 1989), 188.

276   "An incarnation of Fane's": CG, notes for *The Walker*, CGPU.

276   "I ought never," "a major economy": CG to KAP, undated [July 1948], KAPM.

277   "He has to have": CG to WD, undated, DUNC.

277   A house with rammed earth: CG to RL, undated, RLHU.

277-78   "Until it has either acted" to "those gentry": CG to WD, undated, DUNC.

278   "One has always" to "quantities of leisure": CG to WD, undated, DUNC.

278   "Rather like knitting": CG to MT, undated, WTPU.

279-80   "The germ" to "superior to that": CG to WD, undated, DUNC. See also CG to LC, February 23, 1951, CPVU.

280   "Register" to "I've got to die": CG to WD, Octave Day of All Saints, 1950, DUNC.

280   "After all, we all speak": CG to WD, undated, DUNC.

280   "Emerge at the denouement": CG to WD, March 15, 1949, DUNC.

See also the letters from CG to SY, undated and St. Scholastica's Day, 1951, SYPT; CG to AL, undated [fall 1949], LPVU.

280 On Lowell: see Ian Hamilton, *Robert Lowell: A Biography* (New York: Random House, 1982), 149–54; CG to RL, undated, RLHU.

281 "A dangerous state": CG to WD, undated, DUNC.

281 "At arm's length": Hamilton, *Robert Lowell*, 155–58.

281–82 "Run over" to "to be only moderately famous": CG to WD, undated, DUNC.

282 "Visualize the process" to "This is the house": CG to WD, September 14, [1949], DUNC.

282 "One more would push": CG to SY, undated [fall 1949], SYPT.

282 "The upper story": CG to WD, undated, DUNC.

282 "Touches of Benfolly," "on a Lilliputian": CG to FC, undated, CPVU.

282 "It's all most inconvenient": CG to WD, undated, DUNC.

282 "Nip outdoors": CG to WD, September 14, [1949], DUNC.

283 "It's heavenly": CG to WD, undated, DUNC.

283 "Accidental restraints," "what is constant": Andrew Lytle, "Caroline Gordon and the Historic Image," *Sewanee Review* 57 (Autumn 1949): 568.

283 "This makes the period" to "nearest substitute": Lytle, "Historic Image," 569.

283 "If she did not sign": Lytle, "Historic Image," 562.

283–84 "It is a wonderful": CG to AL, undated, LPVU.

284 "What Life" to "Very subtly": Lytle, "Historic Image," 578.

284 "Oh, that Robert": CG to AL, undated, LPVU. For Gordon's later comments on Lytle's misreading, see her letter to William Stuckey, September 25, 1972, CGPU.

285 "Passion, is that" to "The word is 'parnel'": *PY*, 202.

285 "Awfully nice": CG to RL, undated, RLHU.

285–86 "Prepared to say" to "fell back on a trick": CG to WD, undated, DUNC.

286 "Define and, in a sense, crown": CG to James F. Mathias, January 7, 1950, JSGF.

286 "This sort of thing": John Hall Wheelock to CG, February 2, 1950, SAPU.

286 "Moral as well as artistic": Robert Gorham Davis, "Inside the Short Story," *New York Times Book Review*, July 30, 1950, 4.

286 "With Man's relationship": Caroline Gordon and Allen Tate, *The House of Fiction* (New York: Charles Scribner's Sons, 1950), 286.

286 "Failures of form": Davis, "Inside the Short Story," 4.

286 "The editors tend": William Peden, "From Poe to Welty," *Saturday Review of Literature*, June 17, 1950, 18.

287 "It was as if," "establish some": CG to WD, Octave Day of All Saints, 1950, DUNC.

287 "To calculate and translate" to "He had only": CG to WD, March 1, 1950, DUNC.

287 "Those life-giving": Caroline Gordon, "The Story of Ford Madox Ford," review of *Parade's End* by Ford Madox Ford, *New York Times Book Review*, September 17, 1950, 22.

288 "One of the most brilliant" to "in some of Ford's": Gordon "Story of Ford," 1.

288 "If the carpenters": CG to NTW, Tuesday [fall 1950], CGPU.

288 "Artists aren't meant": CG to NTW, Saturday [fall 1950], CGPU.

288 "Transformed because" to "No doubt": CG to NTW, St. Martin's Day, 1950, CGPU.

289 "Characteristic fashion" to "a dither of delight": CG to WD, undated, DUNC.

289 "Entering the Church": CG to Robert Stallman, February 9, 1951, Robert W. Stallman Collection (#6778), Clifton Waller Barrett Library, Manuscripts Division, Special Collections Department, University of Virginia Library, Charlottesville.

289 "As a Catholic," "he might as well": Mary Jarrell, ed., *Randall Jarrell's Letters* (Boston: Houghton Mifflin, 1985), 248.

289 Caroline thought Allen: CG to MC, February 27, 1951, CPNL.

289–90 "He would have joined" to "would like to have some": CG to LC, February 23, 1951, CPVU.

290 "More range": CG to SY, St. Scholastica's Day, 1951, SYPT; Gordon explained that she got the idea when Young came to visit, and she remembered Young's novel *River House*, which changed the point of view at the end of the novel.

290 "Psychiatric errors": CG to LC, February 23, 1951, CPVU.

290 On Percy Wood: interview with PW, September 13, 1988, San Cristóbal de las Casas, Chiapas, Mexico.

291 "Short, sharp yelps": CG to MC, February 27, 1951, CPNL.

291 They could be a buffer: *CC*, 282.

291 "The truth is": CG to LA, undated, LABL.

291 "I knew I ought": CG to LC, Baby Allen's Birthday, [March 27,] 1951, CPVU.

291 "A debauch": CG to WD, July 27, [1951], DUNC.

291 "To soar up" to "a feeling of largeness": CG to LC, undated [September 28, 1951], CPVU.

291 "The sky is the highest": CG to AL, Feast of St. Placidus, [1951], LPVU.

292 "A sizeable chunk" to "plenty of waste space": CG to LC, undated [September 28, 1951], CPVU.

292 "Achieved her worldly ambition": CG to WD, July 27, [1951], DUNC.

292 "Having to set," "positively luxurious": CG to Arthur and Rosemary Mizener, St. Elizabeth of Hungary's Day, 1951, MPVU.

292 "'You-Can't-Take-It-With-You' existence": Wendell Weed, "Artistic Hobbies: Fiddle Playing, Painting Inspire Poet, Novelist," *Minneapolis Star*, October 3, 1951, p. 31, cols. 2–3.

293 "Keep things from happening": *SC*, 228.

293 Sometimes he would joke: *PY*, 199.

293 "Read as much": *SC*, 186.

293 Sarah Lewis resembled: SWK to CG, undated, CGPU.

293–94 Far from anticipating: CG to LC, Baby Allen's Birthday, [March 27,] 1951, CPVU.

294 "A concrete moral focus": Ruth Chapin, "Twilight of the South," *Christian Science Monitor*, October 4, 1951, 15.

294 "Symbolism, high dramatics": Robert Gorham Davis, "An Evil Time for Lucy," *New York Times Book Review*, September 9, 1951, 20.

294 "Something of a pest": review of *The Strange Children*, *New Yorker*, September 15, 1951, 115.

294 "Of all American brats": Anne Fremantle, review of *The Strange Children*, *Commonweal*, November 16, 1951, 156.

294 "Modest contribution": CG to SY, undated, SYPT.

294–95 "Put the woman" to "a period of desolation": *SC*, 226–27.

295–96 "Full of natural grace" to "for any book I write": CG to AL, Feast of St. Placidus, [1951], LPVU.

296 "The old story that is": CG, notes for *Mal*, November 28, 1951, CGPU.

296 On Hart Crane: Gordon had been haunted by the memory of Crane for over a year. While reading the writings of St. Catherine of Siena, she discovered that Crane and St. Catherine had used similar patterns of imagery, particularly a metaphor of a bridge that served as a vehicle of transcendence. She tried to interest some of Tate's colleagues and graduate students in writing a scholarly article on the subject, but when no one seemed interested, she decided to tackle the subject of Crane's religious yearnings in her own fictional terms.

296 "Always craving": CG, notes on *Mal*, St. Dionysius' Day, 1951, CGPU.

296 "She is a person": CG, notes on *Mal*, undated fragment, CGPU.

296 "Seeking love desperately": CG, notes on *Mal*, April 29, 1952, CGPU.

297 "Sharpened by the help" to "movable ways": CG, notes on *Mal*, St. Benedict's Day, 1952, CGPU. Additional information on Cynthia compiled from notes on *Mal*, undated and April 29, 1952, CGPU.

297 "The business": CG to LC, undated [October 5, 1951?], CPVU.

297 "I have got me": CG to NTW, New Year's Eve, 1951, CGPU.

298 "I wish," "already a rare phenomenon": Sally Fitzgerald, "A Master Class: From the Correspondence of Caroline Gordon and Flannery O'Connor," *Georgia Review* 33, no. 4 (Winter 1979): 828.

298 "There are so few," "a Catholic novel": Fitzgerald, "A Master Class," 830.

298 "I feared" to "a sample": CG to LC, undated [December 31, 1951?], CPVU.

298 "Reading that novel": CG to LC, undated [February 16, 1952], CPVU.

298 "Of the first order": Fitzgerald, "A Master Class," 843.

299 "Let this manuscript go" to "They are really": Fitzgerald, "A Master Class," 832.

299 "I am walking": CG to MT, Vigil of St. Thomas, 1951, WTPU.

299 "People who don't": CG to LC, undated [December 31, 1951?], CPVU.

300 When Nancy found out: NTW to CG, undated, CGPU.

300 "Stay put" to "some fixed point": CG to NTW, Holy Saturday, 1952, CGPU.

300 "The truth is": CG to NTW, Wednesday in Holy Week, 1952, CGPU.

300 "It *is* a little rough": AT to Arthur Mizener, December 3, 1951, MPVU.

301 "As Allen remarks": CG to NTW, December 31, [1951], CGPU.

301 "In which virtue": Caroline Gordon, "Mr. Verver, Our National Hero," *Sewanee Review* 63 (Winter 1955): 46.

301 "A green book bag": CG to MT, undated, WTPU.

301 "It lacks": CG to LC, undated [February 16, 1952], CPVU.

301 "What a wonderful thing" to "the Spirit moves him": CG to NTW, Feast of Sts. Faustina and Jovita, [1952], CGPU.

301 "The result of": CG to LC, undated [February 16, 1952], CPVU.

302 "Hopes to have her": CG to MT, undated, WTPU. See the letters between AT and CG, May 1952, CGPU.

302 Allen confided freely: see AT's letters to KAP during this period, KAPM.

302–3 On "Under the Mulberry Tree": Caroline Gordon, "Under the Mulberry Tree," typescript, CGPU.

303 "It is just heavenly": CG to NTW, undated, CGPU.

303 "Tenting about": CG to Morton Zabel, [July 30, 1952], ZPNL.

303 "A new house": CG to LC and FC, undated [October 3, 1952], CPVU.

304 "What I crave": CG to FC, undated [October 28, 1952], CPVU.

304 He wrote Caroline: see, for example, AT to CG, September 14, 1952, CGPU.

304 "The greatest poetic seizure": CG to FC, undated [October 28, 1952], CPVU.

304 "You are damn lucky": CG to Jack Wheelock, undated, SAPU.

304–5 "Brief case bulging" to "on the way to sainthood": CG to NTW, undated [mid-November 1952], CGPU.

305 "The most important talent": CG to Jack Wheelock, undated, SAPU.

305 "Wherever art": Caroline Gordon, "Some Readings and Misreadings," *Sewanee Review* 61 (1953): 384.

305 "A more Christian": CG to NTW, undated [mid-November 1952], CGPU.

305 "Always threatening": CG to PW, undated, CGPU.

306 "The stage gets": CG to NTW, undated, CGPU.

306 "The fountain-head": CG to Jack Wheelock, undated, SAPU.

306 In a local paper: "Judge Studies Case of Very Amorous Bull," unsigned clipping, no known date or source, included in notes on *Mal*, CGPU.

306 "The fact that they have": CG, notes on *Mal*, December 19, 1952, CGPU.

307 "Outwardly very demure": CG, notes on *Mal*, December 16, 1952, CGPU.

307 "Perhaps too direct," "Cynthia has missed out": CG, notes on *Mal*, undated, CGPU.

307 "Not suitable for a woman" to "a woman at intellectual labor": CG to WD, undated, DUNC.

307–8 "'Twas ever thus" to "I consider myself": CG to LC and FC, undated [March 9, 1953], CPVU.

308–9 "Like a cry": CG to LC and FC, St. Fidelis of Singmaringen's Day, 1953, CPVU.

309 "An artist's first duty," "the same as any": *CS*, 337.

309 "Too lonesome": CG to NTW, July 3–21, 1953 [misdated], CGPU.

310 "Darling, there is" to "If you tell me": CG to AT, undated, CGPU.

310 "The Bottomless Pit": CG to MC and Muriel Cowley, Ascension Day, 1953, CPNL.

310 He told friends: see AT to WD, May 11, 1953, DUNC; and *CC*, 298.

310 "If it's not": CG to AT, May 26, 1953, CGPU.

311 "Stirred up," "mother complex": CG to Sam Monk, June 5, 1953, CGPU.

311 "During one of his attacks" to "I'll have much less heart": CG to NTW, July 30, 1953, CGPU.

312 "A perfectly divine terrace": CG to PW and NTW, undated, CGPU.

312 "Benevolent domestic tyrant": CG to LC, undated, CPVU.

312 "You do not love": CG to Amelia Wood, October 29, 1953, CGPU.

313 "Earthy, mystical" to "a broken frieze": CG to LC, undated, CPVU.

313 "Like walking down": CG to LC and FC, undated, CPVU.

313 "In a way" to "in all his life": CG to PW and NTW, undated, CGPU.

314 "I simply love": CG to NTW, undated, CGPU.

314 "An ancient" to "attacks": CG to LC, undated, CPVU.

314–15 "Out of the solid rock" to "I never asked": CG to WD, undated, DUNC.

315 "Tune in on the Rosary": CG to LC and FC, February 19, 1954, CPVU.

315 "What a prodigious," "female identification": CG to NTW, undated [November 1953], CGPU.

CHAPTER 9: THE MALEFACTORS

316 "These spells": CG to WD, February 19, 1954, DUNC.

317 "The text": CG to LA, February 1, 1954, LABL.

317 "The powers necessary": CG to WD, February 19, 1954, DUNC.

317 "This animal too" to "Look, we don't": CG, Notes on Dreams, February 1954, CGPU.

317 "This procession" to "That is not": CG, Notes on Dreams, February 5, 1954, CGPU.

317 "For underground exploration": CG, Notes on Dreams, February 9, 1954, CGPU.

317 "One of the subtlest": CG to PW, St. Paul's Day, [1954], CGPU.

317 "True self": CG to NTW, undated, CGPU.

318 "Feeling-intuition type": CG, Notes on Dreams, undated, CGPU.

318 "Violence, which was": CG, Notes on Dreams, February 1954, CGPU.

318 "My instinctual nature": CG, Notes on Dreams, March 7, 1954, CGPU.

318 "The danger implicit" to "the first person": CG, Notes on Dreams, February 1954, CGPU.

319 "A heavy price": CG, Notes on Dreams, undated, CGPU.

319 "Exactly the desk," "so wonderful": CG, Notes on Dreams, March 9, 1954, CGPU.

319 "The substantial female under-pinning": CG, Notes on Dreams, undated, CGPU.

319 "A real 'new critic'": CG to PW, St. Paul's Day, [1954], CGPU.

319 "Meeting this woman": CG to WD, February 19, 1954, DUNC.

319 "I fear this Italian air": CG to LA, St. Cyril of Jerusalem's Day, 1954, LABL.

319 "We still have a lot of work to do": CG to LA, February 1, 1954, LABL.

319–20 "He was sunk" to "That is a wonderful story": CG to NTW, undated, CGPU.

320 "Mama, I'm sick": CG to AL, January 11, 1955, LPVU.

320 "Detached from reality": interview with PW, September 1988, San Cristóbal de las Casas, Chiapas, Mexico. Information on this period

is based primarily on interviews with PW and NTW, September 1988, San Cristóbal de las Casas. Gordon's views are drawn from Tate's letters to her during this period, CGPU.

321 "A torture chamber" to "They all just walked": CG to LC and FC, August 9, 1954, CPVU.

322 "The house of our dreams" to "the who's who": NTW to CG and AT, November 23, [1953], CGPU.

322 "The ugliest house": CG to Jack and Phyllis Wheelock, Friday, SAPU.

322 "Late Victorian gone pazza": CG to SY, undated [fall 1954], SYPT.

322 "Shaped exactly like the band stand": CG to EL, August 6, 1954, LPVU.

322 An "inter office memo": see CG to PW, undated, CGPU; AT to CG, May 5, 1954, and July 2, 1954, CGPU.

322 Friends who saw Caroline: see letters between Jack Wheelock and AT, May 13, 1954, and May 24, 1954, SAPU.

323 And Caroline worried: see the letters from AT to CG between April and July 1954, especially May 21, 1954, CGPU.

323 "You are more gifted but less intelligent": AT to CG, May 7, 1954, CGPU.

323 Allen agreed he was vulnerable: AT to CG, May 10, 1954, CGPU.

323 Her anxiety found a destructive outlet; Nancy and Percy doubted it: interviews with NTW and PW, September 1988, San Cristóbal de las Casas.

324 "Never to do that again" to "This place is like": CG to Jack Wheelock, June 8, 1954, SAPU.

324–25 "The Battle of Princeton" to "could never have learned": CG to SY, undated, SYPT.

325 "Like a man" to "Everything goes": CG to AL, January 11, 1955, LPVU.

325 "It is hard for Allen and me" to "dived right": CG to FC and LC, April 18, 1955, CPVU.

325 "A listener, not a looker": CG to AL, January 11, 1955, LPVU.

325 "Veiled in snow": CG to SY, undated, SYPT.

325 "Death cell": CG to AL, St. Agatha's Day, [February 5,] 1955, LPVU.

325 "The most wonderful woman": CG to SY, undated, SYPT.

325 "She never learned": CG to LC and FC, St. Fidelis of Singmaringen's Day, 1953, CPVU.

326 "The shadow" to "mother-fixation": CG to SY, November 5, 1954, SYPT.

326–37 "I have worked" to "I'm so damn glad": Danforth Ross, notes on CG, author's collection.

327 "Frightened me": *Mal*, 25.

327 "He had powers": *Mal*, 176.

327 "If only she": *Mal*, 190.

327 "These things—follow patterns": *Mal*, 217.

328 "Uncritical attachment": *Mal*, 165.

329 "When he goes out" to "making him over": CG, notes on *Mal*, undated, CGPU.

329 "I will do": CG, notes on *Mal*, undated, CGPU.

329 "I will just have to wait": CG to AT, March 28, 1955, CGPU.

330 Caroline realized that he was dangerously fatigued, "Caroline can't possibly": CG to LC and FC, April 18, 1955, CPVU.

330 "He could sleep": *Mal*, 312.

330 "A wife is subject": *Mal*, 311.

330 "It is for Adam": see Jacques Maritain, "The Frontiers of Poetry."

331 Nancy even helped: CG to AT, August 21, 1955, CGPU.

331–32 "The dividing line" to "The psychologists say": CG to AT, St. Stephen's Day, 1955, CGPU.

332 "I think that if I could learn": CG to AT, September 10, 1955, CGPU.

333 "Keeping the ground always shifting" to "More and more": CG to AT, November 3, 1955, CGPU.

333 "My longing to have ground," "or, at least, a desk": CG to AT, October 27, 1955, CGPU. In one of the dreams she had before arriving in Rome, Gordon declared that there were three things that she really wanted: "The first thing I want is a garden, second, I want my husband never to deceive me about anything, and third, I want all the dreadful things that have happened to me never to have happened." See Notes on Dreams, December 8, 1954, CGPU.

334 Quotes from "The Buried Lake": Allen Tate, *Collected Poems, 1919–1976* (New York: Farrar, Straus and Giroux, 1977), 138–39.

334 "Pictured as the object": CG to AT, November 9, 1955, CGPU.

334 "Violent reaction" to "I feel a little relieved": CG to AT, November 13, 1955, CGPU.

334 "Even more profound," "You have been sorely": CG to AT, December 5, 1955, CGPU.

335 When George Clay: George R. Clay to Denver Lindley, February 25, 1956, CGPU.

335 "Everybody in Town and Gown": CG to NTW, February 20, 1956, CGPU.

336 "The only way to learn": press release, January 26, 1956, KU News Bureau, University of Kansas, Lawrence.

336 "It was really like writing a book": CG to SY, May 17, 1956, SYPT.

336 "Hope springs eternal": CG to NTW, February 20, 1956, CGPU.

336 "We were born": CG to AT, January 24, 1956, CGPU.

336 Allen not only urged Caroline: AT to CG, January 24, 1956, CGPU.

336–37 "A Still, Small Voice had warned me": CG to SY, May 17, 1956, SYPT.

337 Dorothy wanted Caroline to make major changes: William D. Miller, *Dorothy Day: A Biography* (New York: Harper and Row, 1982), 453–54.

337 Allen comforted her: AT to CG, January 24, 1956, CGPU.

337 "Miss Birdseye was evolved entirely" to "*My* moral conscience": CG to RL, undated, RLHU. Gordon quotes James's comment from his letter to William James, February 14, 1885.

337 "Moral and intellectual striptease": "Ode to the Expatriate Dead," *Time*, March 12, 1956, 124.

337 "Picture of sick intellectuals": Rosemary Benét, "Neurotic People," *Saturday Review*, March 17, 1956, 15.

338 "Most ambitious novel," "great intelligence": Arthur Mizener, "What Matters with Tom," *New York Times Book Review*, March 4, 1956, 4, 32.

338 "The best woman novelist," "profoundly conceived": Vivienne Koch, "Companions in the Blood," *Sewanee Review* 64 (1956): 645–51.

338 Writing for the *New Republic*: Willard Thorp, "The Redemption of the Wicked," *New Republic*, April 30, 1956, 21.

338 Jacques Maritain had profuse praise for *The Malefactors*: Maritain to CG, March 28, 1956, in *Exiles and Fugitives: The Letters of Jacques and Raissa Maritain, Allen Tate, and Caroline Gordon*, ed. John M. Dunaway (Baton Rouge: Louisiana State University Press, 1992), 54.

338 "A pale reflection": CG to AT, November 9, 1955, CGPU.

338 Allen called the book a masterpiece: AT to Mizener, January 16, 1956, MPVU; AT to RPW, January 27, 1956, RPWB; interview with Danforth Ross, August 1987, Clarksville, Tenn.

339 "Unsympathetic and hard" to "A certain enthusiasm": CG to AT, April 11, 1956, CGPU.

339 The reunion of the Fugitives: compiled from CG to LC, undated, CPVU, and AT to Donald Davidson, May 19, 1956, DPVU.

339 He insisted that she was asking too much of him: AT to CG, June 7, 1956, CGPU.

339 "My life here is unnatural and repugnant" to "I'd rather live": CG to AT, Sunday, [1956], CGPU.

339 "Just crawling out": CG to FC, undated [May 19, 1956], CPVU.

340 "Sort of a glorified two storey cabin": CG to Mark Van Doren, May 9, 1958, VDPC.

340 "In the depths of the country": CG to LC, undated, CPVU.

340 "I am not going to cry": CG to SY, St. Ephrem's Day, 1956, SYPT.

341 "This place is as near a farm": CG to Flannery O'Connor, undated, CPVU.

341 "Our last house" to "utterly suited": CG to MC and Muriel Cowley, undated, CPNL.

341 "What of it?": as quoted in CG to LC, undated, CPVU.

341 "Grimly facing our respective fates": CG to Muriel Cowley, undated, CPNL.

342 "There is no good way" to "I want you to consider": AT to CG, undated, CGPU.

342 Years later Caroline would remember that night: CG to Robert W. Barnett, June 8, 1959, CGPU.

342 Allen was afraid: AT to CG, August 30, 1956, September 12, 1956, and undated fragments, CGPU.

342 Caroline was not so sure: see Gordon's notes on AT to CG, October 3, 1956, CGPU.

343 "Since his ills [were] mostly psychic": CG to MC, September 26, 1956, CPNL.

343 "I refuse to believe": MC to CG, September 27, 1956, CPNL.

343 He said that he had arranged for his paycheck: AT to CG, September 3, 1956, CGPU.

343 "Assemble the parts": CG to MC, September 26, 1956, CPNL.

344 The money was coming, he said: AT to CG, October 13, 1956, CGPU. For information on Gordon's financial panic, see CG to MC, December 26, 1956, CPNL; and CG to Robert W. Barnett, June 8, 1959, CGPU.

344 "States" to "not capable of attending to business": CG to MC, December 26, 1956, CPNL.

344 "That of the absconding bank teller": CG to Robert W. Barnett, June 8, 1959, CGPU.

344 Allen was badly shaken: AT to WD, January 1, 1957, DUNC.

344 "First financial security": CG to Robert W. Barnett, December 5, 1958, CGPU.

344–45 "It doesn't look good" to "I hope I can stay": CG to MC, December 26, 1956, CPNL.

345 "I think that you" to "Man is supposed to lead": CG to AT, January 11, 1957, CGPU.

346 "Rounded out properly" to "the bright boys": CG to MC, undated, CPNL.

346–47 "A series of lectures": William Bittner, "For the Ladies," *Saturday Review*, November 16, 1957, 20–21.

347 "You demand more of me than I can give" to "it is you who cannot yet forgive": CG to AT, undated, CGPU.

347–48 "To try to get a formal separation" to "a little better from now on": CG to LC, undated, CPVU.

348 "Attack of hysterics" to "a frantic plea for help": CG to LC and FC, First Sunday in Advent, 1958, and undated [September 1959], CPVU.

348 "I see my own life": CG to AT, undated, CGPU.

348 "I may not make it": CG to AT, St. Paul of the Cross, 1958, CGPU.

348 What he needed was some time to work on his own writing: CG to Mark Van Doren, May 9, 1958, VDPC.

348 Allen told Caroline that he had turned it down: AT to CG, May 5, 1958, CGPU.

349 "Allen's familiar had at last accomplished": CG to FC, undated, CPVU. For information on Tate's intentions and activities during the summer of 1958, see the following: John Clark to AT, August 12, 1958, TPPU; the correspondence between AT and Isabella Gardner, Isabella Gardner Papers, Special Collections, Washington University, St. Louis.

349 "I would not blow my top like that": CG to AT, August 13, 1958, CGPU.

349 Acting the part of an injured but devoted spouse: AT to CG, August 19, 1958, CGPU.

349 Allen was too deep in deception: see AT to CG, August 26, 1958, CGPU; AT to Isabella Gardner, August and September 1958, Gardner Papers.

350 "Necessity and poverty" to "But there is order": CG to MC, St. Elizabeth of Hungary, 1958, CPNL.

350 Caroline wrote Allen that she would no longer stand for his irresponsible behavior: see CG to Father William Lynch, undated [1959], CGPU; AT to Isabella Gardner, November 5, 1959, Gardner Papers.

351 Each priest "has said": CG to AT, First Sunday in Advent, 1958, CGPU.

351 "It would be a great relief" to "consider the place": CG to AT, December 12, 1958, CGPU.

351 Tate's ideas about divorce: AT to RL, November 8, 1958, RLHU; AT to LC, February 19, 1959, CPVU; letters from AT to Isabella Gardner, January to February 1959, Gardner Papers.

352 She found herself looking back: CG to Robert Barnett, March 12, 1959, CGPU.

352 "A man who communicates": CG to Robert Barnett, March 9, 1959, CGPU.

352 "This affair of the missing deed": CG to Robert Barnett, March 12, 1959, CGPU.

352 "I really need you": CG to Marion Meriwether, March 30, 1959, CGPU.

352–53 "Helped to create evil" to "The quickest and best way": CG to Robert Barnett, May 23, 1959, CGPU.

353 "He never meant": MC to CG, June 15, 1959, CPNL.

353 "You are quite right" to "in large part for his protection": CG to MC, June 20, 1959, CPNL.

353 "His plausibility is his curse": CG to Father William Lynch, un-

dated, CGPU. This letter was never mailed, according to Gordon's notations. See also Gordon's correspondence with the Cheneys in 1958–59, CPVU.

354 "Caroline Tate" or "Caroline Gordon Tate": see Gordon's letters to Robert Barnett, CGPU.

354 When she wrote her friends for evidence: CG to LA, undated, LABL.

354 "The mothers of chorus girls": CG to LA, undated, LABL.

354 "The gaff, as my father would say, has been slipped home": CG to LC and FC, May 12, 1959, as quoted in C. Ralph Stephens, ed., *The Correspondence of Flannery O'Connor and the Brainard Cheneys* (Jackson: University Press of Mississippi, 1986), 87.

354 "A woman's life" and "struggle with the daimonic": CG, *Narrow Heart* notebook, undated, CGPU.

355 "The insurance carried": CG to Robert Barnett, June 21, 1959, CGPU.

355 "I pray to God for forgiveness": AT to CG, September 6, 1959, CGPU.

CHAPTER 10: THE SHAPE OF THE RIVER

356 "I have a deep": CG to LC and FC, undated, CPVU.

356 "Only because" to "Any word of comfort": *PY*, 199.

357 "My life, my secret conscious life": "NH," 7.

357 "Thin, undersized child": "NH," 16.

357 "Pursuit of good letters": Caroline Gordon, "To Ford Madox Ford," *Transatlantic Review* 3 (Spring 1960): 5.

357 "Whether you *could* address a letter": CG to AB, undated [early spring 1960], BPPU.

357 "The kind of novel": Gordon, "To Ford Madox Ford," 6.

358 Caroline felt she suffered: see Gordon's notes on her copy of *Recent Southern Fiction: A Panel Discussion*, CGPU.

358 Professor Rubin decided: Louis D. Rubin, Jr., "We Get Along Together Just Fine," *Four Quarters* 12, no. 3 (March 1963): 30–31.

359 Women ought not be allowed to vote: CG, undated note, CGPU.

359 "This computerization of human beings": CG to MG, July 4, 1967, MGPU.

359 "It is my sober and long considered conclusion": CG to AB, May 22, 1962, BPPU.

359 "The *habit* of writing sentences": Caroline Gordon, "On Learning to Write," *Four Quarters* 12, no. 2 (January 1963): 10.

359 "Things about Heracles": CG to AB, undated [December 30, 1960], BPPU. Gordon eventually changed the title of her lecture to "No Snake Gets All the Good Lines."

359 "One of the best stories": CG, "No Snake Gets All the Good Lines," typescript, CGPU.

360 "Discovering some of the joys of scholarship": CG to WT, undated, WTPU.

360 "I'd let them lapse: CG to KAP, Holy Saturday, 1963, KAPM. See CG to Charles Scribner, Jr., July 10, 1962, and Scribner to CG, July 23, 1962, SAPU, as well as CG to LA, St. James' Day, 1962, LABL, for first mention of rumors.

361 "I never saw anything in Europe as grand": CG to MG and Polly Gordon, January 12, 1963, MGPU.

361 "I never saw mountains before": CG to KAP, Holy Saturday, 1963, KAPM.

361 "Inspired by one vision": Caroline Gordon, *A Good Soldier: A Key to the Novels of Ford Madox Ford* (Davis: University of California Library, 1963), 23.

361 Allen thought Greene: see AT to CG, January 18, 1963, March 15, 1963, and October 4, 1963, CGPU.

362 "I adore Indiana": CG to RPW, postmark January 31, 1964, RPWB.

362 "My Boy, you've got" to "the knowledge of the *shape*": CG, "The Shape of the River," typescript, CGPU.

362–63 "Not only useless": CG to AB, April 30, 1964, BPPU.

363 "The doctor says" to "whenever they aren't": Caroline Gordon, "Heresy in Dixie," *Sewanee Review* 76 (Spring 1968): 266.

363 Flannery was amused, and a bit awed: Flannery O'Connor to WD, June 2, 1964, DUNC.

363 "A tendency to rely on statement": CG to AB, September 5, 1964, BPPU.

363 "Did not realize, or perhaps" to "Congratulations": Gordon, "Heresy in Dixie," 266.

364 "Erroneous belief": Caroline Gordon, "Katherine Anne Porter and the ICM," *Harper's*, November 1964, 147.

364 "Apparatus," a "Procrustean couch" or "International Critical Machine": Gordon, "Katherine Anne Porter," 146.

364 "A pilgrim," "But if he settles": Gordon, "Katherine Anne Porter," 147.

365 "Women, of course," "Every one of us": Caroline Gordon, "Cock-Crow," *Southern Review*, n.s., 1 (1965): 560, 562.

365 "These days an aging novelist": CG to KAP, [November 10, 1964], KAPM.

366 "Of course, sixty year old": CG to MG, July 4, 1967, MGPU. For information on Tate's situation, see his letters to AL, February 13 and 21, 1966, LPVU.

367 "Great pre-historic," "so highly gifted": CG to PW and NTW, September 19, 1967, CGPU.

367 "To finish that novel": CG to AB, July 7, 1968, BPPU.

368 "Partly a matter of rhythm," "The alcoholic": CG to AB, May 22, 1962, BPPU.

368 "Just two ounces": *PY*, 201.

368 "Arthritis is a wild beast," "If only I hadn't": CG to AB, Feast of St. Elizabeth of Hungary, 1968, BPPU.

368 "Somewhat diffidently" to "I am too close": CG to Donald Stanford, March [April?] 5, 1969, Donald E. Stanford Papers (M466), Department of Special Collections, Stanford University Libraries, Stanford, Calif.

368 "Woeful condition": Caroline Gordon, "Cloud Nine," *Sewanee Review* 77 (Autumn 1969): 593.

369 "As if an alarm," "It is a damn dull": CG to MG, October 6, 1969, MGPU.

369 "Politicalese," "barbarous jargon": CG to MG, July 18, 1970, MGPU.

369 "Elite," "pragmatical," and "function": CG to MG, October 6, 1969, MGPU.

369 "A real lost generation": CG to MG, June 4, 1968, MGPU. See also CG to MG, July 18, 1970, MGPU.

370 "What one had thought": CG to LA, October 30, 1970, LABL.

370 "Had to deal with an out-sized character": CG to Stewart Richardson, September 1970, CGPU.

370 "My books have never sold": CG to MG and Polly Gordon, October 2, 1970, MGPU.

371 "Clear out of his head": CG to NTW, January 10, 1971, CGPU.

371 "A kind of Kafka's Castle": CG to David McDowell, February 25, 1971, David McDowell Papers, Jean and Alexander Heard Library, Vanderbilt University, Nashville.

371 "Allen's psychosis" to "Also, years of writing": CG to AB, April 8, 1961, BPPU.

371 She apparently destroyed: see letter from Izzy to Marion Meriwether, March 27, 1968, CGPU.

372 "Old Women's Liberation Movement": CG to LA, July 20, 1971, LABL. See the correspondence between CG and Scribner in SAPU, especially Scribner's letter dated August 5, 1971.

3772 "Sold me down": CG to William Stuckey, September 25, 1972, CGPU.

373 "I saw and heard," "I don't want to lose": CG to AB, April 10, 1972, BPPU.

373 "Next to impossible" to "They, as it were": CG, *Narrow Heart* notebook, CGPU.

373 "A masterpiece": AT to CG, April 7, 1972, CGPU.

374 "Nowadays I feel": CG to Eileen Squires, May 1, 1972, SPWU.

374 "heroes have ever": *GH*, 395.

374–75 "The Lord has tempered": CG to William Stuckey, September 25, 1972, CGPU.

375 "Again I am trying": CG to Robert Giroux, July 10, 1972, CGPU.

375 "Restrained by the proper": Gordon, "Cock-Crow," 560.

376 "These early letters": SWK to CG, June 1972, CGPU.

376 "I am afraid" to "quite unconsciously": SWK to CG, August 8, 1972, CGPU.

376–77 "A conscious heiress": Ashley Brown, "The Achievement of Caroline Gordon," *Southern Humanities Review* 2, no. 3 (1968): 279–80.

377 "It seems to me": CG to Sandra Lavin, September 17, 1972, CGPU.

377 "I work every morning": CG to NTW, January 17, 1973, CGPU.

377 "Great Dismal Swamp": CG to Radcliffe Squires, January 12, 1973, SPWU.

377 "Nearer the ideal of Christian education": CG to LC, January 12, 13, or 14, [1973], CGPU.

377 "Center for fictional studies in prose": CG to AB, January 5 or 6, [1973], BPPU.

378 "A foretaste of heavenly bliss": CG to Chauncey Stillman, January 29, [1973], CGPU.

378 "Mama, you have" to "the opportunity of landing": CG to Louise and Don Cowan, January 24, 1973, CGPU.

378 "Just a slip": CG to MC, July 5, 1973, CPNL.

379 "The Red House" to "the shadows of leaves": CG to SWK, December 18, 1973, CGPU.

379 "Professional gambler": CG, "I don't much like air travel," typescript, undated [fall 1973], 3, CGPU.

379 "Writing a novel is a gamble": Mary Brinkerhoff, "Expert at Helm, Sets Course," *Dallas Morning News*, August 10, 1973.

379 "The bedroom of Dallas," "old time professional gamblers": CG to PW and NTW, January 17, 1973, CGPU.

380 "You and I are trying": CG, lecture notes, "Techniques of Fiction, 1973," typescript, September 27, 1973, CGPU.

380 "A good sock in the jaw" to "The kid gloves": CG to SWK, December 18, 1973, CGPU.

380 "A perfect dream-boat": CG to Eileen Squires and RS, February 19, 1974, SPWU.

380 "I am trying hard": CG to Eileen Squires and RS, April 19, 1974, SPWU.

380–81 One day, she called her daughter, to She had seen his cloven foot: interview with NTW, September 13, 1988, San Cristóbal de las Casas, Chiapas, Mexico.

381 "I don't not believe that *Aleck Maury*": CG to Matthew J. Bruccoli, July 19, 1974, CGPU.

382 "They won't interest": quoted in CG to SWK, undated, CGPU.

382 "Discriminating critics": CG to SWK, February 19, 1975, CGPU.

382 "What I'm teaching you": CG, lecture notes, "Techniques of Fiction, Fall 1974," typescript, CGPU.

382 She told her students: CG to Louise Cowan, undated [late fall 1974], CGPU.

382 "Twice as much sunshine": CG to NTW, undated, CGPU.

382 "To check on": CG to FC, April 27, 1975, CPVU.

383 "Nothing like a deadline": CG to Allen Tate Wood, Feast of St. Thomas Aquinas, 1976, general manuscripts, Firestone Library, Princeton University, Princeton, N.J.

383 "Sustaining, with as much": CG to Howard Baker, undated, CGPU.

383–84 On Allen and the Red House: see CG letters to NTW, undated, CGPU; AT to CG, August 19, 1977, CGPU.

384 "The *boredom* of Princeton": CG to FC, July 5, 1977, CGPU.

384 "I cursed loud and deep": CG to Robert Giroux, undated, CGPU.

384–85 "I am so tired," "One's needs must": CG to SWK, February 14, 1978, SWKP.

385–86 "On a slope" to "I want to *see*": CG to SWK, February 28, 1978, CGPU.

386 "Have already seen": telegram from CG to PW, undated, CGPU.

386 "I think this house": interview with NTW, September 11, 1988, San Cristóbal de las Casas.

386 "Who would I talk to": CC, 368.

387 "If you say a word": interview with NTW, September 1988, San Cristóbal de las Casas.

387 "I am not going": CG to NTW, July 10, 1978, CGPU.

387 "I cannot work here," "The language barrier": CG to PW, July 20, 1978, CGPU.

388 "My ignorance" to "I am a prisoner": CG, notebooks, June 3, 1978, CGPU.

388 "This place is beautiful," "I am the only": CG to Robert Liddell Lowe, August 2, 1978, CGPU.

388 "I am too ill": CG to SWK, October 15, 1978, CGPU.

388 "The people here": CG to SWK, undated, CGPU.

388 "Well, thank God": interview with NTW, September 11, 1988, San Cristóbal de las Casas.

389 "Bob Giroux is launching," "I ought to be pleased": CG to SWK, May 18, 1979, SWKP.

389 "I've seen all," "My doctor is determined": CG to AB, December 6, 1979, BPPU.

389 "Weary of this world": CG to SWK, undated [postmarked August 6, 1980], SWKP.

389 "What good times," "I am glad": CG to SWK, undated [postmarked July 25, 1980], SWKP.

389 "Everything I do" to "I read nothing": CG to SWK, undated, SWKP.

389–90 "He just doesn't understand," "He gives me absolution": interviews with NTW, September 1988, San Cristóbal de las Casas.

390 "I like to look at him": NTW to SWK, July 30, 1981, CGPU.

390 She came out of the surgery: interview with NTW, September 11, 1988, San Cristóbal de las Casas.

391 "I know you can't speak": CC, 369.

391 "This look of absolute bliss": interview with NTW, September 11, 1988, San Cristóbal de las Casas. Information on Gordon's death is drawn from this interview and from NTW to SWK, July 30, 1981, CGPU; NTW to Marion Kelleher, May 18, 1981, CGPU.

391 "To warm Doña Carolina": NTW to SWK, July 30, 1981, CGPU.

391 "Listen, Nancy," "Purple is best": NTW to Marion Kelleher, May 18, 1981, CGPU.

391 "It's the custom here": interview with NTW, September 11, 1988, San Cristóbal de las Casas.

392 They also buried ritual packages: SM, 11.

INDEX